AME ENGAGE™

Welcome to the fully integrated and interactive online learning hub for
Financial Accounting Principles, V4.0

Online & Interactive

AME Learning's integrated and interactive online learning hub, AME Engage™, contextualizes the study of accounting in a practical, hands-on online learning environment. Designed to personalize the learning experience and engage students *before* class, our multi-sensory online tutorials guide students through the key accounting concepts for each chapter. These tutorials help students to *learn by doing,* using a variety of effective learning tools ranging from gaming to interactive problem solving.

In order to encourage students to truly understand the concepts rather than simply rely on memorization, AME Engage™ features randomized algorithmic homework questions, allowing students to practice the same concept repeatedly at their own leisure. The "Take me to the text" online homework feature links each question to the relevant examples in the digital textbook, immediately providing students the help they need at any time and from anywhere. Instructors have full control over all resources in AME Engage™, and can therefore effectively tailor their online environment according to their own teaching style.

Unique PIN Code

If you purchased this book brand-new, the PIN Card (image to the right) is attached to the front cover. Open this to get your unique **PIN Code**, then follow the instructions to log in to AME Engage™.

JOFFE/PARKER

FINANCIAL ACCOUNTING PRINCIPLES

V4.0

AME | Learning

AME ENGAGE™
ONLINE STUDENT ACCESS PIN CARD

Unique **PIN Code** for access to:
- Digital Textbook & Workbook
- **AME ENGAGE™** Online Platform
  - Interactive Tutorials
  - Quizzes
  - Homework
  - Tests & Exams

⚠ Don't throw away!

Don't have a PIN Card?

If you **did not** purchase this book brand-new, you will need to purchase your unique PIN Code at www.amelearning.com/store or contact your campus bookstore.

Instructor looking for access?

Please contact your AME Learning or Paradigm Education Solutions representative.

The AME Approach to Learning Accounting

AME utilizes a unique method to simplify accounting concepts, using step-by-step logic to ensure that the subject is extremely easy to understand. Accounting concepts are communicated using straightforward language and AME Accounting Maps™ that make potentially complex transactions simpler and easier to follow.

The AME Accounting Map™ is used throughout the textbook to show the impact of transactions on the financial statements. It is a visual representation of the balance sheet and income statement. The Accounting Map™ is also used in our interactive tutorials. Increases and decreases in values of specific items are clearly shown on the Map without needing to resort to technical accounting terminology.

The Accounting Map™

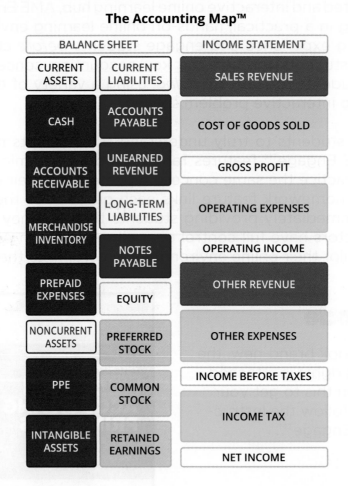

This textbook is part of a larger and blended program that is being used to teach the course. As an instructor it is recommended to follow these steps to ensure your students get the most out of the program.

1. Encourage students to use the interactive online tutorials before attending each class.
2. Use the PowerPoint™ presentations to provide visuals to assist with teaching the material.
3. Online quizzes are available to test student's comprehension of the material. Quizzes can be used either before or after class.
4. Online post-class homework questions are available to test student's ability to complete accounting problems. These should be used after class.

FINANCIAL ACCOUNTING PRINCIPLES

V4.0

Lead Authors
Neville Joffe
Penny Parker, CPA, CGA, MBA

Contributors and Reviewers

Ronnie Carter, CPA
Patrick Henry Community College

Suryakant Desai, Ed.D., CPA, CFP
Dallas County Community College District

Cathy Duffy, Ed.D., M.Sc., B.Sc.
Champlain College

Dr. Regan Garey, D.B.A., M.B.A., B.S., B.A.
Lock Haven University

Sharon O'Reilly, M.B.A., B.A.
Gateway Technical College

Textbook ISBN: 978-1-926751-73-3
Workbook ISBN: 978-1-926751-74-0

Financial Accounting Principles, V4.0
Authors: Neville Joffe/Penny Parker
Publisher: AME Learning Inc.
Content Contributors and Developmental Editors:
    Kobboon Chotruangprasert/Vicki Austin
Production Editors: Graeme Gomes/Lisa McManus/Melody Yousefian
Copy Editor: Lisa McManus
Indexer: Elizabeth Walker
Typesetter: Paragon Prepress Inc.
Vice President and Publishing Manager: Linda Zhang
Cover Design: Pixon Design
Online Course Design & Production: AME Multimedia Team

2 3 4 MCRL 20 19 18

Printed in China

This book is written to provide accurate information on the covered topics.
It is not meant to take the place of professional advice.

For more information contact:

AME Learning Inc.
410-1220 Sheppard Avenue East
Toronto, ON, Canada M2K 2S5
Phone: 416.479.0200
Toll-free: 1.888.401.3881
E-mail: info@amelearning.com
Visit our website at: www.amelearning.com

The AME Learning System™

It started 20 years ago when company founder Neville Joffe developed an innovative game-based methodology to help his employees understand basic financial concepts. Today, the AME Learning System™ is an award-winning teaching strategy. It's unique, patented and most importantly, it works. Designed initially to teach the principles of accounting and financial literacy to people with no previous financial education, the AME Learning System™ has now accelerated learning for hundreds of thousands of students and professionals across North America.

The system incorporates the best of cognitive science, technology and learning principles into an active learning approach that emphasizes constant decision-making, real-world examples and process over memorization.

The patented Accounting Map™ Tutorials are the foundation of the system. Using a logical, visually based approach that translates accounting concepts into common experiences and terminology, the interactive, online tutorials employ the "flipped classroom" strategy that is revolutionizing contemporary learning. Students complete tutorials *before* their in-class instruction consolidates their understanding of the material. Then, plain-language, real-world style exercises help students practice and explore key lessons. When this system meets AME Engage – our distinctive online learning experience – it creates an unmatched connection between learners and content.

Our blended-learning packages offer print and digital resources that can support each other or stand alone to provide the learning experience that best fits everyone's needs. Our system is completely modular, allowing students, learners and clients to customize their learning goals and experiences, even as we continuously update our content and technology.

Full-Cycle Support

The heart of the AME Learning System™ is our connection to you. We customize your experience, your content and your support because we know our customers personally. We ensure our technology is portable and interoperable with your platforms and we organize our materials to match your needs and processes. Behind it all, the AME Assistant Team – our in-house accounting and learning specialists – work as your virtual teaching assistants, helping you build the learning experience, develop tests and exams and refine your curriculum.

Who's It For?

The AME Learning System™ can support everyone looking to enhance their understanding of the financial world, including school-age and higher-education students, people starting their own businesses, employees preparing for their first management roles and people looking for new jobs or retraining in mid-career.

Virtual schools, online universities and traditional colleges are customizing the AME Learning System™ to train accounting majors, entrepreneurs, paralegals, human resources professionals and people working in agriculture, hospitality and sports management. Our system is for anyone who wants to learn more, retain more and understand more about accounting and finance.

Textbook and Workbook Features

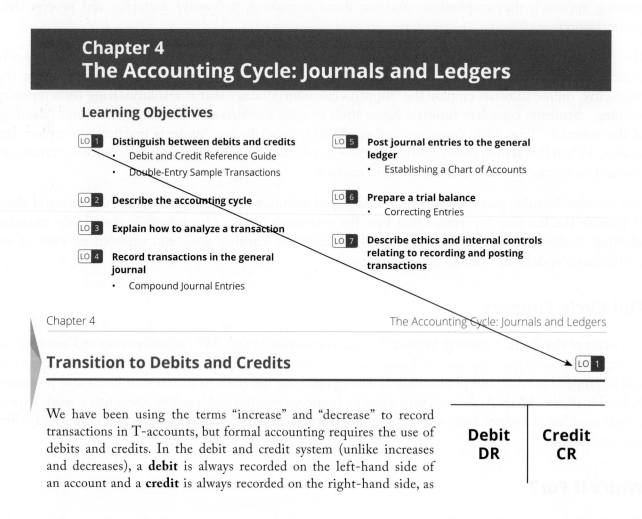 Access **ameengage.com** *for integrated resources including tutorials, practice exercises, the digital textbook and more.*

Every chapter has reminders for students to check their online course for additional resources to help explain the accounting topics.

The learning objectives in each chapter are prepared using Bloom's taxonomy. In the textbook, each heading in the chapters is linked to at least one learning objective. The learning objectives are also linked to all the questions in the workbook.

Chapter 4
The Accounting Cycle: Journals and Ledgers

Learning Objectives

LO 1 **Distinguish between debits and credits**
- Debit and Credit Reference Guide
- Double-Entry Sample Transactions

LO 2 **Describe the accounting cycle**

LO 3 **Explain how to analyze a transaction**

LO 4 **Record transactions in the general journal**
- Compound Journal Entries

LO 5 **Post journal entries to the general ledger**
- Establishing a Chart of Accounts

LO 6 **Prepare a trial balance**
- Correcting Entries

LO 7 **Describe ethics and internal controls relating to recording and posting transactions**

Chapter 4

The Accounting Cycle: Journals and Ledgers

Transition to Debits and Credits
LO 1

We have been using the terms "increase" and "decrease" to record transactions in T-accounts, but formal accounting requires the use of debits and credits. In the debit and credit system (unlike increases and decreases), a **debit** is always recorded on the left-hand side of an account and a **credit** is always recorded on the right-hand side, as

Debit DR	Credit CR

At the end of the chapter is a summary, highlighting key points for each learning objective.

In Summary

LO 1 Distinguish between debits and credits

▶ Debits are recorded on the left side of an account and credits are recorded on the right side. For the accounting equation to stay in balance, the total value of the debits must equal the total value of the credits.

▶ Assets, expenses and owner's withdrawals increase with debits and decrease with credits. Liabilities, revenues and owner's capital increase with credits and decrease with debits.

LO 2 Describe the accounting cycle

▶ The accounting cycle consists of the steps required to prepare financial statements. The cycle repeats every period.

Within each chapter are several Pause & Reflect exercises for students to complete. These break down large chapters into smaller manageable parts to help enforce the concepts learned. Solutions to the Pause & Reflect exercises are in Appendix I of the textbook.

Pause & Reflect

Exercise 4-1

Victor Lee owns and operates a personal training business, which is a sole proprietorship.

a) For each of the following transactions that occurred this month, indicate in Table 1 which two accounts are affected and their category (asset, liability, owner's capital, owner's withdrawal, revenue or expense).

b) Indicate whether the account balance would increase or decrease and whether the account needs to be debited or credited as a result of the transaction. Refer to Figure 4.7 for help, if necessary.

1. Victor invested $10,000 cash in the business.

2. Victor trained a customer for one hour and immediately received a $50 payment.

3. Furniture worth $3,000 was purchased using the business' credit card and will be paid later.

Each chapter has a Review Exercise covering the major topics of the chapter. The Review Exercises are prepared so students can complete them and then compare their answers to the solutions. Solutions to the Review Exercises are in Appendix I of the textbook.

Review Exercise 4-1

Catherine Gordon is running her own sole proprietary business called CG Accounting. CG Accounting provides bookkeeping services to small and mid-sized companies. The company prepares financial statements on a monthly basis and had the following closing balances at the end of May 2018.

CG Accounting **Balance Sheet** **As at May 31, 2018**			
Assets		**Liabilities**	
Cash	$4,200	Accounts Payable	$2,300
Accounts Receivable	3,100	Unearned Revenue	600
Equipment	6,000	Notes Payable	4,000
		Total Liabilities	6,900
		Owner's Equity	
		Gordon, Capital	6,400
Total Assets	$13,300	**Total Liabilities and Owner's Equity**	$13,300

CG Accounting uses a variety of accounts and account numbers in its accounting records.

Account Description	Account #
ASSETS	
Cash	101
Accounts Receivable	105
Prepaid Insurance	110
Equipment	120
Accumulated Depreciation—Equipment	125

Account Description	Account #
REVENUE	
Service Revenue	400
EXPENSES	
Advertising Expense	500
Bad Debt Expense	505
Insurance Expense	510

The workbook is comprised of assessment and application questions.

- Assessment questions (AS) are designed to test theory and comprehension of topics.
- Application questions (AP) are split into Group A and Group B problems. These questions test a student's ability to perform the accounting functions, such as creating journal entries and financial statements.

Chapter 4

THE ACCOUNTING CYCLE: JOURNALS AND LEDGERS

LEARNING OBJECTIVES

LO 1 Distinguish between debits and credits

LO 2 Describe the accounting cycle

LO 3 Explain how to analyze a transaction

LO 4 Record transactions in the general journal

LO 5 Post journal entries to the general ledger

LO 6 Prepare a trial balance

LO 7 Describe ethics and internal controls relating to recording and posting transactions

AMEENGAGE *Access* **ameengage.com** *for integrated resources including tutorials, practice exercises, the digital textbook and more.*

Assessment Questions

AS-1 LO 1

What

A de

Application Questions Group A

AP-1A LO 1 3

Esteem Fitness provides fitness services for its customers. During June 2018, Esteem Fitness had the following

Application Questions Group B

AP-1B LO 1 3

Perfect Party is owned by Candace Rodriguez and provides party planning services. During April 2018, Perfect Party had the following transactions.

Apr 1	The owner invested $5,800 cash into the business
Apr 4	Planned a party for a customer for $740; the customer will pay later
Apr 6	Paid $600 cash for rent for the month

Some Additional Segments

This textbook was designed to make your learning experience productive and engaging. To that end, we have added some segments to each chapter that highlight learning objectives.

A CLOSER LOOK

The *A Closer Look* segments are meant to closely examine a part of the chapter to broaden your understanding of an underlying concept. They may also include an example that applies the concepts being learned, in a way that is easy to understand and follow.

WORTH REPEATING

The *Worth Repeating* segments are meant to remind students of concepts in accounting already learned, and to highlight current concepts being taught that are "worth repeating."

IN THE REAL WORLD

 The *In The Real World* segments are meant to provide applied examples of elements being learned. They are meant to put some of the concepts being learned in context and to drive home the point that eventually, accounting has to be done outside the classroom. We hope that these segments give you a sense of what "the real world" can be like for the accountant or business professional.

GAAP vs IFRS

The *GAAP vs IFRS* segments are meant to discuss differences in the treatment of the topic being covered in the chapter based on the two different *sets* of accounting standards. Not all topics will have a difference between the two.

AME ENGAGE™

Welcome to the fully integrated and interactive online learning hub for *Financial Accounting Principles, V4.0.*

The AME Learning™ Cycle for Students

The AME Learning Cycle is a unique learning method that integrates the textbook seamlessly with the online platform to achieve a fun and interactive learning experience. The online learning hub, AME Engage, guides students every step along the way to achieve successful knowledge retention. The pre-class interactive tutorials allow students to not only better prepare for in-class work but also engage with difficult concepts whenever and wherever. The post-class algorithmic homework provides a platform for students to practice workbook questions online and receive instant feedback.

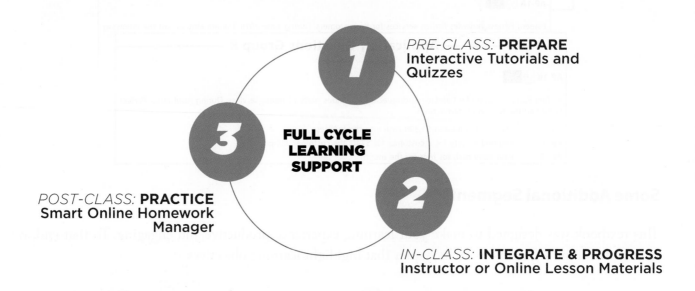

1 *PRE-CLASS:* **PREPARE** Interactive Tutorials and Quizzes

FULL CYCLE LEARNING SUPPORT

2 *IN-CLASS:* **INTEGRATE & PROGRESS** Instructor or Online Lesson Materials

3 *POST-CLASS:* **PRACTICE** Smart Online Homework Manager

AME Engage: Features

Interactive Online Tutorials
Interactive multi-sensory video clips featuring hands on practice with our innovative Accounting Map™.

Online Homework Manager
Algorithmic homework questions, assignments, projects, cases, tests and quizzes.

Resource Library
Focus-in on key lesson objectives with Microsoft Excel™ worksheet templates and our vast PowerPoint™ library.

Digital Textbook
Practical explanations and examples seamlessly integrated with workbook and online homework.

Digital Workbook
Hundreds of questions and cases perfectly integrated with textbook lessons and online homework.

Student Tech Support
Call 1 (888) 401-3881 x 2 from 9am to 5pm EST Monday to Friday or email support@amelearning. com 24 hours a day and 7 days a week.

AME ENGAGE™

Welcome to the fully integrated and interactive online learning hub for
Financial Accounting Principles, V4.0.

Full Cycle Instructor Support

At AME Learning, we proudly provide full cycle instructor support for teaching a stimulating and rewarding class. Our AME Assistant™ Team consists of highly qualified content experts, technical support specialists and resource managers, who can provide you with personalized assistance from custom content development to on-demand training and technical support. Our AME Engage online learning hub offers you a resource center that combines the best content with powerful teaching tools to achieve the desired flexibility and control.

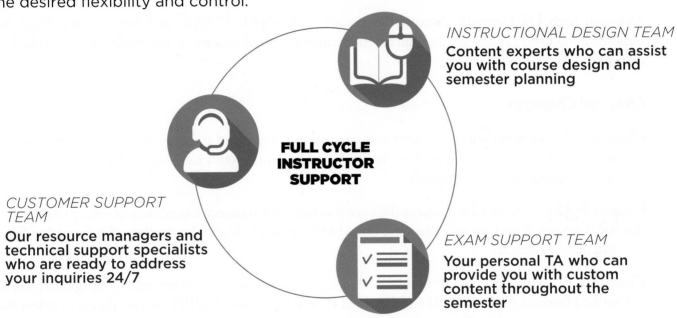

INSTRUCTIONAL DESIGN TEAM
Content experts who can assist you with course design and semester planning

FULL CYCLE INSTRUCTOR SUPPORT

CUSTOMER SUPPORT TEAM
Our resource managers and technical support specialists who are ready to address your inquiries 24/7

EXAM SUPPORT TEAM
Your personal TA who can provide you with custom content throughout the semester

Instructor Support: Features

Personalized Instructional Design.
A unique and personalized service tailors to the needs of each curriculum and each instructor.

Personalized Exam Support
Custom content creation throughout the semester for both paper based and online exams.

Online Question Bank
Over 1,500 questions organized by chapter and include multiple choice, matching, and computational problems.

Workbook Solution Manual
Step-by-step solutions to all workbook questions available in print or in digital format.

Online Resource Library
Powerful online resource center with additional teaching tools such as online cases, Microsoft PowerPoint© and Microsoft Excel© templates.

Instructor Training & Technical Support
On-demand support to integrate our products, technology and services into your course for optimum teaching and results.

Overview of Changes to this Version

Learning objectives better correspond to the depth of the material presented in each chapter, strictly following Blooms Taxonomy.

In addition to the Review Exercises at the end of each chapter, this textbook contains several Pause & Reflect Exercises throughout each chapter. These test an understanding of the content within one learning objective rather than the whole chapter, which allows students to test their knowledge before moving on to the next section. The solutions to the Pause & Reflect Exercises are in an appendix at the end of the textbook.

In the workbook, there are more application questions both in terms of quantity and depth. There is an A set and a B set of questions for each chapter. Instructors can use the A set questions for illustration and allow students to practice with a corresponding B set question.

Although both US Generally Accepted Accounting Principles (GAAP) and International Financial Reporting Standard (IFRS) are introduced, the terminology and content in this textbook are updated to reflect US GAAP.

Chapter Changes

Chapter 1: The presentation of the accounting equation is improved to better explain account increases and decreases. The T-account format is revised to better present account totals and include net worth as an account (i.e. similar to owner's capital).

Chapter 2: All four financial statements (balance sheet, income statement, statement of owner's equity and statement of cash flows) are presented and linked with arrows to highlight the flow of information from one statement to another.

Chapter 3: In addition to the CPA and CMA designations, other accounting-related designations such as Certified Internal Auditor (CIA) and Certified Payroll Professional (CPP) are mentioned to reflect the diverse career opportunities for accountants in the real world.

The role of the SEC and its relationship with the FASB in developing GAAP are discussed.

IFRS is introduced in chapter 3, along with a discussion of its brief developmental history and its most updated status on the convergence with US GAAP.

Chapter 4: For the new V4.0, the accounting cycle is discussed over three chapters (4, 5 and 6). Chapter 4 covers journals and ledgers. Chapter 5 covers adjustments (all discussed with debits and credits) and chapter 6 covers closing the books. The content in the current third edition chapter 4 regarding adjustments with increases/decreases only is eliminated.

For higher clarity, the accounting cycle is broken down in greater detail from the original 6-step cycle to the new 9-step cycle.

Chapter 5: Adjustments and examples for accrued expenses and accrued revenue are added. The topic of depreciation, which is eliminated from the first chapter, is discussed in this chapter. Interest calculation for accrued interest expense is shown and explained in more detail. An emphasis is added that period-end adjustments are different from reversing entries and are not error corrections.

Chapter 6: Sections relating to a classified balance sheet, including an explanation of how assets and liabilities are categorized into current and noncurrent/long-term, are moved from chapter 7 to this chapter.

Discussion of the current ratio and quick ratio is moved from chapters 7 and 13 to this chapter. Working capital is also added.

The content relating to closing entries is reorganized in a way that makes it easier to understand and more convenient to skip one method if an instructor prefers not to cover both the direct and income summary methods.

Chapter 7: More graphics are added to supplement verbal explanations and to improve visual presentation. For instance, an image of a sample invoice is provided to explain how to interpret information on an invoice and how to record journal entries accordingly. An image of a timeline is added for students to more easily visualize credit period and discount period.

Calculation of implied interest rate of purchase discount is shown to explain why it is usually in a buyer's best financial interest to take advantage of a purchase discount.

The net method of journalizing sales discount is added to reflect the FASB's Accounting Standards Update (ASU) 2014-09, Revenue from Contracts with Customers, Topic 606.

Chapter 8: The new chapter 8 covers inventory valuation and lower of cost and net realizable value. These topics are first discussed under perpetual in the main body of the chapter and then under periodic as part of the appendix. Moving the inventory chapter right after the merchandising chapter allows for better continuation of merchandise inventory content.

A new simple, less complex example demonstrating the application of the four inventory valuation methods is added before delving into the existing, more complex example. A figure comparing the four methods is also added.

Chapter 9: The content is modernized to emphasize more information technology by adding QuickBooks® illustrations and an explanation of cloud accounting. Illustrations of how the special journals are used are improved.

Chapter 10: A new section is added at the beginning of the chapter to introduce students to the concept of internal controls before proceeding to the discussion of cash controls.

The content is updated to be more in line with current banking trends. For example, the content related to cash controls in the context of electronic funds transfer (EFT) is added.

A more detailed explanation is included on how the previous month's activity will have an impact on the current month's bank reconciliation (i.e. deposits in transit and outstanding checks).

Chapter 11: The content is improved to be more comprehensive, for example, by adding information about credit card sales, factoring and pledging of receivables. The calculation of note interest and maturity date is illustrated.

Chapter 12: The changes in property, plant and equipment are classified into repair, betterment and extraordinary repairs. Journal entries for all three classifications are illustrated. The Modified Accelerated Cost Recovery System (MACRS) is explained.

Chapter 13: Contingent liabilities are clearly categorized into: a) probable and estimable, b) probable and not estimable, c) reasonably possible, and d) remote. An image is added to summarize accounting practices for different categories of contingent liabilities.

Chapter 14: Discussion of LLC and S Corporation (Sub-Chapter S) is added.

The Uniform Partnership Act, which is currently adopted by many states, is mentioned in this chapter.

Income division in the scenario where salary and interest allowances exceed net income is added.

Chapter 15: This chapter provides in-depth coverage of accounting practices and issues that are unique to a corporate entity. The chapter begins with a discussion of important characteristics, advantages and disadvantages of the corporate form of organization. Common and preferred stocks, along with their features, are highlighted. Then, explanations and any necessary journal entries related to a corporation's stock issuance, cash dividends, stock splits, stock dividends, treasury stock and income tax are provided.

Chapter 16: Following the FASB's issuance of ASU 2015-01, Subtopic 225-20 – Income Statement — Extraordinary and Unusual Items, the extraordinary item section is removed from the income statement, and its related discussions are removed from the textbook. The IFRS financial statements, including the statement of comprehensive income, the statement of changes in equity and the statement of financial position, are demonstrated in addition to the US GAAP financial statements.

Chapter 17: Accounting for notes payable is added. The effective interest rate method of bond amortization is added as an appendix at the end of the chapter.

Chapter 18: Presentation of investments on the financial statements is added as a new section. The financial presentation of unrealized gain or loss on available-for-sale investment is explained.

Chapter 19: The indirect method of statement of cash flows preparation is shown in the main text. The direct method is moved to the appendix at the end of the chapter. Another new appendix is added at the end of the chapter to illustrate how to use a spreadsheet to prepare the statement of cash flows under the direct method.

Chapter 20: Ratios are re-categorized based on what they intend to measure, such as liquidity, profitability, and capital market performance.

Management's Discussion and Analysis (MD&A) is discussed as an information source in addition to the financial statements.

A new summary table containing the formula and purpose of each ratio is added for quick reference.

Brief Table of Contents

Introduction

Detailed Table of Contents

Chapter 3: The Accounting Framework

Chapter 4: The Accounting Cycle: Journals and Ledgers

Chapter 5: The Accounting Cycle: Adjustments

Chapter 6: The Accounting Cycle: Statements and Closing Entries

Chapter 7: Inventory: Merchandising Transactions

Chapter 8: Inventory Valuation

Chapter 11: Accounting For Receivables

Chapter 13: Current Liabilities

Chapter 16: Corporations: The Financial Statements

Chapter 17: Long-Term Liabilities

Chapter 18: Investments

Chapter 19: The Statement of Cash Flows

Chapter 20: Financial Statement Analysis

Chapter 1
Financial Statements: Personal Accounting

Learning Objectives

LO 1 **Describe the purpose of accounting**

LO 2 **Describe the balance sheet**

LO 3 **Describe the income statement**

LO 4 **Define an accounting period**

LO 5 **Explain how the accounting equation works**

- Introduction to T-Accounts

LO 6 **Explain accrual-based accounting**

- Cash Flow vs. Accruals
- Cash-Based vs. Accrual-Based Accounting

LO 7 **Explain how to account for debt**

LO 8 **Explain how to account for assets**

LO 9 **Explain how to account for prepaid expenses**

LO 10 **Define capital**

LO 11 **Demonstrate how double entries are recorded in T-accounts**

The Purpose of Accounting

Accounting is a system to identify, measure and communicate all the financial activities of an individual or a business. Personal accounting tracks how much an individual is worth. Whether you live a simple or luxurious lifestyle, you need money to sustain your personal life. Most people want to save enough money to allow them to retire comfortably. The better you can manage your finances and bring in more money than you spend, the more wealth you have.

It is important to maintain records of the activities that increase or decrease your net worth (i.e. how much you earn, how much you invest and how much you spend). The key concepts that drive your personal economic life are very similar to those used in business. In fact, learning basic accounting is a crucial life skill for everyone.

Most people associate accounting with calculators, computers and long lists of numbers. That may be true to some degree when you are a practicing bookkeeper or accountant; however, understanding accounting involves not only numbers but also a logical way of thinking.

Here is an example of the logic behind one of the concepts you will learn in this course, net worth. Which scenario in Figure 1.1 would you prefer?

Scenario 1

Assets (what you own)	
Cash	$3,000
Contents of Home	6,000
Automobile	15,000
House	80,000
Total Assets	$104,000

Scenario 2

Assets (what you own)	
Cash	$5,000
Contents of Home	8,000
Automobile	20,000
House	100,000
Total Assets	$133,000

FIGURE 1.1

Scenario 2 appears to be preferable. However, some crucial information is missing. You must not only look at how much you own (assets) but also consider how much you owe (liabilities), as shown in Figure 1.2.

Assets = all that you OWN

Value of Assets = $75,000

Liabilities = all that you OWE

Value of Liabilities = $50,000

FIGURE 1.2

In examining the scenarios in Figure 1.3, which one would you now prefer?

Scenario 1

Assets (what you own)

Cash	$3,000
Contents of Home	6,000
Automobile	15,000
House	80,000
Total Assets	$104,000

Liabilities (what you owe)

Bank Loan	$0
Credit Card Account	2,000
Mortgage	60,000
Automobile Loan	5,000
Student Loan	5,000
Total Liabilities	$72,000
Net Worth*	$32,000

Scenario 2

Assets (what you own)

Cash	$5,000
Contents of Home	8,000
Automobile	20,000
House	100,000
Total Assets	$133,000

Liabilities (what you owe)

Bank Loan	$8,000
Credit Card Account	4,000
Mortgage	80,000
Automobile Loan	5,000
Student Loan	10,000
Total Liabilities	$107,000
Net Worth*	$26,000

*Net Worth = amount you own – amount you owe

FIGURE 1.3

Even though you may own more in Scenario 2, you also owe a lot more. The end result is that Scenario 2 is worth less than Scenario 1.

The Balance Sheet   LO 2

The **balance sheet** is a permanent document used to record what you own (assets), what you owe (liabilities) and what you are worth (net worth) on a specific date. An **asset** is something you own that benefits you now and in the future. This includes items such as the cash you have, the house and car you own, the furniture and electronics in your home, and investments you have made. Cash is listed first since it is the asset that can be most conveniently used to exchange for other things.

On the other hand, **liabilities** are obligations. Usually, these obligations mean you owe cash to someone else. One example of a liability is unpaid accounts. Unpaid accounts include amounts owing on credit cards, and bills for items like utilities or cell phones that you have not yet paid. Other longer term liabilities include items such as bank loans and mortgages. Unpaid accounts is listed first on the balance sheet since this is the debt you have to pay first.

Net worth is what is left if you cash out (i.e. successfully sell all your assets and get the value equivalent to the recorded amount) and pay everything you owe (your liabilities). Tracking the amount you are worth is a fundamental component of accounting in both your personal life and your business life.

The balance sheet provides a *snapshot* of your financial position. The difference between the value of what you own and what you owe is your net worth. The date of the balance sheet is presented as "As at..." because it represents a snapshot of your finances at a particular point in time. For example, a balance sheet prepared on December 31, 2018 would have the date "As at December 31, 2018." The next four figures will show different scenarios to illustrate how net worth is determined by both assets and liabilities.

In Figure 1.4, note that you have $7,000 in cash. At this point, if you needed to pay everything that you owe ($105,500), you would need to sell some of your assets (i.e. convert the value of your assets into cash, also known as *liquidating* your assets). Although you may think that you are worth only the $7,000 you have in the bank as cash, your true value (or net worth) is $36,500.

Personal Balance Sheet As at December 31, 2018			
Assets		**Liabilities**	
Cash	$7,000	Unpaid Accounts	$500
Contents of Home	5,000	Mortgage	100,000
Automobile	10,000	Bank Loan	5,000
House	120,000	Total Liabilities	105,500
		Net Worth	36,500
Total Assets	$142,000	Total Liabilities + Net Worth	$142,000

FIGURE 1.4

Net worth is equal to assets minus liabilities. This relationship is discussed later in the chapter.

In Figure 1.5, despite the fact that your cash balance is lower than the scenario in Figure 1.4, your net worth is higher.

Personal Balance Sheet As at December 31, 2018			
Assets		**Liabilities**	
Cash	$1,000	Unpaid Accounts	$5,000
Investments	18,000	Mortgage	100,000
Contents of Home	4,500		
Automobile	10,000	Total Liabilities	105,000
House	120,000	Net Worth	48,500
Total Assets	$153,500	Total Liabilities + Net Worth	$153,500

FIGURE 1.5

In Figure 1.6, you have a negative bank balance, meaning that you have withdrawn more money than you have in your bank account. Note that in accounting, negative numbers are expressed in parentheses. For example, −$2,000 is shown as ($2,000). This is a bank overdraft, which means you owe the bank money and will have to repay the amount with interest. However, your net worth is significantly higher than in Figures 1.4 and 1.5.

Personal Balance Sheet As at December 31, 2018			
Assets		**Liabilities**	
Cash	($2,000)	Unpaid Accounts	$10,000
Investments	30,000	Mortgage	80,000
Contents of Home	5,000	Bank Loan	7,000
Automobile	10,000	Car Loan	6,000
House	180,000	Total Liabilities	103,000
		Net Worth	120,000
Total Assets	$223,000	Total Liabilities + Net Worth	$223,000

FIGURE 1.6

In Figure 1.7, you have a large amount of cash, a valuable home and an expensive car. However, your net worth is lower than the previous three scenarios. This is because you borrowed a large amount from the bank for your house and car, which increased your liabilities.

The net worth reflected in Figure 1.6 (with the negative cash balance) is actually greater than the net worth shown in the other figures.

Personal Balance Sheet As at December 31, 2018			
Assets		**Liabilities**	
Cash	$50,000	Unpaid Accounts	$15,000
Investments	8,000	Mortgage	220,000
Contents of Home	12,000	Bank Loan	60,000
Automobile	50,000	Car Loan	40,000
House	250,000	Total Liabilities	335,000
		Net Worth	35,000
Total Assets	$370,000	Total Liabilities + Net Worth	$370,000

FIGURE 1.7

The Income Statement

The **income statement** is a temporary record used to show and summarize revenue and expenses. **Revenue** is an increase to net worth caused by providing goods or services in exchange for an asset, usually cash. In your personal life, revenue is usually earned by working and earning a salary. **Expenses** are a decrease to net worth caused by day-to-day activities. These costs are incurred and will be paid later or use up an asset, usually cash. In your personal life, expenses can include items such as rent or food.

The purpose of the income statement is to determine the *change* in net worth over a specific period of time. The date of the income statement is presented as "For the Period Ended..." since the statement covers a period of time. For example, an income statement prepared on December 31, 2018 covering a year would have the date "For the Year Ended December 31, 2018."

If you did not want to use an income statement, you could record every transaction in the net worth section on the balance sheet. A **transaction** is a trade or exchange with someone else in order to receive something of value. Since revenue increases net worth and expenses decrease net worth, you could record every revenue and expense amount directly into net worth on the balance sheet. However, this method would not keep track of the specific type of revenue or expense you had. Instead, you could note revenue and expenses on a separate document, the income statement.

Figure 1.8 illustrates a sample personal income statement. This shows that $36,000 was earned during the year and expenses amounted to $29,500. The difference between revenue and expenses is a surplus of $6,500, which is added to the person's net worth. If expenses are more than revenue, a deficit is recorded and subtracted from the person's net worth.

Personal Income Statement For the Year Ended December 31, 2018		
Revenue		$36,000
Expenses		
Food Expense	$12,000	
Insurance Expense	1,000	
Maintenance Expense	800	
Rent Expense	15,000	
Utilities Expense	700	
Total Expenses		29,500
Surplus (Deficit)		**$6,500**

FIGURE 1.8

A CLOSER LOOK

Imagine playing a sport without a scorecard. It would be difficult to play the game effectively without knowing the score during the game. Your economic life is no different. It is crucial to monitor how your day-to-day activities impact your net worth on a monthly basis so you can change your spending behaviors in a timely manner to fit within your income. Remember that there is a difference between cash and your net worth.

Accounting Periods

You can keep recording and calculating changes to net worth continuously; however, for accounting purposes, it is more convenient to record changes to net worth in separate periods. You can use any period you choose as an accounting period. An **accounting period** is the time frame in which the financial statements are prepared and can be one year, six months or one month, as shown in Figure 1.9.

If you use one month as your accounting period, you can look back at previous months (periods) and estimate what your expenses and income will be in

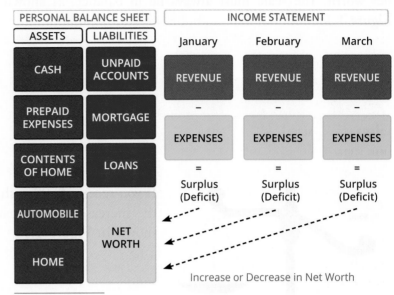

FIGURE 1.9

the coming months. You can also estimate the surplus or deficit you will generate each month. If you are saving for a major purchase, such as a car, computer or entertainment system, you can determine when you will have enough money to buy the desired item or provide a down payment.

Some advantages of using monthly accounting periods for your personal financial statements include

- tracking regular monthly living expenses (e.g. rent, cell phone);
- frequently assessing realistic expectations; and
- controlling errors effectively.

The Accounting Equation

Just as Newton's Third Law applies to science (for every action there is an equal and opposite reaction), the same concept can be applied to the logic of the accounting equation: For every transaction, there is an equal financial consequence. In accounting terms, each transaction has at least two entries of the same value, called a **double entry**. The logic of the double entry is based on the **accounting equation**, shown in Figure 1.10.

Assets = Liabilities + Net Worth

Assets	Liabilities
$1,000	– $700
	= 300 **Net Worth**

Assets	Liabilities
$1,000	$700
	+ 300 **Net Worth**
$1,000	**$1,000**

If assets minus liabilities = net worth, then mathematically… → assets must equal liabilities plus net worth.

FIGURE 1.10

Imagine the accounting equation as a scale; the left side of the scale includes assets and the right side includes liabilities and net worth. The scale must always be in balance, as shown in Figure 1.11.

Assets = Liabilities + Net Worth
$1,000 = $700 + $300

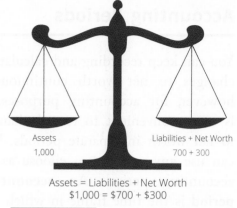

FIGURE 1.11

If you receive $500 cash, it increases your assets. Recording only the increase in cash causes the scale to go out of balance, as shown in Figure 1.12.

Assets = Liabilities + Net Worth
$1,500 ≠ $700 + $300

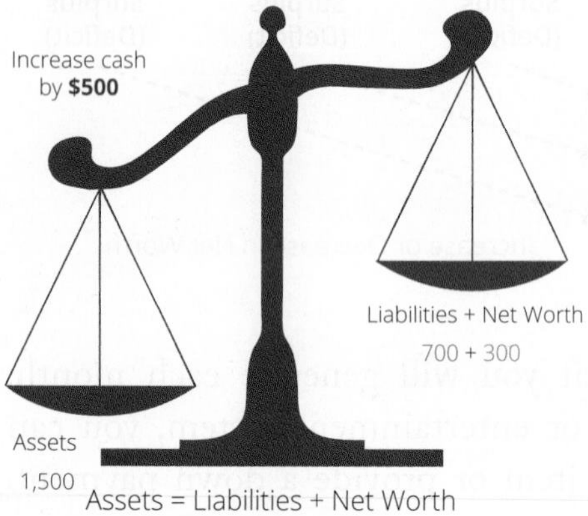

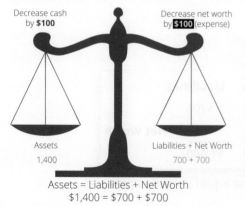

FIGURE 1.12

To balance the scale, you must ask yourself why you received the cash. If you earned it at your job, then the $500 must also increase net worth. This is recorded as revenue and brings the scale back into balance, as shown in Figure 1.13.

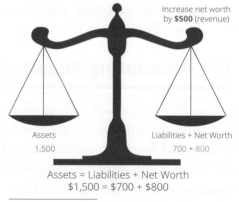

Assets = Liabilities + Net Worth
$1,500 = $700 + $800

FIGURE 1.13

Assets = Liabilities + Net Worth
$1,400 = $700 + $700

FIGURE 1.14

If you make a cash payment of $100, your assets decrease in value. The scale will only balance if you record the $100 somewhere else. Ask yourself why you made a $100 payment. If it was a rent payment for the month, then the $100 must also decrease net worth. This is recorded as an expense and the scale is balanced, as shown in Figure 1.14.

As these examples demonstrate, we can see that without a logical opposite entry, the balance sheet does not balance. Figure 1.15 shows how the transactions are analyzed using an accounting equation. The only way to keep it in balance is to impact at least two accounts. The first two transactions were illustrated in Figures 1.13 and 1.14 in terms of balancing the scale. The Explanation column in Figure 1.15 provides more details on why net worth changes.

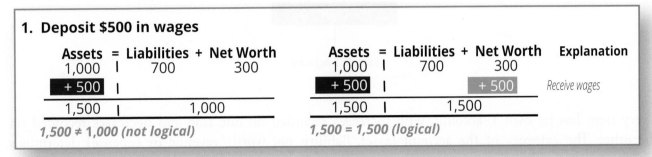

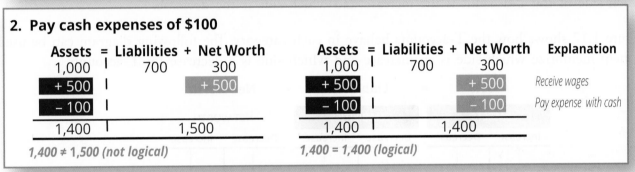

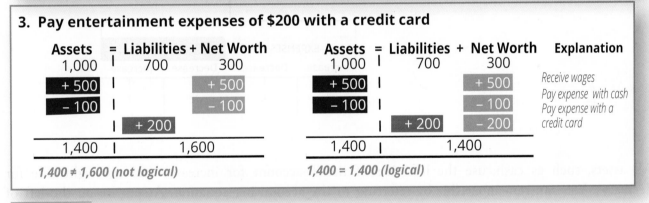

FIGURE 1.15

In the third transaction from Figure 1.15, $200 of expenses were paid with a credit card. The amount owed on the card represents an additional liability, so we increase liabilities by $200. Because the charge was for an expense, we must also decrease net worth by $200 so the accounting equation remains balanced.

Introduction to T-Accounts

An **account** allows us to track detailed information about the values of individual items, such as cash and unpaid accounts. A tool used to record transactions and to keep the accounting equation balanced is a **T-account**, named as such because it looks like a capital T, as shown in Figure 1.16.

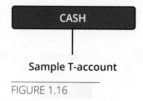

Sample T-account

FIGURE 1.16

Every item has its own T-account, with increases recorded on one side and decreases recorded on the other. The category of the account (asset, liability, net worth, revenue or expense) determines which side of the T-account is the increase and which side is the decrease.

Figure 1.17 shows how the T-accounts behave in each category. The following diagram can be used to help memorize which side is an increase and which side is a decrease for T-accounts.

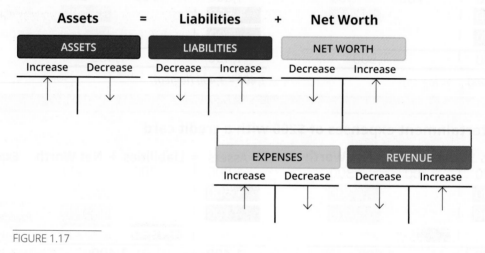

FIGURE 1.17

All assets, such as cash, use the left side of the T-account for increases and the right side for decreases. You can remember this by referring to the accounting equation. Assets are on the left of the accounting equation and assets use the left side of the T-account for increases.

All liabilities, such as unpaid accounts, use the right side of the T-account for increases and the left side for decreases. Again, refer to the accounting equation. Liabilities are on the right side of the accounting equation and liabilities use the right side of the T-account for increases.

Net worth also uses the right side of the T-account for increases and the left side for decreases since it is also on the right side of the accounting equation.

Revenue increases net worth and expenses decrease net worth. The more revenue earned, the more should be added to net worth. Therefore, the revenue T-account increases on the right side and decreases on the left side. The more expenses incurred, the more should be subtracted from net worth. Therefore, the expense T-accounts increase on the left side and decrease on the right side.

Figure 1.18 shows an example of the cash T-account.

Since cash is an asset, the left side of the T-account is for increases and the right side is for decreases. The first thing to enter into a T-account is the **opening balance**, or *beginning balance,* which is the amount left over from the last period carried over to the beginning of the current period. Cash has an opening balance of $1,000, shown at the top of the increase side of the T-account. After all transactions have been recorded, we total both sides of the T-account, shown in red. The increase side includes the opening balance in addition to the transactions. The difference between the increase and decrease sides is $4,400, which is the closing balance of cash. The **closing balance**, or *ending balance,* is the amount remaining in an account at the end of the period. It becomes the opening balance of the account in the next period. The difference is placed on the side that has the larger subtotal, which is the increase side in this example.

INCREASE			DECREASE	
+	CASH			−
Opening Balance	$1,000			
	1.	2,000	2.	1,500
	4.	4,000	3.	1,000
	5.	500	6.	600
Subtotal		7,500		3,100
Closing Balance	$4,400			

FIGURE 1.18

Pause & Reflect

Exercise 1-1

a) Use the accounting equation to calculate your net worth if you have $1,500 in assets and $300 in liabilities at the beginning of the month. Fill your answer in the Beginning Balances row of Table 1 below.

b) Assume that the three transactions listed in Table 1 happened during the current month. Analyze how each transaction affects your assets, liabilities and net worth, and fill in your answers. The first transaction has been started for you.

c) Calculate the ending balances for assets, liabilities and net worth after accounting for the three transactions in part b). Fill your answers in the Ending Balances row of Table 1.

Table 1

	Assets	=	Liabilities	+	Net Worth
Beginning Balances	$1,500	=	$300	+	
1. Paid $100 toward credit card balance	−100		−100		
2. Paid $25 for a meal using cash					
3. Deposited $300 in wages					
Ending Balances		=		+	

d) The cash T-account below shows this month's transactions. Calculate the closing balance of cash and fill in your answer at the bottom of the T-account.

INCREASE			DECREASE	
+	CASH			−
Opening Balance	$200			
	3.	300	1.	100
			2.	25
Closing Balance				

See Appendix I for solutions.

Accrual-Based Accounting   LO 6

A typical reason for personal financial failure (and small business failure) is not understanding accruals. People tend to think intuitively that an increase in cash represents an increase in wealth, and vice versa. The notion of the accrual is recognizing how much you are worth at a point in time.

Accrual-based accounting means that revenue (an increase to net worth) and expenses (a decrease to net worth) are recorded in the period in which they occur, regardless of when cash payment is received or paid.

So far we have assumed that every expense is paid when it is incurred. In reality, many expenses are not paid until a later date.

Assume that you have $1,000 of cash and a net worth of $1,000. If you pay for a $300 expense with cash, your cash and net worth both decrease by $300, as shown in Figure 1.19.

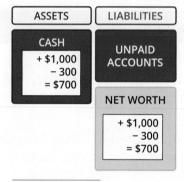

FIGURE 1.19

If, instead, you receive a phone bill for $300 to be paid next month, there is no change in cash in the current month. However, the phone debt (or unpaid accounts) increases by $300 and net worth decreases by $300, as shown in Figure 1.20. You recognize the expense that decreases net worth even if the expense is not paid until a later date.

FIGURE 1.20

In general, keep in mind that the word "expense" relates to a decrease in net worth, which does not necessarily relate to cash.

Cash Flow vs. Accruals

There are two key points to understand when discussing cash flow and accruals. Refer to Figure 1.21, which illustrates the difference between these two key points.

ⓐ Cash flow relates to cash flowing into and out of the bank account. In this instance, you paid $500 for a food expense, which did decrease your net worth. However, if the $500 was to purchase another asset, your net worth would not change because you are simply exchanging one asset (cash) for another asset (computer). Therefore, cash flow does not necessarily connect to net worth.

ⓐ Accruals relate to net worth, which does not necessarily connect to cash flow. In this instance, you received a bill and decided to pay it later. Your unpaid accounts increased by $500, which caused your net worth to decrease by $500. However, because the bill will be paid later, cash flow is not affected.

Both points are important and distinct.

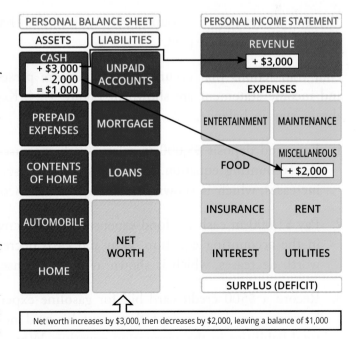

FIGURE 1.21

Cash-Based vs. Accrual-Based Accounting

In **cash-based accounting**, revenue and expenses are recorded only when the cash is received or paid. Since it is more straightforward than accrual-based accounting, individuals tend to use this method of accounting.

As illustrated in Figure 1.22, at the end of January you deposit $3,000 in salary earned that month and pay expenses of $2,000 using cash from the bank. The difference between revenue and expenses results in an increase in net worth of $1,000, which happens to be the same as the increase in cash.

Suppose that you deposit a salary of $3,000 in January, but charge all $2,000 worth of expenses to your credit card, which is to be paid in February. When you use cash-based accounting, your net worth appears to be $3,000 in January, since no cash is used to pay your expenses.

FIGURE 1.22

If, on the other hand, you are using accrual-based accounting, you need to recognize the expense in January, the month in which it was actually incurred. This textbook focuses on accrual-based accounting, since businesses are required to use this method.

In Figure 1.23, the income statement for the month of January shows that you have matched the revenue of $3,000 (an increase in net worth) to the expenses in January of $2,000 (a decrease in net worth), resulting in an overall increase in net worth of $1,000. Cash remains at $3,000 because you have not yet paid any of the expenses incurred.

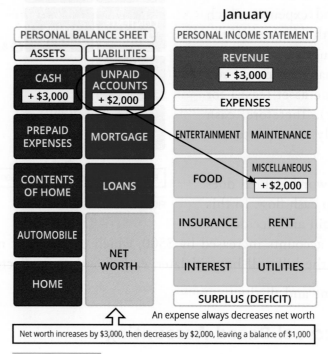

FIGURE 1.23

The accrual system of accounting recognizes the change in net worth even though payment is not necessarily received or paid.

Four transactions that occurred in January are presented below. Their impact on the balance sheet and income statement are shown in Figure 1.24. Keep in mind that the accounting equation must always stay in balance.

1. Earn and deposit $5,000 in salary. Cash increases by $5,000, which increases the total assets in the accounting equation. Why did cash increase? Because you deposited your salary. Net worth increases, which is shown as revenue on the income statement.

2. Pay $1,000 in cash for food expenses. Cash decreases by $1,000, which decreases the total assets in the accounting equation. Why did cash decrease? Because you bought some food. Thus, net worth decreases, which is shown as food expense on the income statement.

3. Record a $500 credit card bill for gasoline expenses (due in one month). Cash is not affected; however, you have a debt that must be paid next month. Debt increases, which increases the total liabilities in the accounting equation. Why did your debt increase? Because you have to pay

for the gasoline at some point in the future. Net worth decreases, which is shown as gasoline expense on the income statement.

4. Record a $1,500 credit card bill for entertainment expenses. Debt increases, which increases the liabilities in the accounting equation. Why did your debt increase? Because you have to pay for the entertainment at some point in the future. Net worth decreases, which is shown as entertainment expense on the income statement.

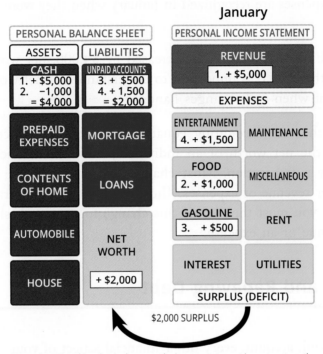

Remember: Everything that is shown on the income statement impacts net worth.

FIGURE 1.24

We can also illustrate these transactions with the accounting equation to ensure that assets equal liabilities plus net worth. This is shown in Figure 1.25.

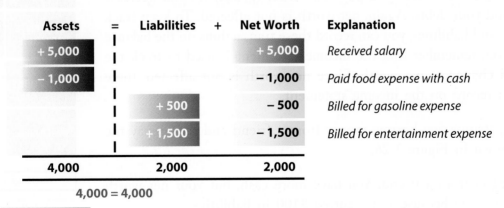

FIGURE 1.25

The accounting equation is balanced.

Assets	=	Liabilities	+	Net Worth
$4,000	=	$2,000	+	$2,000

As the examples in Figures 1.24 and 1.25 illustrate, you need to record your expenses for the month even though cash has not been paid for them in the same month. According to the concept of accruals, the credit card expenses are recognized in January when they were incurred, not in February when they are paid.

It is easy to mistakenly think that since cash increased by $4,000, net worth also increased by the same amount. This is not the case. It is important to understand that net worth is affected by revenue and expenses, regardless of when cash changes hands.

It is important to stress that the accounting equation must be in balance after every transaction. Many transactions affect the net worth of an individual; however, the net worth account itself is rarely directly changed by a transaction. Most changes to net worth are actually recorded in the income statement as either revenue or expenses. Thus, when you analyze transactions and determine that net worth is affected, you must then ask if this change to net worth should be recorded on the income statement as revenue or an expense.

Borrowing Money and Repaying Debt   LO 7

Other than cash in your bank account, every other financial aspect of your life relates to values—not to cash. Your assets have value, but only become cash if you sell them. Your liabilities represent an obligation you have, but they do not affect your cash until you actually pay them.

When you borrow money, you increase your assets and your debts. Net worth is not affected. When you pay your debts (principal), you decrease your assets and your debts. Again, net worth is not affected. To keep track of your assets and liabilities, you can record these transactions on the balance sheet. However, remember that the income statement is used to track the reasons for a change to net worth. Since net worth is not affected, there is nothing to record on the income statement.

For example, assume you borrow money from a friend and then repay the money, as shown in Figure 1.26.

FIGURE 1.26

1. Borrow $100 from a friend: You have more cash, but your net worth does not change because you incurred $100 in liabilities.

2. Repay your friend: You have less cash, but your net worth still does not change because you reduced your liabilities by $100.

The T-account entries related to these two transactions are shown in Figure 1.27.

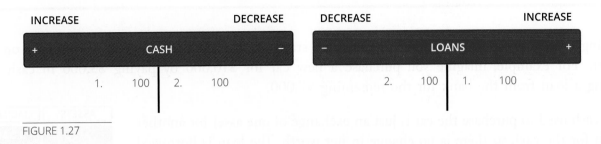

FIGURE 1.27

Only assets and liabilities are affected, so there is no entry on the income statement. There is no change to net worth.

Figure 1.28 demonstrates that not all the cash you spend is used to pay expenses. For example, you arrange for a loan of $15,000 and your loan repayments are $500 each month ($100 toward the principal and $400 in interest). There are three transactions to consider.

1. Receive the loan. Both cash and loans liability are increased. There is no impact to net worth.

2. Pay the interest portion of $400. Net worth has decreased and an expense is recognized.

3. Pay the principal of $100, reducing the amount owing to the loan company. Your net worth does not change and there is no need to record this transaction on the income statement.

The transactions would appear on the T-accounts, as in Figure 1.29.

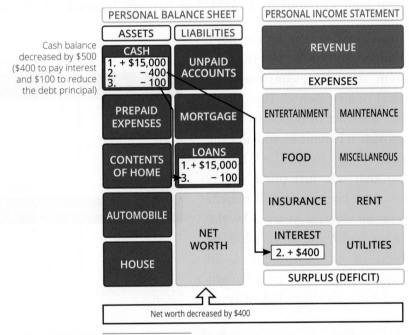

FIGURE 1.28

FIGURE 1.29

Even though your cash decreased by $500 when you made a payment to reduce the loan, your net worth decreased by $400 as a result of the interest expense.

Buying and Selling Assets

LO 8

Buying or selling assets (according to the value stated in the balance sheet) has no impact on net worth. For example, imagine you purchase a new car for $10,000 by paying $3,000 in cash and taking a loan from the bank for the remaining $7,000.

The cash used to purchase the car is just an exchange of one asset for another (cash for the car), so there is no change in net worth. The loan is borrowed to pay for the car, so the liability increases as does the asset (car). Again there is no change in net worth.

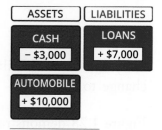

The effect on the accounts is shown in Figure 1.30. Although you now own a $10,000 car, there has been no change in your net worth.

FIGURE 1.30

The transactions appear on the T-accounts as shown in Figure 1.31. Cash decreases by $3,000 and your loan increases by $7,000. You have an increase to your automobile account of $10,000.

If you exchange cash for an item, how do you know whether the item should be considered an asset or an expense? Typically, it is a question of how long it will provide a benefit to you and the cost of the item. The $10,000 car that was just purchased is an asset because it will benefit you for several years. On the other hand, spending $200 on food or entertainment is an expense since they only benefit you for a short period of time.

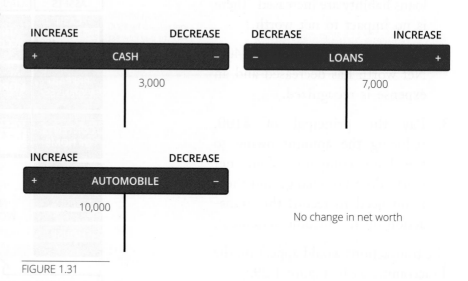

FIGURE 1.31

No change in net worth

A CLOSER LOOK

Over time, the assets you own change in value based on usage and changes in the market. The car you purchased for $10,000 will not always be worth that amount. After several years of use, it is worth less than what you paid for it. Your house, however, may increase in value if you maintain it and the area you live in is desirable. On personal financial statements, there are no rules preventing you from changing the values of these assets as the market values change. In business, though, there are strict rules on how values of assets are recorded. This will be covered in later chapters.

So, borrowing and repaying debt principal does not impact net worth, and neither does buying or selling assets for the value stated on the balance sheet. The primary way you can change your net worth is to have revenue exceed expenses (net worth increases) or have expenses exceed revenue (net worth decreases).

Prepaid Expenses

It is a common practice to pay for various expenses in advance, for example, insurance and rent. These prepayments are not considered an expense at the time they are paid because the services have not yet been provided. The example illustrated in Figure 1.32 explains the prepayment of $1,200 for one year of insurance.

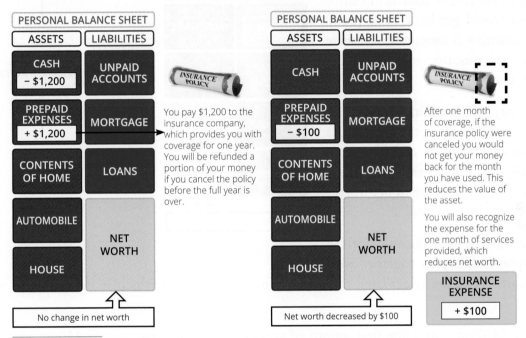

FIGURE 1.32

When you prepay your insurance, you might think that your net worth decreased because the cash is no longer in your bank account. However, what you have really done is purchase a one-year insurance policy, which you now own. Anything you own and will benefit you in the future is considered an asset and recorded as such on the balance sheet. In this case, the amount paid for the insurance policy is considered a prepaid expense. A **prepaid expense** occurs when you pay cash for an expense (like insurance) before you use it. You own the policy for one year and the insurance company must provide you with coverage for that period of time. If you cancel the insurance policy before the year is up, the company has to refund your money for the amount of the policy that you did not use.

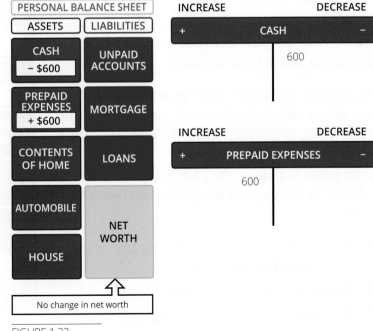

FIGURE 1.33

Figure 1.33 illustrates another example of a prepaid expense. Assume that you hire a gardening service that costs $600 per year ($50 per month). The service provider requests that you prepay the full $600 in January. Ideally, if you were to cancel the contract with the company the next morning, you would receive all the money back because the company has not yet provided the service. In effect, you have simply given the company an interest-free loan. If you were to cancel the contract in three months, you would get back $450 [$600 – ($50 per month × 3 months)]; if it were canceled in six months, you would get back $300; and so on.

When you pay the $600 in advance, the service provider owes you the service. As a result, this payment is considered an asset (which is a prepaid expense). There is no expense (i.e. a decrease in net worth) until the service is provided.

As each month goes by, the value of the prepaid expense decreases together with your net worth. You are *recognizing* the expense in the month in which it is used—not when it is paid.

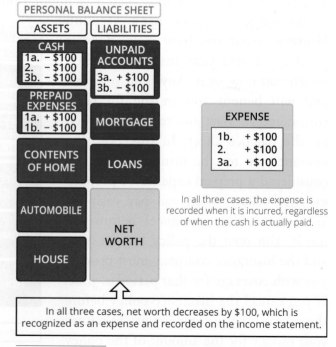

FIGURE 1.34

As Figure 1.34 shows, after the first month of service is provided, you record $50 as an expense for that month, which decreases net worth. The remaining prepaid portion is $550. You will recognize $50 as an expense for each of the next 11 months as the supplier provides the service.

An increase in expenses relates to a decrease in net worth. Cash does not have to be involved to increase an expense and decrease net worth.

According to accrual-based accounting, expenses are always recorded when they are incurred. This has nothing to do with when the cash payment is made. If we assume an expense is $100, there are three possible timings the payment can be made in relation to the expense being incurred (see Figure 1.35).

1. Pay before and recognize the expense when it is incurred (prepaid expense)

2. Pay as the expense is incurred (cash)

3. Pay after the expense is incurred (unpaid account)

FIGURE 1.35

Figure 1.36 shows how to record each possible timing of payment in the relevant T-accounts.

1. Pay before and recognize the expense when it is incurred

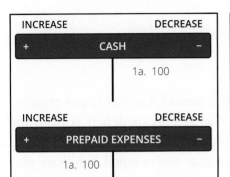
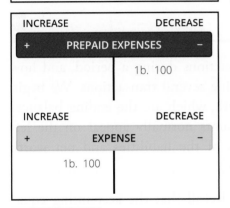

2. Pay as the expense is incurred

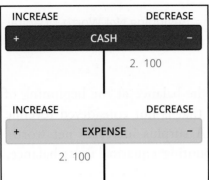

3. Pay after the expense is incurred

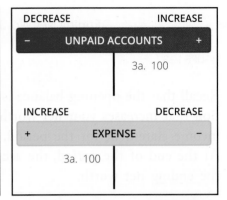

FIGURE 1.36

Capital

So far, we have discussed that the most common way to increase net worth is to earn revenue that exceeds expenses. There are other ways to increase your net worth, such as winning the lottery or receiving a gift. Amounts that increase your net worth but are not earned, and therefore not considered revenue, are known as **capital**.

Capital items are not everyday revenues and are therefore recorded directly to net worth instead of the revenue account. For example, if you win $3,000 cash from a lottery, the transaction is recorded as shown in Figure 1.37. All other changes to net worth are recorded as revenue or expenses on the income statement.

It is important to separate records of revenue received from regular activities (e.g. earning wages) from other infrequent increases to net worth (e.g. gifts) instead of pooling them all together. Keeping them separate allows you to properly manage your finances month-to-month.

FIGURE 1.37

The accounting equation shows net worth at a particular point in time. However, net worth changes over time as you earn revenue, incur expenses or receive capital. The formula in Figure 1.38 shows how to calculate the ending or closing balance of net worth over a period of time.

Ending Net Worth = Beginning Net Worth + Capital + Surplus (Deficit)

FIGURE 1.38

Recall that the opening balance is the balance at the beginning of the period. Capital is any transaction that increases your net worth that is not considered revenue. The surplus or deficit is from the income statement for the period. A surplus increases net worth and a deficit decreases net worth. At the end of the period, the accounting equation must balance, so that assets equal liabilities plus the ending net worth.

T-Account Transactions

To demonstrate how T-accounts are used to record financial transactions during a period, and how the income statement is linked to the balance sheet, we will examine several transactions. We begin the month with opening balances for assets, liabilities and net worth, which are the ending balances from the previous month. The opening balances of the asset accounts normally appear on the left side of the T-accounts (increase side), and the opening balances of the liabilities and net worth normally appear on the right side of the T-accounts (increase side).

The transactions are numbered in the list and in the T-accounts. Recall that the accounting equation must balance, so every transaction has a double entry that affects at least two accounts. To demonstrate how to record transactions in T-accounts, the information in Figure 1.39 will be used.

Opening Balances as at April 1, 2018			
Cash	$1,000	Unpaid Accounts	$1,500
Prepaid Insurance	0	Mortgage	90,000
Contents of Home	6,000	Bank Loan	0
House	150,000	Net Worth	65,500

FIGURE 1.39

The following transactions occurred during the month.
1. Earned and deposited a salary of $2,500
2. Paid $1,200 cash for a one-year insurance policy
3. Paid for $150 of entertainment with a credit card
4. Received a $4,000 loan from the bank
5. Won $800 in a lottery
6. Paid $1,000 toward a mortgage; interest is $100 and the remainder is the principal
7. Purchased new furniture worth $1,400 with a credit card
8. Bought food with $400 cash

The transactions are recorded in T-accounts by using the following steps, illustrated in Figure 1.40.

ⓐ If applicable, enter the opening balances in the appropriate T-account. Then check that the accounting equation is in balance before you begin entering transactions.

ⓑ Enter both sides of the transaction in the correct account on the balance sheet and/or income statement. Be sure to record the transaction number so that you may check your work.

ⓒ Calculate the totals of the T-accounts on the income statement and the surplus or deficit.

ⓓ Calculate the totals of the T-accounts on the balance sheet and complete the accounting equation at the bottom of the balance sheet to check that it balances.

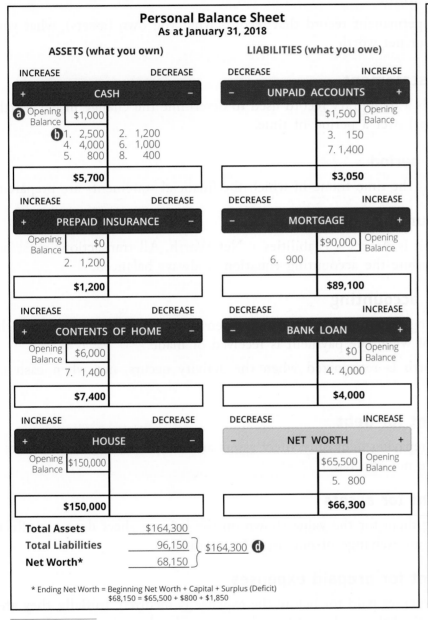
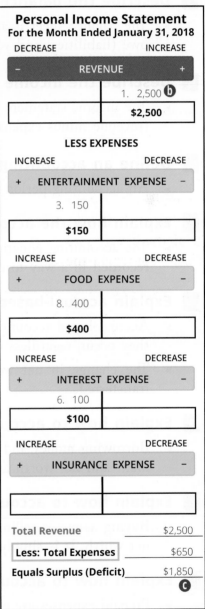

FIGURE 1.40

To calculate net worth, start with the the opening net worth of $65,500 and add the lottery winnings of $800. The surplus of $1,850 from the income statement is added to net worth. This gives a closing net worth balance of $68,150. Note that if there was a deficit on the income statement, this would be subtracted from net worth.

In Summary

LO 1 Describe the purpose of accounting

▶ Accounting identifies, measures and communicates financial activities. This can be done for an individual or a business.

LO 2 Describe the balance sheet

▶ The balance sheet is a permanent record that records what you own (assets), what you owe (liabilities) and your net worth.

LO 3 Describe the income statement

▶ The income statement is a temporary record used to determine the change in net worth (revenue minus expenses) over a period of time.

LO 4 Define an accounting period

▶ An accounting period is the time frame in which the financial statements are prepared.

LO 5 Explain how the accounting equation works

▶ The accounting equation is Assets = Liabilities + Net Worth. All transactions must be recorded in a way to ensure the accounting equation is always balanced.

LO 6 Explain accrual-based accounting

▶ Accrual-based accounting recognizes revenue and expenses in the time period in which they occur, regardless of when the payment is received or made.

▶ The change in net worth is recognized when the activity occurs, not when cash is transferred.

LO 7 Explain how to account for debt

▶ Borrowing money and repaying debt only affect assets and liabilities. The income statement and net worth are not affected.

LO 8 Explain how to account for assets

▶ Buying assets or selling them for the value shown on the balance sheet does not affect net worth. It is simply an exchange of one asset for another.

LO 9 Explain how to account for prepaid expenses

▶ Prepaid expenses are expenses paid for before the expense is incurred. Initially, they are recorded as an asset on the balance sheet. Once the expense has been incurred, the asset is reduced and an expense is recorded on the income statement.

LO 10 **Define capital**

► Capital includes irregular items, such as gifts, that increase net worth. Revenue items also increase net worth but are earned and recorded on the income statement.

LO 11 **Demonstrate how double entries are recorded in T-accounts**

► T-accounts are used to track the increases and decreases in the values of assets, liabilities, net worth, revenue and expenses. Double entries are used to keep the accounting equation balanced.

Review Exercise 1-1

When you woke up in the early morning of January 1, 2018, the opening balances in your personal accounting records appeared as follows.

Cash	$3,000
Contents of Home	3,000
House	100,000
Mortgage	70,000
Net Worth	36,000

The following transactions occurred during the month of January.

1. Earned and deposited $2,000 from salary
2. Earned and deposited $300 from providing tutoring services
3. Paid $300 cash for food
4. Went out for dinner and a show and spent $200 cash
5. Purchased new clothes with $100 cash
6. Paid $500 cash for maintenance on the house
7. Paid $100 cash for utilities
8. Deposited lottery winnings of $600
9. Received a cash gift of $150

Complete the T-account worksheet for the January transactions and calculate ending net worth.

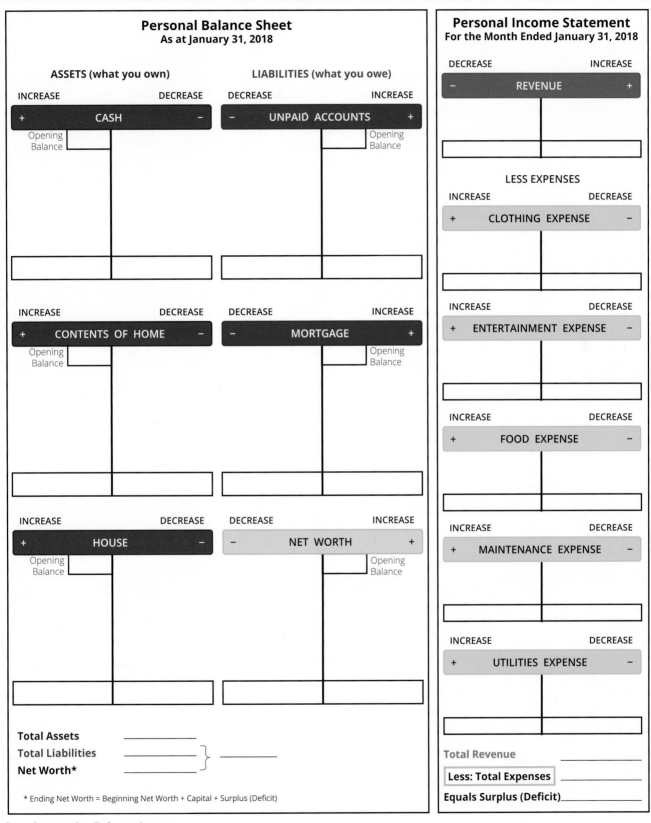

Personal Balance Sheet
As at January 31, 2018

ASSETS (what you own)

INCREASE   DECREASE

+   CASH   −

Opening Balance

INCREASE   DECREASE

+   CONTENTS OF HOME   −

Opening Balance

INCREASE   DECREASE

+   HOUSE   −

Opening Balance

LIABILITIES (what you owe)

DECREASE   INCREASE

−   UNPAID ACCOUNTS   +

Opening Balance

DECREASE   INCREASE

−   MORTGAGE   +

Opening Balance

DECREASE   INCREASE

−   NET WORTH   +

Opening Balance

Total Assets   _____

Total Liabilities   _____ } _____

Net Worth*   _____

* Ending Net Worth = Beginning Net Worth + Capital + Surplus (Deficit)

Personal Income Statement
For the Month Ended January 31, 2018

DECREASE   INCREASE

−   REVENUE   +

LESS EXPENSES

INCREASE   DECREASE

+   CLOTHING EXPENSE   −

INCREASE   DECREASE

+   ENTERTAINMENT EXPENSE   −

INCREASE   DECREASE

+   FOOD EXPENSE   −

INCREASE   DECREASE

+   MAINTENANCE EXPENSE   −

INCREASE   DECREASE

+   UTILITIES EXPENSE   −

Total Revenue   _____

Less: Total Expenses   _____

Equals Surplus (Deficit) _____

See Appendix I for solutions.

Notes

Chapter 2
Linking Personal Accounting To Business Accounting

Learning Objectives

 1 **List the differences between personal accounts and business accounts**

- Equity vs. Net Worth

LO 2 **Describe the three main types of businesses**

- Service Business
- Merchandising Business
- Manufacturing Business

LO 3 **Record revenue based on the concept of accruals**

- Cash Received Before the Service is Performed
- Cash Received When the Service is Performed
- Cash Received After the Service is Performed

LO 4 **Record expenses based on the concept of accruals**

- Cash Paid Before the Expense is Incurred

- Cash Paid When the Expense is Incurred
- Cash Paid After the Expense is Incurred

LO 5 **Record business transactions in T-accounts**

LO 6 **Identify the four required financial statements and prepare three financial statements**

- Income Statement
- Statement of Owner's Equity
- Balance Sheet
- Statement of Cash Flows

LO 7 **Describe ethics relating to financial statement reporting**

- Fraud Triangle

AMEENGAGE™ *Access **ameengage.com** for integrated resources including tutorials, practice exercises, the digital textbook and more.*

29

Business Accounts

Most of what you have learned about accounting in the personal context is similar to accounting in a business context. However, business accounting is more complex than personal accounting. To begin examining the differences, we will look at how terminology differs in business accounting.

1. The personal balance sheet and the personal income statement are called the balance sheet and the income statement, respectively.

2. Cash in a business is like cash in personal accounting. However, businesses may have several different bank accounts and all of these amounts are included in cash.

3. Accounts receivable is a new business asset account. This is used when the business sells services or products to a customer and allows the customer to pay later. **Accounts receivable** is the amount owed to the business by its customers.

4. Merchandise inventory is an asset account used when a business sells products to customers. This account is discussed in detail in later chapters.

5. Equipment, buildings, land and other similar assets that provide the business with benefits for a long period of time are called **property, plant and equipment** or noncurrent assets. These items are not intended to be sold to customers.

6. Unpaid accounts in the personal context are called accounts payable in a business. **Accounts payable** is the obligation the business owes to others.

7. **Unearned revenue** is an obligation the business has to provide products or services to a customer. It is used when a customer prepays the business for products or services.

8. Just as a person may have loans or mortgages, a business may also have long-term debt. Notes payable is a business liability account used when a business signs a written document, such as a bank loan agreement, to borrow money. This account is discussed in detail in later chapters.

9. The category of net worth is referred to as **equity**. The equity may belong to the business owner, the partners, or stockholders, depending on the organization of the business. Business organization is discussed later.

10. Revenue is called either service revenue or sales revenue. If a business provides services to its customers, it uses **service revenue**, a broad term to include various types of revenue, such as interest or fees earned. If it sells products to its customers, it uses **sales revenue**. Some businesses provide both and use both accounts on the income statement.

11. Although there are some similarities in the expense items on the income statement, a business usually has more types of expenses. We will discuss these new expenses as they appear in the textbook. A business typically lists its expenses on the income statement in alphabetical order.

12. Surplus (deficit) on the personal income statement is now called net income (loss). **Net income** occurs when revenue exceeds expenses for the period, which causes equity to increase. A **net loss** occurs when expenses exceed revenue for the period, which causes equity to decrease.

Figure 2.1 shows the comparison between the personal balance sheet and the business balance sheet, and between the personal income statement and the business income statement.

PERSONAL		BUSINESS		PERSONAL		BUSINESS	
PERSONAL BALANCE SHEET		BALANCE SHEET		PERSONAL INCOME STATEMENT		INCOME STATEMENT	
ASSETS	LIABILITIES	ASSETS	LIABILITIES	REVENUE		SERVICE REVENUE	
CASH	UNPAID ACCOUNTS	CASH	ACCOUNTS PAYABLE	EXPENSES		EXPENSES	
PREPAID EXPENSES	MORTGAGE	ACCOUNTS RECEIVABLE	UNEARNED REVENUE	ENTERTAINMENT	INTEREST	DEPRECIATION	RENT
CONTENTS OF HOME	LOANS	MERCHANDISE INVENTORY	NOTES PAYABLE	FOOD	MAINTENANCE	INSURANCE	SUPPLIES
AUTOMOBILE	NET WORTH	PREPAID EXPENSES	EQUITY	INSURANCE	UTILITIES	INTEREST	UTILITIES
HOUSE		PROPERTY, PLANT & EQUIPMENT		SURPLUS (DEFICIT)		NET INCOME (LOSS)	

FIGURE 2.1

Equity vs. Net Worth

Equity is the net worth of a business. Similar to net worth introduced in personal accounting, a business' equity is the leftover value after all assets have been sold and all liabilities have been paid.

WORTH REPEATING

The accounting equation is
Assets = Liabilities + Owner's Equity

There are a few different forms of organizations, and equity has different names based on which form an organization takes. You will learn about different forms of organizations and different names of equity in Chapter 3. In this chapter, we will focus on the sole proprietorship form of business, which is a business owned by a single person. The term "owner's equity" is used to describe the equity of the business. At the end of the accounting period, the ending owner's equity balance can be calculated as shown in Figure 2.2.

Ending Owner's Equity = Beginning Owner's Equity + Owner's Contributions
+ Net Income (Loss) – Owner's Withdrawals

FIGURE 2.2

Owner's contributions is the amount of cash or assets invested in the business by the owner. **Owner's withdrawals** is the amount of cash or assets taken by the owner for personal use. If a company is brand new and has just started operations, then beginning owner's equity will be $0. If a company has been established for at least one accounting period, then the beginning owner's equity is equal to the previous period's ending owner's equity.

In business accounting, owner's equity is a category on the balance sheet but not an account. Separate accounts are required to record transactions such as owner's contributions and owner's withdrawals.

The **owner's capital account** is used to record the amount of the owner's equity including owner's contributions. Owner's contributions are added directly into owner's capital. The owner can also withdraw cash from the business to pay for personal items. These withdrawals are recorded in the **owner's withdrawals account** (or owner's drawings account) and decrease the business' assets and the value of owner's equity. Owner's withdrawals are never an expense and so the account is not included on the income statement. Although a part of equity, it also does not appear on the balance sheet. Instead, it is included on a separate statement, which is introduced later in the chapter.

In the personal T-account worksheet from Chapter 1, we used a single T-account to track the net worth transactions of an individual. In the context of a business, this single T-account is now represented by owner's capital. A separate T-account is used for owner's withdrawals to track the amount removed from the business for personal use. The two T-accounts in Figure 2.3 are the generic capital and withdrawals accounts. In an actual sole proprietary business, these accounts typically have the owner's name attached to them. For example, if John Smith was the owner, the accounts are called "Smith, Capital" and "Smith, Withdrawals."

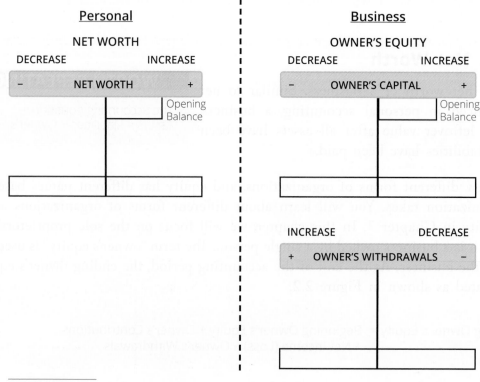

FIGURE 2.3

The T-account increase and decrease map introduced in Chapter 1 needs to be modified to accommodate the new T-accounts that make up owner's equity: capital and withdrawals. Figure 2.4 shows the new T-account map that will be followed throughout the chapter. Notice that owner's withdrawals increases on the left side of the T-account, like an expense, and owner's capital increases on the right side of the T-account, like revenue.

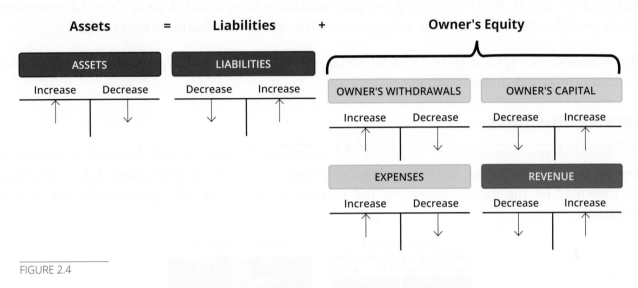

FIGURE 2.4

Figure 2.5 illustrates how T-account entries relate to the owner's capital and owner's withdrawals. Suppose that the owner of a new company invested $10,000 in cash into the company (transaction 1). This increases owner's capital and increases cash. Because this is a newly formed company, all opening account balances are $0.

Also, suppose that the owner withdrew $1,000 from the company for personal use (transaction 2). In this transaction, the capital of the business is distributed to the owner for personal use and not for generating revenue; therefore, owner's withdrawal is different from incurring expenses. It is the reverse of what happens when the owner invests some assets into the business. This transaction decreases cash and increases owner's withdrawals:

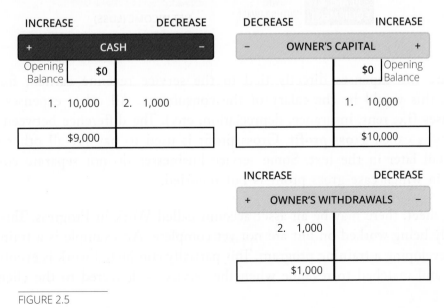

FIGURE 2.5

Financial Statements of Different Types of Businesses   LO 2

Different types of businesses use different financial statement layouts: a small consulting firm uses a very simple income statement and balance sheet compared to a complex manufacturing company that produces goods. A manufacturing company requires a more detailed set of financial statements, which provides the information a manager needs to operate the business effectively.

The following examples display financial statements for three main types of businesses: service, merchandising, and manufacturing.

Service Business

The financial statements shown in Figure 2.6 represent a simple service business. Examples of services include accounting, consulting, lawn maintenance or general contracting. A few new items are presented on the income statement and balance sheet: cost of sales, gross profit and work in progress.

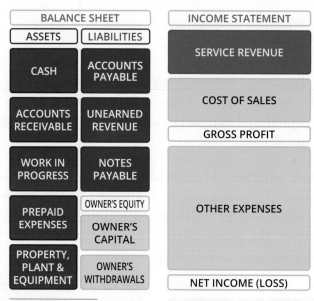

FIGURE 2.6

Cost of sales are the expenses directly tied to the service revenue earned; for example, in a consulting firm, this would be the salary of the consultants. All other expenses are part of the operating expenses (i.e. rent, insurance, depreciation, etc.). The difference between service revenue and cost of sales is called **gross profit**. Gross profit is used to pay for all other expenses and is discussed in detail later in the text. Some service businesses do not separate cost of sales from other expenses, in which case gross profit is not reported.

On the balance sheet, there may be an asset account called Work in Progress. This represents jobs that are currently being worked on but are not yet complete. An example is a training company in the middle of developing a training program. This partially completed work is eventually recognized as cost of sales and matched to revenue when the service is delivered to the client.

Merchandising Business

The financial statements shown in Figure 2.7 represent a merchandising business. Any company that buys goods to resell to customers is considered a merchandising business. A common example is a retail store, such as a hardware, clothing, toy or convenience store.

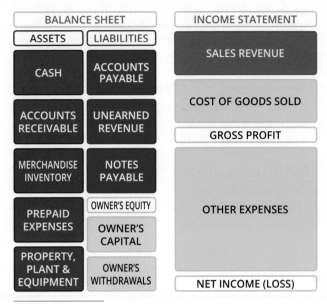

FIGURE 2.7

On the balance sheet, there is a new asset account called Merchandise Inventory. This account tracks the value of all the goods the store has purchased and intends to sell to its customers. Once these items are sold, the value of the inventory is transferred to cost of goods sold on the income statement. **Cost of goods sold (COGS)** is the value of all the goods sold and is subtracted from sales revenue to determine gross profit. Merchandise inventory and COGS are covered in later chapters.

Manufacturing Business

The financial statements of a manufacturing company are shown in Figure 2.8. A manufacturing company makes the products that it sells. Examples of manufacturers include auto makers, steel mills and furniture makers.

The balance sheet has an asset account called Inventory, similar to a retail store. However, a manufacturer has different types of inventory at various stages of production. Raw materials represent items that will be transformed into the product that can be sold (e.g. lumber used to make furniture). Work in progress represents partially completed products, and finished goods represent

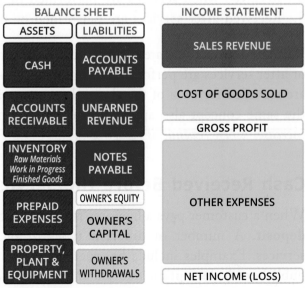

FIGURE 2.8

products that can be sold to customers. Once the items are sold, they are recorded in COGS.

IN THE REAL WORLD

It is simple to grasp the nature of a particular business by labeling it as either a service, merchandising or manufacturing business. However, some companies operate as a combination of two or more of these types of businesses.

Consider Apple Inc., which is a well-known manufacturer of breakthrough technology, such as the Macintosh operating system, iPod, iPhone and iPad. The company also has a merchandising segment; it operates online and retail stores. These stores sell Apple manufactured products, as well as complementary products from other manufacturers, such as security software and computer speakers.

Apple is also a service business because it provides online support as well as warranty and repair services for its products. It also provides online services such as iCloud, a cloud storage and computing service that allows users to store personal data on remote servers, synchronize data, back up key files and so on.

Therefore, Apple is a hybrid of a service, merchandising and manufacturing business. However, it is reasonable to deem the company as primarily a manufacturing business since sales of its own products represent the majority of its total revenue.

Recording Revenue

In business accounting, as in personal accounting, accrual-based accounting is used to record transactions. Revenues are recorded or recognized when they are earned regardless of when cash is received from customers. Cash payment for products or services can be received from customers at three different times.

1. Received before services are performed or products are sold
2. Received when services are performed or products are sold
3. Received after services are performed or products are sold

Revenue transactions are recorded differently depending on whether cash is received before, when, or after services are performed or products are sold. This section illustrates how revenue transactions are recorded for each of the above three scenarios. While a service business is used in our examples, the same concept also applies to merchandising and manufacturing businesses. In all cases, *equity increases when revenue is recognized*.

Cash Received Before the Service is Performed

When a customer pays a business for services before they are performed, it is known as a **customer deposit**. A number of different types of businesses require deposits or prepayments for their services. Examples include banquet halls (hall rental fees), health clubs (memberships), magazine publishers (subscription dues) and insurance companies (insurance premiums). In each case, the business receives cash up front and provides a service at a later date.

Since services have not been performed at the time the cash is received, service revenue cannot be recognized at this time. Instead, the business has an obligation to provide services in the future. You will recall that an obligation of a business is a liability. Thus, a new liability account known as Unearned Revenue must be used.

Suppose a business receives a deposit of $1,100 from a customer one month before services must be provided. Figure 2.9 illustrates the impact on the business accounts at the time the customer paid for the services. The prepayment by the customer is a liability for the business (unearned revenue) because the business now has an obligation to provide services to the customer. The payment is essentially held in trust on behalf of the customer. In this scenario, both cash and unearned revenue are increased by $1,100, meaning that assets and liabilities are both increased by the same amount. At this point, there is no impact on equity because even though cash is received, revenue is not recognized since no work has been completed. If the business fails to provide the services, they must return the deposit to the customer.

It is only when work is completed in the next month that revenue can be recognized. The transaction to record this is covered in a later chapter.

FIGURE 2.9

Cash Received When the Service is Performed

When a company performs a service and the customer pays for it immediately, the transaction is fairly straightforward. From the service provider's perspective, cash increases and equity increases. The increase in equity is recognized as revenue and increases net income.

In this example, a client purchases a service from a business for $1,100. If the client pays cash immediately when the business provides the service, then cash and service revenue are both increased by $1,100. Owner's equity increases by $1,100 as a result of the increase in service revenue. The impact on cash and service revenue is shown in Figure 2.10. Remember that recognizing revenue results in an increase to equity.

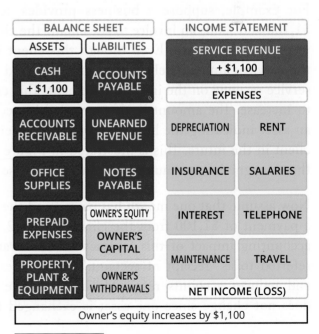

FIGURE 2.10

Cash Received After the Service is Performed

Most businesses provide customers with payment terms, allowing them to pay after they have received the product or service (e.g. 30 days to pay the balance owing). This is sometimes referred to as "selling on account." It may seem that the value of equity would not change when selling with payment terms because cash has not been received from the sale. However, revenue must be recorded at the time the product is sold or the service is delivered, regardless of when the payment is received.

When a company provides payment terms to sell its products or services, the money owed by its customers is recorded as an asset, called Accounts Receivable. After a service is provided, the seller issues an invoice to the buyer. The **invoice** includes the details of the service rendered, the amount owing, and the terms of payment. From the seller's perspective, this is an increase in accounts receivable (an asset) and an increase in equity (recognized as revenue). Later, when the customer actually pays the outstanding amount, the issuing company increases cash and decreases accounts receivable. The decrease in accounts receivable shows that the service provider received cash and is no longer owed any amount from the customer (i.e. nothing is "receivable").

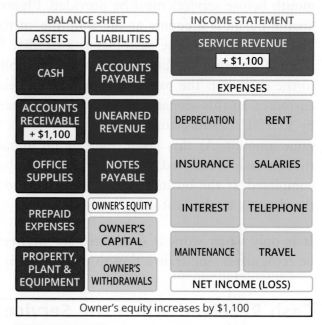

FIGURE 2.11

For example, suppose a business provides services valued at $1,100 and sends an invoice to the client. The client has promised to pay in one month. Even though this client is not paying for the services immediately, equity increases and is recognized as service revenue on the income statement. This causes net income to increase. The amount is also recorded in accounts receivable, an asset indicating the business expects to receive cash from the client in the future. This is illustrated in Figure 2.11. Remember that recognizing revenue results in an increase to equity.

Now assume that one month has passed and the business receives a payment of $1,100 from the client. Figure 2.12 illustrates the accounting impact of this transaction. This transaction is often referred to as "receipt of account." It increases cash by $1,100 and reduces accounts receivable by the same amount. Equity does not change since one asset is exchanged for another.

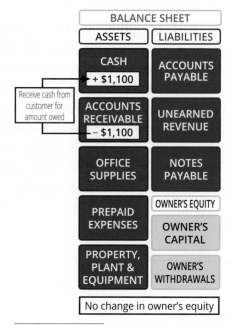

FIGURE 2.12

Pause & Reflect

Exercise 2-1

Felix Graham owns and operates a photography business called Eternity Photography, which is a sole proprietorship. The following transactions occurred this month.

1. A customer paid $3,000 owed for the photographs that Felix had already provided last month.
2. Eternity Photography received $4,000 from a couple immediately after the wedding had been photographed.
3. A customer paid a $1,000 deposit for Eternity Photography to photograph her wedding next year.

For each transaction, indicate which two accounts are affected and the category of each account (asset, liability, owner's capital, owner's withdrawal, revenue or expense). In the final column, indicate whether the account balance would increase or decrease as a result of each transaction.

Fill in your answers in Table 1. The first transaction has been completed as an example.

Table 1

	Name of the Account Affected	Category of Account	Increase or Decrease
1.	Cash	Asset	Increase
	Accounts Receivable	Asset	Decrease
2.			
3.			

See Appendix I for solutions.

Recording Expenses

LO 4

Expenses, similar to revenues, are recorded when they are incurred, not necessarily when they are paid.

An expense is incurred by a company if the activities related to the expense have been used or consumed. You may also see the term "recognized" when it comes to expenses and revenue. **Recognizing** an expense or revenue means recording it on the income statement. For example, if a company has hired a lawn care service company to water the grass on August 16, the expense is incurred once the grass has been watered; the expense is recognized at that time. If a company pays for internet services, the internet expense for a given month is incurred once that month has ended. In all cases, *equity decreases when an expense is recognized.*

There are three different timings of the cash payments for expenses.

1. Pay before the expense is incurred
2. Pay when the expense is incurred
3. Pay after the expense is incurred

This section illustrates how expense transactions are recorded for each of the above three scenarios.

Cash Paid Before the Expense is Incurred

When a company pays before the expense has been incurred, it is a supplier prepayment. This requires increasing an asset account called Prepaid Expense, which was discussed in the context of personal accounting. These prepayments are not considered an expense at the time they are paid because the service or the product has not been used. Some common examples of prepaid expenses are rent and office supplies.

Another example is purchasing an insurance policy. Assume, a business paid cash ahead of time to an insurance company for one year of insurance coverage. At the time of the payment, cash decreases and a prepaid expense called prepaid insurance increases. This prepaid expense is considered an asset because it could be turned back into cash if the entire year of insurance is not used up (e.g. the policy is canceled).

The business paid $3,600 on January 1, 2018 for insurance coverage throughout 2018. On January 1, 2018, when the payment is made, the business' cash (an asset) decreases by $3,600 and prepaid insurance (another asset) increases by $3,600. At this point, equity is not affected. One asset was exchanged for another asset. This is shown in Figure 2.13.

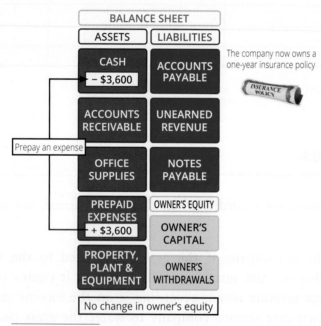

FIGURE 2.13

Notice that expenses, and thus equity, have not been affected yet. Only as the asset is used up is the expense recorded. If the insurance company fails to provide the services, or the business cancels the policy, the insurance company has to return cash to the business for the unused portion of the policy. In this example, a portion of the prepaid insurance becomes an expense as each month passes. The details for this transaction are covered in a later chapter.

Cash Paid When the Expense is Incurred

When a company incurs an expense and pays for it immediately, the transaction is fairly straightforward. From the company's perspective, cash decreases and equity decreases. The decrease in equity is recorded as an expense on the income statement, which reduces net income. Suppose a business paid $800 cash for a salesperson to travel to a client's head office. Figure 2.14 illustrates the accounting treatment when paying immediately in cash for travel expenses. Remember that recognizing an expense results in a decrease to equity. This transaction reduces cash by $800 and increases travel expense by the same amount. The $800 increase in expenses decreases equity by $800.

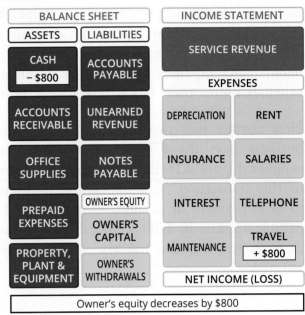

FIGURE 2.14

Cash Paid After the Expense is Incurred

Many expenses are paid after they have been incurred. This form of paying expenses is sometimes referred to as "paying on account" or "on credit." You may think that the value of equity would not change until the expense is paid for. However, accounting standards require expenses to be recorded at the time they are incurred, *regardless of when the payment is made.*

A business that provides products or services to another business is known as a supplier. When a company owes a supplier for a product or service, the money owed is recorded as a liability called Accounts Payable. When an invoice is issued to the company by the supplier (after the expense has been incurred), the value of the invoice is recorded as an increase to the accounts payable account and an increase to the appropriate expense account. Later, when the company actually pays the outstanding amount, the transaction is recorded as a decrease to cash and a decrease to accounts payable. The company used cash to pay and it no longer owes any amount to the supplier (i.e. nothing is "payable").

Suppose a business will pay for a maintenance expense two months after it has been incurred. Even though the business is not paying for the services immediately, the supplier issues an invoice as soon as the maintenance work is done. Assume that the supplier is charging $700 for its maintenance services. Figure 2.15 shows the impact on the

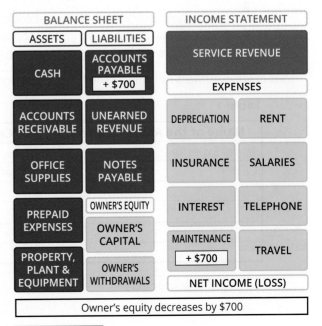

FIGURE 2.15

applicable accounts of the business when the invoice is received from the supplier. Remember that recognizing an expense results in a decrease to equity. This transaction increases both accounts payable and maintenance expenses by $700. The $700 increase in expenses means there is a $700 decrease in equity.

Now assume that two months have passed and the business pays the $700 owed to the maintenance supplier. Figure 2.16 illustrates the accounting impact of this transaction. This transaction is often referred to as a "payment of account." Both cash and accounts payable decrease by $700. Equity does not change. Only an asset (cash) and a liability (accounts payable) are affected.

FIGURE 2.16

Pause & Reflect

Exercise 2-2

Eternity Photography had the following transactions occur during the current month.

1. Eternity Photography paid $50 cash for gas to travel to a client's wedding venue.

2. Eternity Photography received a telephone bill for $120, which will be paid next month.

3. Eternity Photography purchased a one-year insurance policy for $1,400 cash, to insure its photography equipment.

For each transaction, indicate which two accounts are affected and the category of the account (asset, liability, owner's capital, owner's withdrawal, revenue or expense). In the final column, indicate whether the account balance would increase or decrease as a result of the transaction.

Fill in your answers in Table 1. The first transaction has been completed as an example.

Table 1

	Name of the Account Affected	Category of Account	Increase or Decrease
1.	Travel Expense	Expense	Increase
	Cash	Asset	Decrease
2.			
3.			

See Appendix I for solutions.

Business Transactions

The ultimate goal of recording business transactions is to be able to create financial statements and assess how well the business is performing. A transaction occurs when the business trades something of value with another person or business and this causes a change in assets, liabilities or equity. This could include services, products, cash, a promise to pay money or the right to collect money.

However, not everything the business does will be recorded in the T-accounts and appear on the financial statements. An **event** does not involve trading something of value. Since assets, liabilities and equity are not affected by an event, nothing is recorded in the T-accounts. An event can lead to a transaction at a later date, but it is only then that the transaction is recorded in the T-accounts. For example, signing a contract with a customer to provide service in two months' time is an event. At the signing, nothing of value has been traded; therefore, nothing is recorded in the T-accounts. However, two months later after the services have been provided, a transaction has occurred and is recorded in the T-accounts.

The following pages examine several business transactions made by Ace Bookkeepers, a sole proprietorship owned by John Smith, during the month of March 2018. For each transaction that follows, we will show how it is recorded in the T-accounts, how the accounting equation remains in balance, and explain any impact on owner's equity. Keep in mind that every transaction must leave the accounting equation in balance, so every transaction must be recorded in at least two accounts.

1. The owner deposited $30,000 cash into the new business' bank account

When an owner invests his or her own cash into a sole proprietorship, the cash is recorded directly in the owner's capital and regarded as owner's equity. This transaction increases cash by $30,000 (impacting the left side of its T-account), and increases owner's capital by $30,000 (impacting the right side of its T-account). An increase in cash increases assets and an increase in the capital increases owner's equity, balancing the accounting equation, as shown in Figure 2.17.

Record the transaction in the T-accounts

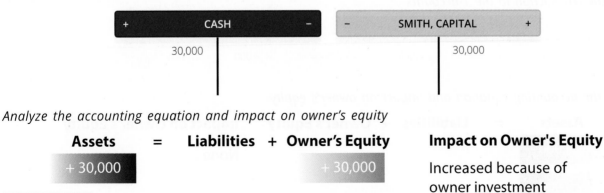

FIGURE 2.17

2. Ace Bookkeepers borrowed $10,000 from the bank

The business has increased its debt by getting a loan from the bank. As shown in Figure 2.18, this transaction increases cash by $10,000 (impacting the left side of its T-account), and increases the value of notes payable by $10,000 (impacting the right side of its T-account). An increase in cash increases assets and the receipt of the bank loan increases liabilities. The transaction has no impact on owner's equity; therefore nothing is recorded on the income statement. The accounting equation is balanced.

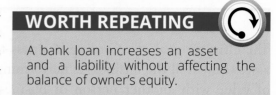

WORTH REPEATING

A bank loan increases an asset and a liability without affecting the balance of owner's equity.

Record the transaction in the T-accounts

+	CASH	−		−	NOTES PAYABLE	+
10,000						10,000

Analyze the accounting equation and impact on owner's equity

Assets	**=**	**Liabilities**	**+ Owner's Equity**	**Impact on Owner's Equity**
+ 10,000		+ 10,000		None

FIGURE 2.18

3. Ace Bookkeepers bought $8,000 worth of furniture with cash

Furniture, computers, cars and other similar items are considered to be property, plant and equipment and are noncurrent assets. These assets are used to run the business and generate sales and should not be sold to customers or to raise cash for day-to-day expenses. Each type of property, plant and equipment is given its own T-account. Cash payment for furniture means that cash is decreased by $8,000 (impacting the right side of its T-account) and furniture is increased by $8,000 (impacting the left side of its T-account). This transaction is simply an exchange of one asset for another with no impact on the owner's equity, as shown in Figure 2.19.

Record the transaction in the T-accounts

+	CASH	−		+	FURNITURE	−
		8,000		8,000		

Analyze the accounting equation and impact on owner's equity

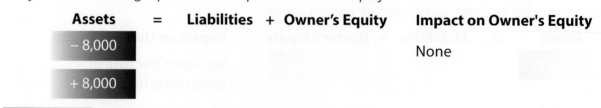

Assets	**=**	**Liabilities**	**+ Owner's Equity**	**Impact on Owner's Equity**
− 8,000				None
+ 8,000				

FIGURE 2.19

4. A customer paid $2,000 cash for bookkeeping services to be provided next month

One way to receive payment for services is for the customer to pay before the services are performed. In this case, when the customer pays cash, the services will not be provided until next month. This means that service revenue cannot be recognized when cash is received. Ace Bookkeepers has accepted an obligation to provide services in one month. An obligation is a liability, meaning the amount received is recorded as an increase to cash and an increase to a liability account called unearned revenue. Unearned revenue represents the obligation the business has to provide services or products to customers in the future. If services are not performed by the business, the cash must be returned to the customer.

In this transaction, cash is increased by $2,000 (impacting the left side of its T-account) and unearned revenue is increased by $2,000 (impacting the right side of its T-account). The transaction is illustrated in Figure 2.20. An increase in cash increases assets and an increase in unearned revenue increases liabilities, balancing the accounting equation. At this time, there is no impact on owner's equity as revenue has not been earned. The transaction to turn this liability into revenue is covered in a later chapter.

Record the transaction in the T-accounts

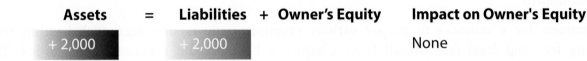

Analyze the accounting equation and impact on owner's equity

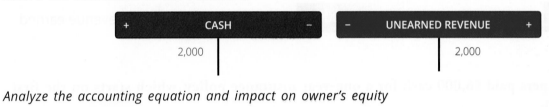

Assets	=	Liabilities	+	Owner's Equity	Impact on Owner's Equity
+ 2,000		+ 2,000			None

FIGURE 2.20

5. Ace Bookkeepers provided services to customers and received $15,000 cash

The sale of services is called revenue and is the primary way a service business increases owner's equity. As shown in Figure 2.21, this transaction is recorded by increasing cash by $15,000 (impacting the left side of its T-account), and increasing service revenue by $15,000 (impacting the right side of its T-account). An increase in cash increases assets and an increase in service revenue increases owner's equity. The accounting equation is balanced.

Record the transaction in the T-accounts

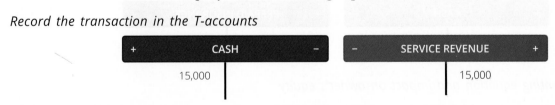

Analyze the accounting equation and impact on owner's equity

Assets	=	Liabilities	+	Owner's Equity	Impact on Owner's Equity
+ 15,000				+ 15,000	Increased because of revenue earned

FIGURE 2.21

6. Ace Bookkeepers provided services for $4,000 on account

Another way to receive payment for services provided is to allow a customer to pay at a later date. Services have been provided, so revenue must be recognized. However, cash is not affected since there has been no payment. Instead, another asset called accounts receivable increases. Recall that accounts receivable is the amount owing to the business from its customers. Since accounts receivable will eventually be collected and become cash, it is regarded as an asset. In this transaction, as shown in Figure 2.22, accounts receivable is increased by $4,000 (impacting the left side of its T-account) and service revenue is increased by $4,000 (impacting the right side of its T-account). The increase in service revenue is also an increase in owner's equity. The accounting equation is balanced.

Record the transaction in the T-accounts

Analyze the accounting equation and impact on owner's equity

FIGURE 2.22

7. Ace Bookkeepers paid $6,000 cash for a one-year insurance policy, which starts on the first of next month

It is common for a business to prepay various expenses such as insurance, web-hosting fees, consulting fees and legal fees. Recall from Chapter 1 how prepaid expenses are recorded. The same concept is practiced in business. The item that is prepaid is initially recorded as an asset on the balance sheet. In this transaction, cash is decreased by $6,000 (impacting the right side of its T-account) and prepaid insurance is increased by $6,000 (impacting the left side of its T-account). Figure 2.23 shows how the prepayment for insurance is recorded by decreasing one type of asset (cash) and increasing another type of asset (prepaid insurance) with no impact on the owner's equity. The accounting equation is balanced. The transaction to convert prepaid insurance (an asset) to an expense is covered in a later chapter.

Record the transaction in the T-accounts

Analyze the accounting equation and impact on owner's equity

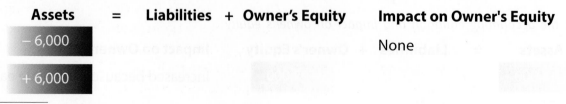

FIGURE 2.23

8. Ace Bookkeepers paid $1,100 cash for rent for the month

9. Ace Bookkeepers paid $6,000 cash to employees for salaries

10. Ace Bookkeepers paid $200 cash for interest on the note payable

All of these transactions relate to cash expenses. As illustrated in Figure 2.24, the transactions are recorded by decreasing the value of the cash account and increasing the value of the appropriate expense accounts. In these transactions, cash is decreased by a total of $7,300 (impacting the right side of its T-account) and the appropriate expense accounts are increased by a total of $7,300 (impacting the left side of their T-accounts). These expenses were incurred by the business in order to run the business and help generate revenue. Remember, the equity in the business decreases and is recorded as an increase to expenses while assets are reduced as cash decreases. The accounting equation is balanced.

Record the transactions in the T-accounts

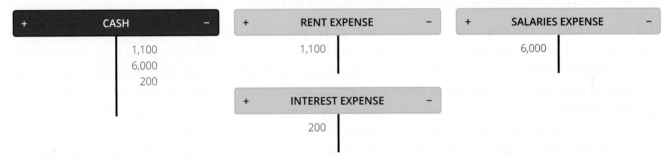

Analyze the accounting equation and impact on owner's equity

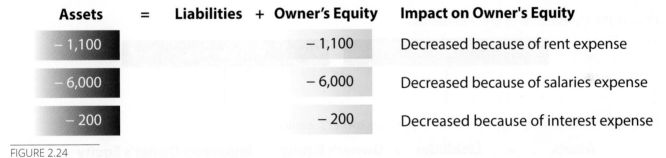

FIGURE 2.24

11. Ace Bookkeepers received a telephone bill for $300, which will be paid later

12. Ace Bookkeepers paid travel expenses of $2,000 with a credit card, which will be paid next month

The telephone expense is due to be paid next month and travel expenses were billed to a credit card that is also to be paid next month. These expenses must be recorded this month because they were incurred and used to generate sales this month; expenses incurred are matched to revenue earned in the same period. In these transactions, accounts payable is increased by $2,300 (impacting the right side of its T-account) and the appropriate expense accounts are increased by a total of $2,300 (impacting the left side of their T-accounts). This transaction is recorded by increasing both liabilities and the appropriate expense accounts, as illustrated in Figure 2.25. The equity in the business decreases and is recorded as an increase to expenses. The accounting equation is balanced.

Record the transactions in the T-accounts

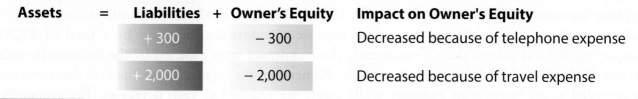

Analyze the accounting equation and impact on owner's equity

Assets	=	Liabilities	+	Owner's Equity	Impact on Owner's Equity
		+ 300		– 300	Decreased because of telephone expense
		+ 2,000		– 2,000	Decreased because of travel expense

FIGURE 2.25

13. Ace Bookkeeping repaid $3,000 toward the note payable

This transaction is the opposite of transaction 2. To pay back part of the note payable principal, cash (an asset) and notes payable (a liability) are both decreased, with no impact on the owner's equity. As illustrated in Figure 2.26, cash is decreased by $3,000 (impacting the right side of its T-account) and the notes payable is decreased by $3,000 (impacting the left side of its T-account). The accounting equation is balanced. Repaying any debt, including accounts payable, is recorded in a similar manner. It is important to be able to pay back loans when they are due. Failure to pay loans on time is called defaulting on the loan and can make it more difficult to borrow in the future. In some cases, defaulting may also cause the business to close down.

Record the transaction in the T-accounts

Analyze the accounting equation and impact on owner's equity

Assets	=	Liabilities	+	Owner's Equity	Impact on Owner's Equity
– 3,000		– 3,000			None

FIGURE 2.26

14. The owner withdrew $2,000 cash for personal use

In a sole proprietorship, the owner is not an employee and does not receive a salary the way that other employees do. Instead, the owner can be compensated in the form of cash withdrawal from the business. As discussed earlier, owner's withdrawals are a direct decrease to owner's equity and are not recorded as expenses. This transaction is recorded by decreasing cash by $2,000 (impacting the right side of its T-account) and increasing owner's withdrawals by $2,000 (impacting the left side of its T-account), as shown in Figure 2.27. The decrease in equity is recorded as an increase to owner's withdrawals and a decrease in cash reduces assets. The accounting equation is balanced.

Record the transaction in the T-accounts

Analyze the accounting equation and impact on owner's equity

Assets	**=**	**Liabilities**	**+ Owner's Equity**	**Impact on Owner's Equity**
− 2,000			− 2,000	Decreased because the owner withdrew cash

FIGURE 2.27

15. A customer paid $500 cash for the amount owing for services provided earlier in the month

In transaction 6, Ace Bookkeepers provided services to a customer and allowed them to pay later. Cash only increases when payment is received. Since amounts owed by customers are recorded in the asset account called accounts receivable, this account decreases when a customer pays the bill. In this transaction, cash is increased by $500 (impacting the left side of its T-account) and accounts receivable is decreased by $500 (impacting the right side of its T-account). An increase in cash increases assets, while a decrease in accounts receivable decreases assets. Notice that service revenue is not affected by this transaction, so owner's equity is not impacted. Service revenue increased in transaction 6 when the service was performed. This transaction is just an exchange of one asset for another, as shown in Figure 2.28. The accounting equation is balanced.

Record the transaction in the T-accounts

Analyze the accounting equation and impact on owner's equity

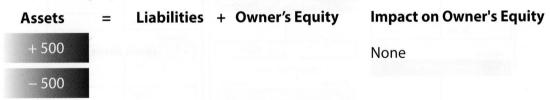

Assets	**=**	**Liabilities**	**+ Owner's Equity**	**Impact on Owner's Equity**
+ 500				None
− 500				

FIGURE 2.28

16. Ace Bookkeepers paid the telephone bill received earlier in the month

In transaction 11, a telephone bill was received but not paid immediately. Cash only decreases when the payment is made. Recall that amounts owed to suppliers are recorded in the liability account called accounts payable. Thus, when Ace Bookkeepers pays the bill, accounts payable decreases. In this transaction, cash decreases by $300 (impacting the right side of its T-account) and accounts payable decreases by $300 (impacting the left side of its T-account). A decrease in cash decreases assets, while a decrease in accounts payable decreases liabilities. Notice that telephone expense is not affected by this transaction. Telephone expense increased in transaction 11 when the bill was received. This transaction is just paying off debt, as shown in Figure 2.29. The accounting equation is balanced.

Record the transaction in the T-accounts

+	CASH	−		−	ACCOUNTS PAYABLE	+
		300				300

Analyze the accounting equation and impact on owner's equity

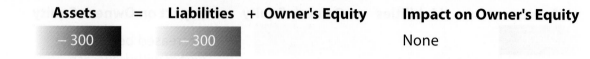

Assets	**=**	**Liabilities**	**+ Owner's Equity**	**Impact on Owner's Equity**
− 300		− 300		None

FIGURE 2.29

All the transactions have been compiled in the T-account worksheet shown in Figure 2.30. Notice that the net income from the income statement is calculated first so it can be added to owner's equity. The owner's equity calculation is at the bottom of the balance sheet and shows an ending balance of $37,400. This calculation is discussed in more detail in the next section.

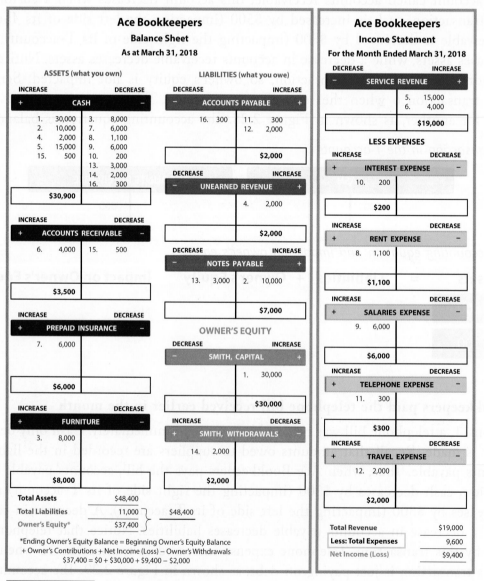

FIGURE 2.30

Pause & Reflect

Exercise 2-3

The following transactions occurred this month at Eternity Photography.

1. Eternity Photography paid last month's telephone bill of $140.
2. Felix Graham deposited an additional $50,000 cash into the business' bank account.
3. Furniture that cost $6,000 was purchased using the business' credit card, which will be paid later.
4. Eternity Photography borrowed $20,000 cash from the bank.
5. Felix Graham withdrew $8,000 cash for personal use.

For each transaction, indicate which two accounts are affected and the category of the account (asset, liability, owner's capital, owner's withdrawal, revenue or expense). In the last column, indicate whether the account balance would increase or decrease as a result of the transaction.

Fill in your answers in Table 1. The first transaction has been completed as an example.

Table 1

	Name of the Account Affected	Category of Account	Increase or Decrease
1.	Cash	Asset	Decrease
	Accounts Payale	Liability	Decrease
2.			
3.			
4.			
5.			

See Appendix I for solutions.

Financial Statements

Now that the T-account worksheet for Ace Bookkeepers is complete, we can prepare formal financial statements. All financial statements follow certain formatting standards when being created.

- Each statement has three lines at the top to identify the company (e.g. Ace Bookkeepers), the type of financial statement (e.g. Income Statement) and the time period or date the statement covers (e.g. For the Month Ended March 31, 2018).

- The first number in each column has a dollar sign to indicate the currency of values presented in the statement.

- The last number in a calculated column has a single underline to indicate a total or subtotal is being calculated.

- The final number on the financial statement, or in the case of the balance sheet the total assets and the total liabilities plus the owner's equity figures, has a dollar sign and is double underlined.

Figure 2.31 on the next page shows the four financial statements discussed in this section: the income statement, the statement of owner's equity, the balance sheet, and the statement of cash flows. All of the statements were prepared based on the transactions completed by Ace Bookkeepers during the month of March 2018. The labeled arrows show you how one statement relates to the next, and each statement is discussed in detail in its relevant section. Please refer back to Figure 2.31 as you read each section, to better understand both the individual statements and how they are connected.

Income Statement

The first statement to complete is the income statement, shown in Figure 2.31. The income statement reports revenue earned and expenses incurred during the period. For Ace Bookkeepers, this income statement is for the month ended March 31, 2018 and shows a net income of $9,400.

Statement of Owner's Equity

The **statement of owner's equity** shows how an owner's equity changed during the month. It covers the same reporting period as the income statement, so Ace Bookkeepers prepares the statement of owner's equity for the month ended March 31, 2018. The basic calculation for the change in equity was shown at the bottom of the T-account worksheet in Figure 2.30. The statement of owner's equity is the formal presentation of this calculation and is the second financial statement shown in Figure 2.31.

Since the business is brand new, the balance of the owner's capital account was $0 at the beginning of the month. The investment made in transaction 1 is added, as is the net income that was calculated from the income statement (indicated by arrow **a**). The amount of withdrawals by the owner is subtracted to give the final balance of the owner's capital of $37,400. The closing balance for March will be the opening balance shown on April's statement of owner's equity.

Balance Sheet

After the statement of owner's equity is prepared, the balance sheet can be created to report on the balances of assets, liabilities and owner's equity on March 31, 2018. The balance sheet is shown as the third financial statement in Figure 2.31. Notice how the value of the owner's capital is taken from the statement of owner's equity (indicated by arrow **b**). Also, the total of the assets is equal to the total of liabilities plus owner's equity. These totals must be the same, otherwise, the accounting equation is not balanced and there is an error either in recording the transactions in the T-accounts or in the calculation of the financial statements.

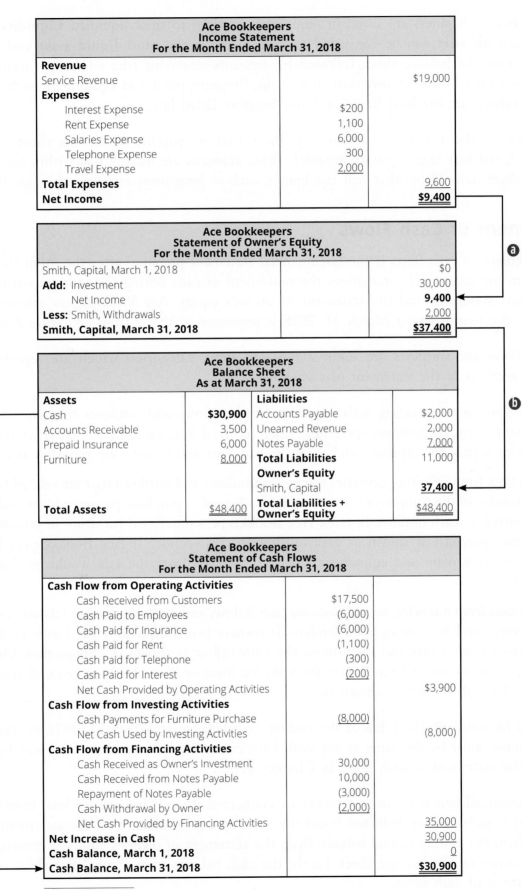

Ace Bookkeepers
Income Statement
For the Month Ended March 31, 2018

Revenue		
Service Revenue		$19,000
Expenses		
Interest Expense	$200	
Rent Expense	1,100	
Salaries Expense	6,000	
Telephone Expense	300	
Travel Expense	2,000	
Total Expenses		9,600
Net Income		**$9,400**

Ace Bookkeepers
Statement of Owner's Equity
For the Month Ended March 31, 2018

Smith, Capital, March 1, 2018		$0
Add: Investment		30,000
Net Income		**9,400**
Less: Smith, Withdrawals		2,000
Smith, Capital, March 31, 2018		**$37,400**

Ace Bookkeepers
Balance Sheet
As at March 31, 2018

Assets		Liabilities	
Cash	**$30,900**	Accounts Payable	$2,000
Accounts Receivable	3,500	Unearned Revenue	2,000
Prepaid Insurance	6,000	Notes Payable	7,000
Furniture	8,000	**Total Liabilities**	11,000
		Owner's Equity	
		Smith, Capital	**37,400**
Total Assets	**$48,400**	**Total Liabilities + Owner's Equity**	**$48,400**

Ace Bookkeepers
Statement of Cash Flows
For the Month Ended March 31, 2018

Cash Flow from Operating Activities		
Cash Received from Customers	$17,500	
Cash Paid to Employees	(6,000)	
Cash Paid for Insurance	(6,000)	
Cash Paid for Rent	(1,100)	
Cash Paid for Telephone	(300)	
Cash Paid for Interest	(200)	
Net Cash Provided by Operating Activities		$3,900
Cash Flow from Investing Activities		
Cash Payments for Furniture Purchase	(8,000)	
Net Cash Used by Investing Activities		(8,000)
Cash Flow from Financing Activities		
Cash Received as Owner's Investment	30,000	
Cash Received from Notes Payable	10,000	
Repayment of Notes Payable	(3,000)	
Cash Withdrawal by Owner	(2,000)	
Net Cash Provided by Financing Activities		35,000
Net Increase in Cash		30,900
Cash Balance, March 1, 2018		0
Cash Balance, March 31, 2018		**$30,900**

FIGURE 2.31

The assets of a business are listed in sequence according to their liquidity. **Liquidity** is the ease with which an asset can be converted to cash. Cash is the most **liquid asset** and is therefore listed first on the balance sheet, followed by accounts receivable (the amount of money owed by customers to the business), inventory and so on. Property, plant and equipment, such as buildings and machinery, are the least liquid and are therefore listed last.

Liabilities are also listed in a similar way. Those that are payable within the shortest amount of time are listed first (e.g. accounts payable). These amounts are usually due within one year of the balance sheet date. Debts that will last longer, such as long-term notes payable, are listed last.

Statement of Cash Flows

The statement of cash flows is the last financial statement prepared after the other three financial statements are created. It summarizes the movement of cash during the same reporting period as the income statement and the statement of owner's equity. Ace Bookkeepers' statement of cash flows for the month ended March 31, 2018 is presented at the bottom of Figure 2.31.

Cash inflows and outflows are summarized into three categories, which are reported in three separate sections in the statement of cash flows.

1. Cash flow from operating activities shows cash inflows and outflows that are related to the company's primary business operations. Cash received from customers is reported as cash inflow, while cash paid for expenses such as insurance, rent and interest are reported as cash outflow.

2. Cash flow from investing activities shows cash inflows and outflows that are related to long-term investments in the company's infrastructure. Cash paid to purchase property, plant and equipment is reported as cash outflow. Because Ace Bookkeepers purchased furniture in transaction 3, the furniture purchase is shown as cash outflow in this section. If Ace Bookkeepers had instead sold property, plant and equipment, the cash received from the sale would be shown as cash inflow.

3. Cash flow from financing activities shows cash inflows and outflows that are related to investments by owners and borrowing from lenders. If owners invest cash into the business or if cash is borrowed from a financial institution, the cash inflow is shown in this section. On the other hand, if the owners withdraw cash from the business or if the business pays off its loan to the bank, the cash outflow is shown here.

As noted by arrow **Ⓒ**, the value of the ending cash balance at March 31, 2018 on the statement of cash flows must be the same as the cash balance on the balance sheet. You will learn how to prepare the statement of cash flows in Chapter 19.

In conclusion, all four financial statements are connected. The net income (or loss) from the income statement is added to (or deducted from) the opening capital balance on the statement of owner's equity. Then, the ending capital balance from the statement of owner's equity is transferred to the capital balance on the balance sheet. Lastly, the cash balance from the balance sheet is shown on the statement of cash flows.

IN THE REAL WORLD

Public US companies are required to periodically file their financial statements with the US Securities and Exchange Commission (SEC). The annual and quarterly report filings are known as Forms 10-K and 10-Q, respectively. These filings are accessible to the public through SEC's online database called EDGAR (www.sec.gov/edgar.shtml). Most large companies also publish their financial statements on their websites.

Ethics

Ethics are a set of guidelines that define if a behavior is moral or not. Sometimes it is hard to make an ethical decision if the path is not clear-cut. An ethical dilemma can occur when a decision may positively affect a group of individuals while negatively affecting another group at the same time. In this type of situation, one should evaluate all possible consequences before making a decision, and then choose the course of action that results in an optimal outcome for the most people involved.

When it comes to ethics in accounting, owners and managers of businesses have some level of control over how revenue and expenses are recorded and reported on the income statement. The owners and managers have an ethical responsibility to record and report revenue and expenses in a way that best represents economic reality, even if doing so means the company reports an unfavorable result. Reporting not "what is," but "what the owners and managers want it to be," is an accounting fraud.

Perhaps the most infamous example of accounting fraud that involves misrepresenting revenue comes from Enron, a large energy company in the United States. Over a period of five years, Enron reported an increase in revenue of more than 750%. This massive increase in revenue was partly due to counting the full amount of trading contracts, instead of just brokerage fees, as revenue.

Another example of corporate fraud was committed by WorldCom, a telecommunications company. In addition to misrepresenting revenue, it took certain expenses and recorded them as assets on the balance sheet. Thus, by increasing revenue and eliminating certain expenses, WorldCom was able to show very large profits. In both the Enron and WorldCom cases, executives were charged and went to jail for their involvement in fraud.

Fraud Triangle

As depicted in Figure 2.32, fraud is caused when three factors are present, including pressure, rationalization and opportunity. To illustrate the three factors, consider this example. The owner of a banquet hall receives deposits from customers to book the hall months in advance. As we learned, customer deposits must be treated as a liability (unearned revenue) until the service is actually performed.

FIGURE 2.32

Suppose the owner requires additional financing from the bank to help pay for an expansion to the hall and feels her income may not be enough to get the loan (pressure). While the owner knows that she's not supposed to manipulate the numbers, she believes that doing so is necessary not only for herself, but also for her employees, who need their jobs at the banquet hall to make their living (rationalization). To make her net income appear higher, the owner records the customer deposits as revenue instead of a liability. Because the owner also acts as the company's accountant, and there's no one else to double check the accuracy of the financial statements (opportunity), she feels that manipulating the numbers is easy to do. By inflating her revenue and profits, she hopes the bank will grant her the loan she needs. This action is unethical.

Consider a sole proprietor who is attempting to minimize the amount of taxes he must pay to the government on his business income. He needs money to pay for his house mortgage (pressure). He argues with himself that he needs to do this so his family has a place to live (rationalization). He has a significant amount of prepaid expenses recorded as assets, and can easily manipulate the numbers (opportunity), and so he reports those assets as expenses. He also overstates the expenses by including personal expenses in his business records. All of these actions reduce his net income and the amount of taxes to be paid. Including personal expenses in business records is illegal, and can lead to charges and penalties imposed by the government.

In Summary

LO 1 **List the differences between personal accounts and business accounts**

▶ Some differences include surplus (deficit) is called net income (loss); revenue is classified as sales revenue or service revenue; and the net worth section is replaced with the owner's equity section.

LO 2 **Describe the three main types of businesses**

▶ A service business provides services to clients.

▶ A merchandising business buys inventory and resells it to customers.

▶ A manufacturing business makes its own products and sells them to customers.

LO 3 **Record revenue based on the concept of accruals**

▶ Revenue is recorded when services have been provided to customers, regardless of when cash is received.

▶ Unearned revenue is used to record cash receipts before services are performed and accounts receivable is used when a customer will pay after services are performed.

LO 4 **Record expenses based on the concept of accruals**

▶ Expenses are recorded when they are incurred, regardless of when cash is paid.

▶ Prepaid expenses are used to record cash payments before expenses are incurred and accounts payable is used when suppliers will be paid after expenses are incurred.

LO 5 **Record business transactions in T-accounts**

▶ When recording transactions in T-accounts, every transaction must be recorded in at least two accounts and the accounting equation must always be balanced.

▶ Revenues and expenses must be recorded when they are incurred, not necessarily when cash is transferred. This creates a need for additional accounts such as accounts receivable, prepaid expenses, accounts payable, and unearned revenue.

LO 6 **Identify the four required financial statements and prepare three financial statements**

▶ The income statement reports the revenue earned and expenses incurred during the period.

▶ The statement of owner's equity shows the changes in owner's equity during the period.

▶ The balance sheet reports the balances of assets, liabilities and owner's equity at the end of the period.

▶ On the balance sheet, assets are listed in order from most to least liquid. Liabilities are listed in order from shortest to longest maturity.

▶ The statement of cash flows reports cash inflows and outflows from operating, investing and financing activities during the period.

LO 7 **Describe ethics relating to financial statement reporting**

▶ A business should report its financial statements in a way that reflects the true substance of business transactions and economic reality. It is unethical to misrepresent financial information.

 *Access **ameengage.com** for integrated resources including tutorials, practice exercises, the digital textbook and more.*

Review Exercise 2-1

Miranda Jones owns a salon called Style House. Below are the balances of the accounts on March 1, 2018.

Cash	$3,000
Equipment	12,000
Accounts Payable	5,000
Jones, Capital	10,000

The following transactions for Style House occurred during the month of March 2018.

1. Borrowed $12,000 from the bank
2. Purchased chairs and dryers with $8,000 cash
3. Paid $333 cash toward the principal of the note payable
4. Paid $50 cash for interest on the note payable
5. Prepaid $600 cash for a monthly maintenance contract that will last six months
6. Provided services to customers and received $8,000 cash
7. Paid $4,000 cash to employees for salaries for the month
8. Received a telephone bill for $250, which will be paid next month
9. Received a bill for $300 for advertising and a bill for $500 for travel, both of which will be paid later
10. Paid monthly rent with $2,000 cash
11. Paid $1,000 owing to a supplier
12. Withdrew $3,000 cash from the business for personal use
13. Provided $400 worth of services to customers on account
14. Received $100 cash from a customer for services to be provided next month

Required

a)   Record the March transactions for Miranda's business on the following T-account worksheet.

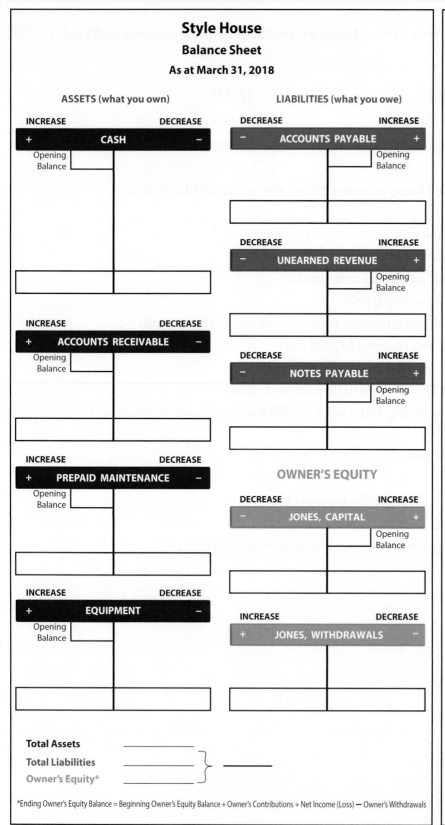

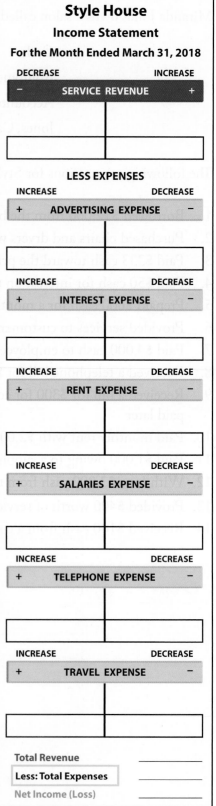

b) Complete the income statement for Style House.

Style House Income Statement For the Month Ended March 31, 2018		

c) Complete the statement of owner's equity for Style House.

Style House Statement of Owner's Equity For the Month Ended March 31, 2018	

d) Complete the balance sheet for Style House.

<table>
<tr><td colspan="4">Style House
Balance Sheet
As at March 31, 2018</td></tr>
<tr><td></td><td></td><td></td><td></td></tr>
<tr><td></td><td></td><td></td><td></td></tr>
<tr><td></td><td></td><td></td><td></td></tr>
<tr><td></td><td></td><td></td><td></td></tr>
<tr><td></td><td></td><td></td><td></td></tr>
<tr><td></td><td></td><td></td><td></td></tr>
<tr><td></td><td></td><td></td><td></td></tr>
<tr><td></td><td></td><td></td><td></td></tr>
<tr><td></td><td></td><td></td><td></td></tr>
</table>

e) The table below lists transactions for Style House. Complete the table to identify which section of the statement of cash flows (operating, investing or financing) each one belongs to.

Transaction	Cash Flow Section
Borrowed $12,000 from the bank	
Purchased chairs and dryers with $8,000 cash	
Paid $333 cash toward the principal of the bank loan	
Paid $50 cash for interest on the bank loan	
Prepaid $600 cash for a six-month maintenance contract	
Provided services to customers and received $8,000	
Paid $4,000 cash to employees for salaries	
Paid monthly rent with $2,000 cash	
Paid $1,000 owing to a supplier	
Miranda withdrew $3,000 cash from the business	

See Appendix I for solutions.

Chapter 3
The Accounting Framework

Learning Objectives

AMEENGAGE *Access **ameengage.com** for integrated resources including tutorials, practice exercises, the digital textbook and more.*

63

Users of Accounting Information

The fundamental objective of accounting is to prepare financial statements to help a wide variety of users make decisions. Users of accounting information can be divided into two categories.

1. **Internal users**, people who own the business and/or work in the business
2. **External users**, people or organizations outside the business, such as suppliers, banks and external accountants

Internal users rely on financial statements to manage the business efficiently. They assess the business by examining the financial results on a regular basis. To an internal user, financial statements serve the same purpose as a scoreboard does to a sports team; the statements give internal users a snapshot of how the business is performing and what needs to be done going forward so the business is successful.

Typically, external users need financial statements to ensure that their investment in the business is protected, whether they provide loans or supply products or services on credit. If a business is poorly managed or not operating profitably, external users can decide whether or not to associate themselves with the business. They want assurance that their loans can be repaid or that they receive a sufficient return on their investment.

There are also indirect external users of financial statements. For example, tax authorities look at the financial statements to confirm that the business is paying the appropriate amount of taxes. Indirect external users also include customers and trade unions.

Fields of Accounting

Accountants measure, record and report on an individual's or a business' financial activities. Businesses large and small need accountants to ensure that internal and external users have the information they need to make informed decisions. There are two general fields of accounting that focus on the needs of different users: financial accounting and managerial accounting.

Financial Accounting

Financial accounting is concerned with keeping records of the business and preparing the financial statements, similar to what has been discussed so far. Financial accounting serves the external users of the business, such as investors, suppliers, customers and lenders, who use financial accounting information to make decisions. For example, an investor may decide to invest more money into a business that reports growing profits, or a supplier may decide to cut ties with a business that reports low cash flows.

Financial accountants make certain that the information in financial statements (income statement, balance sheet, etc.) is accurate and up-to-date so that users can make informed decisions. Financial accountants may be employees of the business, or may work for an accounting firm that services many businesses.

Managerial Accounting

Managerial accounting serves the internal users of the accounting information by preparing specialized reports to assist in decision-making inside the business. Managerial accountants track and classify costs, prepare and analyze budgets, and assist with strategic decision-making. Managers and executives use cost reports and budgets generated by managerial accountants to determine whether certain products, services or business functions are still profitable and how to improve them if necessary. Managerial accountants are often employees of the business.

Accounting Designations

An accounting-related education is required to work in the accounting field. Becoming an accounting clerk requires a college diploma, but many accounting positions (financial or managerial) require further specialized education to obtain an accounting certification. The most common examples of accounting certifications recognized in the US include the following.

- Certified Public Accountant (CPA)
- Certified Internal Auditor (CIA)
- Certified Management Accountant (CMA)
- Certified Payroll Professional (CPP)
- Certified Bookkeeper (CB)
- Certified Fraud Examiner (CFE)

These certifications are each governed by separate profesional organizations. For instance, the CPA certification is governed by the American Institute of Certified Public Accountants (AICPA). Obtaining a CPA designation requires an individual to complete the required educational and practical experience and pass the AICPA's Uniform Certified Public Accountant Examination. Another example of an accounting professional organization is the Institute of Management Accountants (IMA), which governs the CMA certification.

Accountants may work for a single organization, or they may work in a firm that provides accounting services for many other organizations or individuals. The practice of accounting for a single organization is referred to as **private accounting**. A company's bookkeeping is an example of private accounting. A company's bookkeeper is responsible for recording accounting transactions and compiling accounting information into financial statements, and works only for that company. **Public accounting** involves providing services, such as auditing and tax advice, to different companies or individuals. The CPA designation is generally required for an individual to work in the public accounting field.

Forms of Business Organization

So far we have dealt with accounting for sole proprietorships. However, a business could also be organized as a partnership, corporation, or nonprofit organization. The form of organization is important because it determines the laws and accounting standards that must be adhered to. This section discusses each form of organization in detail.

Sole Proprietorship

A **sole proprietorship** is owned and generally operated by one owner. A proprietorship is usually a small business, and could provide products or services, such as bookkeeping, gardening or general contracting. Many proprietorships have only a small amount of money invested by the owner. Starting a sole proprietorship can be an easy process; often it is enough to register a business name and obtain a business license. The proprietorship lasts as long as the owner runs the business, or as long as the owner is alive. Sole proprietorships are examples of private enterprises because ownership of the business is restricted to one person. A **private enterprise** is any business or organization in which ownership is restricted to a select group of people; the general public cannot acquire ownership of the business.

From an accounting perspective, the financial affairs of the business must be separate from the financial affairs of the owner. For example, the proprietor cannot list personal assets, such as home contents, on the same statement as the business' assets. From a legal perspective, however, a sole proprietorship is *not* a separate entity from its owner. This means that the assets and liabilities of the business legally belong to the owner, even though the financial activities are recorded separately. If the business is unable to pay its debts, business creditors can force the owner to sell personal assets to pay the business debts. This is called **unlimited liability**; the owner will receive all the net income, suffer any net loss and be personally liable for all financial obligations of the business.

We will be using a sole proprietorship to illustrate various transactions. Figure 3.1 shows the names of some typical accounts used in a service business in the form of a sole proprietorship.

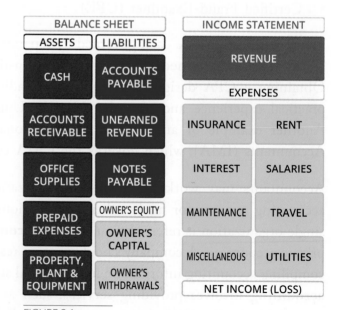

FIGURE 3.1

A CLOSER LOOK

Often, the owner of a sole proprietorship incorrectly records business transactions in the same set of records as his personal records. This makes it almost impossible to monitor the activities of the business to evaluate its performance.

Consider this scenario. Emilio operates a gardening service and combines all his business and personal records. He also has a job at night for extra income. The gardening business has become very busy and he needs to arrange a bank loan to buy more equipment and supplies. By maintaining personal and business records together, Emilio faces the following challenges.

1. He does not know how much the night job and the gardening business are each contributing toward his income.

2. By not separating business and personal expenses, he does not know which expenses are being used to generate sales. This is important because business expenses can be tax deductible.

3. He does not know the expenses of each gardening job, such as insurance and gas, to help identify the profitability of the business.

Before lending money to Emilio, the bank will want to see financial statements to assess if the business is capable of servicing the loan. This will be a problem for Emilio in the current situation.

Partnership

A partnership is a business owned by two or more people, called partners. As in a sole proprietorship, the only legal requirements that must be met to start a partnership are registering the business name and obtaining a business license. To manage a business together, the partners need an oral or written partnership agreement that states how to share profits and losses. Partnerships use the term "partners' equity" as the title of the equity section on the balance sheet, as shown in Figure 3.2. The partnership lasts as long as the partners continue to run the business, or as long as all partners are alive. If the partners end the business, the partnership's assets are sold and existing liabilities are paid. The remaining cash is divided among the partners according to the partnership agreement.

Partnerships are private enterprises. A partnership, like a sole proprietorship, is not legally separated from its owners. Depending on the type of partnership, partners may be subject to unlimited liability, which means that the partners are jointly

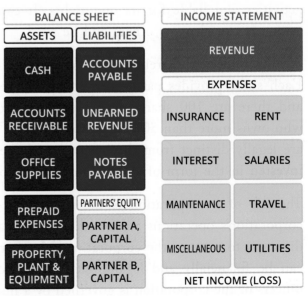

FIGURE 3.2

responsible for all the debts of the partnership. In a partnership, **mutual agency** exists, which means each partner is able to speak for the other partners and bind them to business contracts.

There are four types of partnerships that can be created.

1. A general partnership is a partnership in which all partners are subject to unlimited liability. All partners are considered to be general partners. Unless special provisions are made (as described below), all partnerships are general partnerships.

2. A limited partnership includes at least one general partner who accepts unlimited liability, and one or more limited partners with liability limited to the amount they invested. All limited partnerships must have at least one general partner. The limited partners are sometimes referred to as silent partners because they are not involved in the management of the partnership's daily operations.

3. A limited liability partnership (LLP) allows partners to have limited liability regarding the misconduct or negligence of the other partners. For example, if a partner in a law firm that is an LLP is sued for misconduct, only the partner in question is responsible for paying damages. However, all partners remain personally liable for all other debts of the business.

4. A limited liability company (LLC) is a special type of partnership. It has the same tax treatment as a partnership or a sole proprietorship, but its limited liability and separate legal entity status make it similar to a corporation.

Partnerships are discussed in detail in Chapter 14.

Corporation

A corporation is a business that is registered with the state government as a separate legal entity from its owners. The corporation has all the rights of a person and is responsible for its own activities and liable for its own debts. It can enter into contracts and buy and sell products or assets. It can also sue others and be sued.

A stockholder (or shareholder) is an owner of the business through ownership of stocks (or shares). Each share provides partial ownership of the business. For example, if a person owns one share and there are 100 shares available, the person owns 1/100th of the corporation. A stockholder who owns more than 50% of all the stock of a corporation can control the business. Stockholders are legally distinct from the business and their financial risk is limited to the amount they have invested in the form of stock. Thus, owners or stockholders have limited liability.

The life of a corporation is indefinite and independent of the lives of the stockholders. The corporation's operations are not directly managed by its stockholders, but by an elected board of directors to oversee the corporation. Members of the board of directors and senior management can be financially and legally accountable for the actions of the corporation. The behavior of officers of the corporation is governed by a number of rules, including those relating to responsible accounting and cash management.

As shown in Figure 3.3, the balance sheet of a corporation uses the term "stockholders' equity" for the equity section, and it is equal to the difference between assets and liabilities, just like a sole proprietorship or partnership. For example, a company has assets worth $100,000 and liabilities worth $60,000. If the corporation sells all its assets and pays the liabilities, the remaining $40,000 cash is the stockholders' equity and belongs to the stockholders. The stockholders' equity is divided among the stockholders in proportion to the number of shares that they own. If there are two equal stockholders, each one is paid $20,000. If there are 20 equal stockholders, each one is paid $2,000.

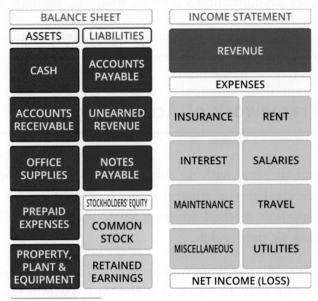

FIGURE 3.3

Corporations can be set up as either public or private enterprises. A public corporation allows its stock to be sold to anyone in the general public. This gives the public corporation access to a large amount of cash to help grow the business. Typically, a public corporation has thousands of individual stockholders. Stock exchanges, such as the NASDAQ Stock Market or the New York Stock Exchange, allow buyers and sellers to trade stock of public corporations.

A private corporation does not allow its stock to be sold to just anyone, and often the stock is held by a few individuals. Private corporations are generally subject to less stringent reporting requirements than public corporations.

The major differences between the three forms of organization are summarized in Figure 3.4.

	Sole Proprietorship	Partnership	Corporation
Title of Owners	Proprietor (One)	Partners (Two or More)	Stockholders (One or More)
Public or Private	Private	Private	Public or Private
Equity Section	Owner's Equity	Partners' Equity	Stockholders' Equity
Owner's Liability	Unlimited	Limited or Unlimited	Limited

FIGURE 3.4

Nonprofit Organizations

As you have learned, the primary objective of a for-profit business is to maximize profits for the business' owner(s). Nonprofit organizations aim to improve or benefit communities by taking profits and redistributing them as services or products. They usually obtain funding from donations and government grants. Nonprofit organizations include religious organizations, community care centers and charitable organizations. They do not have an identifiable owner but require financial statements because they are accountable to donors, sponsors, lenders, tax authorities and so on.

Accounting records provide key information pertaining to the activities of nonprofit organizations, enabling them to operate as permitted. This textbook does not focus on nonprofit organizations.

The Conceptual Framework of Accounting

Imagine a football or baseball game with no rules or consistent method to keep score. The players and spectators would quickly become frustrated because of the lack of consistency. By having rules to follow and a consistent method to keep score, players know how to play the game and spectators can follow along as they watch.

Accounting in a business is similar. If there were no rules to follow, business owners and accountants could make up rules regarding what to report. External users would find the reports unreliable and uncomparable. Thus, the accounting profession has created standards for how financial information should be reported. These standards are commonly referred to as **generally accepted accounting principles (GAAP)**.

In the United States, the development of GAAP is under the legal authority of the **Securities and Exchange Commission (SEC)**, a federal government agency whose mission is to protect investors. The SEC has mostly delegated the writing of GAAP to a private, nonprofit organization called the **Financial Accounting Standards Board (FASB)**. Specifically, the FASB is designated to develop guidelines that all public US companies are required to use in reporting their financial statements according to GAAP. The guidelines developed by the FASB, which are referred to as "US GAAP," encompass both broad and specific accounting issues, and are constantly updated. However, sometimes there are accounting issues that have not been adequately addressed by the FASB, in which case the SEC can step in and issue interpretations and policies to supplement the FASB standards.

In addition to establishing the local accounting standards, the FASB also participates in the development of the **International Financial Reporting Standards (IFRS)** in conjunction with the **International Accounting Standards Board (IASB)**. As the global trend has been intensifying in the business world, the IFRS is designed as the unified set of global accounting standards so that the financial statements of companies from different countries are comparable. IFRS are very well received and widely used around the world. Over 100 governments have required public companies in their countries to adopt IFRS. Figure 3.5 illustrates the various organizations involved with financial accounting standards.

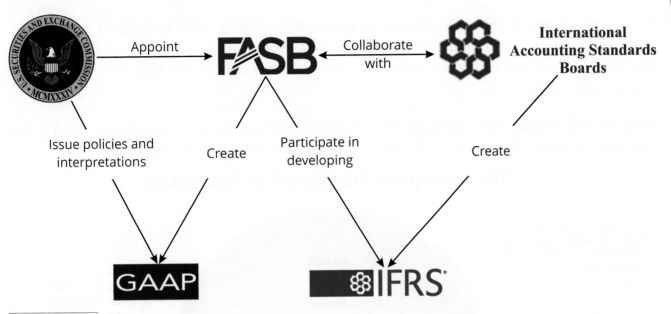

FIGURE 3.5

In the US, private US companies and foreign companies that sell their shares in the US stock markets are permitted to adopt IFRS if they do not want to use US GAAP. However, public US companies are not allowed to adopt the IFRS standards and must use US GAAP. The differences between IFRS and US GAAP will likely have to be reconciled before public US companies are allowed to use IFRS the way public companies in many other countries have already been permitted or required to do.

In 2010, in an attempt to bridge the differences between US GAAP and IFRS, the SEC announced its commitment to one global set of accounting standards. The SEC has also encouraged the FASB to pursue a convergence process with the IASB by incorporating IFRS into US GAAP. Some of the convergence projects between the FASB and the IASB have been completed. However, some important differences between US GAAP and IFRS remain, and it is unclear whether and when the remaining convergence projects will go forward and whether public companies in the US will be permitted or required to use IFRS in the future.

One of the projects that the FASB and the IASB worked on together until 2014 is the Conceptual Framework project. In 2014, the FASB and the IASB decided to continue this project separately (i.e. it's no longer a joint project). However, both US GAAP and IFRS conform to a similar underlying conceptual framework. This **conceptual framework** forms the basis to determine how business transactions should be measured and reported. It ensures external users (e.g. stockholders) have the most consistent, reliable and useful information when reviewing companies' financial reports. US GAAP follows rules-based accounting, meaning the accounting standards are stated as a list of specific, detailed rules that must be followed when preparing financial information. To apply these rules, accountants have little room to make their own judgments. This ensures that accounting standards are applied consistently by all companies.

On the other hand, IFRS is principles-based accounting, meaning IFRS is designed as guidelines and accountants are allowed flexibility to apply these standards when preparing financial information. This removes long lists of detailed rules but requires accountants to use their own judgment on how to apply them.

Next, we will examine the important characteristics, assumptions and principles of GAAP that form the conceptual framework of accounting. Figure 3.6 illustrates the framework.

The Conceptual Framework of Accounting

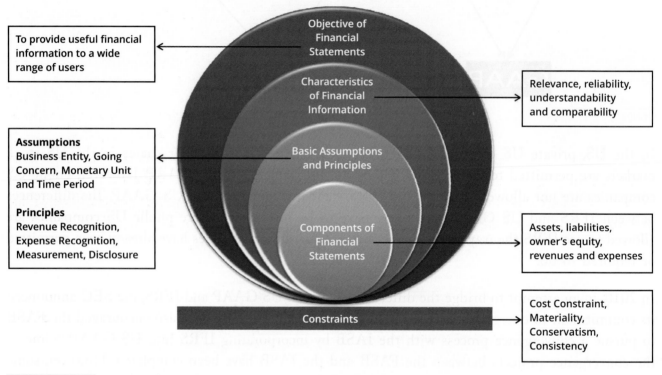

FIGURE 3.6

Objective and Constraints of Financial Information

The fundamental objective of financial reporting is to provide useful and complete information to the users. However, there are four major constraints for a business to consider when trying to achieve this objective. The first underlying constraint in the accounting framework is the cost constraint. The **cost constraint** ensures that the value of reported financial information outweighs the costs incurred to report it, even if the information would improve the accuracy and completeness of the financial statements. For example, a company may find some information that is not required by accounting standards to be somewhat useful but costly to prepare. If the value of this information does not outweigh the costs, the company should not prepare it.

The second constraint in the accounting framework is materiality. **Materiality** refers to the significance of information to users. A piece of information is considered material if it could influence or change a user's decision. Material amounts must be recorded correctly on financial statements. For example, suppose a company paid $100 cash for office supplies. The supplies could be recorded as an asset and expensed as they are used, or they can simply be expensed immediately. While recording them as an asset is more accurate, it is also more complex and more costly to account for. Is this $100 a material amount? It depends on the size of the company. If the company typically lists more than $100,000 in assets, the $100 is not likely to affect any user's decision and is therefore immaterial. On the other hand, if the company typically lists assets totaling $1,000, the treatment of $100 in office supplies may impact the decision of an investor.

The third constraint is **conservatism**, which states that whenever an accountant has several options in applying an accounting standard, the least optimistic or least favorable option should be selected. This means choosing the option that results in a lower balance of assets, lower net income or a higher balance of debt; the accountant should have a *conservative* mindset when making estimates to avoid overstating assets, overstating net income or understating debt.

The last constraint is **consistency**, which prevents businesses from changing accounting methods for the sole purpose of manipulating figures on the financial statements. Accountants must apply the same methods and policies from period to period. For example, a merchandising business must have a method to assign value to its merchandise inventory and use the same method from year to year. When a method changes from one period to another, the change must be clearly explained in notes to the financial statements. The users of financial statements have the right to assume that consistency has been applied if there is no statement to the contrary.

Qualitative Characteristics of Financial Information

Accounting standards are based on fundamental characteristics in the accounting framework. These characteristics form the foundation of the conceptual framework and define how information should be presented in financial statements. For financial statements to be effective, financial information must be relevant, reliable, understandable and comparable.

GAAP vs IFRS

GAAP is more "rules-based" in contrast to IFRS, which is more "principles-based." It could be argued that the strong regulations-based system in the US is a main contributor to all the industry-specific rules enforced by GAAP. The nature of IFRS allows users to have more room for interpretation and judgment, whereas GAAP is stricter and more detailed about proper accounting practices.

Relevance

Relevance means that all information useful for decision-making is present in the financial statements. Information is relevant if it helps users predict future performance or confirms previous predictions. For example, if an investor wants to predict the future cash flows of a company, and the company deliberately avoided reporting a bank loan, the investor cannot understand the company's debt correctly. Therefore, the investor cannot accurately predict the company's interest expenses and available cash flow. In this scenario, the balance of the bank loan would be considered relevant financial information.

A component of relevance is **timeliness**. Information is timely if there is no delay in reporting crucial information. To be useful to a decision maker, information must be received before it is no longer able to influence decisions. For example, if a business only prepares annual statements, the information may be available too late to correct problems with the company. Therefore, a business owner may prefer to have monthly statements prepared to help monitor the company's performance.

Reliability

Reliability means that information is free from significant error and bias, which means different independent people looking at the evidence will arrive at the same values. The activities that a business records must be based on objective evidence. A component of reliability is **verifiability**, which means the ability to see how a company arrived at a certain result. For example, if a company records an expense transaction in its financial records, an invoice must be provided to back it up (i.e. the expense can be verified).

Reliability also depends on the **faithful representation** of the information. This means that transactions must be presented as their true economic substance rather than their legal form. For example, a company that leases a machine for its entire useful life may list the machine as an asset even though it does not legally own the machine.

In order to be reliable, the information must be neutral. The concept of **neutrality** means that financial information must be free from bias. Bias occurs when the information is influenced by the interests of particular users. For example, managers may be tempted to report higher sales and profit figures if they are paid a bonus based on the success of their department.

Understandability

Understandability means that the financial information can be reasonably understood by its users if the users have knowledge of the business and a basic knowledge of accounting. To be understandable, companies include notes in the financial statements to explain the numbers, especially those that are based on company policy. For example, details of long-term debt such as the principal, interest and term would be outlined in the notes.

Comparability

Comparability means that the financial statements of a company must be prepared in a similar way year after year. The accounting policies used should be consistent to prevent misconceptions. This allows a comparison of the current year's performance to past years. By comparing yearly statements, users can identify trends in the company's financial position and performance. For example, an investor may compare a company's debt balance from one year to the next to see if the company incurred additional debt or was able to pay off its creditors. The financial information should also be comparable between companies.

Trade-Offs of Qualitative Characteristics

As discussed, accounting standards dictate that financial information should be relevant, reliable, understandable and comparable. However, sometimes it is difficult to fully represent all of these characteristics. There could be a trade-off among some of the characteristics. A trade-off is an exchange of part of one characteristic for part of another.

A frequently discussed trade-off is the one between relevance and reliability, as shown in Figure 3.7. For information to be relevant, it needs to be timely. For example, presenting information that is a few years old on today's financial statements is likely not very relevant. However, reliable information often requires time to gather.

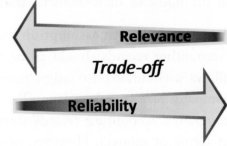

FIGURE 3.7

Suppose that a company chooses to prepare financial statements on a monthly basis instead of a quarterly or semi-annual basis. In this case, the financial statements are very timely and relevant. However, some reliability may be sacrificed since there is less time for the accounting staff to scrutinize and make necessary adjustments to the monthly financial figures. If the financial statements are less frequent (such as quarterly or semi-annually), the accounting staff can allocate more time to verify the accuracy of the statements, but some relevance might be lost since statements are prepared less frequently.

Basic Assumptions and Principles   LO 5

The conceptual framework of accounting also includes several basic accounting assumptions and principles. Accountants must ensure that these assumptions and principles are met by all of the financial information presented by the business.

Assumptions

There are four basic assumptions underlying all accounting information that is prepared in accordance with US GAAP. These assumptions are necessary for users to rely on the information presented.

The **business entity assumption** states that accounting for a business must be kept separate from the personal affairs of its owner or any other businesses. The owner of a business cannot record personal transactions on the income statement or balance sheet of the business. Any personal expenses are charged to the owner and are not allowed to affect the operating results of the business. Financial statements of a business can be assumed to only contain items that pertain to the business and, therefore, reflect the financial position of the business alone.

The **going concern assumption** assumes that a business will continue to operate into the foreseeable future. Determining the value of the assets belonging to a business that is alive and well is not complicated. For example, items such as property, plant and equipment are listed on the balance sheet at their cost, or original purchase price. However, if an accountant deems that the business is unable to continue operating into the foreseeable future, the balance sheet must instead show the value for which the property, plant and equipment could realistically be sold. When a company is going out of business, the value of the assets usually suffers because they have to be sold under unfavorable circumstances. Companies at risk of going out of business must include this information in the notes to their financial statements.

The **monetary unit assumption** requires that accounting records are expressed in terms of money. Accounting records should all be reported in a single currency, such as US dollars or euros. This allows accountants to assign monetary values to business events. For instance, suppose that a company hires a salesperson. The event of officially hiring the employee is not reflected in the company's accounting records since a value cannot be easily assigned to the event (i.e. expressed in terms of money). However, over time, the financial impact of the hiring will be evident (e.g. recognizing the salary expense for the salesperson and realizing an increase in sales). Furthermore, it is also assumed that the unit of measure used in the accounting records remains fairly constant over time and that transactions can be measured relevantly in current monetary units. That is, inflation (a rise in prices) or deflation (a drop in prices) is ignored when comparing dollars of different years.

The **time period assumption** requires that accounting takes place over specific time periods known as fiscal periods. These fiscal periods are of equal length, and are used when measuring the financial progress of a business.

Principles

The following section discusses some of the basic accounting principles and concepts outlined by the conceptual framework of accounting.

Measurement is the process of determining the amount at which an item is recorded in the financial statements. Primarily, items must be recorded at their historical cost. This is sometimes referred to as the *cost principle*. In almost all cases, the historical cost is the amount that appears on the source document for the transaction. If the owner purchased $7,000 worth of office furniture on sale for $5,000, the furniture is recorded as $5,000, as shown on the receipt. There are times when the historical cost of an item is not appropriate. For example, a building could be received as a gift. In such a case, the transaction would be recorded at fair market value, which must be determined by independent appraisals.

Revenue recognition states that revenue can only be recorded (recognized) when goods are sold or services are performed. This means that the item sold must be transferred to the buyer and the buyer has agreed to pay, or has already paid, for the item. If the transaction involves a large project, such as building a dam, it may take a construction company a number of years to complete.

The construction company does not usually wait until the project is entirely completed before it recognizes the revenue. Periodically, it bills for work completed and recognizes this as revenue.

Expense recognition states that an expense must be recorded in the same accounting period in which it is used to generate revenue. For example, suppose a manufacturing business spent $20,000 to produce 1,000 units of inventory in the current accounting period. If 500 units are sold in each of the following two accounting periods, $10,000 would be expensed in each period. This concept is commonly referred to as the *matching principle* because expenses must be matched to the same period as the revenue that they helped to generate. If an expense cannot be tied to revenue, then it should be recorded in the period that it occurs.

Disclosure states that any and all information that affects the full understanding of a company's financial statements must be included with the financial statements. Some items may not affect the accounting records directly. According to the full disclosure principle, these items would be included in the notes accompanying the statements. Examples of such items are outstanding lawsuits, tax disputes and company takeovers.

Pause & Reflect

Exercise 3-1

a) Identify the terminology that matches each description provided in Table 1.

b) Identify each description as characteristic, assumption, principle or constraint.

The first line has been filled in as an example.

Table 1

Description	Terminology	Characteristic, Assumption, Principle or Constraint
1. A piece of information is considered significant if it could influence or change a user's decision.	Materiality	Constraint
2. A company is believed to stay in business for the foreseeable future and not go bankrupt any time soon.		
3. Revenue must be recorded or recognized when goods are sold or when services are performed.		
4. The financial statements of a company must be prepared in a similar way year after year.		
5. Information is free from significant error and bias.		
6. The value of reported financial information outweighs the costs incurred to report it.		
7. An expense must be recorded in the same accounting period in which it was used to produce revenue.		
8. Accounting records are expressed in a single currency, such as US dollars.		

See Appendix I for solutions.

Ethics in Accounting

Users place significant trust in the accuracy of financial records so they can make informed decisions regarding a business. It is an accountant's responsibility to ensure that the financial status of the business is accurately reported. The standards by which these actions are judged as being honest or dishonest, right or wrong, fair or unfair, are also known as **accounting ethics**.

Professional accounting bodies have strict rules governing the behavior of their members. For example, members of the American Institute of Certified Public Accountants (AICPA) must follow the AICPA Code of Professional Conduct. The violation of these rules has resulted in jail sentences in some cases. Two of the most infamous examples are Enron and Worldcom. The senior executives of these companies were found guilty of various offences, including using company funds for personal use and covering up negative financial information.

Typical ethical standards for accountants state the following.

- Members shall act with trustworthiness, integrity and objectivity.

- Members shall not participate in any activity or provide services to any company that the member, or a reasonably prudent person, would believe to be unlawful.

- Members shall not engage in a discriminatory practice prohibited by any antidiscrimination laws.

- Members shall not criticize another professional colleague without first submitting this criticism to the colleague for explanation.

- Members shall act in the interest of their clients, employers and interested third parties, and shall be prepared to sacrifice their self-interest to do so.

- Members shall honor the trust bestowed upon them by others, and shall not use their privileged position without their principal's knowledge and consent.

- Members shall avoid conflicts of interest.

- Members shall not disclose or use any confidential information concerning the affairs of any client, former client, employer or former employer.

- Members shall, when engaged to audit or review financial statements or other information, be free of any influence, interest or relationship with respect to the client's affairs, which impairs the member's professional judgment or objectivity, or which, in the view of a reasonable observer, may have that effect.

- Members shall not, without an employer's or client's consent, use confidential information relating to the business of the member's employer or client to directly or indirectly obtain a personal advantage.

- Members shall not take any action, such as acquiring any interest, property or benefit, that is for unauthorized use, or is confidential relating to an employer's or client's affairs, based on information obtained in the course of his or her duties.

- Members shall strive to continually upgrade and develop their technical knowledge and skills in the areas in which they practice as professionals. This technical expertise shall be employed with due professional care and judgment.

- Members shall adhere to acknowledged principles and standards of professional practice.

- Members shall not be associated with any information that the member knows, or ought to know, to be false or misleading, whether by statement or omission.

- Members shall always act in accordance with the duties and responsibilities associated with being members of the profession, and shall work in a manner that will enhance the image of the profession and the association.

Some of the common concerns about ethics in a business are issues related to the following.

- cash discounts

- operation of a petty cash fund

- manipulation of expenses to manage earnings

- trading a company's shares based on insider information (insider trading)

In 2002, to prevent accounting practices from committing fraudulent activities, the United States Congress passed the **Sarbanes-Oxley Act (SOX)** to be enforced upon all public companies. SOX created an independent oversight body called the Public Company Accounting Oversight Board (PCAOB) to be in charge of ensuring the compliance of all public companies with the specific mandates of SOX. The law requires more stringent policies over codes of conduct, financial disclosure, corporate governance and effectiveness of internal controls. Executive members, such as CEOs and CFOs, along with auditors, could be criminally convicted if the internal control procedures are determined to be ineffective.

There is often a fine line between the law and ethics. A behavior can be quite legal, but unethical. For example, a manager may employ his nephew in the company where he is working. He decides to pay his nephew a higher salary than others in a similar position in the business. While this practice may not be illegal, it could be considered unethical. Many organizations create their own set of rules pertaining to ethics and morals.

In Summary

LO 1 **Describe the users of accounting information**

▶ Internal users include owners and employees of the business. They use accounting information to make internal strategic decisions regarding products, services and business departments.

▶ External users include investors, suppliers, lenders and customers of the business. Financial statements help these users make informed business decisions.

LO 2 **Describe the fields of accounting**

▶ Financial accounting serves the needs of external users by preparing financial statements.

▶ Managerial accounting provides valuable information to internal users to make decisions regarding the future of the business.

LO 3 **Compare the different forms of business organization**

▶ A small business that is owned by one person is generally structured in the form of a sole proprietorship. Sole proprietorships are private enterprises.

▶ A partnership is a business owned by two or more persons operating under a partnership agreement. Partnerships are private enterprises.

▶ A corporation is a business that is registered with the state government and sells ownership of the company to individuals in the form of stock. Corporations may be private or public.

▶ Sole proprietorships and partnerships, excluding LLCs, are subject to unlimited liability, which means that one or more owners are personally and legally accountable for the liabilities of the business.

▶ Corporations (both private and public) are subject to limited liability, which means that their risk is limited to their monetary investment in the business.

▶ Unlike other businesses, profits made by nonprofit organizations are redistributed to the community by providing services or products.

LO 4 **Identify the objective, constraints and qualitative characteristics of financial information**

▶ The objective of financial reporting is to provide useful financial information to both internal and external users.

▶ The four constraints are cost constraint, materiality, conservatism and consistency.

▶ The four qualitative characteristics of financial information are relevance, reliability, understandability and comparability.

▶ Accountants may face a trade-off between two or more characteristics (e.g. relevance and reliability).

LO 5 List and apply basic accounting assumptions and principles

▶ The assumptions of the accounting framework are the business entity, going concern, monetary unit and time period assumptions.

▶ The basic principles of the accounting framework are measurement, revenue recognition, expense recognition and disclosure.

LO 6 Explain the importance of ethics in accounting

▶ Accountants must adhere to a high standard of ethics to ensure that the financial information of a business is accurately reported.

▶ All of a business' users rely on this information to make decisions.

Review Exercise 3-1

Hollinger Runners Inc. (HRI) is a publicly traded manufacturer of high-quality, stylish sneakers with hundreds of stockholders. The company has been in business for more than 20 years and has experienced good and bad economic times. The company's financial performance has usually been aligned with the state of the economy. Lately, the economy has been booming.

The company has a year end of April 30. It is now May 31, 2018. Hollinger produces financial statements on an annual basis. The company's accountant has prepared the balance sheet as at April 30, 2018, using GAAP. The assets portion of this balance sheet is shown below.

Hollinger Runners Inc.
Balance Sheet
As at April 30, 2018

	2018	2017
Assets		
	(in thousands)	
Current Assets		
Cash	$10	$500
Accounts Receivable	10	140
Merchandise Inventory	5	120
Other Current Assets	60	70
Total Current Assets	85	830
Noncurrent Assets		
Available-for-Sale Investments	60	65
Property, Plant and Equipment	1,210	2,120
Goodwill	40	50
Total Noncurrent Assets	1,310	2,235
Total Assets	$1,395	$3,065

On May 1, 2017, the company changed the location of its headquarters from Europe to the United States. Therefore, the 2017 column in the balance sheet is presented in the currency unit of euros and the 2018 column is presented in US dollars. The company did not disclose this information in the notes to the financial statements. The euro was stronger than the US dollar during 2017 and 2018.

Additional information regarding HRI's financial statements and accounting records is shown below.

- HRI indicated in the notes to the financial statements that in 2018 it changed the accounting policy it used for depreciating assets. It did not justify its reason for doing so.

- The cash account is comprised of two sub-accounts: cash related to the business and personal cash savings of a few of the stockholders.

- All assets purchased during the year have been valued at fair market value at the year-end date, which is higher than the amount of money that HRI paid for the purchases.

- Regarding expenses, there are numerous invoices that did not match the cost amounts reported in the accounting records. The amounts on the invoices are significantly greater than the amounts in the accounting records.

- The company's income statement has shown a significant net loss for the past three years.

Required

a) Which of the four qualitative characteristics of financial information has HRI failed to apply? Explain.

_____

_____

_____

_____

_____

_____

_____

_____

_____

_____

_____

_____

_____

_____

_____

b) Which of the basic accounting principles and/or assumptions has HRI violated? Explain.

_____

_____

_____

_____

_____

_____

_____

_____

_____

_____

_____

_____

_____

_____

_____

_____

_____

_____

_____

_____

_____

See Appendix I for solutions.

Learning Objectives

LO 1	**Distinguish between debits and credits**
	• Debit and Credit Reference Guide
	• Double-Entry Sample Transactions

LO 2	**Describe the accounting cycle**

LO 3	**Explain how to analyze a transaction**

LO 4	**Record transactions in the general journal**
	• Compound Journal Entries

LO 5	**Post journal entries to the general ledger**
	• Establishing a Chart of Accounts

LO 6	**Prepare a trial balance**
	• Correcting Entries

LO 7	**Describe ethics and internal controls relating to recording and posting transactions**

AMEENGAGE *Access **ameengage.com** for integrated resources including tutorials, practice exercises, the digital textbook and more.*

85

Transition to Debits and Credits

We have been using the terms "increase" and "decrease" to record transactions in T-accounts, but formal accounting requires the use of debits and credits. In the debit and credit system (unlike increases and decreases), a **debit** is always recorded on the left-hand side of an account and a **credit** is always recorded on the right-hand side, as illustrated in Figure 4.1. Debits are represented by DR, and credits are represented by CR.

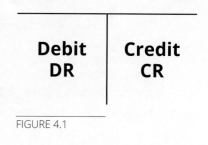

FIGURE 4.1

Debit and Credit Reference Guide

Remember that debit does not always mean decrease and credit does not always mean increase. A credit means an entry on the right side of the account, which may cause the account to increase or decrease, depending on its type. Similarly, a debit means an entry on the left side of the account, which may cause the account to increase or decrease, depending on its type. Recall that the accounting equation is

Assets = Liabilities + Owner's Equity

For the accounting equation to stay in balance, the total value of the debits must always equal the total value of the credits. Throughout this textbook, you may use the Debit and Credit Reference Guide shown in Figure 4.2 to help when analyzing transactions.

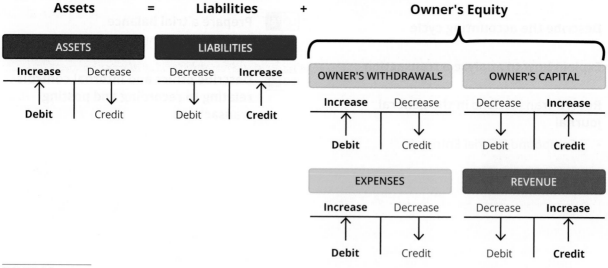

FIGURE 4.2

Every transaction has at least one debit and one credit, referred to as a double entry. The total of all debits in a transaction must equal the total of all credits. If debits do not equal credits, the accounting equation is not balanced.

Each type of account also has a normal balance. A **normal balance** corresponds to the side of the T-account that records the increase and is shown in bold in Figure 4.2. A normal balance indicates a positive balance for the account. For instance, the cash account (an asset) has a debit normal balance.

Double-Entry Sample Transactions

Using the Debit and Credit Reference Guide, let us look at a few sample transactions and see how to translate increases and decreases into debits and credits. The following transactions were completed by Hoffman Company during the month of June 2018.

WORTH REPEATING

In accounting, there are always at least two parts to a transaction. For each transaction, the total value of debits equals the total value of credits. This is known as double entry.

1. Provided services to a customer who paid cash
2. Paid cash to reduce the principal of the bank loan
3. Paid cash for a one-year insurance policy
4. Recorded maintenance expense, which will be paid later

These transactions are summarized in a table and illustrated in T-accounts in Figure 4.3.

| 1. | Cash | Increase | Debit |
| | Service Revenue | Increase | Credit |

| 2. | Notes Payable | Decrease | Debit |
| | Cash | Decrease | Credit |

| 3. | Prepaid Insurance | Increase | Debit |
| | Cash | Decrease | Credit |

| 4. | Maintenance Expense | Increase | Debit |
| | Accounts Payable | Increase | Credit |

| CASH | | SERVICE REVENUE | |
| Debit | | Credit | |

| NOTES PAYABLE | | CASH | |
| Debit | | Credit | |

| PREPAID INSURANCE | | CASH | |
| Debit | | Credit | |

| MAINTENANCE EXPENSE | | ACCOUNTS PAYABLE | |
| Debit | | Credit | |

FIGURE 4.3

The Accounting Cycle

LO 2

As discussed in Chapter 3, the purpose of accounting is to prepare financial statements to help users make informed decisions. There are many transactions during an accounting period and it is important to summarize them all within the financial statements.

Take note of the photo on the first page of Chapter 4. It shows a group of cyclists in a race around a track. The cyclists must go around the track with no break in between each lap (i.e. the end of the first lap is the beginning of the second lap, the end of the second lap is the beginning of the third lap, etc.), and must follow the rules of the race. Similarly, accountants use something called the **accounting cycle,** which is a series of steps required to complete the financial statements. In accounting, the end of the first cycle (the first period's closing balances) is the beginning of the second cycle (the second period's opening balances). Also, accountants have to follow the rules according to GAAP, which you learned about in Chapter 3. Businesses prepare financial statements at the end of each accounting period, whether it is a month, quarter, year, or other period of time. Every period, the cycle repeats. Over the next three chapters, the accounting cycle will be illustrated using a monthly period for a sample company.

Figure 4.4 shows the steps required to generate a formal set of financial statements for a given period. A computerized system either performs most of these steps automatically or has them available immediately, while a manual system requires each step to be completed by hand. The first three steps are performed repeatedly during the accounting period while the remaining steps are all completed at the end of the current period and prepare the accounts for the next period. This chapter covers the first four steps of the accounting cycle (shown in blue).

FIGURE 4.4

Analyze Transactions

The first step of the accounting cycle is to gather and analyze what must be recorded as transactions. All transactions must have **source documents**, or evidence that they actually happened. Source documents can include sales receipts, bills, checks, bank statements, and so on.

As discussed earlier, we must determine which accounts are affected, which parts of the accounting equation the accounts belong to and identify whether these accounts will increase or decrease as a result of this transaction. The extra step now is to match the increase or decrease of each account with a debit or credit entry to the account. Use the Debit and Credit Reference Guide in Figure 4.2 to help with this.

For example, suppose you pay a $100 utility bill with cash. To analyze this, first determine which accounts are affected (utilities expense and cash). Now, for each account, answer the following questions.

- Which category does the account belong to?
- Is the account increasing or decreasing?
- Is the increase or decrease a debit or a credit?

The full analysis for the transaction is shown in Figure 4.5. It is important to note that the analysis is just to determine whether the account will be debited or credited. At this point, which account is analyzed first is irrelevant. Later, in step two of the accounting cycle, we will record the accounts in a standardized format.

Which accounts are affected?	Utilities Expense	Cash
What category does the account belong to?	Expense	Asset
Is the account increasing or decreasing?	Increasing	Decreasing
Is the increase or decrease a debit or a credit? (Use the Debit and Credit Reference Guide)	Debit	Credit

FIGURE 4.5

From this analysis, we can illustrate how the accounts are affected. Notice in Figure 4.6 that utilities expense increases with a debit and cash decreases with a credit.

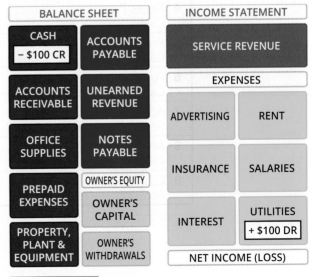

FIGURE 4.6

This type of analysis can be done for any transaction. Keep this in mind as you progress through the textbook and come across new accounts and new types of transactions. To help you analyze how increases and decreases translate into debits and credits, consider these common transactions.

A CLOSER LOOK

If a transaction involves cash, you may find it easiest to analyze cash first for the increase or decrease. Then you can turn your attention to why cash was received or why cash was paid out.

1. Provided consulting services to a customer for cash
2. Received a bill for advertising, which will be paid later
3. Received cash from a customer for work to be completed next month
4. Paid cash toward the principal of a bank loan
5. Prepaid cash for four months' rent
6. Purchased office furniture with cash
7. Provided consulting services to a customer on account
8. Paid cash toward the advertising bill received in transaction 2
9. A customer paid an amount they owed

Using the steps illustrated above on these transactions, we can create a table to determine which accounts will be debited and credited. The table for the nine transactions is shown in Figure 4.7.

	Account Name	Category	Increase or Decrease	Debit or Credit
1	Cash Service Revenue	Asset Revenue	Increase Increase	Debit Credit
2	Advertising Expense Accounts Payable	Expense Liability	Increase Increase	Debit Credit
3	Cash Unearned Revenue	Asset Liability	Increase Increase	Debit Credit
4	Notes Payable Cash	Liability Asset	Decrease Decrease	Debit Credit
5	Prepaid Rent Cash	Asset Asset	Increase Decrease	Debit Credit
6	Furniture Cash	Asset Asset	Increase Decrease	Debit Credit
7	Accounts Receivable Service Revenue	Asset Revenue	Increase Increase	Debit Credit
8	Accounts Payable Cash	Liability Asset	Decrease Decrease	Debit Credit
9	Cash Accounts Receivable	Asset Asset	Increase Decrease	Debit Credit

FIGURE 4.7

Pause & Reflect

Exercise 4-1

Victor Lee owns and operates a personal training business, which is a sole proprietorship.

a)   For each of the following transactions that occurred this month, indicate in Table 1 which two accounts are affected and their category (asset, liability, owner's capital, owner's withdrawal, revenue or expense).

b)   Indicate whether the account balance would increase or decrease and whether the account needs to be debited or credited as a result of the transaction. Refer to Figure 4.7 for help, if necessary.

1.   Victor invested $10,000 cash in the business.

2.   Victor trained a customer for one hour and immediately received a $50 payment.

3.   Furniture worth $3,000 was purchased using the business' credit card and will be paid later.

4.   A customer was trained for a total of eight sessions this month, and promised to pay Victor $400 next month.

5.   Victor paid $5,000 to advertise his business on a billboard.

6.   Victor prepaid $2,000 for two months worth of rent.

Table 1

	Name of the Account Affected	Category	Increase or Decrease	Debit or Credit
1.				
2.				
3.				
4.				
5.				
6.				

See Appendix I for solutions.

Journalize the Transaction

Once the analysis is complete, the transaction must be recorded. The transaction is recorded in a **journal**, which is referred to as a book of original entry. The act of recording in the journal is called **journalizing**. There are various journals available for a company to use, but at this point we will focus solely on the general journal.

The **general journal** lists all the transactions of the business in one place and in chronological order. Keeping all transactions in one place makes them easier to follow and makes it easier to trace any mistakes, compared to only recording them in T-accounts.

As an example, consider a business called MP Consulting, owned by Mark Parish. Mark runs the business as a sole proprietorship and provides financial consulting to his clients. On January 2, 2018, he completed some work for a client who paid $1,500 cash. Our analysis indicates that cash should be debited and service revenue should be credited. Figure 4.8 shows how this is recorded in the journal. The circled letters explain how to properly create a journal entry.

JOURNAL				Page 1
ⓐ Date	**Account Title and Explanation ⓑ**	**PR ⓒ**	**Debit ⓓ**	**Credit**
2018				
Jan 2	Cash ⓑ1		1,500	
	Service Revenue ⓑ2			1,500
	Completed work for client ⓑ3			
	ⓔ			

FIGURE 4.8

ⓐ   **Date**

The date column includes the current year at the top of the column, followed by the month and day of the transaction. The journal entries are entered in chronological order.

ⓑ   **Account Title and Explanation**

This column indicates the names of the accounts being affected. The logic used to indicate which account is affected has not changed. For example, if revenue is earned and cash is received, cash increases (debit) and service revenue increases (credit). The journal places this information in a standard order to keep the information organized.

ⓑ1   Any accounts that are debited in the transaction are listed first.

②   Any accounts that are credited in the transaction are listed after the debited accounts and indented slightly. This is a formatting standard that makes it easier to read long lists of transactions.

③   A brief explanation is listed immediately after the transaction.

If you are given a list of accounts to choose from, use accounts from that list. If you are not provided with a list, use an appropriate name that accurately describes what the account is tracking. For example, repairs performed in the office may be called Repairs Expense, Maintenance Expense or Repairs & Maintenance Expense. Once an account name has been used, the same name should be used for all similar transactions.

ⓒ PR (Posting Reference)

The posting reference column is initially left blank when the journal entry is prepared. We will use this column when we start the third step of the accounting cycle, posting to the ledger accounts.

ⓓ Debit or Credit

These two columns are used to record the amount of the transaction in the appropriate side—debit or credit.

ⓔ   Leave a space between journal entries to make it easier to read and separate them.

Compound Journal Entries

If a journal entry only affects two accounts, one account is debited and one account is credited. This type of entry is fairly straightforward to complete. However, some journal entries may affect three or more accounts. These entries are called **compound journal entries** and have multiple debits or multiple credits.

To illustrate a compound journal entry, suppose you purchase equipment for $5,000 on May 25, 2018. You pay $1,000 cash at the time of the purchase, but will not pay the remainder until some time later (accounts payable). This transaction affects the following accounts: equipment is increased with a debit for the full amount, $5,000; accounts payable is increased with a credit for $4,000; and cash is decreased with a credit for $1,000. The journal entry is illustrated in Figure 4.9.

JOURNAL				Page 1
Date	**Account Title and Explanation**	**PR**	**Debit**	**Credit**
2018				
May 25	Equipment		5,000	
	Accounts Payable			4,000
	Cash			1,000
	Purchased equipment			

FIGURE 4.9

Pause & Reflect

Exercise 4-2

Prepare a compound journal entry for the $1,000 service completed for a client on April 18, 2018. Cash was received in the amount of $600 and the remainder was put on account.

JOURNAL				Page 1
Date	**Account Title and Explanation**	**PR**	**Debit**	**Credit**

See Appendix I for solutions.

Post to Ledger Accounts

Although all the activities for the month have been recorded in the general journal, the ending balance for each account has not yet been determined. For example, there may have been several transactions relating to cash. To calculate the closing cash balance, the accounts need to be sorted into a manageable format where all transactions affecting that account are included and summarized.

The **general ledger** records and organizes the accounts used by the business. Each account is given a unique number to help identify it and is assigned a separate page to track the balance of the account. The list of all the accounts in the general ledger is called a **chart of accounts**. Combined with the journal introduced in the previous section, the journal and ledger can be referred to as the books of the business.

Establishing a Chart of Accounts

To set up a chart of accounts, first define the various accounts used by the business and then give each account an identifying number. For small businesses, three-digit account numbers may be sufficient, although more digits allow for new accounts to be added as the business grows. Large organizations may have thousands of accounts and require longer account numbers. It is important to assign account numbers in a logical manner and to follow specific industry standards. One example of a numbering system is shown in Figure 4.10.

Account Numbering
100–199: **Asset** accounts
200–299: **Liability** accounts
300–399: **Equity** accounts

400–499: **Revenue** accounts
500–599: **Expense** accounts

FIGURE 4.10

Separating each account by several numbers allows new accounts to be added while maintaining the same logical order. Note that the account numbering follows the order of the financial statements: balance sheet (assets, liabilities and equity) and income statement (revenue and expenses).

Different types of businesses use different types of accounts. For example, a manufacturing business requires various accounts for reporting manufacturing costs. A retail business, however, has accounts for the purchase of inventory. Figure 4.11 shows how a service company may set up its accounts. Other accounts can be set up as needed. For example, if the business requires a new expense account, the new account is added to the chart of accounts.

Account Description	Account #
ASSETS	
Cash	101
Accounts Receivable	105
Prepaid Insurance	110
Office Supplies	115
Equipment	120
Accumulated Depreciation—Equipment	125
LIABILITIES	
Accounts Payable	200
Interest Payable	205
Unearned Revenue	210
Notes Payable	215
OWNER'S EQUITY	
Owner's Capital	300
Owner's Withdrawals	310
Income Summary	315

Account Description	Account #
REVENUE	
Service Revenue	400
EXPENSES	
Advertising Expense	500
Bad Debt Expense	505
Insurance Expense	510
Interest Expense	515
Maintenance Expense	520
Miscellaneous Expense	525
Office Supplies Expense	530
Professional Fees Expense	535
Rent Expense	540
Salaries Expense	545
Telephone Expense	550
Travel Expense	555

FIGURE 4.11

Each of the accounts listed in Figure 4.11 has its own ledger account. Think of the ledger as an expanded T-account. In Figure 4.12, notice the red "T" under the debit and credit columns. This is shown to illustrate its similarity to the T-accounts you have been working with.

Account: Cash					GL No: 101
Date	Description	PR	DR	CR	Balance

FIGURE 4.12

Each entry in the journal must be posted to the appropriate ledger account. To maintain up-to-date records, posting should be completed regularly, whether daily, weekly or monthly. The posting of the first journal entry to the general ledger is completed in Figure 4.13. The cash account has an opening balance of $3,000.

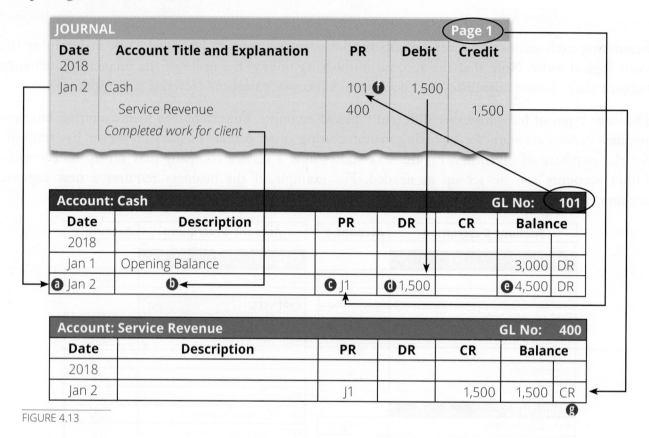

FIGURE 4.13

There are a number of steps to complete when posting items from the journal to the general ledger.

ⓐ Transfer the date of the transaction.

ⓑ The description in the ledger does not have to be completed for every transaction, provided you have a description already recorded in the journal.

ⓒ Transfer the page number of the journal to the posting reference column (PR) in the ledger.

ⓓ Enter the transaction amount into the appropriate debit or credit column.

ⓔ Calculate the new account balance (i.e. the ending, or closing balance). Increase and decrease the previous balance according to the debit and credit rules in Figure 4.1.

ⓕ Enter the ledger number into the posting reference column in the journal as a checking process once the amount has been posted.

ⓖ Repeat the steps for all lines in the journal entry.

IN THE REAL WORLD

Accounting software, such as QuickBooks and Sage, automatically perform the functions of double entries. For example, assume that cash is received by the company and the user identifies the receipt as payment from a customer for services or goods provided. The user is usually the company's bookkeeper or accountant. The software automatically debits the correct asset account and credits the revenue account. After the entry is journalized by the software, the amounts are automatically posted to the general ledger and the trial balance. There is a significant level of automation provided by accounting software, which can reduce the number of accounting errors and misstatements if used correctly.

It is good practice to check that the balance shown in the ledger for each account is a normal balance (e.g. cash has a debit normal balance). If an account does not have a normal balance, an error has likely occurred. Check that the balance was calculated correctly, the amount in the ledger was correctly copied from the journal and the journal entry was created correctly.

In the modern accounting system, the posting process is automatically done by a computer system. Accountants no longer need to refer to a specific page in the journal book to look for transactions.

Return to MP Consulting to see how a full set of journals are prepared and posted to the ledger accounts. First, examine the opening balances from the previous period's balance sheet in Figure 4.14.

MP Consulting Balance Sheet As at December 31, 2017			
Assets		**Liabilities**	
Cash	$3,000	Accounts Payable	$1,000
Accounts Receivable	1,200	Unearned Revenue	900
Equipment	6,000	Notes Payable	3,000
		Total Liabilities	4,900
		Owner's Equity	
		Parish, Capital	5,300
Total Assets	$10,200	**Total Liabilities and Equity**	$10,200

FIGURE 4.14

Note that the balance sheet is dated December 31, 2017. It shows the ending account balances for December 2017, which are the beginning balances for January 2018. These opening balances are already recorded in the ledger accounts. In general, a balance sheet account's ending balance for a given accounting period is the beginning balance of the next period. In this textbook, the term "opening balance" is used synonymously with "beginning balance," and "closing balance" is synonymous with "ending balance."

The income statement is only prepared for the period (the month or year) and always starts the new period with no balances in the accounts. This idea is explained in a later chapter.

MP Consulting had the following transactions for the month of January 2018. The transactions have been entered in the journal in Figure 4.15.

Jan 2   Completed work for a client and the client paid $1,500 cash

Jan 3   Paid $800 cash for January's rent

Jan 4   Prepaid $1,200 cash for a one-year insurance policy

Jan 5   Mark invested $5,000 cash into the business

Jan 7   Paid $2,300 cash for equipment

Jan 10   Completed work for a client, who will pay $1,800 next month

Jan 16   Paid $500 toward the principal of the bank loan

Jan 19   Received $1,100 cash from a client for work to be completed next month

Jan 20   Received a telephone bill for $250 to be paid next month

Jan 30   Mark withdrew $2,000 cash for personal use

JOURNAL				Page 1
Date 2018	**Account Title and Explanation**	**PR**	**Debit**	**Credit**
Jan 2	Cash	101	1,500	
	Service Revenue	400		1,500
	Completed work for client			
Jan 3	Rent Expense	540	800	
	Cash	101		800
	Paid rent for month of January			
Jan 4	Prepaid Insurance	110	1,200	
	Cash	101		1,200
	Prepaid annual insurance policy			
Jan 5	Cash	101	5,000	
	Parish, Capital	300		5,000
	Owner invested cash			
Jan 7	Equipment	120	2,300	
	Cash	101		2,300
	Bought equipment			
Jan 10	Accounts Receivable	105	1,800	
	Service Revenue	400		1,800
	Completed work on account			
Jan 16	Notes Payable	215	500	
	Cash	101		500
	Paid bank loan principal			
Jan 19	Cash	101	1,100	
	Unearned Revenue	210		1,100
	Received customer deposit			
Jan 20	Telephone Expense	550	250	
	Accounts Payable	200		250
	Received telephone bill			
Jan 30	Parish, Withdrawals	310	2,000	
	Cash	101		2,000
	Owner took cash for personal use			

FIGURE 4.15

Figure 4.16 shows how the general ledger would look after posting all the journal entries from Figure 4.15.

GENERAL LEDGER

Account: Cash					GL No:	101
Date	Description	PR	DR	CR	Balance	
2018						
Jan 1	Opening Balance				3,000	DR
Jan 2		J1	1,500		4,500	DR
Jan 3		J1		800	3,700	DR
Jan 4		J1		1,200	2,500	DR
Jan 5		J1	5,000		7,500	DR
Jan 7		J1		2,300	5,200	DR
Jan 16		J1		500	4,700	DR
Jan 19		J1	1,100		5,800	DR
Jan 30		J1		2,000	3,800	DR

Account: Accounts Receivable					GL No:	105
Date	Description	PR	DR	CR	Balance	
2018						
Jan 1	Opening Balance				1,200	DR
Jan 10		J1	1,800		3,000	DR

Account: Prepaid Insurance					GL No:	110
Date	Description	PR	DR	CR	Balance	
2018						
Jan 1	Opening Balance				0	DR
Jan 4		J1	1,200		1,200	DR

Account: Equipment					GL No:	120
Date	Description	PR	DR	CR	Balance	
2018						
Jan 1	Opening Balance				6,000	DR
Jan 7		J1	2,300		8,300	DR

Account: Accounts Payable					GL No:	200
Date	Description	PR	DR	CR	Balance	
2018						
Jan 1	Opening Balance				1,000	CR
Jan 20		J1		250	1,250	CR

Account: Unearned Revenue					GL No:	210	
Date	**Description**	**PR**	**DR**	**CR**	**Balance**		
2018							
Jan 1	Opening Balance				900	CR	
Jan 19		J1		1,100	2,000	CR	

Account: Notes Payable					GL No:	215	
Date	**Description**	**PR**	**DR**	**CR**	**Balance**		
2018							
Jan 1	Opening Balance				3,000	CR	
Jan 16		J1	500		2,500	CR	

Account: Parish, Capital					GL No:	300	
Date	**Description**	**PR**	**DR**	**CR**	**Balance**		
2018							
Jan 1	Opening Balance				5,300	CR	
Jan 5		J1		5,000	10,300	CR	

Account: Parish, Withdrawals					GL No:	310	
Date	**Description**	**PR**	**DR**	**CR**	**Balance**		
2018							
Jan 30		J1	2,000		2,000	DR	

Account: Service Revenue					GL No:	400	
Date	**Description**	**PR**	**DR**	**CR**	**Balance**		
2018							
Jan 2		J1		1,500	1,500	CR	
Jan 10		J1		1,800	3,300	CR	

Account: Rent Expense					GL No:	540	
Date	**Description**	**PR**	**DR**	**CR**	**Balance**		
2018							
Jan 3		J1	800		800	DR	

Account: Telephone Expense					GL No:	550	
Date	**Description**	**PR**	**DR**	**CR**	**Balance**		
2018							
Jan 20		J1	250		250	DR	

FIGURE 4.16

To summarize, the first three steps of the accounting cycle (analyze transactions, journalize transactions and post to the general ledger) are done repeatedly during the period. There may be hundreds of journal entries each period, depending on the size of the business. Once the period ends, the accountant moves on to the rest of the accounting cycle, starting with step 4.

Prepare the Trial Balance

 LO 6

Remember that in every journal entry, the total value of the debits must equal the total value of the credits at *all* times. To ensure that this rule has been adhered to, we need to create a trial balance. A **trial balance** lists all accounts in the general ledger and their balances at a specific date. If the total debits equals total credits, then the trial balance is balanced. The trial balance is created at the end of the accounting cycle and is used as an internal report for the preparation of financial statements. Some accountants choose to total the debit and credit columns in journals as an added control.

The trial balance has a title that indicates the company name, the name of the report (Trial Balance) and the date the trial balance was prepared. It then lists each account in the order they appear in the general ledger and their final balances in the debit or credit column. The trial balance in Figure 4.17 is based on the accounts and balances from Figure 4.16. Only accounts that have a balance are listed in the trial balance.

If the trial balance does not balance, the financial statements cannot be prepared because there is an error somewhere in the accounts. Double check the following items to identify the error.

MP Consulting Trial Balance January 31, 2018		
Account	**DR**	**CR**
Cash	$3,800	
Accounts Receivable	3,000	
Prepaid Insurance	1,200	
Equipment	8,300	
Accounts Payable		$1,250
Unearned Revenue		2,000
Notes Payable		2,500
Parish, Capital		10,300
Parish, Withdrawals	2,000	
Service Revenue		3,300
Rent Expense	800	
Telephone Expense	250	
Total	$19,350	$19,350

1. Do all accounts on the trial balance show a normal balance?

2. Were the balances on the trial balance copied correctly from the ledger accounts?

3. Was the calculation of the ledger account balances done correctly?

4. Were the amounts in the ledger accounts copied correctly from the journal?

5. Were the journal entries created correctly?

FIGURE 4.17

The fact that a trial balance is balanced does not necessarily mean that all transactions were correctly recorded. For example, the following errors can be made but still leave the trial balance in balance.

- The wrong account was used. For example, debiting an asset instead of debiting an expense.

- An entire journal entry was omitted.

- An entire journal entry was recorded or posted twice.

- Incorrect amounts were used for the journal entry.

- Debits and credits were placed on the wrong side of the entry. For example, instead of debiting cash and crediting revenue, the entry may have debited revenue and credited cash.

Locating errors can be a frustrating experience, so it is important to ensure that entries are made correctly the first time.

A CLOSER LOOK

A common error that leaves the trial balance unbalanced is transposition. A transposition error occurs when two numbers are switched (e.g. 530 is written as 350). If the difference between the total debits and total credits is evenly divisible by 9, then it is likely a transposition error has been made. Another common error is a slide error, where the decimal point is slid to the left or right of its correct position (e.g. $1,011.10 is written as $10,111.00).

Correcting Entries

During the process of preparing a trial balance or at any time during the accounting cycle, errors in a journal entry may be discovered in the accounting records. The error could be for the incorrect amount, or the wrong account may have been used. In either case, a correction must be made.

In accounting systems, there must always be a paper trail to document what has happened to affect the ledger balances. Errors cannot be simply erased to be corrected. Instead, a correcting journal entry should be made to reverse the error. Correcting entries can be made at any time during the accounting cycle and are meant to fix an error in a previous journal entry.

For example, suppose an entry was made on March 1, 2018 to prepay a one-year insurance policy for $1,800. Instead of debiting the prepaid insurance account, the prepaid rent account was debited. The incorrect journal entry is shown in Figure 4.18.

JOURNAL				Page 1
Date 2018	**Account Title and Explanation**	**PR**	**Debit**	**Credit**
Mar 1	Prepaid Rent		1,800	
	Cash			1,800
	Pay for one-year insurance policy			

FIGURE 4.18

This journal entry overstates prepaid rent and understates prepaid insurance. The error is discovered on March 8, 2018 and must be corrected. First, a reversing entry is prepared to reverse the original transaction from March 1, and then the correct journal entry is prepared. This is shown in Figure 4.19.

JOURNAL				Page 2
Date 2018	**Account Title and Explanation**	**PR**	**Debit**	**Credit**
Mar 8	Cash		1,800	
	Prepaid Rent			1,800
	To reverse incorrect entry			
Mar 8	Prepaid Insurance		1,800	
	Cash			1,800
	To correctly pay for one-year insurance policy			

FIGURE 4.19

After the correcting entries are made, they are posted to the appropriate general ledger accounts, the balances of which are subsequently transferred to the trial balance. At this point, the ledger account balances and the trial balance is correct.

Pause & Reflect

Exercise 4-3

On September 5, a company paid $5,000 to reduce the principal of the bank loan. The transaction was recorded as a debit to interest expense by mistake. Prepare the correcting entries on September 28, when the error was discovered.

JOURNAL				Page 2
Date	**Account Title and Explanation**	**PR**	**Debit**	**Credit**

See Appendix I for solutions.

Ethics and Internal Controls

Regardless of whether a company uses accounting software or records transactions manually, there is ample opportunity to manipulate the books. Computerized accounting information is only as reliable and accurate as the information that goes into the system. Most of the time, the accounting system used by a company is not fully automated. This means that the user must input information into the system or interact directly with the software at one point or another, which provides opportunity for inaccurate reporting.

For instance, some types of accounting software allow automated recurring entries; they can be set up to repeat the same entry at various time intervals. Some examples of companies that have recurring entries include a rental property company that receives rent from tenants on a monthly basis, an Internet provider that receives subscription payments on a monthly basis, or a bank that receives mortgage payments on a bi-weekly basis.

Consider GG Property Management, which manages and rents out offices in high-rise buildings. Since the company receives rent from its tenants on a monthly basis, it set up its accounting software to record rent revenue automatically at the beginning of each month.

Suppose that a tenant moves out and stops paying rent to GG. However, GG's accounting system continues to record the rent revenue for every subsequent month after the office has been vacated. Allowing the entries to continue being recorded automatically is inaccurate. The additional entries for rent revenue will automatically flow to the general ledger, the trial balance, the income statement and ultimately the balance sheet. Earnings for the period will be inflated. The financial statements will be misstated and this significant error will mislead the users of the financial statements if it goes undetected.

If the above behavior is intentional and management conceals the misstatement, then it is considered highly unethical and fraudulent. However, assume the error was unintentional and the business wants to ensure it does not happen again. A possible control that may detect the error is to compare the current list of tenants to the transaction details in the journal at regular intervals (such as month end). Another method of preventing this error is to program the software to automatically prompt the software administrator to authorize each entry or avoid using automated recurring entries entirely.

Such internal control procedures among US companies have been strengthened as a result of the passage of the Sarbanes-Oxley Act (SOX), which requires statements from every public company's management and external auditor regarding the effectiveness of internal controls.

In Summary

LO 1 Distinguish between debits and credits

- ▶ Debits are recorded on the left side of an account and credits are recorded on the right side. For the accounting equation to stay in balance, the total value of the debits must equal the total value of the credits.

- ▶ Assets, expenses and owner's withdrawals increase with debits and decrease with credits. Liabilities, revenues and owner's capital increase with credits and decrease with debits.

LO 2 Describe the accounting cycle

- ▶ The accounting cycle consists of the steps required to prepare financial statements. The cycle repeats every period.

LO 3 Explain how to analyze a transaction

- ▶ Analysis of a transaction begins with source documents, which indicate that a transaction has occurred. The analysis helps to determine which accounts are affected, whether they are increasing or decreasing and whether they are debited or credited.

LO 4 Record transactions in the general journal

- ▶ A journal is a record in which transactions are recorded before they are posted. Journals are known as books of original entry.

- ▶ Double-entry transactions are called journal entries. Every journal entry must have at least one debit and one credit entry so that the total of the debits equals the total of the credits.

- ▶ Journal entries are dated and listed in chronological order. Accounts that are debited in a journal entry are listed first, followed by the accounts that are credited (indented). A short explanation is included for every journal entry.

LO 5 Post journal entries to the general ledger

- ▶ The general ledger is a book used to record all the accounts and balances of the business. These accounts represent the complete financial position of the business. They also make up the accounting data from which all reports are generated.

- ▶ The listing of all the accounts being used by a business is called a chart of accounts.

- ▶ The general ledger is similar to a collection of T-accounts. The debits and credits of each account are shown along with the current balance of the account.

LO 6 **Prepare a trial balance**

▶ The trial balance lists all accounts in the general ledger and their balances. If the total debits equals total credits, then the trial balance is balanced.

▶ If the trial balance is not balanced, an error has occurred and must be fixed before continuing with the accounting cycle.

▶ Correcting entries are made to fix journal entry errors due to wrong accounts or incorrect amounts.

LO 7 **Describe ethics and internal controls relating to recording and posting transactions**

▶ Accountants should record and post transactions truthfully without manipulating the numbers.

▶ Internal controls, such as double checking and authorization procedures, should be put in place to detect and avoid errors in recording and posting transactions.

AMEENGAGE *Access **ameengage.com** for integrated resources including tutorials, practice exercises, the digital textbook and more.*

Review Exercise 4-1

Catherine Gordon is running her own sole proprietary business called CG Accounting. CG Accounting provides bookkeeping services to small and mid-sized companies. The company prepares financial statements on a monthly basis and had the following closing balances at the end of May 2018.

CG Accounting Balance Sheet As at May 31, 2018			
Assets		**Liabilities**	
Cash	$4,200	Accounts Payable	$2,300
Accounts Receivable	3,100	Unearned Revenue	600
Equipment	6,000	Notes Payable	4,000
		Total Liabilities	6,900
		Owner's Equity	
		Gordon, Capital	6,400
		Total Liabilities and Owner's Equity	
Total Assets	$13,300		$13,300

CG Accounting uses a variety of accounts and account numbers in its accounting records.

Account Description	Account #
ASSETS	
Cash	101
Accounts Receivable	105
Prepaid Insurance	110
Equipment	120
Accumulated Depreciation—Equipment	125
LIABILITIES	
Accounts Payable	200
Interest Payable	205
Unearned Revenue	210
Notes Payable	215
OWNER'S EQUITY	
Gordon, Capital	300
Gordon, Withdrawals	310
Income Summary	315

Account Description	Account #
REVENUE	
Service Revenue	400
EXPENSES	
Advertising Expense	500
Bad Debt Expense	505
Insurance Expense	510
Interest Expense	515
Maintenance Expense	520
Miscellaneous Expense	525
Office Supplies Expense	530
Professional Fees Expense	535
Rent Expense	540
Salaries Expense	545
Telephone Expense	550
Travel Expense	555

During the month of June 2018, CG Accounting made the following transactions.

Jun 1   Paid $900 cash for rent incurred

Jun 3   Prepaid $1,200 cash for a one-year insurance policy

Jun 6   Completed work for a client who immediately paid $2,100 cash

Jun 11   Received a bill for advertising for $450, which will be paid next month

Jun 13   Catherine contributed an extra $3,000 cash to the business

Jun 16   Received $300 from a client for work to be completed in July

Jun 18   Completed work for a client who will pay $1,500 next month

Jun 23   Paid $950 cash toward the principal portion of the bank loan

Jun 30   Catherine withdrew $1,000 cash for personal use

Required

a) Complete the journal entries for each transaction.

JOURNAL				Page 1
Date	Account Title and Explanation	PR	Debit	Credit

JOURNAL				Page 1
Date	Account Title and Explanation	PR	Debit	Credit

b) Post the journal entries to the general ledger.

GENERAL LEDGER

Account: Cash					GL No: 101	
Date	Description	PR	DR	CR	Balance	

Account: Accounts Receivable					GL No: 105	
Date	Description	PR	DR	CR	Balance	

Account: Prepaid Insurance					GL No: 110	
Date	Description	PR	DR	CR	Balance	

Account: Equipment						GL No: 120	
Date	Description		PR	DR	CR	Balance	

Account: Accounts Payable						GL No: 200	
Date	Description		PR	DR	CR	Balance	

Account: Unearned Revenue						GL No: 210	
Date	Description		PR	DR	CR	Balance	

Account: Notes Payable						GL No: 215	
Date	Description		PR	DR	CR	Balance	

Account: Gordon, Capital						GL No: 300	
Date	Description		PR	DR	CR	Balance	

Account: Gordon, Withdrawals						GL No: 310	
Date	Description		PR	DR	CR	Balance	

Account: Service Revenue						GL No: 400	
Date	Description		PR	DR	CR	Balance	

Account: Advertising Expense					GL No:	500
Date	Description	PR	DR	CR	Balance	

Account: Rent Expense					GL No:	540
Date	Description	PR	DR	CR	Balance	

c) Prepare a trial balance.

Account Title	DR	CR

See Appendix I for solutions.

Review Exercise 4-2

On June 28, Jeremy Preston reviewed the transactions that were made for the month. During his review, he came across two errors in the journals.

1. A cash payment of $400 for minor repairs on the company vehicle was debited to the automobile asset account instead of the maintenance expense account.

2. A cash payment of $200 for office supplies was debited to the equipment asset account instead of the office supplies asset account.

Prepare the journal entries to correct the two errors on June 28.

JOURNAL					Page 2
Date	Account Title and Explanation	PR	Debit	Credit

See Appendix I for solutions.

Chapter 5
The Accounting Cycle: Adjustments

Learning Objectives

LO 1 **Describe the purpose of adjustments**

LO 2 **Prepare adjusting entries for accrued revenue**

LO 3 **Prepare adjusting entries for accrued expenses**
- Salaries Expense
- Interest Expense

LO 4 **Prepare adjusting entries for unearned revenue**

LO 5 **Prepare adjusting entries for prepaid expenses**
- Prepaid Rent
- Office Supplies

LO 6 **Prepare adjusting entries for depreciation**
- Contra Account
- Calculation of Depreciation

LO 7 **Prepare an adjusted trial balance**

LO 8 **Describe ethics and internal controls relating to adjusting entries**

Access **ameengage.com** for integrated resources including tutorials, practice exercises, the digital textbook and more.

113

Introduction to Adjustments

As shown in the Chapter Opener photo, when pilots are in flight, they are constantly assessing information from the instruments and gauges and making adjustments to keep the plane on course. Similarly, accountants must regularly analyze transactions, and make adjustments to reflect what is happening before the financial statements can be prepared.

Accrual-based accounting records revenues when they are earned and expenses when they are incurred. However, cash payments and receipts do not always coincide with the recording of revenues and expenses. Thus, cash can change hands in a period before or after recording revenues or expenses.

For example, suppose you prepay $3,000 for a one-year insurance policy in January. In July, the true value of the insurance has decreased by six months and is now worth only $1,500. The value of the prepaid asset must be adjusted to reflect its true value. The decrease in value of the asset decreases equity, which is recorded as an expense on the income statement.

There are a number of adjustments that need to be made to update the values of assets and liabilities. The process to ensure that all accounts are reported accurately at the end of the period is called the adjusting process. This chapter explains the adjusting process and the preparation of an adjusted trial balance. These are the fifth and sixth steps in the accounting cycle, which are shown in blue in Figure 5.1.

*The first three steps are performed repeatedly during an accounting period, while the remaining steps are performed only at the end of the period.

FIGURE 5.1

An accounting period is the period of time covered by the financial statements. A company has a **fiscal year**, which is a consecutive 12-month period that a company chooses for its financial reporting. A company's fiscal year may cover the same time as the calendar year from January 1 to December 31. However, some companies may choose a **natural business year**, which means the fiscal year ends during a slow time of the year. For example, some retail companies, such as Target and Lowe's, have their fiscal year end at the end of January, after the holiday rush is finished. In this case, the fiscal year is from February 1 to January 31.

A company usually prepares a set of financial statements at the end of each fiscal year, although some prepare the statements more frequently to meet statutory requirements or better manage the business. Remember that accrual-based accounting states that revenue and expenses should be recognized in the accounting period when they occur, regardless of when the cash payment is received or made.

Adjusting entries are made at the end of the accounting period to record assets, liabilities, equity, revenue and expenses according to revenue and expense recognition principles. Do not confuse adjusting entries with correcting entries, which you learned about in Chapter 4. A correcting entry is only made when an error is discovered and needs to be corrected. Adjusting entries are prepared at the end of every fiscal period, regardless of whether any errors were made, to update account balances accurately as at the last day of the period. Every adjustment affects both a balance sheet account and an income statement account. Adjusting entries typically fall under five broad categories.

> ## WORTH REPEATING
>
> Revenue recognition states that revenue must be recorded when services are performed, regardless of when cash is received. Expense recognition requires that expenses must be recorded in the same period in which they were used to generate revenue.

1. Accrued revenue
2. Accrued expenses
3. Unearned revenue
4. Prepaid expenses
5. Depreciation

Each category will be examined in detail along with examples of adjustments. It is important to note that all adjustments presented in this chapter are just changes made to the recorded values in the books. At no time will cash be received from customers or paid to suppliers. Therefore, adjusting entries never involve the cash account.

Accrued Revenue   LO 2

Accrued revenue is revenue that has been earned but not yet recorded. There is nothing in the ledger accounts to show for this yet. Revenue can accrue or accumulate over a period of time, such as interest on a loan or collecting rent. Other examples of accrued revenue are where completed services have not been billed or there is a contract for work to be performed over a long period of time. Accrued revenue always increases a receivable asset account and increases a revenue account.

Suppose you have a contract with a client stating you will provide them with services for 30 days. At the end of the contract, you will bill the client and they will pay you. The contract starts on September 21 and is worth $6,000. You will not make a journal entry on September 21, since you have not yet completed any work and no cash has been paid to you.

At the end of September, you want to prepare your financial statements. At this point, there is nothing in the books to indicate that you have done work for this client and that the client owes you money for the work completed so far. As stated by the revenue recognition principle under GAAP, revenue must be recognized (recorded) when goods are sold or services are performed. This means that the portion of the services performed in September must be recognized in September. Between September 21 and September 30, 10 out of 30 days of the services, which are equivalent to one-third of the contract, have been performed. Therefore, an adjusting entry is required on September 30 to accrue the revenue equal to one-third of the $6,000 contract, which is $2,000. Accounts receivable is used to record the amount owing because this is a binding contract and the customer is obligated to pay in the future. Figure 5.2 illustrates the adjusting entry that must be made. Without this adjusting entry, service revenue and accounts receivable would be understated by $2,000 in September. Consequently, both assets and owner's equity would be understated.

JOURNAL					Page 1
Date 2018	**Account Title and Explanation**	**PR**	**Debit**	**Credit**
Sep 30	Accounts Receivable		2,000	
	Service Revenue			2,000
	To accrue revenue on contract			

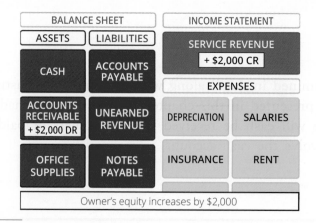

FIGURE 5.2

Once the contract is completed on October 20, you can bill the client. If they pay you immediately, you receive the full $6,000 cash; however, you only record $4,000 worth of revenue earned for the month of October since the other $2,000 was recorded on September 30. There is also a

$2,000 decrease to accounts receivable to indicate that the client has now paid you the amount owed. This is illustrated in Figure 5.3.

JOURNAL				Page 1
Date 2018	Account Title and Explanation	PR	Debit	Credit
Oct 20	Cash		6,000	
	Accounts Receivable			2,000
	Service Revenue			4,000
	To record collection from client			

BALANCE SHEET | INCOME STATEMENT

ASSETS | LIABILITIES | SERVICE REVENUE + $4,000 CR

CASH + $6,000 DR | ACCOUNTS PAYABLE

EXPENSES

ACCOUNTS RECEIVABLE − $2,000 CR | UNEARNED REVENUE | DEPRECIATION | SALARIES

OFFICE SUPPLIES | NOTES PAYABLE | INSURANCE | RENT

Owner's equity increases by $4,000

FIGURE 5.3

IN THE REAL WORLD

In most cases, sales are entered from a sales invoice directly into the accounting records, without looking back to see if there were any adjustments made in the previous period. Thus, the transaction on October 20 could be recorded incorrectly if the adjusted amount in accounts receivable is forgotten and not applied to the transaction. If accounts receivable is not applied, $6,000 would be recorded as service revenue for October instead of $4,000. To eliminate the risk of forgetting about the adjustment for accrued revenue and making an error, an optional step is to record a reversing entry. This is done on the first day of the new accounting period; in this example it would be made on October 1, 2018 so it would not affect the reporting in September. The reversing entry is the opposite of the adjustment on September 30, 2018.

Oct 1	Service Revenue	2,000	
	Accounts Receivable		2,000

By creating this reversing entry, the effect of the adjustment of the previous month is undone for the current month and leaves the service revenue account with a negative (debit) balance of $2,000. On October 20, the full amount of the contract of $6,000 can be recorded, but since service revenue already has a negative balance of $2,000, only $4,000 of revenue is recognized in the month of October.

Oct 20	Cash	6,000	
	Service Revenue		6,000

It is important to note that a reversing entry is just an option businesses can use to make their bookkeeping easier. It does not change anything about the accrual-based accounting and it typically occurs only at the beginning of an accounting period.

Pause & Reflect

Exercise 5-1

Diane Winston owns and operates a pet-sitting business, which is a sole proprietorship. She was hired to care for Angus' dog for 10 days from December 24, 2018 to January 2, 2019, while Angus is away on vacation. Angus signed a contract to pay Diane $600 on January 2. Prepare journal entries for Diane on December 31, 2018 to record revenue accrual, and on January 2, 2019 to record the cash receipt.

JOURNAL				Page 2
Date	Account Title and Explanation	PR	Debit	Credit

See Appendix I for solutions.

Accrued Expenses

Similar to accrued revenue, **accrued expenses** are expenses that have been incurred but have not yet been recorded. Examples of expenses that may accrue at month end include property taxes, salaries, interest on a loan, and rent. Sometimes, a business has to estimate the accrued expense because the bill is not received until later the following month, such as an electricity or water bill. An accrued expense always increases a liability and increases an expense account.

For accrued expenses, the end of the period will report an understated amount of expenses on the income statement without an adjustment. Also, since this expense represents an amount owed, liabilities on the balance sheet will also be understated. The adjusting entry for an accrued expense corrects this. We will examine two examples of accrued expenses: salaries and interest.

Salaries Expense

Salaries to employees are paid after the work has been completed. If the work and the payment for the work occur within the same period, no adjustment has to be made. However, if the work done by the employee occurs in a different period than the payment, an adjustment must be made at the end of the period.

For example, suppose an employee is paid every two weeks. From the calendar in Figure 5.4, we see the first pay period starts on November 12 and ends on November 23, when the employee gets paid. Since the payment on November 23 is for work done in the same month, this is a transaction similar to what you have learned to pay salaries expense with cash.

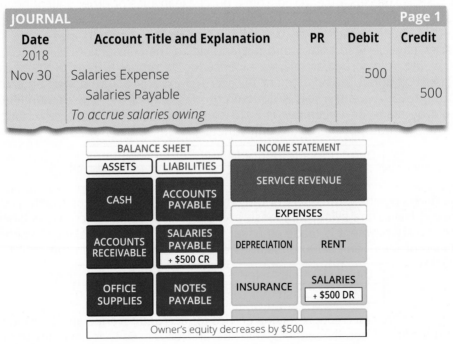

FIGURE 5.4

The employee then works the last week of November but the next pay date is not until December 7. The business accrues a salary expense for the employee for the week worked in November. This expense must be recorded in November, even though the employee is not paid until December.

If the employee earns $1,000 every two weeks, he earns $100 per day ($1,000 ÷ 10 working days). Thus, the business must create an adjusting entry for salaries expense for $500 ($100 per day × 5 days). Figure 5.5 illustrates the adjusting entry. Although the $500 has not been paid to the employee, it has to be accrued. Remember, expenses should be recorded when they are incurred, not necessarily when payments are made. This adjustment is recorded as a salary expense, which decreases equity. Since the salary payment is owed to the employee, a liability account called Salaries Payable tracks the amount owing.

JOURNAL				Page 1
Date	**Account Title and Explanation**	**PR**	**Debit**	**Credit**
2018				
Nov 30	Salaries Expense		500	
	Salaries Payable			500
	To accrue salaries owing			

FIGURE 5.5

On December 7, the business pays the salary of $1,000. The accrued amount of $500 in the liability account is cleared out since the business is paying the debt to the employee. Only $500 is recorded as an expense, since we only need to record the salary expense for the time worked in December. The journal entry for this transaction is shown in Figure 5.6.

JOURNAL				Page 1
Date 2018	**Account Title and Explanation**	**PR**	**Debit**	**Credit**
Dec 7	Salaries Expense		500	
	Salaries Payable		500	
	Cash			1,000
	To record payment of salaries owing			

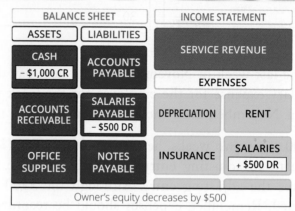

FIGURE 5.6

IN THE REAL WORLD

In most cases, expenses are entered from a purchase invoice or other source documents directly into the accounting records, without checking if any adjustments were made in the previous period. Thus, the transaction on December 7 could be recorded incorrectly if the adjusted amount in salaries payable is forgotten and not applied to the transaction. If salaries payable is not applied, $1,000 would be recorded as salaries expense for December instead of $500. To eliminate the possibility of forgetting about the adjustment for accrued expenses and making an error, an optional step is to record a reversing entry. This is done on the first day of the new accounting period; in this example it would be made on December 1, 2018 so it would not affect the reporting in November. The reversing entry is the opposite of the adjustment on November 30, 2018.

Dec 1	Salaries Payable	500	
	Salaries Expense		500

By creating this reversing entry, the effect of the adjustments of the previous month is undone for the current month and leaves the salaries expense account with a negative (credit) balance of $500. On December 7, the salary payment is made as usual for $1,000, but since salaries expense already has a negative balance of $500, only $500 of salaries expense is recognized in the month of December.

Dec 7	Salaries Expense	1,000	
	Cash		1,000

Some accounting software can create reversing entries for accrued revenue and accrued expenses, thus removing the possibility of double counting revenue and expenses that have already been accrued.

Interest Expense

When borrowing cash, the lender charges interest on the amount borrowed and expects payment at regular intervals. Interest accumulates, or accrues, during the interval before the payment is made. At the end of an accounting period, the borrower must calculate and record the amount of interest that has accumulated to date as an accrued expense. Since it is owed to the lender, it is recorded in a liability account as well.

To calculate interest, three pieces of information must be known.

1. The principal amount (the amount that was originally borrowed)
2. The interest rate (an annual percentage of interest charged on the principal)
3. The term of the loan (how long the debt will last)

The formula to calculate accrued interest is shown in Figure 5.7.

$$\text{Accrued Interest} = \text{Principal} \times \text{Interest Rate} \times \text{Time in Years}$$

FIGURE 5.7

For example, suppose a business borrows $10,000 from the bank on July 1 and must repay the loan in three months on October 1. The bank is charging 5% interest on the loan. Interest rates are always expressed as an annual rate, so any duration that is less than one year must be adjusted accordingly. If the business prepares its statements on September 30, and has not prepared any statements since the loan was received, the entire amount of interest that has accrued in the three months from July 1 to September 30 must be recorded. Using the formula from Figure 5.7, the calculation is shown here.

$$\text{Accrued Interest} = \$10,000 \times 5\% \times {}^{3}/_{12}$$
$$= \$125$$

This means that a $125 interest expense has been incurred between July 1 and September 30 as a result of the $10,000 loan. Because this loan is used to fund the company's revenue-generating operations during the period ending September 30, the interest expense must be accrued in this accounting period. Accruing the interest expense in the same period that the loan is used to generate revenue follows the expense recognition principle under the accrual basis of accounting. The expense recognition principle states that an expense must be recognized in the same accounting period in which it is used to generate revenue. Thus, an adjusting entry to record the accrual of interest of $125 must be made by debiting interest expense and crediting the liability account called interest payable. This account tracks all the interest owed. The adjusting entry is shown in Figure 5.8.

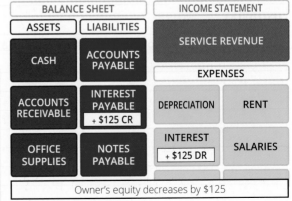

JOURNAL				Page 1
Date 2018	Account Title and Explanation	PR	Debit	Credit
Sep 30	Interest Expense		125	
	Interest Payable			125
	To accrue interest owing			

FIGURE 5.8

After the accrued interest for the loan is recorded, the statements are up-to-date and accurate. When the loan is paid back with interest on October 1, there is no interest expense to record. The payment is a reduction of the bank loan and the interest payable, as shown in Figure 5.9.

JOURNAL				Page 1
Date 2018	**Account Title and Explanation**	**PR**	**Debit**	**Credit**
Oct 1	Notes Payable		10,000	
	Interest Payable		125	
	Cash			10,125
	To pay loan and interest			

	BALANCE SHEET		INCOME STATEMENT

ASSETS	LIABILITIES		INCOME STATEMENT
CASH – $10,125 CR	ACCOUNTS PAYABLE		SERVICE REVENUE
			EXPENSES
ACCOUNTS RECEIVABLE	INTEREST PAYABLE – $125 DR	DEPRECIATION	RENT
OFFICE SUPPLIES	NOTES PAYABLE – $10,000 DR	INTEREST	SALARIES

No change in owner's equity

FIGURE 5.9

Pause & Reflect

Exercise 5-2

Confident Walk Shoe Repair has one employee who works five days a week from Monday to Friday and receives a weekly salary of $550 every Friday. The company borrowed a nine-month bank loan of $8,000 on January 1, 2018. The bank charges an annual interest rate of 6%. The loan interest and principal will be repaid altogether on October 1, 2018. Prepare journal entries on Wednesday, January 31, 2018 to accrue salaries and interest expenses.

JOURNAL				Page 1
Date	**Account Title and Explanation**	**PR**	**Debit**	**Credit**

See Appendix I for solutions.

Unearned Revenue

Unearned revenue is a liability that arises when a customer pays for services or products in advance. For example, when a company sells a gift card, the company receives cash in advance, which increases the cash account. The company also incurs an obligation to later provide products or services to the gift card holder. The amount of this obligation is recorded in unearned revenue, a liability account, until the product or service is provided to the customer. The adjustment to unearned revenue is to account for the earning of revenue for the products or services that were paid for in advance. This adjustment always decreases unearned revenue and increases revenue.

To illustrate the concept of adjustments related to unearned revenue, consider Raina Property Management (Raina). Raina recently bought a large office building and rents out office space for $2,200 a month. The company's policy is to collect the first three months' rent in advance from new tenants. On March 1, 2018, a new tenant moved in and paid $6,600 immediately to Raina to cover rent for March, April and May. Raina makes adjustments to its accounting records at the end of each month because it produces financial statements internally on a monthly basis.

On March 1 when the payment is received, Raina cannot record the $6,600 as revenue because at this point, Raina has not provided any rental service yet. Therefore, on March 1, revenue has not been earned. Instead, Raina makes a journal entry that increases cash (an asset) by $6,600 and increases unearned revenue (a liability) by $6,600. This is shown in Figure 5.10.

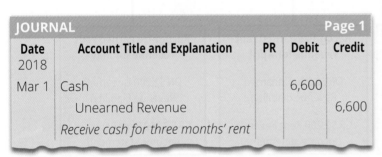

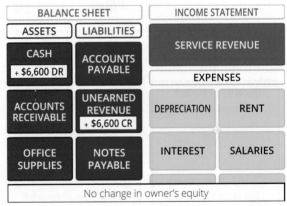

FIGURE 5.10

As of March 31, Raina has earned one month of revenue. On this date, the company decreases unearned revenue (a liability) by $2,200 and increases rent revenue (an income statement account) by $2,200. Waiting until March 31 to recognize the $2,200 rent revenue follows the accrual basis of accounting. Under the accrual basis of accounting, revenue is recognized when it is earned, not when cash is received. After this adjustment is made on March 31, Raina still owes $4,400 worth of rented office space to the tenant, as shown in Figure 5.11.

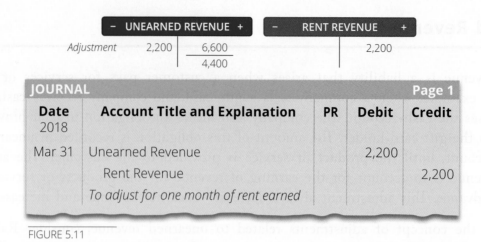

FIGURE 5.11

The same adjustment will be made on April 30 (to recognize April's rent revenue) and May 31 (to recognize May's rent revenue). Figure 5.12 shows the timing of the transactions related to unearned revenue from Raina's perspective.

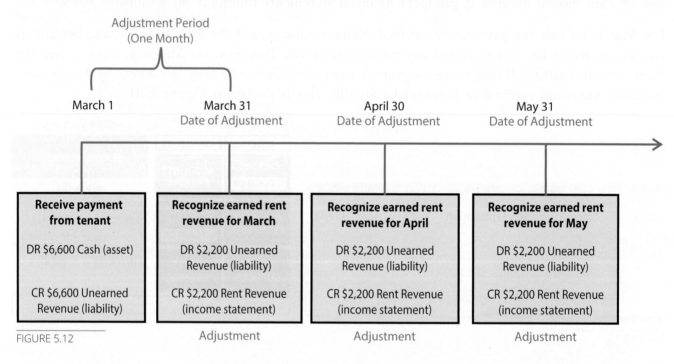

FIGURE 5.12

As shown in Figure 5.12, even though Raina received cash on March 1, the recognition of revenue is deferred to the end of March, April and May, when the revenue has been earned. For this reason, unearned revenue is sometimes referred to as deferred revenue. To "defer" means to put off or delay to a future period. Unearned revenue is different from accrued revenue, which is revenue that is recorded right away when revenue is earned, even though cash has not been received.

Prepaid Expenses

Similar to unearned revenue, accounting for prepaid expenses requires making adjustments as amounts are used. Recall that when a prepaid expense is recognized as an actual expense, prepaid expenses (an asset) decreases and the expense (an income statement account) increases. This is the adjusting entry for prepaid expenses.

Prepaid Rent

We can apply this to the example of Raina Property Management, which was illustrated in the unearned revenue section. Now examine the financial impact of the transactions from the perspective of the tenant who paid Raina three months of rent in advance at $2,200 per month. On March 1, the tenant records a cash payment to Raina for $6,600 as a prepayment for rent, as shown in Figure 5.13. Even though the tenant paid $6,600 cash on March 1, the tenant does not record the transaction as an expense on this date. Under the accrual basis of accounting, expenses are recorded as they are incurred, not when cash is paid. Because rent expense has not been incurred as of March 1, the owner's equity has not decreased on this date. Paying cash for prepaid rent is similar to using cash to purchase another asset. It is simply an exchange of one asset (cash) for another (prepaid rent).

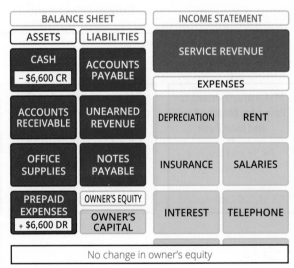

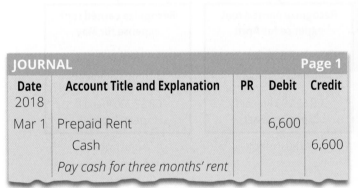

FIGURE 5.13

If the tenant also uses a monthly accounting period, then the prepaid rent is adjusted at the end of each month. In this case, the tenant is adjusting based on what has been used (one month) on March 31. The adjustment decreases the prepaid rent account and increases rent expense on the income statement. As Figure 5.14 shows, after the adjustment on March 31 the prepaid rent account is left with a balance of $4,400, which means two months are still prepaid.

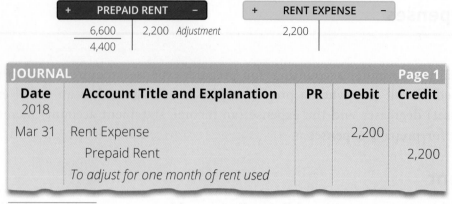

JOURNAL				Page 1
Date 2018	**Account Title and Explanation**	**PR**	**Debit**	**Credit**
Mar 31	Rent Expense		2,200	
	Prepaid Rent			2,200
	To adjust for one month of rent used			

FIGURE 5.14

The same adjustment is made on April 30 (to recognize April's rent expense) and May 31 (to recognize May's rent expense). Figure 5.15 shows the timing of the transactions related to the prepaid rent from the perspective of the tenant.

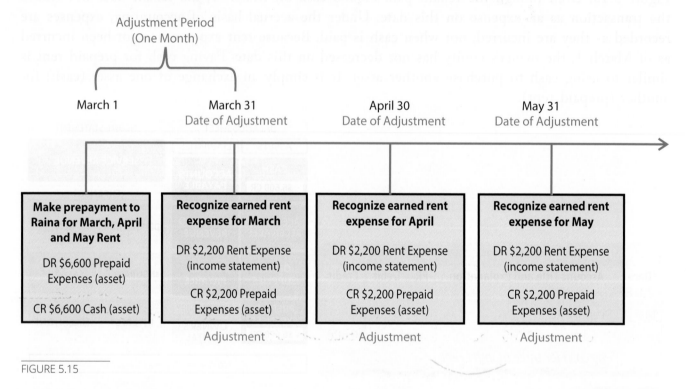

FIGURE 5.15

Prepaid expenses and unearned revenue are opposites. Usually, as in this example, the prepaid expense of one company (the tenant) is the unearned revenue of another company (Raina). The above example illustrated prepaid rent, however the same idea and transactions apply for items such as prepaid insurance or prepaid property taxes.

Office Supplies

Another type of prepaid expense is office supplies. Office supplies are the physical items used to run the office of a business and include paper, photocopy toner, printer toner, pens and so on. When they are initially purchased, these items are recorded as assets on the balance sheet. Instead of recording each item as an expense when it is used, a single adjusting entry is made for the total office supplies used. At the end of the period, a count is made to determine the value of the remaining office supplies and an adjusting entry is created to record the amount of office supplies used as an expense.

To illustrate, suppose a business paid $1,200 cash for office supplies on September 4. This initial purchase of office supplies is just a transfer of one asset (cash) for another (office supplies) and is shown in Figure 5.16.

JOURNAL				Page 1
Date	Account Title and Explanation	PR	Debit	Credit
2018				
Sep 4	Office Supplies		1,200	
	Cash			1,200
	Purchased office supplies			

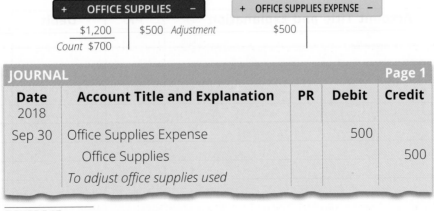

FIGURE 5.16

At the end of the month, a count shows that $700 worth of office supplies remain on hand. This means that office supplies of $500 ($1,200 – $700) were used and must be recorded as an expense. The adjustment is shown in Figure 5.17. Notice that the ending balance of the office supplies account is equal to $700, matching the count that was taken.

+ OFFICE SUPPLIES –		+ OFFICE SUPPLIES EXPENSE –
$1,200	$500 *Adjustment*	$500
Count $700		

JOURNAL				Page 1
Date	Account Title and Explanation	PR	Debit	Credit
2018				
Sep 30	Office Supplies Expense		500	
	Office Supplies			500
	To adjust office supplies used			

FIGURE 5.17

IN THE REAL WORLD

Office supplies are often low-value items, such as paper and pens. In many businesses, keeping track of these small amounts as an asset, then counting them to see what was used, is not viewed as an important procedure. The materiality constraint introduced earlier indicates that if a piece of information could influence a user's decision, it is material and must be accounted for properly according to GAAP. For many businesses, it is easier to simply record office supplies as an expense immediately instead of an asset first. This is done when the amount is not material, since the extra work and detail would not affect users' decisions.

Pause & Reflect

Exercise 5-3

On August 1, Armadillo Property Management collected $36,000 from Beaver Company for 12 months' rent in advance. Beaver Company started its occupancy on August 1. Prepare journal entries for both Armadillo and Beaver on August 1, when cash is received or paid, and on December 31 to recognize rent revenue or expense for the year. Assume no adjusting entries have been made between August 1 and December 31.

Armadillo Property Management's Journal Entries

JOURNAL				Page 1
Date	**Account Title and Explanation**	**PR**	**Debit**	**Credit**

Beaver Company's Journal Entries

JOURNAL				Page 1
Date	**Account Title and Explanation**	**PR**	**Debit**	**Credit**

See Appendix I for solutions.

Depreciation

We learned that items such as land, furniture, computers and automobiles fall under the property, plant and equipment category. These assets are used to run the business and generate sales. However, with the exception of land, these assets eventually become obsolete, unusable or broken. This may not happen for several years, but however long it is, the length of time the asset can be used is called the **useful life**.

These noncurrent assets are like prepaid expenses since the asset is purchased and then used up over time. **Depreciation** is how accountants allocate the cost of a noncurrent asset over its useful life. The reason that land does not depreciate is that land has an unlimited useful life. Depreciation matches the expense of the noncurrent asset to the period in which it generates revenue for the business.

Different types of assets depreciate at different rates. For example, the value of a car tends to depreciate much faster than the value of a desk. For this reason, accountants have come up with multiple depreciation methods that reflect different patterns of depreciation. The most common depreciation methods include the straight-line method, units-of-production method and double-declining-balance method. You will learn about different depreciation methods in Chapter 12. For simplicity, only the straight-line method, which assumes that an asset depreciates equally throughout its useful life, will be used for now.

For example, suppose a machine, which is expected to last for five years and then be thrown out, was purchased for $10,000 one year ago. After one year, a depreciation of $2,000 ($10,000 ÷ 5 years) must be recorded. The $2,000 of depreciation reduces the value of the machine and gives its net book value. The **net book value** of the asset is its original value less the total depreciation that has been recognized. This does not represent what it could be sold for; net book value is just the accounting value of the asset. Thus, the net book value of the machine after recording depreciation is $8,000. However, GAAP requires companies to keep information about the amount assets originally cost and how much they have depreciated so far. Therefore, accounting for depreciation requires a special account called a contra account.

Contra Account

Contra means opposite. A **contra account** is linked to another account and records decreases in the value of that account. This is done so that the original value of the related account remains unchanged. The value of the contra account is subtracted from the related account to arrive at a net book value for the item. In the case of property, plant and equipment (PPE), the contra account is called **accumulated depreciation**. This contra asset account reflects the decrease in the net book value of PPE without changing the original cost of the asset.

With the exception of land, every asset that is considered part of property, plant and equipment has its own separate accumulated depreciation account to track the decrease in net book value.

Suppose an asset was purchased for $10,000 and has accumulated $2,000 worth of depreciation. To preserve the original amount of $10,000, the asset account under PPE is not directly adjusted. Instead, as illustrated in Figure 5.18, accumulated depreciation records the total decrease in net book value of the asset. The contra asset account is called accumulated depreciation because the depreciation accumulates as the asset's cost is allocated to each period. This is different from depreciation expense, an income statement account which only shows the depreciation for the current period.

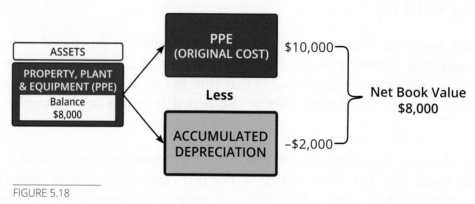

FIGURE 5.18

The contra asset account behaves in a manner opposite to the way a regular asset account behaves. Recall that an asset account increases with a debit and decreases with a credit. The contra asset account (accumulated depreciation) increases with a credit and decreases with a debit. Figure 5.19 illustrates the T-accounts for property, plant and equipment and accumulated depreciation.

FIGURE 5.19

Calculation of Depreciation

As mentioned earlier, we are going to use a simple method called straight-line depreciation. Straight-line depreciation is a method to allocate the cost of the asset evenly over the life of the asset. The calculation for straight-line depreciation is shown in Figure 5.20.

$$\text{Straight-Line Depreciation Rate} = \frac{\text{Cost of Asset} - \text{Residual Value}}{\text{Useful Life}}$$

FIGURE 5.20

There are three parts of this calculation that must be explained.

1. The cost of the asset is the original purchase price of the asset. This is the value shown on the balance sheet in the asset account.
2. Residual value is the estimated value of the asset at the end of its useful life. By subtracting the residual value from the original cost of the asset, we determine the cost that is allocated over the life of the asset. It is possible for an asset to have a residual value of $0, meaning the asset will be fully depreciated and worthless at the end of its useful life.
3. The useful life is how long the asset is expected to be used by the business. Like residual value, this is also an estimate. The useful life can be expressed in years or months, depending on how often depreciation is recorded.

For example, suppose a machine was purchased on January 1, 2018 for $10,000. The machine is expected to last for five years, after which it is expected to have a residual value of $1,000. The calculation for yearly depreciation under the straight-line method is shown below.

$$\text{Straight-Line Depreciation} = \frac{\$10,000 - \$1,000}{5 \text{ Years}}$$

$$= \$1,800/\text{year}$$

The cost allocated over five years is $9,000, which is the original purchase price minus the estimated residual value. Each year, $1,800 is recorded as a depreciation expense and $1,800 is added to accumulated depreciation. The journal entry is shown in Figure 5.21.

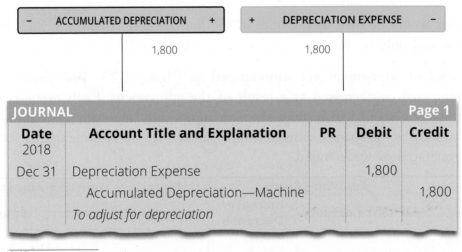

| JOURNAL | | | | Page 1 |
Date 2018	Account Title and Explanation	PR	Debit	Credit
Dec 31	Depreciation Expense		1,800	
	Accumulated Depreciation—Machine			1,800
	To adjust for depreciation			

FIGURE 5.21

Since the income statement resets and starts from scratch each year, a depreciation expense of $1,800 is recorded each year. The accumulated depreciation account, on the other hand, increases by $1,800 each year. As the accumulated depreciation account increases, the net book value of the machine decreases. Net book value is the original cost of the asset less accumulated depreciation. The transaction in Figure 5.19 is recorded at the end of each year. The amount of accumulated depreciation and the net book value of the machine over the five-year useful life are shown in Figure 5.22.

Year	Original Cost of Machine	Depreciation Expense	Accumulated Depreciation	Net Book Value
2018	10,000	1,800	1,800	8,200
2019	10,000	1,800	3,600	6,400
2020	10,000	1,800	5,400	4,600
2021	10,000	1,800	7,200	2,800
2022	10,000	1,800	9,000	1,000
Total	$10,000	$9,000	$9,000	$1,000

FIGURE 5.22

The net book value at the end of 2022 is equal to $1,000, which is the estimated residual value of the machine. This means that $9,000 of the cost of the machine was allocated over five years.

It is possible that depreciation may be recorded for periods of time that are less than one year. For example, suppose the machine was purchased on September 1, 2018 and the business records adjustments at year end, December 31, 2018. In this case, depreciation should only be recorded for four months. The calculation of depreciation is shown below.

$$\text{Straight-Line Depreciation} = \frac{\$10,000 - \$1,000}{5 \text{ Years}} \times \frac{4}{12}$$

$$= \$600 \text{ for 4 months}$$

The same accounts would be used as the ones in the journal entry in Figure 5.21, but the amount of depreciation would only be $600.

The five categories of adjustment are summarized in Figure 5.23. This shows which account categories are increased or decreased as a result of the adjustment. Each category of adjustment affects both income statement and balance sheet accounts (but never the cash account). Therefore, if adjusting entries are not prepared, some accounts in the income statement and the balance sheet will be either overstated or understated.

Category	Adjusting Entry		Impact of Omitting Adjusting Entry	
	Account Category	Increase/Decrease	Income Statement	Balance Sheet
Accrued Revenue	DR Asset	Increase	Revenue understated	Asset understated
	CR Revenue	Increase	Net income understated	Equity understated
Accrued Expenses	DR Expense	Increase	Expense understated	Liability understated
	CR Liability	Increase	Net income overstated	Equity overstated
Unearned Revenue	DR Liability	Decrease	Revenue understated	Liability overstated
	CR Revenue	Increase	Net income understated	Equity understated
Prepaid Expenses	DR Expense	Increase	Expense understated	Asset overstated
	CR Asset	Decrease	Net income overstated	Equity overstated
Depreciation	DR Expense	Increase	Expense understated	Asset overstated
	CR Contra Asset	Increase	Net income overstated	Equity overstated

FIGURE 5.23

The straight-line method of depreciation, as well as other methods, are discussed further in Chapter 12.

Pause & Reflect

Exercise 5-4

Seel Inc. purchased a piece of equipment on January 1, 2018, for $20,000. The useful life of the equipment is estimated to be eight years, after which the company expects to sell it for $4,000. Prepare the adjusting entry on December 31, 2018, to record the equipment's depreciation using the straight-line depreciation method.

JOURNAL					Page 2
Date	**Account Title and Explanation**		**PR**	**Debit**	**Credit**

See Appendix I for solutions.

Adjusted Trial Balance

The sixth step of the accounting cycle is to prepare the adjusted trial balance. To help illustrate this step, return to the sample company MP Consulting introduced in Chapter 4. At the end of the fourth step of the accounting cycle, we had prepared the unadjusted trial balance for the business, shown in Figure 5.24.

MP Consulting Trial Balance January 31, 2018		
Account Titles	**DR**	**CR**
Cash	$3,800	
Accounts Receivable	3,000	
Prepaid Insurance	1,200	
Equipment	8,300	
Accounts Payable		$1,250
Unearned Revenue		2,000
Notes Payable		2,500
Parish, Capital		10,300
Parish, Withdrawals	2,000	
Service Revenue		3,300
Rent Expense	800	
Telephone Expense	250	
Total	**$19,350**	**$19,350**

FIGURE 5.24

This unadjusted trial balance is the balance of the general ledger accounts after all the regular day-to-day transactions have been recorded in the general journal and posted to the general ledger. It is from these balances that MP Consulting will make adjusting entries. Suppose the company has the following adjustments to make at the end of the month. The five adjustments are lettered here and in Figure 5.25 to illustrate how each one is recorded.

ⓐ The company borrowed cash from the bank at a 12% rate of interest. Using the accrued interest calculation from Figure 5.7, accrued interest for the month is calculated as

$$\text{Accrued Interest} = \$2,500 \times 12\% \times \frac{1}{12}$$

$$= \$25 \text{ per month}$$

ⓑ One month of the prepaid insurance has been used. Since the balance of $1,200 represents a one-year policy, $100 ($1,200 ÷ 12 months) must be adjusted as an expense.

ⓒ Based on the records of MP Consulting, $200 worth of unearned revenue had been earned by the end of the month. This amount must be recognized as revenue.

ⓓ All the equipment that MP Consulting owns has an estimated useful life of four years and an estimated residual value of $1,100. Using the depreciation calculation from Figure 5.20, depreciation for the month is calculated as

$$\text{Depreciation} = \frac{\$8,300 - \$1,100}{4 \text{ Years}} \times \frac{1}{12}$$

$$= \$150 \text{ per month}$$

ⓔ On January 2, MP Consulting began a two-month contract with a client. The contract covers work for the months of January and February. On February 28, 2018, the contract will be completed and MP Consulting will bill the client $2,000. An adjusting entry must be made on January 31 to accrue the revenue earned during the month of January. MP Consulting will create an adjusting entry showing revenue of $1,000 earned during the month.

Before recording the adjustments in the general journal, it is helpful to see the impact of the adjustments and to ensure that the accounts will balance after the adjustments are made. To assist in this process, a **spreadsheet**, which is a work sheet prepared using programs like Excel, can be used to display the trial balances before and after the adjustments are made. The trial balance before adjustments are made is called the **unadjusted trial balance**. The trial balance after the adjustments are made is called the **adjusted trial balance**.

The spreadsheet shown in Figure 5.25 shows the unadjusted trial balance at the end of January. Beside this trial balance is a set of debit and credit columns for the adjustments. It is important to ensure the debit and credit columns of the adjustments column balance, otherwise the adjusted trial balance will not balance.

The last set of debit and credit columns is the adjusted trial balance. The amounts in the adjustment columns are added or subtracted from the original balances and placed in the adjusted trial balance columns. This shows what the ledger balances will be after the adjustments are made. If the debit and credit columns balance, then the financial statements can be prepared.

Account Title	Unadjusted Trial Balance DR	Unadjusted Trial Balance CR	Adjustments DR	Adjustments CR	Adjusted Trial Balance DR	Adjusted Trial Balance CR
MP Consulting Spreadsheet January 31, 2018 *New Balances*						
Cash	$3,800				$3,800	
Accounts Receivable	3,000		**e** $1,000		4,000	
Prepaid Insurance	1,200			**b** $100	1,100	
Equipment	8,300				8,300	
Accumulated Depreciation—Equipment		$0		**d** 150		$150
Accounts Payable		1,250				1,250
Interest Payable		0		**a** 25		25
Unearned Revenue		2,000	**c** 200			1,800
Notes Payable		2,500				2,500
Parish, Capital		10,300				10,300
Parish, Withdrawals	2,000				2,000	
Service Revenue		3,300		**c e** 1,200		4,500
Depreciation Expense	0		**d** 150		150	
Insurance Expense	0		**b** 100		100	
Interest Expense	0		**a** 25		25	
Rent Expense	800				800	
Telephone Expense	250				250	
Total	**$19,350**	**$19,350**	**$1,475**	**$1,475**	**$20,525**	**$20,525**

FIGURE 5.25

Once the spreadsheet is prepared and the adjusted trial balance is in balance, the journal entries are recorded in the general journal and posted to the general ledger. The journal entries are shown in Figure 5.26. All the postings to general ledger accounts, including these adjustments, are discussed in Chapter 6.

JOURNAL				Page 1
Date **2018**	**Account Title and Explanation**	**PR**	**Debit**	**Credit**
Jan 31	Interest Expense		25	
	Interest Payable			25
	Record one month of accrued interest			
Jan 31	Insurance Expense		100	
	Prepaid Insurance			100
	Record one month of insurance used			
Jan 31	Unearned Revenue		200	
	Service Revenue			200
	Record revenue now earned			
Jan 31	Depreciation Expense		150	
	Accumulated Depreciation—Equipment			150
	Record depreciation for one month			
Jan 31	Accounts Receivable		1,000	
	Service Revenue			1,000
	Record accrued revenue			

FIGURE 5.26

The preparation of the spreadsheet is optional. It is possible to simply prepare the journal entries as shown in Figure 5.26 and post them to the general ledger, then create the adjusted trial balance without preparing the end-of-period spreadsheet. However, the spreadsheet can be a useful tool to ensure all accounts remain in balance because going back to find errors can be a difficult process.

Ethics and Internal Controls

Reliable and relevant accounting information is important to both internal and external users. Internal users (managers and executives) rely on the information to plan, control and assess business operations. External users (creditors and lenders) rely on accounting information to determine a company is credit-worthy. However, it is possible to intentionally manipulate adjustments to change how the financial performance and position of the company is presented. If the manipulation hides information from users, this is unethical.

Consider the example of a company applying for a bank loan. As a potential lender, the bank's main concern is whether the business generates sufficient cash from its day-to-day operations to repay the loan. Before the bank considers lending to the company it wants to see certain indicators of financial health, such as steady sales, regular collection of accounts receivable, good control over expenses, and the timely payment of debt. If the company's management feels that the company falls short in one or more of these areas, it may be tempted to portray a more favorable picture to the lender by doing one or more of the following.

- adjusting for only accrued revenues and unearned revenues, but not adjusting for depreciation, accrued expenses, or prepaid expenses, which would properly show revenue but understate expenses

- making high estimates of unearned revenue, which would inflate the company's revenues

Unethical practices related to accounting adjustments can take many forms, such as the intentional misstatement of information, abuse in applying accounting principles, underestimation of liabilities and accruals, overstatement of earnings, or the unjustified revision of an asset's estimated useful life in order to alter depreciation figures.

Consider the accrual of interest on a bank loan. Management should not wait until the interest is paid to record interest. Interest should be accrued at the end of an accounting period and thus reflected as interest expense on the income statement. If management fails to accrue interest at the end of an accounting period, the financial statements will understate liabilities (since interest payable is understated) and overstate net income (since interest expense is understated). This will provide investors and creditors an incorrect representation of the company's performance and debt position.

Under the Sarbanes-Oxley Act (SOX), the CEO and CFO of a publicly traded company must certify that the financial statements that are filed with the SEC fairly present the company's operations and financial condition. It is a violation of SOX if management fails to prepare or manipulates the adjusting entries in a way that does not truly present the company's operations and financial condition. Those who violate SOX compliance can be fined or imprisoned.

WORTH REPEATING

The Sarbanes-Oxley Act (SOX) of 2002 was introduced in Chapter 3. It was co-sponsored by Senator Paul Sarbanes and Representative Michael G. Oxley. The bill was passed as a response to major corporate and accounting scandals. SOX requires top levels of management to certify the accuracy of financial information, and has created more severe penalties for committing financial fraud.

Internal control procedures must be in place to ensure that all necessary adjustments are accounted for. For example, the current period's adjusting entries should be compared with the previous period's adjusting entries to check whether any adjusting entries are missing. Any significant deviance from the last period's adjusting entries may need to be investigated. As another example of internal control, management should review the terms of the debt contracts for all outstanding long-term liabilities at the end of an accounting period. This provides management with a reasonable idea of what the interest expense should be for the period after including accrued interest as well.

In Summary

LO 1 **Describe the purpose of adjustments**

► Adjustments are made to ensure that all accounts are accurately reported at the end of the period.

► Adjustments are made before the creation of the financial statements.

LO 2 **Prepare adjusting entries for accrued revenue**

► Accrued revenue is revenue that has been earned but has not yet been recorded. The adjustment is made by debiting (increasing) accounts receivable and crediting (increasing) service revenue.

LO 3 **Prepare adjusting entries for accrued expenses**

► Accrued expenses are expenses that have been incurred but have not yet been recorded. The adjustment is made by debiting (increasing) an expense and crediting (increasing) a liability.

LO 4 **Prepare adjusting entries for unearned revenue**

► Adjustments to unearned revenue is to account for revenue that has now been earned. The adjustment is made by debiting (decreasing) unearned revenue and crediting (increasing) service revenue.

LO 5 **Prepare adjusting entries for prepaid expenses**

► Adjustments to prepaid expenses is to account for expenses that have now been incurred. The adjustment is made by debiting (increasing) an expense and crediting (decreasing) the prepaid expense.

LO 6 **Prepare adjusting entries for depreciation**

► Adjustments for depreciation is to allocate the cost of a noncurrent asset over its useful life. The adjustment is made by debiting (increasing) depreciation expense and crediting (increasing) the contra account called accumulated depreciation.

LO 7 **Prepare an adjusted trial balance**

► The adjusted trial balance is prepared after the adjusting entries have been made. This is to ensure the accounts are still in balance and the financial statements can be prepared.

LO 8 **Describe ethics and internal controls relating to adjusting entries**

► Adjusting entries must be prepared in a way that fairly present the company's operations and financial condition.

► An internal control system must be in place to ensure that all necessary adjustments are accounted for.

 *Access **ameengage.com** for integrated resources including tutorials, practice exercises, the digital textbook and more.*

Review Exercise 5-1

Catherine Gordon is running her own proprietary business called CG Accounting. CG Accounting provides bookkeeping services to small and mid-sized companies. The company prepares financial statements on a monthly basis and was previously introduced. Before you begin this exercise, familiarize yourself with the review exercise in Chapter 4.

The journal entries for the month of June have already been entered in the journal and posted to the ledger. The trial balance, before adjustments, is presented below.

CG Accounting Trial Balance June 30, 2018		
Account Title	**DR**	**CR**
Cash	$5,550	
Accounts Receivable	4,600	
Prepaid Insurance	1,200	
Equipment	6,000	
Accounts Payable		$2,750
Unearned Revenue		900
Notes Payable		3,050
Gordon, Capital		9,400
Gordon, Withdrawals	1,000	
Service Revenue		3,600
Advertising Expense	450	
Professional Fees Expense	900	
Total	**$19,700**	**$19,700**

CG Accounting uses the following accounts and accounting numbers in its accounting records.

Account Description	Account #
ASSETS	
Cash	101
Accounts Receivable	105
Prepaid Insurance	110
Equipment	120
Accumulated Depreciation—Equipment	125
LIABILITIES	
Accounts Payable	200
Interest Payable	205
Unearned Revenue	210
Notes Payable	215
OWNER'S EQUITY	
Gordon, Capital	300
Gordon, Withdrawals	310
Income Summary	315

Account Description	Account #
REVENUE	
Service Revenue	400
EXPENSES	
Advertising Expense	500
Bad Debt Expense	505
Depreciation Expense	510
Insurance Expense	515
Interest Expense	520
Maintenance Expense	525
Office Supplies Expense	530
Professional Fees Expense	535
Rent Expense	540
Salaries Expense	545
Telephone Expense	550
Travel Expense	555

At the end of June 2018, CG Accounting had to make the following adjustments.

Jun 30   The prepaid insurance represents a one-year policy that started in June. One month has now been used.

Jun 30   When examining the balance of unearned revenue, Catherine determined that $450 has now been earned.

Jun 30   Interest has accrued on the balance of the bank loan for the month. The loan interest rate is 10%. (For simplicity, round the interest to the nearest whole number.)

Jun 30   Depreciation on the equipment for the month must be recorded. The equipment is depreciated using the straight-line method. The equipment is expected to last five years and will have no residual value

Jun 30   Catherine started an audit for a new client. The contract is for 20 days of work starting June 21. At the end of the contract, the client will pay CG Accounting $1,800. Accrue the revenue earned for June.

Required

a)   Complete the spreadsheet.

CG Accounting Spreadsheet June 30, 2018						
	Unadjusted Trial Balance		Adjustments		Adjusted Trial Balance	
Account Title	DR	CR	DR	CR	DR	CR
Cash	$5,550					
Accounts Receivable	4,600					
Prepaid Insurance	1,200					
Equipment	6,000					
Accumulated Depreciation—Equipment		$0				
Accounts Payable		2,750				
Interest Payable		0				
Unearned Revenue		900				
Notes Payable		3,050				
Gordon, Capital		9,400				
Gordon, Withdrawals	1,000					
Service Revenue		3,600				
Advertising Expense	450					
Depreciation Expense	0					
Insurance Expense	0					
Interest Expense	0					
Rent Expense	900					
Total	$19,700	$19,700				

b) Prepare the journal entries for the adjusting entries and post them to the general ledger.

JOURNAL				Page 2
Date	Account Title and Explanation	PR	Debit	Credit

GENERAL LEDGER

Account: Cash   **GL No: 101**

Date	Description	PR	DR	CR	Balance	
2018						
Jun 1	Opening Balance				4,200	DR
Jun 1		J1		900	3,300	DR
Jun 3		J1		1,200	2,100	DR
Jun 6		J1	2,100		4,200	DR
Jun 13		J1	3,000		7,200	DR
Jun 16		J1	300		7,500	DR
Jun 23		J1		950	6,550	DR
Jun 30		J1		1,000	5,550	DR

Account: Accounts Receivable   **GL No: 105**

Date	Description	PR	DR	CR	Balance	
2018						
Jun 1	Opening Balance				3,100	DR
Jun 18		J1	1,500		4,600	DR

Account: Prepaid Insurance   **GL No: 110**

Date	Description	PR	DR	CR	Balance	
2018						
Jun 1	Opening Balance				0	DR
Jun 3		J1	1,200		1,200	DR

Account: Equipment   **GL No: 120**

Date	Description	PR	DR	CR	Balance	
2018						
Jun 1	Opening Balance				6,000	DR

Account: Accumulated Depreciation—Equipment   **GL No: 125**

Date	Description	PR	DR	CR	Balance	

Account: Accounts Payable					GL No:	200
Date	**Description**	**PR**	**DR**	**CR**	**Balance**	
2018						
Jun 1	Opening Balance				2,300	CR
Jun 11		J1		450	2,750	CR

Account: Interest Payable					GL No:	205
Date	**Description**	**PR**	**DR**	**CR**	**Balance**	

Account: Unearned Revenue					GL No:	210
Date	**Description**	**PR**	**DR**	**CR**	**Balance**	
2018						
Jun 1	Opening Balance				600	CR
Jun 16		J1		300	900	CR

Account: Notes Payable					GL No:	215
Date	**Description**	**PR**	**DR**	**CR**	**Balance**	
2018						
Jun 1	Opening Balance				4,000	CR
Jun 23		J1	950		3,050	CR

Account: Gordon, Capital					GL No:	300
Date	**Description**	**PR**	**DR**	**CR**	**Balance**	
2018						
Jun 1	Opening Balance				6,400	CR
Jun 13		J1		3,000	9,400	CR

Account: Gordon, Withdrawals					GL No:	310
Date	**Description**	**PR**	**DR**	**CR**	**Balance**	
2018						
Jun 30		J1	1,000		1,000	DR

Account: Service Revenue					GL No:	400
Date	**Description**	**PR**	**DR**	**CR**	**Balance**	
2018						
Jun 6		J1		2,100	2,100	CR
Jun 18		J1		1,500	3,600	CR

Account: Advertising Expense   **GL No: 500**

Date	Description	PR	DR	CR	Balance	
2018						
Jun 11		J1	450		450	DR

Account: Depreciation Expense   **GL No: 510**

Date	Description	PR	DR	CR	Balance	

Account: Insurance Expense   **GL No: 515**

Date	Description	PR	DR	CR	Balance	

Account: Interest Expense   **GL No: 520**

Date	Description	PR	DR	CR	Balance	

Account: Rent Expense   **GL No: 540**

Date	Description	PR	DR	CR	Balance	
2018						
Jun 1		J1	900		900	DR

See Appendix I for solutions.

Chapter 6
The Accounting Cycle: Statements and Closing Entries

Learning Objectives

LO 1 **Prepare financial statements using the adjusted trial balance**
- Income Statement
- Statement of Owner's Equity
- Balance Sheet

LO 2 **Prepare closing journal entries and post them to the general ledger**
- Direct Method: Close Directly to Owner's Capital
- Income Summary Method: Close Using the Income Summary Account

LO 3 **Prepare the post-closing trial balance to complete the accounting cycle**

LO 4 **Prepare the classified balance sheet**
- Current Assets vs. Noncurrent Assets

- Current Liabilities vs. Long-Term Liabilities

LO 5 **Analyze the financial statements using liquidity measures**
- Working Capital
- Current Ratio
- Quick Ratio

LO 6 **Describe the benefits of a computerized accounting system over a manual system**

Appendix

LO 7 **Prepare a 10-column spreadsheet**

AMEENGAGE *Access **ameengage.com** for integrated resources including tutorials, practice exercises, the digital textbook and more.*

145

Preparing the Financial Statements

At this point in the accounting cycle, day-to-day journal entries have been made, adjustments have been recorded, all transactions have been posted to the general ledger and the adjusted trial balance has been completed. It is time to complete the final three steps of the accounting cycle, shown in blue in Figure 6.1, beginning with the preparation of financial statements. Recall that the first three steps of the accounting cycle are repeated many times during the period, while the remaining six steps are only completed at the end of the period.

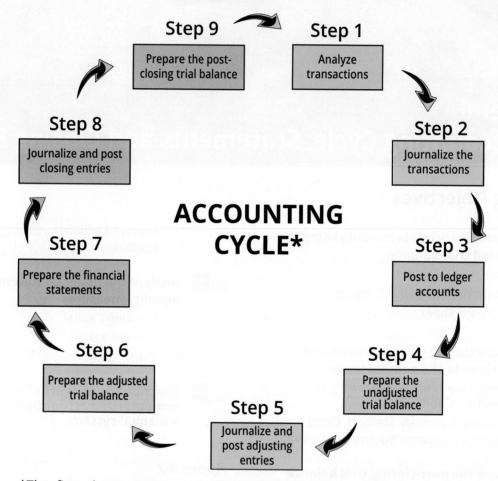

*The first three steps are performed repeatedly during an accounting period, while the remaining steps are performed only at the end of the period.

FIGURE 6.1

The final steps of the accounting cycle are illustrated using the MP Consulting example from Chapter 5. If necessary, refer to Figure 5.25 to recall the steps required to record each adjustment. The spreadsheet has been recreated in Figure 6.2 showing the unadjusted trial balance, adjustments and adjusted trial balance for easy reference. Since the adjusted trial balance is balanced, the accounts are ready to be compiled into the financial statements.

	MP Consulting Spreadsheet January 31, 2018					
	Unadjusted Trial Balance		Adjustments		Adjusted Trial Balance	
Account Title	**DR**	**CR**	**DR**	**CR**	**DR**	**CR**
Cash	$3,800				$3,800	
Accounts Receivable	3,000		$1,000		4,000	
Prepaid Insurance	1,200			$100	1,100	
Equipment	8,300				8,300	
Accumulated Depreciation—Equipment		$0		150		$150
Accounts Payable		1,250				1,250
Interest Payable		0		25		25
Unearned Revenue		2,000	200			1,800
Notes Payable		2,500				2,500
Parish, Capital		10,300				10,300
Parish, Withdrawals	2,000				2,000	
Service Revenue		3,300		1,200		4,500
Depreciation Expense	0		150		150	
Insurance Expense	0		100		100	
Interest Expense	0		25		25	
Rent Expense	800				800	
Telephone Expense	250				250	
Total	$19,350	$19,350	$1,475	$1,475	$20,525	$20,525

FIGURE 6.2

The spreadsheet is only a working paper for accountants; it is not meant to be read by external users of financial information. It is therefore important to create formal documents including an income statement, a statement of owner's equity and a balance sheet.

Income Statement

The income statement takes the values from the adjusted trial balance columns of the spreadsheet and organizes them into a format that shows the net income or loss. To illustrate the importance of preparing the adjustments, first look at the income statement in Figure 6.3. This income statement was prepared before any adjustments were made. The net income is reported as $2,250.

MP Consulting Income Statement (Pre-Adjustment) For the Month Ended January 31, 2018		
Service Revenue		$3,300
Expenses		
Rent Expense	$800	
Telephone Expense	250	
Total Expenses		(1,050)
Net Income (Loss)		$2,250

FIGURE 6.3

After the adjustments, the income statement can be prepared properly. In Figure 6.4, net income is accurately reported as $3,175. If no adjustments had been made, net income would have been understated (as it was in Figure 6.3), which would have caused owner's equity to also be understated. The final net income value (marked **ⓐ**) is transferred to the statement of owner's equity.

MP Consulting Income Statement For the Month Ended January 31, 2018		
Service Revenue		$4,500
Expenses		
Depreciation Expense	$150	
Insurance Expense	100	
Interest Expense	25	
Rent Expense	800	
Telephone Expense	250	
Total Expenses		(1,325)
Net Income (Loss)		$3,175 ⓐ

adjusted entries

FIGURE 6.4

Statement of Owner's Equity

The statement of owner's equity reports any changes in equity during the reporting period. It is presented with a date format of an elapsed time period similar to the income statement. The statement of owner's equity for MP Consulting is shown in Figure 6.5.

MP Consulting Statement of Owner's Equity For the Month Ended January 31, 2018		
Parish, Capital at January 1		$5,300
Add:		
Additional Investment	$5,000	
Net Income	ⓐ 3,175	8,175
Subtotal		13,475
Less:		
Parish, Withdrawals		2,000
Parish, Capital at January 31		$11,475 ⓑ

FIGURE 6.5

WORTH REPEATING

The ending balance of owner's equity for a given period can be calculated as follows.

Ending Owner's Equity = Beginning Owner's Equity + Owner's Contributions + Net Income (Loss) – Owner's Withdrawals

The statement begins with the opening balance of the owner's capital account. In our example, the opening balance was $5,300 on January 1, 2018.

Owner's equity increases if the owner invests more cash or assets into the business, or if the business earns a profit during the period. In our example, the owner invested $5,000 into the business during the month. Notice that the net income (marked **ⓐ**) from the income statement in Figure 6.4 is also added.

Owner's equity decreases if the owner withdraws any capital (cash or assets) from the business for personal use, or if the business suffers a loss during the period. There was no loss in our example, but there was a $2,000 withdrawal, as shown in the spreadsheet under Parish, Withdrawals.

The final closing balance of the capital account (marked **ⓑ**) is transferred to the owner's equity section of the balance sheet.

Balance Sheet

The balance sheet is prepared using the values from the asset and liability accounts from the adjusted trial balance. Previous chapters showed the balance sheet organized horizontally, with assets beside liabilities and owner's equity. This format of the balance sheet presentation is called the account form. An alternate organization, and the way balance sheets are most commonly presented, is vertically, which is known as the report form. Assets are listed above liabilities and owner's equity, as shown in Figure 6.6.

MP Consulting Balance Sheet As at January 31, 2018		
Assets		
Cash		$3,800
Accounts Receivable		4,000
Prepaid Insurance		1,100
Equipment	$8,300	
Accumulated Depreciation	(150)	8,150
Total Assets		$17,050
Liabilities		
Accounts Payable	$1,250	
Interest Payable	25	
Unearned Revenue	1,800	
Notes Payable	2,500	
Total Liabilities		$5,575
Owner's Equity		
Parish, Capital		11,475 **ⓑ**
Total Liabilities and Owner's Equity		$17,050

FIGURE 6.6

Notice that the value of Parish, Capital (marked) comes directly from the statement of owner's equity in Figure 6.5 and not from the spreadsheet. The journal entries used to update the capital account will be demonstrated in the next section.

Notice how equipment is presented. The accumulated depreciation is subtracted from the asset account, giving the net book value of $8,150.

Closing Entries

The statement of owner's equity shows the balance of the owner's capital account after it has been updated with the net income or loss from the period and any withdrawals. Although the ending balance of owner's capital is in the financial statements, the actual account in the general ledger does not yet reflect this new balance and must be updated. This process is called closing the books. **Closing the books** updates owner's capital (the equity of the business) and starts a new income statement for the next accounting period.

An income statement reports net income (or net loss) for a specific period of time. For example, if MP Consulting had a net income of $100,000 for a period ended December 31, 2018, this amount is exclusive to the period ended on that date and is not carried over to the next period.

In a manual accounting system, equity (owner's capital) is only updated at the end of the period. This means that all accounts that affect equity must have their balances transferred to owner's capital. Since these accounts are brought back to a zero balance at the end of each period, they are called **temporary accounts**, or nominal accounts. Revenue and expense accounts are classified as temporary accounts. Once the accounts are cleared, a new income statement can be prepared for the next period.

Besides revenue and expenses, owner's withdrawals is also a temporary account that needs to be closed at the end of the period. This is because owner's withdrawals measures the amount the owner takes from the business during a specific accounting period and is used to calculate the value of equity.

Permanent accounts, or real accounts, are balance sheet items that have their balances carried forward from one accounting period to the next, with no need of being closed. Accounts such as cash, accounts receivables or notes payable are examples of permanent accounts. Figure 6.7 illustrates which accounts are temporary and which are permanent.

FIGURE 6.7

Closing entries are made to revenue, expenses and owner's withdrawals at the end of an accounting period to close out the accounts. We will illustrate the concept of closing entries by walking you through how MP Consulting closes its temporary accounts at the end of January 2018. First, examine MP Consulting's balance sheet at the beginning of January 2018 (i.e. the end of December 2017). At the beginning of the period, MP Consulting's balance sheet is in balance, as shown in Figure 6.8. The T-accounts are also shown to illustrate the overall values of three categories: assets, liabilities and equity.

MP Consulting Balance Sheet As at December 31, 2017		
Assets		
Cash		$3,000
Accounts Receivable		1,200
Equipment		6,000
Total Assets		$10,200
Liabilities		
Accounts Payable	$1,000	
Unearned Revenue	900	
Notes Payable	3,000	
Total Liabilities		$4,900
Owner's Equity		
Parish, Capital		5,300
Total Liabilities and Owner's Equity		$10,200

INCREASE	DECREASE
+ ASSETS	−

10,200

DECREASE	INCREASE
− LIABILITIES	+

4,900

DECREASE	INCREASE
− PARISH, CAPITAL	+

5,300

FIGURE 6.8

Notice what happens in Figure 6.9 when services are provided in January to a customer who pays $1,500 in cash.

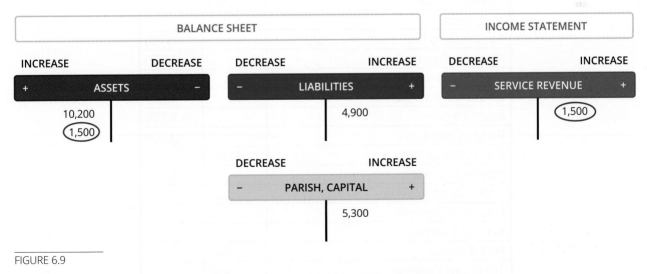

FIGURE 6.9

The balance sheet is now out of balance because assets have increased as a result of the increase in service revenue, but owner's capital has not been updated. A similar discrepancy occurs if a telephone bill is received in January and will be paid later, as shown in Figure 6.10.

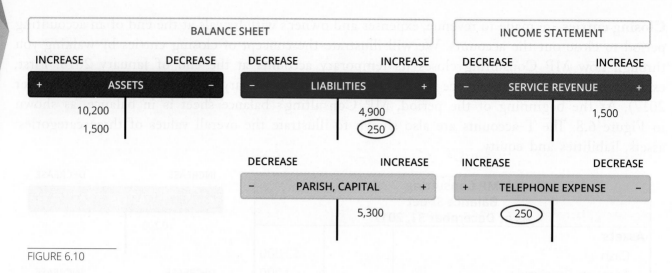

FIGURE 6.10

To get the balance sheet back into balance, owner's capital must be updated with the transactions for revenue and expense. If the owner withdrew cash from the business during the period, owner's capital must be updated with owner's withdrawals as well. In other words, closing entries must be prepared. There are two methods to prepare the closing entries, and MP Consulting will be used to illustrate both methods.

To see how to close the books for MP Consulting, we use the adjusted trial balance from the last column of the spreadsheet in Figure 6.2. The adjusted trial balance is shown again in Figure 6.11.

MP Consulting Adjusted Trial Balance January 31, 2018		
Account Title	**DR**	**CR**
Cash	$3,800	
Accounts Receivable	4,000	
Prepaid Insurance	1,100	
Equipment	8,300	
Accumulated Depreciation—Equipment		$150
Accounts Payable		1,250
Interest Payable		25
Unearned Revenue		1,800
Notes Payable		2,500
Parish, Capital		10,300
Parish, Withdrawals	2,000	
Service Revenue		4,500
Depreciation Expense	150	
Insurance Expense	100	
Interest Expense	25	
Rent Expense	800	
Telephone Expense	250	
Total	**$20,525**	**$20,525**

FIGURE 6.11

Notice that the revenue balance is a credit, the expense balances are debits and the owner's withdrawals balance is also a debit. To reset (close) the balances back to zero to prepare for the next accounting period, we must decrease the value of each of these accounts. Thus, revenue is debited, expenses are credited and owner's withdrawals is credited. In the context of closing entries, the terms "close," "reset" and "zero out" can be used interchangeably.

Direct Method: Close Directly to Owner's Capital

To prepare closing entires under the direct method, the revenue account must be closed by decreasing revenue and increasing owner's capital, as illustrated in Figure 6.12. The revenue account is now reduced to a zero balance.

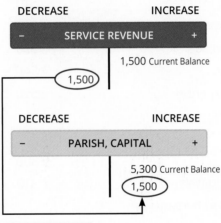

FIGURE 6.12

The telephone expense account must also be closed by decreasing the expense and decreasing owner's capital, as illustrated in Figure 6.13. The expense account is now reduced to zero.

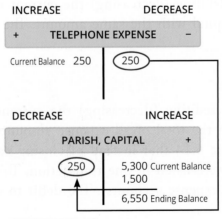

FIGURE 6.13

The end result is that owner's capital has a new balance and assets equal liabilities plus equity.

Returning to the example of MP Consulting, Figure 6.14 illustrates the journal entries to close the accounts directly to the capital account. The steps involved are explained.

JOURNAL					Page 3
Date	**Account Title and Explanation**	**PR**	**Debit**	**Credit**	
2018					
ⓐ Jan 31	Service Revenue	400	4,500		
	Parish, Capital	300		4,500	
	To close revenue				
ⓑ Jan 31	Parish, Capital	300	1,325		
	Depreciation Expense	510		150	
	Insurance Expense	515		100	
	Interest Expense	520		25	
	Rent Expense	540		800	
	Telephone Expense	550		250	
	To close expenses				
ⓒ Jan 31	Parish, Capital	300	2,000		
	Parish, Withdrawals	310		2,000	
	To close owner's withdrawals				

FIGURE 6.14

ⓐ Zero out the revenue account

The transaction is recorded by debiting (decreasing) the current revenue balance with $4,500 and crediting (increasing) owner's capital with the same amount. The revenue account is now reduced to zero.

ⓑ Zero out the expense accounts

The transaction is recorded by crediting (decreasing) the current expense balances and debiting (decreasing) owner's capital with the total of all expense amounts. The expense accounts are now reduced to zero. Notice in Figure 6.14 that instead of closing each expense account individually to owner's capital, all expenses were listed in one transaction. This saves time and effort (imagine if the company had 50 or more expense accounts). The debit to owner's capital is the total of all the expenses.

ⓒ Zero out the owner's withdrawals account

The transaction is recorded by crediting (decreasing) the current owner's withdrawals balance with $2,000 and debiting (decreasing) owner's capital with the same amount. The owner's withdrawals account is now reduced to zero.

Net Result

Owner's capital has increased by the total revenue and decreased by the total expenses and owner's withdrawals. Figure 6.15 shows the new balance is $11,475. This is the same figure shown as the ending value on the statement of owner's equity from Figure 6.5. Note that the direct method of closing accounts is not commonly used in practice; however, the illustration of this method provides you with a better understanding of the next method—the income summary method.

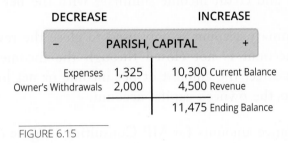

FIGURE 6.15

Income Summary Method: Close Using the Income Summary Account

Instead of debiting and crediting owner's capital directly, it is common to use a temporary holding account called **income summary** to close the revenue and expense accounts. Using our T-account example, in which $1,500 in cash was received for services and a $250 telephone bill was received, Figure 6.16 shows how the income summary account is used.

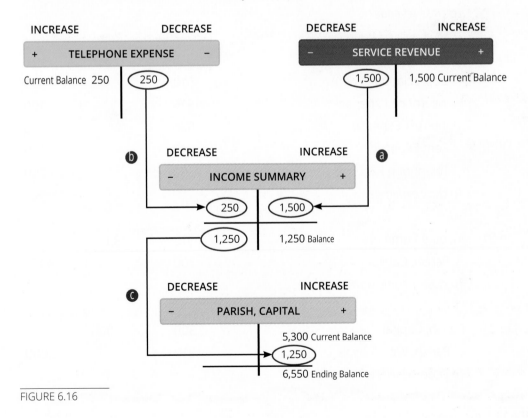

FIGURE 6.16

To close accounts using the income summary method, the following steps are used.

ⓐ Debit each revenue account to clear it and credit the income summary account for the total amount.

ⓑ Credit each expense account to clear it and debit the income summary account for the total amount.

ⓒ Calculate the balance of the income summary account. This is equal to the net income or loss for the period. Credit owner's capital and debit income summary with the net income amount, or debit owner's capital and credit income summary with the net loss amount.

Remember, the income summary account is only used to close the revenue and expense accounts. The owner's withdrawals account is not closed through the income summary account because owner's withdrawals do not affect the amount of net income or net loss. The owner's withdrawals account is closed directly to the owner's capital account.

Using the adjusted trial balance amounts for MP Consulting (Figure 6.11), the closing entries are shown in the journal in Figure 6.17.

	JOURNAL				Page 3
	Date	**Account Title and Explanation**	**PR**	**Debit**	**Credit**
ⓐ	Jan 31	Service Revenue	400	4,500	
		Income Summary	315		4,500
		To close revenue			
ⓑ	Jan 31	Income Summary	315	1,325	
		Depreciation Expense	510		150
		Insurance Expense	515		100
		Interest Expense	520		25
		Rent Expense	540		800
		Telephone Expense	550		250
		To close expenses			
ⓒ	Jan 31	Income Summary	315	3,175	
		Parish, Capital	300		3,175
		To close income summary			
ⓓ	Jan 31	Parish, Capital	300	2,000	
		Parish, Withdrawals	310		2,000
		To close owner's withdrawals			

FIGURE 6.17

ⓐ The first transaction is to zero out the revenue account. Similar to what was discussed in the direct method, the transaction is recorded by debiting (decreasing) the current revenue balance with $4,500; however, instead of crediting (increasing) owner's capital, the income summary account is credited. The revenue account is now reduced to zero.

ⓑ The second transaction is to zero out the expense accounts. The transaction is recorded by crediting (decreasing) the current expense balances and debiting (decreasing) the income summary account with the total of all expense amounts. The expense accounts are now reduced to zero. Notice in Figure 6.17 that instead of closing each expense account individually to income summary, all expenses were listed in one transaction to save time and effort. The debit to the income summary account is the total of all the expenses.

ⓒ The third transaction is to close the income summary to the capital account. The value of $3,175 is the difference between the revenue and expense accounts. Note that this value is the same as the net income reported on the income statement in Figure 6.4.

ⓓ The last transaction is identical to the one shown in the direct method (Figure 6.14). The owner's withdrawals account is closed to the owner's capital account. The withdrawals account decreases with a credit and the capital account decreases with a debit.

Figure 6.18 summarizes how the temporary accounts are closed at the end of an accounting period under each method.

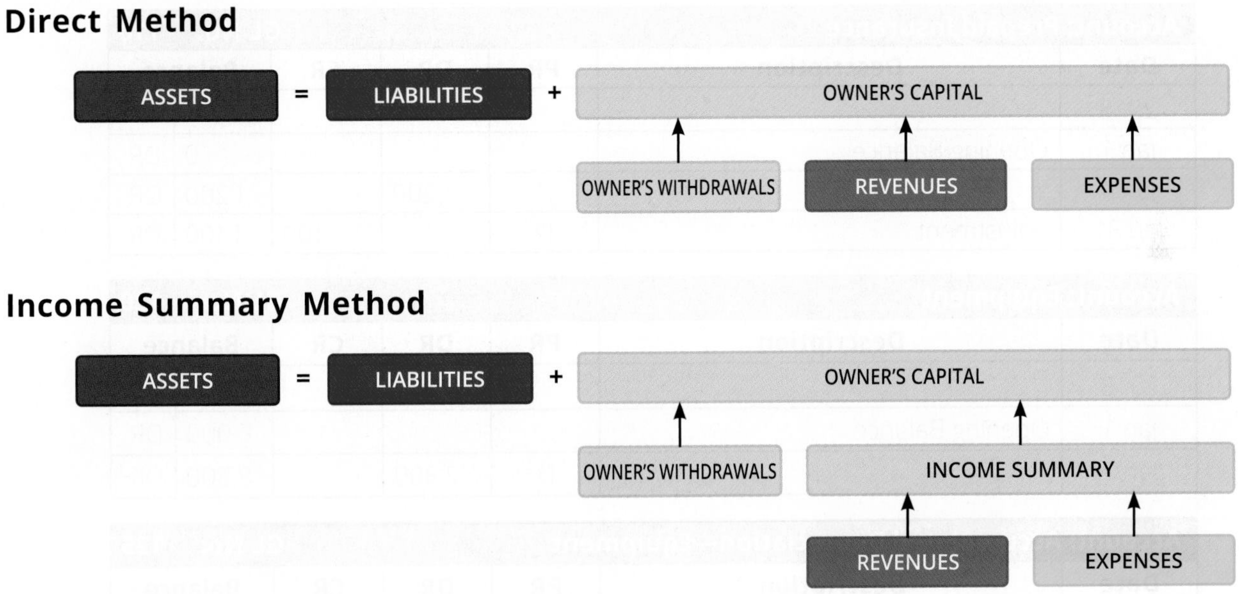

Direct Method

Income Summary Method

FIGURE 6.18

Remember, all journal entries must be posted to the general ledger. Assuming MP Consulting uses the income summary method to close its books, Figure 6.19 shows how the ledger accounts would look at the end of the period. All journal entries from the two previous chapters and the closing entries from this chapter are reflected here. Notice that adjustments and closing entries include a description to make them stand out in the ledger.

GENERAL LEDGER

Account: Cash					GL No:	101	
Date	**Description**	**PR**	**DR**	**CR**	**Balance**		
2018							
Jan 1	Opening Balance				3,000	DR	
Jan 2		J1	1,500		4,500	DR	
Jan 3		J1		800	3,700	DR	
Jan 4		J1		1,200	2,500	DR	
Jan 5		J1	5,000		7,500	DR	
Jan 7		J1		2,300	5,200	DR	
Jan 16		J1		500	4,700	DR	
Jan 19		J1	1,100		5,800	DR	
Jan 30		J1		2,000	3,800	DR	

Account: Accounts Receivable					GL No:	105	
Date	**Description**	**PR**	**DR**	**CR**	**Balance**		
2018							
Jan 1	Opening Balance				1,200	DR	
Jan 10		J1	1,800		3,000	DR	
Jan 31	Adjustment	J2	1,000		4,000	DR	

Account: Prepaid Insurance					GL No:	110	
Date	**Description**	**PR**	**DR**	**CR**	**Balance**		
2018							
Jan 1	Opening Balance				0	DR	
Jan 4		J1	1,200		1,200	DR	
Jan 31	Adjustment	J2		100	1,100	DR	

Account: Equipment					GL No:	120	
Date	**Description**	**PR**	**DR**	**CR**	**Balance**		
2018							
Jan 1	Opening Balance				6,000	DR	
Jan 7		J1	2,300		8,300	DR	

Account: Accumulated Depreciation—Equipment					GL No:	125	
Date	**Description**	**PR**	**DR**	**CR**	**Balance**		
2018							
Jan 31	Adjustment	J2		150	150	CR	

Account: Accounts Payable					GL No:	200	
Date	**Description**	**PR**	**DR**	**CR**	**Balance**		
2018							
Jan 1	Opening Balance				1,000	CR	
Jan 20		J1		250	1,250	CR	

Account: Interest Payable					GL No:	205
Date	Description	PR	DR	CR	Balance	
2018						
Jan 31	Adjustment	J2		25	25	CR

Account: Unearned Revenue					GL No:	210
Date	Description	PR	DR	CR	Balance	
2018						
Jan 1	Opening Balance				900	CR
Jan 19		J1		1,100	2,000	CR
Jan 31	Adjustment	J2	200		1,800	CR

Account: Notes Payable					GL No:	215
Date	Description	PR	DR	CR	Balance	
2018						
Jan 1	Opening Balance				3,000	CR
Jan 16		J1	500		2,500	CR

Account: Parish, Capital					GL No:	300
Date	Description	PR	DR	CR	Balance	
2018						
Jan 1	Opening Balance				5,300	CR
Jan 5		J1		5,000	10,300	CR
Jan 31	Closing Entry	J3		3,175	13,475	CR
Jan 31	Closing Entry	J3	2,000		11,475	CR

Account: Parish, Withdrawals					GL No:	310
Date	Description	PR	DR	CR	Balance	
2018						
Jan 30		J1	2,000		2,000	DR
Jan 31	Closing Entry	J3		2,000	0	DR

Account: Income Summary					GL No:	315
Date	Description	PR	DR	CR	Balance	
2018						
Jan 31	Closing Entry	J3		4,500	4,500	CR
Jan 31	Closing Entry	J3	1,325		3,175	CR
Jan 31	Closing Entry	J3	3,175		0	CR

Account: Service Revenue — GL No: 400

Date	Description	PR	DR	CR	Balance	
2018						
Jan 2		J1		1,500	1,500	CR
Jan 10		J1		1,800	3,300	CR
Jan 31	Adjustment	J2		200	3,500	CR
Jan 31	Adjustment	J2		1,000	4,500	CR
Jan 31	Closing Entry	J3	4,500		0	CR

Account: Depreciation Expense — GL No: 510

Date	Description	PR	DR	CR	Balance	
2018						
Jan 31	Adjustment	J2	150		150	DR
Jan 31	Closing Entry	J3		150	0	DR

Account: Insurance Expense — GL No: 515

Date	Description	PR	DR	CR	Balance	
2018						
Jan 31	Adjustment	J2	100		100	DR
Jan 31	Closing Entry	J3		100	0	DR

Account: Interest Expense — GL No: 520

Date	Description	PR	DR	CR	Balance	
2018						
Jan 31	Adjustment	J2	25		25	DR
Jan 31	Closing Entry	J3		25	0	DR

Account: Rent Expense — GL No: 540

Date	Description	PR	DR	CR	Balance	
2018						
Jan 3		J1	800		800	DR
Jan 31	Closing Entry	J3		800	0	DR

Account: Telephone Expense — GL No: 550

Date	Description	PR	DR	CR	Balance	
2018						
Jan 20		J1	250		250	DR
Jan 31	Closing Entry	J3		250	0	DR

FIGURE 6.19

Pause & Reflect

Exercise 6-1

ZooTak Service has journalized its adjusting entries and prepared the adjusted trial balance. Based on the list of accounts, prepare the closing entries using the income summary account for the month of August.

ZooTak Service List of Accounts August 31, 2018		
Account Title	**DR**	**CR**
ZooTak, Capital		25,310
ZooTak, Withdrawals	3,050	
Service Revenue		9,400
Depreciation Expense	290	
Insurance Expense	260	
Interest Expense	70	
Rent Expense	1,870	
Salaries Expense	2,250	
Telephone Expense	250	

JOURNAL				Page 5
Date	**Account Title and Explanation**	**PR**	**Debit**	**Credit**

See Appendix I for solutions.

Post-Closing Trial Balance

Once the closing entries are completed, it is necessary to ensure that the balance sheet still balances. This is done by completing another trial balance called the **post-closing trial balance**.

The post-closing trial balance only lists accounts that have a balance. Since the closing entries have been journalized and posted, only assets, liabilities and owner's capital should have a balance. The post-closing trial balance is shown in Figure 6.20.

MP Consulting Post-Closing Trial Balance January 31, 2018		
Account Title	**DR**	**CR**
Cash	$3,800	
Accounts Receivable	4,000	
Prepaid Insurance	1,100	
Equipment	8,300	
Accumulated Depreciation—Equipment		$150
Accounts Payable		1,250
Interest Payable		25
Unearned Revenue		1,800
Notes Payable		2,500
Parish, Capital		11,475
Total	$17,200	$17,200

FIGURE 6.20

Once the post-closing trial balance is complete, the entire accounting cycle for the period is done. The company is ready to begin the next accounting cycle for the upcoming accounting period.

Classified Balance Sheet

We have learned that the balance sheet lists assets, liabilities and equity, and have studied the unclassified balance sheet so far. However, it is useful to group together similar assets and similar liabilities on the basis of their financial characteristics. Before we go into the details of a classified balance sheet, we will first discuss the groupings of assets (current assets and noncurrent assets) and liabilities (current liabilities and long-term liabilities).

Current Assets vs. Noncurrent Assets

Assets are divided into two categories.

1. **Current assets** are those that are likely to be converted into cash or used up through the day-to-day operations of the business within the next 12 months or the operating cycle, whichever is longer. The **operating cycle** is the time between the use of cash and the receipt of cash for the business. Since the majority of businesses have operating cycles of a year or less, one year is most often used as the difference between the two categories of current and noncurrent. Some examples of current assets are cash, inventory (products sold to customers), accounts receivable and prepaid expenses.

2. **Noncurrent assets**, also called *long-term assets,* are used to operate a business and are not expected to turn into cash or be used up within the next 12 months (unless they are sold for reasons other than the day-to-day operations of the business). Any asset that is not included in the current asset category is assumed to be noncurrent.

Therefore, the classified balance sheet includes two sections of assets. Current assets are presented under a current asset heading. Noncurrent assets are presented separately.

Certain types of noncurrent assets must be presented separately on the classified balance sheet. Although not all of the noncurrent assets discussed are covered in detail in this textbook, you may come across these terms if you look at the balance sheet of other companies.

Property, plant and equipment are long-term physical assets used to help run the business. This category, also called **plant assets** or **fixed assets**, contains several types of noncurrent assets such as land, building, equipment and furniture. Each of these items must be presented separately along with any accumulated depreciation to show its net book value. Figure 6.21 shows the groupings of assets and liabilities on the balance sheet.

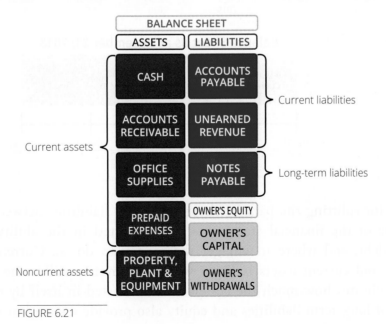

FIGURE 6.21

Current Liabilities vs. Long-Term Liabilities

Liabilities are divided into two categories.

1. **Current liabilities** are amounts due to be paid within the next 12 months. Examples of current liabilities include accounts payable, interest payable and unearned revenue (assuming the related revenue will be earned within the next 12 months).

2. **Long-term liabilities**, also called *noncurrent liabilities*, are amounts due to be paid after 12 months. Examples of long-term liabilities include notes payable and mortgages.

Long-term liabilities usually have a portion that is considered current. That is, a portion must be repaid within the next 12 months. To properly plan for cash payments in the upcoming year, accountants will separate the current portion from the long-term portion on the classified balance sheet.

For example, if a company has a $50,000 bank loan that is supposed to be paid off in five equal installments, $10,000 ($50,000 ÷ 5 years) is due within one year and is considered current. The rest ($40,000) is due after one year and is considered long-term. This separation of current debt from long-term debt is done on the date of the balance sheet. Each year, the amount of long-term debt decreases because a portion becomes due within one year and is classified as current debt. This is illustrated in Figure 6.22.

Balance Sheet as at December 31, 2017

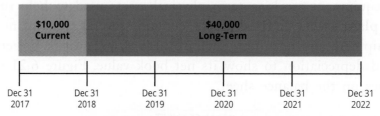

Balance Sheet as at December 31, 2018

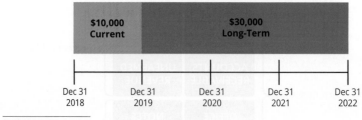

FIGURE 6.22

What is the reason for splitting the balance sheet assets and liabilities between current and long-term items? Readers of the financial statements are interested in the ability of the business to pay the upcoming debt, and where it will get the money to do so. Current liabilities indicate the upcoming debt, and current assets indicate where the money will come from. The classified balance sheet also indicates how much the company has invested in itself by means of noncurrent assets. The amount of long-term liabilities and equity also provide a snapshot of how the company finances its operations.

Now that we have defined current and noncurrent assets, as well as current and long-term liabilities, we can demonstrate the difference between the unclassified balance sheet that we have been using so far and a classified balance sheet.

The classified balance sheet for MP Consulting is illustrated in Figure 6.23. The balance sheet for MP Consulting was shown in Figure 6.6. It was not a classified balance sheet, so all assets and liabilities were grouped as one. The company has a $2,500 bank loan, of which $1,000 will be paid off by January 31, 2019 (one year from the balance sheet date).

MP Consulting Classified Balance Sheet As at January 31, 2018		
Assets		
Current Assets		
Cash	$3,800	
Accounts Receivable	4,000	
Prepaid Insurance	1,100	
Total Current Assets		$8,900
Property, Plant & Equipment		
Equipment	8,300	
Accumulated Depreciation	(150)	
Total Property, Plant & Equipment		8,150
Total Assets		$17,050
Liabilities		
Current Liabilities		
Accounts Payable	$1,250	
Interest Payable	25	
Unearned Revenue	1,800	
Notes Payable, Current Portion	1,000	
Total Current Liabilities		$4,075
Long-Term Liabilities		
Notes Payable, Long-Term Portion	1,500	
Total Long-Term Liabilities		1,500
Total Liabilities		5,575
Owner's Equity		
Parish, Capital		11,475
Total Owner's Equity		11,475
Total Liabilities and Owner's Equity		$17,050

FIGURE 6.23

The balance sheet illustrates the categories used to classify the various assets and liabilities of the business. The order of presentation for the current assets is shown as most liquid (cash) to least liquid (prepaid insurance) followed by noncurrent assets. Liabilities are shown in the order of when they are due, with the debts due earlier listed first. Notice that $1,000 of the note payable is classified as current because it will be paid within the next one-year period.

Analyzing the Financial Statements

LO 5

Financial statements can do more than just tell us how much profit was earned or the total of our assets or liabilities. Financial statement analysis includes calculating ratios between two values to provide insight into the business and how well it is operating. This topic will be covered in more detail later, but for now we will look at a few ratios that indicate how liquid the business is. Liquidity is the ability of the business to convert current assets to cash to pay its debts as they come due.

This presentation of the classified balance sheet, which separates current from long-term items, allows for the easy calculation of working capital, the current ratio and the quick ratio. Each of these looks at how well the company can pay its debts with its liquid, or current, assets.

Working Capital

Working capital is the difference between current assets and current liabilities. This provides a dollar figure, which, if positive, means the business has more current assets than current liabilities and should be able to pay its current debt. If current liabilities are greater than current assets, the business may have difficulty paying its debt as it comes due. The formula to calculate working capital is shown in Figure 6.24.

Working Capital = Current Assets – Current Liabilities

FIGURE 6.24

Using the values from the balance sheet in Figure 6.23, the working capital for MP Consulting is

Working Capital = $8,900 – $4,075

= $4,825

MP Consulting has more than enough current assets to pay for the current liabilities and should have no trouble paying the debts as they come due.

Current Ratio

The **current ratio** measures a company's ability to pay off short-term debt. The higher the current ratio, the more current assets the company has to pay off debt that is due within one year. The formula to calculate the current ratio is shown in Figure 6.25.

$$\text{Current Ratio} = \frac{\text{Current Assets}}{\text{Current Liabilities}}$$

FIGURE 6.25

From the balance sheet in Figure 6.23, the current ratio is calculated as

$$\text{Current Ratio} = \frac{\$8,900}{\$4,075}$$
$$= 2.18$$

This indicates that the company has $2.18 in current assets for every $1.00 in current liabilities. MP Consulting is doing well, since it has enough current assets to cover its upcoming debt payments.

Quick Ratio

The **quick ratio** is similar to the current ratio, but only counts assets that can easily be turned into cash. Thus, assets such as prepaid items are omitted and only cash, accounts receivable and short-term investments are included. (Short-term investments are covered in Chapter 18.) The formula to calculate the quick ratio is shown in Figure 6.26.

$$\text{Quick Ratio} = \frac{\text{Cash + Accounts Receivable + Short-Term Investments}}{\text{Current Liabilities}}$$

FIGURE 6.26

From the balance sheet in Figure 6.23, the quick ratio is calculated as

$$\text{Quick Ratio} = \frac{\$3,800 + \$4,000 + 0}{\$4,075}$$
$$= 1.91$$

This shows that the company has $1.91 of very liquid current assets for every $1.00 of current liabilities. Again, MP Consulting is doing well. If the quick ratio were to drop below 1.00, it could indicate problems with paying back debts.

Pause & Reflect

Exercise 6-2

Health Services has provided you with the financial information in Table 1. Calculate the required ratios. Round your final answers to two decimal places.

Table 1

Account	Balance
Cash	$120,000
Accounts Receivable	90,000
Prepaid Rent	65,000
Equipment	150,000
Accounts Payable	101,000
Unearned Revenue	80,000
Notes Payable, Long-Term	70,000
Health, Capital	45,000

Working Capital	
Current Ratio	
Quick Ratio	

See Appendix I for solutions.

The Evolution from Manual to Computerized Accounting

LO 6

One of the challenges in teaching a modern accounting course is the need to combine traditional concepts and methods with modern technology. However, the reality is that today's accounting students may never see or use a set of paper-based accounting journals and ledgers, such as the ledger shown in Figure 6.27.

Although computerized systems are becoming more common, and while they make gathering and analyzing information easier for the accountant, having a sound knowledge of traditional paper-based systems provides a foundation for understanding what accounting is all about. It also allows for an understanding of how the computerized system stores the information and how to look for errors or anomalies in the data.

FIGURE 6.27

Before computers, bookkeepers used various types of journals to maintain company financial records. Special journals were used to track similar types of transactions, such as sales and purchases. The general journal was used for infrequent transactions, such as adjustments. All of these journals were used to update the general ledger and other accounts.

In manual systems, recording procedures often provide the analytical structure for the accountant. If accounts receivable needs analyzing, the accountant refers to all related journals and ledgers for accounts receivable. If, on the other hand, inventory is being analyzed, the paper trail from receipt to shipping is tracked accordingly.

Similar to the manual system, a computerized system typically has special sections or journals to enter similar types of transactions, such as sales and purchases. There is also a general journal for adjusting entries and other specific types of transactions. All of these journals update the general ledger and other accounts and this information is kept in a database for easy storage and retrieval.

In effect, accountants analyze and create the journal entries for the day-to-day transactions, and journalize the adjusting entries at the end of the period. The day-to-day transactions do not have to be entered in chronological order since the software automatically orders them when reports are prepared. All the postings to the general ledger, preparing the various reports, and even preparing the closing entries are done automatically by the computer.

It is the responsibility of management and the accounting department to work with information technology personnel to buy or design a system that meets organizational objectives. Manual systems help accountants learn the basics of their profession; however, in today's business world, a properly designed computer system, tailored to the needs of a specific company, can make accounting more efficient.

Pause & Reflect

Exercise 6-3

a) List the similarities and differences between a manual accounting system and a computerized accounting system.

_____

_____

_____

b) What are some of the benefits of using a computerized system rather than a manual system?

_____

_____

_____

See Appendix I for solutions.

In Summary

LO 1   **Prepare financial statements using the adjusted trial balance**

▶ The adjusted trial balance provides the updated balances that are used to create the financial statements.

▶ The income statement shows the net income or loss for the period.

▶ The statement of owner's equity shows the change in equity for the period.

▶ The balance sheet shows the financial standing of the business at the period end date.

LO 2   **Prepare closing journal entries and post them to the general ledger**

▶ Closing journal entries zero out the income statement accounts and the owner's withdrawals account. The entries are then posted to the general ledger. After closing these accounts, a new income statement can be started for the next accounting period.

▶ There are two ways to close the income statement accounts: close directly to owner's capital or close to an intermediary income summary account.

LO 3   **Prepare the post-closing trial balance to complete the accounting cycle**

▶ A post-closing trial balance is created after the books are closed. It will only show accounts with a balance, which are assets, liabilities and owner's capital.

LO 4   **Prepare the classified balance sheet**

▶ The classified balance sheet presents assets and liabilities separated into current and long-term items.

▶ Current assets are assets that will be converted to cash or used up within one year. Noncurrent assets are typically used to run the business and will not be used up within one year.

▶ Current liabilities are liabilities that are due within one year. Long-term liabilities are due beyond one year.

LO 5   **Analyze the financial statements using liquidity measures**

▶ Working capital is the difference between current assets and current liabilities.

▶ The current ratio is calculated as current assets divided by current liabilities.

▶ The quick ratio is calculated as liquid assets (cash and accounts receivable) divided by current liabilities.

LO 6   **Describe the benefits of a computerized accounting system over a manual system**

▶ A computerized system automates many of the steps of the accounting cycle, such as posting to the general ledger and preparing reports. It also allows for easy retrieval of the data.

AMEENGAGE   *Access **ameengage.com** for integrated resources including tutorials, practice exercises, the digital textbook and more.*

Review Exercise 6-1

Catherine Gordon is running her own sole proprietary business called CG Accounting. CG Accounting provides bookkeeping services to small and mid-sized companies. The company was introduced in the review exercises from Chapters 4 and 5. Before you begin this exercise, familiarize yourself with the review exercise in Chapter 5 because this is a continuation.

Journal entries for the month have already been completed, as have the adjustments at month end. The adjusted trial balance is presented below.

CG Accounting Trial Balance June 30, 2018		
Account Title	**DR**	**CR**
Cash	$5,550	
Accounts Receivable	5,500	
Prepaid Insurance	1,100	
Equipment	6,000	
Accumulated Depreciation—Equipment		$100
Accounts Payable		2,750
Interest Payable		25
Unearned Revenue		450
Notes Payable		3,050
Gordon, Capital		9,400
Gordon, Withdrawals	1,000	
Service Revenue		4,950
Advertising Expense	450	
Depreciation Expense	100	
Insurance Expense	100	
Interest Expense	25	
Rent Expense	900	
Total	**$20,725**	**$20,725**

The balance of owner's equity as at May 31, 2018 was $6,400. Also, recall from the Chapter 4 review exercise that during June the owner contributed $3,000 cash to the business and withdrew $1,000 cash for personal use. Assume that $800 of the note payable must be paid by June 30, 2019.

CG Accounting uses the following accounts and accounting numbers in its accounting records.

Account Description	Account #
ASSETS	
Cash	101
Accounts Receivable	105
Prepaid Insurance	110
Equipment	120
Accumulated Depreciation—Equipment	125
LIABILITIES	
Accounts Payable	200
Interest Payable	205
Unearned Revenue	210
Notes Payable	215
OWNER'S EQUITY	
Gordon, Capital	300
Gordon, Withdrawals	310
Income Summary	315

Account Description	Account #
REVENUE	
Service Revenue	400
EXPENSES	
Advertising Expense	500
Bad Debt Expense	505
Depreciation Expense	510
Insurance Expense	515
Interest Expense	520
Maintenance Expense	525
Office Supplies Expense	530
Professional Fees Expense	535
Rent Expense	540
Salaries Expense	545
Telephone Expense	550
Travel Expense	555

Required

a) Prepare the income statement, statement of owner's equity and the classified balance sheet.

b) Complete the closing entries using the income summary method and post them to the general
    ledger.

JOURNAL				Page 3
Date	**Account Title and Explanation**	**PR**	**Debit**	**Credit**

GENERAL LEDGER

Account: Cash					GL No:	101
Date	**Description**	**PR**	**DR**	**CR**	**Balance**	
2018						
Jun 1	Opening Balance				4,200	DR
Jun 1		J1		900	3,300	DR
Jun 3		J1		1,200	2,100	DR
Jun 6		J1	2,100		4,200	DR
Jun 13		J1	3,000		7,200	DR
Jun 16		J1	300		7,500	DR
Jun 23		J1		950	6,550	DR
Jun 30		J1		1,000	5,550	DR

Account: Accounts Receivable					GL No:	105
Date	**Description**	**PR**	**DR**	**CR**	**Balance**	
2018						
Jun 1	Opening Balance				3,100	DR
Jun 18		J1	1,500		4,600	DR
Jun 30	Adjusting Entry	J2	900		5,500	DR

Account: Prepaid Insurance					GL No:	110
Date	**Description**	**PR**	**DR**	**CR**	**Balance**	
2018						
Jun 1	Opening Balance				0	DR
Jun 3		J1	1,200		1,200	DR
Jun 30	Adjusting Entry	J2		100	1,100	DR

Account: Equipment					GL No:	120
Date	**Description**	**PR**	**DR**	**CR**	**Balance**	
2018						
Jun 1	Opening Balance				6,000	DR

Account: Accumulated Depreciation—Equipment					GL No:	125
Date	**Description**	**PR**	**DR**	**CR**	**Balance**	
2018						
Jun 30	Adjusting Entry	J2		100	100	CR

Account: Accounts Payable					GL No:	200
Date	**Description**	**PR**	**DR**	**CR**	**Balance**	
2018						
Jun 1	Opening Balance				2,300	CR
Jun 11		J1		450	2,750	CR

Account: Interest Payable					GL No:	205	
Date	Description	PR	DR	CR	Balance	
2018						
Jun 30	Adjusting Entry	J2		25	25	CR

Account: Unearned Revenue					GL No:	210	
Date	Description	PR	DR	CR	Balance	
2018						
Jun 1	Opening Balance				600	CR
Jun 16		J1		300	900	CR
Jun 30	Adjusting Entry	J2	450		450	CR

Account: Notes Payable					GL No:	215	
Date	Description	PR	DR	CR	Balance	
2018						
Jun 1	Opening Balance				4,000	CR
Jun 23		J1	950		3,050	CR

Account: Gordon, Capital					GL No:	300	
Date	Description	PR	DR	CR	Balance	
2018						
Jun 1	Opening Balance				6,400	CR
Jun 13		J1		3,000	9,400	CR

Account: Gordon, Withdrawals					GL No:	310	
Date	Description	PR	DR	CR	Balance	
2018						
Jun 30		J1	1,000		1,000	DR

Account: Income Summary					GL No:	315	
Date	Description	PR	DR	CR	Balance	

Account: Service Revenue					GL No:		400
Date	**Description**	**PR**	**DR**	**CR**	**Balance**		
2018							
Jun 6		J1		2,100	2,100	CR	
Jun 18		J1		1,500	3,600	CR	
Jun 30	Adjusting Entry	J2		450	4,050	CR	
Jun 30	Adjusting Entry	J2		900	4,950	CR	

Account: Advertising Expense					GL No:		500
Date	**Description**	**PR**	**DR**	**CR**	**Balance**		
2018							
Jun 11		J1	450		450	DR	

Account: Depreciation Expense					GL No:		510
Date	**Description**	**PR**	**DR**	**CR**	**Balance**		
2018							
Jun 30	Adjusting Entry	J2	100		100	DR	

Account: Insurance Expense					GL No:		515
Date	**Description**	**PR**	**DR**	**CR**	**Balance**		
2018							
Jun 30	Adjusting Entry	J2	100		100	DR	

Account: Interest Expense					GL No:		520
Date	**Description**	**PR**	**DR**	**CR**	**Balance**		
2018							
Jun 30	Adjusting Entry	J2	25		25	DR	

Account: Rent Expense					GL No:		540
Date	**Description**	**PR**	**DR**	**CR**	**Balance**		
2018							
Jun 1		J1	900		900	DR	

c) Prepare the post-closing trial balance.

Account Title	DR	CR

See Appendix I for solutions.

Appendix 6A: The 10-Column Spreadsheet

 LO 7

In Chapter 5, the six-column spreadsheet was introduced to help track the changes in account balances due to adjustments. Although this spreadsheet is optional, it shows the unadjusted trial balance, the adjustments and the adjusted trial balance all in one place. An extension of this is the optional 10-column spreadsheet. In this spreadsheet, the first six columns are identical to those in the six-column spreadsheet. The extra columns are to show the accounts and balances that will appear on the financial statements. One set of columns is for the income statement accounts and the other set is for the balance sheet and owner's equity accounts. The values shown in these columns are copied directly from the adjusted trial balance columns.

The 10-column spreadsheet is shown in Figure 6A.1, with the new columns shown in red.

Account Title	Unadjusted Trial Balance		Adjustments		Adjusted Trial Balance		Income Statement		Balance Sheet & Equity	
	DR	CR	DR	CR	DR	CR	DR	CR	DR	CR
Cash										
Accounts Receivable										
Prepaid Insurance										
Equipment										

FIGURE 6A.1

In Figure 6A.2, the income statement accounts are separated from the balance sheet and equity accounts. Notice that the initial debit and credit totals of the income statement accounts do not balance. This is expected because the company should report an income or a loss. In this case, MP Consulting shows a greater credit balance (see letters **ⓐ** and **ⓑ**). Since the credit total is higher, MP Consulting generated an income. Find the difference between the two figures and add the difference to the smaller total. In the case of MP Consulting, the difference is $3,175 (see letter **ⓒ**) and is added to the smaller debit total to get $4,500. This ensures the income statement columns balance. If the company had a net loss, the difference would be added to the credit column to ensure the income statement columns balance.

A similar process is completed for the balance sheet and equity columns. The difference is calculated and added to the smaller total (see letter **ⓓ**) to ensure the balance sheet and equity columns balance. Notice that the difference between the income statement columns and the difference between the balance sheet and equity columns are identical. This should always be the case. A net income increases the capital account; therefore it is always a credit to the balance sheet and equity accounts. Conversely, a net loss decreases equity and is placed on the debit side of the balance sheet and equity accounts.

MP Consulting
Spreadsheet
January 31, 2018

Account Title	Unadjusted Trial Balance DR	Unadjusted Trial Balance CR	Adjustments DR	Adjustments CR	Adjusted Trial Balance DR	Adjusted Trial Balance CR	Income Statement DR	Income Statement CR	Balance Sheet & Equity DR	Balance Sheet & Equity CR
Cash	$3,800				$3,800				$3,800	
Accounts Receivable	3,000		$1,000		4,000				4,000	
Prepaid Insurance	1,200			$100	1,100				1,100	
Equipment	8,300				8,300				8,300	
Accumulated Depreciation—Equipment		$0		150		$150				$150
Accounts Payable		1,250				1,250				1,250
Interest Payable		0		25		25				25
Unearned Revenue		2,000	200			1,800				1,800
Notes Payable		2,500				2,500				2,500
Parish, Capital		10,300				10,300				10,300
Parish, Withdrawals	2,000				2,000				2,000	
Service Revenue		3,300		1,200		4,500		$4,500		
Depreciation Expense	0		150		150		$150			
Insurance Expense	0		100		100		100			
Interest Expense	0		25		25		25			
Rent Expense	800				800		800			
Telephone Expense	250				250		250			
Total	$19,350	$19,350	$1,475	$1,475	$20,525	$20,525	**(b)** $1,325	**(a)** $4,500	$19,200	$16,025
Net Income (Loss)							**(c)** 3,175			**(d)** 3,175
Total							$4,500	$4,500	$19,200	$19,200

FIGURE 6A.2

In Summary

LO 7 **Prepare a 10-column spreadsheet**

▶ A 10-column spreadsheet is an extension of a six-column spreadsheet where the four additional columns are for the income statement, balance sheet and owner's equity accounts.

▶ For the income statement columns, the difference between the initial debit and credit totals is equal to the company's reported income or loss.

▶ The debit and credit columns of the balance sheet and equity should have the exact same difference as the income statement columns.

Review Exercise 6A-1

Catherine Gordon is running her own proprietary business called CG Accounting. CG Accounting provides bookkeeping services to small and mid-sized companies. The company prepares financial statements on a monthly basis.

The journal entries for the month of June have already been entered in the journal and posted to the ledger.

At the end of June 2018, CG Accounting had to make the following adjustments.

Jun 30 The prepaid insurance represents a one-year policy that started in June. One month has now been used.

Jun 30 When examining the balance of unearned revenue, Catherine determined that $450 has now been earned.

Jun 30 Interest has accrued on the balance of the bank loan for the month. The loan interest rate is 10%. (For simplicity, round the interest to the nearest whole number.)

Jun 30 Depreciation on the equipment for the month must be recorded. The equipment is depreciated using the straight-line method. The equipment is expected to last five years and will have no residual value

Jun 30 Catherine started an audit for a new client. The contract is for 20 days of work starting June 21. At the end of the contract, the client will pay CG Accounting $1,800. Accrue the revenue earned for June.

Complete the spreadsheet.

CG Accounting
Spreadsheet
June 30, 2018

Account Title	Unadjusted Trial Balance DR	Unadjusted Trial Balance CR	Adjustments DR	Adjustments CR	Adjusted Trial Balance DR	Adjusted Trial Balance CR	Income Statement DR	Income Statement CR	Balance Sheet & Equity DR	Balance Sheet & Equity CR
Cash	$5,550									
Accounts Receivable	4,600									
Prepaid Insurance	1,200									
Equipment	6,000									
Accumulated Depreciation—Equipment		$0								
Accounts Payable		2,750								
Interest Payable		0								
Unearned Revenue		900								
Notes Payable		3,050								
Gordon, Capital		9,400								
Gordon, Withdrawals	1,000									
Service Revenue		3,600								
Advertising Expense	450									
Depreciation Expense	0									
Insurance Expense	0									
Interest Expense	0									
Rent Expense	900									
Total	**$19,700**	**$19,700**								
Net Income (Loss)										
Total										

See Appendix I for solutions.

Notes

Chapter 7
Inventory: Merchandising Transactions

Learning Objectives

LO 1   **Define a merchandising business**

LO 2   **Differentiate between the perpetual and the periodic inventory systems**

LO 3   **Record journal entries under the perpetual inventory system**
- Purchase of Inventory
- Sale of Inventory

LO 4   **Calculate gross profit and gross profit margin percentages**

LO 5   **Prepare the income statement under the perpetual inventory system**
- Single-Step Income Statement
- Multiple-Step Income Statement

LO 6   **Prepare closing entries for a merchandising business under the perpetual inventory system**

LO 7   **Identify inventory controls**
- Compliance with Plans, Policies,

Procedures, Regulations and Laws
- Safeguarding Inventory
- The Economical and Efficient Use of Resources
- Inventory Objectives

Appendix

LO 8   **Record journal entries under the periodic inventory system**
- Purchase of Inventory
- Sale of Inventory

LO 9   **Calculate cost of goods sold under the periodic inventory system**
- FOB and Inventory Counts

LO 10   **Prepare a multiple-step income statement under the periodic inventory system**

LO 11   **Prepare closing entries for a merchandising business under the periodic inventory system**

 *Access **ameengage.com** for integrated resources including tutorials, practice exercises, the digital textbook and more.*

Merchandising Businesses

So far, you have learned the complete accounting cycle of service companies. In reality, many companies not only provide services, but also sell products. A **merchandiser,** or merchandising business, is any business that buys and sells products, referred to as *merchandise* or *goods*, to make a profit. A merchandiser is an intermediary between the manufacturer and the end consumer. Two main categories of merchandisers are wholesalers and retailers. A **wholesaler** buys mostly bulk merchandise from a manufacturer for reselling to retailers, other wholesalers or end consumers. A **retailer** buys merchandise from a wholesaler or manufacturer to sell to end consumers.

There are a number of similarities between a merchandiser and a service provider. Both of them incur expenses to market and sell their products or services. If they hire any employees, both incur salaries expense. In addition, both a merchandiser and a service provider buy items that are classified as property, plant and equipment, and likely incur debt and pay it off. Thus, most of the accounting transactions for service providers that you learned in previous chapters are still applicable to merchandisers.

The main difference between a merchandising business and a service company is that the merchandising business holds an asset called merchandise inventory for sale. **Merchandise inventory,** or simply *inventory,* is a collection of physical goods that a company has purchased or manufactured to sell to its customers. Merchandisers usually have to invest their own cash to buy merchandise inventory, and it may take some time before they are able to resell the inventory and receive cash from customers. Once merchandisers receive cash from customers, the cash can be used to buy more inventory for resale. This cycle of merchandiser's operations is called the operating cycle. As shown in Figure 7.1, the operating cycle involves purchasing inventory and selling it for cash or on account. If merchandise inventory is sold on account, cash collection from the owing customer becomes an additional step in the cycle. The length of the whole cycle depends on the type of merchandise inventory. Merchandisers of perishable items, such as grocery stores, tend to have short operating cycles (usually a few weeks) compared to merchandisers of expensive items, such as jewelry stores, which tend to have a long operating cycle (multiple months or sometimes over a year).

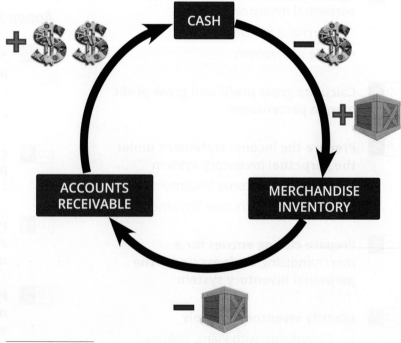

FIGURE 7.1

Carrying inventory presents operational and financial risks for a merchandiser. Inventory value fluctuates based on market demands and the conditions of the goods. Some inventory, such as jewelry, increases in value over time; some inventory, such as technology, decreases over time. In all cases, a merchandiser must sell inventory for more than its cost to make a profit. Senior management and accountants ensure controls are in place to accurately track the value of inventory from the point of purchase to the point of sale. Methods to track the value of inventory are discussed in Chapter 8.

Because merchandisers sell products instead of services, their revenue is called sales revenue, or simply *sales*. An expense account called cost of goods sold (COGS) is used to track the cost of the inventory that was sold during a particular period. For example, if a company purchased a television from a supplier for $200 and sold it for $500, it would have sales revenue of $500 and COGS of $200. The difference between sales revenue and COGS is called gross profit. Figure 7.2 shows the formula to calculate gross profit.

> Gross Profit = Sales Revenue – Cost of Goods Sold

FIGURE 7.2

Gross profit is used to pay for all other expenses in the business. The television sale generated $300 ($500 – $200) of gross profit, which can be used to pay for expenses such as rent, salaries and advertising. After all expenses are deducted, the remaining amount is net income.

Figure 7.3 illustrates the difference in the configuration of the accounts of a merchandising business and a service company. Notice that merchandise inventory is listed as a current asset on the balance sheet right below accounts receivable because it is generally a fairly liquid asset. Cost of goods sold and gross profit are listed on the income statement of the merchandising company. Other income and other expenses will be covered later in this chapter.

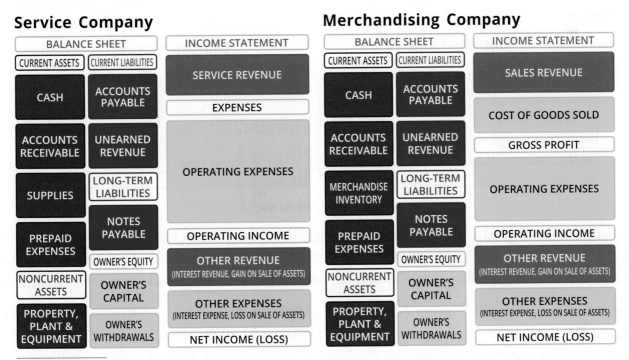

FIGURE 7.3

To see how sales, COGS, gross profit and operating expenses interact, consider the following example. A business purchases T-shirts for $5.00 each and plans to sell them for $7.00 each. The business also incurs a variety of operating expenses, including business travel, printing up business cards, printing up flyers for advertising, and renting office space, which total $700.

Figure 7.4 shows how to calculate net income (loss) if the business sells 200 T-shirts.

Operating expenses of the business

1. Travel	$100
2. Business cards	100
3. Flyers for advertising	300
4. Temporary rental space	200
Total Operating Expenses	**$700**

Every business has various monthly operating expenses that occur regardless of services or products sold. The sale of merchandise, less merchandise cost, contributes toward paying these expenses.

Sell 200 T-shirts

Sales Revenue (200 × $7.00)	**$1,400**
Less COGS	1,000
= Gross Profit	**400**
Less Operating Expenses	700
= Net Income (Loss)	**($300)**

These T-shirts may have been purchased several months earlier. The business is now recognizing (matching) the cost of the shirts against the value of the sale. The COGS for 200 T-shirts is $1,000 (200 x $5.00). To determine gross profit, COGS is subtracted from sales revenue, for a total of $400.

FIGURE 7.4

The business sold 200 T-shirts for a gross profit of $400 ($1,400 – $1,000). However, the business requires $700 to pay for its operating expenses. Selling 200 T-shirts means the company incurs a net loss of $300 ($400 – $700). The business needs to sell more T-shirts to provide enough gross profit to pay for operating expenses. Figure 7.5 shows the results of selling 350 T-shirts and 500 T-shirts.

Sell 350 T-shirts

Sales Revenue (350 x $7.00)	**$2,450**
Less COGS	1,750
= Gross Profit	**700**
Less Operating Expenses	700
= Net Income (Loss)	**$0**

Sell 500 T-shirts

Sales Revenue (500 x $7.00)	**$3,500**
Less COGS	2,500
= Gross Profit	**1,000**
Less Operating Expenses	700
= Net Income (Loss)	**$300**

FIGURE 7.5

If the business sells 350 T-shirts (shown on the left in Figure 7.5), COGS is $1,750 (350 × $5.00). This means the gross profit is $700 ($2,450 – $1,750), which exactly covers the operating expenses. The business did not produce a net income or suffer a net loss, which is known as breaking even.

If the business sells 500 T-shirts (shown on the right in Figure 7.5), COGS is $2,500 (500 × $5.00). This means the gross profit is $1,000 ($3,500 – $2,500), which is more than enough to cover operating expenses. The business produced a net income of $300 ($1,000 – $700).

Pause & Reflect

Exercise 7-1

OnTime Company purchases wall clocks from a supplier for $14 per unit and resells them for $35 each. Calculate this month's sales revenue, COGS, gross profit and net income if OnTime Company sells 300 clocks and incurs $5,000 in operating expenses. Fill in your answers in Table 1.

Table 1

Sales Revenue	
COGS	
Gross Profit	
Net Income	

See Appendix I for solutions.

Perpetual vs. Periodic Inventory Systems

LO 2

Imagine you are shopping for a particular item at a department store. You cannot find it on the shelf, so you ask an employee if there are any left. The employee checks the computer, which says there is one left. The employee finds it in the storage room, gives it to you and you go to the cashier. The cashier scans the item, you pay the bill and you leave the store. If another customer asked for that same item after you bought it, the computer would show that there are none in stock.

This example illustrates the perpetual inventory system. The **perpetual inventory system** updates inventory levels after every purchase and sale. Most merchandising companies use technology, such as scanners, to update their records for inventory, as well as COGS. All the updates happen automatically when the item is scanned.

On the other hand, some small merchandising companies, such as a small convenience store, may not have scanning technology in place. Without the scanning technology, the business can track its sales, but inventory and COGS are not updated automatically. The **periodic inventory system** only updates the inventory and COGS values after physically counting the items on hand. These inventory counts occur periodically, usually at the end of the month or year.

Figure 7.6 highlights the difference between the perpetual and periodic inventory systems. It shows sample revenue and COGS amounts for a company under both systems over a period of three months. Notice that the perpetual system updates COGS continuously while the periodic system updates COGS only when a physical inventory count is performed (at the end of March).

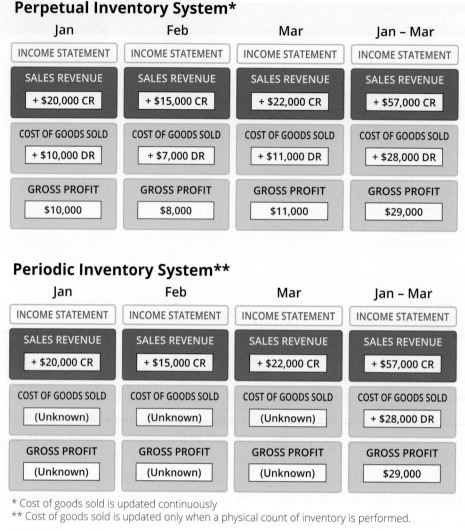

FIGURE 7.6

Perpetual inventory systems are more commonly used in today's computerized environment. In this textbook, unless otherwise stated, assume the perpetual inventory system is used. We will now examine how to record various transactions regarding the purchase and sale of merchandise inventory under the perpetual inventory system.

The Perpetual Inventory System

A perpetual inventory system involves recording all transactions affecting the balance of merchandise inventory on hand, as they occur. In reality, most businesses have separate, detailed records for each type of product they sell. For simplicity, our examples will focus on one type of product, where all transactions affect a single merchandise inventory account directly.

We will demonstrate various inventory-related transactions using an example of a retail store called Tools 4U, which buys and sells tools. Tools 4U is a sole proprietorship owned by Wayne Sanders.

Purchase of Inventory

Tools 4U purchased 100 fall protection kits for resale at a total cost of $10,000 from Roofs and More, which delivered the merchandise and issued an invoice on January 1, 2018. The invoice for this transaction is presented in Figure 7.7. While the supplier (Roofs and More) refers to this invoice as a sales invoice, the customer (Tools 4U) refers to it as a purchase invoice and uses it as a source document to record the purchase transaction.

ROOFS AND MORE
121 Main Street
Paterson NJ 07501

INVOICE

SOLD TO	Tools 4U 1818 1st Avenue Dallas, TX 75210

Invoice #	876-1
Invoice Date	1/1/2018
Customer ID	905

ORDER DATE	YOUR ORDER #	SALES REP.	F.O.B.	SHIP VIA	TERMS
12/29/17	2017122908	52	Destination	ShipPlus	2/10, n/30

QTY.	MODEL NO.	DESCRIPTION	UNIT PRICE	TOTAL
100	DK771R	Fall Protection Kit	100	$10,000

Subtotal	$10,000
Tax	-
Shipping	-
Miscellaneous	-
BALANCE DUE	$10,000

FIGURE 7.7

When merchandise inventory and a purchase invoice are received under the perpetual inventory system, the merchandise inventory account is debited and the cash or accounts payable account is credited. Assume all purchases and sales are made on account. Figure 7.8 shows how this purchase is journalized.

JOURNAL			
Date	**Account Title and Explanation**	**Debit**	**Credit**
2018			
Jan 1	Merchandise Inventory	10,000	
	Accounts Payable		10,000
	Purchased inventory on account		

FIGURE 7.8

Purchase Returns

Sometimes, goods are returned for reasons such as incorrect product, over-shipments or inferior product quality.

When the manager of Tools 4U examined the new shipment of inventory from the company's supplier, Roofs and More, he noticed that there were some damaged goods in the shipment. The damaged goods cost $500. The goods were returned and a journal entry for $500 was recorded to reverse part of the original purchase transaction, as shown in Figure 7.9.

BALANCE SHEET	
CURRENT ASSETS	CURRENT LIABILITIES
CASH	ACCOUNTS PAYABLE − $500 DR
ACCOUNTS RECEIVABLE	UNEARNED REVENUE
MERCHANDISE INVENTORY − $500 CR	LONG-TERM LIABILITIES
PREPAID EXPENSES	NOTES PAYABLE
	OWNER'S EQUITY
NONCURRENT ASSETS	OWNER'S CAPITAL
PROPERTY, PLANT & EQUIPMENT	OWNER'S WITHDRAWALS

No change in owner's equity

JOURNAL			
Date	**Account Title and Explanation**	**Debit**	**Credit**
2018			
Jan 2	Accounts Payable	500	
	Merchandise Inventory		500
	Goods returned to Roofs and More		

FIGURE 7.9

Purchase Allowances

Purchase allowances occur when the buyer agrees to keep the undesirable goods at a reduced cost. When a buyer encounters undesirable goods, the buyer issues a **debit memorandum**, or a *debit memo* in short, to inform the seller about the purchase returns or allowances. The document is called a debit memorandum because accounts payable is debited in the buyer's books, meaning that the buyer's liabilities decrease. Assume Tools 4U found another $500 worth of unsatisfactory goods and the supplier offered a 20% allowance for the company to keep the goods, rather than returning them. The journal entry is recorded by debiting accounts payable and crediting merchandise inventory as shown in Figure 7.10. The transaction amount is $100 ($500 × 20%).

A balance of $9,400 ($10,000 – $500 – $100) is still owing to Roofs and More.

JOURNAL			
Date	Account Title and Explanation	Debit	Credit
2018			
Jan 4	Accounts Payable	100	
	Merchandise Inventory		100
	Allowance from Roofs and More		

FIGURE 7.10

Purchase Discounts

Various types of discounts exist when purchasing products or services. Sellers often give discounts to encourage customers to purchase more and to encourage early payments.

Two types of common discounts given are trade discounts and cash discounts.

Trade discounts represent the discount from the *manufacturer's suggested retail price* that is usually given by manufacturers to merchandisers in order to resell their products. The manufacturer's suggested retail price is usually printed in a catalog, so it is sometimes called a *catalog price* or a *list price*. Merchandisers, who act as intermediaries between manufacturers and end consumers, make a profit by paying less than the list price. The difference between the list price and the price that the merchandiser has to pay for the product is the trade discount.

For example, suppose the list price of the fall protection kit, according to Roofs and More's catalog, is $250. Roofs and More gives a 60% trade discount to Tools 4U. The purchase price that Tools 4U has to pay is $100 [$250 - ($250 × 60%)]. The buyer records the price net of trade discount in its inventory purchase journal entry. In this example, if Tools 4U purchased one fall protection kit on account, it records a debit to merchandise inventory and a credit to accounts payable of $100.

Merchandisers sometimes encourage prompt payment from customers by offering a **cash discount**, which is a percentage off the final bill if it is paid in a specified amount of time. **Credit terms** are the terms indicating when a buyer has to pay for the merchandise and whether there are any discounts for paying early. The **credit period** is the maximum number of days that the buyer can wait before paying the full amount due. The **discount period** is the number of days within which the buyer has to pay to receive the cash discount.

In our example, the invoice in Figure 7.7 has a "Terms" field, which shows 2/10, n/30 (read as "two-ten, net thirty," the credit terms). This means that Roofs and More will apply a 2% discount if payment is received within 10 days (the discount period); otherwise the net amount of $10,000 is due within 30 days (the credit period).

Another example is 3/15, n/30, which means a 3% discount is applied if payment is received within 15 days, otherwise the net amount owing is payable within 30 days. While sellers refer to these discounts as **sales discounts**, buyers refer to them as **purchase discounts**. The following example illustrates how to record a purchase discount.

Tools 4U made the original purchase from Roofs and More on January 1, 2018 for $10,000. The amount Tools 4U owes has been reduced by $600 due to returns and allowances, so only $9,400 remains to be paid. The supplier (Roofs and More) allows 2/10, n/30 on all invoices. The discount period and credit period for this transaction are shown in Figure 7.11. The amount owing during the discount period is $9,212 ($9,400 – [$9,400 × 2%]). The amount owing after the discount period (10 days), is the full amount of $9,400. Since Tools 4U has excess cash at this time, the manager decides to take advantage of the cash discount by paying the invoice within 10 days.

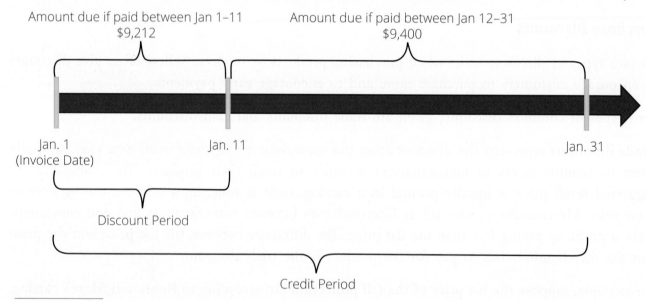

FIGURE 7.11

A CLOSER LOOK

Some credit terms contain EOM, which stands for end of month. For example, if the credit term is n/EOM or "net EOM", it means that the buyer has to pay the full amount by the last day of the same month as the invoice date. If the credit term is n/10 EOM or "net 10 EOM", it means that the buyer has to pay the full amount within 10 days after the end of the month that is written on the invoice.

Since Tools 4U makes the payment on January 11, the amount for the bill is $9,400 less the $188 discount ($9,400 × 2%). Since the business is paying less for the inventory, the value of the inventory needs to decrease by the value of the discount. The entry to record the payment is shown in Figure 7.12.

JOURNAL			
Date	**Account Title and Explanation**	**Debit**	**Credit**
2018			
Jan 11	Accounts Payable	9,400	
	Cash		9,212
	Merchandise Inventory		188
	Paid invoice and took purchase discount		

FIGURE 7.12

The discount of $188 is credited to merchandise inventory because the adjustment is made to reflect the true cost of the goods.

If Tools 4U decides not to pay the amount owing within 10 days, then it is not entitled to the discount. It must pay the full amount of $9,400 within 30 days of the invoice date. This payment is just like paying any other amount that is owed to a supplier. Cash decreases and accounts payable decreases by the amount owed. The entry is shown in Figure 7.13. Notice the date is more than 10 days past the invoice date.

JOURNAL			
Date	**Account Title and Explanation**	**Debit**	**Credit**
2018			
Jan 31	Accounts Payable	9,400	
	Cash		9,400
	Paid amount owing to Roofs and More		

FIGURE 7.13

A buyer's failure to take advantage of a purchase discount is often very costly. On the surface, the 2% discount that Tools 4U must forfeit if it pays on January 31 instead of January 11 may seem insignificant. However, the 2% discount for 20 days can be converted to a very high annual percentage. Specifically, the annual interest rate for the 2% higher price in order to pay 20 days later is 36.5% [(365 days ÷ 20 days) × 2%]. Because a commercial bank usually charges much lower interest than 36.5% annually for a loan, it is in the buyer's best interest to pay within the discount period, even if a bank loan has to be taken out to do so.

A CLOSER LOOK

Realistically, most buyers take advantage of all available purchase discounts to avoid paying an interest rate that is much higher than a bank loan. Buyers that do this may use an alternative accounting method to record the inventory purchase and cash payment transactions called the *net method*, instead of the *gross method* shown in Figure 7.12.

Under the net method, inventory purchase and cash payment transactions are always recorded at the amount that is net of purchase discount. To illustrate, if Tools 4U had made a purchase from Roofs and More on January 1 for $9,400 under the credit term of 2/10, n/30, and if it had paid $9,212 for the purchase on January 11, the transactions are recorded as shown here.

Jan 1	Merchandise Inventory	9,212	
	Accounts Payable		9,212
	Purchased inventory on account		
Jan 11	Accounts Payable	9,212	
	Cash		9,212
	Paid invoice and took purchase discount		

Regardless of which method is use, account balances are the same. In Tools 4U's case, merchandise inventory increases by $9,212 and cash decreases by $9,212 under both methods when the payment is made during the discount period.

Freight Cost

When one company purchases goods from another, the items must be transported from the seller's place of business to the buyer's place of business. There are a number of ways to transport goods (sea, rail, truck, etc.). The selling company may have its own fleet of vehicles to deliver goods to customers, or it may use a common carrier. A common carrier in this context is a company that provides shipping services to the general public. Examples include railroad companies, trucking companies, local couriers, or the postal service.

In addition to arranging transport of the goods, ownership of the goods must be legally transferred from the seller to the buyer. The term used to determine when ownership of the goods changes hands is called the FOB point. "FOB" stands for Free On Board. There are two possible FOB points. FOB shipping point and FOB destination. Each of these points have implications regarding who pays for shipping, when ownership passes from the buyer to the seller and who bears the risk for the goods during transport.

FOB Shipping Point

FOB shipping point indicates that ownership of the purchased items changes as soon as the goods leave the seller's place of business (i.e. when shipping begins). In this case, a common carrier is often used to deliver the items to the buyer. The buyer pays for shipping and is responsible to insure the items while they are in transport. If anything happens to the items while they are being transported, the buyer bears the risk of loss.

The seller records revenue earned and the buyer records an increase to merchandise inventory as soon as the goods are loaded on the truck (or other transport). Under FOB shipping point, the delivery expense that the buyer pays is often referred to as *freight-in* or *transportation-in*, and it increases the cost of merchandise inventory on the buyer's balance sheet. The reason the buyer includes shipping costs in merchandise inventory is that the value of the goods must include all costs that are incurred to get the goods ready to sell, such as transportation. Figure 7.14 illustrates who pays the shipping costs for FOB shipping point.

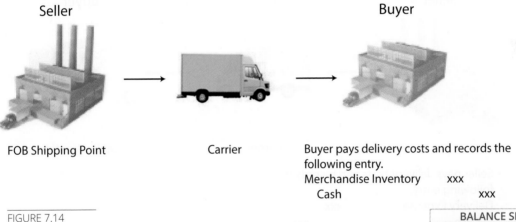

Seller   Buyer

FOB Shipping Point   Carrier   Buyer pays delivery costs and records the
                                              following entry.
                                              Merchandise Inventory   xxx
                                                  Cash   xxx

FIGURE 7.14

Assume that Tools 4U had inventory shipped FOB shipping point. This means that Tools 4U must pay the cost of shipping. Suppose the shipping charge totaled $100 and was paid in cash on January 2. This amount must be included in the merchandise inventory account. The journal entry is shown in Figure 7.15.

JOURNAL			
Date	**Account Title and Explanation**	**Debit**	**Credit**
2018			
Jan 2	Merchandise Inventory	100	
	Cash		100
	Paid for freight costs		

BALANCE SHEET

CURRENT ASSETS	CURRENT LIABILITIES
CASH − $100 CR	ACCOUNTS PAYABLE
ACCOUNTS RECEIVABLE	UNEARNED REVENUE
MERCHANDISE INVENTORY + $100 DR	LONG-TERM LIABILITIES
PREPAID EXPENSES	NOTES PAYABLE
	OWNER'S EQUITY
NONCURRENT ASSETS	OWNER'S CAPITAL
PROPERTY, PLANT & EQUIPMENT	OWNER'S WITHDRAWALS

No change in owner's equity

FIGURE 7.15

FOB Destination

FOB destination indicates that ownership of the purchased items changes when the goods arrive at the buyer's place of business. In other words, ownership changes at the point of destination. In this case, the seller may have a fleet of vehicles and use them to deliver goods to its customers. Thus, the seller pays for the shipping and is responsible for the items while they are in transport. If anything happens to the items while they are being transported, the seller bears the risk of loss.

The seller records revenue earned and the buyer records an increase to merchandise inventory once the goods reach their destination (the buyer's place of business). Under FOB destination, the delivery expense that is paid by the seller is often referred to as *freight-out* or *transportation-out*, and it is recorded as a selling expense on the seller's income statement. Figure 7.16 illustrates who pays the shipping cost for FOB destination.

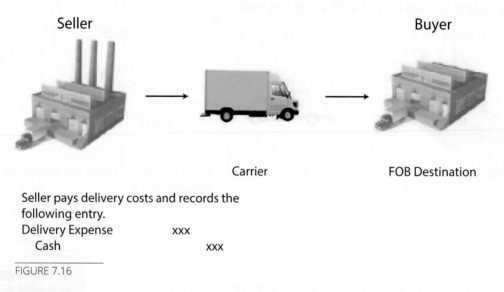

FIGURE 7.16

Suppose that Tools 4U shipped inventory to a customer FOB destination on January 3. Tools 4U must pay the cost of shipping because it is the selling company. The shipping cost is a delivery expense. Suppose that it costs Tools 4U $120 to ship the order and this amount was paid in cash. The journal entry for this transaction is shown in Figure 7.17.

JOURNAL			
Date 2018	**Account Title and Explanation**	**Debit**	**Credit**
Jan 3	Delivery Expense	120	
	Cash		120
	To record shipping expenses on a customer order		

FIGURE 7.17

A CLOSER LOOK

Sometimes the party that is not responsible for paying the delivery cost may prepay it and then charge it back to the responsible party later. To illustrate, assume that Tools 4U purchases $10,000 worth of merchandise from Roofs and More under FOB shipping point, which means that Tools 4U is responsible for paying the delivery cost. If Roofs and More prepays the $100 delivery cost, this is added to the invoice. The prepaid delivery portion of the invoice is not covered in the discount terms. For example, if the terms are 2/10, n/30 and if Tools 4U pays within 10 days, it receives a $200 discount ($10,000 x 2%) and has to pay a total of $9,900 ($10,000 merchandise inventory − $200 discount + $100 prepaid delivery cost) to Roofs and More.

A summary of FOB shipping point and FOB destination is presented in Figure 7.18.

	FOB Shipping Point	**FOB Destination**
Ownership Change	When goods leave the seller on a common carrier	When goods arrive at the buyer's place of business
Transportation Costs	Paid by the buyer and recorded in merchandise inventory	Paid by the seller and recorded as an expense
Risk of Loss	Buyer bears risk of loss during transport	Seller bears risk of loss during transport

FIGURE 7.18

Sale of Inventory

WORTH REPEATING

When goods are shipped from the selling company to the buyer's company, whoever pays for shipping owns the goods while they are being transported. They also bear the risk of loss during transport.

Suppose on January 15, Tools 4U sells $7,200 worth of inventory for $15,000 on account. The sale of inventory is recorded by using two journal entries.

1. Accounts receivable is debited and sales revenue is credited for $15,000 to show the sale on account. This records the proceeds from the sale. If the sale was made for cash, then the cash account is debited instead of accounts receivable.

2. COGS is debited and merchandise inventory is credited for $7,200 to show that inventory has been reduced. This entry is necessary because it removes the inventory sold from the balance sheet and records its cost on the income statement as a cost of doing business for the period.

These transactions are shown in Figure 7.19. Note that the gross profit generated by this sale is equal to $7,800 ($15,000 − $7,200).

JOURNAL			
Date	**Account Title and Explanation**	**Debit**	**Credit**
2018			
Jan 15	Accounts Receivable	15,000	
	Sales Revenue		15,000
	To record product sales on account		
Jan 15	Cost of Goods Sold	7,200	
	Merchandise Inventory		7,200
	Sold inventory to a customer		

FIGURE 7.19

When inventory is sold by a merchandiser, it is no longer an asset of the company because it is owned by the customer. This is the reason for the second journal entry in Figure 7.19. In a service company, this entry is not recorded because assets are not sold in the ordinary course of business.

Debit and Credit Card Transactions

In addition to receiving cash from customers for payment, many businesses allow customers to pay using debit or credit cards. From the business' perspective, these payments are like cash since they are deposited into the business' bank account. The business may have the amounts from debit and credit card sales transferred into the bank account each day or less frequently if it does not have many daily sales.

A debit card sale transfers cash from the customer's bank account to the business' bank account. This limits customers to spending only what they have in their account. A credit card sale gives the customer access to credit, usually available through the bank. This is like a loan from the bank to the customer.

In both cases, a sale paid for by credit card or debit card includes a small transaction fee the business must pay to the bank or processing company. This fee covers the bank's cost of providing the equipment and technology to allow these transactions. In the case of credit card fees, it also covers the risk that the customer may not repay the borrowed money to the bank. From the business' perspective, this fee is a cost of processing the sale and is recorded as an expense.

For example, suppose that instead of buying on account, Tools 4U's customer paid $15,000 using a credit card. The bank charges the business 2.5% of total sales as the transaction fee. Thus, $375 ($15,000 × 2.5%) is kept by the bank and $14,625 is deposited to the business bank account. The transaction is illustrated in Figure 7.20. The COGS transaction is omitted from Figure 7.20 because it would be the same as in Figure 7.19.

JOURNAL			
Date	**Account Title and Explanation**	**Debit**	**Credit**
2018			
Jan 15	Debit/Credit Card Expense	375	
	Cash	14,625	
	Sales Revenue		15,000
	To record credit card sales		

FIGURE 7.20

On the other hand, a bank can charge a fixed percentage of all debit transactions, such as 1% or 2%, or charge a per-transaction fee, such as $0.006 per transaction, depending on the terms of the bank account. This debit card expense is recorded in the journal under the Debit/Credit Card Expense account as shown in Figure 7.20.

Sales Returns

Goods are sometimes returned to a merchandiser for any number of reasons: excess quantity ordered, defective goods received, goods arrived too late, product specifications were incorrect, and so on. A merchandiser must track returns over a period of time. High return levels may indicate serious problems with the products being sold. Therefore, instead of reversing the revenue account with a debit when recording returns, a contra-revenue account called **sales returns and allowances** is used to track the number of returns. Recall that "contra" means opposite and a contra account holds an opposite normal balance of its related account.

Sales returns and allowances is a contra-revenue account with a normal debit balance. It is generally used to record both sales returns and sales allowances. **Sales returns** occur when undesirable products are returned to the seller. **Sales allowances** occur when the customer decides to keep such undesirable products at a reduced price. When sales returns and allowances occur, a seller issues a **credit memorandum**, or a *credit memo* in short, to inform the buyer that the accounts receivable balance has been credited (or decreased) in the seller's books.

Continuing with our example, suppose that a customer returned $4,000 worth of undesirable goods to Tools 4U (the original cost of the inventory was $3,000). There is nothing wrong with the goods and they can be resold. The journal entries to record this return, using the contra-revenue account, are shown in Figure 7.21. Note that two entries are required: one to record the reduction in sales and accounts receivable (or cash, if applicable) and one to reverse the reduction of merchandise inventory.

JOURNAL			
Date 2018	**Account Title and Explanation**	**Debit**	**Credit**
Jan 18	Sales Returns & Allowances	4,000	
	Accounts Receivable		4,000
	Customer returned items		
Jan 18	Merchandise Inventory	3,000	
	Cost of Goods Sold		3,000
	Restock returned inventory		

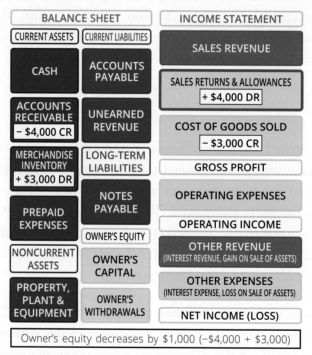

FIGURE 7.21

There is a $4,000 increase in the sales returns and allowances account. This amount decreases revenue since the contra-revenue account has the opposite effect than the revenue account.

In the example in Figure 7.21, the inventory that was returned was not what the customer wanted. There was nothing wrong with the product in terms of quality, so it was placed back on the shelf to be sold again. If the items returned by the customer were damaged, then the inventory cannot be sold again. In that case, Tools 4U would not record the second journal entry from Figure 7.21 because the damaged inventory is worthless.

Sales Allowances

There are circumstances where a reduction to the original selling price is given to a customer.

Assume the customer from January 15 discovered that some goods were damaged during shipping. Instead of returning the items, the customer agreed to accept an allowance of 5% on the price of the goods kept. The customer kept $11,000 worth of goods ($15,000 original sale – $4,000 return), so there is a $550 reduction ($11,000 × 5%) on what is owed to Tools 4U.

The journal entry is shown in Figure 7.22. The amount is recorded as a debit to sales returns and allowances and a credit to accounts receivable. The transaction decreases equity by $550.

A balance of $10,450 ($15,000 – $4,000 – $550) is still owed by Tools 4U's customer.

JOURNAL			
Date	**Account Title and Explanation**	**Debit**	**Credit**
2018			
Jan 18	Sales Returns & Allowances	550	
	Accounts Receivable		550
	Sale allowance for damaged goods		

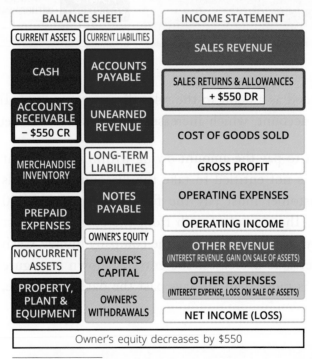

FIGURE 7.22

Sales Discounts

When selling products or services, it is common to offer sales discounts to customers for early payment. The concept works in the same way as the purchase discount. Assume that Tools 4U offered its customer from January 15 terms of 2/10, n/30 on the invoice. If the customer pays by January 25, a 2% discount is applied to the amount owing of $10,450.

Assume the customer made the payment on January 20; the amount is $10,241 ($10,450 less the 2% discount). The journal entry to record this transaction is shown in Figure 7.23.

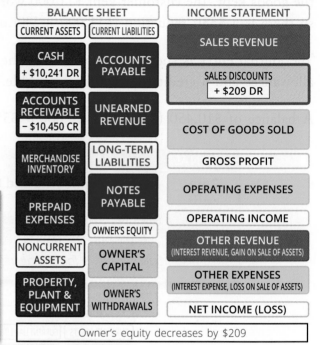

JOURNAL			
Date	Account Title and Explanation	Debit	Credit
2018			
Jan 20	Cash	10,241	
	Sales Discounts	209	
	Accounts Receivable		10,450
	Payments received from customer less discount		

FIGURE 7.23

The $209 discount is recorded as a debit to the sales discounts account. The **sales discount account** is another contra-revenue account, which increases with a debit and decreases with a credit.

If the customer decides not to pay the amount owing within the discount period, then the customer is not entitled to take the discount that Tools 4U offers. Instead, the customer must pay the full amount of $10,450 within 30 days of the sale. The receipt of cash from the customer is just like receiving cash from any customer that owes the company money. Cash increases and accounts receivable decreases. The entry is shown in Figure 7.24. Notice that the date is more than 10 days past the date of the sale.

JOURNAL			
Date	Account Title and Explanation	Debit	Credit
2018			
Feb 2	Cash	10,450	
	Accounts Receivable		10,450
	Payment received from customer		

FIGURE 7.24

A CLOSER LOOK

Because a sales discount normally represents a very high annual percentage, as shown in the purchase discount calculation, it is in the buyer's best interest to take advantage of the discount. Therefore, it is reasonable for a seller to expect that the buyer will pay within the discount period and that the seller will receive the amount net of sales discount. One of the options under GAAP is for the seller to record the sale transaction at the most likely amount to be collected, or the amount net of the sales discount in this case, rather than the total amount of the goods sold.

To illustrate, assume that on January 15, Tools 4U sells $15,000 worth of merchandise inventory under the terms 2/10, n/30. If Tools 4U expects the customer to pay within the discount period, and if the customer in fact pays on January 25, Tools 4U can record the sale and the cash receipt transactions at $14,700, which is the amount net of the $300 ($15,000 x 2%) sales discount as shown here. (The COGS transaction is omitted for simplification.)

Jan 15	Accounts Receivable	14,700	
	Sales Revenue		14,700
	To record product sales on account		
Jan 25	Cash	14,700	
	Accounts Receivable		14,700
	Payment received from customer		

Figure 7.25 summarizes the required journal entries in the buyer's and the seller's books for the merchandising transactions covered in this chapter so far. Every merchandising transaction affects both the buyer and the seller, except for the freight transaction, which affects only the party that is responsible for paying the freight cost.

Transactions	Seller's Journal Entries	Buyer's Journal Entries

Sale/purchase of merchandise on account	Accounts Receivable
	   Sales Revenue
	Cost of Goods Sold
	   Merchandise Inventory
		Merchandise Inventory
		   Accounts Payable

Sale/purchase returns	Sales Returns & Allowances
	   Accounts Receivable
	Merchandise Inventory
	   Cost of Goods Sold
		Accounts Payable
		   Merchandise Inventory

Sale/purchase allowance	Sales Returns & Allowances
	   Accounts Receivable
		Accounts Payable
		   Merchandise Inventory

Cash receipt/payment with sale/purchase discount	Cash
	Sales Discounts
	   Accounts Receivable
		Accounts Payable
		   Cash
		   Merchandise Inventory

Cash receipt/payment without sales discount	Cash
	   Accounts Receivable
		Accounts Payable
		   Cash

Freight cost: FOB shipping point	No entry	Merchandise Inventory Cash
Freight cost: FOB destination	Delivery Expense Cash	No entry

FIGURE 7.25

Pause & Reflect

Exercise 7-2

On May 10, 2018, Caterpy Company sold merchandise that originally cost the company $3,000 to Weezle Company for $5,000 cash. The delivery term was FOB shipping point, and the freight cost was $130. Journalize the necessary transactions for both Caterpy and Weezle.

Caterpy Company

Date	Account Title and Explanation	Debit	Credit
JOURNAL			

Weezle Company

Date	Account Title and Explanation	Debit	Credit
JOURNAL			

See Appendix I for solutions.

Gross Profit Margin: A Profitability Ratio

Recall that net sales is equal to the difference between sales revenue and any sales returns, allowances and discounts. Gross profit is the difference between sales revenue and COGS. Gross profit expressed as a percentage of sales is called **gross profit margin**, or simply gross margin. The gross profit margin represents the percentage of sales left over to pay for all the operating expenses.

When gross profit is expressed as a percentage, it is calculated as shown in Figure 7.26.

$$\text{Gross Profit Margin (\%)} = \frac{\text{Gross Profit}}{\text{Net Sales}}$$

FIGURE 7.26

Gross profit margin is more meaningful when comparing the results from one period to another or between different companies. For example, suppose Company A has sales revenue of $100,000 and its COGS is $60,000, which means it has a gross profit of $40,000. It does not have any sales returns, allowances or discounts, so its sales revenue is equal to its net sales. If Company B has sales of $500,000, with a gross profit of $175,000, which of the two companies is performing better? You may think that Company B is performing better because a gross profit of $175,000 is greater than a gross profit of $40,000. However, to assess the results properly, it is important to compare the two percentages.

Company A: $\dfrac{\$40,000 \text{ Gross Profit}}{\$100,000 \text{ Sales}}$ = 0.40 or 40%

Company B: $\dfrac{\$175,000 \text{ Gross Profit}}{\$500,000 \text{ Sales}}$ = 0.35 or 35%

The results show that Company A is more efficient because it used only 60% of revenue to cover the cost of the product, leaving $0.40 of every dollar to contribute toward its operating expenses. Company B, on the other hand, used 65% of its revenue to cover the COGS, leaving only $0.35 of each dollar to contribute toward its operating expenses.

Keep in mind that ratios should be compared within industry groups, taking industry norms into account. Suppose Company A and Company B are both hardware stores and other hardware stores have a gross profit margin of 38%. In this situation, Company A is doing better than the industry average and Company B is doing worse than the industry average.

Pause & Reflect

Exercise 7-3

a) In 2018, Cochran Company has net sales of $400,000 and its COGS is $220,000. What is the company's gross profit margin?

_____

_____

b) If Cochran expects its net sales to increase to $500,000 in 2019, what is the maximum COGS required to maintain the same gross profit margin as in 2018?

_____

_____

See Appendix I for solutions.

Income Statement

Single-Step Income Statement

The income statement of a merchandising business follows the same principles as those of a service business. Until now, we have been grouping revenue accounts together and listing all expenses together, without further categorizing. The income statement that is presented in this format is referred to as the **single-step income statement**. This is shown in Figure 7.27. This format of the income statement classifies expenses by their nature, which means that expenses are presented based on their purposes, without further categorizing them by function.

Tools 4U Income Statement For the Year Ended December 31, 2018		
Revenues		
Net Sales		$194,000
Interest Revenue		8,000
Total Revenues		202,000
Expenses		
Cost of Goods Sold	$100,000	
Depreciation Expense	8,000	
Interest Expense	4,000	
Rent Expense	10,000	
Salaries Expense	40,000	
Office Supplies Expense	4,000	
Advertising Expense	3,500	
Delivery Expense	1,300	
Insurance Expense	1,200	
Total Expenses		(172,000)
Net Income		$30,000

FIGURE 7.27

Multiple-Step Income Statement

A **multiple-step income statement** is an income statement that further divides specific revenues and expenses to show subtotals like gross profit, operating expenses and income from operations (also referred to as operating income). This format classifies expenses by function, which means that related expenses are grouped together. Also, important measures such as gross profit and income from operations are clearly shown. A multiple-step income statement is illustrated in Figure 7.28.

1. Calculate Net Sales and Gross Profit	**Tools 4U** **Income Statement** **For the Year Ended December 31, 2018**			
	Sales Revenue			$200,000
	Less: Sales Returns & Allowances		$4,000	
	Sales Discounts		2,000	(6,000)
	Net Sales			194,000
	Cost of Goods Sold			(100,000)
	Gross Profit			94,000
2. Calculate Selling Expenses	**Operating Expenses**			
	Selling Expenses			
	Depreciation Expense—Store Equipment	$5,000		
	Rent Expense—Retail Space	8,000		
	Salaries Expense—Sales	32,000		
	Advertising Expense	3,500		
	Delivery Expense	1,300		
	Total Selling Expenses		49,800	
3. Calculate Administrative Expenses and Income from Operations	**Administrative Expenses**			
	Depreciation Expense—Office Equipment	3,000		
	Rent Expense—Office Space	2,000		
	Salaries Expense—Office	8,000		
	Supplies Expense	4,000		
	Insurance Expense	1,200		
	Total Administrative Expenses		18,200	
	Total Operating Expenses			(68,000)
	Income from Operations			26,000
4. Calculate Non-Operating Activities and Net Income	**Other Income and Expenses**			
	Interest Revenue		8,000	
	Interest Expense		(4,000)	4,000
	Net Income			$30,000

FIGURE 7.28

The multiple-step income statement further groups the revenues and expenses that are not part of the main operations of the business, such as interest expense, interest revenue or loss from a lawsuit, under a separate category called Other Income and Expenses or Other Revenues and Expenses.

The expenses incurred as part of the main operations of the business that are beyond the cost of goods sold are referred to as **operating expenses**. Operating expenses can be further divided by function into selling and administrative expenses. **Selling expenses** are those related to actually selling inventory. Examples include sales salaries, rent for retail space, and advertising. **Administrative expenses**, sometimes referred to as *general expenses* or *general and administrative expenses*, are those related to running the business, which are not directly tied to selling inventory. Examples include office salaries, office supplies and depreciation of office equipment.

The multiple-step income statement is particularly useful for the company's internal analysis. It allows managers and executives to clearly see a detailed breakdown of costs by function and compare performance in different areas against competitors and its own financial history.

GAAP vs IFRS

GAAP provides no guidance on whether a company has to present its expenses on an income statement by nature or by function. However, the SEC requires its registrants to present the expenses by function.

Under IFRS, expenses can be classified either by nature or by function on an income statement. Using a mixture of nature and function is prohibited.

IN THE REAL WORLD

An actual company's income statement usually looks similar to what we have seen up to this point. However, it will also have additional columns to show amounts from the previous fiscal years, as required by GAAP. For instance, a company reporting for the 2018 fiscal year will have a column with the header "2018" in its income statement to report revenue and expense information for the most recent fiscal year. There would also be additional columns with the headers "2017" and "2016" to show amounts from the previous fiscal years. This form of financial reports is referred to as comparative financial statements. This allows users to easily compare the financial performance and position of a company to that of the previous years.

Closing Entries

When using a perpetual inventory system, merchandise inventory is immediately updated after each purchase and sale transaction. However, the value of merchandise inventory on the balance sheet may not accurately represent the value of inventory actually on hand. To verify the accuracy of the accounting records, a physical inventory count should be performed at the end of the reporting period. If the count does not match the records, an adjustment must be made to bring the merchandise inventory to its correct balance. A physical inventory count that is lower than the recorded amount in the merchandise inventory account is often referred to as **inventory shrinkage**, resulting either from an error in recording transactions, theft or breakage. The journal entry to adjust for inventory shrinkage of $200 is shown in Figure 7.29.

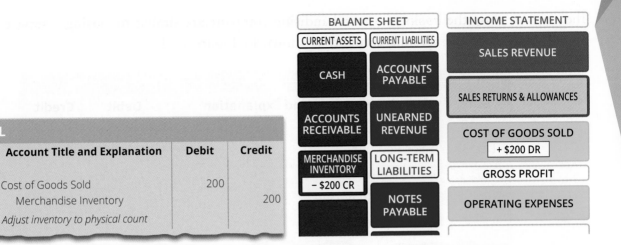

FIGURE 7.29

After this adjustment and all other adjustments have been made, assume Tools 4U has the adjusted trial balance shown in Figure 7.30.

Tools 4U Adjusted Trial Balance December 31, 2018		
Account Title	**DR**	**CR**
Cash	$25,000	
Accounts Receivable	18,000	
Merchandise Inventory	45,000	
Prepaid Expenses	12,000	
Equipment	180,000	
Accumulated Depreciation—Equipment		$60,000
Accounts Payable		34,000
Unearned Revenue		8,000
Notes Payable		100,000
Sanders, Capital		48,000
Sales Revenue		200,000
Interest Revenue		8,000
Sales Returns & Allowances	4,000	
Sales Discounts	2,000	
Cost of Goods Sold	100,000	
Depreciation Expense	5,000	
Interest Expense	4,000	
Rent Expense	10,000	
Salaries Expense	40,000	
Supplies Expense	7,000	
Utilities Expense	6,000	
Total	**$458,000**	**$458,000**

FIGURE 7.30

The steps to close the books of a merchandising company are similar to closing a service company. Step 1 is to close the revenue account, as shown in Figure 7.31.

JOURNAL			
Date	**Account Title and Explanation**	**Debit**	**Credit**
2018			
Dec 31	Sales Revenue	200,000	
	Interest Revenue	8,000	
	Income Summary		208,000
	Close revenue accounts		

FIGURE 7.31

Step 2 is to close expenses. In this step, shown in Figure 7.32, the two contra-revenue accounts (sales returns and allowances and sales discounts) are also closed because they have debit balances like the rest of the expense accounts.

JOURNAL			
Date	**Account Title and Explanation**	**Debit**	**Credit**
2018			
Dec 31	Income Summary	178,000	
	Sales Returns & Allowances		4,000
	Sales Discounts		2,000
	Cost of Goods Sold		100,000
	Depreciation Expense		5,000
	Interest Expense		4,000
	Rent Expense		10,000
	Salaries Expense		40,000
	Supplies Expense		7,000
	Utilities Expense		6,000
	Close expense and contra-revenue accounts		

FIGURE 7.32

Step 3 closes the income summary account. Recall from Chapter 6 that the income summary account is closed to owner's capital, as shown in Figure 7.33.

JOURNAL			
Date	**Account Title and Explanation**	**Debit**	**Credit**
2018			
Dec 31	Income Summary	30,000	
	Sanders, Capital		30,000
	Close income summary		

FIGURE 7.33

The end result, just as in a service company, is that the equity in the business is updated with the net income as shown in Figure 7.34.

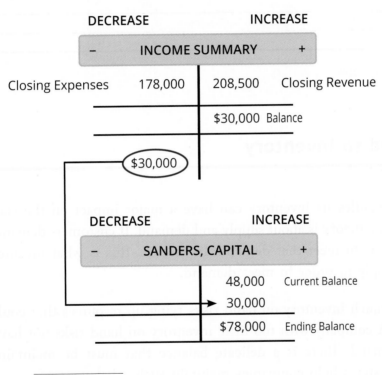

FIGURE 7.34

Similar to a service company, if the owner of a merchandising company withdraws money from the business during the year, the owner's withdrawals account also has to be closed. In Tools 4U's case, the owner's withdrawals account does not have to be closed because the owner did not withdraw any money during the year, and it has a zero balance.

Pause & Reflect

Exercise 7-4

During the year-end physical inventory count, Squaker Company realized that a portion of its merchandise must have been stolen. Squaker Company used the perpetual inventory system and its accounting records showed the merchandise inventory balance of $53,000 as at December 31. However, the actual value of the physical inventory in the warehouse on December 31 was only $50,000. Prepare the journal entry to record the inventory shrinkage.

JOURNAL			
Date	Account Title and Explanation	Debit	Credit

See Appendix I for solutions.

Controls Related to Inventory

The way a company handles its inventory can have a major impact on the state of the business. After all, basic economic theory is about supply and demand. If customers demand goods or services, the goal of a business is to meet that demand. In essence, this is what inventory management is about—to manage supply in order to meet demand.

A company with too much inventory on hand risks tying up resources that could be used productively in other areas. A company with too little inventory on hand risks not having enough supply to meet customer demand. There is a delicate balance that must be maintained by a company. Perpetual inventory systems help companies maintain such a balance.

Keeping track of a company's inventory can be a challenge, but computer software can help. However, every accountant should have an understanding of how merchandise inventory is tracked and recorded manually.

First, even with the use of technology, errors can be made. It is the responsibility of the accounting department and management to ensure that inventory information is accurate and reliable.

Second, a thorough knowledge of manual accounting procedures helps the accountant develop the necessary controls to ensure that this type of asset is managed responsibly and with integrity.

We will provide examples to show how an accountant can develop a personal method of controlling inventory manually. We will then take a closer look at the kinds of controls needed when dealing with the merchandise inventory section of the balance sheet.

Compliance with Plans, Policies, Procedures, Regulations and Laws

All aspects of doing business should be governed by the appropriate plans, policies, procedures, regulations and laws. This is certainly true regarding a company's handling and control of inventory.

All businesses should have plans that are formalized through general policies that lead to specific procedures. These should all comply with the regulations and laws in place within the jurisdiction of the business.

For example, a company can have a plan to train all inventory personnel. This plan can include detection controls to identify instances of procedures not being followed. An example of such a procedure could be to have all items tagged and scanned at the checkout. If this procedure is not followed, then a backup measure could be implemented, such as alarms going off at the exit.

All plans, policies and procedures must adhere to relevant regulations and laws, as illustrated in Figure 7.35. For example, customers cannot be strip-searched because the alarm goes off as they are leaving the store because this would be a violation of their rights. In addition to the human rights law, there are laws and regulations specific to inventory, especially for the industries whose inventory is potentially harmful. For example, companies in the chemical industry must comply with the Toxic Substances Control Act, which regulates distribution and use of chemicals. The companies in food, medical and cosmetic industries must comply with the Federal Food, Drug, and Cosmetic Act. Each company is responsible for observing and complying with the industry-specific laws and continually keeping up-to-date with any amendments.

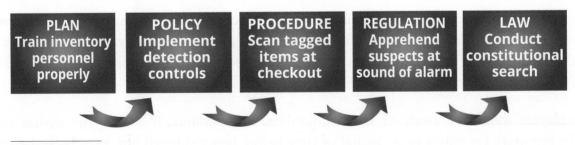

FIGURE 7.35

All employees should be trained in the inventory procedures that are in place. For example, the receiver should count all goods that enter the premises and match the count with the one initially written on the purchase order. The supervisor should ensure that this procedure is followed. Internal auditors can conduct field visits to ensure that both the supervisor and the receiver are implementing procedures according to plans and policies.

Safeguarding Inventory

All company assets must be physically protected. Cash is generally deposited in a bank; securities can be kept with the brokerage house. Inventory, on the other hand, is often located on company premises in a warehouse or onsite storage facility. The location needs to be easily accessible for receiving or shipping, but it also needs to be protected from the possibility of theft; at the most basic level of safeguarding, inventory facilities are locked up after closing. The more valuable the inventory, the more elaborate the security measures needed to protect it. Examples of the measures to safeguard inventory include inspecting the inventory and comparing it against the company's purchase order and the supplier's invoice when the inventory is received, building fences, and installing alarm systems and video cameras. Other measures can include hiring security guards, guard dogs and inventory custodians, who are charged specifically with protecting the inventory.

The Economical and Efficient Use of Resources

The concept that resources should be used economically and efficiently is especially applicable to inventory. First, financial ratios—which are examined later in this textbook—can be used to determine if there is too much or too little inventory on hand. If there is too much inventory, then money is tied up that could be used more efficiently elsewhere. If there is too little inventory, then customer demand will not be met.

Second, the physical condition of the inventory should be checked regularly. This can be done visually or through inventory reports. Any inventory items that are old or in disrepair, and therefore difficult to sell at market value, can be sold at reduced prices or disposed of so that valuable storage space can be maximized.

Inventory Objectives

All aspects of a business should be guided by the objectives set by management. This not only allows for the accomplishment of specific objectives, but allows all organizational objectives to be properly coordinated. For example, sales objectives can be tied to inventory objectives, and profit objectives can be tied to those set by the marketing department.

All employees should be aware of stated objectives. For example, if a company wishes to keep items in inventory for only a short period of time before being shipped out, then both the receiver and shipper should be aware of this. This objective would guide much of their short-term and long-term activities.

Meeting inventory objectives must be a total team effort. If inventory levels are not maintained close to management's objectives, then initiatives should be implemented to ensure that objectives are reassessed or changed. For example, if inventory levels are higher than expected, the sales department can view it as a challenge to get items moving out faster. The more sales increase, the less inventory builds up in the warehouse.

In Summary

LO 1 **Define a merchandising business**

- A merchandising business, or merchandiser, is any business that buys and sells products for the purpose of making a profit.

LO 2 **Differentiate between the perpetual and the periodic inventory systems**

- The perpetual inventory system constantly updates merchandise inventory whenever a purchase or sale is made.

- The periodic inventory system only updates merchandise inventory when a physical count of the inventory is taken, usually at the end of a period.

LO 3 **Record journal entries under the perpetual inventory system**

- Purchase returns and allowances cause accounts payable and merchandise inventory to decrease.

- Purchase discounts allow the buyer to save money by paying early. Merchandise inventory value is reduced by the amount of the discount to reflect the actual cost of the inventory.

- Goods shipped FOB shipping point are owned by the buyer as soon as they are loaded onto the carrier. The buyer pays for shipping costs and records them in merchandise inventory.

- Goods shipped FOB destination are owned by the seller until they arrive at the buyer's destination. The seller pays for shipping costs and records them as a delivery expense.

- Inventory sales require two journal entries: one to record the sales revenue and one to remove the merchandise inventory from the balance sheet.

- Sales returns and allowances cause an increase to a contra-revenue account called sales returns and allowances. If returned merchandise can be resold, an additional entry must be recorded to increase merchandise inventory and decrease COGS.

- Sales discounts allow customers to save money by paying early. Another contra-revenue account called sales discounts is used to track the amount of discounts taken by customers.

LO 4 **Calculate gross profit and gross profit margin percentages**

- Gross profit is the amount of profit remaining after the COGS is deducted from revenue. Gross profit is used to cover operating expenses.

- Gross profit margin is the gross profit as a percentage of sales. It is calculated by dividing gross profit by sales revenue.

LO 5 **Prepare the income statement under the perpetual inventory system**

▸ A single-step income statement reports all revenues together, followed by all expenses.

▸ A multiple-step income statement further categorizes revenues and expenses to show subtotals, such as gross profit and income from operations. Expenses are categorized into selling expenses and administrative expenses. Other income and expenses that are not part of regular operations are presented separately.

LO 6 **Prepare closing entries for a merchandising business under the perpetual inventory system**

▸ If there is inventory shrinkage, an adjusting entry must be made by debiting COGS and crediting merchandise inventory.

▸ All revenue accounts are closed to the income summary account.

▸ All expense accounts and contra-revenue accounts are closed to the income summary account.

▸ The income summary account is closed to the owner's capital account.

▸ If there are owner's withdrawals, they are closed directly to the owner's capital account.

LO 7 **Identify inventory controls**

▸ All aspects of doing business should be governed by the appropriate plans, policies, procedures, regulations and laws.

▸ All businesses should have plans that are formalized through general policies that lead to specific procedures.

▸ All company assets must be physically protected.

▸ The concept that resources should be used economically and efficiently is especially applicable to inventory.

AMEENGAGE™ *Access **ameengage.com** for integrated resources including tutorials, practice exercises, the digital textbook and more.*

Review Exercise 7-1

Part 1

The following transactions occurred between George's Gardening Supplies, owned by George Gregg, and Michael's Distributing, owned by Michael Aberdeen, during the month of December 2018.

Dec 3   George's Gardening Supplies purchased $50,000 worth of inventory on account from Michael's Distributing. The purchase terms were 2/10, n/30. The cost of the goods to Michael's Distributing was $35,000.

Dec 6   Freight charges of $200 were paid in cash by the company that incurred them.

Dec 8   George's Gardening Supplies returned $2,000 of incorrect merchandise from the purchase on December 3. Michael's Distributing put the merchandise back into inventory. The cost of the goods to Michael's Distributing was originally $700.

Dec 11   George's Gardening Supplies paid the balance owing to Michael's Distributing.

Assume that both companies use the perpetual inventory system.

Required

a) Journalize the December transactions for George's Gardening Supplies. Assume the goods from December 3 were shipped FOB shipping point.

JOURNAL			
Date	**Account Title and Explanation**	**Debit**	**Credit**

b) Journalize the December transactions for Michael's Distributing. Assume the goods from December 3 were shipped FOB destination.

JOURNAL			
Date	Account Title and Explanation	Debit	Credit

See Appendix I for solutions.

Part 2

Below is the adjusted trial balance for George's Gardening Supplies at the end of the year.

George's Gardening Supplies Adjusted Trial Balance December 31, 2018		
Account Title	**DR**	**CR**
Cash	$54,830	
Accounts Receivable	33,500	
Merchandise Inventory	33,440	
Prepaid Insurance	3,600	
Equipment	45,000	
Accumulated Depreciation—Equipment		$5,000
Accounts Payable		10,000
Notes Payable		30,000
Gregg, Capital		90,000
Gregg, Withdrawals	5,000	
Sales Revenue		113,500
Interest Revenue		6,500
Sales Returns & Allowances	1,000	
Sales Discounts	1,580	
Cost of Goods Sold	44,700	
Depreciation Expense	5,000	
Insurance Expense	2,500	
Interest Expense	2,600	
Rent Expense	6,000	
Salaries Expense	11,000	
Supplies Expense	4,500	
Utilities Expense	750	
Total	**$255,000**	**$255,000**

Note: $10,000 of the notes payable will be paid by December 31, 2019.

Required

a) Prepare a single-step income statement for George's Gardening Supplies for the year ended December 31, 2018.

b) Calculate the gross profit margin.

Gross Profit Margin = _____

c) Prepare a multiple-step income statement for George's Gardening Supplies for the year ended December 31, 2018 using the following information.

- The equipment is used solely for selling purposes.

- Supplies are used for administrative purposes only.

- Insurance, salaries, rent and utilities are allocated 70% to selling and 30% to administration.

d) Journalize the closing entries for George's Gardening Supplies for 2018 using the income summary method.

JOURNAL			
Date	**Account Title and Explanation**	**Debit**	**Credit**

See Appendix I for solutions.

Appendix 7A: The Periodic Inventory System   LO 8

The periodic inventory system determines the quantity of merchandise inventory on hand only periodically, not on a regular basis as a perpetual inventory system does. A physical count is taken at the end of the period to determine the value of the ending inventory and update a new list of income statement accounts, which are used to calculate COGS.

Consider the differences between the perpetual and the periodic inventory systems. Figure 7A.1 illustrates the perpetual inventory system. A business that has the technology to properly implement the perpetual inventory system records purchases, discounts, allowances and other adjustments into the merchandise inventory asset account. Merchandise inventory is then transferred to COGS when a sale is made. Cost of goods sold is immediately matched to sales, and gross profit is reported every month, although gross profit may be slightly incorrect if an inventory count is not performed.

A business that does not have the technology to use the perpetual inventory system must instead use the periodic inventory system. Figure 7A.2 illustrates the periodic inventory system. Merchandise inventory shows an opening value at the beginning of the period, but is only adjusted up or down at the end of the period when an inventory count is performed. All purchases, discounts, allowances and other adjustments are recorded directly into the income statement as part of COGS.

If purchases were recorded in the merchandise inventory account on the balance sheet, they would always remain in merchandise inventory since merchandise inventory is not transferred to COGS when a sale is made. This would leave a large amount of merchandise inventory remaining on the balance sheet and no COGS on the income statement. It is more practical to record purchases directly on the income statement, and adjust the merchandise inventory account only at year end.

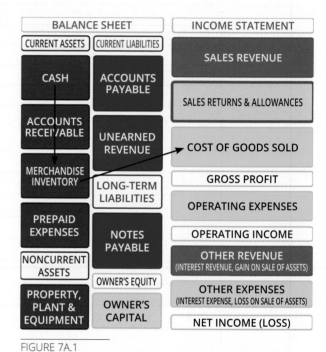

FIGURE 7A.1

FIGURE 7A.2

Keep the concept of the periodic inventory system in mind as the journal entries are presented. The transactions are very similar to the perpetual inventory system, except that income statement accounts are affected instead of merchandise inventory.

Purchase of Inventory

When inventory is purchased for resale using a periodic inventory system, the merchandise inventory account is not debited. Instead, we debit an account called purchases on the income statement, which is part of COGS. If the inventory was paid for on credit, then accounts payable is credited. If the inventory was paid for with cash, then the cash account is credited. In this example, Tools 4U purchased inventory of $10,000 on January 1, 2018, as shown in Figure 7A.3. Assume all purchases and sales are made on account and Tools 4U uses a periodic inventory system.

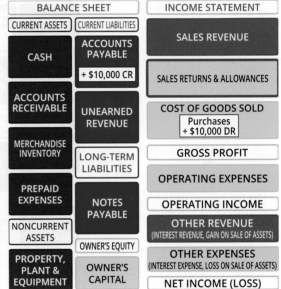

JOURNAL			
Date	Account Title and Explanation	Debit	Credit
2018			
Jan 1	Purchases	10,000	
	Accounts Payable		10,000
	Record purchase of inventory		

FIGURE 7A.3

The purchases account is a temporary account located on the income statement as part of COGS. It records all the inventory purchased by a company during a specific period of time under the periodic inventory system.

The values of merchandise inventory and COGS are not adjusted until the end of the period when the physical inventory count is taken. As a result, we need to track the costs related to merchandise inventory in separate accounts.

Purchase Returns

Assume Tools 4U returned $300 worth of inventory to its supplier. Instead of crediting the purchases account, it tracks the return by using a temporary contra account to purchases called **purchase returns and allowances**. This new account is also part of COGS. The journal entry to record the return is shown in Figure 7A.4.

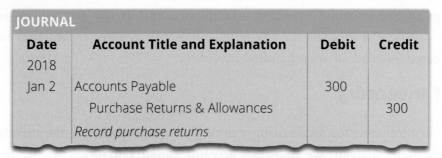

JOURNAL			
Date	**Account Title and Explanation**	**Debit**	**Credit**
2018			
Jan 2	Accounts Payable	300	
	Purchase Returns & Allowances		300
	Record purchase returns		

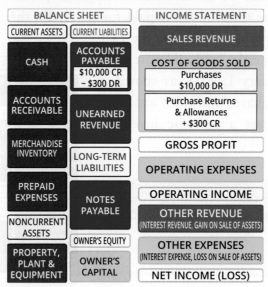

FIGURE 7A.4

Purchase Allowances

Assume Tools 4U found another $300 worth of unsatisfactory inventory. The supplier offers a 20% allowance to Tools 4U to keep the goods, rather than return them. This results in an allowance of $60 ($300 × 20%). The credit is recorded in the purchase returns and allowances account as shown in Figure 7A.5.

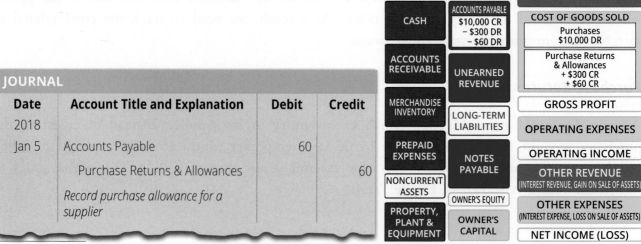

JOURNAL			
Date	**Account Title and Explanation**	**Debit**	**Credit**
2018			
Jan 5	Accounts Payable	60	
	Purchase Returns & Allowances		60
	Record purchase allowance for a supplier		

FIGURE 7A.5

Purchase Discounts

The supplier may offer credit terms and a discount period to encourage early payments. In a periodic inventory system, the amount of the discount is credited to another contra expense account to purchases called **purchase discounts**. This is another account that is part of COGS. By crediting this account, instead of simply crediting the merchandise inventory account as in the perpetual inventory system, management is able to track the amount it is saving by paying suppliers within the discount period. We will now show the journal entries for both the purchase and payment from Tools 4U, who bought goods from Roofs and More in the amount of $4,200 on January 10.

The supplier allows 2/10, n/30 on all invoices. Since Tools 4U had excess cash at this time, the manager chose to take advantage of the cash discount by paying the invoice within 10 days.

The original entry for the purchase is shown in Figure 7A.6.

JOURNAL			
Date	Account Title and Explanation	Debit	Credit
2018			
Jan 10	Purchases	4,200	
	Accounts Payable		4,200
	Purchase of goods from Roofs and More		

FIGURE 7A.6

The payment amount for the bill is $4,200 less the $84 discount ($4,200 × 2%). Since the business is paying less for the purchase of inventory, the value of the purchase must decrease by the discount amount. The entry to record the discount when the payment was made to Roofs and More on January 12 is shown in Figure 7A.7.

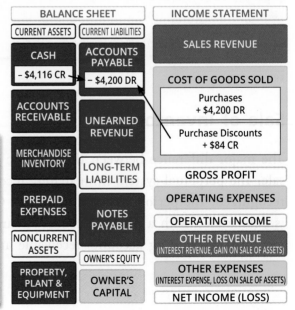

JOURNAL			
Date	Account Title and Explanation	Debit	Credit
2018			
Jan 12	Accounts Payable	4,200	
	Cash		4,116
	Purchase Discounts		84
	Paid invoice owing to Roofs and More less discount for early payment		

FIGURE 7A.7

Both purchase returns and allowances and purchase discounts are known as contra accounts, as they have the opposite balance to the account they are related to. They reduce the balance of purchases when reported on the financial statements.

From the above journal entries, the amount of net purchases is determined in Figure 7A.8.

Purchases		$14,200
Less: Purchase Returns & Allowances	$360	
Purchase Discounts	84	(444)
Net Purchases		$13,756

FIGURE 7A.8

Freight-In and Freight-Out

In a periodic inventory system, shipping charges on inventory shipped FOB shipping point is recorded by the purchaser debiting the **freight-in account**, which is an income statement account that is part of COGS. Similarly, the shipping charges on inventory that is shipped FOB destination are recorded by the seller by debiting the **freight-out account**. Assume Tools 4U paid a $100 freight cost for the inventory on January 10. The journal entry is shown in Figure 7A.9.

BALANCE SHEET		INCOME STATEMENT
CURRENT ASSETS	CURRENT LIABILITIES	SALES REVENUE
CASH – $100 CR	ACCOUNTS PAYABLE	COST OF GOODS SOLD
ACCOUNTS RECEIVABLE	UNEARNED REVENUE	Freight-In + $100 DR
MERCHANDISE INVENTORY	LONG-TERM LIABILITIES	GROSS PROFIT
PREPAID EXPENSES	NOTES PAYABLE	OPERATING EXPENSES
		OPERATING INCOME
NONCURRENT ASSETS		OTHER REVENUE (INTEREST REVENUE, GAIN ON SALE OF ASSETS)
PROPERTY, PLANT & EQUIPMENT	OWNER'S EQUITY OWNER'S CAPITAL	OTHER EXPENSES (INTEREST EXPENSE, LOSS ON SALE OF ASSETS)
		NET INCOME (LOSS)

JOURNAL

Date	Account Title and Explanation	Debit	Credit
2018			
Jan 10	Freight-In	100	
	Cash		100
	Record the payment of freight cost		

FIGURE 7A.9

Sale of Inventory

The major difference between the periodic and perpetual inventory systems occurs at the point of sale. The perpetual system immediately records COGS when revenue from the sale of inventory is recognized. The periodic system calculates COGS at the end of the period when ending inventory is determined with a physical count. Assuming inventory is sold on account, the entry should be recorded by debiting accounts receivable and crediting revenue.

Assume Tools 4U sold $13,000 worth of goods for $20,000 on January 15. The entry is recorded by debiting accounts receivable and crediting sales. The COGS and merchandise inventory accounts are updated at the end of the period when the physical count is taken. Figure 7A.10 shows the transaction.

JOURNAL			
Date	Account Title and Explanation	Debit	Credit
2018			
Jan 15	Accounts Receivable	20,000	
	Sales		20,000
	Record sales on account		

FIGURE 7A.10

Sales Returns

If a customer returns goods, only one journal entry is required to record the sales return and credit the amount owing from the customer (assuming the goods were sold on account). On January 16, a customer returned $4,000 worth of goods to Tools 4U.

The journal entry is recorded by debiting sales returns and allowances and crediting accounts receivable. Unlike the perpetual inventory system, the COGS and merchandise inventory are not updated immediately. Figure 7A.11 shows the journal entry for this transaction.

JOURNAL			
Date	Account Title and Explanation	Debit	Credit
2018			
Jan 16	Sales Returns & Allowances	4,000	
	Accounts Receivable		4,000
	Record sales return		

FIGURE 7A.11

Sales Allowances

Sales allowances are recorded in the same way as when a perpetual inventory system is used. Assume that Tools 4U granted a $300 sales allowance on January 18. The journal entry is recorded as shown in Figure 7A.12.

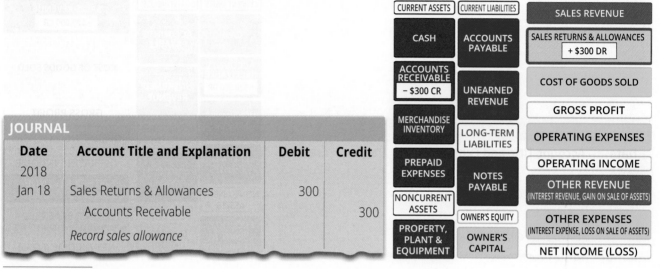

JOURNAL

Date	Account Title and Explanation	Debit	Credit
2018			
Jan 18	Sales Returns & Allowances	300	
	Accounts Receivable		300
	Record sales allowance		

FIGURE 7A.12

Sales Discounts

Sales discounts are recorded in the same way as when a perpetual inventory system is used. In our example, the customer paid within the discount period and received a $314 discount, which is 2% of the amount owing, as shown in Figure 7A.13.

JOURNAL

Date	Account Title and Explanation	Debit	Credit
2018			
Jan 20	Cash	15,386	
	Sales Discounts	314	
	Accounts Receivable		15,700
	Record collection less discount		

FIGURE 7A.13

Net sales is determined by deducting sales returns and allowances and sales discounts from sales revenue as follows.

$$\$20,000 - \$4,000 - \$300 - \$314 = \$15,386$$

Reporting the Cost of Goods Sold

In a periodic system, the COGS is not known until the end of the period, when the ending inventory is known. This is because the costs that make up the cost of goods available for sale are kept in separate accounts (beginning inventory, purchases and freight-in). Once ending inventory is determined, it is subtracted from the cost of goods available for sale to determine the COGS, as shown in Figure 7A.14.

Cost of Goods Sold = Beginning Inventory + Net Purchases + Freight-In − Ending Inventory

FIGURE 7A.14

Assuming the beginning inventory in our example is $20,000 and the ending inventory is $22,856, the COGS is determined on the income statement as shown in Figure 7A.15.

Cost of Goods Sold = Beginning Inventory + Net Purchases + Freight-In − Ending Inventory		
Beginning Inventory		$20,000
Net Purchases	$13,756	
Freight-In	100	13,856
Cost of Goods Available for Sale		33,856
Less: Ending Inventory		22,856
Cost of Goods Sold		$11,000

FIGURE 7A.15

The freight-in is added to net purchases to determine cost of goods available for sale. The value of ending inventory is determined by a physical count and subtracted from cost of goods available for sale to determine COGS. The amounts included in the merchandise inventory and COGS is no different from the example under the perpetual inventory system. It is mainly a timing difference regarding when these amounts are updated.

FOB and Inventory Counts

The shipping terms have an impact on period-end inventory counts. An inventory count is supposed to include all inventory that is owned by the company, and this can include items that are not physically at the place of business. All companies must pay careful attention to items in the process of being shipped when counting inventory.

For example, suppose Company A purchases items with a cost of $10,000 with terms of FOB shipping point. This means that Company A takes ownership of the goods as soon as they are loaded onto the carrier, and should include these as part of its inventory. If Company A's balance sheet includes only the merchandise in its warehouse and excludes the merchandise in transit under

FOB shipping point, the value of ending inventory on the balance sheet will be understated by $10,000. If Company A uses the periodic inventory system, an understated ending inventory will cause COGS to be overstated and net income to be understated. This is shown in Figure 7A.16.

	Correct		Incorrect	
Sales		$160,000		$160,000
Cost of Goods Sold				
Beginning Inventory	$50,000		$50,000	
Net Purchases	65,000		65,000	
Cost of Goods Available for Sale	115,000		115,000	
Less: Ending Inventory	45,000		35,000	
Cost of Goods Sold		70,000		80,000
Gross Profit		90,000		80,000
Operating Expense		50,000		50,000
Net Income		$40,000		$30,000

FIGURE 7A.16

Similar problems occur if a company sells inventory with terms of FOB destination. Although the items are not in the seller's warehouse, the seller still owns the items while they are in transit and must include them as part of the merchandise inventory.

To summarize the differences between the perpetual and periodic journal entries, Figure 7A.17 indicates which accounts are affected by the types of transactions we have learned.

Transaction	Perpetual*		Periodic*	
	Debit	Credit	Debit	Credit
Purchase	Merchandise Inventory (B/S)	Cash or Accounts Payable	Purchases (I/S)	Cash or Accounts Payable
Purchase Return	Cash or Accounts Payable	Merchandise Inventory (B/S)	Cash or Accounts Payable	Purchase Returns & Allowances (I/S)
Purchase Allowance	Cash or Accounts Payable	Merchandise Inventory (B/S)	Cash or Accounts Payable	Purchase Returns & Allowances (I/S)
Payment with Discount	Accounts Payable	Cash Merchandise Inventory (B/S)	Accounts Payable	Cash Purchase Discounts (I/S)
Freight	Merchandise Inventory (B/S)	Cash or Accounts Payable	Freight-In (I/S)	Cash or Accounts Payable
Sales	Cash or Accounts Receivable	Sales Revenue (I/S)	Cash or Accounts Receivable	Sales Revenue (I/S)
	Cost of Goods Sold (I/S)	Merchandise Inventory (B/S)		

Transaction	Perpetual*		Periodic*	
	Debit	Credit	Debit	Credit
Sales Returns	Sales Returns & Allowances (I/S)	Cash or Accounts Receivable	Sales Returns & Allowances (I/S)	Cash or Accounts Receivable
	Merchandise Inventory (B/S)	Cost of Goods Sold (I/S)		
Sales Allowance	Sales Returns & Allowances (I/S)	Cash or Accounts Receivable	Sales Returns & Allowances (I/S)	Cash or Accounts Receivable
Receipt with Discount	Cash Sales Discounts (I/S)	Accounts Receivable	Cash Sales Discounts (I/S)	Accounts Receivable

*B/S = Balance Sheet
 I/S = Income Statement

FIGURE 7A.17

In essence, the mechanisms behind recording these transactions under both inventory tracking methods are the same. They only differ in that Merchandise Inventory and Cost of Goods Sold accounts are not present under the periodic inventory transactions.

A CLOSER LOOK

The accurate financial performance of a company that uses the periodic system can only be calculated when an inventory count is performed and COGS is calculated. If a business wants to see how it is performing between inventory counts, it may have to make some adjustments to the reports before the numbers are useful for decision-making.

For example, a nursery selling flowers and plants operates from May to October. After closing in October, it performs a physical count of inventory and prepares formal financial statements.

Before it opens in May, it has to purchase soil and seeds and start growing plants in the greenhouses in preparation for spring. These purchases are made before any sales are made. Recall that under a periodic inventory system, cost of goods sold = beginning inventory + purchases – ending inventory. If the company uses the periodic inventory system and wants to see its performance after one month of operations (May) without counting inventory, only the beginning inventory and purchases amount are available to calculate COGS. That is, ending inventory would be missing. By not deducting ending inventory, the information presented is distorted and it would appear the company is operating at a loss.

To prevent the distortion of the financial statements, management can estimate what COGS was using the gross profit method, which will be discussed in a later chapter.

For example, if the nursery typically operates at 40% gross profit during the sales season, the income statement on the next page illustrates how the income statement could be estimated without doing a physical inventory count.

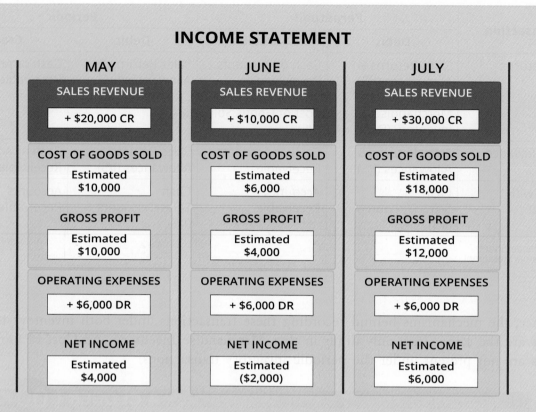

This estimation can only be used for management purposes and interim statements. Formal financial statements can only be prepared after a physical count has been performed.

Multiple-Step Income Statement

The multiple-step income statement under a periodic inventory system is much like that of a perpetual inventory system, except when it comes to COGS. Recall that there is a single line for COGS on the income statement for a perpetual inventory system. However, this line is replaced with a COGS section for a periodic inventory system. The section is taken from the schedule of COGS introduced earlier.

Note that the periodic and perpetual inventory systems both produce the same values for COGS, gross profit and net income. The only difference is the way in which COGS is calculated. The multiple-step income statement for Tools 4U is shown in Figure 7A.18 using the same values from the perpetual inventory system example.

Tools 4U Income Statement For the Year Ended December 31, 2018				
Sales Revenue				$200,000
Less: Sales Returns & Allowances			$4,000	
Sales Discounts			2,000	(6,000)
Net Sales				194,000
Cost of Goods Sold				
Merchandise Inventory, January 1, 2018			20,000	
Purchases		$140,000		
Less: Purchase Returns & Allowances	$9,000			
Purchase Discounts	13,000	(22,000)		
Net Purchases		118,000		
Freight-In		6,000	124,000	
Cost of Goods Available for Sale			144,000	
Merchandise Inventory, December 31, 2018			44,000	
Cost of Goods Sold				(100,000)
Gross Profit				94,000
Operating Expenses				
Selling Expenses				
Depreciation Expense—Store Equipment		5,000		
Rent Expense—Retail Space		8,000		
Salaries Expense—Sales		32,000		
Advertising Expense		3,500		
Delivery Expense		1,300		
Total Selling Expenses			49,800	
Administrative Expenses				
Depreciation Expense—Office Equipment		3,000		
Rent Expense—Office Space		2,000		
Salaries Expense—Office		8,000		
Supplies Expense		4,000		
Insurance Expense		1,200		
Total Administrative Expenses			18,200	
Total Operating Expenses				(68,000)
Income from Operations				26,000
Other Revenues and Expenses				
Interest Revenue			8,000	
Interest Expense			(4,000)	4,000
Net Income				$30,000

Bracket annotations (left margin):

1. Calculate Net Sales
2. Calculate Cost of Goods Sold and Gross Profit
3. Calculate Income from Operations
4. Calculate Non-Operating Activities and Net Income

FIGURE 7A.18

Closing Entries

Although there are a few variations of how merchandise inventory is adjusted through the closing entries when a periodic system is used, the main objective is the same: to remove the beginning inventory balance and add the new ending inventory balance.

One approach that is frequently used is shown in Figure 7A.19.

When closing the accounts with a credit balance on the income statement, the new ending inventory balance of $22,856 is debited to the merchandise inventory account. To understand the logic of this entry, refer to the detailed COGS section previously discussed. The ending inventory is deducted from the cost of goods available for sale to determine the amount of COGS because ending inventory represents the amount a company still has on hand at the end of the accounting period. It is available for sale at the beginning of the next accounting period.

JOURNAL

Date	Account Title and Explanation	Debit	Credit
2018			
Dec 31	Sales Revenue	20,000	
	Merchandise Inventory	22,856	
	Purchase Returns & Allowances	360	
	Purchase Discounts	84	
	Income Summary		43,300
	Close revenue and credit balances and update merchandise inventory		

FIGURE 7A.19

JOURNAL

Date	Account Title and Explanation	Debit	Credit
2018			
Dec 31	Income Summary	40,360	
	Merchandise Inventory		20,000
	Sales Returns & Allowances		4,300
	Sales Discounts		250
	Purchases		14,200
	Freight-in		100
	Operating Expenses		1,510
	Close expenses and debit balances and update merchandise inventory		

FIGURE 7A.20

In closing the expense accounts, notice in Figure 7A.20 that the beginning inventory balance of $20,000 is credited. The detailed COGS section is shown. What effect does the beginning inventory have on the cost of goods available for sale? It is added together with purchases and therefore represents an expense of the period. The logic is that expenses are credited through the closing entries; therefore, the beginning inventory balance of $20,000 must be credited.

After the closing entries are posted to the accounts, the merchandise inventory account will be updated to reflect the actual amount of inventory on hand, $22,856.

The final step of the closing entry process is to close the income summary account to the owners' capital account. The journal entry to do this on December 31 is shown in Figure 7A.21. If the owner withdraws money from the business during the year, the owner's withdrawals account also has to be closed. In Tools 4U's case, the owner did not withdraw any money during the year, so the owner's withdrawals account already has a zero balance and does not have to be closed.

JOURNAL			
Date	**Account Title and Explanation**	**Debit**	**Credit**
2018			
Dec 31	Income Summary	2,940	
	Sanders, Capital		2,940
	To close income summary account		

FIGURE 7A.21

The T-accounts in Figure 7A.22 summarize the closing entries under the periodic inventory system. Note how the merchandise inventory account is updated following the physical inventory count. Each item that is closed to the income summary account is shown separately so the opening and ending inventory amounts can be highlighted.

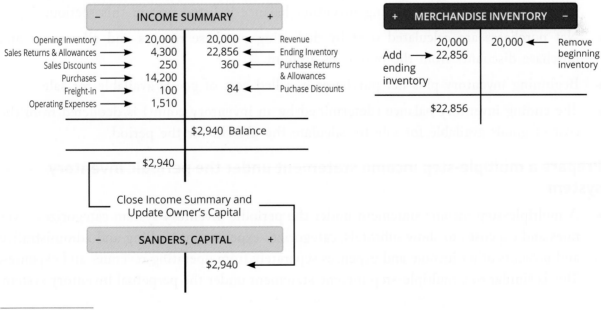

FIGURE 7A.22

In Summary

LO 8   **Record journal entries under the periodic inventory system**

- When buying inventory, the purchases account is debited.

- When returning inventory or taking an allowance on purchased goods, the contra-expense account called purchase returns and allowances is credited.

- When discounts are taken advantage of on inventory purchases, the contra-expense account called purchase discounts is credited for the amount of the discount.

- Shipping costs paid on goods purchased FOB shipping point are recorded in the freight-in account.

- When selling inventory, only the sales transaction is recorded. The merchandise inventory is not removed from the balance sheet at the time of sale.

- When customers return goods or take allowances on their purchases, the contra-revenue account called sales returns and allowances is debited.

- Sales discounts allow customers to save money by paying early. This causes a debit to the contra-revenue account called sales discounts.

- Shipping costs paid on goods sold FOB destination are recorded in the freight-out account.

LO 9   **Calculate cost of goods sold under the periodic inventory system**

- Cost of goods sold appears as a separate section below net sales on the multiple-step income statement. The beginning inventory balance is listed first in this section.

- Net purchases are calculated next by deducting purchase returns and allowances and purchase discounts from the purchases account.

- Beginning inventory plus net purchases is called cost of goods available for sale.

- The ending inventory balance (determined by an inventory count) is deducted from the cost of goods available for sale to calculate the COGS for the period.

LO 10   **Prepare a multiple-step income statement under the periodic inventory system**

- A multiple-step income statement under the periodic inventory system categorizes revenues and expenses to show subtotals, categorizes expenses into selling and administrative and presents other income and expenses separately from operating revenues and expenses. This is similar to a multiple-step income statement under the perpetual inventory system.

- ▶ Under the periodic inventory system, the COGS is presented with its calculation in a multiple-step income statement. This is different from the perpetual inventory system's multiple-step income statement, which presents COGS as a one-line item with no calculation.

LO 11 Prepare closing entries for a merchandising business under the periodic inventory system

- ▶ All revenue and contra-expense accounts are closed to the income summary account. The balance of ending inventory is also added to the income summary account in this entry.

- ▶ All expense and contra-revenue accounts are closed to the income summary account. The balance of beginning inventory is also removed from the income summary account in this entry.

- ▶ The income summary is closed to the owner's capital account.

- ▶ If there are owner's withdrawals, they are closed directly to the owner's capital account.

AMEENGAGE™ *Access **ameengage.com** for integrated resources including tutorials, practice exercises, the digital textbook and more.*

241

Review Exercise 7A-1

Part 1

The following transactions occurred between George's Gardening Supplies, owned by George Gregg, and Michael's Distributing during the month of December 2018.

Dec 3   George's Gardening Supplies purchased $50,000 worth of merchandise inventory on account from Michael's Distributing. The purchase terms were 2/10, n/30. The cost of the goods to Michael's Distributing was $35,000.

Dec 6   Freight charges of $200 were paid in cash by the company that incurred them.

Dec 8   George's Gardening Supplies returned $2,000 of incorrect inventory from the purchase on December 3. Michael's Distributing put the merchandise back into inventory. The cost of the goods to Michael's Distributing was originally $700.

Dec 11   George's Gardening Supplies paid the balance owing to Michael's Distributing.

Assume that both companies use the periodic inventory system.

Required

a) Journalize the December transactions for George's Gardening Supplies. Assume the goods from December 3 were shipped FOB shipping point.

JOURNAL			
Date	**Account Title and Explanation**	**Debit**	**Credit**

b) Journalize the December transactions for Michael's Distributing. Assume the goods from December 3 were shipped FOB destination.

JOURNAL			
Date	Account Title and Explanation	Debit	Credit

See Appendix I for solutions.

Part 2

Below is the adjusted trial balance for George's Gardening Supplies at the end of the year.

George's Gardening Supplies Adjusted Trial Balance December 31, 2018		
Account Title	**DR**	**CR**
Cash	$54,830	
Accounts Receivable	33,500	
Merchandise Inventory	16,140	
Prepaid Insurance	3,600	
Equipment	45,000	
Accumulated Depreciation—Equipment		$5,000
Accounts Payable		10,000
Notes Payable		30,000
Gregg, Capital		90,000
Gregg, Withdrawals	5,000	
Sales Revenue		113,500
Interest Revenue		6,500
Sales Returns & Allowances	1,000	
Sales Discounts	1,580	
Purchases	70,000	
Purchase Returns & Allowances		5,800
Purchase Discounts		3,200
Freight-In	1,000	
Depreciation Expense	5,000	
Insurance Expense	2,500	
Interest Expense	2,600	
Rent Expense	6,000	
Salaries Expense	11,000	
Supplies Expense	4,500	
Utilities Expense	750	
Total	**$264,000**	**$264,000**

Notes:

• The balance in the merchandise inventory account is the value at January 1, 2018. An inventory count revealed that $33,440 of merchandise inventory is on hand at December 31, 2018.

• $10,000 of the notes payable will be paid by December 31, 2019.

Required

a) Prepare a multiple-step income statement for George's Gardening Supplies for the year ended December 31, 2018.

b) Calculate the gross profit margin.

Gross Profit Margin = _____

c) Journalize the closing entries for George's Gardening Supplies for 2018 using the income summary method.

JOURNAL			
Date	Account Title and Explanation	Debit	Credit

See Appendix I for solutions.

Chapter 8
Inventory Valuation

Learning Objectives

*Access **ameengage.com** for integrated resources including tutorials, practice exercises, the digital textbook and more.*

Inventory Valuation Methods

In Chapter 7, we saw how merchandising businesses account for various transactions involving inventory. A perpetual inventory system updates the merchandise inventory and cost of goods sold (COGS) accounts after every sales transaction. This is straightforward when identical inventory is purchased for the same price, but prices for identical goods often fluctuate. This can make it difficult to calculate the COGS for a particular sale.

For example, suppose that Tools 4U purchased 10 steel hammers for $20 each as inventory in March. When one of these hammers is sold to a customer, merchandise inventory is credited for $20 and COGS is debited for $20. Due to an increase in the price of steel, Tools 4U must pay $25 per hammer in April. Now it has a mix of identical hammers, some with a unit cost of $20 and some with a unit cost of $25. When a hammer is sold during April, which unit cost should be used to update merchandise inventory and COGS? Ideally, it would be possible to tell which hammer came from which shipment, but the cost and effort of tracking such information often outweigh the benefits.

There are different methods that companies can use, based on the nature of the goods, to determine how inventory costs are handled. These are called **inventory valuation methods** because they determine the value of inventory on hand at any given time. The four methods used in the United States are specific identification; first-in, first-out; last-in, first-out; and weighted-average cost.

- The **specific identification method** is used when a business sells goods that are not identical or are customized in some way. This method accurately tracks the unit cost and value of merchandise inventory, but it can be costly to apply. Highly valuable items such as cars, houses and diamonds are often valued under this method.

- The **first-in, first-out (FIFO) method** is used when a business assumes that the first items received in inventory are also the first items moved out of inventory. Perishable items that expire within a relatively short period of time, such as fruits and vegetables, are often valued under this method.

- The **last-in, first-out (LIFO) method** is used when a business assumes that the last items received in inventory are the first items moved out. Think of a product that is kept in a pile, with newer inventory being added to the top of the pile, such as interlocking paving stones. The oldest inventory is left at the bottom of the pile and sold last.

- The **weighted-average cost method** is used when a business simply applies an average unit cost to all of the units of a particular inventory item. Homogenous (standardized) materials, such as plastic used to make garbage bags, or oil used to make gasoline, are often valued under this method.

The method chosen does not need to perfectly match the actual physical movement of goods. For example, if a business chooses the FIFO method to value its lawn chairs, it is still acceptable to sell newer lawn chairs before older ones in the course of business.

Figure 8.1 illustrates a simple example where the values of COGS and ending inventory do not match the actual physical movement of merchandise except when the specific identification method is used.

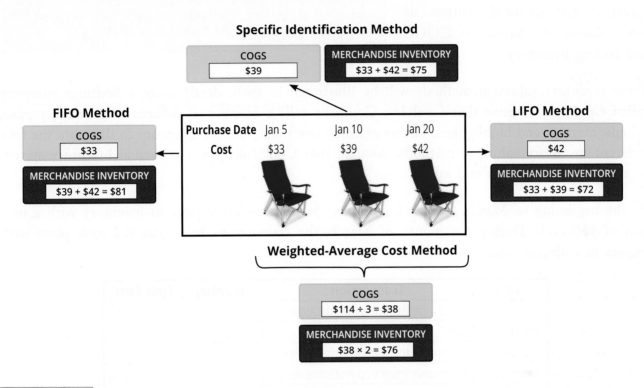

FIGURE 8.1

Assume that a company purchased three identical lawn chairs at three different costs and dates: $33 on January 5, $39 on January 10, and $42 on January 20. The company sold one chair to a customer on January 31; it was purchased by the company on January 10 for $39. The company would report COGS as $39 only if it uses the specific identification method. If the company uses the FIFO method, it would report COGS as $33 because this method assumes that the oldest unit of inventory, which was purchased on January 5 at $33, was sold first. If the company uses the LIFO method, it would report COGS as $42 because this method assumes that the newest item, which was purchased on January 20 at $42, was sold first. If the company uses the weighted-average cost method, it would report COGS as $38 because this method assumes that the unit cost is equal to the average cost of all three units in the inventory.

With each inventory valuation method used, both the COGS figures and the ending balances of merchandise inventory are different. While the specific identification method shows the actual cost of physical units remaining in the company's warehouse, other methods show different inventory values. FIFO assumes that the remaining inventory is comprised of the newest units. LIFO assumes that the remaining inventory is comprised of the oldest units. Lastly, the weighted-average cost method assumes that the value of the remaining inventory is equal to the average cost multiplied by the number of units remaining.

Once a valuation is chosen, accounting standards dictate that the business must use it consistently unless a change can be properly justified. This prevents businesses from arbitrarily changing inventory valuation methods for the purpose of manipulating the values of COGS and ending inventory.

WORTH REPEATING

The consistency constraint prevents businesses from changing accounting methods for the sole purpose of manipulating figures on the financial statements.

These inventory valuation methods will be illustrated in more detail using a fictitious company called Cool Ink. Assume that Cool Ink Company sells a number of different high-quality pens, pencils, markers and highlighters. Let us examine one item from its inventory to illustrate the four different inventory valuation methods. Assume that Cool Ink uses a perpetual inventory system to account for purchases and sales.

At the beginning of March, Cool Ink Company has ten collector pens in inventory with a unit cost of $10 each. During the month of March, the transactions in Figure 8.2 took place with respect to collector pens.

Date	Transaction	Quantity	Unit Cost
March 5	Purchase from Pen Distributers	50	$12
March 7	Sale	15	
March 15	Purchase from Promotional Pens	40	$14
March 19	Purchase from Promotional Pens	20	$16
March 27	Sale	50	

FIGURE 8.2

During the month, the unit cost of the pens increased, as shown in the Unit Cost column. This means that COGS applied to each sale can be different, based on which pens are actually sold. We can apply the four methods of valuing inventory to the transactions to arrive at different values for merchandise inventory and COGS, which will affect the financial statements of a company.

Specific Identification Method

The specific identification method is used when a company sells goods that are unique in some way and can be distinguished from each other. For example, a jewelry retailer may use this method to value its engagement rings because each ring is unique, with different diamond settings and different metals used to make the bands.

When using specific identification, it is helpful to list the purchases separately from each other to easily identify the unit cost associated with each batch of inventory. This is done by using a table as shown in Figure 8.3. The opening balance and the transactions from Figure 8.2 are listed, and the corresponding letters explain how to complete the table. Purchases increase the balance of merchandise inventory and sales decrease it. At the bottom of the table is the value of ending inventory.

	Date	Purchases			Sales			Balance		
		Quantity	Unit Cost	Value	Quantity	Unit Cost	Value	Quantity	Unit Cost	Value
a	March 1							10	$10	$100
b	March 5							10	$10	$100
		50	$12	$600				50	$12	$600
c	March 7				8	$10	$80	2	$10	$20
					7	$12	$84	43	$12	$516
d	March 15							2	$10	$20
								43	$12	$516
		40	$14	$560				40	$14	$560
e	March 19							2	$10	$20
								43	$12	$516
								40	$14	$560
		20	$16	$320				20	$16	$320
f	March 27				2	$10	$20	0	-	-
					33	$12	$396	10	$12	$120
					15	$14	$210	25	$14	$350
								20	$16	$320
g	**Ending Inventory**									$790

FIGURE 8.3

ⓐ Record the opening balance of merchandise inventory of 10 pens at $10 each.

ⓑ The purchase of 50 pens on March 5 is added to the value of merchandise inventory. These are listed on a separate line from the 10 opening units because they were purchased at a different unit cost.

ⓒ The sale of 15 pens on March 7 can be specifically identified. Eight of the pens came from opening inventory and seven of the pens came from the purchase on March 5. As a result, the opening balance of 10 pens is reduced to two and the batch of 50 pens is reduced to 43. The value of COGS for this sale is $164 ($80 + $84).

ⓓ The purchase of 40 pens on March 15 is added to the value of merchandise inventory. A new row is used because the unit cost is different from the current inventory.

ⓔ The purchase of 20 pens on March 19 is added to the value of merchandise inventory. A new row is used because the unit cost is different from the current inventory.

ⓕ The sale of 50 pens on March 27 can be specifically identified. Two came from opening inventory, 33 from the purchase on March 5 and 15 from the purchase on March 15. The value of COGS for this sale is $626 ($20 + $396 + $210).

g The value of ending inventory is made up of 10 pens remaining from the March 5 purchase, 25 pens remaining from the March 15 purchase and 20 pens remaining from the March 19 purchase. The total value of ending inventory is $790 ($120 + $350 + $320).

First-In, First-Out (FIFO) Method

The FIFO method is used when the inventory items that are purchased first (first-in) are generally sold first (first-out). For example, a supermarket will try to sell its oldest dairy products first before they expire on the shelf.

When using the FIFO method, it is helpful to list the purchases in the order they were received. This clearly shows which items were the first ones purchased, and assumed to be the first ones sold. This is done by using a table as shown in Figure 8.4. The opening balance and the transactions from Figure 8.2 are listed, and the corresponding letters explain how to complete the table. This is similar to the specific identification method. At the bottom of the table is the value of ending inventory.

	Date	Purchases			Sales			Balance		
		Quantity	Unit Cost	Value	Quantity	Unit Cost	Value	Quantity	Unit Cost	Value
a	March 1							10	$10	$100
b	March 5							10	$10	$100
		50	$12	$600				50	$12	$600
c	March 7				10	$10	$100	0	-	-
					5	$12	$60	45	$12	$540
d	March 15							45	$12	$540
		40	$14	$560				40	$14	$560
e	March 19							45	$12	$540
								40	$14	$560
		20	$16	$320				20	$16	$320
f	March 27				45	$12	$540	0	-	-
					5	$14	$70	35	$14	$490
								20	$16	$320
g	**Ending Inventory**									$810

FIGURE 8.4

a Record the opening balance of merchandise inventory of 10 pens at $10 each.

b The purchase of 50 pens on March 5 is added to the value of merchandise inventory. These are listed on a separate line from the 10 opening units because they were purchased with a different unit cost from the current inventory.

c The sale of 15 pens on March 7 must first use the units from the opening balance. Since there were only 10 pens in the opening balance, another five are taken from the purchase on

March 5. This means that the entire opening balance of merchandise inventory has been sold and 45 units remain from the purchase on March 5. The value of COGS for this sale is $160 ($100 + $60).

d The purchase of 40 pens on March 15 is added to the value of merchandise inventory. A new row is used because they were purchased with a different unit cost from the current inventory.

e The purchase of 20 pens on March 19 is added to the value of merchandise inventory. A new row is used because they were purchased with a different unit cost from the current inventory.

f The sale of 50 pens on March 27 must first use the units from the purchase on March 5. Since there are only 45 pens left from that purchase, another five are taken from the purchase on March 15. The value of COGS for this sale is $610 ($540 + $70).

g The value of ending inventory is made up of 35 pens remaining from the March 15 purchase and 20 pens from the March 19 purchase. The total value of merchandise inventory is $810 ($490 + $320).

Last-In, First-Out (LIFO) Method

When using the LIFO method, it is helpful to list the purchases in the order they were received. This allows you to easily see which items were the last ones purchased and will be the first ones sold. The opening balance and the transactions from Figure 8.2 are listed in Figure 8.5, and the corresponding letters explain how to complete the table. At the bottom of the table is the value of ending inventory.

	Date	Purchases			Sales			Balance		
		Quantity	Unit Cost	Value	Quantity	Unit Cost	Value	Quantity	Unit Cost	Value
a	March 1							10	$10	$100
b	March 5							10	$10	$100
		50	$12	$600				50	$12	$600
c	March 7							10	$10	$100
					15	$12	$180	35	$12	$420
d	March 15							10	$10	$100
								35	$12	$420
		40	$14	$560				40	$14	$560
e	March 19							10	$10	$100
								35	$12	$420
								40	$14	$560
		20	$16	$320				20	$16	$320
f	March 27							10	$10	$100
								35	$12	$420
					30	$14	$420	10	$14	$140
					20	$16	$320	0	-	-
g	**Ending Inventory**									$660

FIGURE 8.5

ⓐ Record the opening balance of inventory of 10 pens at $10 each.

ⓑ The purchase of 50 pens on March 5 is added to the value of merchandise inventory. A new row is used because they were purchased with a different unit cost from the current inventory.

ⓒ The sale of 15 pens on March 7 must first use the units from the purchase on March 5. Since it had 50 pens, the entire 15 units will come from that purchase. This means that 35 units from the purchase on March 5 and the entire opening balance remain. The value of COGS for this sale is $180.

ⓓ The purchase of 40 pens on March 15 is added to the value of merchandise inventory. A new row is used because they were purchased with a different unit cost from the current inventory.

ⓔ The purchase of 20 pens on March 19 is added to the value of merchandise inventory. A new row is used because they were purchased with a different unit cost from the current inventory.

ⓕ The sale of 50 pens on March 27 must first use the units from the purchase on March 19. Since there are only 20 pens from that purchase, another 30 are taken from the purchase on March 15. The value of COGS for this sale is $740 ($420 + $320).

ⓖ The value of ending inventory is made up of 10 pens from the opening inventory, 35 pens remaining from the March 5 purchase and 10 pens remaining from the March 15 purchase. The total value of ending inventory is $660 ($100 + $420 + $140).

Weighted-Average Cost Method

The weighted-average cost method is used when inventory items are identical and the order in which they are sold is irrelevant. For example, when a gas station has its gasoline holding tank filled, and the new product is mixed with the old product.

When using the weighted-average cost method, the total inventory value is divided by the total quantity on hand to arrive at an average cost for each unit, as shown in Figure 8.6.

$$\text{Average Unit Cost} = \frac{\text{Total Value}}{\text{Total Quantity}}$$

FIGURE 8.6

Using the Cool Ink example, let's calculate the average unit cost of the pens after the purchase on March 5.

$$\text{Average Unit Cost} = \frac{(\$600 + \$100)}{(50 + 10)}$$

$$= \$11.67$$

The unit cost of each pen has increased from $10.00 to $11.67.

The opening balance and transactions from Figure 8.2 are listed in Figure 8.7, and the corresponding letters explain how to complete the table. The average unit cost changes after every purchase, but not after a sale. At the bottom of the table is the value of ending inventory.

Date	Purchases			Sales			Balance		
	Quantity	Unit Cost	Value	Quantity	Unit Cost*	Value	Quantity	Unit Cost*	Value**
ⓐ March 1							10	$10.00	$100.00
ⓑ March 5	50	$12	$600				60	$11.67	$700.00
ⓒ March 7				15	$11.67	$175.05	45	$11.67	$524.95
ⓓ March 15	40	$14	$560				85	$12.76	$1,084.95
ⓔ March 19	20	$16	$320				105	$13.38	$1,404.95
ⓕ March 27				50	$13.38	$669.00	55	$13.38	$735.95
ⓖ **Ending Inventory**									$735.95

*Unit cost is rounded to two decimal places.
**Balance values are calculated by subtracting the value of COGS from the value of total inventory.

FIGURE 8.7

ⓐ Record the opening balance of merchandise inventory of 10 pens at $10 each.

ⓑ The purchase of 50 pens on March 5 is added to the quantity on hand. The value of the 50 pens is first added to the value of the opening inventory. The average unit cost is $11.67 ($700 ÷ 60 units).

ⓒ The sale of 15 pens on March 7 is taken from merchandise inventory. The most recent unit cost of $11.67 is used to calculate COGS as $175.05 ($11.67 × 15 units). Both the quantity and value of merchandise inventory decrease, but the unit cost is still $11.67 ($524.95 ÷ 45 units). The unit cost of merchandise inventory only changes after a purchase, not after a sale.

ⓓ The purchase of 40 pens on March 15 is added to the quantity on hand. The value of the 40 pens is added to the current value of merchandise inventory. The unit cost is now $12.76 ($1,084.95 ÷ 85 units).

ⓔ The purchase of 20 pens on March 19 is added to the quantity on hand. The value of the 20 pens is added to the current value of merchandise inventory. The unit cost is now $13.38 ($1,404.95 ÷ 105 units).

ⓕ The sale of the 50 pens on March 27 is taken from merchandise inventory. The most recent unit cost of $13.38 is used to calculate COGS as $669.00 ($13.38 × 50 units).

ⓖ The value of ending inventory is 55 pens at the average unit cost of $13.38. The total value of ending inventory is $735.90 (55 × $13.38).

Note that multiplying 55 units by an average unit cost of $13.38 results in an ending inventory $0.05 less than what is shown in the table. This is due to rounding.

The Effect of Different Valuation Methods: Perpetual

As the inventory valuation methods demonstrate, different ending inventory figures are produced using different valuation methods. The chart in Figure 8.8 summarizes these differences when applied to the Cool Ink example.

	Specific Identification	FIFO	LIFO	Weighted Average
Inventory Available for Sale (beginning inventory + purchases)	$1,580	$1,580	$1,580	$1,580
Ending Inventory	790	810	660	736
Value of COGS	790	770	920	844

FIGURE 8.8

From Figure 8.8, we can make the following observations.

1. When product cost increases over the period, FIFO results in the highest value of ending inventory and LIFO results in the highest value of COGS.

2. While specific identification provides the true value of ending inventory and COGS, it is costly to implement and therefore not practical for items of small value.

3. FIFO reports a more accurate value of ending inventory than weighted average, as it is based on the most recent purchases.

4. LIFO matches current revenues with the closest current unit cost since it uses the unit costs of the most recent purchases, resulting in a lower profit than when other methods are used, if the inventory unit cost increases over time.

Figure 8.8 illustrates an important point when the unit cost of inventory increases over a period of time. LIFO uses COGS from the most recent purchases, so COGS, gross profit and net income are all the most up-to-date under this method. The merchandise inventory balance is the least up-to-date because it assumes the oldest inventory remains. In contrast, FIFO uses COGS from the oldest purchases, so COGS, gross profit and net income are the least up-to-date under this method. The merchandise inventory balance is the most up-to-date because this method assumes the newest inventory remains.

GAAP vs IFRS

Accounting software usually allows you to select which inventory method you wish to use—specific identification, FIFO, LIFO or weighted average. The LIFO valuation method is not allowed under IFRS, but is allowed under GAAP.

In conclusion, when ending inventory amounts change, COGS, gross profit and net income also change. Therefore, two identical companies using different inventory valuation methods will show different financial results.

Determining the Actual Quantity of Inventory

Goods are moved in and out of inventory all the time, which is why recording the amount and quantities bought and sold is so important. This is done when the goods enter the premises after a purchase and when they leave the premises after a sale. The reliability of the information recorded at these points must be assured.

For example, the items must be counted when they are received, and these amounts should be compared to the amounts listed on the original purchase order. Any discrepancies must be noted and investigated. Once the inventory count is complete, the company's records should be updated immediately.

Before goods can leave the premises, a release order, such as a packing slip, must be written up and authorized. The shipper should note which goods are leaving and forward the documents to the accounting department to ensure the information is entered into the system.

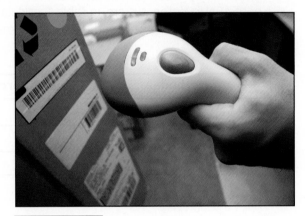

FIGURE 8.9

Some of this paperwork can take time using a manual system. Computer scanning software can eliminate much of the paperwork and time involved in recording the movement of goods in inventory. Whether items are coming in or moving out, a swipe of the scanner can immediately track their location and status while in inventory, as shown in Figure 8.9.

The Physical Inventory Count

A company must take a physical count of its inventory at least once a year. Companies using the periodic inventory system must take a physical count as it is the only way to accurately determine the amount on hand at the end of a period. Companies using the perpetual inventory system must count inventory to ensure the accuracy of their records. While a business may have its own policies and procedures for the process of taking a physical inventory count, the following steps are generally included.

1. Designate an area to a specific person.

2. Count and record each item on pre-numbered sheets that are distributed and controlled by the accounting department.

3. Return completed sheets to the accounting department where items are valued and summarized.

4. Where a perpetual system is used, the inventory record (ledger account) is compared to the physical count. Differences are noted and any necessary adjustments are recorded.

5. Where major differences occur between the inventory record and the physical count, further investigation is required.

Pause & Reflect

Exercise 8-1

The following inventory data is available for the month of April for King Company.

Date	Description	Quantity	Unit Cost	Total
April 1	opening	20	$8.15	$163
April 10	purchase	300	$8.20	$2,460
April 20	purchase	210	$8.40	$1,764
April 25	purchase	110	$8.50	$935
Total		640		$5,322

King Company sold 630 units on April 30 for $15 per unit on account. Assume that King Company uses a perpetual inventory system. In Table 1, calculate the value of ending merchandise inventory and COGS under FIFO, LIFO and weighted-average cost methods.

Table 1

Method	Ending Merchandise Inventory	Cost of Goods Sold
FIFO		
LIFO		
Weighted-Average Cost		

See Appendix I for solutions.

Effect of Inventory Errors

Inventory is a type of asset that differs somewhat from other assets discussed in previous chapters. Unlike cash, the value of which is quite definitive (except when it comes to exchange rates between currencies), or accounts receivable, which is also quite definitive, the value of merchandise inventory can be subjective to a certain extent.

Attaching a value to inventory involves a different kind of challenge. A warehouse can be full of various products that were bought at a certain price and will be sold at another price, with no clarity as to which items moved when. Matching physical items in inventory to specific dollar values using any valuation method can be complicated. Consequently, the inventory valuation process is prone to errors such as miscalculating inventory value, miscounting physical inventory and wrongly including or excluding inventory in transit.

In Chapter 7, you learned that goods that are being shipped from suppliers under FOB shipping point and goods that are being shipped to customers under FOB destination must be included in merchandise inventory even though they are not physically in the warehouse. Likewise, consigned inventory must be included in the consignor's merchandise inventory even when it is not in the consignor's warehouse. **Consigned inventory** refers to the merchandise that the **consignor,** who retains ownership of the merchandise, lets the **consignee,** who acts as the consignor's selling agent, carry in order to resell it to customers for a commission. Because the merchandise belongs to the consignor until it is sold to a customer, the merchandise must be included as merchandise inventory in the consignor's books and cannot be included in the consignee's books. Errors occur when the consignor forgets to include or when the consignee wrongly includes the consigned inventory. These errors can impact the way a company presents its financial figures—both internally and externally.

Next, examine the impact that an inventory error can have on gross margin and other aspects of financial reporting.

The Impact of Cost of Goods Sold on Gross Profit

Although merchandise inventory is a balance sheet account, it can have an immediate impact on the income statement because COGS is used to calculate gross profit. Gross profit is then used to calculate the gross margin. The gross margin represents the percentage of sales left to pay the remaining operating expenses of the company.

The relationship between merchandise inventory and gross profit is demonstrated in Figure 8.10. The COGS of $6,000 is subtracted from the revenue of $10,000 to reach a gross profit of $4,000. The gross margin is 40%, which means the company has 40% of its revenue left to pay any remaining operating expenses.

It should become clear that COGS is a focal point when dealing with merchandise inventory on a company's financial statements.

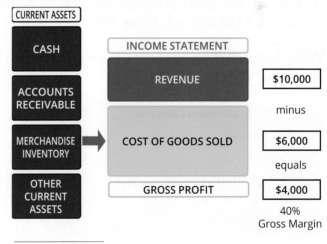

FIGURE 8.10

In a periodic inventory system, COGS is calculated by adding total inventory purchases to the value of inventory on hand at the beginning of the period, then deducting the closing value of inventory at the end of the period. The closing value of inventory is determined by a physical count. An example of the calculation is shown in Figure 8.11.

Errors in valuing closing inventory can affect COGS and, as a result, gross profit. Beyond affecting the current period's COGS and gross profit, an incorrect merchandise inventory value affects opening inventory for the next period. We will examine the impact on gross profit while ignoring the effects on net income for the year.

Inventory Calculation	
Opening Inventory	$10,000
Plus: Purchases	60,000
Cost of Goods Available for Sale	70,000
Less: Closing Inventory	20,000
Cost of Goods Sold	$50,000

FIGURE 8.11

The Effect of Overstating Merchandise Inventory

To understand the effect of overstating merchandise inventory, we will use two examples. One set of charts includes the correct amount for closing inventory; the other set of charts includes an incorrect amount for closing inventory.

Figure 8.12 shows the correct inventory numbers and the correct income statement.

Inventory Calculation	
Opening Inventory	$5,000
Plus: Purchases	75,000
Cost of Goods Available for Sale	80,000
Less: Closing Inventory	9,000
Cost of Goods Sold	$71,000

Income Statement Year 1	
Sales	$100,000
Less: Cost of Goods Sold	71,000
Gross Profit	$29,000

FIGURE 8.12

When closing inventory is correctly valued at $9,000, COGS is correctly calculated as $71,000. As a result, the gross profit for the year is $29,000. The gross margin for the reporting period is $29,000 ÷ $100,000 = 0.29 or 29%.

What happens if we overstate closing inventory by $1,000? This is shown in Figure 8.13, and the impact on the income statement.

Inventory Calculation	
Opening Inventory	$5,000
Plus: Purchases	75,000
Cost of Goods Available for Sale	80,000
Less: Closing Inventory	10,000
Cost of Goods Sold	$70,000

Income Statement Year 1	
Sales	$100,000
Less: Cost of Goods Sold	70,000
Gross Profit	$30,000

FIGURE 8.13

When closing inventory is incorrectly valued at $10,000, the COGS value is understated by $1,000. This causes gross profit to be overstated by $1,000. The gross margin for the reporting period is $30,000 ÷ $100,000 = 0.30 or 30%. Gross margin is overstated by 1%. The same error while performing a physical count for a company that uses the perpetual inventory system will lead to the same problem.

If this error is found and corrected before the end of the period, a journal entry must be recorded to correct the balances of merchandise inventory and COGS, as shown in Figure 8.14. If inventory was understated by $1,000, the journal entry would debit merchandise inventory and credit COGS.

JOURNAL			
Date	**Account Title and Explanation**	**Debit**	**Credit**
2018			
Dec 31	Cost of Goods Sold	1,000	
	Merchandise Inventory		1,000
	Corrected overstated inventory		

FIGURE 8.14

Inventory errors are *self-correcting*, which means an inventory error made in one year will create an offsetting effect to correct itself in the next year. Figure 8.15 illustrates how the inventory error reverses itself in 2019 if the overstatement of closing inventory in 2018 is never detected or corrected, provided that the closing inventory in 2019 is correctly stated.

Income Statement (Partial)

	2018		2019	
	Correct	**Incorrect**	**Correct**	**Incorrect**
Sales	$100,000	$100,000	$120,000	$120,000
Cost of Goods Sold Calculation				
Opening Inventory	$5,000	$5,000	$9,000	$10,000
Plus: Purchases	75,000	75,000	90,000	90,000
Cost of Goods Available for Sale	80,000	80,000	99,000	100,000
Less: Closing Inventory	9,000	10,000	7,000	7,000
Cost of Goods Sold		71,000	70,000	92,000	93,000
Gross Profit		$29,000	$30,000	$28,000	$27,000

Gross profit overstated by $1,000   Gross profit understated by $1,000

Inventory error self-corrected in 2019 and 2-year net effect on gross profit is zero.

FIGURE 8.15

The overstatement of closing inventory in 2018 by $1,000 causes COGS to be understated and thus gross profit to be overstated by $1,000. The overstated closing inventory balance in 2018 then becomes the overstated opening inventory balance in 2019. The overstatement of opening inventory balance causes COGS to be overstated by $1,000 for 2019. As a result, gross profit is understated by $1,000 in 2019. The understatement of gross profit in 2019 offsets the overstatement of gross profit in 2018, resulting in a net effect of zero. This is why inventory errors are said to be self-correcting.

However, the fact that inventory errors are self-correcting does not mean that companies can carelessly make inventory errors and assume the errors will self-correct, because accurate inventory information is important for internal and external users of financial statements. This is discussed in the next section.

The Impact on Financial Statement Users

Both internal and external stakeholders are affected by inventory errors. Such errors can affect business decision-making, tax reporting and adherence to accounting procedures.

A company that requires debt financing may try to make its financial statements appear better by overstating merchandise inventory, which understates COGS and causes gross profit to be overstated. If merchandise inventory is overstated unintentionally, it can give management a false sense of confidence in the company. This could lead to bad decisions about pricing, discounts, target market share or other aspects of business performance. The reverse is true for understated numbers, which could create unnecessary panic and desperation.

An inaccurate gross profit figure can also have consequences when it comes to paying taxes. An incorrect higher gross profit shows a higher net income, which means that a company is paying more tax than it should. On the other hand, understating merchandise inventory would overstate COGS, which causes gross profit and net income to be understated. This means that the government would get less in taxes from the company than it should.

Finally, a company could use its inflated financial figures to create a false impression of its performance for external stakeholders, or for banks when trying to secure loans. This can represent an ethical violation of the accounting principle of disclosure.

Pause & Reflect

Exercise 8-2

On December 31, 2018, Silver Duck International miscounted its inventory as $48,000, when the correct balance was $53,000. Assuming that the inventory error in 2018 was never detected or corrected, indicate the impact of the inventory error by filling in the word "overstated" or "understated" in the following sentences. Assume that the inventory count at the end of 2019 was correct.

a) The company's COGS in 2018 would be _____ .

b) The company's gross profit in 2018 would be _____ .

c) The company's opening balance of merchandise inventory in 2019 would be _____ .

d) The company's COGS in 2019 would be _____ .

e) The company's gross profit in 2019 would be _____ .

See Appendix I for solutions.

The Lower of Cost and Net Realizable Value

Market conditions can fluctuate. With respect to inventory, this means that sometimes a company sells its inventory for a lower price than what it was purchased for (i.e. the selling price is lower than cost). This could be due to an advancement in technology or a change in industry trends, rendering older products obsolete or outdated.

The conservatism constraint asserts that, given a choice, the accounting alternative that produces a lower value for assets must always be used. This prevents companies from providing an overly optimistic statement of their finances. This is a trade-off with the accounting principle of measurement, which states that merchandise inventory should be recorded at the cost identified by the inventory value method used.

When a company determines that inventory must be sold at a price below cost, this asset must be recorded at its net realizable value. **Net realizable value (NRV)** is the price that a company can realistically expect to sell the item for, less any costs incurred to make the item ready for sale, such as repair costs. This method is known as the **lower of cost and net realizable value (LCNRV)**.

For example, suppose that Elan's Camera Shop sells point-and-shoot cameras, DSLR cameras and camera bags. Cost and net realizable values are shown in Figure 8.16.

	Cost	NRV	Individual	Merchandise Category	Total
Point-and-Shoot					
Camera 1	$40,000	❶ $12,000	❷ $12,000		
Camera 2	35,000	45,000	35,000		
Total Point-and-Shoot	75,000	57,000		❹ $57,000	
DSLR					
Camera A	80,000	85,000	80,000		
Camera B	90,000	100,000	90,000		
Total DSLR	170,000	185,000		170,000	
Camera Bags	15,000	16,000	15,000	15,000	
Total	❶ $260,000	$258,000	$232,000	$242,000	❺ $258,000

FIGURE 8.16

❶ The total cost of $260,000 is the current balance of the merchandise inventory account and is broken down between the various groups of inventory items carried by the store.

❷ NRV is the net realizable value of the different inventory items. Notice that the group of Camera 1 point-and-shoot cameras has an NRV significantly less than cost. The camera model may be outdated and thus difficult to sell.

c Usually, LCNRV is applied to individual inventory items. Only Camera 1 shows an NRV less than cost, so $12,000 is recorded in the Individual column. The difference between its cost and its NRV is $28,000 ($40,000 − $12,000). Since NRV is less than cost, inventory must be written down by $28,000. The write-down decreases merchandise inventory and increases COGS. The journal entry is shown in Figure 8.17.

JOURNAL			
Date	**Account Title and Explanation**	**Debit**	**Credit**
2018			
Dec 31	Cost of Goods Sold	28,000	
	Merchandise Inventory		28,000
	Adjust inventory to LCNRV		

FIGURE 8.17

The journal entry in Figure 8.17 debits COGS. However, if the amount of the adjustment is deemed material, the company can instead debit another income statement account called Loss on Write-Down of Inventory.

d In certain circumstances, LCNRV can be applied to categories of inventory. In this instance, the value of the entire point-and-shoot camera inventory takes into account the lower NRV value for Camera 1, for a total of $57,000 ($12,000 + $35,000).

The difference between cost and NRV for the point-and-shoot category is $18,000 ($75,000 − $57,000). If LCNRV had been applied to inventory categories, the value used in the journal entry would have been $18,000.

e A third option for a company to determine LCNRV is to take into account the total inventory. If Elan's Camera Store takes this approach, it records the NRV value of total inventory, which is $258,000. The total inventory cost of $260,000 is compared to the total NRV of $258,000. Since NRV is lower by $2,000 ($260,000 − $258,000), the merchandise inventory is written down by $2,000 in the journal entry.

GAAP vs IFRS

If the NRV of an inventory item increases after it has already been written down, a company is not allowed to reverse the write-down according to GAAP. Under IFRS, however, the company may reverse the write-down, but the reversal cannot exceed the amount of the original write-down; the value recorded for any inventory item cannot exceed its historical cost.

The application of LCNRV is also different. Under IFRS, applying LCNRV can be either based on individual inventory items (in general cases) or a category (only when certain criteria are met). Applying LCNRV at the total inventory level is never allowed under IFRS. Under GAAP, in addition to applying LCNRV at the item and the category level, the total inventory level can also be used if specific criteria are met.

Pause & Reflect

Exercise 8-3

Sun Fashion sells its own brand of sunglasses. The cost and NRV of each individual type of product in the company's ending inventory as at December 31, 2018 are shown in Table 1.

a) Complete the LCNRV column for individual types of product.

Table 1

	Cost	NRV	LCNRV (Individual)
Cat Eye	$6,000	$7,500	
Rimless	10,000	9,000	
Total	$16,000	$16,500	

b) Prepare the journal entry to adjust merchandise inventory to LCNRV.

JOURNAL			
Date	Account Title and Explanation	Debit	Credit

See Appendix I for solutions.

Measuring Inventory Using Inventory Ratios

Generally speaking, a business wants to be as precise as possible when buying inventory for resale. Ideally, inventory should be sold as soon as it is bought; the less time that an item spends in inventory, while still meeting customer demand, the better.

A company can measure the extent to which it is moving inventory through the use of two ratios: inventory turnover and days' sales in inventory.

Inventory Turnover Ratio

The extent to which an organization can quickly sell inventory on hand is known as inventory turnover. Specifically, the **inventory turnover ratio** estimates how many times a year a company is buying inventory. The more often a company buys inventory, the less likely it is that the inventory sits for extended periods of time, and the more likely it is that the turnover is high.

The inventory turnover ratio is calculated by taking COGS for a year and dividing it by average inventory, as shown in Figure 8.18.

$$\text{Inventory Turnover Ratio} = \frac{\text{Cost of Goods Sold}}{\text{Average Inventory}}$$

FIGURE 8.18

Average inventory is calculated by adding the opening and closing inventory numbers and dividing the total by 2.

New Tech Mobile makes mobile devices. Its merchandise inventory and COGS are shown in Figure 8.19 (numbers are in the millions). For 2018, it had an inventory turnover of 6.2. This means the company bought and sold its entire inventory just over six times during the year.

Merchandise Inventory—December 31, 2017	$501.5
Merchandise Inventory—December 31, 2018	$428.3
Cost of Goods Sold	$2,882.8
Average Inventory ($501.5 + $428.3) ÷ 2 = $464.9	
Turnover $2,882.8 ÷ $464.9 = 6.2	

FIGURE 8.19

Inventory turnover is useful when it is compared to another company within the same industry. Suppose a competitor has an inventory turnover of 9.0. This is higher than that of New Tech Mobile and more desirable. The higher turnover indicates that inventory is moving faster at the competitor than at New Tech Mobile. Inventory that moves fast is less likely to become outdated.

Days' Sales in Inventory

There is another way of looking at inventory turnover. Instead of estimating how often a company sells and replaces inventory over a period of time (as indicated by the inventory turnover ratio), turnover can be calculated by estimating how many days it takes to move items out of inventory. **Days' sales in inventory**, sometimes called *inventory days on hand*, is a calculation of how many days inventory will last given the current rate of sales.

The number of days in a year (365) is divided by the inventory turnover ratio, resulting in the days' sales in inventory, as shown in Figure 8.20.

$$\text{Days' Sales in Inventory} = \frac{365}{\text{Inventory Turnover Ratio}}$$

FIGURE 8.20

The days' sales in inventory divides the calendar year into equal-sized portions. The number of portions equals the inventory turnover ratio. The size of the portions translates into the days' sales in inventory.

For example, if a company's inventory turnover ratio is 10, then inventory is completely purchased and sold 10 times throughout the year. Since there are 365 days in the year, each portion is 36.5 days long (365 ÷ 10).

Therefore, the days' sales in inventory is 36.5 days. This means that, on average, it takes 36.5 days to "turn over" inventory. This is shown in Figure 8.21.

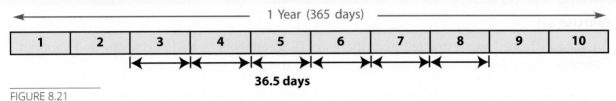

FIGURE 8.21

Returning to the example, New Tech Mobile calculates its days' sales in inventory to be 58.9 days (365 ÷ 6.2). Since its competitor had an inventory turnover of 9.0, the competitor's days' sales in inventory is 40.6 days (365 ÷ 9.0). The competitor's lower ratio means it has a better rate of inventory turnover; it takes less time for the company to move its inventory.

Another way of calculating days' sales in inventory is shown in Figure 8.22.

$$\text{Days' Sales in Inventory} = \frac{\text{Average Inventory}}{\text{Cost of Goods Sold}} \times 365$$

FIGURE 8.22

The relationship (ratio) is between how much inventory is in stock and the amount of inventory used for the year (which is COGS). Dividing the average inventory by how much was used and multiplying this number by 365 (number of days in the year) converts the ratio to the number of days on hand based on how much was used.

Using the values for New Tech Mobile, we can calculate days' sales in inventory using the formula in Figure 8.22.

$$\text{Days' Sales in Inventory} = \frac{\$464.9}{\$2,4882.8} \times 365$$

$$= 58.9$$

Management should not make decisions regarding inventory based on ratios alone. There could be many factors that affect such numbers. For example, some industries might require companies to wait longer periods of time to have goods shipped to them. High turnover in these instances may lead to empty warehouses and customer demands not being met.

As an example, a grocery store will have higher inventory turnover than an appliance store. Car engines will move out of an auto plant warehouse much slower than light bulbs in a hardware store.

It is the responsibility of accountants and management to know what inventory levels are best for business. Ratios can help but they are only one of many tools that can be used.

Pause & Reflect

Exercise 8-4

The data in Table 1 was extracted from the financial statements of Nado Company and Vaporen Company. These two companies are competitors in the same industry.

a) Calculate average inventory, inventory turnover and days' sales in inventory for both companies and fill in your answers in Table 1. Round your answers to whole numbers.

Table 1

	Nado	Vaporen
Cost of Goods Sold	$600,000	$960,000
Opening Merchandise Inventory	100,000	270,000
Closing Merchandise Inventory	140,000	210,000
Average Inventory		
Inventory Turnover		
Days' Sales in Inventory		

b) Which company has more favorable ratios? _____

See Appendix I for solutions.

An Ethical Approach to Inventory Estimation and Valuation

As mentioned earlier, management is able to choose the method used to value inventory. Thus, merchandise inventory may be open to manipulation. A company can purchase, store and sell many items throughout the course of a business year, and how all these items are valued can have a significant impact on a company's bottom line.

The impact of inflating closing inventory is significant. It reduces COGS and increases net income for the year. It also inflates COGS and reduces net income for the following year. Therefore, any manipulation of inventory value has negative consequences that extend beyond the current fiscal year. The ethical responsibility of management is to ensure this does not happen by detecting errors and the causes behind them.

Who Commits Fraud and Why?

Companies need to know the kinds of inventory fraud that can be perpetrated and understand who would be most likely to commit fraud.

Inventory fraud from the top down

Various methods can be used to pad a company's inventory value. One method is to overstate the value of items deemed obsolete, shop-worn or generally unsaleable, instead of writing them down to the appropriate amount. This overstates the overall value of inventory. Similarly, various overhead costs can be attributed to inventory. These figures can also be manipulated in a way that affects the company's bottom line. In addition, a manufacturer might be tempted to overstate the completion of work-in-progress inventories.

Generally speaking, these kinds of attempts to pad inventory numbers tend to come from the top. Unlike determining fixed costs, such as rent, determining inventory costs is a more subjective exercise. Accountants and executives can abuse the subjectivity involved in some of these decisions and errors can be rationalized as a matter of opinion.

When a manager's bonus depends on earnings, such as gross profit or net income, the manager may be tempted to choose the inventory valuation method that maximizes earnings in order to maximize the bonus, even if the method is not in the best interest of the company. For example, during a period of inflation, when the cost of inventory keeps rising, the manager may choose the FIFO inventory valuation to maximize income figures and therefore maximize the bonus. However, by choosing FIFO the company would pay higher taxes, which is not in the company's best interest. Instead, the manager should choose the LIFO inventory valuation, which minimizes the company's taxes, assuming that the company is profitable. (Corporate income tax is discussed in Chapter 15.) Even though choosing FIFO as the company's inventory valuation method is completely legal and not considered fraud, doing so is not in the company's best interest and is therefore unethical.

Situations like this can be avoided by establishing bonus policies that encourage a manager to always act in the best interest of the company. For example, a policy can be established that the manager's bonus is calculated based on FIFO valuation even if the company's financial statements report inventory using a different valuation method. Similarly, other forms of inventory abuse can be avoided by establishing specific policies and guidelines for handling and valuing inventory. Controls should be in place to ensure that these policies are followed. Companies can also have both internal and external auditors review the design and effectiveness of inventory controls and detect any possible ethical breaches.

In the end, management is responsible for any errors arising from the way its financial situation is reported. There is no excuse for manipulating the value of inventory. Any wrongful reporting should be dealt with at the earliest opportunity.

Inventory fraud from the bottom up

Employees below the executive level can also commit inventory fraud. Their motivation is often associated with greed.

Inventory items are goods that have value and that people want to buy. That is why companies purchase these items and eventually sell them. People who have routine access to such items, such as employees, might be tempted to take them without paying for them. Alternatively, an employee might take funds from the company, buy the inventory, then resell it and pocket the profits. Even borrowing an item without permission, such as a car on a sales lot, is theft and needs to be prevented.

There are red flags that help a company monitor and prevent inventory shrinkage. One such red flag occurs when sales lag inventory levels. In other words, the company is buying more than it is selling. Another potential inventory red flag occurs when shipping costs lag inventory. This indicates that the company is not shipping out as many items as it is receiving in inventory. In either case, inventory counts can verify if the amount of inventory purchased is equal to the amount of inventory sold plus inventory on hand. If there is missing inventory, then the items may have been stolen.

All companies should be in the practice of noting these red flags and ensuring measures are in place to prevent or detect theft. Furthermore, all businesses should implement security measures that properly safeguard inventory on their premises.

IN THE REAL WORLD

Perhaps no business philosophy captures the spirit of high inventory turnover more than Just In Time, also known as JIT.

Japan first started developing JIT in their manufacturing industries after Word War II. The goal was to gain a competitive advantage by reducing the amount of inventory a company had in storage at any given time, since inventory is often a larger but less liquid asset than other assets on the balance sheet. JIT made its way to North America and has been used to improve manufacturing efficiency in many different industries.

At the heart of JIT is a comprehensive approach not just to reduce inventory, but to manage a business. Under JIT, it is the customer that drives the manufacturing process. That is why JIT systems are often implemented in conjunction with what is known as Total Quality Management, or TQM. Under such philosophies, everything is done to ensure that the customer gets quality goods and services on time, every time.

To that end, JIT systems mobilize efforts to coordinate manufacturing processes and reduce waste. The goal is to have virtually no excess inventory on hand at any time. This can only be achieved if a company thoroughly understands what the customer wants and when they want it. Receiving and shipping schedules, assembly parts and labor flexibility are all adapted to ensure that customer demands are met while enhancing organizational efficiency and profitability.

JIT stresses the importance of reducing a company's inventory while enhancing customer service. It is a comprehensive approach that has achieved success on a global scale.

In Summary

LO 1 **Determine the value of merchandise inventory under the perpetual inventory system**

- The specific identification method tracks the cost of each item in inventory separately and is used for unique or custom products, such as vehicles and jewelry.

- A schedule is used to track the different costs of purchased inventory and the costs of specific items sold. The value of merchandise inventory is made up of the costs of the actual physical items remaining in inventory.

- The FIFO method assumes that the first items purchased are also the first items sold, even if this is not the actual flow of inventory. This method is used for many types of inventory, especially perishable goods.

- Under FIFO, a schedule is used to track the different costs of purchased inventory. Cost of goods sold is calculated using the costs of the earliest purchased inventory. The value of merchandise inventory is made up of the costs of the most recently purchased inventory.

- The LIFO method assumes that the last items purchased are also the first items sold, even if this is not the actual flow of inventory.

- Under LIFO, a schedule is used to track the different costs of purchased inventory. Cost of goods sold is calculated using the costs of the most recent purchased inventory. The value of merchandise inventory is made up of the costs of the earliest purchased inventory.

- The weighted-average cost method uses an average unit cost to calculate the value of inventory and COGS. It is used when inventory items are identical and when the order in which they are sold is irrelevant.

- Under this method, a schedule is used to track the weighted-average cost of purchased inventory. The unit cost is updated after every purchase and is calculated by dividing the total value of the inventory by the total number of units on hand. The value of merchandise inventory is calculated using the unit cost at the end of the period.

LO 2 **Explain the impact of inventory errors**

- An overstatement of ending inventory results in an understatement of COGS and an overstatement of net income.

- An understatement of ending inventory results in an overstatement of COGS and an understatement of net income.

LO 3 **Apply the lower of cost and net realizable value (LCNRV) rule to value merchandise inventory**

- Merchandise inventory must be recorded at the lower of its cost and net realizable value. That is, if the value of merchandise inventory is calculated to be higher than the amount that could be recovered by selling it, then it must be written down.

▶ LCNRV may be applied to either individual inventory items or categories of inventory.

LO 4 Measure a company's management of inventory using inventory ratios

▶ The inventory turnover ratio is calculated by dividing COGS by the average value of inventory over the period. This ratio is equal to the number of times inventory was completely purchased and sold (turned over) during the period.

▶ A higher inventory turnover ratio means that inventory is less likely to become obsolete because it is sold more quickly.

▶ The days' sales in inventory is calculated by dividing 365 by the inventory turnover ratio. This figure is equal to the number of days on average it takes to sell inventory.

▶ A lower days' sales in inventory means that inventory is less likely to become obsolete because it is sold in fewer days.

LO 5 Describe ethics relating to inventory

▶ Management has the ability to manipulate inventory values reported on financial statements. Inventory values that are deliberately manipulated to deceive users of the financial statements is unethical and could be considered fraud.

AMEENGAGE Access **ameengage.com** for integrated resources including tutorials, practice exercises, the digital textbook and more.

Review Exercise 8-1

The following transactions took place at Mike's Tikes Toys during the month of June 2018. The company uses a perpetual inventory system. There are 100 items in opening inventory that cost $12 each.

Jun 3   Purchased 500 items at a cost of $15 each on credit (on account)

Jun 10   Sold 200 items at $45 each on credit

Jun 12   Purchased 300 items at $18 each on credit

Jun 20   Sold 300 items at $50 each for cash

Required

a) Using FIFO, prepare the inventory record to show the closing inventory balance after the above transactions have occurred.

Date	Purchases			Sales			Balance		
	Quantity	Unit Cost	Value	Quantity	Unit Cost	Value	Quantity	Unit Cost	Value
Ending Inventory									

b) Prepare the top step of the multiple-step income statement showing sales revenue, COGS and gross profit for the month ended June 30, 2018. Use the information from part a).

c) Using the LIFO method, prepare the inventory record to show the closing inventory balance after the above transactions have occurred.

Date	Purchases			Sales			Balance		
	Quantity	Unit Cost	Value	Quantity	Unit Cost	Value	Quantity	Unit Cost	Value
Ending Inventory									

d) Prepare the top step of the multiple-step income statement showing sales revenue, COGS and gross profit for the month ended June 30, 2018. Use the information from part c).

e) Using the weighted-average cost method, prepare the inventory record to show the closing inventory balance after the above transactions have occurred.

Date	Purchases			Sales			Balance		
	Quantity	Unit Cost	Value	Quantity	Unit Cost	Value	Quantity	Unit Cost	Value
Ending Inventory									

f) Prepare the top portion of the multiple-step income statement showing sales revenue, COGS and gross profit for the month ended June 30, 2018. Use the information from part e).

See Appendix I for solutions.

Appendix 8A: Periodic Inventory Valuation

In this chapter you were introduced to Cool Ink Company, which sells a number of different pens, pencils, markers and highlighters. We will examine one item from its inventory to illustrate the four different inventory valuation methods. However, this time we will look at how Cool Ink uses a periodic inventory system to account for purchases and sales.

Cool Ink Company currently has 10 pens in inventory with a unit cost of $10 each. During the month of March, the transactions in Figure 8A.1 took place with respect to collector pens.

Date	Transaction	Quantity	Unit Cost
March 5	Purchase from Pen Distributers	50	$12
March 7	Sale	15	
March 15	Purchase from Promotional Pens	40	$14
March 19	Purchase from Promotional Pens	20	$16
March 27	Sale	50	

FIGURE 8A.1

During the month, the unit cost of the pen increased. This means that COGS applied to the sales will likely be different, based on which pens are actually sold. We can apply the four methods of valuing inventory to the transactions to determine the different values for merchandise inventory and COGS. This will demonstrate that the choice of inventory valuation method can make a difference to the financial statements of a company.

The main difference between the perpetual and the periodic inventory systems is when unit costs are assigned to the sales. The perpetual system assigns unit costs as the sales are made. The periodic system only assigns unit costs at the end of the period, when a physical count of the inventory is made.

Specific Identification Method

When using the specific identification method, the purchases are listed separately from each other to easily identify the unit cost associated with each batch of inventory. Sales for the period are listed underneath since inventory costs are not recorded until the end of the period. This is done by using a table as shown in Figure 8A.2. The opening balance and the transactions from Figure 8A.1 are listed, and the corresponding letters explain how to complete the table. Purchases cause the balance of merchandise inventory to increase and sales cause it to decrease. At the bottom of the table is the value of ending inventory.

Date	Purchases			Sales			Balance		
	Quantity	Unit Cost	Value	Quantity	Unit Cost	Value	Quantity	Unit Cost	Value
ⓐ March 1							10	$10	$100
ⓑ March 5							10	$10	$100
	50	$12	$600				50	$12	$600
ⓒ March 15							10	$10	$100
							50	$12	$600
	40	$14	$560				40	$14	$560
ⓓ March 19							10	$10	$100
							50	$12	$600
							40	$14	$560
	20	$16	$320				20	$16	$320
ⓔ Sales for the Month				10	$10	$100	0	-	-
				40	$12	$480	10	$12	$120
				15	$14	$210	25	$14	$350
							20	$16	$320
ⓕ **Ending Inventory**									$790

FIGURE 8A.2

ⓐ Record the opening balance of inventory of 10 pens at $10 each.

ⓑ The purchase of 50 pens on March 5 is added to the value of merchandise inventory. A new row is used because the unit cost is different from the current inventory.

ⓒ The purchase of 40 pens on March 15 is added to the value of merchandise inventory. A new row is used because the unit cost is different from the current inventory.

ⓓ The purchase of 20 pens on March 19 is added to the value of merchandise inventory. A new row is used because the unit cost is different from the current inventory.

ⓔ The sales are tallied at the end of the month and are identified based on which batch of inventory the merchandise came from. In this example, the entire amount of opening inventory was sold, 40 items from the March 5 purchase were sold and 15 items from the March 15 purchase were sold. The total COGS is $790 ($100 + $480 + $210).

ⓕ The value of ending inventory includes 10 pens from the March 5 purchase, 25 pens from the March 15 purchase and 20 pens from the March 19 purchase. The total value of ending inventory is $790 ($120 + $350 + $320).

WORTH REPEATING

When an inventory valuation method is used with a perpetual inventory system, the unit cost is applied after every sale. When a periodic inventory system is used, the unit cost is only assigned at the end of the period when a physical inventory count is made.

First-In, First-Out (FIFO) Method

When using the FIFO method, merchandise inventory is listed in the order it is purchased. This clearly shows which items were the first ones purchased and assumed to be the first ones sold. The sales for the period are listed underneath since merchandise inventory costs are not recorded until the end of the period. This is done by using a table as shown in Figure 8A.3. The opening balance and the transactions from Figure 8A.1 are listed, and the corresponding letters explain how to complete the table. This is similar to the specific identification method. At the bottom of the table is the value of ending inventory.

	Date	Purchases			Sales			Balance		
		Quantity	Unit Cost	Value	Quantity	Unit Cost	Value	Quantity	Unit Cost	Value
ⓐ	March 1							10	$10	$100
ⓑ	March 5							10	$10	$100
		50	$12	$600				50	$12	$600
ⓒ	March 15							10	$10	$100
								50	$12	$600
		40	$14	$560				40	$14	$560
ⓓ	March 19							10	$10	$100
								50	$12	$600
								40	$14	$560
		20	$16	$320				20	$16	$320
ⓔ	Sales for the Month				10	$10	$100	0	-	-
					50	$12	$600	0	-	-
					5	$14	$70	35	$14	$490
								20	$16	$320
ⓕ	**Ending Inventory**									$810

FIGURE 8A.3

ⓐ Record the opening balance of inventory of 10 pens at $10 each.

ⓑ The purchase of 50 pens on March 5 is added to the value of merchandise inventory. A new row is used because they were purchased with a different unit cost from the current inventory.

ⓒ The purchase of 40 pens on March 15 is added to the value of merchandise inventory. A new row is used because they were purchased with a different unit cost from the current inventory.

ⓓ The purchase of 20 pens on March 19 is added to the value of merchandise inventory. A new row is used because they were purchased with a different unit cost from the current inventory.

ⓔ There was a total of 65 items sold (15 units on March 7 and 50 units on March 27). Unit costs are taken from the balance of merchandise inventory, starting with the first item at the top of the list. The entire amount of opening inventory, the entire amount of the March 5 purchase, and five items from the March 15 purchase are considered sold. The total COGS is $770 ($100 + $600 + $70).

ⓕ The value of ending inventory is made up of 35 pens from the March 15 purchase and 20 pens from the March 19 purchase. The total value of ending inventory is $810 ($490 + $320).

Last-In, First-Out (LIFO) Method

When using the LIFO method, it is helpful to list the purchases in the order they were received. This allows you to easily see which items were the last ones purchased and will be the first ones to be sold. The opening balance and the transactions from Figure 8A.1 are listed in Figure 8A.4. The corresponding letters explain how to complete the table. At the bottom of the table is the value of ending inventory.

	Date	Purchases			Sales			Balance		
		Quantity	Unit Cost	Value	Quantity	Unit Cost	Value	Quantity	Unit Cost	Value
ⓐ	March 1							10	$10	$100
ⓑ	March 5							10	$10	$100
		50	$12	$600				50	$12	$600
ⓒ	March 15							10	$10	$100
								50	$12	$600
		40	$14	$560				40	$14	$560
ⓓ	March 19							10	$10	$100
								50	$12	$600
								40	$14	$560
		20	$16	$320				20	$16	$320
ⓔ	Sales for the Month							10	$10	$100
					5	$12	$60	45	$12	$540
					40	$14	$560	0	-	-
					20	$16	$320	0	-	-
ⓕ	**Ending Inventory**									$640

FIGURE 8A.4

ⓐ Record the opening balance of inventory of 10 pens at $10 each.

ⓑ The purchase of 50 pens on March 5 is added to the value of merchandise inventory. A new row is used because they were purchased with a different unit cost from the current inventory.

ⓒ The purchase of 40 pens on March 15 is added to the value of merchandise inventory. A new row is used because they were purchased with a different unit cost from the current inventory.

ⓓ The purchase of 20 pens on March 19 is added to the value of merchandise inventory. A new row is used because they were purchased with a different unit cost from the current inventory.

ⓔ There was a total of 65 items sold (15 units on March 7 and 50 units on March 27). The unit costs are taken from the list of inventory, starting with the item at the bottom of the list. The entire amount of the March 19 purchase, the entire amount of the March 15 purchase, and five items from the March 5 purchase are considered sold. The total COGS is $940 ($320 + $560 + $60).

f The value of ending inventory is made up of 10 pens from the opening inventory and 45 pens from the March 5 purchase. The total value of ending inventory is $640 ($100 + $540).

Weighted-Average Cost Method

When using the weighted-average cost method, the average cost per unit is only calculated once, at the end of the period. This is done by using a table as shown in Figure 8A.5. Recall that average unit cost is calculated by dividing the total value of inventory by the total quantity.

The opening balance and the transactions from Figure 8A.1 are listed, and the corresponding letters explain how to complete the table. At the bottom of the table is the value of ending inventory.

	Date	Purchases			Sales			Balance		
		Quantity	Unit Cost	Value	Quantity	Unit Cost*	Value	Quantity	Unit Cost*	Value**
a	March 1							10		$100.00
b	March 5	50	$12	$600				60		$700.00
c	March 15	40	$14	$560				100		$1,260.00
d	March 19	20	$16	$320				120		$1,580.00
	Average Inventory for the Month							120	$13.17	$1,580.00
e	Sales for the Month				65	$13.17	$856.05	55	$13.17	$724.95
f	**Ending Inventory**									$724.95

*Unit cost is rounded to two decimal places.
**Balance values are calculated by subtracting the value of COGS from the value of total inventory.

FIGURE 8A.5

a Record the opening balance of merchandise inventory of 10 pens at $10 each.

b The purchase of 50 pens on March 5 is added to the quantity on hand. The value of the 50 pens is added to the value of the opening inventory.

c The purchase of 40 pens on March 15 is added to the quantity on hand. The value of the 40 pens is added to the current value of merchandise inventory.

d The purchase of 20 pens on March 19 is added to the quantity on hand. The value of the 20 pens is added to the current value of merchandise inventory.

e At the end of the month, there are 120 pens available for sale with a total cost of $1,580. The average cost per pen is $13.17 ($1,580 ÷ 120 units). This average cost is applied to the total sales of 65 pens for the month. The total COGS is $856.05 (65 units × $13.17).

f The ending inventory is 55 pens with an average unit cost of $13.17. The total value of ending inventory is $724.35 (55 units × $13.17).

Note that multiplying 55 units by an average unit cost of $13.17 results in an ending inventory $0.60 less than what is shown in the table. This is due to rounding.

The Effect of Different Valuation Methods: Periodic

As the example with Cool Ink Company demonstrates, different valuation methods under the periodic inventory system produce different ending inventory values. The chart in Figure 8A.6 summarizes these differences when applied to the Cool Ink examples.

Periodic Inventory System	Specific Identification	FIFO	LIFO	Weighted Average
Inventory Available for Sale (beginning inventory + purchases)	$1,580	$1,580	$1,580	$1,580
Ending Inventory	790	810	640	724
Value of COGS	790	770	940	856

FIGURE 8A.6

From Figure 8A.6, we can make the following observations.

1. In times where the product unit cost increases over the period, FIFO results in the highest value of ending inventory and LIFO results in the highest value of COGS.

2. While specific identification provides the true value of ending inventory and COGS, it is costly to implement and therefore not practical for items of small value.

3. FIFO reports a more accurate value of ending inventory than weighted average, as it is based on the most recent purchases.

4. LIFO matches current revenues with the closest current unit cost since it uses the unit costs of the most recent purchases, resulting in a lower profit than when other methods are used, if the inventory unit cost increases over time.

When ending inventory amounts change, so does COGS, gross profit and net income. Therefore, two identical companies using different inventory valuation methods will show different financial results.

When comparing inventory valuation methods between the perpetual and periodic systems in Figures 8A.6 and 8A.7, notice the ending inventory and COGS.

Perpetual Inventory System	Specific Identification	FIFO	LIFO	Weighted Average
Inventory Available for Sale (beginning inventory + purchases)	$1,580	$1,580	$1,580	$1,580
Ending Inventory	790	810	660	736
Value of COGS	790	770	920	844

FIGURE 8A.7

Specific identification will always provide the same values since the company is able to specifically identify which items are being sold, regardless of the inventory system being used. FIFO will also provide the same values because the most recent purchases are always in ending inventory.

LIFO and the weighted average method show different values for ending inventory and COGS. This is because the perpetual inventory system assigns unit costs as the items are sold, whereas the periodic inventory system only assigns unit costs at the end of the period.

Methods of Estimating Inventory

In a perpetual inventory system, a company maintains a continuous record of the changes to merchandise inventory. This means that, at any given point in time, a company can take an instant snapshot of its merchandise inventory value, including the amounts for COGS and ending inventory. Modern scanning and computer technology can help a company update its financial situation quickly and accurately.

A periodic inventory system poses greater challenges in obtaining up-to-date merchandise inventory information, since the value of the merchandise inventory cannot be tracked from start to finish. Taking a physical count of inventory can be very costly; therefore, a physical count may be done only for year-end reports. If inventory values are required at other times for internal reporting, they have to be estimated.

We will examine two methods of estimating inventory under a periodic inventory system: the gross profit method and the retail method.

The Gross Profit Method

The **gross profit method** uses a company's gross profit figure to estimate the value of inventory. More specifically, a company analyzes the gross profit numbers of prior years to come up with a current gross profit number to apply to estimation figures.

IN THE REAL WORLD

Every now and then, you might see the term *pro forma* financial statements. These are statements prepared by a company that do not necessarily adhere to GAAP or IFRS.

There are various reasons why companies prepare such reports. They can be used in an informal way to temporarily guide managerial decision-making. They can also be used to present financial figures that might otherwise be distorted by accounting principles. For example, costs associated with a previous accounting scandal must be included in formal reports, yet such numbers may inaccurately reflect how the company is currently performing.

Pro forma statements can provide the public with a clearer snapshot of current organizational performance. In fact, *pro forma* financial figures were reported publicly and often during the dot-com boom of the late 1990s. However, regulators began to crack down on such practices, since even *pro forma* statements have their limitations and are not a substitute for documents that adhere to GAAP or IFRS. For example, critics of *pro forma* statements argue that financial stresses from previous periods happen often and are part of the capitalist economic system. Leaving them out can distort a company's status and not fully reflect its performance.

Nevertheless, *pro forma* financial statements serve as a tool for company management when it wants a financial snapshot of the company that isn't as formal, or potentially cumbersome, as accounting principles require.

Other figures a company needs to complete the gross profit method that can be taken from the general ledger are sales, opening inventory and purchases. Once an accountant has these numbers, the rest of the numbers needed to estimate inventory can be determined.

For example, suppose that a company called Van Der Linden must prepare financial statements for the quarter and needs to value its inventory. It will use the gross profit method.

Based on an analysis of gross margin in previous years, a figure of 50% is used for current calculations, shown in Figure 8A.8. The cells with a question mark are those that must be calculated step-by-step to complete the estimation process.

Sales Revenue		$100,000
Cost of Goods Sold		
Opening Inventory	$3,000	
Purchases	70,000	
Cost of Goods Available for Sale	73,000	
Closing Inventory	?	
Cost of Goods Sold		?
Gross Profit (Gross Margin = 50%)		?

FIGURE 8A.8

Additionally, the following financial numbers were taken from the accountant's general ledger.

Sales Revenue: $100,000
Opening Inventory: $3,000
Purchases: $70,000

Van Der Linden's accountant will use these numbers to estimate the value of inventory.

If the gross margin is 50% (marked in red), then it is applied to the sales figure (marked in blue) to calculate the estimated gross profit, shown in Figure 8A.9 ($100,000 × 50% = $50,000).

Sales Revenue		$100,000
Cost of Goods Sold		
Opening Inventory	$3,000	
Purchases	70,000	
Cost of Goods Available for sale	73,000	
Closing Inventory	?	
Cost of Goods Sold		?
Gross Profit (Gross Margin = 50%)		$50,000

FIGURE 8A.9

Next, COGS is estimated by subtracting the estimated gross profit from sales revenue, as shown below.

COGS = Sales − Gross Profit
     = $100,000 − $50,000
     = $50,000

The $50,000 COGS is added to the chart and marked in gray in Figure 8A.10.

The final step is to estimate the balance of closing inventory. This is done by subtracting COGS from the cost of goods available for sale as shown in Figure 8A.11.

Sales Revenue		$100,000
Cost of Goods Sold		
Opening Inventory	$3,000	
Purchases	70,000	
Cost of Goods Available for Sale	73,000	
Closing Inventory	?	
Cost of Goods Sold		50,000
Gross Profit (Gross Margin = 50%)		$50,000

FIGURE 8A.10

Closing Inventory = Cost of Goods Available for Sale − Cost of Goods Sold

FIGURE 8A.11

Using the values from Figure 8A.10, closing inventory is calculated as shown here.

Closing Inventory = $73,000 − $50,000
= $23,000

Therefore, the gross profit method yields a closing inventory estimate of $23,000, which is marked in gray in Figure 8A.12. This figure will be used on the quarterly balance sheet for Van Der Linden.

Sales Revenue		$100,000
Cost of Goods Sold		
Opening Inventory	$3,000	
Purchases	70,000	
Cost of Goods Available for Sale	73,000	
Closing Inventory	23,000	
Cost of Goods Sold		50,000
Gross Profit (Gross Margin = 50%)		$50,000

FIGURE 8A.12

In summary, the gross profit method starts with a historical analysis that yields a gross profit margin. This is applied to sales revenue, which yields a gross profit figure. Each subsequent step calculates an additional piece of information until a value for closing inventory is obtained. This is the estimation that is used for the quarterly financial statements.

The Retail Method

The **retail method** of estimating inventory requires less information and fewer steps than the gross profit method. Specifically, it requires two things: (1) the value of sales at retail prices (which is why it is called the retail method); and (2) the company's COGS section on the income statement.

For example, refer to Leung Retail Company's information in Figure 8A.13.

	At Cost	At Retail
Cost of Goods Sold		
Opening Inventory	$3,000	$6,000
Purchases	70,000	134,000
Cost of Goods Available for Sale	73,000	140,000
Less: Sales at Retail		70,000
Closing Inventory at Retail		70,000

FIGURE 8A.13

The COGS section is shown in brown, and the sales at retail figure is shown in red. The cost of goods available for sale (shown in green), is calculated by adding opening inventory and purchases together. This section is important because the cost and retail figures for cost of goods available for sale will be used in ratio format as shown in Figure 8A.14.

Cost of Goods Available for Sale at Cost
Cost of Goods Available for Sale at Retail

FIGURE 8A.14

Using the values from Figure 8A.13, the ratio of cost of goods available for sale at cost compared to retail is shown here.

$$\frac{\$73,000}{\$140,000} = 0.521 \text{ or } 52.1\%$$

This ratio must be applied to the closing inventory at retail figure to calculate the closing inventory at cost.

$$\$70,000 \times 52.1\% = \$36,500$$

Figure 8A.15 shows the closing inventory at cost (in red), using the retail method of inventory estimation, which is added to the bottom of the Leung Retail Company chart.

	At Cost	At Retail
Cost of Goods Sold		
Opening Inventory	$3,000	$6,000
Purchase	70,000	134,000
Cost of Goods Available for Sale	73,000	140,000
Less Sales at Retail		70,000
Closing Inventory at Retail		70,000
Closing Inventory at Cost	$36,500	

FIGURE 8A.15

Companies can choose either the gross profit or the retail method to estimate physical inventory. If a company sells products with a consistent markup, retail inventory is a simple and effective choice, and requires less steps than the gross profit method. However, if a company sells a range of products with different markups, gross profit is a better choice, although it does involve the extra step of determining the gross profit margin.

Remember that these methods are only estimations, and are not intended to be relied upon for a long period of time. They should be used only as an interim alternative to a physical inventory count, and are not accurate enough to be used for year-end financial statements.

In Summary

LO 6 **Determine the value of merchandise inventory under the periodic inventory system**

► The specific identification method is similar to the same method used under the perpetual inventory system except that sales are grouped at the bottom of the schedule because COGS is not known until the end of the period.

► The first-in, first-out (FIFO) method is similar to the same method used under the perpetual inventory system except that sales are grouped at the bottom of the schedule because COGS is not known until the end of the period.

► The last-in, first-out (LIFO) method shows different values for ending inventory and COGS. This is because the perpetual inventory system assigns unit costs as the items are sold, whereas the periodic inventory system only assigns unit costs at the end of the period.

► The average unit cost is only calculated once at the end of the period when the weighted-average cost method is used under the periodic inventory system.

► Under the weighted-average cost method, sales are grouped at the bottom of the schedule because COGS is not known until the end of the period.

LO 7 **Estimate the value of merchandise inventory under the periodic inventory system**

► The gross profit method is applied by using the estimated gross profit margin for the period to calculate the value of ending inventory.

► Under the gross profit method, first multiply the gross profit margin by sales revenue to estimate gross profit. Second, subtract gross profit from sales revenue to estimate COGS. Third, subtract the cost of goods available for sale from COGS to estimate ending inventory.

► The retail method is applied by first calculating the ratio of cost to retail for the cost of goods available for sale. Next, this ratio is multiplied by the retail price of ending inventory to estimate the cost of ending inventory.

AMEENGAGE™ *Access **ameengage.com** for integrated resources including tutorials, practice exercises, the digital textbook and more.*

Review Exercise 8A-1

The following transactions took place at Mike's Tikes Toys during the month of March 2018. The company uses a periodic inventory system. There are 100 items in opening inventory with a unit cost of $12 each.

Mar 3   Purchased 500 items with a unit cost of $15 on credit (on account)

Mar 10   Sold 200 items at $45 each on credit

Mar 12   Purchased 300 items with a unit cost of $18 on credit

Mar 20   Sold 300 items at $50 each for cash

Required

a) Using the specific identification method, prepare the inventory record to determine the closing inventory balance after the above transactions have occurred. Assume that 50 items were sold from opening inventory, 350 items were sold from the purchase on March 3 and 100 items were sold from the purchase on March 12.

Date	Purchases			Sales			Balance		
	Quantity	Unit Cost	Value	Quantity	Unit Cost	Value	Quantity	Unit Cost	Value
Sales for the Month									
Ending Inventory									

b) Using the FIFO method, prepare the inventory record to determine the closing inventory balance after the above transactions have occurred.

Date	Purchases			Sales			Balance		
	Quantity	Unit Cost	Value	Quantity	Unit Cost	Value	Quantity	Unit Cost	Value
Sales for the Month									
Ending Inventory									

c) Using the LIFO method, prepare the inventory record to determine the closing inventory balance after the above transactions have occurred.

Date	Purchases			Sales			Balance		
	Quantity	Unit Cost	Value	Quantity	Unit Cost	Value	Quantity	Unit Cost	Value
Sales for the Month									
Ending Inventory									

d) Using the weighted-average cost method, prepare the inventory record to determine the closing inventory balance after the above transactions have occurred.

Date	Purchases			Sales			Balance		
	Quantity	Unit Cost	Value	Quantity	Unit Cost	Value	Quantity	Unit Cost	Value
Average Inventory for the Month									
Sales for the Month									
Ending Inventory									

Note: Numbers may vary due to rounding.

See Appendix I for solutions.

Chapter 9
Accounting Information Systems

Learning Objectives

Access **ameengage.com** for integrated resources including tutorials, practice exercises, the digital textbook and more.

289

The Accounting Paper Trail   LO 1

Throughout this textbook we have learned how the accounting cycle behaves. We have followed the values from source documents to journals and ledgers, then to trial balances and financial statements. This is the paper trail accountants create to ensure all values are stated correctly. Together, the documents and procedures that are used to collect, classify, summarize and report on a business' transactions and operations all make up an **accounting system**.

Source documents, which provide evidence that a business transaction has occurred, come in many different forms. The most common examples of source documentation are usually associated with accounts payable and accounts receivable. Source documents includes purchase orders, sales invoices, cash receipts and contracts.

Accountants use source documents (in addition to other sources of information) to update the accounting records of an organization. For example, when the accounting department issues a sales invoice, the corresponding journal entry should be made. The procedures to make this entry differ slightly between manual and computerized accounting systems. Our focus in this section is on manual accounting systems; computerized accounting systems are discussed later in the chapter.

Figure 9.1 outlines the traditional accounting paper trail. Once source documentation is received, the accountant updates the journal. At specified times, this information is transferred to the general ledger. At the end of the accounting period, a trial balance is produced. A trial balance lists all the company's accounts and their corresponding balances. The main purpose of a trial balance is to ensure that all debits equal all credits. The trial balance may need to be adjusted (e.g. to take into account recognition of prepaid expenses, depreciation of assets, etc.) before the financial statements are produced. The financial statements are then organized into a financial report for management to review.

The Traditional Accounting Paper Trail

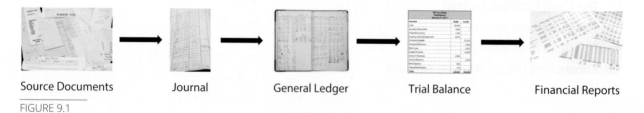

| Source Documents | Journal | General Ledger | Trial Balance | Financial Reports |

FIGURE 9.1

Regardless of whether one is dealing with a manual or a computerized system, an effective accounting system should ensure

- adequate internal controls to prevent misuse of assets;
- accurate information is provided on a timely basis;
- effective communication across the various components of the system;
- flexibility to allow for changes as the organization grows and evolves; and
- maximum benefits at a reasonable cost.

In this section, we will focus on two components of the traditional accounting information system: special journals and subsidiary ledgers.

Special Journals

If we follow the manual accounting paper trail, after the source documentation has been received the next step for the accountant is to record the transaction in journal format.

In a traditional accounting system, recording all business transactions in one journal can be very time consuming, especially when there are lots of activities concerning specific transactions. For transactions that occur regularly, it is wise to maintain a separate book called a **special journal**. Examples of regular transactions include sales, purchases, cash payments, cash receipts and payroll. These journal entries are essentially the same entries already covered, except we will sort them by type and condense the amount of information to be recorded.

WORTH REPEATING

All transactions must be recorded in a journal before being posted to the ledgers, regardless of whether special journals are used or not.

Maintaining these events in a separate set of books organizes accounting information in separate categories, allowing users easy access to specific information. For example, if a sales manager wants to see the amount of credit sales generated in May, she could examine the sales journal and add up all the sales for that month. Examples of special journals include the following.

- **Sales Journal**—This journal is used to record all sales made on account.

- **Cash Receipts Journal**—This journal is used to record all cash deposits (e.g. cash sales) and collections from outstanding accounts receivable.

- **Purchases Journal**—This journal is used to record all purchases (products or services) made on account.

- **Cash Payments Journal**—This journal is used to record all cash payments made by the business (e.g. rent and wages) including payments made to suppliers.

The general journal is the journal that has been used throughout the textbook up until this point. It is used to record any entry that does not belong in one of the special journals. Typical entries recorded in the general journal include the following.

- purchase and sales returns

- adjustments

- correcting entries

Subsidiary Ledgers

The general ledger was first introduced in Chapter 4. It records and organizes the accounts used by a business, which are then used to create the financial statements. However, the general ledger does not list specific information, such as details about individual suppliers or customers, since too much information would clutter up the general ledger accounts. **Subsidiary ledgers** (also called **subledgers**) are a group of similar accounts used to keep track of specific information related to the general ledger account.

For example, subsidiary ledgers for accounts receivable contain all of the information on credit sales to each customer, such as the date of the sale, invoice number, amount of the sale, terms of the sale, and so on. This information can help a company better control its financial information and help with decision-making.

The related account in the general ledger acts as a **controlling account** (sometimes referred to as a *control account*) for the subledgers. It summarizes the information and reports the combined balance of every related subsidiary ledger. For example, the accounts receivable general ledger is the controlling account for all of the accounts receivable subsidiary ledgers.

Transactions are initially recorded in one of the five journals—general, sales, purchases, cash payments, or cash receipts—and are then posted to the general ledger or the subledgers as needed. Examples of transactions that are first posted to subledgers are accounts receivable, accounts payable and merchandise inventory. Examples of transactions that are posted directly to the general ledger are increases or decreases to a company's assets, liabilities or owner equity accounts.

The subledgers are usually updated after each transaction, while the general ledger is usually updated at the end of the period, such as the end of the month. Since subledger accounts only contain details about specific customers or suppliers, and are not used in preparing financial statements, they are not assigned account numbers.

For example, suppose a company has the following list of customers who each owe a certain amount:

- Customer A owes $4,600;

- Customer B owes $500; and

- Customer C owes $300.

The subsidiary ledger tracks each customer and the amount owing, while the accounts receivable controlling account shows the total amount of $5,400, as shown in Figure 9.2.

Subsidiary Ledgers

Accounts Receivable Subsidiary Ledgers

Account: Customer A

Date	PR	DR	CR	Balance (DR or CR)	
O/B				2,400	DR
Apr 1			2,400	0	
Apr 12		4,600		4,600	DR

Account: Customer B

Date	PR	DR	CR	Balance (DR or CR)	
Apr 12		500		500	DR

Account: Customer C

Date	PR	DR	CR	Balance (DR or CR)	
Apr 8		400		400	DR
Apr 12			100	300	DR

Controlling Account

General Ledger

Account: Accounts Receivable				GL No: 110	
Date	PR	DR	CR	Balance	
Apr 12		5,400		5,400	DR

Customer A	$4,600
Customer B	$500
Customer C	$300
Accounts Receivable	$5,400

> A **subsidiary ledger** is a group of accounts.
>
> The total of the subsidiary ledger accounts is equal to the **controlling account**.

FIGURE 9.2

It is important to note that amounts are not posted from the subledger to the general ledger. Subledgers simply keep a record of detailed information about specific general ledger accounts. All amounts in the general ledger are posted from either the special journal or the general journal.

At the end of a period, the total of the subledger accounts is compared with the respective controlling account balance. If the sum of the subsidiary ledger accounts is not equal to the controlling account, an error has occurred and must be identified and corrected.

Just as the accounts receivable subsidiary ledger ensures customer amounts to collect are properly recorded, the accounts payable subsidiary ledger ensures supplier amounts owed are properly recorded. For example, a manager may want to know how much product was purchased from a particular supplier, over which time period, when it was paid for, what discounts were allowed for early payment, and so on. To have easy access to this information, an individual subsidiary ledger is maintained for each supplier. The ledger, which records the activities for each individual supplier, is called the accounts payable subsidiary ledger. The total of all the closing balances for the accounts payable subsidiary ledger must be equal to the accounts payable general ledger balance, which is the controlling account.

There are different subsidiary ledgers to control various assets or liabilities (e.g. inventory, noncurrent assets, accounts receivable). Figure 9.3 illustrates how the accounts payable, accounts receivable and merchandise inventory subsidiary ledgers are totaled and reconciled to their corresponding controlling accounts in the general ledger.

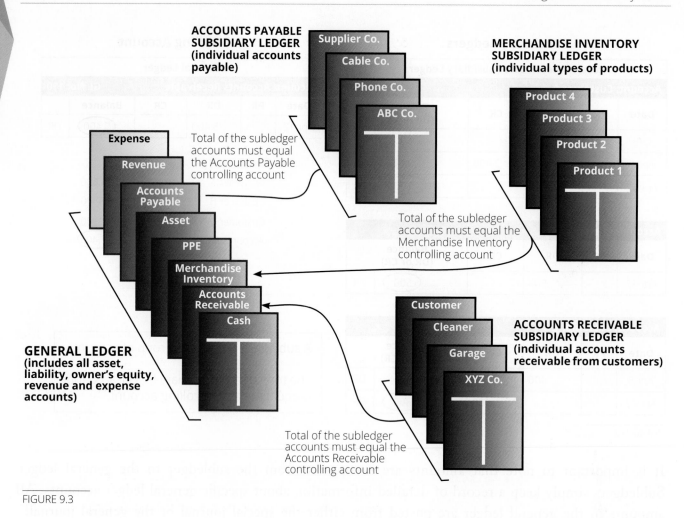

FIGURE 9.3

Once the subledgers have been reconciled to the controlling accounts in the general ledger, a trial balance can be created with the general ledger accounts and balances. The rest of the accounting cycle continues as previously described.

Using Special Journals and Subsidiary Ledgers

It is important to emphasize that the special journals are used to group similar transactions that would normally appear in the general journal. Transactions are entered into the appropriate journal when they occur. For the most part, the subledgers are immediately updated from the special journals while the general ledger is updated at the end of the accounting period. The details of posting from the special journals to the ledgers will be discussed with each journal.

To help with the posting to the general ledger as we discuss the special journals, we will use the selected accounts from Jill Hanlon Retailer, shown in Figure 9.4. You will notice these account numbers being used as we progress through the special journal examples.

Account Description	Account #	Account Description	Account #
Cash	101	Hanlon, Capital	300
Accounts Receivable	110	Hanlon, Withdrawals	310
Merchandise Inventory	120	Sales Revenue	400
Accounts Payable	200	Sales Discount	405
Notes Payable	220	Cost of Goods Sold	500
		Maintenance Expense	525

FIGURE 9.4

The Sales Journal

The sales journal records all the details of sales on account. (Cash sales are not included in this journal; they appear in the cash receipts journal, which records all cash received). The sales journal includes information such as the date of the sale, name of the customer, invoice number and the value of both the sale and the merchandise inventory. Let us look at an example of Jill Hanlon Retailer selling a couch to a customer, Joe Blog.

When a sale is made, the transaction is first recorded in the sales journal. Then, the customer subledger account is updated immediately. Updating the subledger account follows these steps.

ⓐ Transfer the date from the sales journal to the date column in the subledger account.

ⓑ Make a note of the journal and page number in the PR column of the subledger.

ⓒ Transfer the amount of the accounts receivable column from the sales journal to the debit column in the subledger.

ⓓ Indicate the posting is complete by entering a check mark in the PR column of the sales journal.

The steps are illustrated and labeled with the corresponding letters in Figure 9.5.

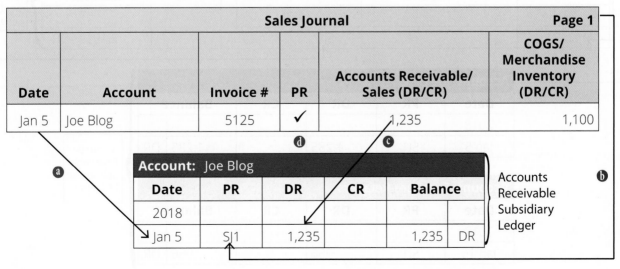

FIGURE 9.5

Note that companies often offer sales discounts to their customers (i.e. 2/10, n/30). The terms of each sale should be recorded in the sales journal. However, if a company provides the same sales terms to all its customers, there is no need to record the terms in the sales journal.

At the end of the month, the totals of all the columns in the sales journal are posted to the appropriate general ledger accounts. The numbers in brackets under the totals represent the ledger numbers of the accounts used. In this example, we are focusing on accounts receivable, account number 110. The posting to the accounts receivable controlling account in Figure 9.6 follows these steps.

ⓐ Transfer the date from the sales journal to the date column in the general ledger account.

ⓑ Make a note of the journal and page number in the PR column of the general ledger.

ⓒ Transfer the total of the accounts receivable column from the sales journal to the debit column in the general ledger account.

ⓓ Indicate the posting is complete by writing the general ledger number(s) under the total in the sales journal.

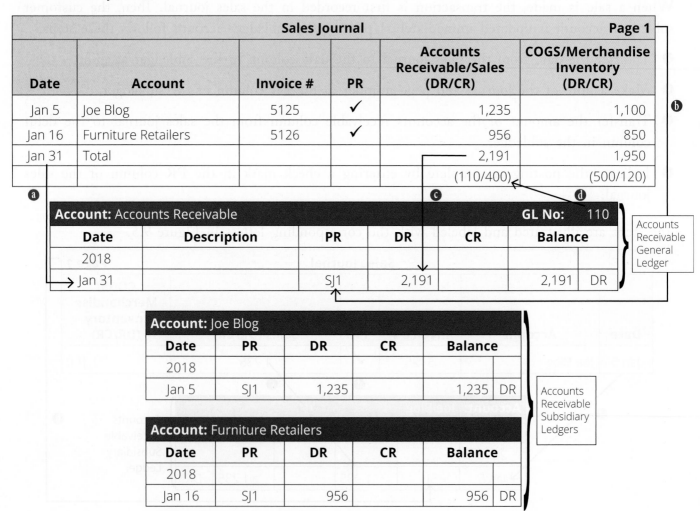

FIGURE 9.6

The total for Accounts Receivable/Sales from the sales journal ($2,191) is posted to the accounts receivable controlling account, and to the sales revenue account (not shown). The total for COGS/Merchandise Inventory ($1,950) is posted to both the cost of goods sold and merchandise inventory accounts (not shown). Note that the total of the two customer subsidiary ledgers ($1,235 + $956) equals the balance of the accounts receivable controlling account ($2,191).

The Cash Receipts Journal

The cash receipts journal records all receipts of cash. Typical reasons for the receipt of cash are listed in the column headings (e.g. Accounts Receivable, Sales, Notes Payable), which vary depending on the company. A column titled Other is used to record cash receipts that do not fall under one of the frequently used categories. Any amount recorded in the Other column is immediately posted to the appropriate general ledger account. The Sales Discount column is used if customers make a payment within the discount period specified by the company.

Cash sales are first recorded in the cash receipts journal, as shown in Figure 9.7. Because accounts receivable is not affected, nothing is posted to the subledger accounts. Because the Other column was not used, no entry is posted to the general ledger at this time. For the remaining columns, the general ledger is only updated at the end of the month, when the columns are totaled.

Cash Receipts Journal									Page 3
Date	Account	PR	Cash (DR)	Sales Discount (DR)	Accounts Receivable (CR)	Sales (CR)	Notes Payable (CR)	Other (CR)	COGS/ Merchandise Inventory (DR/CR)
Jan 2	Cash Sale		350			350			280

FIGURE 9.7

The transaction on January 4 in Figure 9.8 is an investment into the company by the owner. There is no column with Hanlon, Capital as a heading, so the amount is recorded in the Other column. The post reference (300) indicates that the amount of the investment shown is immediately updated to owner's capital in the general ledger. At the end of the month, the total of the Other column will not be posted because any amount in this column was posted immediately to the appropriate general ledger account.

Cash Receipts Journal									Page 3
Date	Account	PR	Cash (DR)	Sales Discount (DR)	Accounts Receivable (CR)	Sales (CR)	Notes Payable (CR)	Other (CR)	COGS/ Merchandise Inventory (DR/CR)
Jan 2	Cash Sale		350			350			280
Jan 4	Hanlon, Capital	300	4,000					4,000	

This posting reference means the amount in the Other column has been immediately updated in the general ledger.

FIGURE 9.8

Let us look at another type of transaction posted to the cash receipts journal. When a payment is made from a customer who made a purchase on credit, the subledger account is immediately updated because the payment affects the accounts receivable account. Updating the subledger account follows these steps.

ⓐ Transfer the date from the cash receipts journal to the date column in the subledger account.

ⓑ Make a note of the journal and page number in the PR column of the subledger.

ⓒ Transfer the amount of the accounts receivable column from the cash receipts journal to the credit column in the subledger.

ⓓ Indicate the posting is complete by entering a check mark in the PR column of the cash receipts journal.

For example, suppose Joe Blog makes a partial payment on January 10. Since the payment is made within 10 days of the original sale, Joe receives a 2% discount on the amount paid. The discount therefore reduces the amount of cash received, but does not reduce the amount of accounts receivable that is paid off. The steps required to post from the cash receipts journal to the subledger accounts are shown in Figure 9.9.

Cash Receipts Journal									Page 3
Date	Account	PR	Cash (DR)	Sales Discount (DR)	Accounts Receivable (CR)	Sales (CR)	Notes Payable (CR)	Other (CR)	COGS/ Merchandise Inventory (DR/CR)
Jan 2	Cash Sale		350			350			280
Jan 4	Hanlon, Capital	300	4,000					4,000	
Jan 10	Joe Blog	✓	588	12	600				

Account: Joe Blog					
Date	PR	DR	CR	Balance	
2018					
Jan 5	SJ1	1,235		1,235	DR
Jan 10	CR3		600	635	DR

FIGURE 9.9

At the end of the month, when all transactions have been recorded, all columns in the cash receipts journal are totaled and posted to the appropriate general ledger accounts. The posting to the accounts receivable controlling account follows these steps.

ⓐ Transfer the date from the cash receipts journal to the date column in the general ledger account.

ⓑ Make a note of the journal and page number in the PR column of the general ledger.

ⓒ Transfer the total of the accounts receivable column from the cash receipts journal to the credit column in the general ledger account.

ⓓ Indicate the posting is complete by writing the general ledger number under the total in the cash receipts journal.

These steps are illustrated and labeled in Figure 9.10.

Cash Receipts Journal									Page 3
Date	Account	PR	Cash (DR)	Sales Discount (DR)	Accounts Receivable (CR)	Sales (CR)	Notes Payable (CR)	Other (CR)	COGS/ Merchandise Inventory (DR/CR)
Jan 2	Cash Sale		350			350			280
Jan 4	Hanlon, Capital	300	4,000					4,000	
Jan 10	Joe Blog	✓	588	12	600				
Jan 22	Granger Bank		2,000				2,000		
Jan 31	Total		6,938	12	600	350	2,000	4,000	280
			(101)	(405)	(110)	(400)	(220)	(X)	(500/120)

Account: Accounts Receivable — **GL No:** 110

Date	Description	PR	DR	CR	Balance	
2018						
Jan 31		SJ1	2,191		2,191	DR
Jan 31		CR3		600	1,591	DR

Account: Joe Blog

Date	PR	DR	CR	Balance	
2018					
Jan 5	SJ1	1,235		1,235	DR
Jan 10	CR3		600	635	DR

Account: Furniture Retailers

Date	PR	DR	CR	Balance	
2018					
Jan 16	SJ1	956		956	DR

FIGURE 9.10

In this example, $600 is posted as a credit to accounts receivable, $6,938 is posted as a debit to cash (not shown), $12 is posted as a debit to sales discounts (not shown), and so on. Since the entry in the Other column—the investment made by the owner—was immediately posted to the general ledger when the transaction was recorded, an (X) is used to indicate that no posting is required.

The Purchases Journal

The purchases journal records all purchases on account. Several columns are provided to keep track of common items that the company purchases on account (e.g., merchandise inventory and office supplies). If anything else is purchased, it is recorded in the Other column.

When a purchase is made, the supplier subledger account must be updated immediately. Notice that the purchases journal has a column for terms, which is used to keep track of any terms offered by each supplier. Updating the subledger account with the transactions posted to the purchases journal follows these steps.

ⓐ Transfer the date from the purchases journal to the date column in the subledger account.

ⓑ Make a note of the journal and page number in the PR column of the subledger.

ⓒ Transfer the amount of the accounts payable column from the purchases journal to the credit column in the subledger.

ⓓ Indicate the posting is complete by entering a check mark in the PR column of the purchases journal.

Figure 9.11 shows the steps to update the subledger account when a purchase is made.

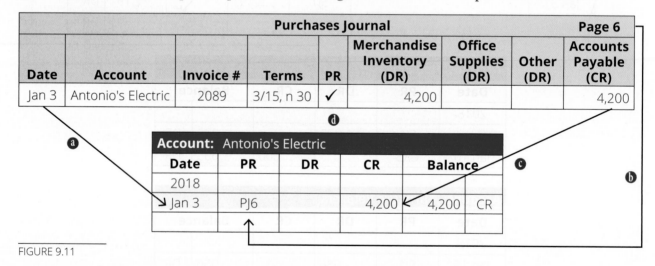

FIGURE 9.11

At the end of the month, after all transactions have been posted, the totals of the columns from the purchases journal are posted to the general ledger accounts. The totals of the individual subledger accounts must equal the balance of the accounts payable controlling account. The posting to the accounts payable controlling account follows these steps.

ⓐ Transfer the date from the purchases journal to the date column in the general ledger account.

ⓑ Make a note of the journal and page number in the PR column of the general ledger.

ⓒ Transfer the total of the accounts payable column from the purchases journal to the credit column in the general ledger account.

ⓓ Indicate the posting is complete by writing the general ledger number under the total in the purchases journal.

The posting of the transactions from the purchases journal to the accounts payable general ledger account is shown in Figure 9.12.

Purchases Journal								Page 6
Date	Account	Invoice #	Terms	PR	Merchandise Inventory (DR)	Office Supplies (DR)	Other (DR)	Accounts Payable (CR)
Jan 3	Antonio's Electric	2089	3/15, n 30	✓	4,200			4,200
Jan 19	Maintenance Expense/Doug's Maintenance	6091		525/✓			80	80 ⓒ
Jan 31	Total				4,200		80	4,280
					(120)		(X)	(200) ⓓ

Account: Accounts Payable   **GL No:** 200 ⓐ ⓑ

Date	Description	PR	DR	CR	Balance	
2018						
Jan 31		PJ6		4,280	4,280	CR

Account: Antonio's Electric

Date	PR	DR	CR	Balance	
2018					
Jan 3	PJ6		4,200	4,200	CR

Account: Doug's Maintenance

Date	PR	DR	CR	Balance	
2018					
Jan 19	PJ6		80	80	CR

FIGURE 9.12

Note that if an item is purchased that does not have a heading in the journal, it is placed in the Other column. Suppose the company had maintenance repairs done for the office, and received an invoice for $80. The $80 is placed in both the Other column and the Accounts Payable column of the purchases journal. Since the amount in the Other column must be posted immediately to the general ledger for the maintenance expense account, the GL number (525) is placed in the PR column. Additionally, since the $80 must also be posted to the relevant accounts payable subledger, a check mark is placed in the PR column of the purchases journal.

The Cash Payments Journal

The cash payments journal records all cash payments made by the company. There is a column to record the check number, since a good control is to have all payments made by check. Various columns are provided for the most common reasons for paying with cash, and an Other column is used to record cash payments for items that do not fall under one of the given columns. Merchandise Inventory includes both debit and credit columns. The debit side is used if merchandise inventory is purchased with cash (check) and the credit side is used if the company pays a supplier of merchandise inventory early and receives a discount.

Cash purchases are recorded in the cash payments journal, as shown in Figure 9.13. Since accounts payable is not affected, no entry should be posted to the subledger accounts. The Other column was not used, so no entry should be posted to the general ledger at this time. The general ledger is only updated at the end of the month when the columns are totaled.

Cash Payments Journal								Page 4
Date	Account	Check #	PR	Accounts Payable (DR)	Other (DR)	Merchandise Inventory (DR)	Merchandise Inventory (CR)	Cash (CR)
Jan 6	Electro Parts	748				1,500		1,500

FIGURE 9.13

The transaction on January 15 in Figure 9.14 is a withdrawal from the company by the owner. Since there is no column with Hanlon, Withdrawals as a heading, the amount is recorded in the Other column. The post reference (310) indicates that the amount of the withdrawal shown is immediately updated to owner's withdrawals in the general ledger. At the end of the month, the total of the Other column will not be posted because any amount in this column is posted immediately to the appropriate general ledger account.

Cash Payments Journal								Page 4
Date	Account	Check #	PR	Accounts Payable (DR)	Other (DR)	Merchandise Inventory (DR)	Merchandise Inventory (CR)	Cash (CR)
Jan 6	Electro Parts	748				1,500		1,500
Jan 15	Hanlon, Withdrawals	749	310		500			500

FIGURE 9.14

Updating the transactions posted in the cash payments journal to the relevant subledger account in Figure 9.15 follows these steps.

a Transfer the date from the cash payments journal to the date column in the subledger account.

b Make a note of the journal and page number in the PR column of the subledger.

c Transfer the amount of the accounts payable column from the cash payments journal to the debit column in the subledger.

d Indicate the posting is complete by entering a check mark in the PR column of the cash payments journal.

Cash Payments Journal								Page 4
Date	Account	Check #	PR	Accounts Payable (DR)	Other (DR)	Merchandise Inventory (DR)	Merchandise Inventory (CR)	Cash (CR)
Jan 6	Electro Parts	748				1,500		1,500
Jan 15	Hanlon, Withdrawals	749	310		500			500
Jan 18	Antonio's Electric	750	✓	4,200			126	4,074

Account: Antonio's Electric

Date	PR	DR	CR	Balance	
2018					
Jan 3	PJ6		4,200	4,200	CR
Jan 18	CP4	4,200		0	CR

FIGURE 9.15

Note that the payment to Antonio's Electric (a supplier) on January 18 immediately updates the subledger account since it affects accounts payable. Similar to the other journals, a check mark is placed in the PR column of the cash payments journal to show the transaction has been posted to the subledger account. Since the original purchase was on January 3, and the terms of the purchase were 3/15, n/30, the company can take a 3% discount on the payment. The discount amount is recorded as a credit to merchandise inventory and reduces the amount of cash that must be paid to the supplier.

At the end of the month, all columns from the cash payments journal are totaled and the amounts are posted to the appropriate general ledger accounts. The posting to the accounts payable controlling account follows these steps.

a Transfer the date from the cash payments journal to the date column in the general ledger account.

b Make a note of the journal and page number in the PR column of the general ledger.

c Transfer the total of the accounts payable column from the cash payments journal to the debit column in the general ledger account.

d Indicate the posting is complete by writing the general ledger number under the total in the cash payments journal.

Figure 9.16 illustrates the steps required to post from the cash payments journal to the accounts payable controlling account.

Cash Payments Journal								Page 4
Date	Account	Check #	PR	Accounts Payable (DR)	Other (DR)	Merchandise Inventory (DR)	(CR)	Cash (CR)
Jan 6	Electro Parts	748				1,500		1,500
Jan 15	Hanlon, Withdrawals	749	310		500			500
Jan 18	Antonio's Electric	750	✓	4,200			126	4,074
Jan 31	Total			4,200	500	1,500	126	6,074
				(200)	(X)	(120)	(120)	(101)

ⓐ

Account: Accounts Payable					GL No: 200	
Date	Description	PR	DR	CR	Balance	
2018						
Jan 31		PJ6	**ⓒ**	4,280	4,280	CR
Jan 31		CP4	4,200		80	CR

ⓑ

ⓓ

Account: Antonio's Electric				
Date	PR	DR	CR	Balance
2018				
Jan 3	PJ6		4,200	4,200 CR
Jan 18	CP4	4,200		0 CR

Account: Doug's Maintenance				
Date	PR	DR	CR	Balance
2018				
Jan 19	PJ6		80	80 CR

FIGURE 9.16

In this example, $4,200 is posted as a debit to accounts payable, $1,500 is posted as a debit to merchandise inventory (not shown), and so on. Since the transaction in the Other column was immediately posted to the general ledger, an (X) indicates that no posting is required.

Figure 9.17 summarizes the types of special journals.

Type of Special Journal	Purpose	Examples of Related General Ledger Accounts
Sales Journal	to record all sales made on account	Accounts Receivable, COGS, Merchandise Inventory
Cash Receipts Journal	to record all cash deposits and collections from outstanding accounts receivable	Accounts Receivable, Cash, Sales Discounts
Purchases Journal	to record all purchases made on account	Accounts Payable, Office Supplies, Merchandise Inventory
Cash Payments Journal	to record all cash payments made by the business	Accounts Payable, Cash, Merchandise Inventory

FIGURE 9.17

At times, a transaction recorded in the special journal may require two amounts to be placed in the Other column. When this happens, it is acceptable to use two rows of the special journal to record the transaction. For example, suppose a company makes a $1,050 payment to its bank to pay back a note payable that includes $50 in interest. If the cash payments journal does not have a column for notes payable or for interest expense, both amounts must be recorded in the Other column. The journal below shows how this is recorded.

| | Cash Payments Journal | | | | | Merchandise Inventory | | Page 4 |
Date	Account	Check #	PR	Accounts Payable (DR)	Other (DR)	(DR)	(CR)	Cash (CR)
Aug 31	Notes Payable	263	210		1,000			1,050
	Interest Expense		530		50			

Notice that cash is credited for the total amount of the payment on the first line. The amount of the notes payable principal and interest are listed on two separate lines and the PR column indicates that both amounts were updated in the appropriate general ledger accounts.

Reconciling the Controlling Account

Remember that at the end of the month, when the general ledger is updated by the journals, the total of all the subledger accounts must equal the balance of the appropriate controlling account (e.g. accounts receivable or accounts payable).

To confirm that the total of the individual subledger accounts is equal to the respective controlling account balance in the general ledger, a reconciliation is prepared. From Figure 9.10, the balance of accounts receivable was $1,591. By finding the total of the accounts receivable subsidiary ledger, called a schedule of accounts receivable, we can confirm that the controlling account and subledger balance, as shown in Figure 9.18.

Jill Hanlon Retailer January 31, 2018 General Ledger	
Accounts Receivable	$1,591

Controlling account in the general ledger

Jill Hanlon Retailer Schedule of Accounts Receivable January 31, 2018	
Joe Blog	$635
Furniture Retailers	956
Total Accounts Receivable	$1,591

The total of all subledger accounts

FIGURE 9.18

A similar schedule can be done for the accounts payable subsidiary ledger. From Figure 9.16, the balance of accounts payable was $80. The total of the accounts payable subledger is shown in Figure 9.19.

Jill Hanlon Retailer January 31, 2018 General Ledger	
Accounts Payable	$80

Controlling account in the general ledger

Jill Hanlon Retailer Schedule of Accounts Payable January 31, 2018	
Antonio's Electric	$0
Doug's Maintenance	80
Total Accounts Payable	$80

The total of all subledger accounts

FIGURE 9.19

If the comparison of the general ledger controlling account and the total of the subledger accounts shows that they do not balance, the difference must be investigated and resolved before the trial balance can be completed.

Returns

The special journals are designed to record specific types of transactions, but some transactions that must be recorded do not fit into these special journals. In this case, the transaction must be recorded in the general journal. For example, sales and purchase returns do not fit into the special journals and must be recorded in the general journal. The only change to the way these transactions are recorded from what was learned earlier is how the posting is processed for accounts receivable or accounts payable.

Suppose Furniture Retailers, a customer from the example in Figure 9.6, returned $300 worth of items on January 18 that cost $170. The general journal entry is shown in Figure 9.20. The PR for accounts receivable updates the general ledger (shown by the account number 110) and the subsidiary ledger for the customer (shown by the check mark).

JOURNAL					Page 5
Date 2018	Account Title and Explanation	PR	Debit	Credit	
Jan 18	Sales Returns & Allowances	410	300		
	Accounts Receivable	110/✔		300	
	Customer returned items				
	Merchandise Inventory	120	170		
	Cost of Goods Sold	500		170	
	Returned items to supplier				

FIGURE 9.20

Also, suppose Jill Hanlon Retailer returned $500 of the merchandise inventory it purchased from Antonio's Electric on January 10 (from the example in Figure 9.12). This purchase return is completed in the general journal, as shown in Figure 9.21. The PR for accounts payable updates the general ledger (shown by the account number 200) and the subsidiary ledger for the supplier (shown by the check mark).

JOURNAL				Page 5
Date 2018	**Account Title and Explanation**	**PR**	**Debit**	**Credit**
Jan 10	Accounts Payable	200/✔	500	
	Merchandise Inventory	120		500
	Returned items to supplier			

FIGURE 9.21

Pause & Reflect

Exercise 9-1

Simmons Inc., a small consulting business, recorded the following transactions for June 2018.

Jun 4	Issued Invoice #325 for $1,200 to Derek Smith for consulting services
Jun 8	Purchased $75 worth of office supplies on account from Supply Depot
Jun 10	Issued Invoice #326 for $800 to Soft Cell Enterprises for consulting services
Jun 15	Paid in full the June 8th invoice from Supply Depot
Jun 20	Purchased a printer for $140 on account from Buzz Electronics
Jun 22	Received $800 cash from Soft Cell Enterprises for payment of Invoice #326
Jun 26	Issued Invoice #327 for $525 to Bill Waites for consulting services
Jun 30	Received $700 cash from Derek Smith for partial payment of Invoice #325

Reconcile that the totals of the individual subledger accounts (Accounts Receivable, Accounts Payable) are equal to their respective account balances in the controlling accounts in the general ledger. Enter the appropriate information in the general ledgers and the schedules below.

Simmons Inc. June 30, 2018 General Ledger	
Accounts Receivable	

Simmons Inc. Schedule of Accounts Receivable June 30, 2018	

Simmons Inc. June 30, 2018 General Ledger	
Accounts Payable	

Simmons Inc. Schedule of Accounts Payable June 30, 2018	

See Appendix I for solutions.

Computerized Accounting

So far in this chapter, all journals, ledgers and subledgers have been illustrated using a manual accounting system. For a small business with a small number of transactions, a manual system may be adequate. However, as the number of transactions increases, so does the amount of information that is kept. In a manual accounting system, storing, tracking and finding information can become tedious and difficult.

These days, even the smallest businesses are opting to use computerized accounting systems. Computerized accounting systems offer numerous benefits, including the following.

- automating and simplifying the record-keeping and posting processes
- providing an intuitive and user-friendly interface for entering and extracting information
- providing current account balances and account activity
- producing timely financial statements and management reports
- allowing the user to customize and format financial statements and reports
- providing features for budgeting and data analysis
- enabling users to account for multiple companies, as well as multiple currencies

Many computerized accounting systems can be tailored to the size of a business, its particular industry, and its specific accounting and reporting requirements, such as payroll or inventory control. Accounting systems are also available for different platforms, or operating environments, such as desktop accounting software installed directly on the user's computer hard drive; desktop software with mobile capabilities so it can be accessed via a wireless portable device; or cloud-based systems that provide access to accounting applications on a subscription basis. (Cloud accounting is discussed later in this section.)

A computerized system is typically set up in a similar manner to the special journals just described. Sales are entered in one section of the software, while receipts are entered in another. Purchases and payments are also separated into different sections. The general journal is available for any transaction that does not fit into any of the special journals.

Although entries can be recorded in different sections, the system updates the appropriate subledgers and the general ledger accounts at the time they are posted. By updating all appropriate ledgers after every posting, reports can be viewed or printed at any time and be up-to-date.

Details about customers and suppliers are available from the subledgers. Contact information and billing information can be stored. Reports on each customer or supplier can be easily generated to show all transactions and any amounts outstanding.

A computerized system keeps track of the terms of a purchase and indicates to the user when a payment should be made to take advantage of discounts. If no discounts are available, the system indicates when the bill should be paid so it is not late. For sales, the system can indicate when a customer is overdue for payment so a letter or email can be sent to remind the customer that payment is required.

Many accounting system vendors offer different levels of their software so that a business can upgrade an application as the business evolves. One of the most popular accounting software programs that offer this capability is QuickBooks®. Intuit and QuickBooks are trademarks and service marks of Intuit Inc., registered in the United States and other countries. We will use QuickBooks to demonstrate the typical functions of a computerized accounting system.

QuickBooks Illustration

We will illustrate how QuickBooks works using the example of Jill Hanlon Retailer from our discussion of manual accounting systems. To simplify things, we will limit our illustration to transactions involving invoicing, cash sales, and customer payments. As you follow the figures in this example, note that the screen titles and the function names (for example, "Create Invoices") may differ depending on the particular accounting program used. However, the accounting principles and procedures are common across all accounting software programs. For our example, we are using the desktop version of the QuickBooks Premier Edition for multiple users. There is also a QuickBooks online version that uses cloud technology, which is discussed later.

The following steps are involved when using a computerized accounting system.

1. Record a sale.

2. Record a payment received by a customer.

3. Print reports.

The first step is to record a sale. Many small businesses offer their customers different methods of making a purchase: by the business invoicing the customer on account (1a.), or by the customer paying cash for goods or services (1b.). We will look at both methods.

1a. Record a sale on account by creating an invoice

From the QuickBooks "Create Invoices" screen, the user selects a customer job from the customer records using a pull-down list. The customer job is usually the customer's name. The program fills in the customer's name and address from the information entered when the customer account was set up. Similarly, the remaining fields of the invoice are completed by using pull-down menus and (for some fields) entering the information manually.

To demonstrate, recall from Figure 9.5 that on January 5, Jill Hanlon sold a couch on account to Joe Blog and issued Invoice #5125 for the value of the sale, $1,235. Figure 9.22 shows how the transaction is recorded in QuickBooks.

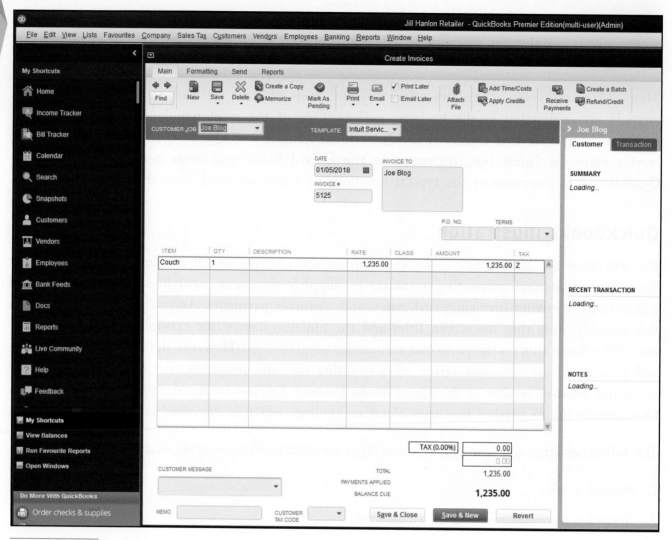

FIGURE 9.22

When the entry is saved and closed, the transaction is automatically posted as a debit to the accounts receivable customer account for Joe Blog, and a credit to the sales revenue account. The equivalent journal entry is shown in Figure 9.23.

JOURNAL				Page 5
Date 2018	**Account Title and Explanation**	**PR**	**Debit**	**Credit**
Jan 5	Accounts Receivable—Joe Blog		1,235	
	Sales Revenue			1,235

FIGURE 9.23

The invoice can then be printed and mailed to the customer, or saved in an electronic form (such as a PDF file) and emailed to the customer.

1b. Record a cash sale

When a customer pays in full for a product or service, accounts receivable is not affected. Most businesses, however, like to create customer records for cash-paying customers for several reasons: to simplify transactions for repeat customers, to maintain records of a customer's previous purchases, and to electronically communicate with customers for marketing purposes. Most importantly, a customer's record can be used to print a personalized sales receipt for the customer. Details of the transaction are entered in the QuickBooks "Sales Receipt" screen using a combination of pull-down menus and manual entries.

To demonstrate, recall from Figure 9.7 that on January 2, Jill Hanlon sold a product to a customer and received $350 in cash. The item was a small table sold to "Customer A," since Jill does not maintain individual customer records for cash sales. Because this is a sale of a product (as opposed to a service), the item must also be accounted for in Jill's merchandise inventory. QuickBooks includes an "Inventory Center" that allows the user to keep detailed records on each item that is purchased, tracked and resold. Figure 9.24 shows how the sales receipt is generated, and Figure 9.25 shows the related merchandise inventory record for the small table.

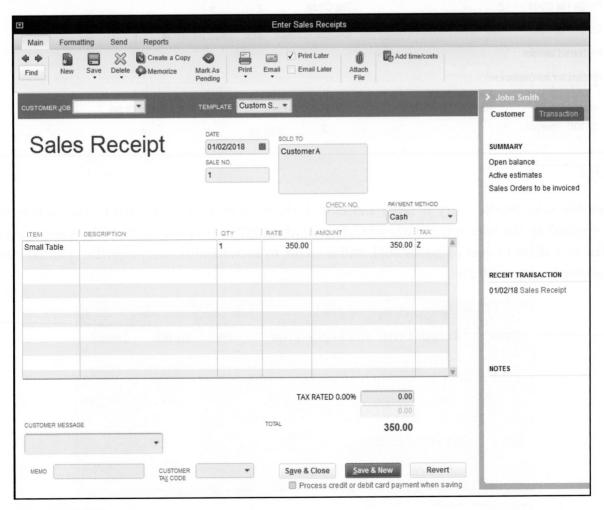

FIGURE 9.24

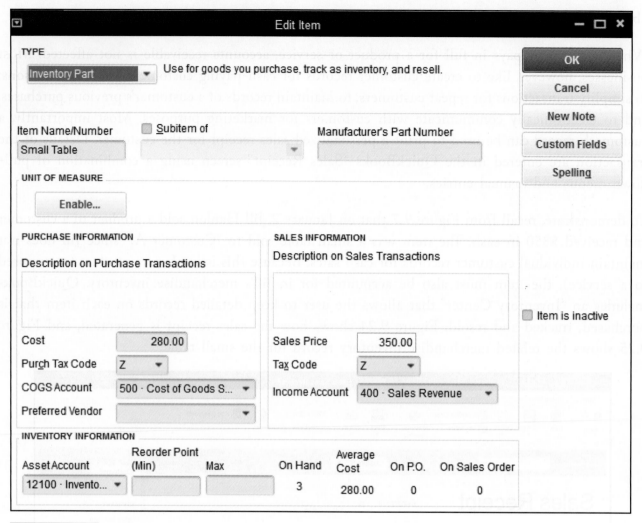

FIGURE 9.25

When the sales receipt entry is saved and closed, the total of $350 is debited to the cash account and credited to the sales revenue account. As well, the $280 cost of the small table is automatically posted as a debit to cost of goods sold, and a credit to merchandise inventory. The journal entries are shown in Figure 9.26.

JOURNAL				Page 5
Date **2018**	**Account Title and Explanation**	**PR**	**Debit**	**Credit**
Jan 2	Cash		350	
	Sales Revenue			350
Jan 2	Cost of Goods Sold		280	
	Merchandise Inventory			280

FIGURE 9.26

2. Record a payment received from a customer

Customer payments are entered from the QuickBooks "Customer Payment" screen. As with the "Create Invoices" screen, the user selects the customer job (name) and the program fills in the customer's name and address. Similarly, the fields of the invoice are completed by using pull-down menus and entering any remaining information manually.

To demonstrate, recall from Figure 9.9 that on January 10, Jill Hanlon received partial payment from customer Joe Blog for Invoice #5125. Of the $1,235 owing, Joe can pay $600. Because he is paying within the 10-day discount period, he receives a 2% discount on the amount paid, or $12 ($600 × 0.02). So he will actually pay $588 ($600 − $12). Recall that the discount reduces the amount of cash received, but it does not reduce the amount of accounts receivable that is paid off. Figure 9.27 shows how the transaction is recorded in QuickBooks.

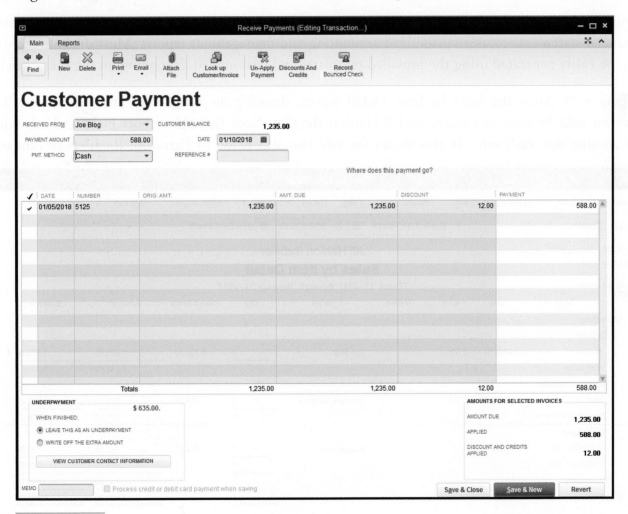

FIGURE 9.27

When the customer payment entry is saved and closed, the payment of $588 is debited to the cash account, the discount of $12 is posted to the sales discounts account, and $600 is credited to accounts receivable. The equivalent journal entry is shown in Figure 9.28.

JOURNAL				Page 5
Date 2018	**Account Title and Explanation**	**PR**	**Debit**	**Credit**
Jan 10	Cash		588	
	Sales Discounts		12	
	Accounts Receivable—Joe Blog			600

FIGURE 9.28

After the partial payment, Joe Blog's accounts receivables will have a balance of $635.

3. Print reports

Computerized accounting systems provide numerous options to print reports, ranging from standard financial statements to user-customized accounting and management reports. Most of these reports can be easily generated using the provided templates and customized depending on the users' needs.

Figure 9.29 shows the Sales by Item Detail report, showing the number of units and the dollar amount sold by item in January by Jill Hanlon Retailer. Note that this report includes both sales on account and cash sales. It also shows the sale that was made to Furniture Retailers in January.

								Sales by Item Detail			— □
Customize Report		Comment on Report		Memorize		Print	E-mail ▼	Excel ▼	Hide Header	Refresh	

Dates Custom ▼ From 03/17/2017 ▦ To 01/31/2018 ▦ Sort By Default ▼

1:18 PM
03/17/17
Accrual Basis

Jill Hanlon Retailer
Sales by Item Detail
March 17, 2017 through January 31, 2018

Type	Date	Num	Memo	Name	Qty	Sales Price	Amount	Balance
Inventory								
Couch								
Invoice	01/05/2018	5125		Joe Blog	1	1,235.00	1,235.00	1,235.00
Total Couch					1		1,235.00	1,235.00
Electric Fireplace								
Invoice	01/16/2018	5126		Furniture Retailers	1	956.00	956.00	956.00
Total Electric Fireplace					1		956.00	956.00
Small Table								
Sales Receipt	01/02/2018	1		Customer A	1	350.00	350.00	350.00
Total Small Table					1		350.00	350.00
Total Inventory					3		2,541.00	2,541.00
TOTAL					3		**2,541.00**	**2,541.00**

FIGURE 9.29

Figure 9.30 shows the Open Invoices report, listing the customers who still owe money to the company as at the end of January, including the dollar amount that each customer owes. Note that the line item for Joe Blog shows his outstanding balance at January 31 (i.e. after he made his partial payment).

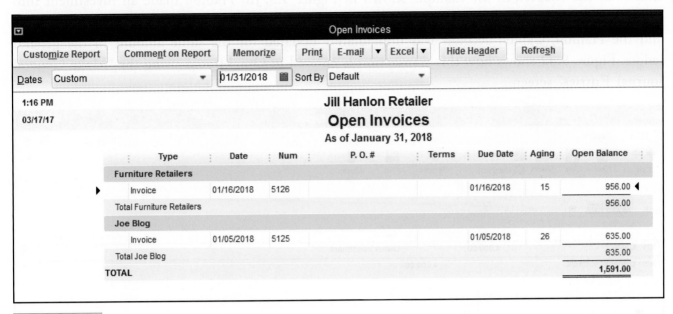

FIGURE 9.30

Figure 9.31 shows the Transactions by Account report, listing all cash transactions, including cash receipts and cash payments, during the month of January. Note that the investment made by the owner is also listed here, since it was a cash investment.

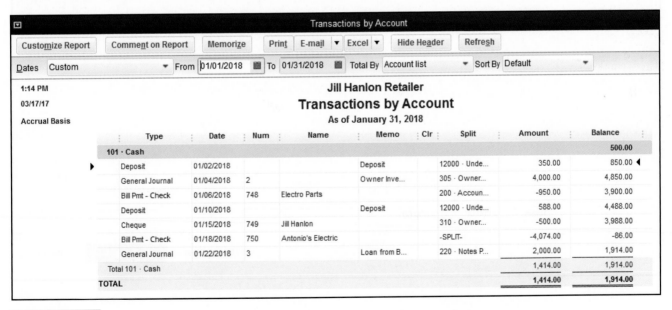

FIGURE 9.31

Transactions by Account reports can be made for any account in the company, allowing users to see transactions related to expenses, merchandise inventory, accounts receivable, and so on. These reports can also be customized, for example, to show only transactions that occurred between specific dates, or transactions related to a specific customer.

General Journal Entries in QuickBooks

Earlier in the chapter, in the example shown in Figure 9.8, Jill Hanlon made an investment into the company as the owner. On January 4, a journal entry was made for the cash receipt of $4,000, and the Hanlon, Capital account was immediately updated for the same amount in the general ledger. Figure 9.32 shows how this transaction is entered in QuickBooks using the "Make General Journal Entries" screen.

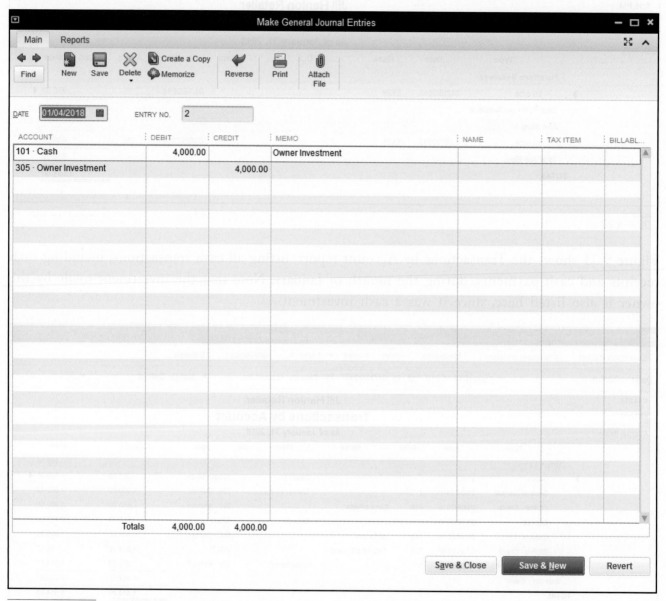

FIGURE 9.32

Also, note that this general journal entry relating to Jill's $4,000 cash investment into the company is included in the Transactions by Account report in Figure 9.31.

Cloud Accounting

Cloud accounting, also known as cloud-based accounting, refers to accounting software that is hosted remotely on the vendor's computer servers and accessed by users through the cloud. Data is entered via a user interface on the client's desktop, and then sent through the cloud (via the Internet or a large computer network) to be processed on the vendor's server. The information is then returned to the client by the same method. Cloud accounting is a service that is usually offered as a monthly or annual subscription for a set fee.

Cloud accounting provides many benefits to businesses of all sizes. Because the software resides remotely there is no need for the client to purchase or upgrade hardware, or to install and maintain the accounting software on its own desktop computers. Since the application is not on-site, the client company does not require specially trained IT staff to maintain it. All users at the client site have access to the same version of the software and can retrieve current financial information and produce customized reports. Accounting data is updated automatically so that account balances and reports provide the users with real-time information. When the accounting software is updated on the provider's server, all users have immediate access to the newest version of the application. Cloud accounting also enables users to access the software via mobile devices anywhere there is an Internet connection or Wi-Fi (known as "wireless networking").

Cloud-based systems provide a secure environment in which to store financial information, which is a definite advantage over traditional on-site accounting software. Data is encrypted and protected on the provider's system, and most providers maintain several backup servers in different locations in case of emergencies, such as major system outages or natural disasters.

Some of the most popular cloud-based accounting services for small businesses are QuickBooks Online (Intuit), Sage Accountant Solutions (The Sage Group), and Xero (Xero Limited), as well as FreshBooks (for self-employed service professionals, such as consultants and agencies). For mid-sized and larger companies with more complex accounting, reporting, and enterprise resource planning (ERP) needs, some popular cloud-based solutions are NetSuite (NetSuite Inc.), SageCRM (The Sage Group), and Oracle Cloud (Oracle). All of the accounting services listed here are registered trademarks.

There are a number of accounting software vendors that provide cloud accounting as part of their entire range of accounting software solutions. This enables a company to start with accounting software that meets its current needs and to upgrade to the vendor's more advanced applications as its business evolves.

In Summary

LO 1 **Explain the flow of accounting information through the accounting paper trail**

▶ Source documents provide evidence for journal entries, which are then posted to the general ledger accounts. The values from the general ledger accounts are used to create a trial balance and the financial statements.

LO 2 **Describe and record transactions in special journals and subsidiary ledgers**

▶ The sales journal is used to record all sales on account.

▶ The cash receipts journal is used to record all cash received.

▶ The purchases journal is used to record all purchases on account.

▶ The cash payments journal is used to record all cash paid.

▶ The general journal is used to record all transactions that do not fit into the other special journals.

▶ Subsidiary ledgers are used to track details that would clutter the general ledgers.

▶ All special journals are totaled at the end of the month and the totals are posted to the general ledger accounts.

▶ If a transaction in the sales journal or cash receipts journal affects accounts receivable, the accounts receivable subledger for that customer is updated immediately.

▶ If a transaction in the purchases journal or cash payments journal affects accounts payable, the accounts payable subledger for that supplier is updated immediately.

LO 3 **Identify features of a computerized accounting system**

▶ Computerized accounting systems have many benefits, including simplifying record-keeping and posting, providing a user-friendly interface for entering and extracting information, allowing the user to customize and format financial statements and reports, and producing timely financial statements and reports.

▶ Computerized accounting systems are available for different platforms such as desktop, desktop with mobile capabilities, and cloud-based applications on a subscription basis.

▶ A computerized accounting system has sections like the special journals to enter transactions. Transactions automatically update general and subsidiary ledgers.

▶ Subsidiary ledgers keep information about suppliers and customers and can be used to generate reports.

 *Access **ameengage.com** for integrated resources including tutorials, practice exercises, the digital textbook and more.*

Review Exercise 9-1

Lin-Z is an owner-operated office furniture retailer. Lin-Z uses the perpetual inventory system. The following is a list of transactions for the month of June.

Jun 4   Received $4,000 from a cash sale to Gus Van Sand (sold office furniture costing $2,015)

Jun 5   Lin-Z received Invoice #4053 for $100 worth of supplies from Stapl-EZ Inc.

Jun 6   Received $480 from Bo Didley regarding outstanding accounts receivable

Jun 9   Received $2,160 for the cash sale of a lounge suite (costing $1,050) to Rita Patterson

Jun 9   Lin-Z received a bill from Building Services Inc. (Invoice #124) for $350 for repairs and maintenance of the office building

Jun 10   Received $25 in interest from a loan to Kurt Domino

Jun 12   Paid amount owing (Invoice #4053) to Stapl-EZ Inc. (Check #465)

Jun 15   Received a loan of $2,400 from the bank

Jun 18   Sold goods on account (Invoice #10022) to Richard Starkey, for office furniture for $3,000 (costing $2,000)

Jun 21   Purchased $4,000 worth of inventory from Noel's Inc. using Check #466

Jun 22   Paid amount owing (Invoice #124) to Building Services Inc. for repairs (Check #467)

Jun 25   Paid $175 to SKG Inc., for general expenses (Check #468)

Jun 26   Received a bill from Brick & Mortar Inc. (Invoice #404241) for $3,500 worth of inventory

Jun 28   Sold $5,000 worth of inventory (costing $3,700) on account to Pete Best (Invoice #10023)

Required

a) Record the transactions in the relevant cash receipts, sales, purchases, and cash payments journals.

Cash Receipts Journal									**Page 1**
Date	Account	PR	Cash (DR)	Sales (CR)	Accounts Receivable (CR)	Interest Revenue (CR)	Notes Payable (CR)	Other (CR)	COGS/ Merchandise Inventory (DR/CR)
	Total								

Sales Journal					Page 1
Date	Account	Invoice #	PR	Accounts Receivable/Sales (DR/CR)	COGS/ Merchandise Inventory (DR/CR)
	Total				

Purchases Journal							Page 1
Date	Account	Invoice #	PR	Repairs Expense (DR)	Office Supplies (DR)	Purchases (DR)	Accounts Payable (CR)
	Total						

Cash Payments Journal							Page 1
Date	Account	Check #	PR	Other (DR)	Purchases (DR)	Accounts Payable (DR)	Cash (CR)
	Total						

b) Post from the special journals to the accounts receivable subledger. At the end of the month, post the following opening subledger balances from the special journals to the general ledger controlling account.

- Bo Didley: $2,000 (DR)
- Richard Starkey: $1,000 (DR)
- Pete Best: $1,500 (DR)

Note that Lin-Z's accounts receivable records consist of only these three subledgers. Assume no entries were made directly to accounts receivable through the general journal. Reconcile the subledger to the controlling account at the end of the month.

Accounts Receivable Subsidiary Ledger
Bo Didley

Date	PR	DR	CR	Balance

Accounts Receivable Subsidiary Ledger
Richard Starkey

Date	PR	DR	CR	Balance

Accounts Receivable Subsidiary Ledger
Pete Best

Date	PR	DR	CR	Balance

Post to the general ledger.

Account: Accounts Receivable					GL No: 110
Date	Description	PR	DR	CR	Balance

Lin-Z
June 30, 2018
General Ledger

Lin-Z
Schedule of Accounts Receivable
June 30, 2018

c) Post from the special journals to the accounts payable subledger and then to the general ledger controlling account at the end of the month. Assume the following opening subledger balances.

- Stapl-EZ: $500 (CR)
- Building Services Inc: $750 (CR)
- Brick & Mortar Inc: $2,500 (CR)

Note that Lin-Z's accounts payable records consist of only these three subledgers. Assume no entries were made directly to accounts payable through the general journal. Reconcile the subledger to the controlling account at the end of the month.

	Accounts Payable Subsidiary Ledger Stapl-EZ Inc.			
Date	PR	DR	CR	Balance

	Accounts Payable Subsidiary Ledger Building Services Inc.			
Date	PR	DR	CR	Balance

	Accounts Payable Subsidiary Ledger Brick & Mortar Inc.			
Date	PR	DR	CR	Balance

Post to the general ledger.

Account: Accounts Payable					GL No: 200	
Date	Description	PR	DR	CR	Balance	

Lin-Z June 30, 2018 General Ledger	

Lin-Z Schedule of Accounts Payable June 30, 2018	

See Appendix I for solutions.

Appendix 9A: Special Journals and Periodic Inventory

Special journals and subledgers can also be used if the company uses the periodic inventory system instead of the perpetual inventory system. Most of the processes covered in Chapter 9 still apply. This includes posting totals at the end of the month to the appropriate general ledger accounts, immediately posting amounts in the Other column to the general ledger accounts, and updating the accounts receivable or accounts payable subledger accounts.

Figure 9A.1 illustrates the sales journal and cash receipts journal for a periodic inventory system using the same sample transactions from Chapter 9.

Sales Journal				Page 1
Date	Account	Invoice #	PR	Accounts Receivable/Sales (DR/CR)
Jan 5	Joe Blog	5125	✓	1,235
Jan 16	Furniture Retailers	5126	✓	956
Jan 31	Total			2,191
				(110/400)

Cash Receipts Journal								Page 3
Date	Account	PR	Cash (DR)	Sales Discount (DR)	Accounts Receivable (CR)	Sales (CR)	Notes Payable (CR)	Other (CR)
Jan 2	Cash Sale		350			350		
Jan 4	Hanlon, Capital	300	4,000					4,000
Jan 10	Joe Blog	✓	588	12	600			
Jan 22	Granger Bank		2,000				2,000	
Jan 31	Total		6,938	12	600	350	2,000	4,000
			(101)	(405)	(110)	(400)	(220)	(X)

FIGURE 9A.1

The journals used in a periodic inventory system are very similar to those used in a perpetual inventory system. The biggest difference is the absence of a column to record merchandise inventory and COGS.

Recall that the periodic inventory system does not update merchandise inventory or COGS until a physical count is performed at the end of the period. Therefore, the sales and cash receipts journals do not have this column.

Figure 9A.2 shows the purchases journal and cash payments journal for a periodic inventory system using the same sample transactions from Chapter 9.

	Purchases Journal							Page 6
Date	Account	Invoice #	Terms	PR	Purchases (DR)	Office Supplies (DR)	Other (DR)	Accounts Payable (CR)
Jan 3	Antonio's Electric	2089	3/15, n 30	✓	4,200			4,200
Jan 19	Maintenance Expense/Doug's Maintenance	6091		525/✓			80	80
Jan 31	Total				4,200		80	4,280
					(120)		(X)	(200)

	Cash Payments Journal							Page 4
Date	Account	Check #	PR	Accounts Payable (DR)	Other (DR)	Purchases (DR)	Purchase Discounts (CR)	Cash (CR)
Jan 6	Electro Parts	748				1,500		1,500
Jan 15	Hanlon, Withdrawals	749	310		500			500
Jan 18	Antonio's Electric	750	✓	4,200			126	4,074
Jan 31	Total			4,200	500	1,500	126	6,074
				(200)	(X)	(120)	(120)	(101)

FIGURE 9A.2

Similar to the sales and cash receipts journals, there is no column to record merchandise inventory or COGS, since they are only updated at the end of the period when a physical inventory count is made. Instead, both journals have a column to record purchases. The cash payments journal has an additional column to record purchase discounts.

In Summary

LO 4 **Prepare special journals under a periodic inventory system**

▸ Special journals using the periodic inventory system will not update inventory or COGS. The purchases and cash payments journal update purchases, and the cash payments journal also updates purchases discounts.

▸ Posting to the general ledger and subledger accounts is the same as in the perpetual inventory system.

 *Access **ameengage.com** for integrated resources including tutorials, practice exercises, the digital textbook and more.*

Review Exercise 9A-1

Lin-Z is an owner-operated office furniture retailer. Lin-Z uses the periodic inventory system. The following is a list of transactions for the month of June.

Jun 4   Received $4,000 from a cash sale to Gus Van Sand (sold office furniture costing $2,015)

Jun 5   Lin-Z received Invoice #4053 for $100 worth of supplies from Stapl-EZ Inc.

Jun 6   Received $480 from Bo Didley regarding outstanding accounts receivable

Jun 9   Received $2,160 for the cash sale of a lounge suite (costing $1,050) to Rita Patterson

Jun 9   Lin-Z received a bill from Building Services Inc. (Invoice #124) for $350 for repairs and maintenance of the office building

Jun 10   Received $25 in interest from a loan to Kurt Domino

Jun 12   Paid amount owing (Invoice #4053) to Stapl-EZ Inc. (Check #465)

Jun 15   Received a loan of $2,400 from the bank

Jun 18   Sold goods on account (Invoice #10022) to Richard Starkey, for office furniture for $3,000 (costing $2,000)

Jun 21   Purchased $4,000 worth of merchandise inventory from Noel's Inc. using Check #466

Jun 22   Paid amount owing (Invoice #124) to Building Services Inc. for repairs (Check #467)

Jun 25   Paid $175 to SKG Inc. for general expenses (Check #468)

Jun 26   Received a bill from Brick & Mortar Inc. (Invoice #404241) for $3,500 worth of merchandise inventory

Jun 28   Sold $5,000 worth of merchandise inventory (costing $3,700) on account to Pete Best (Invoice #10023)

Required

a) Record the transactions in the relevant cash receipts, sales, purchases and cash payments journals.

Cash Receipts Journal								Page 1
Date	Account	PR	Cash (DR)	Sales (CR)	Accounts Receiv-able (CR)	Interest Revenue (CR)	Notes Payable (CR)	Other (CR)
	Total							

Sales Journal				Page 1
Date	Account	Invoice #	PR	Accounts Receivable/ Sales (DR/CR)
	Total			

Purchases Journal							Page 1
Date	Account	Invoice #	PR	Repairs Expense (DR)	Office Supplies (DR)	Purchases (DR)	Accounts Payable (CR)
	Total						

Cash Payments Journal							Page 1
Date	Account	Check #	PR	Other (DR)	Purchases (DR)	Accounts Payable (DR)	Cash (CR)
	Total						

b) Post from the special journals to the accounts receivable subledger. At the end of the month, post from the special journals to the general ledger controlling account. Assume the following opening subledger balances.

- Bo Didley: $2,000 (DR)
- Richard Starkey: $1,000 (DR)
- Pete Best: $1,500 (DR)

Note that Lin-Z's accounts receivable records consist of only these three subledgers. Assume no entries were made directly to accounts receivable through the general journal. Reconcile the subledger to the controlling account at the end of the month.

Accounts Receivable Subsidiary Ledger Bo Didley					
Date	PR	DR	CR	Balance	

Accounts Receivable Subsidiary Ledger Richard Starkey					
Date	PR	DR	CR	Balance	

Accounts Receivable Subsidiary Ledger Pete Best					
Date	PR	DR	CR	Balance	

Post to the general ledger.

Account: Accounts Receivable					GL No: 110	
Date	Description	PR	DR	CR	Balance	

Lin-Z June 30, 2018 General Ledger	

Lin-Z Schedule of Accounts Receivable June 30, 2018	

c) Post from the special journals to the accounts payable subledger and then to the general ledger controlling account at the end of the month. Assume the following opening subledger balances.

- Stapl-EZ: $500 (CR)
- Building Services Inc: $750 (CR)
- Brick & Mortar Inc: $2,500 (CR)

Note that Lin-Z's accounts payable records consist of only these three subledgers. Assume no entries were made directly to accounts payable through the general journal. Reconcile the subledger to the controlling account at the end of the month.

Accounts Payable Subsidiary Ledger Stapl-EZ Inc.					
Date	PR	DR	CR	Balance	

Accounts Payable Subsidiary Ledger Building Services Inc.					
Date	PR	DR	CR	Balance	

Accounts Payable Subsidiary Ledger Brick & Mortar Inc.					
Date	PR	DR	CR	Balance	

Post to the general ledger.

Account: Accounts Payable					GL No: 200	
Date	Description	PR	DR	CR	Balance	

Lin-Z June 30, 2018 General Ledger	

Lin-Z Schedule of Accounts Payable June 30, 2018	

See Appendix I for solutions.

Notes

Chapter 10
Cash and Internal Controls

Learning Objectives

 *Access **ameengage.com** for integrated resources including tutorials, practice exercises, the digital textbook and more.*

331

Internal Controls

While cash controls are extremely important for any business, there are many control aspects pertaining to businesses that are not related to cash. Figure 10.1 shows examples of some controls you likely have in your personal life. You have locks on the doors and windows to your house or apartment. You have a PIN on your bank card or credit card. You have access to a bank statement that allows you to monitor all the deposits and withdrawals from your bank account. The locks, PIN and bank statement are all considered controls. Why do you have controls? You want to protect the things you own and make sure that all payments and transactions are authorized. Businesses also implement controls to protect what they have.

FIGURE 10.1

Definition of Internal Controls

Internal controls are the policies and procedures that a business uses to

- protect its assets
- encourage effectiveness and efficiency of operations
- ensure that the accounting records are accurate
- ensure adherence to company practices as well as compliance to laws and regulations

Internal controls are designed to

- align managers and employees with the objectives of the business
- safeguard assets against loss, misuse and theft
- prevent and detect fraud and error
- encourage good management
- allow appropriate action to be taken
- reduce exposure to risks
- ensure compliance with financial reporting standards, such as generally accepted accounting principles (GAAP)
- ensure accuracy and validity of the accounting records

Internal controls can include, but are not limited to, the following measures.

- cash controls
- budgetary controls
- credit controls
- working procedures
- inventory controls
- production processes
- hiring policies
- safety standards
- environmental regulations

The Sarbanes–Oxley Act

Chapter 3 discussed how, as a result of the financial scandals in the early 2000s, the US Congress passed the Sarbanes–Oxley Act (SOX) in 2002. SOX outlines specific requirements for the managers and auditors of any company whose stocks are publicly traded on a stock exchange. Its purpose is to maintain public confidence in the accounting practices and financial reporting of public companies by improving financial disclosure. However, it also emphasizes the importance of effective internal controls in all companies, regardless of their size.

Section 404 of SOX is a key mandate that requires a company's senior management and auditors to establish internal controls. Furthermore, the managers and auditors must assess and certify to the effectiveness of the internal controls, as well as the record-keeping and reporting practices based on those controls.

The following specific requirements are included under SOX.

- Auditors are subject to independent oversight by the Public Company Accounting Oversight Board (PCAOB).
- Auditors (i.e. auditing companies) must be external to, and independent from, the client (the audited company) in order to limit any conflict of interest.
- Auditors are restricted from providing other consulting services to the client company.
- A company's senior management (its corporate officers) must take responsibility for the accuracy and completeness of the financial reports.
- Severe penalties exist for non-compliance with SOX. Non-compliance includes the destruction, alteration or manipulation of financial records.

The requirements under SOX are very costly for a company to implement and maintain; however, the benefits are greater public confidence in the company's financial accounting and reporting.

Figure 10.2 shows a portion of Target Corporation's SOX internal control report from management, taken from its 2015 annual report to stockholders. This report must be included with the company's annual 10-K report that is filed with the Securities and Exchange Commission (SEC).

Report of Management of Internal Control over Financial Reporting

Our management is responsible for establishing and maintaining adequate internal control over financial reporting, as such term is defined in Exchange Act Rules 13a-15(f). Under the supervision and with the participation of our management, including our chief executive officer and chief financial officer, we assessed the effectiveness of our internal control over financial reporting as of January 30, 2016, based on the framework in *Internal Control—Integrated Framework (2013)*, issued by the Committee of Sponsoring Organizations of the Treadway Commission (2013 framework). Based on our assessment, we conclude that the Corporation's internal control over financial reporting is effective based on those criteria.

Our internal control over financial reporting as of January 30, 2016, has been audited by Ernst & Young LLP, the independent registered public accounting firm who has also audited our consolidated financial statements, as stated in their report which appears on the page.

Brain C. Cornell
Chairman and Chief Executive Officer
March 11, 2016

Catherine R. Smith
Executive Vice President and
Chief Financial Officer

FIGURE 10.2

Elements of Internal Control

The Sarbanes–Oxley Act emphasizes the need for internal controls to promote the accuracy and reliability of financial reports.

The **Committee of Sponsoring Organizations (COSO)** of the Treadway Commission (www.coso.org) provides a framework to help companies design and implement internal controls. This framework, known as the *Internal Control—Integrated Framework (2013)* provides tools and guidance on the five key **elements of internal control**, which are as follows.

- Control Environment—This refers to corporate management's overall attitude toward the importance of internal controls. The control environment takes into account the company's structural organization, its human resources policies and its management style.

- Risk Assessment—This refers to assessing the common risks that businesses encounter in day-to-day operations, such as competition, regulatory changes, changes in the economy and changing customer trends.
- Control Procedures—These are the activities that help the company stay on track to meet its goals and to safeguard its assets. Control procedures are a key element of internal control. They include such practices as
  - hiring competent and properly trained staff;
  - rotating staff duties, and ensuring that all employees take regular vacations (it is during such changes that any fraudulent behavior can often become evident);
  - separating responsibilities so that no single employee handles all related activities (e.g. one person receives the checks in the mail, another person records the payments in the accounting records, and another person deposits the checks in the bank, so that three checkpoints exist in the system);
  - implementing and maintaining effective security measures; and
  - separating the custody of assets from responsibilities for recordkeeping (e.g. an employee that handles cash should not also be responsible for the bookkeeping activities).
- Monitoring Activities—This refers to management's regular evaluation of business operations to identify any weaknesses and to improve the company's internal controls. It includes measures such as observing staff behavior, having internal auditors monitor day-to-day operations and using external auditors to perform regular reviews and audits of the financial records.
- Information and Communication—This is a key element that encompasses the other four key elements of internal control. Within the organization, management uses information about the control environment, risk assessment, control procedures and monitoring activities to guide the company's operations and ensure adherence and compliance to standards, laws and regulations. Management also evaluates external information such as economic conditions, competition, industry trends and other factors that could affect reporting and decision-making.

Limitations of Internal Control

The objectives of internal controls are to safeguard assets, encourage efficiency in operations, ensure accuracy of accounting records and encourage companies to comply with laws and regulations. Still, internal controls are not a guarantee against errors, omissions or intentional misuse of company resources. As you learned earlier in this section, there is a cost-benefit element since it can be very expensive to implement and maintain internal controls, and the costs may outweigh the expected benefits.

Policies and procedures are devised and applied by humans, and so there are potential limitations to internal control. The human element of internal control takes into account that errors can occur from things such as fatigue, carelessness, insufficient training or misjudgment. The human element also takes into account intentional breaches of procedure, or fraud. **Fraud** is defined as any illegal intentional act of deception that results in a financial benefit or gain. Fraud may not always be easy to identify because the intention is to hide the fraudulent act within normal business activities.

Fraudulent behavior can arise from opportunity (insufficient controls that enable someone to easily carry out fraud), from an attitude of rationalization (the perpetrator feels justified in carrying out fraud), or from personal stressors such as financial difficulties, family pressure or social pressure. One individual may carry out fraud or there may be collusion between two or more employees who agree to override the internal controls.

Warning Signs of Internal Control Problems

One of the key elements of internal control is the monitoring of activities, which refers to management's regular evaluation of business operations to identify any weaknesses in internal controls. Warning signs of internal control problems often become evident from several sources.

- by observing staff behavior—behaviors such as excessive alcohol or drug use, resistance to taking vacation, overly-close relationships with suppliers or service providers, a sudden change in lifestyle, or constantly borrowing money from fellow employees can be signs of potential internal control problems
- by detecting changes within the company's accounting system—behaviors such as slow or missing payments to suppliers, frequent or regular discrepancies in cash receipt records and bank deposits, missing documents, gaps or backlogs in the financial records, or a sudden increase in refunds to customers can all be signs of possible internal control problems

A properly designed internal control system can reduce the potential for loss due to fraud as well as help detect problems in their earliest stages, when corrective actions can be taken.

Implementing Internal Controls

Under an adequate system of internal controls, each business transaction is complete, accurate, authorized, real (i.e. it exists) and valid. In addition, when internal controls are present, errors in the system are automatically identified and corrected, duties are segregated and financial reports are timely.

Generally, internal controls can be classified as preventive (i.e. to stop an incident before it happens), or detective (i.e. to discover an incident after it happens). Obviously, it is better to prevent incidents than to discover them after they occur.

Consider the following situation. Michael purchased a family restaurant, which he managed himself. He bought supplies, paid bills, and opened and closed the restaurant himself each day. He was doing so well that he decided to open a second location. He promoted an employee, who had worked with him for the past three years, to manage the old location while he focused on setting up the new location.

Michael disliked anything to do with accounting. He operated a simple hands-on business and his bookkeeper updated the books each month to ensure that sales taxes and payroll were paid in full and on time. Other than these two functions, the bookkeeper relied on the accountant to complete the financial statements at the end of each year and complete Michael's annual tax return.

Michael's business was performing well, so Michael and his wife decided to take a vacation. Not long after they returned, Michael discovered that a payment he had issued a few days before he left to his supplier was returned by the bank because of insufficient funds in the business account. Michael was not only frustrated but also extremely embarrassed. He had to transfer money from his personal savings account to cover the shortfall in his business account and immediately started looking into what happened.

Since Michael knew very little about accounting, he contacted his accountant to investigate. An entire year had passed since the accountant had worked with Michael's financial statements, so the investigation was no easy task. The following issues were discovered.

1. Cash was only being deposited every few days, rather than daily, and the cash receipts did not match the cash register.

2. Payroll was considerably higher, relative to sales, than it had been in previous years. It appears that the manager was paying ghost employees—he was making payments to contract staff that did not actually exist.

3. His trusted manager was stealing food supplies and selling them for cash. This increased the food costs and decreased profits.

4. Some of the servers were "sweet-hearting" customers—meaning that friends and family were being given free meals or extras at no charge.

As a result of a lack of controls, poor bookkeeper oversight and his employees' fraudulent behavior, Michael nearly went bankrupt. He hired a new manager, and with the help of his accountant he implemented the following controls to prevent problems from happening again.

1. The new manager does not handle any sales and deposits the cash every day. Any discrepancies between the cash receipts and the register are investigated by the manager immediately.

2. The new manager is responsible for scheduling and keeping payroll costs to a certain percentage of sales.

3. The head chef at the restaurant counts food supplies at the beginning of each day and is responsible for ordering replacement food. The manager compares the daily inventory counts to the inventory used in the daily sales to ensure there are no anomalies.

4. A hiring package was created to collect personal information on new employees (such as name, address, SIN, bank account number). Michael has to approve all new hires and payroll is deposited directly into employees' bank accounts.

5. A computerized system is now used to record sales. All servers have their own pass code to record sales. Discounts or free meals must be approved by the manager, who then has to enter a special code to allow the discount or free meal.

6. Overall, the bookkeeper still updates the books every month, but also prepares financial statements on a monthly basis for Michael to examine.

As this example shows, when controls are not in place, organizations are vulnerable to fraudulent or harmful activities. Once Michael uncovered how theft and fraud were taking place, he was able to implement controls and policies to better monitor business activities and identify problems before they caused financial harm.

Cash Controls

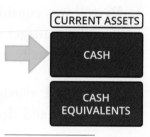

FIGURE 10.3

We will now turn our attention to controlling cash. As illustrated in Figure 10.3, the current assets section of the balance sheet starts with cash because it is the most liquid asset. **Cash** is defined as currency (paper money), coins, checks, money orders, and money on deposit in a bank account. Cash is essentially anything that a bank or other financial institution will accept for deposit in an account. A business receives cash for providing services or selling products to customers and uses that cash to purchase assets and pay for expenses. Without cash, a business will likely fail. Thus, it is important for a business to ensure that controls are in place to protect this valuable asset.

While it is important to have sufficient cash on hand, if a business earns more cash than it currently needs, leaving it in a checking account earns little return. Instead of having the cash sitting idle, some companies choose to invest their excess cash into highly liquid investments, known as **cash equivalents**, which are expected to generate a higher return. Cash equivalents are considered a short-term investment, usually shorter than three months (or 90 days). They are highly liquid and can be quickly converted into cash when needed. Therefore, they get recorded under cash in the current assets section of the balance sheet. Some examples of cash equivalents are treasury bills, money market funds, commercial paper and short-term government bonds. Investments, both short-term and long-term, are covered in Chapter 18.

Alternatively, a business may have less cash than it currently needs. This can create a negative balance in the bank account, which is known as a bank overdraft.

Control of Cash Receipts

Businesses usually receive cash from customers in two different ways.

- from cash sales—at the cash counter when the products or services are sold
- from credit sales—when a customer pays on account after an invoice has been issued for products or services; payment may be made by sending it in the mail, or by sending it electronically

We will look at each of these types of payment in more detail.

Cash Received from Cash Sales

In a retail sales environment where a cash register is used, proper internal controls should be used to safeguard cash and prevent its misuse.

1. At the beginning of a work shift, provide each cash register clerk with his or her own cash drawer with a predetermined amount of cash. This cash amount, known as a cash float, is used to make change for customers. The cash float normally consists of a range of bills and coins.

2. When a sale is made, the clerk keys the amount of the sale into the cash register. The amount is usually displayed so the customer can see it, to ensure that the clerk has entered the correct amount. Once the sales clerk has received the payment, the customer receives a printed cash register receipt showing the date, amount and method of payment.

3. At the end of the work shift, the cash register clerk and the manager or supervisor count the amount of cash in the cash drawer to verify that it equals the amount of the original cash float plus the cash sales for that shift.

4. The cash is taken to the cashier's department by the supervisor, and is placed in a safe. The manager or supervisor then sends the cash register receipts to the accounting department.

5. The cashier prepares a bank deposit slip in duplicate and sends (or takes) it, along with the cash, to deposit in the bank. In many companies where there is a considerable amount of cash involved, the deposit may be picked up and delivered to the bank by an armored vehicle service.

6. The accounting department uses the cash register receipts to prepare a summary report to record the cash sales for the day.

7. When the bank deposit is made, the bank clerk stamps one copy of the deposit slip to verify that the correct amount of cash has been received. The stamped deposit slip is returned to the company's accounting department, where it is verified against the amount recorded per the cash register receipts. It is at this point that any cash shortages can be immediately detected.

Cash Received in the Mail

Customers sometimes pay their bills by sending cash (usually checks or money orders) by mail. Most companies send an invoice that includes a remittance advice, a detachable part of the invoice that is returned along with the customer's payment. A remittance advice includes details such as the customer's account number, the amount of payment requested and the date the payment is due. The remittance advice is an important part of the internal controls that a business uses as part of the following process.

1. The employee who opens the mail compares the amount of payment with the amount on the remittance advice. If the business does not provide remittance advices with their invoices, the employee prepares one. This ensures that the amount actually received is immediately recorded upon receipt. The employee also stamps the back of the check or money order "For Deposit Only." As extra protection, the stamp often includes the name of the business as well as its bank account number.

2. The checks and money orders are taken to the cashier's department. The remittance advice and a summary report of payments received are delivered to the accounting department.

3. The cashier prepares a bank deposit slip in duplicate and sends (or takes) it, along with the checks and money orders, to deposit in the bank. If there is a considerable amount of money involved, the deposit may be picked up and delivered to the bank by an armored vehicle service.

4. The accounting department records the amount received and posts it to the customer's account.

5. When the bank deposit is made, the bank clerk stamps one copy of the deposit slip to verify that the correct amount of checks and money orders have been received. The stamped deposit slip is returned to the company's accounting department, where it is verified against the amount recorded per the accounting records. It is at this point that any cash shortages can be immediately detected.

As you learned in the section on internal controls, these control procedures reinforce the importance of the separation of duties between those who receive, record and deposit the cash. When these control procedures are consistently enforced it is much easier to detect fraud or misuse as soon as it occurs.

Cash Received by Electronic Funds Transfer

Many businesses accept payment on account using **electronic funds transfer (EFT)**, which is a method of sending payment online directly from the customer's bank account into the bank account of the supplier. EFT is a secure, inexpensive and fast method of paying bills for things such as internet services, cell phone plans and utilities. It is also convenient for the customer and the supplier because their respective financial institutions automatically prepare and send all required documentation. The customer can set up and authorize a regular monthly transfer so that the payment is made automatically on a specified date.

EFT provides a reliable internal control over cash payments because transactions are recorded accurately and the receipt is posted directly to the customer's account. It also avoids late payments, and eliminates the need for any intermediaries to handle cash. EFT is also particularly well suited for debit and credit card transactions, because the actual funds from debit or credit card sales are automatically and electronically deposited into the company's bank account.

Remote Deposit

Many financial institutions allow customers to deposit checks directly into their bank accounts remotely (such as from home) without having to physically deposit the check at a bank machine or bank branch. Such a deposit is known as a **remote deposit**. This is different from an online deposit, which requires that the customer later mail or physically deposit the check into the bank.

A remote deposit allows the customer to scan the image of the check, front and back, into a computer or handheld digital device. The images are then electronically transmitted to the bank via a special computer application and deposited directly into the customer's designated account. Both businesses and individuals can use remote deposit.

Remote deposit was introduced in the US in the mid-2000s under the *Check Clearing for the 21st Century Act (the Check 21 Act)*. The act enables the country's financial system to continue operating even if mobility is limited, such as in the case of a catastrophic event. However, it has also become a secure, convenient, time-saving and accurate way to conduct transactions. It reduces paperwork and travel time, and eliminates the risk of losing checks in transit, or having them entered incorrectly into the system. It also eliminates the longer waiting period for a check to clear the issuer's bank, because checks are both cashed and cleared electronically.

Cash Over and Short

Any cash that a business receives must be properly recorded and protected until it is deposited to the business' bank account. Occasionally, a cashier may make an error when making change, causing the count of cash and the actual amount to be different. If the difference is a large amount, the business should investigate the reason for the discrepancy.

For very small differences, the discrepancy is recorded in an account known as **cash over and short**. At the end of the accounting period, a debit balance in this account is reported as part of miscellaneous expenses on the income statement. A credit balance in the account is reported in the other income section of the income statement.

To illustrate how the cash over and short account is used, suppose a store had cash sales on May 25, 2018 of $1,425.56, but counted only $1,425.55 in the cash drawer. In this example, $0.01 is missing and is not worth the effort to track down. The difference is recorded in the cash over and short account, as shown in Figure 10.4.

JOURNAL			
Date	**Account Title and Explanation**	**Debit**	**Credit**
May 25	Cash Over and Short	0.01	
	Cash	1,425.55	
	Sales Revenue		1,425.56
	To record cash sales		

FIGURE 10.4

Control of Cash Payments

In a small owner-operated business, there may be only one person responsible for all aspects of managing the business, so separation of responsibility is not possible. The owner-operator is intimately involved with the day-to-day operations of the business, from buying and receiving inventory to the payment of suppliers. In larger businesses, however, it is possible that different employees handle these related functions. Internal controls can help a larger business ensure that cash is not misused and payments are properly issued to suppliers and creditors. Good internal controls for cash payments should aim at ensuring the following.

- all transactions that involve cash payments have been authorized
- cash payments take advantage of all allowable discounts (such as discounts for early payment)

Transactions that use the corporate account's debit and credit cards are also considered to be cash payments, and are subject to the same control policies. For example, all purchases using corporate debit and credit cards must be itemized and substantiated by original receipts with a description of the business purpose of each purchase. Similar to cash payments, there must be a segregation of duties. For example, the person who makes a purchase using the company's debit or credit card should be different from the person receiving and inspecting the goods, and there should be a third person approving the purchase.

Voucher System

One common internal control for cash payments is a voucher system. A **voucher system** is a set of control procedures that a business uses to authorize, record and disburse cash payments. The documentation used to authorize and record the cash payment is called a **voucher**. A voucher can be as official as a special form designed by the company to record all the necessary information, or as simple as an invoice that has been approved by a designated employee for payment.

A voucher is normally prepared using the input from a supplier's invoice, as well as any related purchase orders and receiving slips that accompany the goods received. After a voucher has been approved by the designated employee, it is recorded in the books and then eventually paid as a normal account payable. If the voucher system is an electronic one, all required information is entered directly into the system and a payment is issued on the specified due date. For a small business on a manual system, payment may be made by check. Many larger companies now use EFT to make payments. Once the payment has been made, the related voucher is filed in the company's accounts payable system.

Cash Payments by Electronic Funds Transfer

Many businesses opt for the security and convenience of paying vendors and creditors by EFT. You may be familiar with EFT from using an automated teller machine (ATM) to withdraw cash from your bank account. It is also very common for businesses to pay their employees by EFT. When employees hired, they are asked to provide their bank branch and account information. This authorizes the employer to transfer payment directly from the company's system into an employee's designated bank account. Cash payments by EFT are examples of payments made by direct deposit.

Pause & Reflect

Exercise 10-1

Stacy Dixon operates a convenience store and has two employees. One employee is the cashier and the other stocks the shelves with inventory. Stacy orders inventory, manages day-to-day operations, looks after bills and helps elsewhere as the need arises.

Since this is a small business, the cashier looks after most of the paperwork related to creating the float for the cash drawer, totaling the day's sales and preparing the deposit at the end of the day. Stacy will give a quick glance at the deposit slip and bring the deposit to the bank.

Some inventory is delivered and stocked by suppliers, such as soda and chips. These suppliers present an invoice to the cashier and are paid cash upon delivery from the cash drawer by the cashier.

Identify areas that can be improved with better controls.

_____

_____

_____

_____

_____

See Appendix I for solutions.

Bank Reconciliations

A **bank statement** is a record of all activity (the transactions) in a bank account for a given period, usually a month. The bank statement is provided to the account owner (the depositor) by the bank at the end of the period. The format of a bank statement varies by bank, but they all provide the same basic information. The statement shows the beginning balance for the period, all additions and deductions during the period, and the ending balance as of the statement date. A bank reconciliation is a simple internal control that compares, reconciles and explains the difference between a company's bank statement and its own cash accounting records. This is usually done at the end of a statement period.

To understand bank statements and bank reconciliations, we must first look at the records from the different perspectives of the bank and the company (the depositor). Figure 10.5 illustrates the differences. For the bank, the depositor's account balance represents a liability. This is because the money belongs to the depositor and the bank has an obligation to pay the balance to the depositor on demand. Therefore, in the bank's records, the depositor's account shows a credit balance. From the bank's point of view, any increase to the depositor's account requires a credit memo entry. Conversely, any decrease to the depositor's account requires a debit memo entry. From the depositor's perspective, a credit memo from the bank increases the asset cash on the depositor's books, and a debit memo from the bank decreases the asset cash on the depositor's books.

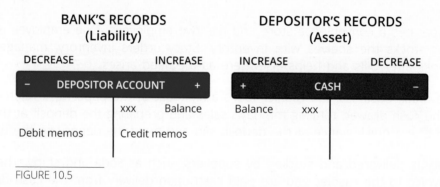

FIGURE 10.5

Typical reasons for the bank making debit entries (issuing debit memos) to the company's cash account include the following.

- loan interest charges
- repayment of a bank loan (note payable)
- bank charges
- payments by electronic funds transfer (EFT)
- automatic cash payments to other accounts
- non-sufficient funds (NSF) checks

Typical reasons for the bank making credit entries (issuing credit memos) to the depositor's cash account include the following.

- interest earned on the depositor's account
- payment from a customer deposited directly into the account
- deposits by electronic funds transfer (EFT)
- automatic cash deposits from other accounts
- proceeds from collection of notes receivable
- corrections of bank errors

The bank statement balance and the cash ledger balance at the end of the month may not be the same. The bank reconciliation is prepared to reconcile these two balances and ensure no errors have been made by either the bank or the company bookkeeper. If an error has been made, it must be corrected.

In the process of comparing the items in your records with the items shown on the bank statement, you may notice that some items shown correctly on the bank statement may not appear in your records. Similarly, some items shown correctly in your records may not appear on the bank statement.

As illustrated in Figure 10.6, a bank reconciliation compares the bank statement balance (shown on the left side of the bank reconciliation) and the company's actual bank account (i.e. cash) balance per its accounting records (shown on the right side of the bank reconciliation). The bank reconciliation adjusts both balances to the correct cash balance based on GAAP principles. To determine the correct cash balance, cash balance per bank statement must be adjusted in the bank reconciliation by adding and deducting transactions that are missing from the bank statement due to timing differences or errors.

Example Bank Reconciliation Month of October, 2018			
Cash balance per bank statement	$1,000	Cash balance per company books	$1,500

Add
    Debits to cash not included on bank statement (e.g. outstanding deposits, errors)
	800	Add
		    Credits to bank account not included in company books (e.g. notes receivable collected by bank)
			400

Deduct
    Credits to cash not included on bank statement (e.g. EFT payments, outstanding checks, errors)
	200	Deduct
		    Debits to bank account not included in company books (e.g. bank charges, NSF checks)
			300

Adjusted bank balance	$1,600	Adjusted book balance	$1,600

Balances must be equal

FIGURE 10.6

For example, if a company deposits checks worth $800 on October 31, the bank processes these checks at the beginning of November, and the deposits appear in the November bank statement, not in the October bank statement. However, because the checks were deposited in October, the $800 balance has to be added to the cash balance per bank statement in the bank reconciliation in October. Likewise, check payments in October that have not been processed by the bank and thus do not appear in the October bank statement have to be deducted from the cash balance per bank statement in the October bank reconciliation.

Conversely, cash balance per company books must be adjusted to reflect the items that appear on the bank statement but have not been recorded in the company's books, such as bank charges. After adjusting both cash balance per bank statement and cash balance per company books, these two adjusted balances must match because there can only be one correct cash balance at a specific point in time.

In the following sections, different scenarios will be presented illustrating how discrepancies in bank reconciliations can occur, and how to correct them. A complete bank reconciliation statement is presented at the end of the discussion.

Unrecorded Deposits from the Bank Statement

From time to time, the bank may automatically record a deposit in the company's bank account. The company would be unaware of the amount until it receives the bank statement. For example, compare HR Clothing Company's cash ledger entries to the company's bank statement, shown in Figure 10.7.

Company's Records

GENERAL LEDGER

Account: Cash				GL No:	101
Date	Description	DR	CR	Balance	
Jun 1	Opening Balance			5,000	DR
Jun 2	Check #1		300	4,700	DR
Jun 3	Check #2		500	4,200	DR
Jun 10	Check #3		700	3,500	DR

Bank's Records

Bank Statement				June 1–June 30, 2018
Date	Description	Withdrawal	Deposit	Balance
Jun 1	Opening Balance			5,000
Jun 2	Check #1	300		4,700
Jun 3	Check #2	500		4,200
Jun 10	Check #3	700		3,500
Jun 30	Interest		5	3,505

FIGURE 10.7

All of the checks have been recorded by the bank as well as by the company. However, notice that on June 30 the bank has recorded a $5 deposit to HR Clothing because of interest. Since the interest earned is correctly shown on the bank statement, it should also be recorded in the general ledger by debiting (increasing) cash and crediting (increasing) interest revenue.

Assume that HR Clothing's ledger balance is $3,500, and the bank statement for the month shows a balance of $3,505. The bank reconciliation for this is shown in Figure 10.8.

HR Clothing Company Bank Reconciliation June 30, 2018			
Cash balance per bank statement	$3,505	Cash balance per books	$3,500
		Add unrecorded deposit	
		Interest received June 30	5
Adjusted bank balance	$3,505	Adjusted book balance	$3,505

FIGURE 10.8

Since the adjusting amount is in the cash balance per books, or general ledger column, the general ledger balance must be corrected with an adjusting journal entry. The entry is shown in Figure 10.9. Notice that the journal entry includes interest revenue. On the Accounting Map, interest revenue is listed under other revenue on the income statement.

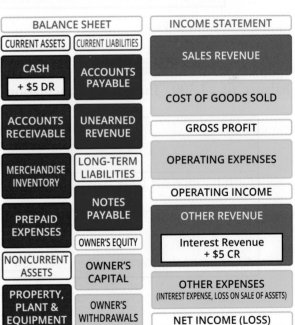

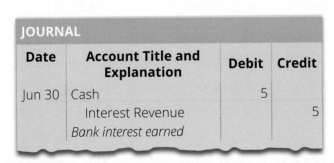

JOURNAL			
Date	Account Title and Explanation	Debit	Credit
Jun 30	Cash	5	
	Interest Revenue		5
	Bank interest earned		

FIGURE 10.9

Another type of deposit occurs when a note receivable is collected on behalf of the depositor. For example, in Figure 10.10, the bank has recorded the proceeds of a $1,000 note receivable from Models Inc. in HR Clothing's account on June 30. Compare HR Clothing's cash ledger entries to the company's bank statement.

Company's Records

GENERAL LEDGER

Account: Cash					GL No:	101
Date	Description	DR	CR	Balance		
Jun 1	Opening Balance			5,000	DR	
Jun 2	Check #1		300	4,700	DR	
Jun 3	Check #2		500	4,200	DR	
Jun 10	Check #3		700	3,500	DR	

Bank's Records

Bank Statement			June 1–June 30, 2018	
Date	Description	Withdrawal	Deposit	Balance
Jun 1	Opening Balance			5,000
Jun 2	Check #1	300		4,700
Jun 3	Check #2	500		4,200
Jun 10	Check #3	700		3,500
Jun 30	Proceeds of note receivable—Models Inc.		1,000	4,500

FIGURE 10.10

Assume that HR Clothing's ledger balance is $3,500 and the bank statement for the month shows a balance of $4,500. The bank reconciliation for this is shown in Figure 10.11.

HR Clothing Company Bank Reconciliation June 30, 2018			
Cash balance per bank statement	$4,500	Cash balance per books	$3,500
		Add unrecorded deposits	
		Note receivable collected June 30	1,000
Adjusted bank balance	$4,500	Adjusted book balance	$4,500

FIGURE 10.11

The adjusting amount is in the cash balance per books, or general ledger column. This means that the general ledger balance must be corrected with an adjusting journal entry. The entry is shown in Figure 10.12. The journal entry includes the receipt of the cash (a debit) and the corresponding decrease in notes receivable (a credit). For the sake of simplicity, we will disregard any interest earned on the note receivable as well as any bank charges for collection expense. On the Accounting Map, the transaction is shown in the two related balance sheet accounts.

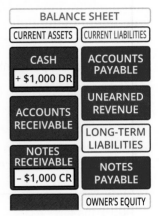

JOURNAL			
Date	Account Title and Explanation	Debit	Credit
Jun 30	Cash	1,000	
	Note Receivable—Models Inc.		1,000
	Proceeds of note receivable		

FIGURE 10.12

Unrecorded Charges from the Bank Statement

As with unrecorded deposits, there may be charges shown on the bank statement that are not yet recorded in the general ledger. Typical examples are a monthly bank charge for using account services, such as an ATM withdrawal, or an annual fee for a safe deposit box. Such charges should be adjusted in the ledger.

Figure 10.13 shows that HR Clothing has a cash ledger balance of $3,500. The bank statement shows a balance of $3,450. All checks are recorded in both the bank statement and the general ledger. Upon comparison, the bookkeeper of the company notices that the bank recorded bank charges of $50 on the last day of the month. This change must be updated in the general ledger.

GENERAL LEDGER

Account: Cash				GL No: 101	
Date	Description	DR	CR	Balance	
Jun 1	Opening Balance			5,000	DR
Jun 2	Check #1		300	4,700	DR
Jun 3	Check #2		500	4,200	DR
Jun 10	Check #3		700	3,500	DR

Bank Statement			June 1–June 30, 2018	
Date	Description	Withdrawal	Deposit	Balance
Jun 1	Opening Balance			5,000
Jun 2	Check #1	300		4,700
Jun 3	Check #2	500		4,200
Jun 10	Check #3	700		3,500
Jun 30	Bank Charges	50		3,450

FIGURE 10.13

The bank reconciliation for this item is shown in Figure 10.14.

HR Clothing Company Bank Reconciliation June 30, 2018			
Cash balance per bank statement	$3,450	Cash balance per books	$3,500
		Deduct unrecorded charges	
		Bank service charge	50
Adjusted bank balance	$3,450	Adjusted book balance	$3,450

FIGURE 10.14

The adjustment is shown in the cash balance per books, or general ledger column, so it must be updated with a journal entry as shown in Figure 10.15. The journal entry includes the account Bank Charges Expense. On the Accounting Map, bank charges are listed under other expenses on the income statement.

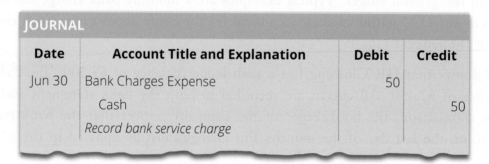

JOURNAL			
Date	Account Title and Explanation	Debit	Credit
Jun 30	Bank Charges Expense	50	
	Cash		50
	Record bank service charge		

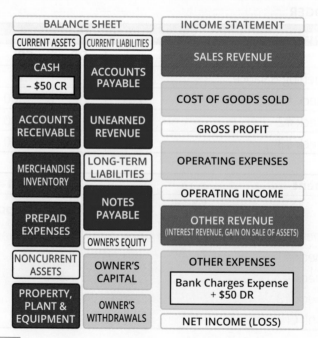

FIGURE 10.15

The journal entry is recorded by debiting (increasing) bank charges expense and crediting (decreasing) cash (an asset).

Another type of bank charge is for **non-sufficient funds (NSF) checks,** which are payments made to the company by a customer who does not have sufficient funds in his or her bank account to cover the amount of the check. If this is the case, the bank charges the customer an NSF fee. The company's bank also charges the company with an NSF fee. The fee is to cover the bank's administrative costs of dealing with the NSF check.

For example, HR Clothing receives a $400 check from a customer and deposits the check into the company's bank account on June 17. However, the bank cannot successfully collect the $400 from the customer's account because the customer does not have enough money in his account to support this withdrawal. The bank would return the check to the company and charge an additional service fee.

Figure 10.16 shows the deposit of the check in both the general ledger and bank statement, and the two additional transactions (withdrawing the NSF check and the NSF charge) in the bank statement.

GENERAL LEDGER

Account: Cash				GL No:	101	
Date	Description	DR	CR	Balance		
Jun 1	Opening Balance			5,000	DR	
Jun 2	Check #1		300	4,700	DR	
Jun 3	Check #2		500	4,200	DR	
Jun 10	Check #3		700	3,500	DR	
Jun 17	Deposit	400		3,900	DR	

Bank Statement				June 1–June 30, 2018
Date	Description	Withdrawal	Deposit	Balance
Jun 1	Opening Balance			5,000
Jun 2	Check #1	300		4,700
Jun 3	Check #2	500		4,200
Jun 10	Check #3	700		3,500
Jun 17	Deposit		400	3,900
Jun 19	NSF Check	400		3,500
Jun 19	NSF Charge	10		3,490

FIGURE 10.16

The bank reconciliation for this item is shown in Figure 10.17.

HR Clothing Company Bank Reconciliation June 30, 2018			
Cash balance per bank statement	$3,490	Cash balance per books	$3,900
		Deduct unrecorded charges	
		Check returned NSF	$400	
		Bank charges for NSF check	10	410
Adjusted bank balance	$3,490	Adjusted book balance	$3,490

FIGURE 10.17

This adjustment should also be recorded in the journal and updated in the ledger. Since an NSF check represents the amount of cash receipts unsuccessfully collected, this amount should be added to the company's Accounts Receivable account. In addition, the bank charge associated with the NSF check should also be recorded. The journal entries are shown in Figure 10.18.

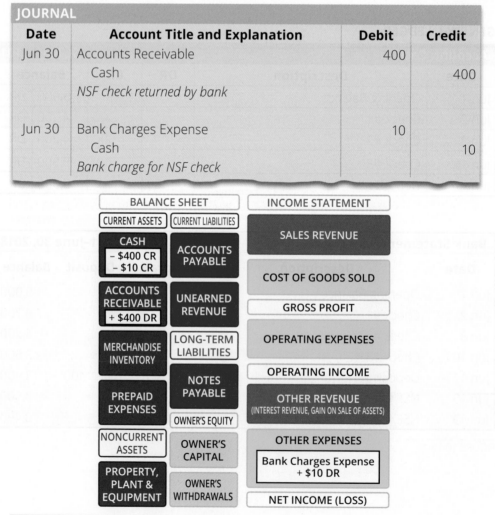

JOURNAL			
Date	Account Title and Explanation	Debit	Credit
Jun 30	Accounts Receivable	400	
	Cash		400
	NSF check returned by bank		
Jun 30	Bank Charges Expense	10	
	Cash		10
	Bank charge for NSF check		

FIGURE 10.18

HR Clothing was charged because the customer was unable to honor the check. The company will not want to pay the extra fee for the customer's error. HR Clothing will create a new invoice charging the customer an extra amount to cover the NSF fee. Some companies charge the exact amount of the bank's NSF fee, in this case $10. Other companies charge the customer a flat fee greater than the NSF charge to cover both the NSF fee and the administrative process of handling the NSF check.

IN THE REAL WORLD

 Non-sufficient funds checks are commonly known as bad checks or bounced checks. In our example, it is assumed that NSF checks occur because the issuer of the check does not have enough money in his or her own bank account to support the check. However, NSF checks can result from a variety of reasons including the following.

1. The issuer purposely cancels the check.
2. The account is frozen.
3. The account does not exist (i.e. the issuing party engaged in a fraudulent act).
4. The account is under investigation.

Outstanding Deposits

An outstanding deposit is one that has been recorded in the company's general ledger but not shown on the bank statement. These are also referred to as *deposits in transit*. This can occur when the company makes a deposit in the bank (perhaps using the night deposit box) on the last day of the month, but the bank does not record the deposit until the following business day—in the next month. The bank statement and the company's ledger account may appear as shown in Figure 10.19.

GENERAL LEDGER

Account: Cash				GL No:	101
Date	Description	DR	CR	Balance	
Jun 1	Opening Balance			5,000	DR
Jun 2	Check #1		300	4,700	DR
Jun 3	Check #2		500	4,200	DR
Jun 10	Check #3		700	3,500	DR
Jun 30	Deposit	1,000		4,500	DR

Bank Statement			June 1–June 30, 2018	
Date	Description	Withdrawal	Deposit	Balance
Jun 1	Opening Balance			5,000
Jun 2	Check #1	300		4,700
Jun 3	Check #2	500		4,200
Jun 10	Check #3	700		3,500

FIGURE 10.19

The balance on the bank statement is $3,500. The balance in the general ledger is $4,500. There was a deposit of $1,000 on June 30 that was not recorded by the bank. Since the balance is missing from the bank statement, it should be added to the bank balance as shown in Figure 10.20.

HR Clothing Company Bank Reconciliation June 30, 2018			
Cash balance per bank statement	$3,500	Cash balance per books	$4,500
Add outstanding deposit June 30	1,000		
Adjusted bank balance	$4,500	Adjusted book balance	$4,500

FIGURE 10.20

Notice that the reconciled balances are the same for the bank and the cash balance per books, or general ledger columns. There is no adjustment required in the ledger because the entry is only in the bank account column of the bank reconciliation worksheet. The outstanding deposit is a timing difference; it should appear on the bank statement that includes the following business day (in July). If the deposit does not show up within one or two business days, further investigation should be made to rule out theft or fraud.

Outstanding Checks

The next item to consider is outstanding checks. An outstanding check (issued by the company) has been recorded in the general ledger, but has not been recorded on the bank statement. This can happen because after the company records the check, it is mailed to the supplier. The supplier then records it in its books, prepares the deposit and takes it to the bank. The process can take several days, so a check mailed on June 29 may not appear on the bank statement until July 2 or 3.

Consider the following example. Six checks have been recorded in the ledger for the month of June, as shown in Figure 10.21. Three of the checks (Check #1, Check #2 and Check #3) appear on the bank statement. The checks that were written at the end of the month (Check #4, Check #5 and Check #6) have not yet been processed by the bank as of June 30.

GENERAL LEDGER

Account: Cash				GL No:	101	
Date	**Description**	**DR**	**CR**	**Balance**	
Jun 1	Opening Balance			5,000	DR
Jun 2	Check #1		300	4,700	DR
Jun 3	Check #2		500	4,200	DR
Jun 10	Check #3		700	3,500	DR
Jun 15	Deposit	1,000		4,500	DR
Jun 28	Check #4		400	4,100	DR
Jun 29	Check #5		800	3,300	DR
Jun 30	Check #6		700	2,600	DR

Bank Statement			June 1–June 30, 2018	
Date	**Description**	**Withdrawal**	**Deposit**	**Balance**
Jun 1	Opening Balance			5,000
Jun 2	Check #1	300		4,700
Jun 3	Check #2	500		4,200
Jun 10	Check #3	700		3,500
Jun 15	Deposit		1,000	4,500

FIGURE 10.21

To reconcile the ledger account with the bank statement, we must treat the checks as if the transaction had been completed by the bank (i.e. deduct the amounts from the bank record).

The bank reconciliation for outstanding checks is shown in Figure 10.22.

HR Clothing Company Bank Reconciliation June 30, 2018				
Cash balance per bank statement		$4,500	Cash balance per books	$2,600
Deduct outstanding checks				
Check #4 (June 28)	400			
Check #5 (June 29)	800			
Check #6 (June 30)	700	1,900		
Adjusted bank balance		$2,600	Adjusted book balance	$2,600

FIGURE 10.22

No adjustment is required in the ledger account because the checks are correctly recorded in the general ledger but have not been cashed by the bank. The bank will eventually include them on the bank statement.

Bank Errors

Although rare, it is possible that banks will make errors, such as charging the company incorrectly with a check belonging to another company. In this case, the company's ledger balance is correct and the bank must correct the error.

Consider the following example. When the bookkeeper for HR Clothing Company receives the bank statement and compares it with the company records, she notices that the bank processed a check for $800 on June 8, but the company has no knowledge of the check. This is shown in Figure 10.23.

GENERAL LEDGER

Account: Cash				GL No:	101	
Date	Description	DR	CR	Balance		
Jun 1	Opening Balance			5,000	DR	
Jun 2	Check #1		300	4,700	DR	
Jun 3	Check #2		500	4,200	DR	
Jun 10	Check #3		700	3,500	DR	

Bank Statement			June 1–June 30, 2018	
Date	Description	Withdrawal	Deposit	Balance
Jun 1	Opening Balance			5,000
Jun 2	Check #1	300		4,700
Jun 3	Check #2	500		4,200
Jun 8	Check #108	800		3,400
Jun 10	Check #3	700		2,700

FIGURE 10.23

At this point, the bookkeeper calls the bank and discovers that the check belongs to another bank client. The bank reconciliation for this item is shown in Figure 10.24.

HR Clothing Company **Bank Reconciliation** **June 30, 2018**			
Cash balance per bank statement	$2,700	Cash balance per books	$3,500
Add bank error			
Check incorrectly charged to account on June 8	800		
Adjusted bank balance	$3,500	Adjusted book balance	$3,500

FIGURE 10.24

Since the adjustment is in the bank column, it does not need to be adjusted in the company's books. The amount is the bank's error, not a timing difference, and the bank must correct the error by depositing funds back into HR Clothing Company's account. The company needs to follow up to ensure that the bank corrects the error.

An incorrect deposit may also appear on the bank statement, which would incorrectly overstate the bank balance. In that case, the bank reconciliation would show a deduction from the bank balance to correct the error. The company would follow up to ensure that the amount was deducted from its bank account.

Ledger Errors

It is possible for bookkeepers to make errors that appear in the company's records.

Consider the following example. Upon investigating the difference between the bank statement and the ledger, HR Clothing Company's bookkeeper discovers that Check #2 was recorded as $950 in the ledger and should have been recorded as $590. The bank cashed the correct amount of the check ($590), as shown in Figure 10.25.

GENERAL LEDGER

Account: Cash				GL No:	101	
Date	**Description**	**DR**	**CR**	**Balance**		
Jun 1	Opening Balance			5,000	DR
Jun 2	Check #1		300	4,700	DR
Jun 3	Check #2		950	3,750	DR
Jun 10	Check #3		700	3,050	DR

Bank Statement		June 1–June 30, 2018		
Date	**Description**	**Withdrawal**	**Deposit**	**Balance**
Jun 1	Opening Balance			5,000
Jun 2	Check #1	300		4,700
Jun 3	Check #2	590		4,110
Jun 10	Check #3	700		3,410

FIGURE 10.25

In this situation, the deduction from the general ledger was greater than the amount of the check. To correct this error, the difference between what was recorded and the amount deducted by the bank ($950 – $590 = $360) is added to the general ledger. The bank reconciliation is shown in Figure 10.26.

HR Clothing Company Bank Reconciliation June 30, 2018			
Cash balance per bank statement	$3,410	Cash balance per books	$3,050
		Add recording error on Check #2	360
Adjusted bank balance	$3,410	Adjusted book balance	$3,410

FIGURE 10.26

Because the correcting entry is in the cash balance per books, or general ledger column, an adjusting entry must be recorded in the journal. Assuming the original check was written to purchase inventory by using a perpetual method, the journal entry to correct the ledger is shown in Figure 10.27.

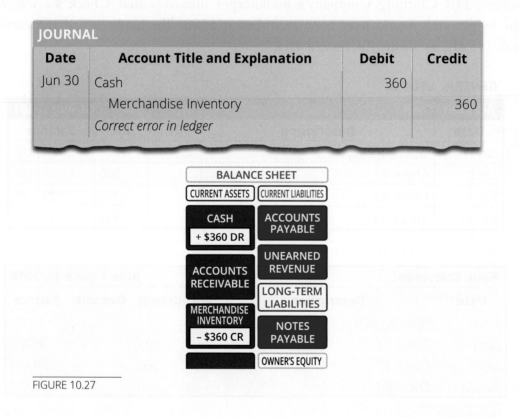

JOURNAL			
Date	Account Title and Explanation	Debit	Credit
Jun 30	Cash	360	
	Merchandise Inventory		360
	Correct error in ledger		

BALANCE SHEET

CURRENT ASSETS   CURRENT LIABILITIES

CASH
+ $360 DR

ACCOUNTS PAYABLE

ACCOUNTS RECEIVABLE

UNEARNED REVENUE

MERCHANDISE INVENTORY
– $360 CR

LONG-TERM LIABILITIES

NOTES PAYABLE

OWNER'S EQUITY

FIGURE 10.27

When an error is made by the bookkeeper, the bookkeeper must go back into the records to determine what the original entry was for. This determines which account will be used to offset the cash account. In our example, the payment was for inventory, so the merchandise inventory account is used. If the payment was to pay off an account, accounts payable would be used; if it was to pay this month's rent, rent expense would be used, and so on.

As with the previous examples, any discrepancy between the bank statement and the ledger record should be examined and then corrected with the appropriate entries.

Incorrect amounts in the ledger can be more or less than the amounts shown on the bank statement. Each error must be analyzed carefully for appropriate adjustments.

A CLOSER LOOK

In a computerized accounting system, errors in the ledger, such as the one described in Figure 10.25, are corrected using two entries instead of one. The first entry is a $950 debit to cash and a $950 credit to merchandise inventory. This entry reverses the original incorrect entry. The second entry is a $590 debit to merchandise inventory and a $590 credit to cash to record the correct amount of the June 3 check. The net result is the same as the single entry in the amount of $360 shown in Figure 10.27. Manual accounting systems may not use this method because it requires more entries, which means more room for error.

Bank Reconciliation Summary

Once all the items on a bank statement and the ledger have been matched up, only a few items should remain that need to be reconciled. Figure 10.28 summarizes how items will be treated on a bank reconciliation. Remember that all items that must be added to or subtracted from the ledger balance must be recorded in a journal entry.

Add to Ledger Balance*	Add to Bank Balance
• Interest earned • Direct deposit from customer • Receipts through EFT • Notes receivable collected • Bookkeeper error	• Outstanding deposits • Bank error
Subtract from Ledger Balance*	**Subtract from Bank Balance**
• Loan interest charges • Repayment of bank loan • Bank service charges • Payments through EFT • NSF checks • Bookkeeper error	• Outstanding checks • Bank error

*Must also create a journal entry to update the ledger balance.

FIGURE 10.28

To illustrate, we will complete a bank reconciliation with journal entries for HR Clothing for the month of October 2018. Before comparing the new items, it is always important to consider the outstanding items from the last period. We need to ensure these items have been cleared. The completed bank reconciliation from September is shown in Figure 10.29. There are three items in the bank column that are outstanding as of September 30, 2018: the deposit for $2,200 and checks #57 and #59. It is likely that these will clear the bank in October and must be compared to the October bank statement. If they appear on the bank statement, we will check the items on the September bank reconciliation and the October bank statement.

HR Clothing Company Bank Reconciliation September 30, 2018					
Cash balance per bank statement		$4,930	Cash balance per books		$7,360
Add outstanding deposit		✓2,200	Add EFT deposit		250
Deduct outstanding checks			Deduct charges		
Check #57	✓350		EFT—Rent	1,300	
Check #59	✓480	830	Bank service charge	10	1,310
Adjusted bank balance		$6,300	Adjusted book balance		$6,300

FIGURE 10.29

The cash ledger account and the bank statement for October are shown in Figure 10.30.

GENERAL LEDGER

Account: Cash				GL No: 101	
Date	Description	DR	CR	Balance	
Oct 1	Opening Balance			6,300	DR
Oct 2	Check #62		✓ 140	6,160	DR
Oct 4	Deposit M. Smith	✓ 200		6,360	DR
Oct 7	Check #63		570	5,790	DR
Oct 15	Check #64		820	4,970	DR
Oct 17	Deposit	✓ 1,200		6,170	DR
Oct 21	Check #65		✓ 540	5,630	DR
Oct 25	Check #66		320	5,310	DR
Oct 29	Check #67		410	4,900	DR
Oct 31	Deposit	900		5,800	DR

Bank Statement			October 1–October 31, 2018		
Date	Description	Withdrawal	Deposit	Balance
Oct 1	Opening Balance			4,930
Oct 1	EFT Rent	1,300		3,630
Oct 2	Deposit		✓ 2,200	5,830
Oct 4	Check #57	✓ 350		5,480
Oct 5	Deposit		✓ 200	5,680
Oct 6	NSF Check ⓐ	200		5,480
Oct 6	NSF Fee	15		5,465
Oct 8	Check #62	✓ 140		5,325
Oct 10	Check #59	✓ 480		4,845
Oct 15	EFT Deposit ⓑ		300	5,145
Oct 18	Deposit		✓ 1,200	6,345
Oct 23	Check #63 ⓒ	750		5,595
Oct 25	Check #65	✓ 540		5,055
Oct 31	Service Charge	10		5,045

ⓐ The NSF Check was from a customer as payment of her account.
ⓑ The EFT deposit was a customer paying his account.
ⓒ Check #63 was for advertising and was cashed for the correct amount by the bank.

FIGURE 10.30

The October bank statement is compared to the October general ledger and the September bank reconciliation. The green check marks, in Figures 10.29 and 10.30, indicate that the item on the October bank statement matches an item from the ledger or September's bank reconciliation. As shown in Figure 10.31, only the items on the October bank statement without a check mark need to be included on the bank reconciliation for October.

HR Clothing Company Bank Reconciliation October 31, 2018					
Cash balance per bank statement		$5,045	Cash balance per books		$5,800
Add outstanding deposit		900	Add EFT deposit		300
Deduct outstanding checks			Deduct charges		
Check #64	820		EFT—Rent	1,300	
Check #66	320		NSF Check	200	
Check #67	410	1,550	Bank charges for NSF Check	15	
			Bank service charge	10	
			Error on Check #63	180	1,705
Adjusted bank balance		$4,395	Adjusted book balance		$4,395

FIGURE 10.31

Once the bank is reconciled to the ledger, all items that increase or decrease the ledger balance must be recorded in the journal. The journal entries are shown in Figure 10.32.

JOURNAL			
Date	**Account Title and Explanation**	**Debit**	**Credit**
Oct 31	Cash	300	
	Accounts Receivable		300
	Collection from customer		
Oct 31	Rent Expense	1,300	
	Cash		1,300
	Payment for rent		
Oct 31	Accounts Receivable	200	
	Cash		200
	NSF check from customer		
Oct 31	Bank Charges Expense	15	
	Cash		15
	Record NSF fee		
Oct 31	Bank Charges Expense	10	
	Cash		10
	Record bank service charge		
Oct 31	Advertising Expense	180	
	Cash		180
	Correct error on check		

FIGURE 10.32

An alternative way to record the journal entries is to make compound journal entries to combine similar transactions. All transactions that credit cash can be combined into a single transaction. Each debited account is still listed, but there is a single credit to cash for $1,705.

Pause & Reflect

Exercise 10-2

Prescott Marketing received its bank statement for the month of September 2018. The accountant compared the bank statement to the general ledger cash account and made a list of the items that remained unchecked after the comparison. The accountant also included the ending balances of both the bank statement and the cash ledger account.

1. Balance of cash at September 30, 2018 is $9,260

2. Balance of the bank account at September 30, 2018 is $8,570

3. Deposit of $2,480 is unrecorded in the bank statement

4. Checks #287 for $650 and #291 for $870 do not appear on the bank statement

5. The bank showed an EFT deposit from a customer for $1,560

6. There was an NSF check from a customer for $1,240

7. Total service charges were $50

Prepare the bank reconciliation for the month of September 2018.

See Appendix I for solutions.

Petty Cash

At times, a business may require small amounts of cash to pay for petty (small) expenses, such as parking, postage stamps and courier fees. Instead of issuing a check each time, the business will set up a petty cash fund to pay for these small amounts in cash.

Petty cash is usually operated on what is known as an *imprest system*. An imprest system for petty cash ensures that spending is limited to the amount available in the petty cash fund. For example, if a petty cash fund starts with $100, that is the maximum amount that can be spent. When the amount spent approaches the $100 limit, the petty cash fund is replenished up to $100. In any case, the petty cash fund should always be replenished at the end of the accounting year so that expenses paid from petty cash are recorded in the year in which they were incurred.

Setting Up a Petty Cash Fund

1. **Designate one individual as the petty cash custodian.** There are many ways in which petty cash can be mishandled. Having one person responsible for the fund increases transparency and accountability. The petty cash custodian ensures that petty cash is properly safeguarded and disbursed for legitimate reasons and that an accurate record is maintained for all activities related to the fund.

2. **Establish the amount of the fund.** The petty cash custodian needs to determine the amount of the fund as well as the frequency with which it is replenished.

3. **Record the initial petty cash transaction.** The establishment of a petty cash fund requires one initial transaction. The journal entry is shown in Figure 10.33.

JOURNAL			
Date	**Account Title and Explanation**	**Debit**	**Credit**
Dec 10	Petty Cash	100	
	Cash		100
	To set up the petty cash fund		

CURRENT ASSETS

CASH

– $100 CR

PETTY CASH

+ $100 DR

FIGURE 10.33

4. **Require users of petty cash to provide receipts.** Any employee who requires petty cash must provide a receipt from the supplier indicating the amount of money spent and the reason for the purchase. The petty cash custodian will require the person to sign the receipt, indicating that the person has been reimbursed. Figure 10.34 shows a petty cash receipt.

RECEIVED IN PETTY CASH

Date: *December 13, 2018*

Description	Amount	
Office supplies	7	00
TOTAL	7	00

Received By

Rebecca McGillivray
Approved By

FIGURE 10.34

5. **Provide a summary of petty cash.** At the end of the period, which in this example is one week, the petty cash custodian prepares a summary that lists the details of the fund before it is reimbursed. The summary sheet is shown in Figure 10.35.

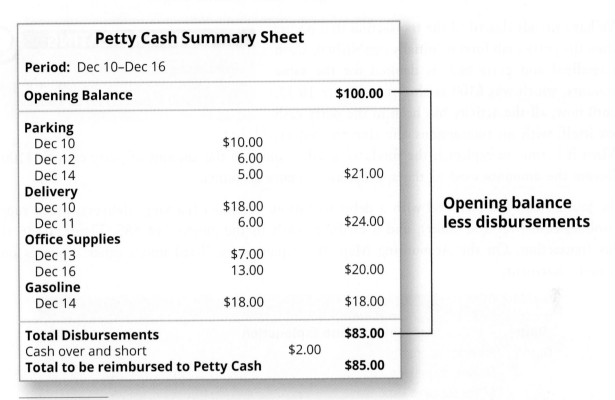

FIGURE 10.35

The petty cash summary should include a list of all the items, in groups, paid with the petty cash fund. Both subtotals and a grand total should be calculated. In this example the grand total comes to $83. The amount of cash remaining in the petty cash box should be equal to the opening balance minus the total spent, which in this case is $17 ($100 – $83).

6. **Reconcile any overage or shortage.** The petty cash custodian must take care of any amounts over or short in the petty cash box. This is done by making additions or subtractions to the account called Cash Over and Short. In our current example, there was only $15 in the petty cash box at the end of the week, meaning there was a $2 shortage. Such discrepancies can result from a miscount of coins or an overpayment during the period. The total disbursements recorded, along with any cash over or short, constitute the total amount to be reimbursed to petty cash to restore it to its original value of $100. In this case, the amount is $85.

7. **Present a summary slip to a supervisor.** The petty cash custodian presents the supervisor with a summary slip and all supporting vouchers. After reviewing these documents, the supervisor provides the petty cash custodian with a check to reimburse the petty cash fund. The receipts are stamped "paid" so that they cannot be reused.

8. **Reimburse the petty cash fund.** The petty cash custodian cashes the check (in this example the check is for $85) and replenishes the fund to its original amount ($100).

Posting Petty Cash to the General Ledger

We have examined the steps that an organization must take when establishing a petty cash fund. Now look at how this process affects the organization's general ledger.

We have already described the transaction that occurs when the petty cash fund is initially established. Cash is credited and petty cash is debited for the same amounts, which was $100 as shown in Figure 10.33. Until now, all the activity has been in the petty cash box itself, with no transactions affecting the ledger.

WORTH REPEATING

Transferring assets from one account (e.g. cash) to another account (e.g. petty cash) has no impact on owner's equity.

When it is time to replenish the fund, we need to increase the amount of petty cash to $100 and allocate the amounts used to the appropriate expense accounts.

The journal entry is recorded with a debit to various expenses (parking, delivery, office supplies, gasoline, cash over and short), and a credit to cash in the amount of $85. Figure 10.36 shows this transaction. On the Accounting Map, the expenses are listed under other expenses on the income statement.

JOURNAL			
Date	**Account Title and Explanation**	**Debit**	**Credit**
Dec 17	Parking Expense	21	
	Delivery Expense	24	
	Office Supplies Expense	20	
	Gasoline Expense	18	
	Cash Over and Short	2	
	Cash		85
	Replenish the petty cash fund		

FIGURE 10.36

The cash over and short account behaves like an expense account when there is a shortage. It will be debited in the journal entry. If there is an overage, the cash over and short account behaves like a revenue account. It will be credited in the journal entry.

No change is made to the amount of the petty cash ledger account when the reimbursement check is issued, and the reimbursed cash is placed in the petty cash box. You may think that the transaction should be recorded by debiting expenses and crediting petty cash, followed by a debit to petty cash and a credit to cash. However, in practice, when the bookkeeper records the check there is no change to the petty cash account.

It is important to note that the *only* time the petty cash account in the ledger is debited or credited is when the account is established or when the amount in the petty cash fund is increased or decreased.

Assume that on December 31, the manager decided to increase the petty cash fund to $150. The journal entry to record the $50 increase is shown in Figure 10.37.

JOURNAL			
Date	**Account Title and Explanation**	**Debit**	**Credit**
Dec 31	Petty Cash	50	
	Cash		50
	Increase the petty cash fund		

FIGURE 10.37

When the petty cash fund is increased, the petty cash account should be debited (increased) and the cash account should be credited (decreased).

Petty cash can also increase at the same time it is replenished. If on December 17 petty cash was replenished and increased at the same time, Figures 10.36 and 10.37 would be combined, meaning cash would be credited by a total of $135. The combined transaction is shown in Figure 10.38.

JOURNAL			
Date	**Account Title and Explanation**	**Debit**	**Credit**
Dec 17	Parking Expense	21	
	Delivery Expense	24	
	Office Supplies Expense	20	
	Gasoline Expense	18	
	Cash Over and Short	2	
	Petty Cash	50	
	Cash		135
	Replenish and increase petty cash		

FIGURE 10.38

A spreadsheet may be maintained listing the various expenses so that each month the general ledger can be updated with the correct allocation of expenses. An example is shown in Figure 10.39.

Description	Receipt #	Amount	Office	Travel	Meals	Marketing
HR Clothing **Petty Cash Expenses Paid** **July 2018**						
Photo Developing	1	$8.07				$8.07
Taxis	2	65.00		$65.00		
Meals	3	33.00			$33.00	
Batteries	4	11.00				11.00
Photocopying—brochures	5	23.32				23.32
Photocopying—general	6	3.05	$3.05			
Parking	7	1.87		1.87		
Parking	8	10.26		10.26		
Parking	9	3.00		3.00		
Parking	10	4.00		4.00		
Parking	11	6.50		6.50		
Parking	12	7.00		7.00		
Parking	13	6.00		6.00		
Parking	14	3.94		3.94		
Parking	15	1.00		1.00		
Gas	16	10.00		10.00		
Meals	17	8.10			8.10	
Travel	18	49.01		49.01		
TOTALS		**$254.12**	**$3.05**	**$167.58**	**$41.10**	**$42.39**

Cash will be credited with this amount.
(assuming no cash over/short).

= $254.12
Each of these amounts will be debited to the respective GL expense accounts.

FIGURE 10.39

Pause & Reflect

Exercise 10-3

Empire Architects created a petty cash fund on November 1, 2018 with $500. By November 15, there was only $56 left in the petty cash box. The petty cash custodian had the following receipts.

1. Postage, $58

2. Delivery expense, $94

3. Entertainment expense, $242

4. Maintenance, $46

Prepare the journal entry to establish the petty cash fund on November 1 and to replenish the petty cash fund on November 15.

JOURNAL			
Date	Account Title and Explanation	Debit	Credit

See Appendix I for solutions.

Petty Cash Controls

Using petty cash funds can be a convenient way to purchase small items. However, the funds also provide opportunities for abuse. It is therefore important to regulate the use of the petty cash fund to ensure that it is not mishandled. Here are some steps to ensure that petty cash is used appropriately.

1. **Establish guidelines.** The first step in ensuring that petty cash is used properly is to draw up a list of items that can be purchased with petty cash. Determine what purchases may be made with purchase orders, and then make a list of other types of regular purchases. The fund should be reserved strictly for small ("petty") expenses and not for items such as noncurrent assets or inventory, or for paying accounts payable and independent contractors.

2. **Maintain documentation.** It is difficult to keep accurate records unless you have a uniform documentation system. Establish an easy-to-use system and follow it consistently. The easiest way to do this is by keeping track of all receipts, whether they are register receipts or written invoices. Each receipt should have the date of purchase, the name of the vendor, a list of the items or services purchased, the price of each item and the total cost. Accurate recordkeeping also requires the following measures.

- the person who made the purchase signs the receipt

- all receipts are filed correctly so they can be checked for discrepancies

3. **Review the rules with employees.** If the regulations are not well known, abuse of the petty cash fund becomes easier. Keep everyone up-to-date and do not allow exceptions to the rules.

4. **One person should be responsible for petty cash—the petty cash custodian.** The appointment of one person to administer and be exclusively responsible for the fund limits the opportunities for mismanagement.

5. **Periodically count the petty cash fund.** Have one person independent from the petty cash custodian, such as a manager, count the fund with the custodian present. This discourages misuse of the funds and can detect shortages early.

This chapter discusses cash equivalents and petty cash as separate functions within a business. At this point, we can look at the impact of these two items and how they affect the balance sheet and its presentation. Figure 10.40 shows a partial balance sheet of Donatello's restaurant.

Donatello's Restaurant Balance Sheet As at December 31, 2018	
Assets	
Current Assets	
Cash and Cash Equivalents	
Bank Account—Checking	$13,220
Bank Account—Savings	4,700
Petty Cash Fund	300
Cash Equivalents	6,500
Total Cash and Cash Equivalents	24,720

FIGURE 10.40

Figure 10.40 shows the presentation of cash items shown in order of liquidity, with actual cash items listed before cash equivalents. Specifically, petty cash and cash equivalents are shown as separate line items.

In Summary

LO 1 **Describe and apply internal controls for a business**

▶ Controls are procedures and methods used to protect assets, monitor cash payments, ensure transactions are authorized and generally make sure the accounting records are accurate.

▶ Generally, internal controls can be classified as preventive (i.e. to stop an incident before it happens), or detective (i.e. to discover an incident after it happens).

LO 2 **Apply cash controls**

▶ Cash must be recorded immediately when it is received so it can be tracked from receipt to deposit in the business bank account.

▶ Cash should be stored in a secure place until it can be deposited to the business bank account.

▶ Regular bank deposits should be made to ensure a minimal amount of cash is kept on site.

▶ All payments must have an authorization. This includes checks as well as debit and credit cards.

▶ Cash payments should take advantage of payment discounts if they are offered.

▶ An account to track the cash over and short should be used. Any small discrepancies between expected cash and actual cash is recorded in this account.

LO 3 **Prepare a bank reconciliation and related journal entries**

▶ A bank reconciliation compares the bank statement to the cash ledger account to ensure no errors have been made.

▶ Amounts added or deducted by the bank that do not appear in the ledger must be added or deducted from the cash ledger balance. These amounts must also be recorded in the journal to update the cash ledger account.

▶ Amounts added or deducted by the business that do not appear in the bank statement must be added or deducted from the bank balance.

LO 4 **Prepare a petty cash fund and record related journal entries**

▶ A petty cash fund is used to pay for small, incidental expenses. A check is cashed and the money is kept by a petty cashier in a secure location.

▶ As cash is spent, receipts are placed in the petty cash box to explain why the cash was spent.

▶ A comparison of remaining cash and the total receipts may indicate a cash overage or shortage. The receipts and any over or short is recorded in a journal entry.

 *Access **ameengage.com** for integrated resources including tutorials, practice exercises, the digital textbook and more.*

Review Exercise 10-1

JP has been running his dry cleaning business, called Clean 4U, since he purchased it last year. It is a small business with eight employees. He has run into some difficulty with his business. His cash flow has declined every month, but he is as busy as last year.

Every single order has its own multiple-part receipt: the office gets a copy, the cash drawer gets a copy, and customers get a copy when they pay. Customers get a ticket stub as part of the receipt based on their first and last names only. The garments get tagged and matched to the receipt to get processed and returned with the receipt.

The company has only a cash drawer to accept cash payments. The drawer does not lock, and the cash cannot be locked away when the business is closed. Cash is deposited when large quantities of cash are on hand. The company uses a manual point-of-sale terminal to accept debit and credit payments and the counter clerk must enter the dollar amount before the customer can complete the transaction.

Recently, JP discovered a small pile of cash-drawer receipts in the garbage while he was cleaning the storefront. He knows that many of the customers are regulars and always pay cash. JP discovers that the counter clerk has been stealing cash when customers pay and throwing out the cash-drawer receipts. He has been committing fraud.

Required

a) What recommendations should be made with respect to cash controls for a company this size?

_____

_____

_____

_____

_____

_____

_____

_____

_____

b) What is the overall goal for cash controls?

_____

_____

_____

_____

c) What recommendations should be made for Clean 4U in general?

_____

_____

_____

_____

_____

_____

_____

_____

_____

_____

_____

_____

_____

_____

_____

_____

See Appendix I for solutions.

Review Exercise 10-2

The following is the general ledger and bank statement for Martin Furniture.

GENERAL LEDGER

Account: Cash				GL No:	101
Date	**Description**	**DR**	**CR**	**Balance**	
Jun 1	Opening Balance			3,100.50	DR
Jun 6	Check #541		900.50	2,200.00	DR
Jun 9	Reo's Interiors Inc.	1,925.00		4,125.00	DR
Jun 10	Check #543		1,600.00	2,525.00	DR
Jun 16	Check #542		400.00	2,125.00	DR
Jun 16	Check #256	2,000.00		4,125.00	DR
Jun 19	Check #544		110.00	4,015.00	DR
Jun 19	Check #545		500.00	3,515.00	DR
Jun 28	Eric Draven Enterprises	1,300.00		4,815.00	DR
Jun 30	Closing Balance			4,815.00	DR

Reserve Bank
146 Lineage Avenue, Springfield

Martin Furniture
234 Lakeview Drive
Springfield, Oregon

Date	Explanation	Withdrawal	Deposit	Balance
Jun 1	Balance Forward			3,100.50
Jun 8	Check #541	900.50		2,200.00
Jun 9	Deposit		1,925.00	4,125.00
Jun 10	Check #543	1,600.00		2,525.00
Jun 16	Deposit		2,000.00	4,525.00
Jun 16	Check #542	400.00		4,125.00
Jun 18	NSF Check #256	2,000.00		2,125.00
Jun 18	NSF Charge	6.00		2,119.00
Jun 21	Check #544	110.00		2,009.00
Jun 27	Interest on Bank Account		5.00	2,014.00
Jun 29	Service Charge	14.00		2,000.00
Jun 30	Ending Balance			2,000.00

Required

a) Reconcile the ledger and bank statement.

Martin Furniture **Bank Reconciliation** **June 30, 2018**					

b) Record the relevant transactions in the general journal.

JOURNAL			
Date	**Account Title and Explanation**	**Debit**	**Credit**

See Appendix I for solutions.

Review Exercise 10-3

On April 1, 2018, Clayton Company established a petty cash fund of $200.

During the month, the custodian placed the following receipts in the petty cash box.

Apr 6   Paid $40 for postage
Apr 8   Paid $20 to FedEx for delivery of a package
Apr 10   Paid $25 for travel expenses of employees on company business
Apr 14   Paid $8 for coffee and donuts for a client meeting
Apr 15   Paid $7 for paper for the photocopier

The custodian counted the fund on April 16 and found $95 in the petty cash box.

Required

a) Prepare the journal entry to record the establishment of the fund.

JOURNAL			
Date	Account Title and Explanation	Debit	Credit

b) Prepare the journal entry to record the reimbursement of the fund on April 16.

JOURNAL			
Date	Account Title and Explanation	Debit	Credit

See Appendix I for solutions.

Chapter 11
Accounting For Receivables

Learning Objectives

LO 1 **Explain the importance of accounts receivable**
- Accounts Receivable
- Credit Card Sales

LO 2 **Account for bad debt using the allowance method and the direct write off method**
- The Allowance Method
- The Direct Method

LO 3 **Estimate bad debt using the income statement and balance sheet approaches**
- The Income Statement Approach
- The Balance Sheet Approach

LO 4 **Record promissory notes and notes receivable**

LO 5 **Utilize reports, including the accounts receivable subledger, to manage accounts receivable information**
- The Accounts Receivable Subledger

- Alternative Presentation Formats

LO 6 **Calculate financial ratios pertaining to accounts receivable**
- Accounts Receivable Turnover Ratio
- Days' Sales Outstanding

LO 7 **Account for the disposal of receivables using factoring and pledging**
- Factoring Receivables
- Pledging Receivables

LO 8 **Apply internal controls relating to accounts receivable**
- Credit Approval
- Credit Information
- Credit Terms
- Credit Collection

LO 9 **Apply ethics relating to accounts receivable and notes receivable**

 *Access **ameengage.com** for integrated resources including tutorials, practice exercises, the digital textbook and more.*

Accounts Receivable: An Introduction

You have been introduced to many common assets and liabilities on the balance sheet. You know their definitions and how to record them as debits and credits. However, there are more complex accounts and processes that companies use to account for assets and liabilities. These topics will be covered in depth as we explore the balance sheet in more detail.

Accounts Receivable

On a company's balance sheet, presented below cash, is a category of current assets known as receivables, which are amounts due from other businesses, customers or financial institutions. As with other assets on the balance sheet, receivables are listed in order of liquidity, from most to least liquid. Common types of receivables are notes receivable, interest receivable, taxes receivable and accounts receivable. This chapter focuses on one of the largest of these amounts: accounts receivable.

Accounts receivable are amounts owing from customers for credit sales; that is, sales billed on account for goods and services. You may recall that when a sale is made on account, it is recorded as a debit to accounts receivable and a credit to sales. The debit to accounts receivable increases the asset of the company, while the credit to sales increases equity. When the customer pays the amount owed to the company, the company records the transaction as a debit to cash and a credit to accounts receivable. The remaining amount that has not been received from customers at the end of an accounting period is reported as accounts receivable on the balance sheet. Accounts receivable amounts are normally due to be paid within 30 or 60 days; hence, they are current assets.

When customers purchase a product or service from a company, they are issued an invoice that shows the **payment terms**, which are the conditions by which the vendor expects to be paid by the customer. Also known as credit terms (covered in Chapter 7), they specify the payment due date and any other conditions on that payment, such as the discount rate for early payment. For example, the term 2/10, n/30 means that the customer will get a 2% discount if payment is received within 10 days; otherwise, the full amount is due within 30 days. Payment terms ensure that the customer pays the invoice in a reasonable amount of time. They are an example of an internal control that a company uses to manage its assets (a concept discussed in Chapter 10).

Figure 11.1 highlights a portion of the current assets section of the classified balance sheet. Starting with cash and cash equivalents, as we move down the accounts, there is a decrease in liquidity. Accounts receivable is less liquid than cash because it takes some time for accounts receivable to be converted into cash through collection from customers. In addition, there is some risk that customers will not pay the amount they owe.

FIGURE 11.1

Nevertheless, accounts receivable is an integral part of doing business in a modern economy. Sales may be increased by allowing customers to pay at a later date since some customers may be unable to pay for their purchases immediately.

Many businesses have accounts receivable on their books, so it is important to know how to record and manage them. Throughout this chapter, we will look at how this is achieved.

Compared to cash and cash equivalents, accounts receivable requires more hands-on administration, because it involves debt collection and management of debtor information.

IN THE REAL WORLD

 One of the most prominent business trends of the past decade has been outsourcing, whereby one company hires another company to take over a certain business function, whether it is call center duties or specialized manufacturing capabilities.

The accounts receivable department has not escaped this outsourcing trend. Accounts receivable may represent only a small percentage of a company's total assets; yet the administrative burdens associated with this asset can be overwhelming, and a company's resources in dealing with it are often inadequate.

To handle this challenge, companies have the option of hiring firms that specialize in taking over the accounts receivable function. Such specialists possess the technical hardware, expertise and experience to maximize this important asset.

Outsourcing accounts receivable offers certain advantages, especially for companies that have a poor history of managing this asset. Outsourcing can

- improve a company's profitability by having the asset managed and controlled more efficiently;

- make a company's accounts receivable function more consistent, thereby making customers more satisfied;

- ensure financial reporting is more accurate; and

- allow a company to focus on its core business, while leaving some of the administrative duties to specialists.

Accounts receivable is an important asset for most companies. Ensuring they are collected is necessary for business success, whether the company itself handles this, or it is outsourced to a third party.

Administration of accounts receivable requires some basic information to be collected and managed. The information can include a debtor's company name, full address, contact information, what the company bought, the cost of the item(s) bought, delivery and payment or credit terms.

Employees need to spend a significant amount of time on the day-to-day administration of accounts receivable. Even a business with a relatively small number of customers has many transactions to record and manage on a daily basis. To reduce the amount of time spent on administering accounts receivable, many companies opt for the services of third-party credit card companies, as will be discussed next.

Credit Card Sales

Many businesses offer customers the choice to pay for goods and services using credit cards. Major credit cards such as VISA, MasterCard, and American Express are known as third-party credit cards, because they accept customer payments on behalf of other businesses in return for a service fee. When a customer pays for a purchase using a third-party credit card, the sale is recorded as a cash sale by the vendor. The actual funds from the credit card sale are automatically and electronically deposited into the vendor company's bank account by the third party, so the sale is not a receivable for the vendor. The credit card company bills the customer directly, shifting the risk of uncollectible debt to that credit card issuer. For the vendor, this a good method of internal control because it reduces the overall risk to its cash flow.

Many large retailers, such as Best Buy, Target, IKEA and some department stores, offer their own credit cards. These retailer-specific or store-issued credit cards are for use exclusively at that card issuer's physical and online stores. That is, a Target credit card can only be used at Target and not at any other retailer. However, these cards usually offer benefits, such as rewards points, product discounts and advance sales to cardholders. With store-issued credit cards, the retailer is responsible for approving and issuing credit as well as for collecting the customers' balances. Interest is charged to the customer on any unpaid balance after the payment due date. Store-issued credit cards carry a risk of uncollectible debt for the issuer, but by issuing cards that are specific to its store, the company hopes to promote customer loyalty.

Accounting for Bad Debt

There is an upside and a downside to selling goods and services to customers on credit. The upside is that selling on credit encourages people to buy. For the most part, people pay their bills when they are due. The downside is that there are inevitably customers who delay paying their bills. There are also customers who never pay their bills, resulting in an uncollectible account known as **bad debt**.

Bad debt is considered an operating expense, and must be recorded in a way that is consistent with GAAP principles. Because GAAP's expense recognition principle requires recording expenses during the same period in which the related revenue is generated, bad debt expense must be recorded during the same period in which credit sales are generated. Accurately determining the amount of bad debt in the same period as credit sales can be challenging, because it is sometimes difficult to know if a customer is just late with the payment or is unable to pay. Assumptions must be made in this regard because the records must reflect the company's current financial position as accurately as possible. GAAP provides two accounting methods for doubtful accounts and bad debt: (1) the allowance method, and (2) the direct write off method. The direct method can only be allowed in very specific circumstances, which is discussed later in this section.

The Allowance Method

To record bad debt in a way that satisfies expense recognition, accountants have created an account called **allowance for doubtful accounts (AFDA)**. It is located directly beneath accounts receivable on the Accounting Map, and is a contra account. Recall that a contra account is linked directly to another account and is used to decrease the account balance. In this case, the AFDA contra account is linked directly to accounts receivable. The AFDA account has a normal credit balance, unlike accounts receivable, which has a normal debit balance. The use of the AFDA account in recording bad debt is referred to as the allowance method of accounting for bad debt.

The **allowance method** estimates an amount that will be bad debt and records it in the books. Recording bad debt decreases the equity of the company by recognizing an expense on the income statement, and decreases assets by using the AFDA account. Bad debt is recorded in the same period in which revenue is generated in order to adhere to expense recognition.

For example, assume that at the end of 2018, Columbo Company has an outstanding accounts receivable balance of $100,000. After analyzing the existing data and the current economy, it is determined that $5,000 of the accounts receivable may not be collectable. However, since there is still a chance that Columbo will collect, the accounts are not removed from the accounts receivable list. Note that the amount estimated to be uncollectable is not based on one specific customer but is an overall estimate for the entire accounts receivable.

The accounts receivable account of $100,000 does not change. It remains as a debit on the balance sheet. Instead, the AFDA contra account is credited with $5,000, resulting in a net realizable value of $95,000. The net realizable value of accounts receivable is the amount of cash that the accounts receivable are likely to turn into; in other words, the accounts receivable balance net of the AFDA. For the debit side of this transaction, bad debt expense is increased by $5,000 and this amount is reported as an expense for the period on the income statement. The journal entry at the end of 2018 for this transaction is shown in Figure 11.2.

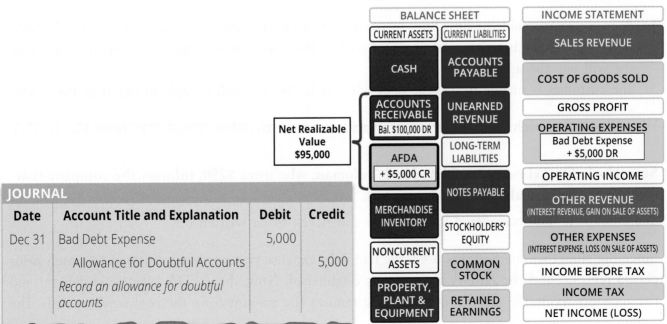

FIGURE 11.2

The net realizable value of accounts receivable is $95,000 and is presented on the balance sheet. The partial balance sheet for Columbo Company is shown in Figure 11.3.

Columbo Company Balance Sheet (partial) As at December 31, 2018		
Current Assets		
Cash		$12,500
Accounts Receivable	$100,000	
Allowance for Doubtful Accounts	(5,000)	
Net Accounts Receivable		95,000
Merchandise Inventory		210,000
Prepaid Insurance		12,000
Total Current Assets		329,500

FIGURE 11.3

The AFDA contra account allows for the possibility that some of the accounts receivable generated in the current period will not be collected. The debit to bad debt expense supports expense recognition since this amount is deducted as an expense in the period when the sale was recorded. Note that the company's equity decreases as a result of recognizing the bad debt expense.

A company must have a good reason to believe that some amounts will not be paid in order to justify the adjustments made to the assets and expenses. There should be some documentation to justify the amount of bad debt estimated. Such measures are warranted because estimates such as AFDA are easy targets for manipulation by management.

After companies anticipate bad debt by setting up the AFDA contra account, several scenarios can exist.

1. A customer is unable or unwilling to pay the debt and the amount is considered uncollectible.
2. After an account is written off as uncollectible, the customer informs the company that he or she will pay the amount.
3. The customer is unable to pay the debt when it is due, but will be able to pay it in the future.

We will examine each scenario as a continuation of the estimation of bad debt from Figure 11.3.

Scenario 1: On February 16, 2019, Jacob Soloman, who owes $250, informs the company that he is unable to pay his account.

The amount is now considered uncollectible and needs to be written off.

Since the allowance method was used, the bad debt expense was previously entered to match prior period revenue, and the AFDA account was established. Now, the AFDA account is debited and the accounts receivable account is credited to remove the amount from the company's records. The entry shown in Figure 11.5 has no impact on the company's equity, since the amount was already accounted for by the original debit to bad debt expense in 2018.

Usually, a company attempts to collect outstanding payments from a customer for many months. If it is unsuccessful, the company writes off that account. The journal entry is shown in Figure 11.4.

ACCOUNTS RECEIVABLE				
– $250 CR				

JOURNAL

Date	Account Title and Explanation	Debit	Credit
Feb 16	Allowance for Doubtful Accounts	250	
	Accounts Receivable—Jacob Soloman		250
	To write off account as uncollectible		

AFDA
– $250 DR

FIGURE 11.4

Scenario 2: Jacob Soloman is now able to pay his account (which was previously written off as uncollectible). He pays the amount on June 25, 2019.

Two journal entries must be made in this scenario. The first journal entry is to reinstate the customer's account balance (by reversing the entry in Figure 11.4). The second journal entry records the amount being paid. These journal entries are shown in Figures 11.5 and 11.6, respectively.

1. Reinstate the customer's account balance.

ACCOUNTS RECEIVABLE
+ $250 DR

JOURNAL

Date	Account Title and Explanation	Debit	Credit
Jun 25	Accounts Receivable—Jacob Soloman	250	
	Allowance for Doubtful Accounts		250
	To reinstate amount previously written off		

AFDA
+ $250 CR

FIGURE 11.5

2. Record receipt of payment on account.

CASH
+ $250 DR

JOURNAL

Date	Account Title and Explanation	Debit	Credit
Jun 25	Cash	250	
	Accounts Receivable—Jacob Soloman		250
	To record receipt of payment from customer		

ACCOUNTS RECEIVABLE
– $250 CR

FIGURE 11.6

Scenario 3: Jacob Soloman is unable to pay the debt by the due date, but will be able to pay in the future.

Even customers with a good credit record sometimes take time to settle their bills. After many months of attempting to collect from a customer, a company faces the decision of writing off the account as uncollectable. If the amount is written off, the transaction in scenario 1 is made. If the customer finally does pay, the two transactions in scenario 2 are made.

However, if it is relatively certain that the customer will pay eventually, the company can decide to take no action, except to periodically issue a reminder to the customer. The original amount in accounts receivable remains on the books and is credited when the account is finally paid. Another alternative is to convert the accounts receivable into a notes receivable, which is covered later in this chapter.

Pause & Reflect

Exercise 11-1

Using the allowance method, Sybil Company estimated $6,500 in bad debt for the year ending December 31, 2018. On March 5, 2019, its customer, Basil's Hotel, declared bankruptcy. Basil's Hotel owed $2,100, which was written off.

Prepare the journal entries for these two events. Assume that before any adjusting entries were made on December 31, 2018, AFDA has a zero balance.

JOURNAL			
Date	**Account Title and Explanation**	**Debit**	**Credit**

See Appendix I for solutions.

The Direct Method

When a sale is made on account, it is recorded as a debit to accounts receivable and a credit to sales revenue. The debit to accounts receivable increases the assets of the company, while the credit to sales increases equity and is recorded as sales revenue.

However, consider this example. A customer informs you on March 3 that her company, Sweet Treats, has filed for bankruptcy and is unable to pay its outstanding account balance of $5,000.

When it is determined that the bill will not be paid, the direct method requires a journal entry to increase (debit) bad debt expense and decrease (credit) accounts receivable. Note that the AFDA account is never used when the direct method is used, thus it never shows up in the journal entries. Figure 11.7 shows the required journal entry for this transaction.

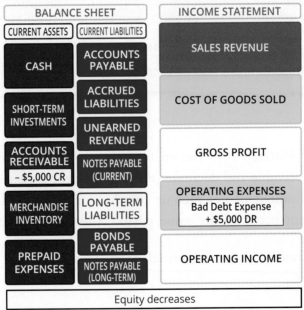

FIGURE 11.7

One drawback of using the direct method to write off bad debt is that it does not always satisfy expense recognition. Recall that expense recognition states that expenses must be recorded during the same period in which the related revenue is generated.

The write off should be made in the same accounting period in which the sale was recorded in order to properly recognize the expense; however, it is more likely to be made in a later period, which violates expense recognition. The write off under the direct method is usually made in later periods because it takes time to determine whether or not a customer will pay. For businesses that experience very few bad debts or if the dollar amount involved is considered immaterial to the business, the direct method may be used. In the above example, assume that the year-end balance of accounts receivable was $50 million and credit sales for the year were $650 million. The company experiences very few write offs and management considers $5,000 immaterial. In this case, using the direct method is acceptable.

The second drawback to using this method arises if the customer is able to repay the account *after* the account has been written off. For example, suppose the owner of Sweet Treats is able to pay her account of $5,000 on August 7, after the account has already been written off. Figure 11.8 shows the journal entries that are recorded if this occurs.

JOURNAL			
Date	**Account Title and Explanation**	**Debit**	**Credit**
Aug 7	Accounts Receivable—Sweet Treats	5,000	
	Bad Debt Expense		5,000
	To reinstate the customer's account		
Aug 7	Cash	5,000	
	Accounts Receivable—Sweet Treats		5,000
	To record receipt of payment on account		

FIGURE 11.8

The amount needs to be reinstated into the customer's account. This requires a journal entry to increase (debit) accounts receivable and decrease (credit) bad debt expense, which causes a reduction in expenses and an overstatement of net income for the current period. Unless the write off and the subsequent reinstatement occur in the same period, the expense recognition is violated.

After the amount is reinstated, a second journal entry is required to record the receipt of the payment from the customer.

Approaches to Estimate Bad Debt

 LO 3

Managing accounts receivable includes assessing how much of it will end up as bad debt. This has an impact on how a company reflects its financial position on a timely basis, and also has implications for meeting GAAP requirements. Business should always have good reasons for their treatment of bad debt and must maintain the necessary documentation to justify it.

We will examine two approaches for estimating bad debt under the allowance method: the income statement approach and the balance sheet approach.

The Income Statement Approach

The **income statement approach**, or the percentage of sales method, uses credit sales from the income statement as a basis to predict future bad debt. More specifically, the current year's bad debt expense is calculated by multiplying credit sales by a percentage. Different companies use different percentages based on their own collection history and credit policy.

For example, if the collection history of a company suggests that 1% of credit sales will result in bad debt, that rate is used to estimate the portion of each period's sales that will not be collectible.

Total credit sales for Columbo Company in 2018 amounted to $1,000,000, of which $200,000 is currently owed by customers. On the basis of historical sales, 1% of credit sales is expected to be uncollectible, which is $10,000 ($1,000,000 × 1%). The bad debt expense for the period is shown in Figure 11.9.

JOURNAL			
Date	**Account Title and Explanation**	**Debit**	**Credit**
Dec 31	Bad Debt Expense	10,000	
	Allowance for Doubtful Accounts		10,000
	To record bad debt expense based on percentage of credit sales		

FIGURE 11.9

As previously discussed, the accounts receivable account, or controlling account, maintains the same debit amount, which in this case is $200,000. The $10,000 that is expected to be uncollectible is added to the current balance in the AFDA account. Assuming that the AFDA starts with a zero balance, it now has a $10,000 credit balance. This leaves a net realizable value of $190,000 in accounts receivable. The AFDA credit balance of $10,000 represents a decrease in the company's assets. The income statement includes a debit balance of $10,000 for bad debt expense. This is shown in Figure 11.10.

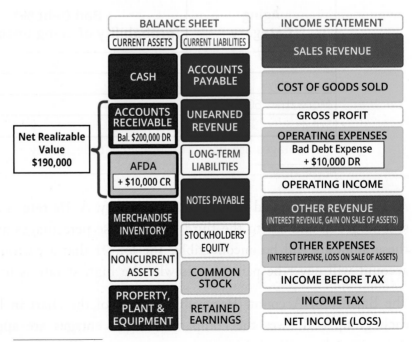

FIGURE 11.10

This approach is called the income statement approach because bad debt expense is calculated based on the credit sales figure from the income statement. Nevertheless, adjustments must be made to both the income statement and the balance sheet accounts when accounting for bad debt expense.

The Balance Sheet Approach

Under the **balance sheet approach**, a company can calculate allowance for bad debt using either the percentage of total accounts receivable method or the aging method. The **percentage of total accounts receivable method**, as the name implies, uses a percentage of receivables to estimate bad debt. The percentage is applied to the ending accounts receivable balance. For example, if the accounts receivable balance at the end of the period is $200,000, and the company estimates, based on its experience, that 4% of total accounts receivable will become uncollectible, the allowance for bad debt in this period is $8,000 ($200,000 × 0.04). Therefore, the AFDA account must be adjusted to have a credit balance of $8,000. We will show entries to adjust the AFDA balance later in this section.

Under the **aging method**, percentages are applied to groupings based on the age of outstanding accounts receivable amounts. We will use an example to illustrate this procedure.

The chart in Figure 11.11 contains three groups of customers and their outstanding balances on December 31, 2018.

1. Those who have not paid within 30 days
2. Those who have not paid for 31 to 60 days
3. Those who have not paid for more than 60 days

Aging Category	Bad Debt %* (probability of being uncollectible)	Balance of Accounts Receivable
30 days	2%	$80,000
31–60 days	3%	90,000
More than 60 days	5%	30,000
Total		$200,000

*Percentages are based on historical collectability.

FIGURE 11.11

A percentage is applied to each aging category. A 2% rate is applied to the first group, 3% to the second group and 5% to the third group. These percentages are the probability, or likelihood, that these amounts will be uncollectible. The longer that a customer takes to pay, the more likely the account will never be paid; that is why the highest rate is used for the third group.

The Balance of Accounts Receivable column of the chart in Figure 11.12 shows the amount that each group still owes the company. The percentages are applied to these amounts to calculate the expected total bad debt per customer group. These amounts are then added to give the total amount of estimated bad debt.

Aging Category	Bad Debt % (probability of being uncollectible)	Balance of Accounts Receivable	Estimated Bad Debt*
30 days	2%	$80,000	$1,600
31–60 days	3%	90,000	2,700
More than 60 days	5%	30,000	1,500
Total		$200,000	$5,800

*Balance of Accounts Receivable x Bad Debt %

FIGURE 11.12

In this example, $5,800 of the gross accounts receivable balance of $200,000 is estimated to be uncollectible. The $5,800 of estimated bad debt becomes the ending balance of AFDA for the period regardless of AFDA's existing balance or which method was used: the percentage of total accounts receivable method or the aging method. Under the balance sheet approach, the adjustments required could be grouped into three different scenarios based on AFDA having a credit, zero or debit balance. These scenarios are presented through the following examples.

Scenario 1: AFDA has a credit balance of $3,000.

If there is already a credit balance in the AFDA account, it needs to be subtracted from the $5,800 total to give us the bad debt expense for the period. A credit balance indicates the company has overestimated bad debt expense in the past. In this example, the AFDA account already has a credit balance of $3,000. Subtracting that from the calculated amount of $5,800 leaves us with an adjustment in the AFDA account of $2,800. In effect, this "tops up" the AFDA account, because we are adjusting it to reflect the total amount of bad debt expected. Figure 11.13 shows the journal entry for this transaction and Figure 11.14 shows its impact on the balance sheet and income statement.

Scenario 1

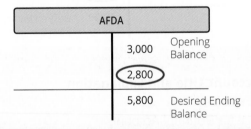

JOURNAL			
Date	**Account Title and Explanation**	**Debit**	**Credit**
Dec 31	Bad Debt Expense	2,800	
	Allowance for Doubtful Accounts		2,800
	To adjust the AFDA account to the correct balance		

FIGURE 11.13

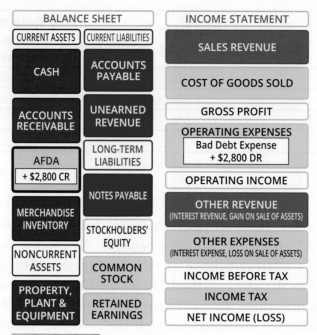

FIGURE 11.14

Scenario 2: AFDA has a balance of zero.

If AFDA has a zero balance, then the amount calculated as uncollectible becomes the amount of the adjustment. In our example, the amount of the credit to the AFDA account is $5,800. Figure 11.15 shows the journal entry for this transaction.

Scenario 2

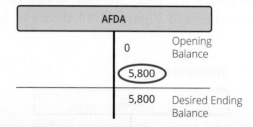

JOURNAL			
Date	**Account Title and Explanation**	**Debit**	**Credit**
Dec 31	Bad Debt Expense	5,800	
	Allowance for Doubtful Accounts		5,800
	To adjust the AFDA account to the correct balance		

FIGURE 11.15

Scenario 3: AFDA has a debit balance of $1,000.

If there is already a debit balance in the AFDA account, it is added to the $5,800 total to give us the bad debt expense for the period. A debit balance indicates the company has underestimated bad debt expense in the past. In this example, the AFDA account already has a debit balance of $1,000. Adding that to the calculated amount of $5,800 leaves us with an adjustment in the AFDA account of $6,800. Figure 11.16 shows the journal entry for this transaction.

Scenario 3

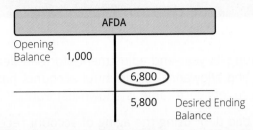

AFDA		
Opening Balance 1,000		
	6,800	
	5,800	Desired Ending Balance

JOURNAL

Date	Account Title and Explanation	Debit	Credit
Dec 31	Bad Debt Expense	6,800	
	Allowance for Doubtful Accounts		6,800
	To adjust the AFDA account to the correct balance		

FIGURE 11.16

Note that the net adjustment of accounts receivable adheres to conservatism, which requires assets to be valued at the lower amount of possible alternatives and, as a result, reflects a reduced net income for the period. This approach allows the business to make decisions based on figures that do not overstate assets, net income or the financial position of the company.

Rather than using only the income statement approach or only the balance sheet approach, a company can use a mix of procedures. The mix of procedures involves the initial use of the income statement approach and later adjusting AFDA using the balance sheet approach. Specifically, in the initial stage, bad debt is calculated as a percentage of sales while ignoring the existing AFDA balance. At the end of the period, accounts receivable is reviewed to check the appropriateness of the AFDA balance, and adjustments to the AFDA balance are made as required.

A CLOSER LOOK

For the income statement approach, the calculated amount is recorded as the bad debt expense regardless of what the existing balance of AFDA is. The calculated amount for the balance sheet approach is the ending balance of AFDA and not necessarily the amount of adjustment required.

Under the income statement approach, after the amount based on a percentage of credit sales is calculated, it is debited to bad debt expense and credited to AFDA. The expense is based on sales to appropriately match the bad debt expense with the credit sales of the period. The total amount of the allowance is essentially ignored. If the percentage of credit sales used realistically reflects the actual amount of bad debt experienced, the allowance account reflects a reasonable balance.

If the actual bad debt experienced is materially lower than the estimate (based on a percentage of sales), the allowance for doubtful accounts may build to an unrealistically large amount. This would occur because the increase in AFDA based on the estimate of bad debt is not consistent with a reduction from actual bad debt write offs.

If the allowance account is becoming unusually large, you could forego recording additional bad debt expenses (and the corresponding credit to the allowance account), until debits (i.e. actual bad debt write offs) reduce the allowance account to a reasonable balance. What is a reasonable balance? As with many items in accounting, the answer is based on professional judgment.

Pause & Reflect

Exercise 11-2

Manuel Enterprise is preparing its year-end adjustments for bad debt. Accounts receivable has a debit balance of $400,000 and allowance for doubtful accounts has a credit balance of $3,400. The aging breakdown of accounts receivable is shown below.

a) Calculate the esimated bad debt using the aging of account receivable method and complete the final column of the table.

Aging Category	Bad Debt %	Balance of Accounts Receivable	Estimated Bad Debt
30 days	1%	$200,000	
31-60 days	5%	120,000	
More than 60 days	10%	80,000	
Total		$400,000	

b) Prepare the journal entry to record the bad debt expense on December 31, 2018.

JOURNAL			
Date	Account Title and Explanation	Debit	Credit

See Appendix I for solutions.

The Promissory Note and Notes Receivable

There is another way to look at accounts receivable. In a sense, the transaction is much like a loan. Since the customers do not initially pay for the goods or services they receive from the company, the selling company is in effect lending customers money until the loan is due. However, this loan usually does not come with interest within the credit period.

A **promissory note**, or **note receivable,** makes an account receivable resemble a formal loan by adding precise terms of repayment, to which the customer adds her signature. The customer (the borrower) is known as the **maker** of the note, because she is the one making a promise to pay. The company (the lender) is known as the **payee**, because it is the one to whom the note is payable. Figure 11.17 shows an example of a promissory note. The face of a promissory note usually contains the information about the maker, the payee, the issuance date, the due date, the principal amount and the interest rate. The term of the note can be calculated as the duration between the issuance date and the maturity date. The term is sometimes specified on the face of the note in addition to the issuance date and the maturity date.

PROMISSORY NOTE

_____, 20____

At any time after the above date, the undersigned promises to pay the lender the sum of $_____ with _____ % interest until _____ 20___.
The makers, endorsers, and guarantors hereof waive presentment, demand of payment, notice of nonpayment, protest, notice of protest, and all exemptions.

_____   _____
NAME OF LENDER   NAME OF BORROWER

_____   _____
LENDER'S SIGNATURE   BORROWER'S SIGNATURE

FIGURE 11.17

If a customer is overdue on his account, the company may request that the customer sign a promissory note to formalize the arrangements of the debt repayment, similar to how a formal loan specifies its terms of repayment. Both a loan and a promissory note can set terms that include naming the parties to the document, the amount to be paid (the *face value*), the rate of interest to be paid on the note, and the *maturity date* or *due date* when the face amount of the note (plus interest) is to be paid.

A promissory note is used to formalize an accounts receivable item and also to extend unusual credit terms to a specific customer. For example, an agreement may involve lengthening the terms of repayment to more than one year. In addition, the note can be used to extend credit to a customer with no formal credit history. The stronger legal claim associated with a note provides greater protection for the selling company when dealing with uncertain or riskier customer accounts. Provided that the seller is confident the customer will eventually pay the note, there should be no objection to issuing the note.

Notes are often issued on a date other than the first or last day of the month. They can also have maturity dates that are less than a full year, such as 30, 60 or 90 days. In such cases, special calculations determine both the note's maturity date and the interest amount to be paid.

For example, assume a promissory note between two parties is issued on January 15, 2018. The face value of the note is $1,000 and the annual interest rate is 8%. The term of the note is 60 days. First, we will determine the maturity date.

The note has a maturity date of March 16, 2018, which is calculated as follows.

Days in January	31
Deduct: Note issuance date	15
Days remaining in January	16
Add: Days in February	28
Add: Days in March until due date	16
Term of note (in days)	60

Next, we can calculate the interest amount on the note.

The formula to calculate interest is shown in Figure 11.18.

$$\text{Interest} = \text{Face Amount of Note} \times \text{Annual Interest Rate} \times \left(\frac{\text{Term of Note}}{365 \text{ days}} \right)$$

FIGURE 11.18

The note's interest rate is given as 8%, stated on an *annual* basis, but the term of the note is stated in *days* (60). Therefore, the interest needs to be adjusted for the partial year. Interest is calculated as shown here.

$$\text{Interest} = \$1,000 \times 8\% \times \left(\frac{60}{365} \right)$$

$$= \$13.15$$

Therefore, $13.15 in interest, along with the principal or face amount of the note ($1,000), is due on March 16, 2018.

To keep things simple, we will use a maturity date exactly one year away, and use the number of months instead of the number of days to calculate accrued interest in the following example.

On April 1, 2018, Kay Alonso has $1,000 of outstanding accounts receivable with Columbo Company. Columbo's year end is October 31. Kay cannot pay the amount immediately, but is willing to sign a promissory note. The interest is 6% per annum, to be collected when the note is due. Kay promises to pay on April 1, 2019. The entry to record the conversion of the accounts receivable to a note receivable on April 1, 2018 is shown in Figure 11.19.

| JOURNAL | | | |
Date	Account Title and Explanation	Debit	Credit
Apr 1	Notes Receivable	1,000	
	Accounts Receivable		1,000
	Converted accounts receivable to a note receivable		

ACCOUNTS RECEIVABLE
– $1,000 CR

NOTES RECEIVABLE
+ $1,000 DR

FIGURE 11.19

On October 31, when Columbo Company prepares its financial statements, it needs to accrue the interest earned from Kay. The interest is 6% of $1,000 that has been earned from April 1 to October 31, 2018, which is seven months ($1,000 × 6% × 7/12 = $35). Notice from Figure 11.20 that the interest earned is classified as "other revenue" rather than sales revenue.

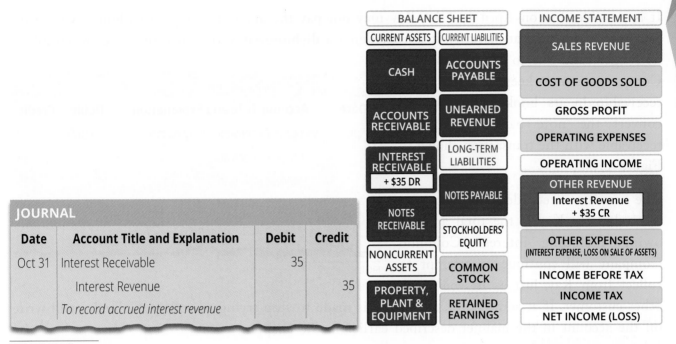

JOURNAL

Date	Account Title and Explanation	Debit	Credit
Oct 31	Interest Receivable	35	
	Interest Revenue		35
	To record accrued interest revenue		

FIGURE 11.20

When Kay pays the amount due on April 1, 2019, the entry in Figure 11.21 is recorded on the statements of Columbo Company.

JOURNAL

Date	Account Title and Explanation	Debit	Credit
Apr 1	Cash	1,060	
	Interest Receivable		35
	Interest Revenue		25
	Notes Receivable		1,000
	Record the receipt of note principal and interest		

FIGURE 11.21

The explanation for this transaction is as follows.

- Kay paid $1,060 (debit to cash).
- An amount of $25 was recorded as interest revenue earned from November 1, 2018 to April 1, 2019 ($1,000 × 6% × 5/12) by crediting interest revenue.
- The interest receivable of $35, which was recorded on October 31, 2018, was eliminated by crediting the account.
- The note receivable of $1,000 was eliminated by crediting the notes receivable account.

It is possible that on April 1, 2019, Kay may not pay the amount owing to Columbo Company. If a note is not paid at maturity, it is considered a **dishonored note**. Since the notes receivable is no longer valid due to expiry, Columbo Company cannot keep it as a notes receivable in its books. Thus, it will convert the note back to accounts receivable with the transaction shown in Figure 11.22.

The amount recorded in accounts receivable for Kay is the total amount owing, including interest. Columbo Company will continue to attempt to collect from Kay, just as it would any other customer. If at some point, a decision is made to stop trying to collect, Columbo will write off the account in the manner described earlier in the chapter.

JOURNAL			
Date	**Account Title and Explanation**	**Debit**	**Credit**
Apr 1	Accounts Receivable—Kay Alonso	1,060	
	Interest Receivable		35
	Interest Revenue		25
	Notes Receivable		1,000
	To record a dishonored note		

FIGURE 11.22

Pause & Reflect

Exercise 11-3

Polly Company converted an accounts receivable from its customer, Fawlty Company, into a notes receivable on November 1, 2018. The note is for $6,000 and is due in six months on April 30, 2019. Fawlty Company will pay 5% annual interest on the note. Polly Company has a year end on December 31, 2018. Fawlty Company pays the note plus interest on April 30, 2019.

Prepare the journal entries for Polly Company for the issuance of the note receivable, the accrual of interest at year end and receiving the note plus interest.

JOURNAL			
Date	**Account Title and Explanation**	**Debit**	**Credit**

See Appendix I for solutions.

Managing Accounts Receivable Information Using Reports

 LO 5

Much of our analysis of accounts receivable has involved accounting for receivables in the company's books. This is important because these records give management accurate information with which to make good business decisions. This also allows companies to adhere to external reporting standards and principles.

Another important aspect of accounts receivable is managing or controlling them. It is important for a business to know not only the amount of its accounts receivable but also which policies and procedures will lead to collecting the maximum possible amount.

Having too many customers owing the company too much money on overdue bills restricts cash flow and working capital. Among other things, it limits the ability of the company to meet its commitments, such as accounts payable and loans.

Since accounts receivable plays such a prominent role in the financial well-being of a company, it is important that information about this asset is efficiently organized.

Computer software is available to collect, organize and process information in different ways. Reports can be produced to give management insight into financial affairs in ways that raw data cannot.

A CLOSER LOOK

A number of strategies ensure that a company effectively manages and controls its accounts receivable. These include the following.

- **Commitment to efficiency**—Management commits to ensuring that accounts receivable are handled efficiently.

- **Measuring results**—After using ratios and reports to manage information, it is essential to determine whether these measures are working.

- **Cutting-edge technology**—Having the company's technology up-to-date to provide accurate and useful information about accounts receivable assists in informed decision-making.

The Accounts Receivable Subledger

Accounts receivable is considered a controlling account, since it is the sum total of all amounts owed by customers to the company and controls the accounts receivable subledgers. The subledgers are individual customer accounts to track the amounts each customer owes. The list in Figure 11.23 is a customer-by-customer list of outstanding amounts owing to a company; these amounts represent the total in the accounts receivable controlling account.

Accounts Receivable listing as at July 31					
	Current	31–60 days	61–90 days	91 days +	Total
Archer Limited	1,300	900	1,500		**3,700**
Beta Company	1,200	1,800	1,300	150	**4,450**
Cooper Limited	1,800	150			**1,950**
Dunwoody Company	200	500	200		**900**
Harry's Supplies	4,000	3,000	1,600	1,200	**9,800**
Lino Inc.	400	600	100		**1,100**
Total	**8,900**	**6,950**	**4,700**	**1,350**	**21,900**
	40.64%	31.74%	21.46%	6.16%	

FIGURE 11.23

Presenting the data in this form facilitates the analysis of accounts receivable by customer. It also highlights the figures that stand out from the others. In this case, the areas to note are marked in yellow, red and green in the revised chart in Figure 11.24.

Accounts Receivable listing as at July 31					
	Current	31–60 days	61–90 days	91 days +	Total
Archer Limited	1,300	900	1,500		3,700
Beta Company	1,200	1,800	1,300	150	4,450
Cooper Limited	1,800	150			1,950
Dunwoody Company	200	500	200		900
Harry's Supplies	4,000	3,000	1,600	1,200	9,800
Lino Inc.	400	600	100		1,100
Total	8,900	6,950	4,700	1,350	21,900
	40.64%	31.74%	21.46%	6.16%	

FIGURE 11.24

As the yellow and red areas show, two customers have bills outstanding more than 90 days.

The yellow area shows an amount of $150 from Beta Company that has not been paid for more than 90 days. However, this is a relatively small amount, especially in comparison with Beta's total amount owing. It could be the result of an invoice discrepancy or some other minor issue. Although Beta is one of only two customers with balances owing for more than 90 days, management may not be too concerned about this balance. There should still be controls in place to follow up with the customer either to correct or adjust the amount.

The other customer with a balance exceeding 90 days, Harry's Supplies, is certainly cause for concern. The amount marked in red, $1,200, represents a significant portion of the outstanding balance. Furthermore, the amount might be even more problematic, given that the same customer was given $4,000 in credit in the current month. This account is not being well managed, and management should follow up with the company and reconsider the credit policies that allowed this situation to develop.

The green area of this chart is notable because, unlike all the other customers on the list, Cooper Limited does not have an outstanding balance for the 61–90 day period. Furthermore, it has only $150 outstanding for the 31–60 day period. Therefore the $1,800 credit given to Cooper in the current period appears to be justified; this customer has paid bills promptly, and providing more credit for this customer makes good business sense.

Alternative Presentation Formats

The preceding examples represent just a few ways in which accounts receivable information can be organized and presented. Computer software allows for multiple methods of analysis. Management should tailor computer programs to meet the specific needs and objectives of the company with regard to information about accounts receivable, bad debt, internal controls and all other related issues.

The reports that can be generated involving accounts receivable include the following.

- Current active customers
- Past customers not active for the last 12 months
- Customer activities listing value of sales per month
- Customer activities listing value of sales per product
- Categorization of customers according to sales representative or geographic location
- Overdue accounts

Measuring the Effectiveness of Collections Using Ratios

Another approach to measuring the effectiveness of the company's collection efforts is financial ratios. This section examines two types of ratios: accounts receivable turnover and days' sales outstanding.

Accounts Receivable Turnover Ratio

The **accounts receivable turnover ratio (ART)** measures how often during the year a company collects its entire accounts receivable amount. This is done by using two basic figures from the financial records: average net accounts receivable and net credit sales for the past 12 months. Recall that the net accounts receivable is equal to the gross accounts receivable less allowance for doubtful accounts. The net credit sales is equal to the total of credit sales less sales discounts, returns and allowances. The formula to calculate ART is shown in Figure 11.25.

$$\text{Accounts Receivable Turnover (ART)} = \frac{\text{Net Credit Sales}}{\text{Average Net Accounts Receivable}}$$

FIGURE 11.25

The following two examples illustrate the use and function of this particular ratio.

Example 1: Juniper Company

Assume that Juniper Company has an average net accounts receivable of $200,000 and net credit sales of $1,200,000. The accounts receivable turnover is calculated as shown.

$$\text{ART} = \frac{\$1,200,000}{\$200,000}$$

$$= 6 \text{ times}$$

The turnover of six times per year means Juniper Company collects the entire amount of accounts receivable six times a year, or approximately every two months.

Example 2: Willow Company

Assume that Willow Company has an average net accounts receivable of $135,000 and net credit sales of $1,650,000. The accounts receivable turnover is calculated as shown.

$$ART = \frac{\$1,650,000}{\$135,000}$$

$$= 12.2 \text{ times}$$

The turnover of 12 times per year means Willow Company collects the entire amount of accounts receivable 12 times a year, or every month.

Days' Sales Outstanding

Another way of organizing accounts receivable information is to use days' sales outstanding. **Days' sales outstanding (DSO)** tracks how long customers take to pay their bills. The formula is shown in Figure 11.26.

$$\text{Days' Sales Outstanding (DSO)} = \frac{\text{Average Net Accounts Receivable}}{\text{Net Credit Sales}} \times 365$$

FIGURE 11.26

As shown in the formula, the average net accounts receivable figure is divided by the net credit sales of the past 12 months. The result is then multiplied by 365 (days in the year). The result provides the company with the average number of days that customers take to pay their bills.

Example 1: Juniper Company

From the previous example, the total average net accounts receivable amount for Juniper Company is $200,000, and the total net credit sales amount for the past year is $1,200,000. The DSO ratio is calculated as shown.

$$DSO = \frac{\$200,000}{\$1,200,000} \times 365$$

$$= 61 \text{ days}$$

Juniper Company collects amounts outstanding in an average of 61 days, or approximately two months.

Example 2: Willow Company

From the previous example, the total average net accounts receivable amount for Willow Company is $135,000, and the total net credit sales for the past year was $1,650,000. The DSO ratio is calculated as shown.

$$\text{DSO} = \frac{\$135,000}{\$1,650,000} \times 365$$

$$= 30 \text{ days}$$

Willow Company collects amounts oustanding in an average of 30 days, or approximately one month. On the basis of these calculations, Willow Company is collecting its accounts receivable from customers twice as fast as Juniper Company. Because of the importance of cash in operating a business, it is in the company's best interest to collect outstanding accounts receivable as quickly as possible. By quickly turning sales into cash, a company can effectively use the cash for reinvestment and to produce more revenue. One of the most important factors that affect both ART and DSO is a company's credit terms.

If both companies allow customers 30 days to pay for their purchases on account, Willow Company is doing well in terms of collection whereas Juniper Company is doing poorly.

Pause & Reflect

Exercise 11-4

The Practical Company obtained the following information from its financial records for 2018.

Net Credit Sales	$278,000
Average Net Accounts Receivable	$23,000

a) Calculate the accounts receivable turnover ratio. Explain what this result means.

b) Calculate the days' sales outstanding. Explain what this result means.

See Appendix I for solutions.

Disposal of Receivables   LO 7

Sometimes a company may want to speed up the collection of accounts receivable by converting them to cash before they are due. The cash may be needed to purchase assets, cover operating expenses or pay debts. Or perhaps the expense and time-intensive collection duties are a strain on the company's staffing resources. Companies can dispose of their accounts receivable by converting them into cash using different methods: (1) by *factoring* (selling them); or (2) by *pledging* them as collateral (security) for a loan.

Factoring Receivables

A company can sell all or a portion of its accounts receivable to a factor, such as a bank or financial institution, in exchange for cash. The factor becomes the owner of the receivables and assumes the responsibility for collecting the amounts owing directly from the company's customers. It also assumes the risk of any bad debt. The seller may also choose to have the factor take over the cost of the billing function. The factor charges a factoring fee, usually a percentage of the total receivables sold. For example, Zeta Inc. wants to dispose of $50,000 of its receivables by selling them to the bank in exchange for cash. The bank charges a 5% factoring fee. Figure 11.27 shows the journal entry for this transaction.

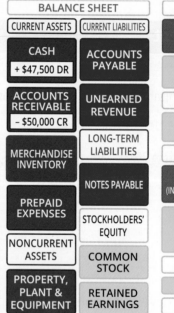

JOURNAL			
Date	Account Title and Explanation	Debit	Credit
Oct 1	Cash	47,500	
	Factoring Expense	2,500	
	Accounts Receivable		50,000
	To record sale of accounts receivable for cash, less 5% factoring fee		

FIGURE 11.27

In a factoring arrangement, the company's customers are instructed to remit their payments directly to the factor. Because factoring expense is incurred in order to receive cash sooner, it is normally considered a part of the company's financing cost. Therefore, factoring expense, similar to interest expense, is classified as "other expenses" on the income statement.

Pledging Receivables

A company can also exchange its receivables for cash by pledging them as collateral for a loan. Unlike factoring, the borrower retains ownership of the pledged receivables. If the borrower is unable to pay back the loan, the lender is entitled to the cash receipts when the receivables are collected. For example, Jackman Company wants to borrow $45,000 from the bank, and pledges $50,000 of its receivables as collateral for the loan. The journal entry for this transaction is shown in Figure 11.28.

JOURNAL			
Date	**Account Title and Explanation**	**Debit**	**Credit**
Oct 1	Cash	45,000	
	Notes Payable		45,000
	To borrow cash with a note payable secured by pledging receivables		

BALANCE SHEET

CURRENT ASSETS	CURRENT LIABILITIES
CASH + $45,000 DR	**ACCOUNTS PAYABLE**
ACCOUNTS RECEIVABLE	**UNEARNED REVENUE**
MERCHANDISE INVENTORY	**LONG-TERM LIABILITIES**
PREPAID EXPENSES	**NOTES PAYABLE** + $45,000 CR
NONCURRENT ASSETS	**STOCKHOLDERS' EQUITY**
PROPERTY, PLANT & EQUIPMENT	**COMMON STOCK**
	RETAINED EARNINGS

FIGURE 11.28

In addition to journal entries, Jackman Company is required to disclose the pledging of its accounts receivable in the notes to its financial statements. The note would be something similar to "Accounts receivable of $50,000 has been pledged as security for a $45,000 note payable."

Internal Controls for Accounts Receivable

 LO 8

Now that we have examined various ways of organizing, presenting and managing accounts receivable information, the information can be used to implement sound control policies. There is no value in collecting all that data unless it is used to better manage a company's accounts receivable.

This is the purpose of accounts receivable internal controls—to help a company get the most out of one of its largest and most crucial assets. We will look specifically at how a credit policy can serve as a control mechanism to ensure that the accounts receivable asset is managed, protected and maximized in value.

Credit Approval

Providing payment terms to customers involves making unsecured loans to the customers so that they can buy the company's product or service. Instead of automatically offering these terms, a company can implement various measures to better understand its customers and follow up when necessary. This is the essence of credit approval. The company can have the customer complete a credit application and update the information regularly. It can also request a customer's financial statements to ensure the customer is in a position to pay the bills.

Credit Information

Of course, customers may not always be completely open about their financial health or ability to pay their bills. Companies, therefore, get independent credit information about customers from credit reporting agencies, financial institutions or other vendors.

Credit agency reports can be very useful in getting up-to-date information on current and potential customers. They can provide payment history, claims against the customer, banking information, existing credit granted, a record of recent inquiries as well as any credit ratings.

Credit Terms

One of the first decisions a company should make when establishing a credit policy is whether to adopt a lenient or restrictive approach to providing credit. This is an important decision because the company's credit policy can have a significant impact on sales volume. The more lenient a company's credit policy, the more likely it is to generate additional sales. A lenient credit policy provides potential customers with the incentive to buy goods without having to pay for them immediately. However, it also increases the risk of bad debt for the company. In order to make credit policy decisions effectively, a company should take the following factors into consideration.

Firstly, the company should consider its own financial situation. The stronger its financial situation is, the better the company can afford to make sales on credit. If a company is financially constrained, it probably cannot risk extending credit to customers. Similarly, low sales volumes for custom-made products leave a company with less room to extend generous credit terms.

Secondly, a company should consider its competitive situation. The more competition the company has, the greater the pressure to extend credit in order to increase sales. A company with little or no competition does not need to increase market share, and has little incentive to adopt lenient credit policies.

In conclusion, a competitive market environment, homogeneous products and high sales volumes are greater incentives for a company to extend more lenient credit terms to customers.

After analyzing the factors above, the company can set its credit terms, which are often an integral component of credit control. A certain period, such as 30 days, can be used and enforced with all approved customers.

A company should try to assess whether its collection period is stringent enough. Accounts receivable should not remain uncollected for more than 10 or 15 days beyond the credit terms. Industry standards differ, so assessing what the competition is doing, then setting a benchmark to meet or surpass those expectations, may be a wise business strategy. Setting a high standard and routinely enforcing it might improve the collection of accounts.

Credit Collection

Finally, deciding on the methods of collecting from customers is another control in credit policy. The invoice is always the first tool of collection. If a customer is overdue with payment, the company can send a copy of the invoice as a reminder. If that is unsuccessful, other measures such as letters, phone calls and even personal visits can be used to put pressure on the customer. If all else fails, a collection agency can be hired to enforce payment, especially when the account is long overdue.

Other controls for accounts receivable that may be implemented include the following.

- Keeping individual records for each customer.

- Following up on large accounts that are overdue.

- Writing off a bad debt when all reasonable measures have been exhausted to collect the debt.

- Ensuring that the original write off is reversed when payments are received for a previously written off account.

A CLOSER LOOK

An important objective for any successful business is to maximize its control and management of accounts receivable. To that end, a company can establish a checklist of items to monitor how well it is doing in meeting this objective. Such a checklist may include the following items.

- Is the staff fully trained to handle accounts receivable issues?
- Is all sensitive accounts receivable information adequately secured?
- Are invoices being processed accurately?
- Are customers informed quickly enough of credit decisions made by the company?
- Are third-party collection agencies being properly monitored?

An Ethical Approach to Managing Accounts Receivable   LO 9

The company and its accounting department are responsible for managing accounts receivable accurately and ethically. This includes properly recording credit sales and receipt of cash, as well as properly estimating bad debt. Accounts receivable is an important asset on the balance sheet and managing and accounting for this asset is open to manipulation.

Various ethical principles and standards have been established to prevent or detect manipulation of accounts receivable. The following case study illustrates unethical behavior, which violates the full disclosure principle.

Case Study 11-1

Charles owns a manufacturing business, which has been growing steadily. His bank wants to examine his financial statements before approving his loan to finance his increasing need for capital. His records show a total of $250,000 in accounts receivable, and he has earned a net income of $80,000 for the current year. Charles is also aware that there is an amount of $50,000 that is likely to be uncollectible; however, he knows that if he allows for the bad debt in his statements, he may not be successful in securing the loan. Charles justifies his non-disclosure by committing himself to allowing for the bad debt the following year because there is a slight chance that he may still get paid.

What Charles did was unethical. He deliberately overstated the value of his assets to try to secure the loan. He believed that the debt was not going to be paid, but he represented it otherwise to distort the current value of the accounts receivable.

Charles consciously violated the full disclosure principle by withholding information relevant to the valuation of these assets.

Consider another example of unethical behavior. This time we will examine the importance of maintaining the integrity of the accounts receivable information that a company collects and manages. Failure to do so can put into doubt the accuracy of the company's books, and the ethics of the people in charge.

Case Study 11-2

Sophie is hired by the controller, Rick, to manage the company's accounts receivable. Upon assuming the job, Sophie notices that the company's accounts receivable has been poorly managed. The computer system was old and the invoices were not detailed enough, thus leading to customers questioning their invoices. Furthermore, the company would increase prices on the date of shipment instead of using the prices on the date the order was placed. Customers complained and did not want to pay invoices showing prices they had not agreed to.

Sophie brings her concerns to Rick, who asks her to keep quiet and do the best she can. Rick is afraid that he will be held accountable if upper management finds out, so he has tried to hide the problems. Sophie does not know what to do about the unethical accounting practices. If she remains silent, the integrity of the company's accounts receivable is in serious jeopardy.

An accountant is responsible for maintaining the integrity of the information in the books. Rick should have dealt with these problems as soon as he became aware of them. Instead, when these problems were identified, he tried to hide them and absolve himself of any responsibility. The company's customers are being treated unfairly, the integrity of the financial information of the company is compromised and the tactics used in response to the problems are ethical violations. Furthermore, Rick has imposed an unacceptable dilemma on his employee, Sophie, requiring her to choose between her job and the proper management of the company's assets. Unless Rick accepts responsibility for the problems and corrects them, he puts both himself and his company in a vulnerable position both financially and ethically.

In Summary

LO 1 Explain the importance of accounts receivable

▶ Accounts receivable often represents a significant percentage of a company's assets.

▶ Allowing the existence of accounts receivable is instrumental in increasing sales in a modern economy. This includes allowing customers to buy on credit or make purchases using credit cards.

▶ While most companies find day-to-day administration of accounts receivable burdensome, effective and efficient management of accounts receivable by factoring (selling) them can help improve cash flows and customer satisfaction.

LO 2 Account for bad debt using the allowance method and the direct write off method

▶ When accounts receivable are deemed uncollectible, they can be accounted for as bad debt using two different methods: the allowance method, and the direct write off method.

▶ The expense recognition principle requires bad debt expense to be estimated and accounted for in the same period that sales are recorded.

▶ The allowance method satisfies expense recognition through the use of an allowance for doubtful accounts (AFDA), which is a contra account attached to the accounts receivable account.

▶ Under the direct write off method, as soon as a receivable is determined to be uncollectible, it is written off by a debit (increase) to bad debt expense and a credit (decrease) to accounts receivable.

LO 3 Estimate bad debt using the income statement and balance sheet approaches

▶ The income statement approach estimates bad debt based on credit sales of the year.

▶ The balance sheet approach estimates bad debt based on the balance of accounts receivable or on the aging of accounts receivable at year end.

LO 4 Record promissory notes and notes receivable

▶ Accounts receivable can be converted into promissory notes, or notes receivable, which are legally binding documents. The conversion from accounts receivable to notes receivable is recorded in the journal with a debit to notes receivable and a credit to accounts receivable.

▶ The company that issued the notes receivable must record accrued interest revenue at the end of an accounting period.

LO 5 **Utilize reports, including the accounts receivable subledger, to manage accounts receivable information**

▶ The accounts receivable subledger shows accounts receivable balances by customer and by the length of time the debt has been outstanding. Detailed examination of the accounts receivable subledger can help the company highlight important areas that require management focus or changes in credit policies.

▶ Using computer software, a company can generate various accounts receivable reports that are tailored to management's needs.

LO 6 **Calculate financial ratios pertaining to accounts receivable**

▶ The effectiveness of accounts receivable collections can be gauged with the use of two ratios: accounts receivable turnover (ART) and days' sales outstanding (DSO).

LO 7 **Account for the disposal of receivables using factoring and pledging**

▶ A company can sell all or a portion of its accounts receivable to a factor, such as a bank or financial institution, in exchange for cash. The factor becomes the owner of the receivables and assumes responsibility for collecting them.

▶ A company can also exchange its receivables for cash by pledging them as collateral for a loan. The borrower retains ownership of the pledged receivables, but must forfeit the proceeds to the lender if it defaults on the loan.

LO 8 **Apply internal controls relating to accounts receivable**

▶ Credit controls and policies are necessary to manage and protect the accounts receivable asset.

▶ Examples of controls relating to accounts receivable include setting competitive yet firm credit terms and getting independent credit information about customers before approving their credit.

LO 9 **Apply ethics relating to accounts receivable and notes receivable**

▶ Management must ensure that accounts receivable is properly managed and any estimates for bad debt are recorded as accurately as possible.

AMEENGAGE™ *Access **ameengage.com** for integrated resources including tutorials, practice exercises, the digital textbook and more.*

Review Exercise 11-1

ABC Company uses the allowance method to account for bad debt. During 2018, the company had $350,000 in sales, of which 80% were on account and 20% were cash sales. During the year, the company received $250,000 from customers as payment on their accounts. In June, it wrote off $1,500 for a customer who filed for bankruptcy and would not pay. However, some time after the account was written off, the customer notified ABC Company that she would to pay the account early in the new year. The company expects that $5,000 of the accounts receivable balance at the end of the year may be uncollectible.

Note: Do not consider cost of goods sold in any of the transactions.

Required

a) Using the general journal and December 31 as the date for all transactions, record the sales, collections for customers on account, write off of accounts and bad debt expense for 2018. You may omit explanations for each entry. Assume accounts receivable had a debit balance of $35,000 and that the AFDA had a credit balance of $2,500 at the beginning of the year (January 1, 2018).

JOURNAL			
Date	Account Title and Explanation	Debit	Credit

b) Show how the transactions from part a) are posted in the related T-accounts.

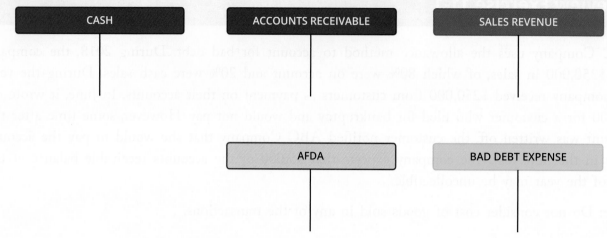

c) Show how accounts receivable is reported on the December 31, 2018 balance sheet after the entries from part a) are posted.

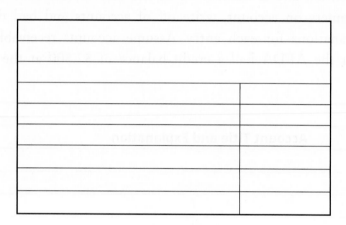

d) Assume that instead of using the balance sheet approach, the company uses the income statement approach and expects that 1% of credit sales may be uncollectible. Record the journal entry to estimate bad debt on December 31. Assume that AFDA has a credit balance of $2,500 at the beginning of the year.

JOURNAL			
Date	Account Title and Explanation	Debit	Credit

See Appendix I for solutions.

Review Exercise 11-2

You are the accountant for Braham Company. Record the following transactions assuming the company has an August 31 year end.

1. Sale to Guy Tygart on account—1,000 gadgets for $5,000 on June 30, 2018.
2. Guy Tygart cannot pay on July 31, but signs a note with an annual 6% interest rate, to be collected on December 31, 2018.
3. Guy Tygart pays the amount due on December 31.
4. Assume instead that Guy dishonored the note on December 31.

Prepare the journal entries for the transactions. Do not record cost of goods sold

JOURNAL			
Date	Account Title and Explanation	Debit	Credit

See Appendix I for solutions.

Notes

Chapter 12
Noncurrent Assets

Learning Objectives

 *Access **ameengage.com** for integrated resources including tutorials, practice exercises, the digital textbook and more.*

Noncurrent Assets

Current assets are defined as those owned for the short term. Noncurrent assets are those that are owned and used by a company as part of normal operations for the long term. Specifically, noncurrent assets must possess the following three characteristics.

1. They provide the infrastructure necessary for operating the business.

2. They are expected to be used on an ongoing basis. Typically, this means longer than the business' operating cycle or one year.

3. They are not intended to be sold to customers.

Noncurrent assets are also commonly referred to as *long-term assets*, *long-lived assets*, *fixed assets* or *capital assets*.

Noncurrent assets can be either tangible or intangible by nature. Tangible assets have physical substance, which can be perceived with our senses, especially by touch. Intangible assets have no physical substance and can only be perceived by the mind or imagination. The noncurrent assets section of the Accounting Map is divided into separate parts containing tangible and intangible assets. As shown in Figure 12.1, Property, Plant & Equipment, which are also called *plant assets*, pertains to a company's noncurrent tangible assets, such as buildings, machinery, vehicles and computer equipment. The intangible part is labeled Intangible Assets and includes items such as patents and trademarks. Goodwill is also intangible by nature, but it has distinctive characteristics deserving of its own section. Each group of assets is covered in this chapter. Long-term investments, while considered a part of noncurrent assets, are covered in Chapter 18.

A company must have noncurrent tangible assets to accomplish physical tasks. Examples include machines that package bottles, trucks that deliver products and computers that scan and calculate inventory data. Noncurrent tangible assets often form the physical backbone of a company. Without them, a business will not have the property, buildings and machinery it needs to deliver goods and services to its customers. This is particularly true for manufacturers or companies involved in the transportation industry, whose noncurrent assets are often the largest group of assets on the balance sheet.

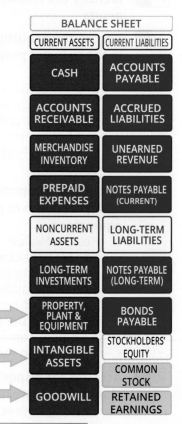

FIGURE 12.1

For example, Figure 12.2 shows an excerpt of a balance sheet for Amtrak—an American passenger railroad company. The balance sheet shows values for the years ended September 30, 2015 and September 30, 2014.

National Railroad Passenger Corporation and Subsidiaries (Amtrak) Consolidated Balance Sheet (partial) For the Year Ended September 30 (In Thousands of Dollars)	2015	2014
ASSETS		
Current Assets		
Cash and cash equivalents	$523,028	$424,041
Restricted cash and cash equivalents	4,978	5,149
Accounts receivable, net of allowances of $5,067 and $4,429 as of September 30, 2015 and 2014, respectively	308,875	307,917
Materials and supplies, net of allowances of $27,782 and $46,074 at September 30, 2015 and 2014, respectively	272,689	268,410
Prepaid expenses	27,721	15,396
Other current assets	36,653	44,219
Total Current Assets	**1,173,944**	**1,065,132**
Property and Equipment		
Locomotives	1,944,706	1,709,439
Passenger cars and other rolling stock	3,168,946	2,992,737
Right-of-way and other properties	12,124,468	11,733,797
Construction-in-progress	1,410,974	1,311,304
Leasehold improvements	556,327	527,439
Property and equipment, gross	19,205,421	18,274,716
Less: Accumulated depreciation and amortization	(7,502,347)	(7,016,382)
Total Property and Equipment, Net	**11,703,074**	**11,258,334**
Other Assets, Deposits and Deferred Charges		
Notes receivable on sale-leasebacks	55,210	54,440
Deferred charges, deposits and other	362,356	76,020
Total Other Assets, Deposits and Deferred Charges	**417,566**	**130,460**
Total Assets	**$13,294,584**	**$12,453,926**

FIGURE 12.2

For both fiscal years 2015 and 2014, the company's largest assets were its property, plant and equipment. Figure 12.3 illustrates this important relationship for some other American companies. As you can see, noncurrent assets often make up a large percentage of many companies' total assets. These are important investments for the business and need to be properly managed to achieve success. Because noncurrent assets tend to be worth large amounts of money and constitute major items on a company's balance sheet, it is tremendously important for accountants to properly classify, record and monitor the value of noncurrent assets. This chapter will discuss in detail how accountants perform these tasks.

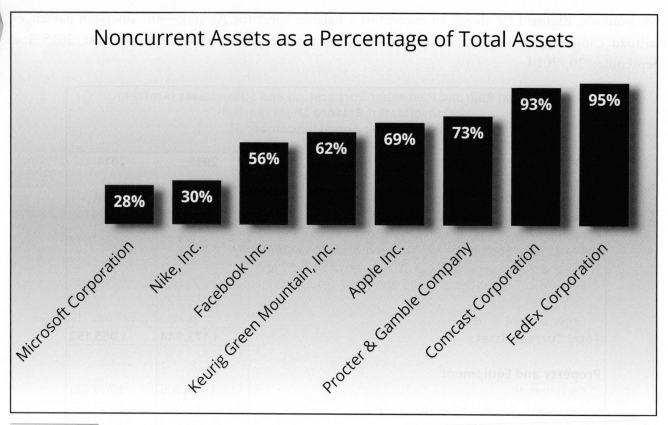

FIGURE 12.3

Tangible assets that last longer than one year and are used in normal operations are classified as part of property, plant and equipment. Items that are still used, even if only some of the time (e.g. equipment at peak periods of activity), are also reported as property, plant and equipment. However, there are instances of tangible assets that last longer than one year but are not reported in the same way on the balance sheet. Specifically, tangible assets that are not used at all for operations are not reported as property, plant and equipment; for example, old equipment that was once used for manufacturing but is now sitting unused waiting to be sold as scrap metal.

Long-lived assets that are held for sale to customers but not used in normal operations are classified as merchandise inventory. For example, vehicles held in merchandise inventory by an automotive dealership are intended for sale and therefore not considered as noncurrent assets of the dealership. Conversely, a delivery truck that is used in the daily operations of the dealership is classified as a noncurrent asset.

Land that is not used for daily operations but is held for resale or future expansion is classified on the balance sheet as a long-term investment. However, if the land holds a building that is used in normal operations, then that land is classified as a plant asset and is reported as part of property, plant and equipment on the balance sheet.

The Acquisition and Changes in Value of Noncurrent Assets

 LO 2

The initial purchase of property, plant and equipment requires a journal entry to record the value of the asset purchased. Following the cost principle, an asset must be recorded at its actual cost. The first step in accounting for the acquisition of property, plant and equipment is to determine the cost of the acquired item.

WORTH REPEATING

Buying assets as well as selling assets at book value has no impact on the value of equity.

When a company purchases physical items, such as land, buildings and equipment, the company usually pays additional costs associated with acquiring the assets. For example, when a company buys land with the intention of building a factory, it may have to pay for land drainage before the factory can be built. When a company buys a vehicle, it must pay for the vehicle's insurance and license before the vehicle can be legally driven. Some of these expenditures have to be included in the cost of the asset and reported on the balance sheet, while others must be expensed and reported on the income statement. Accountants must pay attention to the nature of the expenditures related to asset acquisition to properly classify which costs should be included in the asset cost and which costs should be expensed.

The costs necessary for getting the asset ready for use are those directly related to having the asset set up at its intended location and in a ready-to-use condition. These expenditures benefit the company not only in the current period, but also in future periods as long as the noncurrent asset is still being used. Figure 12.4 lists the items that are usually included in the costs of acquiring the following classifications of noncurrent assets: (1) buildings, (2) machinery and equipment, and (3) land and land improvements.

Buildings	Machinery and Equipment	Land and Land Improvements
• Purchase price • Sales taxes • Brokerage fees • Legal fees • Title fees • Design fees • Building permits • Betterments and extraordinary repairs of existing buildings • Insurance while under construction • Finance costs related to construction • Electrical system • Lighting fixtures • Plumbing • Flooring • Painting and wall coverings • Materials, labor and overhead costs of new building construction	• Purchase price • Sales taxes • Freight and delivery charges • Government permits • Insurance while in transit • Betterments and extraordinary repairs of existing machinery and equipment • Installation • Assembly • Testing prior to use	• Purchase price • Sales taxes • Brokerage fees • Delinquent property taxes • Legal fees • Title insurance • Government permits • Reclamation or remediation of land (if contaminated) to make it suitable for use • Removal of any existing structures • Land surveying fees • Preparation of land, such as clearing, grading, leveling, drainage, government assessments, installing sewers • Land improvements, such as driveways, walkways, paving, fences, landscaping, sprinkler systems, outdoor lighting

FIGURE 12.4

Since these expenditures are directly related to the asset itself, they are not treated as expenses but as part of the cost of the asset. This cost is then recorded on the company's balance sheet. Other costs that are not directly attributable to getting the asset ready for use, such as the costs of advertising products that a recently acquired machine will be producing, or unnecessary costs such as errors or damage in the installation of machinery, are expensed rather than capitalized. Recurring costs that benefit the company only in the current period (without providing long-term benefits, such as the costs of a vehicle's license and insurance) are also expensed.

The value of a noncurrent asset also dictates whether its purchase should be capitalized or expensed. The materiality constraint allows the company to expense low-cost, noncurrent assets that are below the company's materiality threshold; an item can be considered an expense on the income statement instead of a noncurrent asset on the balance sheet if it has no material value relative to the size of the business.

Recording the Acquisition of Property, Plant and Equipment

The asset's purchase price and the costs necessary for getting the asset ready for use are combined into a single amount representing the cost of the asset. The amount is then debited to the appropriate asset account.

For example, the Sunshine Juice Company has purchased a new bottling machine for its orange juice line on February 1, 2018. It was purchased for $120,000, shipped at a cost of $5,000, and had installation costs of $2,000. Assuming one invoice for all these costs, Figure 12.5 shows the journal entry for the acquisition of this noncurrent asset.

JOURNAL			
Date	**Account Title and Explanation**	**Debit**	**Credit**
Feb 1	Machine	127,000	
	Accounts Payable		127,000
	Record the purchase of a machine for $120,000 plus $2,000 for installation and $5,000 for shipping		

FIGURE 12.5

When totaled, the costs amount to $127,000. This is debited to an account that is part of property, plant and equipment and credited to accounts payable, since the company was invoiced and owes this amount to the bottling machine manufacturer. Of course, once the bill is paid, accounts payable is debited and cash is credited.

Although some prepared financial statements may show a single property, plant and equipment line item, there are actually separate accounts for each noncurrent asset within that category.

Lump Sum Purchases of Property, Plant and Equipment

Companies sometimes purchase property, plant and equipment in bundles, or what is known as a "basket of assets." Instead of buying property, plant and equipment individually from different vendors, a company may get a good price for a basket of assets by buying them from the same vendor in one transaction, called a **lump sum purchase** or a **basket purchase**.

The accounting challenge with this type of transaction is that by paying a lower price for the assets, the buyer acquires them for less than their appraised value. In this case, the lump sum paid for all the assets is divided and allocated to each item according to percentages based on the appraised values or fair values. For example, on August 1, 2018, the Huge Bargain Store purchased land, a building and a parking lot to open a new store. It bought the assets in a bundle for the lump sum payment of $800,000. However, each asset has its own appraised value, as listed in Figure 12.6.

Item	Appraised Value
Land	$600,000
Building	300,000
Parking Lot	100,000
Total	**$1,000,000**

FIGURE 12.6

The total of all the appraised values is $1,000,000, which is $200,000 more than the purchase price. The first step is to take each item's appraised value and divide it by the total appraised value. This produces a percentage that should be allocated to each asset and is shown in Figure 12.7.

Land	600,000 ÷ 1,000,000 × 100%	60%
Building	300,000 ÷ 1,000,000 × 100%	30%
Parking Lot	100,000 ÷ 1,000,000 × 100%	10%

FIGURE 12.7

These percentages are now allocated to the amount actually paid, which was $800,000. For example, land made up 60% of the total appraised value, so it makes up 60% of the price paid, which is $480,000. The allocated amounts for the land, building and parking lot are shown in Figure 12.8.

Land	800,000 × 60%	$480,000
Building	800,000 × 30%	240,000
Parking Lot	800,000 × 10%	80,000
Total		**$800,000**

FIGURE 12.8

Figure 12.9 shows the journal entry after calculating the actual value applied to the assets. Each asset is debited by the value calculated and cash is credited by the purchase price of $800,000.

JOURNAL			
Date	Account Title and Explanation	Debit	Credit
Aug 1	Land	480,000	
	Building	240,000	
	Parking Lot	80,000	
	Cash		800,000
	Record the purchase of land, building and parking lot		

FIGURE 12.9

Pause & Reflect

Exercise 12-1

On May 1, 2018, Bristol Holding Company purchased land valued at $600,000, a building valued at $1,000,000 and a parking lot valued at $400,000. Bristol Holding paid $1,800,000 cash for these three assets.

a) Calculate the book value that should be recorded for these assets.

Asset	Appraised Value	Percentage	Book Value
Building	$1,000,000		
Land	600,000		
Parking Lot	400,000		
Total	$2,000,000		

b) Prepare the journal entry for this purchase.

JOURNAL			
Date	Account Title and Explanation	Debit	Credit

See Appendix I for solutions.

Changes in Property, Plant and Equipment

Property, plant and equipment can change in value as a result of two factors: depreciation, which will be examined shortly, and changes made to the asset itself. One challenge with property, plant and equipment is determining whether an item should be classified as a noncurrent asset or simply recorded as an expense in the current year. This challenge is even more difficult when there is a change to the asset. If the change results in beneficial consequences to the asset that extend beyond the current period, the expenses paid for the change are classified as a **capital expenditure**. Two types of capital expenditures are betterments and extraordinary repairs. Capital expenditures increase the net book value of the related asset accounts and are reported on the balance sheet. On the other hand, an expense that benefits the current period is known as a **revenue expenditure**. Revenue expenditures include ordinary repairs and maintenance, and are reported on the income statement.

We will look at the different types of both capital expenditures and revenue expenditures in this section, starting with betterments.

Betterments

A betterment is an improvement that increases an asset's efficiency or effectiveness without necessarily increasing the asset's useful life. Some examples of betterments are plant expansions or major upgrades to equipment or vehicles used in the business. Betterments are capital expenditures and benefit future periods, so they are debited to the asset account (capitalized) and depreciated over the asset's remaining useful life. To illustrate, suppose a company replaces the engine in its existing equipment with a more powerful engine that will improve its efficiency. The new engine, including installation, costs $6,000. The journal entry is shown in Figure 12.10.

JOURNAL			
Date	**Account Title and Explanation**	**Debit**	**Credit**
Oct 1	Equipment	6,000	
	Cash		6,000
	To record installation of upgraded engine to equipment		

BALANCE SHEET

CURRENT ASSETS	CURRENT LIABILITIES
CASH − $6,000 CR	**ACCOUNTS PAYABLE**
ACCOUNTS RECEIVABLE	**UNEARNED REVENUE**
MERCHANDISE INVENTORY	**LONG-TERM LIABILITIES**
PREPAID EXPENSES	**NOTES PAYABLE**
NONCURRENT ASSETS	**STOCKHOLDERS' EQUITY**
PROPERTY, PLANT & EQUIPMENT + $6,000 DR	**COMMON STOCK** / **RETAINED EARNINGS**

FIGURE 12.10

Extraordinary Repairs

Extraordinary repairs, unlike asset betterments, are costs incurred to extend an asset's useful life past the original estimate. Some examples are replacing the existing roof of a building or repaving a parking lot. Extraordinary repairs are capital expenditures and benefit future periods, so they are recorded as a debit to the accumulated depreciation account for that asset. To illustrate, suppose a company overhauls the engine in its 10-year-old delivery van and now expects to get another four years of use from it. The overhaul, including materials and labor, costs $5,000. The journal entry is shown in Figure 12.11.

BALANCE SHEET	
CURRENT ASSETS	CURRENT LIABILITIES
CASH – $5,000 CR	ACCOUNTS PAYABLE
ACCOUNTS RECEIVABLE	UNEARNED REVENUE
MERCHANDISE INVENTORY	LONG-TERM LIABILITIES
PREPAID EXPENSES	NOTES PAYABLE
NONCURRENT ASSETS	STOCKHOLDERS' EQUITY
PROPERTY, PLANT & EQUIPMENT	COMMON STOCK
ACCUMULATED DEPRECIATION – $5,000 DR	RETAINED EARNINGS

JOURNAL

Date	Account Title and Explanation	Debit	Credit
Oct 1	Accumulated Depreciation—Delivery Van	5,000	
	Cash		5,000
	To record cost of engine overhaul for delivery van		

FIGURE 12.11

Because this journal entry changes the value of the delivery van's accumulated depreciation, the depreciation charge needs to be recalculated and adjusted for the delivery van's remaining useful life. The concept of depreciation is explained later in the chapter.

Ordinary Repairs and Maintenance

Ordinary repairs and maintenance are expenditures made for the upkeep of existing assets, but they do not materially improve an asset's efficiency or effectiveness, nor do they extend the asset's useful life. Some examples are painting, minor wall and floor repairs, cleaning, and minor adjustments to equipment and machinery. Ordinary repairs and maintenance are revenue expenditures and benefit the current period, so they are debited to the related expense account. To illustrate, suppose a company pays for repairs to a hole in the drywall in one of its offices. The repairs, including materials and labor, cost $325. The journal entry is shown in Figure 12.12.

GAAP vs IFRS

Under GAAP, accounting treatments are different for ordinary repairs, extraordinary repairs and betterments. Under IFRS, the cost is typically capitalized as part of the cost of the asset if future economic benefit is probable and can be reliably measured.

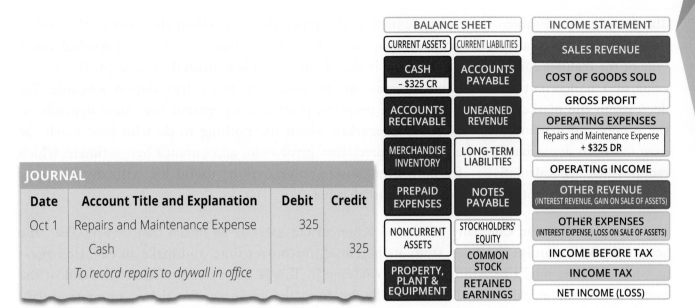

BALANCE SHEET		INCOME STATEMENT
CURRENT ASSETS	CURRENT LIABILITIES	SALES REVENUE
CASH – $325 CR	ACCOUNTS PAYABLE	COST OF GOODS SOLD
ACCOUNTS RECEIVABLE	UNEARNED REVENUE	GROSS PROFIT
		OPERATING EXPENSES
		Repairs and Maintenance Expense + $325 DR
MERCHANDISE INVENTORY	LONG-TERM LIABILITIES	OPERATING INCOME
PREPAID EXPENSES	NOTES PAYABLE	OTHER REVENUE (INTEREST REVENUE, GAIN ON SALE OF ASSETS)
NONCURRENT ASSETS	STOCKHOLDERS' EQUITY	OTHER EXPENSES (INTEREST EXPENSE, LOSS ON SALE OF ASSETS)
	COMMON STOCK	INCOME BEFORE TAX
PROPERTY, PLANT & EQUIPMENT		INCOME TAX
	RETAINED EARNINGS	NET INCOME (LOSS)

JOURNAL

Date	Account Title and Explanation	Debit	Credit
Oct 1	Repairs and Maintenance Expense	325	
	Cash		325
	To record repairs to drywall in office		

FIGURE 12.12

The Concept of Depreciation

In any discussion of expenses arising from assets, expense recognition must be considered. Expenses associated with assets need to be matched with associated revenues. Property, plant and equipment are typically used for long periods of time. Depreciation is the allocation of an asset's cost over its life span. We will examine various aspects of depreciation and how noncurrent assets on the balance sheet are affected.

Residual Value

Before discussing specific methods of depreciation, we should first examine what an asset's residual value is and how it affects depreciation calculations. **Residual value** is the estimated value of an asset at the end of its useful life. An asset may still have some value, even if it is no longer useful to the company, or it may have a residual value of $0. Residual value is also referred to as *salvage value* or *scrap value*.

For example, a company has a delivery truck that has been on the road for many years and can no longer be fixed to continue running. A buyer might see some residual value in the truck, buy it, and sell its spare parts or scrap metal. Sometimes, a noncurrent asset carries a residual value even after it is unable to do what it was designed for.

The total amount depreciated for a noncurrent asset is affected by the residual value that is expected to remain at the end of the asset's useful life. An asset's residual value is not depreciated. For example, if a company purchases an item of property, plant and equipment for $5,000, and estimates its residual value as $1,000, the amount depreciated over the useful life of the asset is $4,000. Even though the asset can no longer be used for business after its useful life expires, the company may be able to get some money for it and this price should be subtracted from the depreciation calculations made by the company.

The *actual* residual value of an asset, defined as the proceeds from selling the asset at the end of its useful life less its disposal cost, may turn out to be different from the *estimated* residual value. One of the realities confronting accountants is that depreciation is a theoretical concept. The market value of a noncurrent asset may not decrease at the same rate as its depreciation schedule. The decrease in the market value of an item of property, plant and equipment over time depends on the supply and demand mechanism of the market, which has nothing to do with how much the item has been depreciated in the books. Depreciation involves an accountant's best estimate, which requires justified calculations of a noncurrent asset's value over its useful life with the company. Depreciation does not dictate an asset's market value.

For example, Skyscape Company purchased a noncurrent asset at an initial cost of $100,000. The accountant will examine the asset, study its potential worth over time, and make an educated guess at what someone might be willing to pay to salvage it. This is not an easy task. At the end of the asset's life, if the actual residual value is different from the accountant's original estimate, a gain (or loss) on asset disposal is recorded.

Assume that the accountant estimates an item's residual value to be $10,000. Ten years later, the item is sold for $6,000. Since the selling price was lower than the estimated residual value, the accountant records a loss of $4,000. The overestimation is not an issue as long as the accountant was justified in making the initial estimate and adjusts for a loss once the asset is sold. Similarly, if the asset is sold for more than its estimated residual value, the difference is recorded as a gain.

In addition to estimating the residual value, an accountant must also decide which of the three depreciation methods to use. The accountant should try to choose the depreciation method that best reflects the pattern in which the asset will be used by the company in practice. The same depreciation method should be used throughout the life of the asset. However, there are times when an accountant may change the method used, which is acceptable as long as there is justification in doing so.

We will now examine three methods of depreciation related to noncurrent assets. The three methods and their assumptions are listed in Figure 12.13.

Depreciation Method	Assumption
Straight-Line Method	Asset depreciates equally every year
Declining-Balance and Double-Declining-Balance Method	Asset depreciates faster at the beginning
Units-of-Production Method	Asset depreciates based on activity level

FIGURE 12.13

The Straight-Line Method

The straight-line method of depreciation was first introduced in Chapter 5. The **straight-line method of depreciation** produces an average depreciation expense, which is applied each year until the asset is sold or reaches the end of its useful life. Figure 12.14 shows the formula to calculate the amount of depreciation under the straight-line method.

$$\text{Straight-Line Depreciation} = \frac{\text{Cost of Asset} - \text{Residual Value}}{\text{Useful Life}}$$

FIGURE 12.14

There are three components of the calculation.

1. The total cost of the asset is the original purchase price of the asset and any additional costs required to get it in a ready-to-use condition.

2. The residual value is the estimated value of the asset at the end of its useful life. Since the residual value is not depreciated, it is subtracted from the total cost of the asset.

3. The useful life is an estimate of how long the asset is expected to be used by the business. Useful life is usually expressed in years.

For example, Smith Tools buys a machine for $5,000. The machine is expected to have a useful life of five years and its residual value is estimated to be $1,000. The calculation to determine the amount of depreciation applied annually for the machine is shown below.

$$\text{Straight-Line Depreciation} = \frac{\$5,000 - \$1,000}{5 \text{ years}}$$

$$= \$800/\text{year}$$

If the machine was purchased on January 1, 2018, the annual depreciation is applied to the machine as shown in Figure 12.15.

Year	Cost of Machine	Depreciation Expense	Accumulated Depreciation	Net Book Value
2018	$5,000	$800	$800	$4,200
2019	5,000	800	1,600	3,400
2020	5,000	800	2,400	2,600
2021	5,000	800	3,200	1,800
2022	5,000	800	4,000	**1,000**

FIGURE 12.15

A depreciation of $800 is accumulated each year until the end of the asset's useful life. At that time, all that is left of the asset's book value is its residual value. In this case, the amount is $1,000, the final net book value (shown in green in Figure 12.15).

Now, assume that the asset has no residual value at the end of its useful life. This means that the total amount to be depreciated is $5,000, which was the original cost of the asset. The annual depreciation amount is calculated as $1,000 ($5,000 ÷ 5).

As is common in accounting, the calculations are only part of the process. The next step is to record the results of those calculations in the financial statements.

Accountants want to see the original value of the asset on the balance sheet and the net book value change over time. Contra accounts allow both values to be reflected on the balance sheet. Remember, a contra-asset account is linked to another asset account to reduce the value of the asset. The contra account for a noncurrent asset is called accumulated depreciation. It reflects the decrease in value of the noncurrent asset over time. The original cost of the noncurrent asset account remains constant.

Figure 12.16 shows the corresponding journal entry for recording $1,000 of depreciation expense of the machine on December 31, 2018.

JOURNAL			
Date	**Account Title and Explanation**	**Debit**	**Credit**
Dec 31	Depreciation Expense	1,000	
	Accumulated Depreciation—Machine		1,000
	Record the depreciation of machine for the first year		

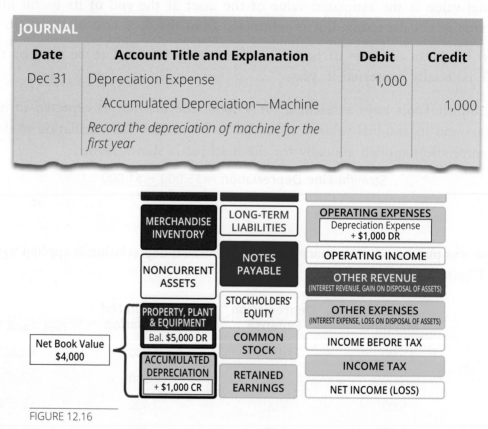

FIGURE 12.16

The initial purchase of the asset on January 1 is shown as a $5,000 debit balance in property, plant and equipment. The entry for depreciation on December 31 is recorded as a $1,000 credit to accumulated depreciation. This reduces the net book value of the machine to $4,000. Equity decreases with the depreciation expense that is recorded on the income statement under operating expenses.

Each year depreciation is recorded, the amount of accumulated depreciation increases and the net book value of the noncurrent asset decreases. This is illustrated in Figure 12.17. Notice that as accumulated depreciation increases by $1,000 each year, the net book value decreases by $1,000.

Year	Cost of Noncurrent Asset	Depreciation Expense	Accumulated Depreciation	Net Book Value
2018	$5,000	$1,000	$1,000	$4,000
2019	5,000	1,000	2,000	3,000
2020	5,000	1,000	3,000	2,000
2021	5,000	1,000	4,000	1,000
2022	5,000	1,000	5,000	0

FIGURE 12.17

The Declining-Balance and Double-Declining-Balance Methods

One drawback to the straight-line method is that it may not realistically reflect how the cost of the asset should be allocated, thus showing an inaccurate net book value for the asset. This is because the net book value of noncurrent assets does not always decrease by the same amount each year. Alternative depreciation methods have been developed by the accounting profession. One of them is the declining-balance method.

The most common real-life example of asset depreciation is a car. Usually, the largest decrease in the net book value of a car occurs the moment it is driven off the dealership's lot. Since the greatest depreciation in value occurs during the early years of the car's useful life, the declining-balance method is used. This concept applies to many noncurrent assets.

While the straight-line method simply applies an average depreciation rate, the **declining-balance method** applies an annual percentage for the calculation of depreciation against the net book value of the asset. Since the net book value decreases each year, a higher level of depreciation is recorded in the early years of the asset's useful life. The formula to calculate annual depreciation rate under the declining-balance method is shown in Figure 12.18.

$$\text{Declining-Balance Depreciation Rate} = \frac{100\%}{\text{Years of Useful Life}}$$

FIGURE 12.18

Consider the purchase of equipment worth $10,000 that has a useful life of five years with no residual value. The percentage for the declining-balance method is calculated as shown below.

$$\text{Declining-Balance Depreciation Rate} = \frac{100\%}{5}$$
$$= 20\%$$

An annual depreciation rate of 20% is applied to the net book value of the asset to calculate depreciation for each year. In the first year, depreciation can be calculated by multiplying the depreciation rate of 20% with the asset's original cost of $10,000. Therefore, the first year's depreciation is equal to $2,000. The net book value of the asset after deducting the first year's depreciation is $8000 ($10,000 – $2,000). In the second year, depreciation is equal to $1,600 (20% × net book value of $8,000). As the asset's net book value decreases, the depreciation amount also gradually decreases from year to year.

Unlike the straight-line method, which applies the same dollar amount of depreciation every year, the declining-balance method applies the same depreciation *percentage rate* to the net book value every year. If the useful life of the asset is 10 years instead of the 5 years shown in the above example, the depreciation rate applied each year is 10% (100% ÷ 10); if the useful life is 20 years, the depreciation rate applied each year is 5% (100% ÷ 20); and so on.

The depreciation rate can be multiplied based on the accountant's estimation of how fast the asset's value will depreciate. One of the most commonly used depreciation rates is the **double-declining-balance method**, which doubles the declining-balance rate of depreciation. For example, a double-declining depreciation rate of 40% (20% × 2) is used when the useful life of an asset is five years. When the useful life is 10 years, a double-declining depreciation rate of 20% is used (10% × 2). For a useful life of 20 years, an annual rate of 10% is used (5% × 2).

The formula for calculating the double-declining depreciation rate is shown in Figure 12.19.

Double-Declining Depreciation Rate = Declining-Balance Depreciation Rate × 2

FIGURE 12.19

Using a double-declining rate exaggerates the declining effect by two. This ensures that much of the depreciation occurs during the early years of an asset's life span.

In the example of the $10,000 piece of equipment with a useful life of five years, assume the company uses the double-declining-balance method. The depreciation for the first year is calculated as follows.

$10,000 x 40% = $4,000

The net book value for the beginning of the second year is calculated as follows.

$10,000 – $4,000 = $6,000

The double-declining depreciation rate of 40% is applied to this new balance to determine the depreciation amount for the second year.

$6,000 x 40% = $2,400

The same double-declining rate is applied to a decreasing net book value on an annual basis. This means that over the years, the depreciation amounts are reduced substantially, which generally reflects the way noncurrent assets decline in value.

The rest of the depreciation amounts in the example are shown in Figure 12.20.

Year	Beginning of Year Book Value	@ 40% Double-Declining Depreciation Rate	Remaining Book Value
1	$10,000	minus $4,000 equals	$6,000
2	6,000	2,400	3,600
3	3,600	1,440	2,160
4	2,160	864	1,296
5	1,296	518.40	777.60

FIGURE 12.20

Applying a percentage rate to a balance every year means there will always be a remaining balance when the declining-balance or double-declining-balance methods are used. In this example, the remaining book value at the end of five years under the double-declining-balance method is $777.60 despite the asset having a zero estimated residual value. Because a noncurrent asset is not fully depreciated by the end of its useful life under the double-declining-balance method, companies usually switch from the double-declining-balance method to the straight-line method when the asset reaches half of its useful life so the asset will be fully depreciated. If the asset has a residual value when the declining-balance (or double-declining-balance) method is used, the asset should not be depreciated below the residual value. For example, if the residual value is $1,000 for the example shown above, Figure 12.21 shows the depreciation amounts. Notice that in the last year, depreciation can only be $296 to drop the net book value to the residual amount of $1,000.

WORTH REPEATING

The straight-line method applies the same depreciation amount to the net book value of a noncurrent asset for each year of its useful life.

The declining-balance and double-declining-balance methods apply a depreciation percentage to the net book value of a noncurrent asset. Therefore, a larger amount of depreciation is applied in the early years of the asset's useful life. For many assets, this is a more realistic estimation of how the asset will depreciate each year.

Year	Beginning of Year Book Value	@ 40% Double-Declining Depreciation Rate	Remaining Book Value
1	$10,000	$4,000	$6,000
2	6,000	2,400	3,600
3	3,600	1,440	2,160
4	2,160	864	1,296
5	1,296	296*	1,000

*Only $296, instead of $518.40, is subtracted from the beginning of the year book value to avoid having the remaining book value drop below a residual value of $1,000.

FIGURE 12.21

Pause & Reflect

Exercise 12-2

On January 1, 2018, London Bridge Company purchased a hydraulic stamping machine for $5,000,000. It is expected to last five years and estimated to have a residual value of $400,000 at the end of the five years. London Bridge Company will depreciate the machine using the double-declining-balance method. Prepare the following chart to calculate the depreciation for each year.

Year	Beginning of Year Book Value	Depreciation	Remaining Book Value
2018			
2019			
2020			
2021			
2022			

See Appendix I for solutions.

The Units-of-Production Method

The **units-of-production method** involves a different procedure for depreciating property, plant and equipment. The level of asset usage is the basis for calculating depreciation. The methods studied so far use a predetermined formula that is not based on usage.

The following steps are involved when using the units-of-production method.

1. Choose a unit for measuring the usage of the noncurrent asset. For example, if the asset is a vehicle, the unit can be the number of miles driven. If the asset is a machine, the unit can be the number of hours operated. These measures are known as units-of-production, hence the name of this method.

2. Estimate the number of units used for the entire life of the asset. For example, an estimate for a vehicle may be 200,000 miles, or for a machine may be 600,000 hours.

3. Divide the total cost of the asset by the estimated number of units from step 2. This gives the cost per unit.

4. The cost per unit determined in step 3 is multiplied by the number of units produced in a year to determine that year's depreciation amount.

Step 4 is repeated each year until the end of the asset's estimated useful life. Figure 12.22 shows how to calculate the cost per unit amount.

$$\text{Cost per Unit Amount} = \frac{\text{Cost} - \text{Residual Value}}{\text{Total Units of Production}}$$

FIGURE 12.22

Here is an example to illustrate how the units-of-production method is applied in the depreciation of property, plant and equipment.

Fenway Delivery bought a delivery truck for $110,000. The truck has an estimated residual value of $10,000. The company chooses a mile (mi) as the unit for measuring usage (step 1). The company wants its trucks to be in top condition, so it retires them after 200,000 miles of usage (step 2). The calculation for the per unit amount (step 3) is shown here.

$$\text{Cost per Unit Amount} = \frac{\$110,000 - \$10,000}{200,000 \text{ mi}}$$

$$= \$0.50/\text{mi}$$

Using the cost per unit amount, the amount of depreciation applied for that period is shown in Figure 12.23

Units-of-Production Depreciation = Units of Production Used for Year x Cost per Unit Amount

FIGURE 12.23

If the truck is driven 30,000 miles for the first year, the depreciation for that year (step 4) is calculated as shown here.

$$\text{Units-of-Production Depreciation} = 30,000 \text{ mi} \times \$0.50/\text{mi}$$

$$= \$15,000$$

The amount of depreciation for a year is entirely dependent on the asset's usage. For example, if the truck was driven for 25,000 miles in the second year, the depreciation for that year is calculated as follows.

$$25,000 \text{ mi} \times \$0.50/\text{mi} = \$12,500$$

If the truck was driven for 35,000 miles in the third year, the depreciation for that year is calculated as follows.

$$35,000 \text{ mi} \times \$0.50/\text{mi} = \$17,500$$

This depreciation procedure is applied annually until the truck has been driven for 200,000 miles, the initial estimation for the life of the truck. Once the usage exceeds the estimated units of production, no additional depreciation expense should be allocated to the units produced.

Choosing a Depreciation Method

As is common in accounting, no single method of calculating a balance sheet item is necessarily better than or preferable to another. The challenge for the accountant is to choose a method that best reflects the nature of the asset involved. For example, a company might use the straight-line method to depreciate an advertising sign, but use the declining-balance method to depreciate a company-owned vehicle, since the value of cars and trucks decreases most during their early years.

A Comparison of Depreciation Methods

Figure 12.24 compares depreciation expense under the three different depreciation methods. Using numbers from our previous examples, although the depreciation expense for each period is different, the total over the asset's useful life remains the same under all methods.

Refer to the example of Fenway Delivery, who bought a delivery truck for $110,000. The truck's estimated residual value is $10,000. The company retires all of its trucks after 200,000 miles of use. The cost per unit of production (in which "production" was stated in miles of usage) was calculated as $0.50/mi. For our example, the number of miles the truck was driven per year is shown in brackets under the units-of-production method. Assume that the 200,000 miles occur during a five-year period. This allows a comparison of all the depreciation methods based on an estimated useful life of five years.

	Depreciation Expense		
Year	Straight-Line Method $20,000/year[1]	Double-Declining-Balance Method 40%/year[2]	Units-of-Production Method
2018	$20,000	$44,000 ($110,000 x 40%)	$15,000 ($0.50 x 30,000 mi)
2019	20,000	26,400 ($66,000 x 40%)	12,500 ($0.50 x 25,000 mi)
2020	20,000	15,840 ($39,600 x 40%)	17,500 ($0.50 x 35,000 mi)
2021	20,000	9,504 ($23,760 x 40%)	30,000 ($0.50 x 60,000 mi)
2022	20,000	4,256[3]	25,000 ($0.50 x 50,000 mi)
Total	$100,000	$100,000	$100,000

[1] ($110,000 – $10,000)/5
[2] 100%/5 years x 2
[3] The net book value of $14,256 x 40% gives a depreciation of $5,702; however, only $4,256 is applied because the truck cannot be depreciated beyond a residual value of $10,000.

FIGURE 12.24

Depreciation for Partial Years

Our examination of depreciation has been based on the assumption that property, plant and equipment are purchased on the first day of a year and sold on the last day of another year. Of course, depreciation methods do not dictate when assets are bought and sold. Various tactics can be employed to accommodate the realities of the calendar year when depreciating a company's noncurrent assets. Once a noncurrent asset has been purchased, the accountant must choose a depreciation schedule that accommodates the timing of asset ownership.

A number of possible combinations are available to the accountant to depreciate during the year (or month) of purchase or sale. One common approach, illustrated below, is to calculate the depreciation of the asset purchased between the first and 15th day of a month for the full month of purchase, as if the asset was purchased on the first day of the month, and to not apply any depreciation in the month of purchase if the asset is purchased between the 16th day and the last day of the month, as if the asset was purchased on the first day of the next month. These combinations provide the accountant with the flexibility to develop a depreciation schedule that best reflects the business reality of the company.

Examine the situation that arises from the purchase of a $120,000 packaging machine by the Jones Cookie Factory on March 27, 2011. The company determines that the packager has a useful life of 10 years, after which it will not be salvageable; thus no residual value needs to be estimated. The machine will be depreciated by $12,000 annually, which is equivalent to $1,000 monthly. The machine is eventually sold on October 19, 2018 for $32,000. The fiscal year end for the Jones Cookie Factory is November 30.

The company decides to use the following depreciation rules: the asset is depreciated for a whole month of purchase if it is purchased by the 15th day of the month, and not depreciated in the month of purchase if it is purchased after the 15th day of the month. If the asset is sold by the 15th day of the month, it is not depreciated in the month of sale. If the asset is sold after the 15th day of the month, it is depreciated for a whole month of sale.

Figure 12.25 displays the annual depreciation calculated after the application of the chosen schedule. For fiscal years 2012 to 2017, each year includes 12 full months and has $12,000 of annual depreciation at $1,000 per month. That is the easy part. The challenge is dealing with the partial years of 2011 (year of purchase) and 2018 (year of sale).

	Months	Depreciation
2011	8	$8,000
2012	12	12,000
2013	12	12,000
2014	12	12,000
2015	12	12,000
2016	12	12,000
2017	12	12,000
2018	11	11,000
	Total	$91,000

FIGURE 12.25

In fiscal year 2011, although the actual month of purchase was March, it is assumed that the machine was purchased on April 1. The chosen schedule dictates that there is no depreciation in the month of purchase if the asset is purchased after the 15th day of the month, as illustrated in Figure 12.26. That leaves eight months of depreciation in the fiscal year, or $8,000.

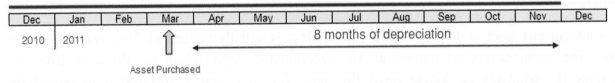

Fiscal Year 2011

FIGURE 12.26

In fiscal year 2018, the month of sale was October. The chosen schedule dictates that since the sale occurred within the second half of the month, depreciation for the entire month is calculated, as shown in Figure 12.27. This means there are 11 months of depreciation for the fiscal year, for a total of $11,000.

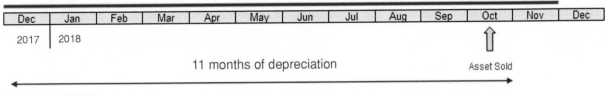

Fiscal Year 2018

FIGURE 12.27

As Figure 12.28 shows, the total amount depreciated for the packaging machine is $91,000. Subtracting this amount from the original purchase price of $120,000 produces a net book value of $29,000. If the machine is sold for $32,000, it generates a gain of $3,000 on the sale. A different depreciation method would likely result in a different amount for the gain, or even a loss on the sale.

Packaging Machine

Original Purchase Price $120,000

Depreciated $91,000

Net Book Value at Disposal $29,000

$32,000 Sale Price – $29,000 Book Value = $3,000 Gain

FIGURE 12.28

Another common practice of the partial depreciation is a half-year of depreciation in the year of acquisition and a half-year of depreciation in the year of sale. If the company chooses to use this method, the gain or loss on the sale will likely change. Although depreciation is an estimate, the accountant should try to make the estimate as accurate as possible.

Disposal of Assets and Revision of Depreciation

When a noncurrent asset is disposed of, a gain or loss is usually generated from the disposal of the asset. The accountant must remove all the accumulated depreciation for the asset from the books, since the company no longer owns the item. The first step of disposal is to record the depreciation expense for the current year.

For example, a company has equipment that costs $5,000, with a useful life of five years and a residual value of $1,000. Assume that the company has not yet recorded depreciation expense for the year ended December 31, 2018. The first step is to update the depreciation as at the disposal date. For this scenario, we will assume an annual straight-line depreciation of $800 ([$5,000 – $1,000] ÷ 5). The journal entry to update the depreciation before disposal is shown in Figure 12.29. This entry brings the balance in the accumulated depreciation account to $4,000.

JOURNAL			
Date	**Account Title and Explanation**	**Debit**	**Credit**
Dec 31	Depreciation Expense	800	
	Accumulated Depreciation—Equipment		800
	To record current period depreciation on equipment for disposal		

FIGURE 12.29

The asset is eventually sold after five years on December 31, 2018 for $1,000. When the asset is sold, the journal entry to record the transaction is shown in Figure 12.30.

JOURNAL			
Date	**Account Title and Explanation**	**Debit**	**Credit**
Dec 31	Cash	1,000	
	Accumulated Depreciation—Equipment	4,000	
	Equipment		5,000
	To record the sale of used asset for $1,000		

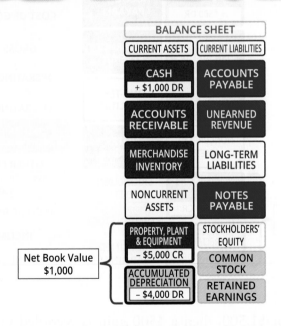

FIGURE 12.30

The amount of $1,000 is received for the asset and debited to cash. An amount of $4,000 is debited to the accumulated depreciation account, which initially had a credit balance of $4,000 due to adjusting entries made over the years. This amount is now cleared. Lastly, $5,000 is credited to the property, plant and equipment account to clear the value of the asset since the company no longer owns it.

Now assume that the equipment was sold for $500, half the estimated residual value. As shown before, depreciation is first updated as at the disposal date. The $4,000 in accumulated depreciation is debited to that account, and the initial cost of $5,000 is credited to the property, plant and equipment asset account. Since only $500 was received for the asset, this amount is debited to cash and the $500 loss is recorded as an other expense on the income statement. The transaction is shown in Figure 12.31.

JOURNAL			
Date	**Account Title and Explanation**	**Debit**	**Credit**
Dec 31	Cash	500	
	Accumulated Depreciation—Equipment	4,000	
	Loss on Disposal of Asset	500	
	Equipment		5,000
	To record the sale of used asset for $500		

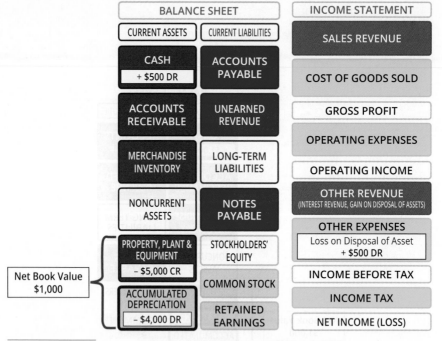

FIGURE 12.31

If the equipment was sold for $1,500, then a $500 gain is recorded under other revenue, since it was sold for more than the net book value. This is shown in Figure 12.32.

JOURNAL			
Date	**Account Title and Explanation**	**Debit**	**Credit**
Dec 31	Cash	1,500	
	Accumulated Depreciation—Equipment	4,000	
	Gain on Disposal of Asset		500
	Equipment		5,000
	To record the sale of used asset for $1,500		

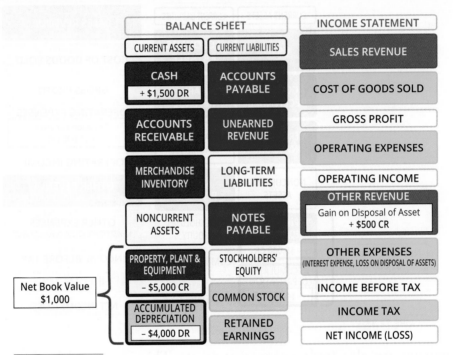

FIGURE 12.32

Instead of trying to sell the noncurrent asset, a company may decide to donate it to charity. The transaction involves a loss for the company and is recorded as a donation expense under other expenses on the income statement.

Assume the company donated the equipment from the previous example to a local charity. The first step, as in the other examples, is to update the depreciation for the period prior to disposal of the asset. This brings the balance in the accumulated depreciation account to $4,000. The journal entry to record the donation is shown in Figure 12.33.

JOURNAL			
Date	**Account Title and Explanation**	**Debit**	**Credit**
Dec 31	Accumulated Depreciation—Equipment	4,000	
	Donation Expense	1,000	
	Equipment		5,000
	To record the donation of used asset		

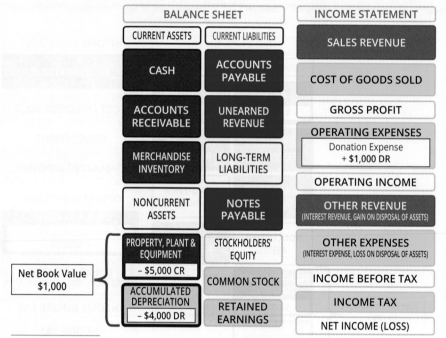

FIGURE 12.33

Note that a company can also trade noncurrent assets. This is covered in Appendix 12A at the end of this chapter.

As explained earlier, a noncurrent asset can be disposed of in many ways that do not involve selling the item. For the purpose of this textbook, we have discussed only the routine methods of disposal and provided a solid foundation for understanding the accounting concept in general. Here is one final change to the initial example in this section. Instead of five years, the life of the equipment ends up being four years, and the asset is sold for $500.

When the useful life was five years, $4,000 of total depreciation had to be spread out over those five years, using the straight-line method. This amounted to $800 of depreciation per year. If the actual life of the asset ends up being four years, then only four years' worth of depreciation has accumulated, for a total of $3,200 ($800 × 4). The remaining book value, which is the residual value ($1,000) plus the amount yet to be depreciated ($800) is $1,800. Since the asset was sold for $500, this results in a loss of $1,300.

To record this as a journal entry, $500 is debited to cash; $3,200 in accumulated depreciation is taken off the books by debiting that amount; $1,300 is debited as a loss on the income statement; and the original cost of the asset ($5,000) is removed from the books by crediting that amount to the account. The journal entry for this is shown in Figure 12.34.

JOURNAL

Date	Account Title and Explanation	Debit	Credit
Dec 31	Cash	500	
	Accumulated Depreciation—Equipment	3,200	
	Loss on Disposal of Asset	1,300	
	Equipment		5,000
	To record the sale of used asset for $500		

FIGURE 12.34

If the company wants to retire this equipment at the end of the fourth year but cannot find a buyer for the equipment, the transaction still needs to be recorded even though the company does not gain any proceeds from the asset retirement. As a first step, we must record the depreciation expense for the current year before removing the asset from the books. Recall that the annual depreciation expense for the truck is $800. The journal entry prior to disposal is shown in Figure 12.35. This entry brings the balance in the accumulated depreciation account to $3,200.

JOURNAL

Date	Account Title and Explanation	Debit	Credit
Dec 31	Depreciation Expense	800	
	Accumulated Depreciation—Equipment		800
	To record current period depreciation on equipment for disposal		

FIGURE 12.35

When the equipment is retired, the accumulated depreciation of $3,200 and the original cost of $5,000 are removed from the books, while the loss on disposal of asset increases to $1,800. The journal entry for disposal of the equipment is shown in Figure 12.36.

JOURNAL

Date	Account Title and Explanation	Debit	Credit
Dec 31	Accumulated Depreciation—Equipment	3,200	
	Loss on Disposal of Asset	1,800	
	Equipment		5,000
	To record disposal of equipment		

FIGURE 12.36

If there is no gain or loss on the disposal of the asset, the journal entry still needs to be made whenever a noncurrent asset is retired. The retirement of an asset that has been fully depreciated without any residual value simply involves debiting accumulated depreciation and crediting the asset account at the original cost of the asset, as shown in Figure 12.37.

JOURNAL			
Date	**Account Title and Explanation**	**Debit**	**Credit**
Dec 31	Accumulated Depreciation—Equipment	5,000	
	Equipment		5,000
	To record disposal of fully-depreciated equipment		

FIGURE 12.37

This completely removes the asset and its accumulated depreciation from the company's books.

One final note using our original example. If the company uses the asset for longer than the estimated useful life of five years, the remaining book value is $1,000, which is the estimated residual value. In this case, no adjustments are made and the company continues to use the asset without further depreciation.

Pause & Reflect

Exercise 12-3

Whitechapel Manufacturing sold an old piece of equipment on December 31, 2018 for $360,000. The company purchased it on January 1, 2010 for $3,000,000. It was estimated to last 10 years and have a residual value of $400,000. The depreciation for 2018 has not yet been recorded. Prepare the journal entries to record the yearly depreciation and the disposal of the asset on December 31, 2018.

JOURNAL			
Date	**Account Title and Explanation**	**Debit**	**Credit**

See Appendix I for solutions.

Revising Depreciation

Our examination of depreciation in this chapter has included numerous references to estimates. We have also looked at examples in which the residual value, the asset's useful life, or both, were incorrectly estimated. Let us take a closer look at these scenarios with a more comprehensive example.

Brian's Bricks bought a new brick molding machine for its factory at a cost of $300,000. It is expected to have a useful life of 10 years and a residual value of $20,000, as shown in Figure 12.38.

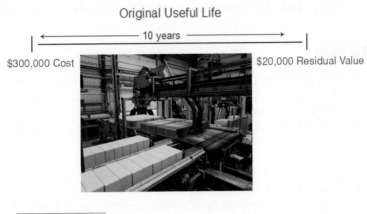

FIGURE 12.38

After five years of use, the molding machine is not deteriorating as quickly as expected. After consulting with the machine's manufacturer, management determines that the useful life of this asset could be extended to 15 years, and the residual value increased to $40,000, as illustrated in Figure 12.39.

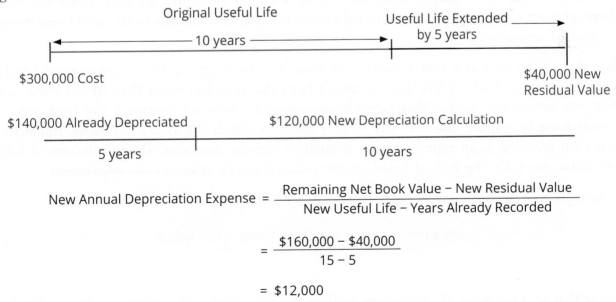

FIGURE 12.39

Using the straight-line method, the company's accountants had already recorded a total depreciation of $140,000 over five years [(($300,000 − $20,000) ÷ 10) × 5], which produced a net book value of $160,000 ($300,000 − $140,000).

Brian's Bricks then started a new depreciation schedule, assuming the straight-line method again, in which the amount to be depreciated for the rest of the asset's new useful life would be $120,000 ($160,000 – $40,000), where $40,000 is the new residual value. This amount is divided by the number of years left in the new useful life of 10 years (15 years – 5 years already recorded), to produce an annual depreciation amount of $12,000.

Note that the company should not change the depreciation already accumulated during the first five years of using the molding machine. An accountant should only make or change depreciation estimates for the future. Any changes that are made need to be justified with the appropriate documentation. In this case, that documentation would include a consultation with the asset's manufacturer.

GAAP vs IFRS

There are two ways for a company to re-measure the value of noncurrent assets: the cost model and the revaluation model. Under GAAP, only the cost model is allowed, so noncurrent assets must always be recorded at cost (less accumulated depreciation and impairment). This means that if the market value of an asset increases, GAAP prohibits companies from recording the corresponding increase in the asset's book value.

However, under IFRS, companies may choose to account for noncurrent assets using either the cost model or the revaluation model. Under the revaluation model, assets are revalued periodically to reflect their fair market value. This means that if the market value of a noncurrent asset is higher than the asset's net book value, under IFRS' revaluation model, the company increases the book value of the asset to match its market value. Unlike GAAP, IFRS requires an annual review of useful life and residual value estimates.

Depreciation also needs to be revised when the value of the asset decreases due to impairment. **Impairment** occurs when the asset's fair value appears to permanently drop to a point that is below its net book value. Both external factors (i.e. changes in technology that reduce the older-technology asset's market price) and internal factors (i.e. physical damage to the asset) may provide indicators of impairment.

When there is an indicator that a noncurrent asset may be impaired, the company must conduct impairment tests to find out whether the asset's fair value is in fact lower than its net book value. When any noncurrent asset, either tangible or intangible, becomes impaired, the book value of the asset must be written down on the balance sheet to match the asset's fair value. Impairment loss is then recorded as an expense on the company's income statement. The calculations of future depreciation must also be revised based on the reduced asset's value due to impairment.

The formula to calculate impairment loss is shown in Figure 12.40.

Impairment Loss = Net Book Value – Fair Value

FIGURE 12.40

Assume that on December 31, a company realizes that the value of its factory machinery has been impaired due to physical damage. The machinery's fair value is determined to be $60,000 while the machinery's original cost was $130,000. Up to this date, the accumulated depreciation is recorded as $40,000. The company must first determine the net book value of the machinery, as shown here.

$$\text{Net Book Value} = \$130{,}000 - \$40{,}000$$
$$= \$90{,}000$$

Using this value and the formula from Figure 12.40, impairment loss is calculated as follows.

$$\text{Impairment Loss} = \$90{,}000 - \$60{,}000$$
$$= \$30{,}000$$

The fair value of $60,000 is $30,000 less than the net book value of $90,000. Figure 12.41 shows that the $30,000 impairment is recorded by debiting the impairment loss account and crediting the accumulated depreciation account. As indicated by the Accounting Map, on the income statement, the loss increases the operating expenses; on the balance sheet, it decreases the net book value of the machinery by increasing the accumulated depreciation account.

JOURNAL			
Date	**Account Title and Explanation**	**Debit**	**Credit**
Dec 31	Impairment Loss	30,000	
	Accumulated Depreciation—Machinery		30,000
	To record impairment loss		

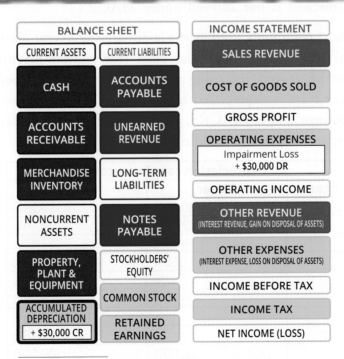

FIGURE 12.41

GAAP vs IFRS

Under GAAP, the book value of an impaired plant asset is written down to its fair value. An impairment loss that has been previously recorded can never be reversed.

Under IFRS, the book value of an impaired plant asset is written down to its recoverable amount. An asset's recoverable amount is equal to the asset's market price less costs of disposal, or its future value, whichever is higher. Future value represents future revenue that the asset will generate for the company. IFRS allows reversal of previously recorded impairments for all tangible and intangible assets, except goodwill. Impairment reversal is recorded in income, while any increase in market value over the asset's original cost is recorded in comprehensive income.

Depreciation for Federal Income Tax Purposes

In the US, businesses usually keep separate depreciation records for financial accounting purposes versus tax accounting purposes. Simply put, "book depreciation" is different from "tax depreciation." This is because the purpose of financial accounting is to report a company's financial position and performance, while tax accounting is intended to adhere to the federal Internal Revenue Code. The depreciation rules under US federal income tax law are known as the **Modified Accelerated Cost Recovery System (MACRS)**. MACRS specifies both the method of depreciation to be used (declining-balance methods or the straight-line method) and the lives of the different asset classes. (The units-of-production method is not allowed under MACRS.)

For instance, two of the most commonly used asset classes are the 5-year class (which covers lighter vehicles, such as cars and trucks) and the 7-year class (for heavier machinery and equipment). Both of these classes must be depreciated using a declining-balance method, as shown in Figure 12.42. Note that the 5-year class is depreciated over six years, and the 7-year class is depreciated over eight years. This is because under MACRS, all fixed assets are considered to be entered into service, and removed from service, in the middle of the year.

	Depreciation rate for recovery period	
Year	5-Year	7-Year
1	20.00%	14.29%
2	32.00%	24.49%
3	19.20%	17.49%
4	11.52%	12.49%
5	11.52%	8.93%
6	5.76%	8.92%
7		8.93%
8		4.46%
	100.00%	100.00%

FIGURE 12.42

Because MACRS allocates costs over an arbitrary useful life that is often less than the asset's useful life, it is not considered suitable for financial accounting purposes. It also does not take into account an asset's residual value when computing depreciation. Details of depreciation under MACRS are beyond the scope of this course.

Natural Resources

Natural resources have a physical nature, but are different from the nature of property, plant and equipment. In fact, some companies place natural resources in a separate asset category on the balance sheet. **Natural resources** include things such as metal ores, minerals, timber, petroleum and natural gas. We will examine these types of assets in our broader discussion of noncurrent assets and how we account for natural resources in the company's books.

First, natural resources come at a cost. This includes any expenditures to acquire the asset, such as preparing resources for extraction. It also includes any expenditure for restoring the land upon completion of use. The total cost is recorded in the appropriate asset account on the balance sheet.

Second, the value of natural resources decreases over time as more natural resources are extracted from the ground or harvested from the land. As the resources are collected and sold, they must be allocated, or expensed, to the period in which they are consumed. This is called **depletion**, and needs to be accounted for in the books just as depreciation is with property, plant and equipment. The resources must also be reported on the balance sheet at cost less accumulated depletion.

> ## A CLOSER LOOK
>
> Some companies still use the terms *amortization* or *depreciation* instead of *depletion*.
>
> Not all companies use the accumulated depreciation or depletion account. Instead, they credit the natural resource account directly and debit the expense account.

Our examination of depreciation introduced us to the units-of-production method of depreciation; the method that involves actual usage of an asset. It is appropriate for calculating the depletion of natural resources, where actual units, such as ounces, barrels or metric tons, can be used in the calculation.

We can use the example of a mining company to illustrate how the units-of-production method is applied to a natural resource asset. The company has bought land containing an estimated 8,000,000 tons of ore (rock from which minerals can be extracted), at a total cost of $10 million. It estimates that once all the ore has been extracted, the land will have zero residual value. Using this information, we can calculate depletion as follows.

1. Determine the depletion rate per unit using the formula shown in Figure 12.43.

$$\text{Depletion Rate} = \frac{\text{Total Cost} - \text{Residual Value}}{\text{Estimated Total Units of Resource}}$$

FIGURE 12.43

Using the values from the mining company example, the depletion rate is calculated as follows.

$$\text{Depletion Rate} = \frac{\$10,000,000 - \$0}{8,000,000 \text{ tons}}$$
$$= \$1.25/\text{ton}$$

2. If 2,000,000 tons were mined and sold in the first year, the depletion expense for the year is calculated using the formula shown in Figure 12.44.

Depletion Expense = Depletion Rate × Quantity Extracted and Sold

FIGURE 12.44

Using the depletion rate of $1.25/ton, depletion expense is calculated as shown here.

Depletion Expense = $1.25/ton × 2,000,000 tons
= $2,500,000

Figure 12.45 shows the journal entry at the end of the year.

JOURNAL			
Date	Account Title and Explanation	Debit	Credit
Dec 31	Depletion Expense—Mineral Deposit	2,500,000	
	Accumulated Depletion—Mineral Deposit		2,500,000
	To record depletion of mineral deposit for year		

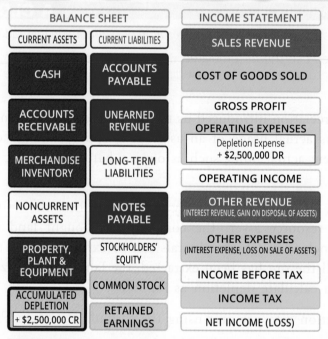

FIGURE 12.45

The $2,500,000 accumulated depletion for the year is reported on the year-end balance sheet as a contra asset to the mineral deposit account. The same amount is reported as an expense on the income statement at the end of the period.

This example assumes that all 2,000,000 tons of the ore mined in the year are sold within that same period. But suppose that in the second year, 1,000,000 tons of ore are mined but only 700,000 tons are sold, leaving 300,000 tons of ore unsold. The depletion on the unsold portion of ore must be carried forward as a current asset, called Ore Inventory, on the balance sheet. The depletion for the second year is calculated as follows.

$$\text{Depletion Expense} = \$1.25/\text{ton} \times 700,000 \text{ tons}$$

$$= \$875,000$$

The remaining 300,000 tons is carried as ore inventory, with a value of $375,000 ($1.25/ton × 300,000 tons).

The journal entry is shown in Figure 12.46.

JOURNAL			
Date	**Account Title and Explanation**	**Debit**	**Credit**
Dec 31	Depletion Expense—Mineral Deposit	875,000	
	Ore Inventory	375,000	
	Accumulated Depletion—Mineral Deposit		1,250,000
	To record depletion and inventory of mineral deposit for year		

FIGURE 12.46

On the balance sheet, the mineral deposit is reported at its original cost less the accumulated depletion. The ore inventory is carried as a separate asset. The depletion of $875,000 is reported as an expense on the income statement at the end of the period.

Pause & Reflect

Exercise 12-4

GoldCorp has just purchased a gold mine for $21,000,000. At the end of its life, the land for the gold mine is expected to be worth $1,000,000. GoldCorp estimates that it will mine 500,000 ounces of gold. During its first year of operation, 14,000 ounces were mined and sold.

a) Calculate the depletion rate per unit.

b) Prepare the journal entry for the first year of depletion on December 31, 2018.

JOURNAL			
Date	**Account Title and Explanation**	**Debit**	**Credit**

See Appendix I for solutions.

Since we have learned the calculations and journal entries for natural resource transactions, we can look at how the information is presented by an American mining company in the real world. Newmont Mining Corporation is one of the world's leaders in the gold mining industry. Headquartered in Colorado and founded in 1921, Newmont has operations in the US, Australia, New Zealand, Peru, Indonesia and Ghana. Gold mining requires a lot of investments in terms of property, plant and equipment. Figure 12.47 represents the components of Newmont's property, plant and equipment.

Note 22: Property, Plant and Mine Development (dollars in millions)

	Depreciable Life (in years)	At December 31, 2015			At December 31, 2014		
		Cost	Accumulated Depreciation	Net Book Value	Cost	Accumulated Depreciation	Net Book Value
Land	–	$222	$ –	$222	$222	$ –	$222
Facilities and equipment	1 – 22	16,848	(9,720)	7,128	16,022	(9,076)	6,946
Mine development	1 – 22	4,832	(2,554)	2,278	4,502	(2,374)	2,128
Mineral interests	1 – 22	1,990	(528)	1,462	1,989	(556)	1,433
Asset retirement cost	1 – 22	1,001	(615)	386	1,043	(529)	514
Construction-in-progress	–	2,827	–	2,827	2,407	–	2,407
		$27,720	$(13,417)	$14,303	$26,185	$(12,535)	$13,650
Leased assets included above in facilities and equipment	1 – 22	$30	$(4)	$26	$8	$(1)	$7

Mineral Interests	Depreciable Life (in years)	At December 31, 2015			At December 31, 2014		
		Cost	Accumulated Depreciation	Net Book Value	Cost	Accumulated Depreciation	Net Book Value
Production stage	1 – 22	$713	$(528)	$185	$733	$(556)	$177
Development stage	–	215	–	215	190	–	190
Exploration state	–	1,062	–	1,062	1,066	–	1,066
		$1,990	$(528)	$1,462	$1,989	$(556)	$1,433

FIGURE 12.47

Figure 12.47 shows the balances included in Note 22 in the Notes to the Financial Statements section of Newmont Mining Corporation's 2015 annual report. It provides the details of Newmont's property, plant and equipment, which show net book values (in millions) of $14,303 and $13,650 on the 2015 and 2014 balance sheets, respectively. Remember, all costs involved in preparing resources for extraction are capitalized. For Newmont, the costs of mine development include items such as expenses in constructing equipment used in mining natural resources. Construction may take more than a year to complete. At the end of the year, the costs associated with constructing assets that have not been finished are capitalized as Construction-in-Progress. Once construction is complete and the asset is ready for use, the balance is transferred from the construction-in-progress account to the appropriate account.

For example, if the company is constructing equipment, the balance is transferred from construction-in-progress to facilities and equipment once the equipment is ready for use. This is why the assets under construction are not depreciated, while all other four components of property, plant and equipment are. Depreciation does not start until the asset under construction is complete and ready for its intended use. Once this happens, the asset must be depreciated or depleted as discussed earlier.

Intangible Assets and Goodwill

The previous discussion of noncurrent assets covered tangible assets, which are physical in nature and can be touched or sensed. In contrast, **intangible assets** are conceptual in nature. They are *identifiable* assets that have no physical form and largely constitute intellectual property, such as patents and trademarks. An asset is considered to be identifiable if it

1. is separable, meaning it is capable of being separated from the company and sold; or

2. emerges from contractual or legal rights, regardless of whether it is separable or transferable from the company.

An asset that is not identifiable does not count as an intangible asset. Goodwill, for example, is not identifiable, since it does not fit either of the above two criteria. Therefore, it is accounted for differently and reported separately from other intangible assets. Goodwill is discussed at the end of this section.

Different intangible assets differ in their lengths of useful life. Some intangible assets benefit the company for a finite number of years, while others benefit the company indefinitely. Just as property, plant and equipment need to be depreciated, intangible assets with finite useful lives need to go through a similar process. However, the process of allocating the cost of intangible assets over their useful lives is usually called **amortization** instead of depreciation. In addition to amortization, the value of intangible assets (including both those with finite useful lives and those with infinite useful lives) may also decrease due to impairment, which is similar to the impairment of property, plant and equipment discussed earlier.

Intangible Assets with Finite Useful Lives

Patents and copyrights are the most obvious examples of intangible assets that have limited useful lives.

Patents

Individuals and companies invent and develop innovative products, usually at an enormous cost of both money and time. Inventors need to protect their intellectual property and this is achieved through patenting.

A **patent** grants the patentee the exclusive right, for a set period of time, to prevent others from making, using, selling or distributing the patented invention without permission. In most international jurisdictions, a patent term lasts for 20 years, but the duration can differ according to the type of patent. This gives the inventor or inventing company the right to enjoy the rewards of creating a new and successful product.

A patent can be purchased from another party or filed by the company. If the company purchases the patent from another party, the cost of the patent is equal to the purchase price plus any legal costs involved. If the company files its own patent, the application process typically requires the use of patent lawyers (as does the defense and management of a patent). All legal and associated costs in acquiring and defending a patent are capitalized in the noncurrent assets section of the balance sheet. The value of the patent is then amortized for the amount of time left in the patent's legal term or its estimated useful life, whichever is shorter.

This example illustrates how to record journal entries for patent acquisition and amortization. Assume Henry's Lights purchases a patent from Pixie Light Bulbs for $28,000 on January 1, 2018. The patent has seven years remaining in its term and is expected to bring in revenues to the company for the whole seven years. The entries to record the purchase on January 1, 2018, as well as one year's amortization for the year ending December 31, 2018, are recorded as shown in Figure 12.48.

JOURNAL

Date	Account Title and Explanation	Debit	Credit
Jan 1	Patents	28,000	
	Cash		28,000
	To record purchase of patent with seven years remaining		
Dec 31	Amortization Expense—Patents	4,000	
	Accumulated Amortization—Patents		4,000
	To record amortization expense for one year		

FIGURE 12.48

The $4,000 annual amortization amount is calculated using the straight-line method. The straight-line method divides the amortizable amount ($28,000 less a residual value of zero) by the number of years remaining (7 years). This method is often used for amortizing patents and other intangible assets.

Copyright

Copyright is similar to a patent in that it gives exclusive rights of ownership to a person or group that has created something. The difference with copyright is that it applies to artistic work, such as music and literature, and can exist even if the work has not been registered. For example, it is automatically assumed that an article or photo posted on the Internet is protected by copyright.

A person cannot simply assume that he has unlimited rights to use or copy a work from the Internet. Registration with the US Copyright Office, however, puts a copyright holder in a stronger position if litigation arises over the copyright. In the United States, the laws regarding copyrights are governed by the *Copyright Act,* which states that, generally, the life of a copyright lasts throughout the life of the author plus 70 years from the end of the calendar year of his or her death. This means that estimates of a copyright's legal life depend on when the work was first created and how long the author lived. The copyright's useful life, however, is usually shorter than its legal life in practice.

Overall, copyright is treated in much the same way as a patent. The costs may include the purchase price in obtaining the copyright from someone else, legal fees paid to register and defend the copyright, and any other fees involved in its acquisition and defense. The cost of the copyright is amortized over the number of years of its legal term, or its estimated useful life, whichever is shorter.

GAAP vs IFRS

Under GAAP, research and development costs are always expensed as they are incurred.

Under IFRS, research costs are expensed and development costs are capitalized once technical and economic feasibility is attained.

Intangible Assets with Infinite Useful Lives

Some intangible assets do not have an expiry date, and will keep generating economic benefits for the company as long as the company still owns them. Some examples of these assets include trademarks, trade names, franchises and licenses.

Trademark and Trade Name

A **trademark** is similar to a patent and copyright except that it grants ownership rights for a recognizable symbol or logo. A **trade name** grants exclusive rights to a name under which a company or product trades for commercial purposes, even though its legal or technical name might differ. Some corporations have numerous trademarks and trade names that they protect on a continuing basis. For example, McDonald's is not only a trade name that the company protects, but it serves as an umbrella brand for numerous other trademarks, such as the Golden Arches, the Extra Value Meal and Hamburger University.

Any internal costs incurred for developing and maintaining a trademark or trade name, such as those involved with advertising, are considered indistinguishable from other costs of developing the company's business, and are expensed during the year they are incurred. However, just as with patents and copyrights, legal fees for registering the name or logo are capitalized. Alternatively, trademarks and trade names can be purchased from someone else. Because these can be separately measured, they are capitalized as intangible assets on the balance sheet.

Franchises and Licenses

A **franchise** is a contract that allows the franchisee to operate a branch using the franchisor's brand name and business model. For example, one can buy a franchise to run a KFC branch, Learning Express Toys store, or Midas service station. The franchisee receives operating support from the franchisor, such as marketing and training, while the franchisor maintains some control of how the franchisee operates the branch.

A **license** is a contract that permits the licensee to use the licensor's product or brand name under specified terms and conditions. For example, one can buy a license from Marvel to sell T-shirts with Iron Man printed on them. A license usually does not come with an ongoing formal support from the licensor, and the licensor usually does not have much control over how the licensee operates the business.

The franchisee usually has to pay initial fees when acquiring the franchise. These initial fees are capitalized as noncurrent assets on the balance sheet. Normally, there is no expiry date on the franchise, meaning the franchisee can keep operating the branch under the contract, as long as annual payments called royalties are made. Because there is no expiry date, if the franchisee plans to operate the franchise indefinitely, the initial fees are not amortized. Royalties that are paid annually are expensed. The same principles described here also apply to a licensee obtaining and using a license.

Goodwill

Goodwill arises when a company purchases another company at a cost that is greater than the market value of that company's net assets. The excess of the cost of the company over the total market value of its assets, less its total liabilities, is recorded as goodwill.

Goodwill can be attributed to factors such as a recognizable brand name, experienced management, a skilled workforce or a unique product. Unlike other assets, items representing goodwill do not come with an easily determinable market price to be amortized over time. Nevertheless, businesses are willing to pay for goodwill, and it increases equity on the balance sheet. We will use an example to explain how goodwill works and how accountants should record such items in the company's books.

Vicky's Entrepreneurial Enterprises decides to buy Jack's Sweets, a relatively new but established candy maker on June 1, 2018. The purchase price is $1 million. At the time of purchase, Jack's Sweets has assets with a market value of $1.5 million and liabilities totaling $700,000, giving the purchased company a net asset value of $800,000.

The extra $200,000 in the company's purchase price constitutes goodwill. Vicky is willing to pay for the brand name, because Jack's Sweets is known for great tasting candies. In addition, Jack's Sweets' memorable commercials featured a fictional "Uncle Jack" handing out treats to beloved customers. Vicky considers $200,000 for this brand to be a bargain and is willing to pay this amount for goodwill. However, she also expects a good return on her investment for the premium paid for the business.

To record the purchase of Jack's Sweets, Vicky's accountant adds the value of the assets and liabilities to Vicky's balance sheet. This results in a debit to assets of $1,500,000 and a credit to liabilities of $700,000. The cash payment amount of $1,000,000 is recorded as a credit to cash. The premium paid is recorded as goodwill and increases that asset account by $200,000. Figure 12.49 shows this transaction.

JOURNAL			
Date	**Account Title and Explanation**	**Debit**	**Credit**
Jun 1	Assets	1,500,000	
	Goodwill	200,000	
	Liabilities		700,000
	Cash		1,000,000
	Purchase net assets of Jack's Sweets, including goodwill		

Note: We use the title "Assets" and "Liabilities" in this journal for demonstration purpose. In reality, each asset and liability are recorded in its specific account.

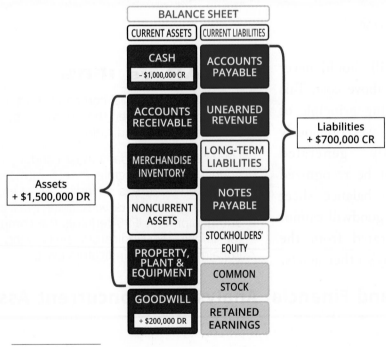

FIGURE 12.49

Unlike other intangible assets with infinite useful lives, items categorized as goodwill do not have their value amortized over time. However, this does not mean that the value of goodwill cannot decrease. Events may occur that impair the value of goodwill.

For example, assume that Company A bought Company B because the latter was producing a unique product that the rest of the market could not match. Company A paid a premium of $150,000 over the net asset value of Company B, so this premium is goodwill. However, since the purchase, advances in technology allowed a competitor to create a new product to compete with the one produced by Company B. The new product is still undergoing development and testing, but will almost certainly enter the market within a year.

The value of goodwill associated with the innovative quality of Company B's product will be seriously reduced. But it will not be negated altogether, since it is estimated that the product will still be competitive, even after the introduction of another product.

A decrease in the value of goodwill for the current year is estimated at $50,000. The journal entry to record this is shown in Figure 12.50. The impairment of goodwill is recorded as an expense on the income statement, which reduces the equity of the company.

JOURNAL			
Date	Account Title and Explanation	Debit	Credit
Dec 31	Impairment Loss	50,000	
	Goodwill		50,000
	Loss on impairment of goodwill		

FIGURE 12.50

The value of goodwill should never be adjusted upward above cost. This violates the accounting principle of conservatism, which was previously covered. Internally generated goodwill also cannot be recognized or recorded on the balance sheet because the value of goodwill cannot be objectively separated from the value of the company's other assets.

GAAP vs IFRS

Under GAAP, a company must conduct impairment tests whenever the company becomes aware of an impairment indication.

Under IFRS, a company must conduct impairment tests on goodwill and intangible assets with indefinite lives every year, even if there is no indication of impairment. However, for intangible assets with finite lives and property, plant and equipment, IFRS requires the company to actively look for impairment indicators every year, and only conduct impairment tests if indicators exist.

Presentation and Financial Analysis of Noncurrent Assets

The details of Newmont Mining Corporation's property, plant and equipment were examined in Figure 12.47. We will return to Newmont Mining to see how the company's noncurrent assets and their depreciation and amortization are presented on its financial statements. Figure 12.51 shows the assets portion of Newmont's balance sheet (called Consolidated Balance Sheets). Note that Newmont uses the term "long-term assets" instead of noncurrent assets.

NEWMONT MINING CORPORATION
STATEMENTS OF CONSOLIDATED OPERATIONS

	Years Ended December 31,		
	2015	2014	2013
	(in millions, except per share)		
Sales	$7,729	$7,292	$8,414
Costs and expenses			
Costs applicable to sales [1]	4,312	4,457	5,299
Depreciation and amortization	1,239	1,229	1,362
Reclamation and remediation (Note 5)	266	154	81
Exploration	156	164	247
Advanced projects, research and development	133	161	222
General and administrative	183	186	203
Impairment of long-lived assets (Note 6)	56	26	4,352
Other expense, net (Note 7)	221	205	300
	6,566	6,582	12,066
Other income (expense)			
Other income, net (Note 8)	128	157	349
Interest expense, net of capitalized interest of $40, $23 and $88, respectively	(325)	(361)	(303)
	(197)	(204)	46
Income (loss) before income and mining tax and other items	966	506	(3,606)
Income and mining tax benefit (expense) (Note 9)	(644)	(133)	755
Equity income (loss) of affiliates (Note 10)	(45)	(4)	(5)
Income (loss) from continuing operations	277	369	(2,856)
Income (loss) from discontinued operations (Note 11)	27	(40)	61
Net income (loss)	304	329	(2,795)
Net loss (income) attributable to noncontrolling interests (Note 12)	(84)	179	261
Net income (loss) attributable to Newmont stockholders	$220	$508	$(2,534)

CONSOLIDATED BALANCE SHEETS

	At December 31,	
Assets	2015	2014
	(in millions)	
Cash and cash equivalents	$2,782	$2,403
Trade receivables	260	186
Other accounts receivables	185	290
Investments (Note 18)	19	73
Inventories (Note 19)	710	700
Stockpiles and ore on leach pads (Note 20)	896	666
Deferred income tax assets (Note 9)	—	240
Other current assets (Note 21)	131	881
Current assets	4,983	5,439
Property, plant and mine development, net (Note 22)	14,303	13,650
Investments (Note 18)	402	334
Stockpiles and ore on leach pads (Note 20)	3,000	2,820
Deferred income tax assets (Note 9)	1,718	1,790
Other long-term assets (Note 21)	776	883
Total assets	$25,182	$24,916

FIGURE 12.51

As illustrated in Newmont's balance sheet, long-term assets are below current assets in the assets section. Tangible assets (property, plant and equipment) are separate from intangible assets. Notice that Newmont presented its noncurrent assets on the balance sheet at their net book value. The $14,303 balance of Newmont's property, plant and equipment on the company's 2015 balance sheet is the net book value, less accumulated depreciation. A company must always present the costs and accumulated depreciation or amortization of its noncurrent assets either in the notes or on the balance sheet itself. Newmont included this detail in the notes. Because Newmont's intangible assets constitute a relatively small portion of its total assets, Newmont includes intangible assets as part of their "other long-term assets."

Figure 12.51 also shows Newmont's income statement (called Statements of Consolidated Operations). The statement shows depreciation and amortization under costs and expenses as well as impairment of long-lived assets. Details of the depreciation methods and the impairments would be explained in the notes and are part of the complete set of financial statements.

The details of Newmont's other long-term assets are provided in Note 21 in Figure 12.52. Notice how Newmont reports goodwill separately from other intangible assets in Note 21.

NEWMONT MINING CORPORATION
NOTES TO CONSOLIDATED FINANCIAL STATEMENTS
(dollars in millions, except per share, per ounce and per pound amounts)

NOTE 21 OTHER ASSETS (Other long-term assets portion only)

	At December 31,	
	2015	**2014**
	(in millions, except per share)	
Other long-term assets		
Income tax receivable	$222	$215
Prepaid royalties	140	125
Restricted cash	117	127
Intangible assets	94	109
Goodwill	58	105
Debt issuance costs	46	58
Taxes other than income and mining	15	59
Other	84	85
Total other long-term assets	$776	$883

FIGURE 12.52

The values of the assets on the balance sheet provide an idea of the amount invested in the company to run its operations. However, these values alone do not indicate whether these assets are being used effectively and efficiently. We will examine two ratios that can provide insight on how well assets are being used: asset turnover and return on assets.

Asset Turnover

A turnover ratio measures how rapidly an asset's status changes and becomes productive. Recall that inventory turnover measures how quickly an asset converts from inventory to becoming a sale. **Asset turnover** measures how quickly a company converts its total assets, including noncurrent assets, into revenue.

To calculate asset turnover, we need net sales from the income statement and the average total assets, which is produced by taking the average of beginning and ending total assets. The equations to do this are shown in Figure 12.53.

$$\text{Asset Turnover } = \frac{\text{Net Sales}}{\text{Average Total Assets*}}$$

*Average Total Assets = (Beginning of Year Total Assets + End of Year Total Assets) ÷ 2

FIGURE 12.53

Return on Assets

A company's return on assets is similar to asset turnover except that its focus is on net income instead of revenue. **Return on assets** measures the relationship between net income and assets. In other words, is the company making enough profit from investment in its total assets? Figure 12.54 shows the formula to calculate return on assets.

$$\text{Return on Assets } = \frac{\text{Net Income}}{\text{Average Total Assets}}$$

FIGURE 12.54

Note that the ratios to calculate asset turnover and return on assets both have the same denominator: average total assets. It is the numerators that differ. Asset turnover uses net sales, while return on assets uses net income. Another difference is that asset turnover is expressed as a decimal number, while return on assets is expressed as a percentage.

Using the Ratios

We can calculate and compare these two ratios by using the financial information made available by Amtrak, a US company in the railway transportation industry, and Coastal Rail, a fictitious US company in the same industry. Using the formulas already outlined, the ratios are calculated in Figure 12.55.

Selected Financial Information (in millions)			
Year 2015		**Amtrak**	**Coastal Rail**
A	Net Sales	$3,211	$21,813
B	Total Assets—Beginning of Year	$12,454	$52,372
C	Total Assets—End of Year	$13,295	$54,600
D = (B+C) ÷ 2	Average Total Assets	$12,875	$53,486
E = A ÷ D	Asset Turnover	0.25	0.41
F	Net Income (Loss)	($1,233)	$4,772
G = F ÷ D	Return on Assets	(9.58%)	8.92%

FIGURE 12.55

For Amtrak and Coastal Rail, both net sales and net income were divided by average total assets to produce the two financial ratios.

With regard to asset turnover, Amtrak has a figure of 0.25 and Coastal Rail has a figure of 0.41. This means that Coastal Rail generated more revenue dollars per investment in assets than Amtrak.

With regard to return on assets, Amtrak has a rate of –9.58% and Coastal Rail's rate is 8.92%. This means that Coastal Rail generated more net income per investment in assets than Amtrak.

All financial ratios represent a simple snapshot of company performance; each ratio tends to focus on one aspect of a business. Calculation and interpretation of multiple ratios can provide a bigger picture of an overall well-being of a company, which will be discussed in Chapter 20.

Controls Related To Noncurrent Assets

Tangible assets are purchased by a company, used to earn an income and eventually disposed of. In the meantime, the value of a noncurrent asset depreciates over the period of its estimated useful life. Accounting procedures are used to control and safeguard all tangible assets while the company possesses them. Different companies and industries depend on noncurrent assets to varying degrees. For instance, auto manufacturers General Motors and Ford rely heavily on noncurrent assets, such as machines, robots and factories. It is sometimes possible for people to steal large assets of a company. Security measures, such as physical barriers and security personnel, can protect large items from theft.

Insurance is a more useful measure to protect large noncurrent assets. Insurance can protect not only in the event of theft, but also in the event of catastrophic situations, such as extreme weather or unforeseen breakdowns. It is important for management to make sure that the best possible insurance policies are in place and are updated or adjusted when needed. Some companies may even want to consider some self-insurance options to help protect their noncurrent assets from catastrophic risk.

IN THE REAL WORLD

Although businesses should make certain that all their assets are insured and that potential liabilities are also covered, this does not always mean that an insurance company needs to be involved. Businesses can self-insure to cover various risks. Companies that self-insure are sometimes regarded as being uninsured. In other words, "self-insurance" can be seen as an attempt to avoid paying for insurance. Indeed, this can be true, since some companies fail to adequately self-insure.

Proper self-insurance involves a company setting aside enough capital reserves to cover itself in case of a catastrophic event. If something happens to a company's noncurrent assets, these capital reserves can be used to cover the loss. The advantage of self-insurance is that a company avoids paying premiums that are often very high.

The disadvantage of self-insurance is that a company needs to tie up a certain amount of its capital to cover a disaster, and even that is sometimes insufficient. To minimize this disadvantage, there are alternative self-insurance strategies. For example, a business can still buy some insurance, but add self-insurance. Alternatively, businesses can form collaborative self-insurance groups, whereby a group of companies contributes to a pool of funds that can be used if one or more of them suffer a catastrophic event.

As with most aspects of today's business environment, various innovative solutions can be found to resolve inadequacies in the market. Self-insurance is an example of one of these innovations.

Big or small, expensive or inexpensive, all types of tangible assets should be tracked properly and relevant transactions recorded accurately in the company's books. Experienced accountants should perform these control procedures.

Each noncurrent asset should be tagged in some way, perhaps by a bar code and scanner. The tags should be read and compared with accounting records, and vice versa. Physical audits should be performed on a regular basis to ensure that all assets on the books are on the premises, still in use and accounted for.

For all company assets, paperwork and records should be completed correctly and handled securely. The first priority is to record the correct amount of cost for the noncurrent asset. As always, any costs related to the acquisition of the asset must be included in the total cost. These can include freight, installation and testing costs.

As emphasized throughout our discussion of asset controls, policies, plans and procedures need to be in place, and regulations and laws followed. For example, a large company may have a policy of classifying items as noncurrent assets only if they cost more than $1,000. A smaller company may have a lower threshold for its policy. These policies need to be clearly communicated to the staff responsible for their implementation. Adherence to all related policies, plans, procedures, regulations and laws should be monitored, with audits when necessary.

Economical and efficient use of tangible assets involves purchasing assets at the best possible price. Internal controls should include a bidding process for suppliers, which helps to ensure the best possible price. Financial ratios, discussed earlier in this chapter, can be used on a regular basis to monitor the efficient use of a company's noncurrent assets. If the ratios indicate an inefficient use of these assets, measures can be taken to either dispose of or make better use of them. If sales are slow, this may mean that noncurrent assets are not being used to their full capacity. A business may also find that too much money has been invested in its noncurrent assets. Leasing them could free up some capital. As always, company goals and objectives related to noncurrent assets should be stated, implemented, reviewed and changed when necessary.

Controls related to intangible assets are not very different from those relating to tangible assets. Qualified staff should be available to ensure that transactions are recorded and classified properly in the company's books and all payments are properly documented. Costs should be objectively verified and any supporting documentation should be properly maintained. The procedures involved are similar for both tangible and intangible assets.

However, with intangible assets, the only physical evidence of their existence often comes in the form of contracts, accompanying invoices and supporting cost documentation. That is why it is so important to physically protect such documents. They can be placed in a vault on the premises or a safe deposit box in a bank. These documents can be referenced when changes are made or when the company's books need updating.

Beyond initial registration or purchase, ongoing valuation of intangible assets needs to take place. For example, market conditions may affect the value of goodwill, or competing trademarks may diminish the value of a brand name. Furthermore, companies that own patents, copyright and trademarks should be on the lookout for entities that are using such intellectual property without permission. Any such use diminishes the value of the protected asset. All proper legal avenues should be pursued, including legal action or the threat of legal action, when improper use of protected intellectual assets has taken place.

An Ethical Approach To Noncurrent Assets   LO 9

Accounting for a firm's noncurrent assets can be manipulated to produce fraudulent figures. Decisions regarding classifying noncurrent assets, depreciating them and estimating residual values can have a significant impact on a company's financial statements. It is important for accountants to understand the ethical principles that help prevent abuse.

When accountants are faced with a decision, they should ask if it should be done because it is an accurate reflection of the business or for some other reason. Other reasons could be to hide one's own incompetence, seek financial gain, succumb to pressure from management or meet public expectation of company performance.

A good accountant always raises a red flag when the answer to the question is anything other than, "This is being done because it is an accurate reflection of the financial condition of the business."

Figures for noncurrent assets can be manipulated to present a financial picture that does not accurately reflect the financial state of the company. One of the first decisions that an accountant must make is whether a noncurrent asset in question is in fact a noncurrent asset. An attempt to falsely classify a noncurrent asset as an expense understates the company's net income in the current period. Conversely, an attempt to classify an expense as a noncurrent asset overstates the company's equity in the current period. Any result that does not reflect the true nature of the asset is an ethical breach and should always be avoided.

IN THE REAL WORLD

The year 2001 saw the beginning of numerous corporate and accounting scandals that breached ethical standards. Authorities began investigating some of America's largest corporations regarding, among other things, accounting fraud. The corporations investigated included three telecommunications companies—Global Crossing, Qwest and WorldCom.

Some of these investigations found a distortion of gains and expenses as a result of misclassifying noncurrent assets. For example, both Global Crossing and Qwest engaged in billions of dollars of what are known as swaps. These companies purchased telecom capacity from customers who then bought it back from the companies. These were falsely treated as noncurrent assets rather than as current operating expenses. The result was that both companies recorded the revenue upfront, then expensed the amount over a period of time. This violates, among other things, the expense recognition principle.

In addition, WorldCom classified billions of dollars of current operating expenses as noncurrent assets. This was done over a period of 15 months. The auditing firm Arthur Andersen failed to raise any red flags over the practice.

Estimating the useful life of a noncurrent asset is also open to manipulation. Intentionally shortening an asset's life span can unduly increase the annual depreciation charges recorded in the company's books. Intentionally increasing a noncurrent asset's residual value decreases the amount to be depreciated and the depreciation charges. An accountant has an ethical obligation to avoid, or detect and correct, these abuses at all times.

Ethical considerations of intangible assets relate mostly to their correct reporting in financial statements. This includes determining the appropriate cost, calculating the correct amortization and impairment and accurately reporting all amounts on the income statement and balance sheet.

Companies should always set up internal controls to ensure that ongoing transactions involving intangible assets are expensed or capitalized properly. Following review procedures ensures that annual amortization is verified and properly reported. Any review procedure should be the joint responsibility of both management and company auditors. Executives and accountants must take responsibility for the company's books; not doing so can lead to serious consequences.

In Summary

LO 1 Identify the characteristics of noncurrent assets

- ▶ Noncurrent (long-term) assets provide the infrastructure necessary for operating a business.

- ▶ They are expected to be used on an ongoing basis, typically longer than one year, and are not intended to be sold to customers.

LO 2 Record the acquisition and changes in the value of property, plant and equipment

- ▶ Cost of property, plant and equipment includes purchase price and expenditures necessary to get the asset ready for operation. The whole cost is debited to the appropriate noncurrent asset account.

- ▶ In a lump sum purchase, the amount paid for all the assets is divided and allocated to each item according to percentages based on the appraised values or fair values.

- ▶ After acquisition, changes made to property, plant and equipment are classified as a betterment, an extraordinary repair, or ordinary repairs and maintenance.

- ▶ Property, plant and equipment (except land) decrease in value (depreciate) over time. Depreciation is the process of allocating the cost of the asset over its useful life.

LO 3 Apply and compare the three methods of depreciation of property, plant and equipment

- ▶ The straight-line method of depreciation uses a simple average, resulting in the same amount of depreciation every year.

- ▶ The declining-balace and double-declining-balance methods apply a depreciation rate to the remaining balance of the book value of the asset.

- ▶ The units-of-production method utilizes the level of asset usage as the basis for calculating depreciation.

- ▶ Accountants choose the depreciation method that best reflects the nature of the asset.

LO 4 Account for disposal of assets and changes in depreciation estimates

- ▶ The disposal of an asset usually involves a gain or loss relative to the item's book value. Gains and losses appear on the income statements.

- ▶ Revisions can be made to a depreciation schedule. However, proper justification should always be used and prior depreciation deductions should never be changed.

- ▶ "Book depreciation" is different from depreciation for federal income tax purposes. The depreciation rules under US federal income tax law are known as the Modified Accelerated Cost Recovery System (MACRS).

LO 5 Account for natural resources

- ▶ The natural resources that a company owns—such as minerals, oil or timber—are physical in nature, and are capitalized under the noncurrent assets section on the balance sheet. Some companies categorize them separately from other noncurrent assets.

- ▶ A natural resource's value is depleted over time using the units-of-production method.

LO 6 Define and account for intangible assets and describe the different types of intangible assets

▶ Intangible assets are defined as identifiable assets that have no physical form. An asset is considered to be identifiable if it either is separable from the company or emerges from contractual or legal rights.

▶ The decrease in an intangible asset's value due to amortization and impairment is recorded as an expense or a loss on the income statement. While impairment loss may be recorded directly against the asset account, amortization must be recorded in an accumulated amortization account.

▶ A patent gives the inventor the exclusive right to use a product. The cost of the patent is for legal fees or the purchase of rights from someone else. This cost is amortized over the remaining term of the patent, or its expected useful life, whichever is shorter.

▶ Copyright gives exclusive rights of a creation to its creator. Copyright is granted automatically to works produced and published.

▶ A trademark gives exclusive rights to logos and other company symbols. A trade name provides exclusive rights to names of companies and products.

▶ A franchise is a contract that allows the franchisee to operate a branch using the franchisor's brand name and business model. A license is a contract that permits the licensee to use the licensor's product or brand name under the specified terms and conditions. The initial franchise fees or license fees are capitalized.

▶ Goodwill arises when a company purchases another company at a cost that is greater than the market value of that company's net assets. Unlike other intangible assets, goodwill is considered to be unidentifiable. Therefore, it is reported separately from other intangible assets.

LO 7 Calculate and interpret asset turnover and return on assets ratios

▶ Asset turnover measures the revenue a company generates relative to its investment in total assets.

▶ Return on assets measures the net income a company generates relative to total assets.

LO 8 Describe controls related to noncurrent assets

▶ Controls to protect a company's noncurrent assets can include accurate recording and tracking procedures, or proper insurance in case of catastrophic events. Qualified accounting personnel should always supervise the policies and measures that a company implements.

LO 9 Describe ethical approaches related to noncurrent assets

▶ Net income figures and net asset values can be distorted by manipulating decisions regarding the classification of noncurrent assets, the estimation of residual value and useful life, and other aspects of depreciation. Unethical manipulations must always be avoided.

 *Access **ameengage.com** for integrated resources including tutorials, practice exercises, the digital textbook and more.*

Review Exercise 12-1

Nelson Rugasa is an entrepreneur who has just started a consulting business. On December 31, 2018, Nelson used cash to purchase a laptop computer for $3,000 and office equipment for $10,000.

Required

a) Record the purchase of noncurrent assets.

JOURNAL			
Date	Account Title and Explanation	Debit	Credit

Research Component (to be done outside of class time)

b) Research the useful life of noncurrent assets, and suggest the useful life for the computer and office equipment.

_____

_____

_____

_____

_____

_____

_____

_____

_____

c) Research the way in which the value of noncurrent assets decline, and suggest the depreciation method(s) that should be used for the computer and office equipment.

_____

_____

_____

_____

_____

_____

d) Based on your research on useful life, and the ways in which the value of noncurrent assets decline, prepare a table showing the cost, depreciation, accumulated depreciation, and net book value of the computer and office equipment for the first three years.

Year	Cost	Depreciation	Accumulated Depreciation	Net Book Value

Year	Cost	Depreciation	Accumulated Depreciation	Net Book Value

e) Explain how you calculate the profit or loss on the disposal of a noncurrent asset.

_____

_____

_____

_____

_____

_____

_____

_____

_____

_____

_____

_____

_____

_____

_____

_____

_____

_____

See Appendix I for solutions.

Review Exercise 12-2

Rulison Company had the following transactions during 2018.

Jan 1   Paid $250,000 to purchase Regnier Ltd., which had $500,000 in assets and $300,000 in liabilities.

Jan 1   Purchased patents from Sandra Raymond for $50,000. The remaining life of the patents is four years.

Jan 1   Purchased a trademark, which will be applied to the patented product for $20,000. Management believes that the trademark's remaining useful life will be double that of the patent's, and the trademark will have a residual value of $100.

Jan 30 Purchased a mineral deposit for $100,000. The company needs to extract a mineral that goes into the patented product. Rulison Company expects to extract 500,000 pounds of mineral before the rights expire.

Jun 30 The senior executives that came from Regnier Ltd. resigned en masse. The directors felt that the loss of the senior executives decreased the value of goodwill by $25,000.

Rulison Company prepares its financial statements with a year end of December 31. Amortization policy states that one half-year's amortization is taken in both the year of purchase and year of sale. Depletion is based on units extracted. The company extracted and sold 10,000 pounds of mineral from the beginning of February to the end of December. Assume all purchases are made with cash and that the straight-line method of depreciation is used for the patent and trademark.

Prepare the journal entries to record the above transactions. Also prepare the year-end adjusting entries associated with the noncurrent assets.

JOURNAL			
Date	Account Title and Explanation	Debit	Credit

See Appendix I for solutions.

Appendix 12A: Trading Noncurrent Assets

Rather than selling or donating an old asset that the company no longer wants, it may trade the old asset with its supplier for a newer one with a similar use. The supplier usually offers the buyer what is known as a trade-in allowance on the old asset that is being exchanged. The trade-in allowance may be either greater than or less than the old asset's book value. Often, the company has to pay cash in addition to giving up the old asset. Accounting for the exchange transaction depends on whether or not the exchange has commercial substance. Commercial substance exists when the exchange results in a change to the company's future cash flows.

As with all disposal scenarios, the first step is to update the depreciation as of the date of disposal. To record the exchange transaction, the old asset and its accumulated depreciation are removed from the company's books by crediting the original cost of the old asset and debiting the associated accumulated depreciation balance. Cash is credited for the amount paid. If the exchange has commercial substance, the new asset is debited at the fair value of the old asset plus the cash paid. The difference between the fair value of the old asset and its net book value is then recorded as a gain or loss on exchange of assets.

An asset exchange with commercial substance can result in a gain or a loss. We will look at both of these cases, starting with a gain on exchange. We will then discuss how to handle an asset exchange with no commercial substance.

Commercial Substance: Gain on Exchange

To illustrate a gain on exchange of assets, assume that the company exchanged its old truck for a new one valued at $120,000 at a truck dealership on June 1. The company's old truck and an additional $85,000 cash were given in exchange. The old truck originally cost $100,000. It had a fair market value of $35,000 and an accumulated depreciation of $70,000 on the day of the trade. (To keep things simple, we will assume that the $70,000 accumulated depreciation already includes the updated depreciation for the current period.) The gain on the exchange can be calculated in two different ways, both of which yield the same result.

The gain on exchange can be determined as the difference between the fair market value of the new asset received and the book value of the old asset given up plus cash paid on exchange, as shown in Figure 12A.1.

Price (Fair Market Value) of New Truck		$120,000
Less: Assets Given Up in Exchange		
Book Value of Old Truck ($100,000 – $70,000)	$30,000	
Cash Paid on Exchange	85,000	$115,000
Gain on Exchange of Assets		$5,000

FIGURE 12A.1

Alternatively, the gain on exchange can be determined as the difference between the fair market value (the trade-in allowance) of the asset given up and the book value of that asset, as shown in Figure 12A.2.

Fair Market Value (Trade-In Allowance) of Old Truck	$35,000
Less: Book Value of Old Truck ($100,000 – $70,000)	$30,000
Gain on Exchange of Assets	$5,000

FIGURE 12A.2

If the exchange is determined to have commercial substance, the journal entry in Figure 12A.3 is made to record the truck exchange.

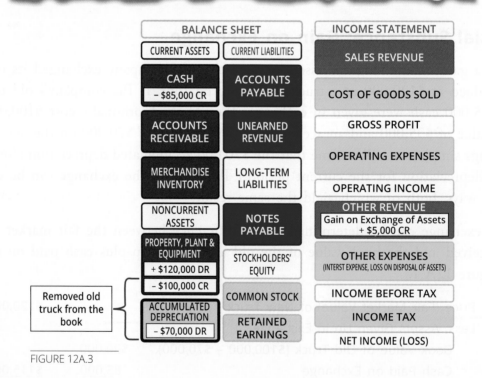

JOURNAL			
Date	Account Title and Explanation	Debit	Credit
Jun 1	Truck (new)	120,000	
	Accumulated Depreciation—Truck	70,000	
	Gain on Exchange of Assets		5,000
	Truck (old)		100,000
	Cash		85,000
	To record exchange of old truck and cash for new truck		

FIGURE 12A.3

Commercial Substance: Loss on Exchange

Now assume that the company exchanged its old truck for the new one valued at $115,000. The company's old truck and an additional $95,000 cash were given in exchange. The old truck originally cost $100,000. It had a fair market value of $20,000 and an accumulated depreciation of $70,000 on the day of the trade. (Assume that the $70,000 accumulated depreciation already includes the updated depreciation for the current period.) The loss on the exchange can be calculated in two different ways, both of which yield the same result.

The loss on exchange can be determined as the difference between the fair market value of the new asset received and the book value of the old asset given up plus cash paid on exchange, as shown in Figure 12A.4.

Price (Fair Market Value) of New Truck		$115,000
Less: Assets Given Up in Exchange		
Book Value of Old Truck ($100,000 – $70,000)	$30,000	
Cash Paid on Exchange	95,000	$125,000
Loss on Exchange of Assets		($10,000)

FIGURE 12A.4

Alternatively, the loss on exchange can be determined as the difference between the fair market value (the trade-in allowance) of the asset given up and the book value of that asset, as shown in Figure 12A.5.

Fair Market Value (Trade-In Allowance) of Old Truck	$20,000
Less: Book Value of Old Truck ($100,000 – $70,000)	$30,000
Loss on Exchange of Assets	($10,000)

FIGURE 12A.5

If the exchange is determined to have commercial substance, the journal entry in Figure 12A.6 is made to record the truck exchange.

JOURNAL			
Date	**Account Title and Explanation**	**Debit**	**Credit**
Jun 1	Truck (new)	115,000	
	Accumulated Depreciation—Truck (old)	70,000	
	Loss on Exchange of Assets	10,000	
	Truck (old)		100,000
	Cash		95,000
	To record exchange of old truck and cash for new truck		

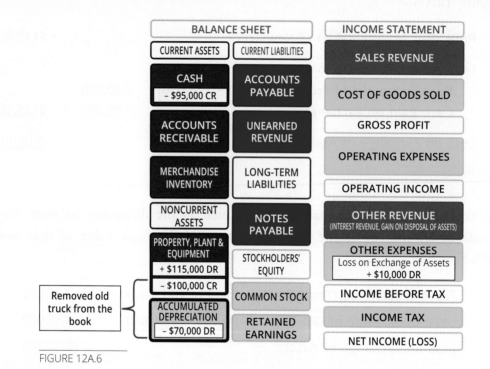

FIGURE 12A.6

Asset Exchange with No Commercial Substance

If an asset exchange has no commercial substance (i.e. the exchange will have no effect on the company's future cash flows), no gain or loss is recorded. Instead, the book value of the new asset received is based on the book value of the old asset given up. We can use the previous example to illustrate what happens when the exchange lacks commercial substance.

As before, the company exchanged its old truck for the new one valued at $115,000. The company's old truck and an additional $95,000 cash were given in exchange. The old truck originally cost $100,000. It had a fair market value of $20,000 and an accumulated depreciation of $70,000 on the day of the trade. (Assume that the $70,000 accumulated depreciation already includes the updated depreciation for the current period.)

The cost of the new equipment when there is no commercial substance can be determined as shown in Figure 12A.7.

Cost of Old Truck	$100,000
Less: Accumulated Depreciation	70,000
Book Value of Old Truck	30,000
Cash Paid on Exchange	95,000
Cost of New Truck	$125,000

FIGURE 12A.7

The journal entry in Figure 12A.8 is made to record the truck exchange.

JOURNAL			
Date	**Account Title and Explanation**	**Debit**	**Credit**
Jun 1	Truck (new)	125,000	
	Accumulated Depreciation—Truck	70,000	
	Truck (old)		100,000
	Cash		95,000
	To record exchange of old truck and cash for new truck		

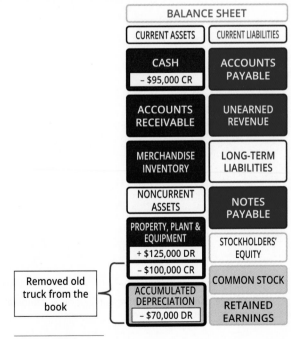

FIGURE 12A.8

In Summary

LO 10 **Account for trading of noncurrent assets**

► Accounting for the exchange transaction depends on whether or not the exchange has commercial substance. Commercial substance exists when the exchange results in a change to the company's future cash flows.

► An asset exchange with commercial substance can result in a gain or loss.

► An asset exchange with no commercial substance does not produce a gain or a loss.

 *Access **ameengage.com** for integrated resources including tutorials, practice exercises, the digital textbook and more.*

Review Exercise 12A-1

On November 30, Absolute Manufacturing exchanged a unit of old machinery for some new machinery valued at $150,000. The company gave its old machinery plus $120,000 cash in exchange for the new machine. The old machinery originally cost $125,000. It had a fair market value of $30,000 and accumulated depreciation of $103,750 on the day of the trade. (Assume that the accumulated depreciation includes the updated depreciation for the month of November.) Assume that the transaction has commercial substance.

Required

a) On a separate piece of paper, calculate the gain (loss) on the exchange.

b) Record the journal entry for the above transaction.

JOURNAL			
Date	**Account Title and Explanation**	**Debit**	**Credit**

c) Journalize the exchange transaction, assuming instead that the transaction has no commercial substance.

JOURNAL			
Date	**Account Title and Explanation**	**Debit**	**Credit**

See Appendix I for solutions.

Review Exercise 12A-2

On April 30, Victory Fabrications exchanged an old delivery vehicle for a new one valued at $60,000. The company gave its old vehicle plus $55,000 cash in exchange for the new vehicle. The old delivery vehicle originally cost $45,000. It had a fair market value of $5,000 and accumulated depreciation of $39,000 on the day of the trade. (Assume that the accumulated depreciation includes the updated depreciation for the month of April.) Assume that the transaction has commercial substance.

Required

a) On a separate piece of paper, calculate the gain (loss) on the exchange.

b) Record the journal entry for the above transaction.

JOURNAL			
Date	Account Title and Explanation	Debit	Credit

c) Journalize the exchange transaction, assuming instead that the transaction has no commercial substance.

JOURNAL			
Date	Account Title and Explanation	Debit	Credit

See Appendix I for solutions.

Chapter 13
Current Liabilities

Learning Objectives

LO 1 **Define and differentiate between determinable and non-determinable liabilities**
- Bank Overdraft and Operating Line of Credit

LO 2 **Record accounts payable**

LO 3 **Record transactions with sales tax**

LO 4 **Record unearned revenue**

LO 5 **Record short-term notes payable**
- Extending Credit Terms
- Borrowing from a Bank
- Accrued Interest and Notes Payable

LO 6 **Record transactions related to the current portion of long-term liabilities**

LO 7 **Record payroll liabilities**
- Payroll as an Accrued Liability
- Gross Pay to Net Pay

- Employee Payroll Deductions—Statutory
- Employee Payroll Deductions—Voluntary
- Employer Payroll Contributions
- Responsibility for Paying Taxes and Benefits
- Payroll Example
- Payroll Register
- Payroll Records
- Paying the Liabilities

LO 8 **Record estimated liabilities**
- Employee Benefits
- Product Warranties
- Customer Loyalty Programs

LO 9 **Explain the accounting treatment for contingent liabilities**

LO 10 **Apply internal controls relating to current liabilities**
- Payroll Controls

 *Access **ameengage.com** for integrated resources including tutorials, practice exercises, the digital textbook and more.*

Current Liabilities

This chapter deals with current liabilities, which are obligations expected to be paid within one year of the balance sheet date or the company's normal operating cycle. Obligations due beyond one year are classified as long-term liabilities, which are covered in Chapter 17.

The balance sheet presentation of current liabilities is comparable to the balance sheet presentation of current assets. The main difference is that the order of liabilities is dictated by the timing of settlement, whereas assets are placed in order of liquidity. Figure 13.1 illustrates this difference. Bank overdraft and operating line of credit are listed first among the current liabilities, followed by accounts payable, which is a common type of trade payable. Accrued liabilities include payroll liabilities, sales taxes payable to the government and interest payable on notes and loans. Unearned revenue and the current portion of long-term notes payable are also listed as current liabilities.

FIGURE 13.1

A company's liabilities can be divided into two categories: known liabilities and unknown liabilities. These categories are sometimes referred to as *determinable liabilities* and *non-determinable liabilities*, respectively.

Determinable liabilities have a precise value; businesses that have determinable liabilities know exactly who they owe, how much they owe and when they are supposed to pay. Amounts owed to suppliers (trade payables), employees (payroll liabilities) and the government (sales taxes) are determinable liabilities. All determinable liabilities should leave an easily recognizable and traceable paper trail, and may include documents

GAAP vs IFRS

 A "liability" or "payable" under GAAP is usually referred to in IFRS as a "provision."

such as invoices and contracts. The exact amounts due, and when they are due, should be clearly identified.

A company's unknown or **non-determinable liabilities** include estimated and contingent liabilities. They are non-determinable because the exact amount owing or whether and when they are supposed to be paid is unknown on the date of financial statement issuance. This is similar to a topic that was studied on the assets side of the balance sheet, where the exact amount of bad debt for the year was unknown on the date of financial statement issuance.

We will first discuss each important type of determinable liability, starting with bank overdraft and operating line of credit. Non-determinable liabilities, as well as controls and ethics related to current liabilities, are examined at the end of the chapter.

Bank Overdraft and Operating Line of Credit

A company faced with short-term financial needs can borrow from a financial institution through a bank overdraft or a line of credit. **Bank overdraft** is a financial institution's extension of credit to cover the portion of cash withdrawal that is more than the account's balance. The financial institution will automatically deposit amounts into the company's cash account if it goes into a negative balance up to a pre-specified amount. The negative balance could be due to issues with cash flow or simply timing differences between deposits and withdrawals.

Alternatively, many businesses have an operating line of credit with their financial institution. An **operating line of credit** is the maximum loan balance that a business may draw upon at any time without having to visit or request approval from the bank. The business negotiates a predetermined maximum balance that it is allowed to owe as well as the interest rate charged on the outstanding balance of the account.

If the company's cash account has a negative balance as of the balance sheet date, the bank overdraft is reported as a current liability. Likewise, if the company owes a financial institution on its line of credit as of the balance sheet date, the line of credit is reported as a current liability. Both bank overdraft and line of credit are reported ahead of accounts payable and any other determinable liabilities on the balance sheet.

Accounts Payable

Accounts payable is a determinable liability. A company purchases goods or services from a vendor and that vendor issues the company an invoice, which must be paid by a certain date. The terms of the liability are easily recognized and recorded by the company.

In previous chapters, we pointed out that selling an item on account means debiting accounts receivable and crediting sales. With accounts payable, there is a mirror transaction; an asset or expense account is debited and the accounts payable account is credited.

The amount of money owed by customers is controlled by using an accounts receivable subledger (or subsidiary ledger, introduced in Chapter 9). The same principle applies to the amount of money owed to suppliers, which is controlled by using the accounts payable subledger.

For accounts payable, the controlling account in the general ledger includes the total amount of credit balances in an individual subledger accounts.

Figure 13.2 shows the required journal entry when a company buys a repair service on credit from Plumbers Inc. for $1,000 on September 30, 2018.

BALANCE SHEET	INCOME STATEMENT
CURRENT LIABILITIES	SALES REVENUE
BANK OVERDRAFT & OPERATING LINE OF CREDIT	SALES REVENUE
ACCOUNTS PAYABLE + $1,000 CR	COST OF GOODS SOLD
ACCRUED LIABILITIES	GROSS PROFIT
UNEARNED REVENUE	OPERATING EXPENSES Repairs Expense + $1,000 DR
NOTES PAYABLE (CURRENT)	OPERATING INCOME
LONG-TERM LIABILITIES	OTHER REVENUE (INTEREST REVENUE, GAIN ON SALE OF ASSETS)
NOTES PAYABLE (LONG-TERM)	OTHER EXPENSES (INTEREST EXPENSE, LOSS ON SALE OF ASSETS)
STOCKHOLDERS' EQUITY	OTHER EXPENSES (INTEREST EXPENSE, LOSS ON SALE OF ASSETS)
COMMON STOCK	INCOME BEFORE TAX
RETAINED EARNINGS	INCOME TAX
RETAINED EARNINGS	NET INCOME (LOSS)

Stockholders' equity decreases by $1,000

JOURNAL

Date	Account Title and Explanation	Debit	Credit
Sep 30	Repairs Expense	1,000	
	Accounts Payable		1,000
	Record repairs expense owing to Plumbers Inc.		

FIGURE 13.2

Since the purchase was for repairs, the repairs expense account is debited for $1,000 and is listed under operating expenses on the income statement. Accounts payable is credited for the same amount, showing that an invoice was received and must be paid in the future.

Sales Tax

Sales tax is a tax that is applied by the state government to goods or services that are sold. They are calculated as a percentage of a sale, and the percentages can vary from state to state. Figure 13.3 shows some examples of states and the amount of sales tax they charge.

California
7.25%

Utah
4.7%

Pennsylvania
6%

Note: Local sales tax may be added to state sales tax, causing actual sales tax in certain jurisdictions to be higher.

FIGURE 13.3

Although sales tax must be paid to the government, it would be impractical, if not impossible, for individual customers to send the sales tax money to the government every time they bought something. Imagine buying a coffee and having to send the government a few cents in sales tax.

Instead, businesses act as tax collectors for the government by collecting the sales tax from their customers and sending it to the government. For example, imagine a business receives $1,650 from a customer for the purchase of a TV. Of that amount, $1,500 is for the actual TV and $150 is the amount of sales tax. The business has to eventually remit the $150 sales tax to the government. Figure 13.4 demonstrates a simplified version of this process.

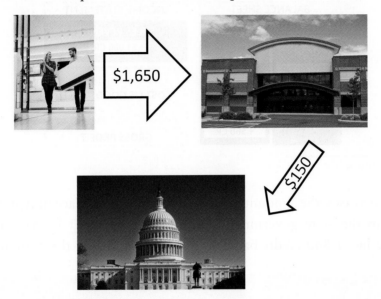

FIGURE 13.4

The retailer is responsible for collecting sales tax from the customer and eventually sending (remitting) the amount collected to the state government. The amount collected does not belong to the company and is considered a liability until it is paid to the government. Therefore, sales tax is recorded in a current liability account until it is remitted.

The range of sales tax varies by each state, from 0% to 7.25%. Some cities and counties impose additional sales tax on top of the state sales tax. The Federal Tax Administration publishes sales tax rates for all states and cities. It is important to note that for certain items that are resold more than once, (e.g. used cars), sales tax can be applied indefinitely. Each state has a list of tax exempt goods and services or items that are taxed at a reduced rate.

The due date to send the collected sales tax to the government varies from business to business. Companies that have a very small amount of sales may be required to send in the sales tax once a year. As the amount of sales increases and the amount of sales tax collected increases, the business may be required to send in the money on a quarterly or monthly basis. The government charges interest and penalties to businesses that fail to send the money or send it late.

As an example, assume Hardware Store Inc. sells inventory to a customer for $1,000 cash on June 15, 2018. The state sales tax rate is 6%. The transaction is shown in Figure 13.5. For this example, ignore COGS. Notice that while cash increased by $1,060, equity only increased by $1,000.

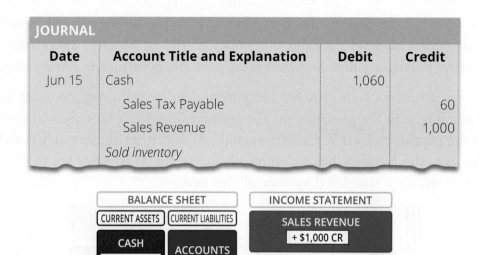

FIGURE 13.5

Each sale gradually increases the amount in the sales tax payable account until it is time for the company to send it to the state government. Assume the payment is made on August 31, 2018 and the account only has a $60 credit balance. Figure 13.6 shows the transaction.

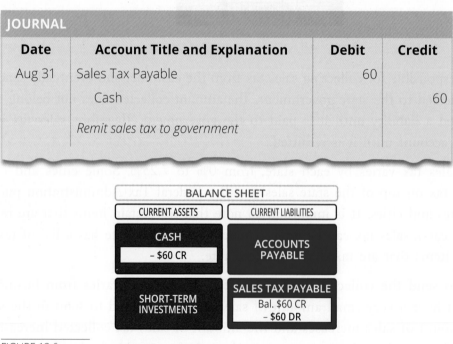

FIGURE 13.6

The sales tax payable account essentially acts as a clearing account. It accumulates the sales tax collected over a period of time, and then is cleared to $0 when a payment is made to send the sales tax to the state government.

Sales tax that is paid on purchased items is often added to the value of the asset or expense purchased. For example, suppose a company purchases $100 worth of inventory in a state where sales tax is 6%. The sales tax amount of $6 is added to the $100 worth of inventory, so merchandise inventory actually increases by $106 and is recorded as such.

Pause & Reflect

Exercise 13-1

On March 13, 2018, Jerrod Furniture Shop sold products for $50,000 cash. The products cost Jerrod $22,000. Jerrod Furniture Shop operates in a state that charges 5% sales tax. Assume Jerrod Furniture Shop uses a perpetual inventory system. Prepare the journal entries for the sale of the products.

JOURNAL			
Date	Account Title and Explanation	Debit	Credit

See Appendix I for solutions.

Unearned Revenue

LO 4

The accrual basis of accounting applies to both expenses and revenues. As you have learned, expenses are recognized during the period in which they are incurred, and not when they are actually paid. The same applies to unearned revenue: it is recognized in the period in which it was earned, and not when payment was actually received. As shown in Figure 13.7, for both accrued expense and unearned revenue, current liabilities are recorded in the first period. For accrued expense, accounts payable is recorded in the first period because the expense is incurred in the first period, but the company has not yet paid for it. Accounts payable has been covered in a previous section in this chapter. This section focuses on unearned revenue, which is recorded when the company receives cash before rendering goods or services to customers.

Accrued Expense		Unearned Revenue	
Expense Incurred	Expense Paid	Cash Received	Revenue Earned
Period 1	Period 2	Period 1	Period 2

DR Expense
    CR Accounts Payable
	DR Accounts Payable
	    CR Cash
		DR Cash
		    CR Unearned Revenue
			DR Unearned Revenue
			    CR Revenue

FIGURE 13.7

For example, a publishing company might receive payment in advance for a one-year subscription to its magazine. The money is received, but the magazine has not yet been supplied to the customer. Until the product exchanges hands, the amount received in advance cannot be recognized as revenue. The advanced cash receipt is therefore considered unearned revenue, which is a liability.

Business owners sometimes misunderstand how accruals work. This can lead to mistakes and bad decisions. For example, management may be tempted to treat unearned revenue as though it is already earned. Using the example of a magazine subscription again, what would happen if a customer decided to cancel the subscription and the magazine publisher had considered the money as earned? Until the product has been delivered, no transaction has been finalized with the customer. The money should be paid back to the customer when the subscription is canceled.

With a non-refundable subscription, the same principle would apply. It is still the obligation of the company to deliver goods or services that have been paid for and to treat the money as unearned until completion of the transaction.

What happens if a customer voluntarily cancels the rights to the goods or services and notifies the company to that effect? An example of this might be a subscriber moving overseas and informing the publisher that delivery of the magazine is no longer necessary. If the subscription is non-refundable, the customer has no right to request repayment and the company can continue to recognize revenue as it is earned. Of course, if the subscription is refundable, the publisher has to reverse all or part of the initial transaction and refund the subscriber for any remaining unused months of the subscription.

Here is an example to illustrate the concept of accruals and revenue. Tracking Time is the publisher of a magazine with a fiscal year end of December 31. In December, Tracking Time receives $120,000 from subscribers to cover the monthly delivery of magazines for one year, starting on January 1. The transaction is recorded in the company's books as shown in Figure 13.8.

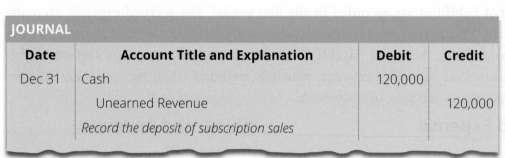

JOURNAL			
Date	**Account Title and Explanation**	**Debit**	**Credit**
Dec 31	Cash	120,000	
	Unearned Revenue		120,000
	Record the deposit of subscription sales		

FIGURE 13.8

The money is received and debited to the cash account in December. However, the revenue is yet to be earned (i.e. it is earned when the magazines are delivered), so the amount is credited to the unearned revenue account. Since revenue is not yet earned, there is no change to the company's equity.

On January 1, the magazine is delivered to customers for that month. This means that Tracking Time's obligation to the customers has been met for the month and the corresponding revenue is now earned. One month of subscriptions equals one-twelfth of the annual subscription; therefore, $10,000 is recognized as revenue for the month of January, as shown in Figure 13.9.

JOURNAL			
Date	**Account Title and Explanation**	**Debit**	**Credit**
Jan 1	Unearned Revenue	10,000	
	Sales Revenue		10,000
	Record delivery of magazines for January		

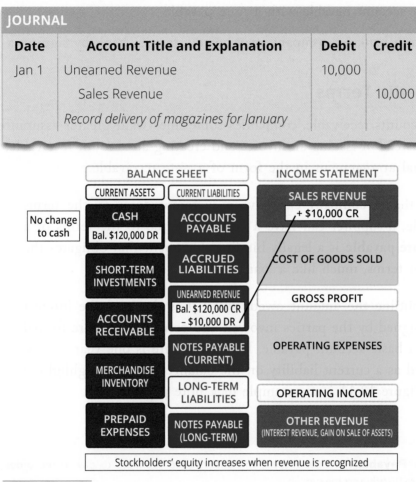

FIGURE 13.9

Unearned revenue originally had a credit balance of $120,000. Of that amount, $10,000 is now debited to the unearned revenue account and credited to the sales revenue account on the income statement. Although cash remains the same, the recognition of the unearned revenue means that equity has increased by $10,000. The obligation that Tracking Time now has to its customers is reduced from $120,000 to $110,000.

Another type of unearned liability gaining popularity in recent years is for gift cards or gift certificates. Similar to the Tracking Time example above, when a business sells a gift card or certificate, it debits the cash account and credits an unearned revenue account. The sales revenue account is only credited, and the unearned revenue account debited, when the gift card or certificate is redeemed for a product or service.

Short-Term Notes Payable

Short-term notes payable (notes payable that are considered current) can be issued for several different reasons.

- To extend credit terms—a company that purchases goods on credit can extend its credit term by replacing an account payable with a note payable

- To borrow from a bank—a company may borrow from a bank by signing a note payable

Extending Credit Terms

With regard to accounts receivable, companies sometimes want greater assurance that a customer will pay the bill. Instead of issuing an invoice and creating an account receivable, a company might make a more formal arrangement in the form of a note receivable.

In the same way that a company can have a customer agree to the terms of a note receivable, a supplier can have a company agree to the terms of a note payable. A **note payable** is a legally binding document that obligates the borrower to certain terms, much like a loan.

Such documents outline the amount owed, when it is due and the interest payable. They are signed by the parties involved and constitute a more formal arrangement than a basic account payable. If the due date is one year or less, the note is reported as a current liability on the balance sheet, as highlighted in Figure 13.10. Figure 13.11 is an example of a note payable.

FIGURE 13.10

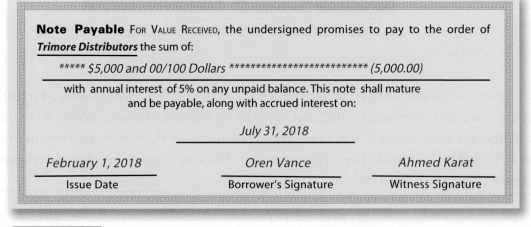

Note Payable FOR VALUE RECEIVED, the undersigned promises to pay to the order of *Trimore Distributors* the sum of:

***** $5,000 and 00/100 Dollars ************************* (5,000.00)

with annual interest of 5% on any unpaid balance. This note shall mature and be payable, along with accrued interest on:

July 31, 2018

February 1, 2018 — Issue Date

Oren Vance — Borrower's Signature

Ahmed Karat — Witness Signature

FIGURE 13.11

In the note payable from Figure 13.11, Oren Vance borrowed $5,000 from Trimore Distributors on February 1, 2018. The annual interest rate is 5% and both principal and interest are payable in six months. The journal entry used by the debtor (borrower) to record the extension of the credit term and the conversion of the original account payable to a note payable is shown in Figure 13.12.

JOURNAL			
Date	Account Title and Explanation	Debit	Credit
Feb 1	Accounts Payable	5,000	
	Notes Payable		5,000
	Record a six-month, 5% note payable		

FIGURE 13.12

When the note payable is due, Vance pays the principal and interest to Trimore. The journal entry for this transaction is shown in Figure 13.13.

JOURNAL			
Date	Account Title and Explanation	Debit	Credit
July 31	Notes Payable	5,000	
	Interest Expense	125	
	Cash		5,125
	Paid $5,000 note payable with interest		

FIGURE 13.13

Borrowing from a Bank

When a company borrows from a bank, the loan is documented with a note payable. To illustrate, suppose that on February 1, 2018, Oren Vance borrows money from Carson Bank to purchase merchandise. A $5,000, six-month, 5% note payable is issued. Note that the 5% is an annual interest rate. The journal entry for this transaction is shown in Figure 13.14.

JOURNAL			
Date	Account Title and Explanation	Debit	Credit
Feb 1	Cash	5,000	
	Notes Payable		5,000
	Borrowed $5,000 cash with a six-month,		
	5% note payable to Carson Bank		

FIGURE 13.14

When the note payable is due, Vance pays the principal and interest to the bank. The journal entry for this transaction is shown in Figure 13.15.

JOURNAL			
Date	Account Title and Explanation	Debit	Credit
July 31	Notes Payable	5,000	
	Interest Expense	125	
	Cash		5,125
	Paid $5,000 note payable with interest		

FIGURE 13.15

Accrued Interest and Notes Payable

Using the above example, let us assume the borrower has a June 30 year end date. Expense recognition dictates that we must report expenses in the period in which they helped to earn revenue; since no payment has been made or interest expense recognized, we must accrue the interest owing on the note to June 30. The calculated interest is $104 ($5,000 × 5% × 5/12, rounded to the nearest dollar amount). The journal entry in Figure 13.16 would be required.

JOURNAL			
Date	Account Title and Explanation	Debit	Credit
Jun 30	Interest Expense	104	
	Interest Payable		104
	Record interest on a six-month, 5% note payable		

FIGURE 13.16

In addition to the note payable for $5,000, the company would report interest payable of $104 on its June 30 year-end balance sheet within the accrued liabilities sections.

On July 31, both principal and interest will be paid to Carson Bank. The remaining interest expense is calculated as $21 ($5,000 × 5% × 1/12) since interest was already accrued up until June 30. The entry to record repayment of the note, plus interest, is presented in Figure 13.17.

JOURNAL				
Date	Account Title and Explanation	PR	Debit	Credit
Jul 31	Interest Payable		104	
	Interest Expense		21	
	Notes Payable		5,000	
	Cash			5,125
	Record interest and payment for a six-month, 5% note payable			

FIGURE 13.17

Note that the interest payable account is debited to remove the accrual recorded in the previous period and interest expense is debited with $21, which represents the interest expense for the month of July. In total, six months worth of interest has been recorded: five months in the previous period and one month in the current period.

Pause & Reflect

Exercise 13-2

Bach Supplies has a short-term cash flow problem. It approaches its bank and receives a $20,000 short-term note payable on September 1, 2018. The note is due in six months on February 28, 2019. The annual interest rate on the note payable is 6%. Bach Supplies has a December 31 year end. Record the journal entries for the issuance of the note payable, the accrued interest and the payment of the note when it is due.

JOURNAL			
Date	Account Title and Explanation	Debit	Credit

See Appendix I for solutions.

Current Portion of Long-Term Liabilities

When the term of a note payable is longer than one year, there will be two components to the note payable. The portion of the loan principal that will be paid within the next 12 months is considered current. This amount must be reported separately when the balance sheet is prepared, in a section under current liabilities called Notes Payable, Current Portion. The remaining amount of the note payable that is due beyond one year is reported on the balance sheet under long-term liabilities as Notes Payable, Long-Term Portion. (Note that this account can also be called Notes Payable, Noncurrent Portion.)

For example, a company manufactures a wide range of products for consumers. It wants to purchase a new processing machine to keep up with growing demand for its product. The company has insufficient cash reserves on hand to finance the purchase. Management decides to obtain a loan from a bank to finance an important capital investment.

On January 2, 2018, the company negotiates a loan from the bank of $50,000 with a term of five years, bearing an annual interest rate of 5%. Of that debt, $10,000 plus interest is payable every December 31. The full amount of the loan is recorded as a notes payable in the journal entry. When the balance sheet is prepared, the current portion of $10,000 is presented separately from the long-term portion of $40,000. Figure 13.18 shows how the note payable is recorded in the company's books.

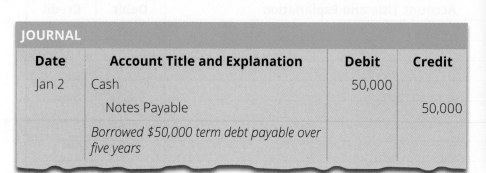

JOURNAL			
Date	**Account Title and Explanation**	**Debit**	**Credit**
Jan 2	Cash	50,000	
	Notes Payable		50,000
	Borrowed $50,000 term debt payable over five years		

FIGURE 13.18

On December 31, the first installment plus interest was paid. The transaction is recorded as shown in Figure 13.19.

JOURNAL			
Date	**Account Title and Explanation**	**Debit**	**Credit**
Dec 31	Notes Payable	10,000	
	Interest Expense	2,500	
	Cash		12,500
	Record payment for first notes payable installment plus interest		

FIGURE 13.19

After the first payment, the balance of the note payable decreases to $40,000, $10,000 of which is still considered current. When the balance sheet is prepared at the year end, $10,000 is included as part of current liabilities and $30,000 is included as part of long-term liabilities.

Payroll Liabilities

Payroll as an Accrued Liability

Payroll is one of the most important business obligations of any organization. Employees are entitled to receive payment for services they have provided to the company. Similar to interest expense, which must be accrued in the same period that it is incurred, payroll expenses must also be accrued when they are incurred even when cash has not yet been paid. In fact, payroll expense is an excellent example of accrued liabilities because payroll journal entries are often recorded in one period, but amounts are not paid until the next period. For example, if an employee works in December 2018 but will not receive her salary until January 2019, the company still has to accrue December payroll expenses and liabilities in the fiscal year 2018.

The amount of payroll that a company has to accrue is determined partly by employment law and legislation that the company must follow. The law requires not only that a company pay its employees fairly, but also that the employer submit payroll-related taxes to the government. Some taxes are deducted from the employee's paychecks, while others are paid by the employer or are paid jointly by both employee and employer. Therefore, payroll accounting involves three types of payroll liabilities: (1) the net pay owed to an employee, (2) amounts deducted from employee paychecks and owed to the government and other relevant organizations, and (3) employer payroll contributions. Any business that hires people to work on its behalf will incur these liabilities and related expenses.

The net pay owed to an employee amounts to the gross pay minus employee payroll deductions. These deductions can include the following.

- Social Security tax
- Medicare tax
- federal, state and local income taxes
- other voluntary deductions

Gross pay represents the total amount actually earned by the employee, and **net pay** represents the amount after the various deductions have been made.

The amount of gross pay and deductions on each paycheck is affected by the pay period (pay frequency). Pay period refers to the number of times an employee is paid during one year. The table in Figure 13.20 shows how many pay periods there are in a year for the common pay frequencies.

Pay Frequency	Number of Pay Periods in a Year
Weekly	52
Bi-weekly	26
Semi-monthly	24
Monthly	12

FIGURE 13.20

Gross Pay to Net Pay

There are two ways to pay an employee: salaries and wages.

Generally speaking, employees who work full-time in a company, such as in the administrative, sales or management roles, are paid a salary. A salary is a *fixed annual* amount that is divided by the number of pay periods in a calendar year to determine the gross pay for each pay period.

For example, a sales manager who is paid $52,000 per year earns $1,000 per week. If he is paid on a bi-weekly basis, his gross pay is $2,000 for each pay period.

Individuals employed on a part-time basis (e.g. in the retail sector, in factories, or as manual laborers), are more likely to be paid a wage (hourly rate), where the pay for any given pay period is determined by the number of hours worked in that period.

As an example, if a factory worker is paid $17.00 per hour and works for 65 hours in a two-week period, the gross pay is $1,105.00 (65 hours × $17.00 per hour).

Some of the key differences between salaries and wages are payments for overtime and sick pay. In most cases, employees who are paid by salary *do not* receive overtime pay. Salaried employees may continue to receive their pay if they are absent for a few days with legitimate reasons.

Hourly employees are entitled to extra pay when they work on statutory holidays, such as New Year's Day, or if they work overtime. Generally, hourly employees do not receive any pay if they are absent for personal reasons.

The US Department of Labor, under the *Fair Labor Standards Act,* requires employers to pay overtime pay at a rate of at least 1.5 times an employee's regular rate of pay after 40 hours of work in one week. Certain categories of employees are exempt from this stipulation, such as many executive, management and administrative positions.

To illustrate, we can look at the overtime pay calculation for employee Amy Wood of Roofus Construction. Amy normally works a standard 40-hour work week at a rate of $23.75 an hour. During the last week of June, Amy worked a total of 44 hours, which is four hours over her normal work week. Her employer pays 2 times the regular rate (sometimes referred to as "double time") for all hours worked in excess of 40 hours per week. The calculation to determine Amy's gross pay for that week is shown in Figure 13.21.

Earnings at regular rate (40 hrs × $23.75/hr)	$950.00
Earnings at overtime rate* (4 hrs × $47.50)	190.00
Gross pay for last week of June	$1,140.00

*Overtime rate = $47.50 ($23.75 × 2)

FIGURE 13.21

There are at least two different amounts shown on a pay stub. Gross pay is the amount of pay an employee receives before any deductions—statutory or voluntary—are made. The amount remaining after deductions have been made is the net pay, or an employee's "take home pay." Payroll deductions are discussed next.

Employee Payroll Deductions—Statutory

Every business is required to withhold amounts from an employee's gross pay, called statutory deductions. These deductions are eventually paid to the appropriate tax authority in the country. In the Unites States, the tax authorities are the Internal Revenue Service (IRS) for federal income tax purposes and various state authorities for state income tax purposes, such as the California Employment Development Department or the New York State Department of Taxation and Finance. Statutory deductions in the United States include the following.

- federal income tax
- state and local income taxes
- Social Security tax
- Medicare tax

Each of the above statutory deductions is calculated using annual tax tables. The calculated amounts are then subtracted from an employee's pay. The business is responsible for keeping track of payroll and the associated deductions to prepare tax forms for the employee at the end of each calendar year. The tax forms are then used by the employee when preparing a personal tax return for the government.

It is important to note that these deductions are made on the employee's behalf. When the employee files an annual income tax return, the deducted amounts show as payments already made and reduce the final tax amount owed. The system is designed this way to reduce the financial burden on individuals who would otherwise have to pay huge amounts when they file their tax returns every year. As well, businesses withhold and remit these amounts to the tax authorities on behalf of employees to assist in paying for the government services provided all year. Examples of these services include education programs, unemployment programs and transportation funding. Regardless of the level of government that provides or contributes to these services, the majority of the funding comes throughout the year from tax installments.

The amounts withheld are required under law, and failure to withhold the amounts from the employee's pay and remit them to the tax authorities can result in severe penalties. Therefore, payroll liabilities warrant their own account, separate from accounts payable.

Federal Income Taxes

Every business is required to withhold income tax from an employee's gross pay. There is no age limit for paying taxes and no maximum on the total earnings for which taxes must be paid. The more an employee earns, the more tax is deducted from the pay.

Income tax is a major source of revenue for the federal government. The personal income tax rates depend on three factors.

- gross pay
- marital status

- withholding allowances

Every employee must complete an *Employee's Withholding Allowance Certificate,* also known as **Form W-4,** and submit it to the employer. The employer uses the information provided on the W-4, along with the employee's gross salary or gross wages, to calculate the amount of taxes to deduct, or *withhold,* from an employee's earnings.

On a W-4, an employee provides a social security number, marital status, and the withholding allowances to which he or she is entitled. Generally, the more withholding allowances an employee has, the lower the amount of federal income tax withheld. For instance, an employee who is single receives one withholding allowance, whereas a married employee may be entitled to an additional allowance for his or her spouse. Figure 13.22 shows the employee's portion of a W-4.

-------------------------------- **Separate here and give Form W-4 to your employer. Keep the top part for your records.** --------------------------------

Form **W-4**	**Employee's Withholding Allowance Certificate**	OMB No. 1545-0074
Department of the Treasury Internal Revenue Service	▶ **Whether you are entitled to claim a certain number of allowances or exemption from withholding is subject to review by the IRS. Your employer may be required to send a copy of this form to the IRS.**	20**16**

1 Your first name and middle initial	Last name		2 **Your social security number**

Home address (number and street or rural route)	3 ☐ Single ☐ Married ☐ Married, but withhold at higher Single rate.
	Note: If married, but legally separated, or spouse is a nonresident alien, check the "Single" box.
City or town, state, and ZIP code	4 **If your last name differs from that shown on your social security card, check here. You must call 1-800-772-1213 for a replacement card.** ▶ ☐

5	Total number of allowances you are claiming (from line **H** above **or** from the applicable worksheet on page 2)	5	
6	Additional amount, if any, you want withheld from each paycheck	6	$
7	I claim exemption from withholding for 2016, and I certify that I meet **both** of the following conditions for exemption.		

• Last year I had a right to a refund of **all** federal income tax withheld because I had **no** tax liability, **and**
• This year I expect a refund of **all** federal income tax withheld because I expect to have **no** tax liability.
If you meet both conditions, write "Exempt" here . . . . ▶ | 7 |

Under penalties of perjury, I declare that I have examined this certificate and, to the best of my knowledge and belief, it is true, correct, and complete.

Employee's signature
(This form is not valid unless you sign it.) ▶ _____   Date ▶ _____

8	Employer's name and address (Employer: Complete lines 8 and 10 only if sending to the IRS.)	9 Office code (optional)	10 Employer identification number (EIN)

For Privacy Act and Paperwork Reduction Act Notice, see page 2.   Cat. No. 10220Q   Form **W-4** (2016)

FIGURE 13.22

There are various methods for calculating federal income taxes. Each year, the Internal Revenue Service (IRS) issues income tax withholding tables to help employers calculate the amount of federal income tax to withhold, such as the **wage bracket method tables** for income tax withholding (a portion of a table for a single taxpayer is shown in Figure 13.23). This information is annually published by the IRS as the *(Circular E), Employer's Tax Guide.*

Wage Bracket Method Tables for Income Tax Withholding

SINGLE Persons—WEEKLY Payroll Period

(For Wages Paid through December 31, 2016)

And the wages are—		And the number of withholding allowances claimed is—										
At least	But less than	0	1	2	3	4	5	6	7	8	9	10
		The amount of income tax to be withheld is—										
$0	$55	$0	$0	$0	$0	$0	$0	$0	$0	$0	$0	$0
55	60	1	0	0	0	0	0	0	0	0	0	0
60	65	2	0	0	0	0	0	0	0	0	0	0
65	70	2	0	0	0	0	0	0	0	0	0	0
70	75	3	0	0	0	0	0	0	0	0	0	0
75	80	3	0	0	0	0	0	0	0	0	0	0
80	85	4	0	0	0	0	0	0	0	0	0	0
85	90	4	0	0	0	0	0	0	0	0	0	0
90	95	5	0	0	0	0	0	0	0	0	0	0
95	100	5	0	0	0	0	0	0	0	0	0	0
100	105	6	0	0	0	0	0	0	0	0	0	0
105	110	6	0	0	0	0	0	0	0	0	0	0
110	115	7	0	0	0	0	0	0	0	0	0	0
115	120	7	0	0	0	0	0	0	0	0	0	0
120	125	8	0	0	0	0	0	0	0	0	0	0
125	130	8	1	0	0	0	0	0	0	0	0	0
130	135	9	1	0	0	0	0	0	0	0	0	0
135	140	9	2	0	0	0	0	0	0	0	0	0
140	145	10	2	0	0	0	0	0	0	0	0	0
145	150	10	3	0	0	0	0	0	0	0	0	0
150	155	11	3	0	0	0	0	0	0	0	0	0
155	160	11	4	0	0	0	0	0	0	0	0	0
160	165	12	4	0	0	0	0	0	0	0	0	0
165	170	12	5	0	0	0	0	0	0	0	0	0
170	175	13	5	0	0	0	0	0	0	0	0	0

FIGURE 13.23

The withholding table in Figure 13.23 is for single persons, but withholding tables are also issued for married persons, and for different pay periods, such as semi-monthly and monthly. To use the table, the employer locates the employee's wage bracket from the first two columns, and then follows that row across to the column showing the number of withholding allowances claimed by that particular employee. The amount shown in that column is what should be withheld from the employee's gross salary (or wages). For example, if an employee earns a weekly salary of $163, and has claimed one withholding allowance, the employer withholds $4 from the employee's gross salary, as indicated by the highlight in Figure 13.23.

For simplicity in calculating federal income tax deductions, we will use a standard rate. In the real world, withholding tables or accounting software is used to get a precise figure. Figure 13.24 shows the simplified way of calculating how much federal income tax to deduct from an employee's pay.

Federal Income Tax Deduction = Gross Pay × Income Tax Rate

FIGURE 13.24

At the end of the year, the employer must complete a *Wage and Tax Statement* for each employee, also known as a **Form W-2**. This form indicates the employees' gross pay and all the statutory deductions taken from the gross pay for the year. This form is given to the employee and sent to the IRS.

State and Local Income Taxes

Like federal income taxes, most states require employers to withhold income taxes from employee earnings. The calculation criterion is similar to that of federal taxes. Each state issues its own tax table similar to *Circular E*.

As with federal income tax, for simplicity in calculating state income tax deductions, we will use a standard rate. In the real world, withholding tables or accounting software is used to get a precise figure. Figure 13.25 shows the simplified way of calculating how much state income tax to deduct from an employee's pay.

State Income Tax Deduction = Gross Pay × Income Tax Rate

FIGURE 13.25

Federal Insurance Contributions Act

Every business is required to withhold a portion of an employee's earnings in accordance with the Federal Insurance Contributions Act (FICA) from an employee's gross pay. The amount withheld is known as **FICA tax**. The statutory deduction is to pay for federal Social Security and Medicare benefits programs. The business is also required to match the amount withheld from the employee. For example, if an employee has $50 deducted from gross pay for FICA, the business has to pay an additional $50 towards FICA.

Both Social Security and the Medicare portion have their own rates applied to the gross pay of an employee. The rates usually change annually, but in recent years the typical rate for Social Security is 6.2% and the typical rate for Medicare is 1.45%, for a total FICA deduction of 7.65%. Since the employer must match this amount, the employer pays an additional 7.65% of the employee's gross pay to the federal government for FICA.

FICA Tax Threshold

The amount withheld for an employee is based on the employee's earnings for the calendar year. The amount withheld is also subject to a wage base limit above which additional taxes are withheld. This limit is updated annually. Using 2016 rates and limits, an employee is required to pay FICA taxes (on the calendar year salary/wages) as follows.

- Social Security tax of 6.2% on the first $118,500 of salary/wages, up to a maximum of $7,347 ($118,500 × 6.2%)

  plus

- Medicare tax of 1.45% on the first $200,000 of salary/wages, up to a maximum of $2,900 ($200,000 × 1.45%).

  plus

- An additional Medicare tax of 0.9% on salary/wages in excess of $200,000*

*The wage base limit for couples filing a joint tax return is $250,000; for married taxpayers filing separate tax returns, each is allowed a $125,000 wage base limit.

In the case of additional Medicare tax, this is only imposed on the employee and not on the employer. Also note that additional Medicare tax must be withheld from the point in the pay period that the employee's salary reaches the $200,000 threshold and for the remainder of that calendar year.

Figure 13.26 illustrates the application of the FICA base wage limits for an employee earning $210,000 in wages for the 2016 calendar year.

FICA Taxes (based on 2016 rates and base wage limits)

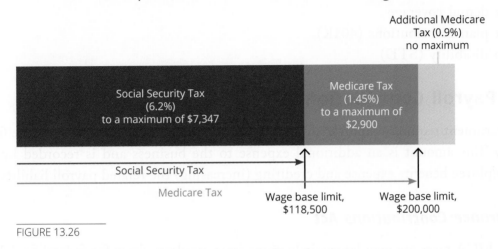

FIGURE 13.26

For our examples, we will use the 2016 FICA rates of 6.2% (Social Security tax), and 1.45% (Medicare tax) and assume that all employees are paid wages that fall within the wage base limits. Figure 13.27 shows the formula to calculate the amount of FICA deducted from an employee's pay.

FICA Deduction = Gross Pay × FICA Rate

FIGURE 13.27

Employee Payroll Deductions—Voluntary

An employer may also deduct other amounts from an employee's pay with the employee's permission; these amounts are referred to as voluntary deductions. In each case, the employee is advised of the potential deductions and signs a contract indicating his or her agreement.

While these deductions are generally considered voluntary, they may be required by an employer as part of the employment agreement (typical examples would be union dues, medical and dental coverage).

Unions are organizations that employees can belong to that create better working conditions for the employees. Sometimes belonging to a union is the only way an employee can get a job. Charitable donations can include national and international charities, such as the US Fund for

UNICEF, Direct Relief, or a registered local charity to which employees would like to contribute. The donations may be tax deductible.

There are many different types of voluntary deductions, all of which depend on what the business is willing to offer employees. The business deducts these amounts and eventually sends them to the appropriate institution. Examples of other voluntary deductions include the following.

*   Accidental death and dismemberment coverage (AD&D)
*   Employee Stock Purchase Plan (ESOP and ESPP)
*   Roth IRA
*   Long-term disability (LTD)
*   Medical or dental coverage
*   Retirement plan contributions (401K)
*   Short-term disability (STD)

Employer Payroll Contributions

Often, the government requires employers to match or contribute to the deductions made from their employee's pay. This amount is an additional expense to the business and is recorded by debiting (increasing) employee benefits expense and crediting (increasing) the related payroll liability account.

Federal Insurance Contributions Act

As mentioned, FICA taxes are mandatory deductions from employees' pay for federal Social Security and Medicare benefits programs. The employer must also match the employee's deduction.

Federal Unemployment and State Unemployment Taxes

The business has to contribute towards federal and state unemployment taxes on behalf of employees. The Federal Unemployment Tax Act (FUTA) rate is 6.0% of gross pay, but only applies to the first $7,000 of gross pay an employee earns in the year.

The State Unemployment Tax (SUTA) rate changes from state to state. The rate fluctuates based on factors such as the number of unemployment claims in the state and the overall "good standing" of the state with the federal government. For this textbook, assume the SUTA rate is 5.4%. The employer is allowed to reduce the federal unemployment tax rate by the state unemployment tax rate. In this example, the FUTA rate of 6.0% is reduced to 0.6% (6.0% - 5.4%).

Figure 13.28 shows the formula to calculate the amount of FUTA that is payable to the government. The formula for SUTA payable is the same, except it uses the SUTA rate.

FUTA Payable = Gross Pay × FUTA Rate

FIGURE 13.28

Employee Benefits

Some employers will pay for some or all of the benefits they provide their employees. This is an extra cost to the business. If the employer decides to pay for all of a benefit (for example a health benefit), then the employee would not see any deduction from his or her pay.

Responsibility for Paying Taxes and Benefits

We have just discussed the employee payroll deductions (statutory and voluntary) and the employer payroll contributions. Figure 13.29 summarizes these responsibilities according to who pays them.

Employee Payroll Deductions	Employer Payroll Contributions
• FICA tax—Social security taxes • FICA tax—Medicare taxes • Federal income taxes • State and local income taxes • Portion of medical coverage (if applicable) • Portion of pension plan (if applicable) • Portion of other benefits (if applicable, e.g. insurance) • Charitable donations and union dues (if applicable)	• FICA tax—Social security taxes • FICA tax—Medicare taxes • FUTA tax—Federal unemployment taxes • SUTA—State unemployment taxes • Portion of medical coverage (if applicable) • Portion of pension plan (if applicable) • Portion of other benefits (if applicable)

FIGURE 13.29

Payroll Example

Assume that Roofus Construction's gross payroll for the period ending January 31, 2018 is $15,000, consisting of $11,200 in sales salaries and $3,800 in office salaries. Employees are paid every month and have statutory deductions withheld from their pay. In addition, there are voluntary deductions from their gross earnings including union dues, charitable contributions, health insurance plan and retirement savings. As part of their benefits package, Roofus Construction matches employee contributions to health insurance and retirement plans.

Payroll Register

Since businesses usually have multiple employees, a payroll register is often used rather than preparing individual entries. A payroll register lists every employee along with his or her gross pay, deductions and net pay. The bottom of the payroll register calculates totals that can be used to complete the journal entries. Computer accounting software has a similar tool for creating paychecks for multiple employees at one time.

Figure 13.30 shows a sample payroll register. Glen Booth earns $5,000 gross pay per month as a salary. The rest of the employees are paid various hourly wages and work a different number of hours. We will assume all employees must pay monthly union dues of $25 and monthly health insurance of $15. The monthly health insurance premiums are actually $30 per person, but the business pays half. By completing the rest of the payroll information for all the employees, we can use the totals to create the journal entries.

PAYROLL PERIOD JANUARY 1 TO JANUARY 31, 2018

Name	Hourly Wage	Hours	Gross Earnings
Booth, Glen		160	$5,000.00
Dickens, Charlie	$27.35	100	$2,735.00
Smith, Adam	23.10	150	$3,465.00
Wood, Amy	23.75	160	$3,800.00
Total			$15,000.00

Payroll Register

Gross Earnings	Deductions							Total Deductions	Net Pay
	Federal Income Tax	State Income Tax	FICA Tax	Charitable Donations	Union Dues	Retirement Savings Plan	Health Insurance		
$5,000.00	$500.00	$250.00	$382.50	$50.00	$25.00	$250.00	$15.00	$1,472.50	$3,527.50
$2,735.00	$273.50	$136.75	$209.23	$50.00	$25.00	$250.00	$15.00	$959.48	$1,775.52
$3,465.00	$346.50	$173.25	$265.07	$50.00	$25.00	$250.00	$15.00	$1,124.82	$2,340.18
$3,800.00	$380.00	$190.00	$290.70	$50.00	$25.00	$250.00	$15.00	$1,200.70	$2,599.30
$15,000.00	$1,500.00	$750.00	$1,147.50	$200.00	$100.00	$1,000.00	$60.00	$4,757.50	$10,242.50

FIGURE 13.30

Payroll Records

The business must keep a record of gross pay, deductions, hours worked and a variety of other information about every employee. This information is collected at the time the employee is hired and updated every pay or when any important piece of information relating to payroll changes. A computerized system updates the payroll record automatically after every pay, as shown in Figure 13.31.

Booth, Glen 5234 North Street Springfield, IL 62704-1234 Single Number of Withholding Allowances: 1	Phone: (217) 555-1212 Date of Birth: February 16,1977 Soc. Sec. No.: 123-45-6789 Pay Rate: $5,000.00 per month Occupation: Sales	Employee No.: 2218 Date of Hire: June 20, 2008 Date of Termination:

Month Ended	Hours	Gross Earnings	Deductions							Total Deductions	Net Pay
			Federal Income Tax	State Income Tax	FICA Tax	Charitable Donations	Union Dues	Retirement Saving Plan	Health Insurance		
Jan 31, 2018	160	$5,000.00	$500.00	$250.00	$383.50	$50.00	$25.00	$250.00	$15.00	$1,472.50	$3,527.50
Feb 28, 2018	160	$5,000.00	$500.00	$250.00	$383.50	$50.00	$25.00	$250.00	$15.00	$1,472.50	$3,527.50
Mar 31, 2018	160	$5,000.00	$500.00	$250.00	$383.50	$50.00	$25.00	$250.00	$15.00	$1,472.50	$3,527.50
Apr 30, 2018	160	$5,000.00	$500.00	$250.00	$383.50	$50.00	$25.00	$250.00	$15.00	$1,472.50	$3,527.50
May 31, 2018	160	$5,000.00	$500.00	$250.00	$383.50	$50.00	$25.00	$250.00	$15.00	$1,472.50	$3,527.50

FIGURE 13.31

The steps to create the journal entry to record payroll (wages and/or salaries) with deductions are as follows.

- Record gross pay by debiting (increasing) the salaries expense account.
- Record the amounts withheld to various payable accounts by crediting (increasing) each of the payable accounts; these amounts are paid to the IRS and others at a later date.
- Record the net amount actually paid to the employees as a credit (decrease) to cash if the employee is paid immediately. If payment is delayed a few days, post the net amount as a credit (increase) to the salaries payable account for later payment.

The journal entry to record these transactions is shown in Figure 13.32. Note that amounts have been rounded to the nearest dollar for simplicity. The deductions have been calculated based on the gross pay and the calculations presented earlier.

JOURNAL			
Date	Account Title and Explanation	Debit	Credit
Jan 31	Sales Salaries Expense	11,200	
	Office Salaries Expense	3,800	
	Federal Income Tax Payable		1,500
	State Income Tax Payable		750
	FICA Tax Payable		1,148
	Charitable Donations Payable		200
	Union Dues Payable		100
	Retirement Savings Plan Payable		1,000
	Health Insurance Payable		60
	Salaries Payable		10,242
	Record salaries and deductions		

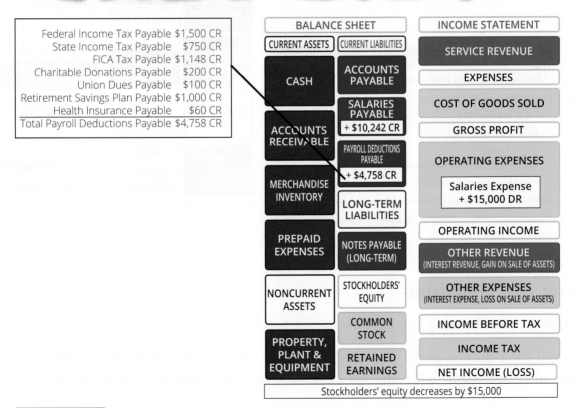

Federal Income Tax Payable $1,500 CR
State Income Tax Payable $750 CR
FICA Tax Payable $1,148 CR
Charitable Donations Payable $200 CR
Union Dues Payable $100 CR
Retirement Savings Plan Payable $1,000 CR
Health Insurance Payable $60 CR
Total Payroll Deductions Payable $4,758 CR

BALANCE SHEET

| CURRENT ASSETS | CURRENT LIABILITIES |

CASH — ACCOUNTS PAYABLE

SALARIES PAYABLE + $10,242 CR

ACCOUNTS RECEIVABLE — PAYROLL DEDUCTIONS PAYABLE + $4,758 CR

MERCHANDISE INVENTORY — LONG-TERM LIABILITIES

PREPAID EXPENSES — NOTES PAYABLE (LONG-TERM)

NONCURRENT ASSETS — STOCKHOLDERS' EQUITY

PROPERTY, PLANT & EQUIPMENT — COMMON STOCK — RETAINED EARNINGS

Stockholders' equity decreases by $15,000

INCOME STATEMENT

SERVICE REVENUE

EXPENSES

COST OF GOODS SOLD

GROSS PROFIT

OPERATING EXPENSES

Salaries Expense + $15,000 DR

OPERATING INCOME

OTHER REVENUE (INTEREST REVENUE, GAIN ON SALE OF ASSETS)

OTHER EXPENSES (INTEREST EXPENSE, LOSS ON SALE OF ASSETS)

INCOME BEFORE TAX

INCOME TAX

NET INCOME (LOSS)

FIGURE 13.32

Net pay is calculated by subtracting all the deductions from the gross pay. The employee's net pay is recorded in salaries payable. This indicates that the business has recorded the payroll journal entry but pays the employee at a later date. If the employee is paid immediately, the employee's net pay is recorded to cash.

The business now has to record its own payroll expenses. In addition to paying for FICA, remember that this business pays for half of the health insurance coverage for its employees.

The steps to record the business expenses as a journal entry are as follows.

- Record total expenses to the business by debiting (increasing) employee benefits expense.
- Record individual amounts by crediting (increasing) the various payable (liability) accounts.

The journal entry to record these transactions is shown in Figure 13.33. The employer amounts have been calculated based on the calculations presented earlier.

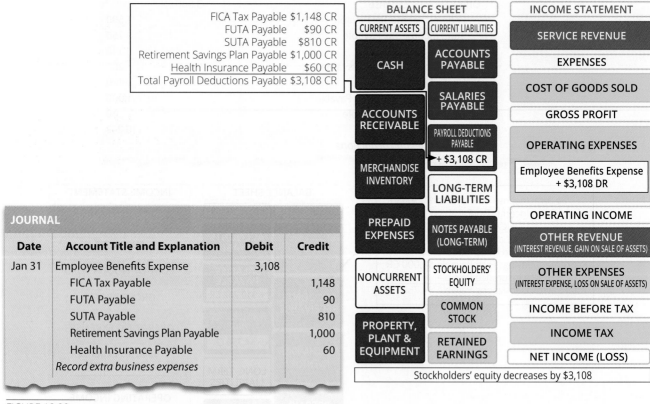

FIGURE 13.33

Paying the Liabilities

The steps to record paying the liabilities as journal entries are as follows.

- Record the reduction of the liabilities by debiting (decreasing) each of the payable accounts.
- Record the payment to the appropriate individual or institution by crediting (decreasing) cash.

Once the journal entries are made and the decreases to the liability accounts are complete, the liability accounts have a zero balance. All the amounts that were payroll debts to the company are completely paid off. Notice that there is no change to the income statement or equity when the liabilities are paid.

Salaries Payable

Employees do not always receive a paycheck on the same day that the payroll entry is recorded. For our example, the journal entry to record salaries and deductions in Figure 13.32 was made on January 31, 2018, and the journal entry to record paying the employee in Figure 13.34 was made on February 1, 2018. When the employees receive their salaries, we can decrease the liability and reduce cash.

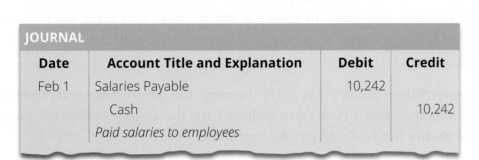

JOURNAL			
Date	**Account Title and Explanation**	**Debit**	**Credit**
Feb 1	Salaries Payable	10,242	
	Cash		10,242
	Paid salaries to employees		

FIGURE 13.34

BALANCE SHEET

CURRENT ASSETS	CURRENT LIABILITIES
CASH – $10,242 CR	**ACCOUNTS PAYABLE**
ACCOUNTS RECEIVABLE	**SALARIES PAYABLE** – $10,242 DR
	PAYROLL DEDUCTIONS PAYABLE
MERCHANDISE INVENTORY	**LONG-TERM LIABILITIES**
PREPAID EXPENSES	**NOTES PAYABLE (LONG-TERM)**
NONCURRENT ASSETS	**STOCKHOLDERS' EQUITY**
PROPERTY, PLANT & EQUIPMENT	**COMMON STOCK**
	RETAINED EARNINGS

No change to stockholders' equity

Statutory Deductions Payable

Figure 13.35 shows the journal entry to record statuatory deductions payable.

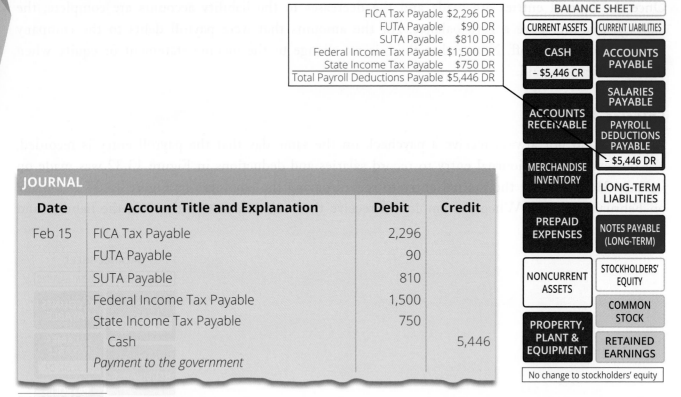

| FICA Tax Payable $2,296 DR |
| FUTA Payable $90 DR |
| SUTA Payable $810 DR |
| Federal Income Tax Payable $1,500 DR |
| State Income Tax Payable $750 DR |
| Total Payroll Deductions Payable $5,446 DR |

JOURNAL

Date	Account Title and Explanation	Debit	Credit
Feb 15	FICA Tax Payable	2,296	
	FUTA Payable	90	
	SUTA Payable	810	
	Federal Income Tax Payable	1,500	
	State Income Tax Payable	750	
	Cash		5,446
	Payment to the government		

FIGURE 13.35

The government has strict guidelines for when the payroll liabilities are due. Businesses must pay close attention to these dates. If payments are late, the business must pay penalties and interest on top of the amount owed. It is usually best to send payment through the bank. The bank teller's stamp indicates the date the payment was made to record if the payment was made on time or made late. Most moderate size businesses have to pay their statutory deduction liabilities by the 15th of the following month.

In this example, payroll was recorded on January 31, 2018; therefore the government must receive payment by February 15, 2018. Notice that FICA taxes include both the amounts deducted from the employee's pay and the amounts the business had to contribute.

Charitable Donations and Union Dues Payable

Any voluntary amounts deducted from an employee's pay must be sent to the institution to which they are owed. Businesses merely act as an intermediary, taking the money from the employee and sending it to the institution. In this example, union dues must be sent to the union hall by the end of the following month, as

JOURNAL

Date	Account Title and Explanation	Debit	Credit
Feb 28	Union Dues Payable	50	
	Cash		50
	Payment to union hall		

FIGURE 13.36

indicated by the journal entry in Figure 13.36. Charitable donations are paid in a similar manner to the appropriate charity.

Health and Retirement Plan Payable

Some voluntary amounts are split between the employee and the business. In this example for health insurance, the business combines the amount deducted from the employee in Figure 13.32 and the amount the business contributes in Figure 13.33. The journal entry is shown in Figure 13.37. The payment is being made to the health insurance company. The process to record the payment for the retirement plan is similar.

An important point to note is that the $15,000 in gross payroll actually costs the business $18,108, which is the total cash flow impact of paying all the payroll journal entries. In our example, for every $1 of gross payroll, the actual cost to the business is approximately $1.21 because of the employer contributions and taxes. This actual cost can be higher if higher rates for federal and state income taxes are used, or the employer pays the full amount for items like health insurance and retirement plans. This shows that payroll can be much more expensive to a business than just the amount received by employees, depending upon the types and amounts of benefits that a business pays.

JOURNAL			
Date	**Account Title and Explanation**	**Debit**	**Credit**
Feb 28	Health Insurance Payable	120	
	Cash		120
	Payment for health insurance		

FIGURE 13.37

Pause & Reflect

Exercise 13-3

Cranberry Pickers is determining the payroll amounts for the month ending April 30, 2018. Its employees earned a total of $10,000 in gross pay. Assume the following rates.

Federal Income Tax	10%
State Income Tax	5%
FICA	7.65%
FUTA	0.6%
SUTA	5.4%

Calculate the net pay to be paid to the employees, as well as the total employer payroll contributions.

See Appendix I for solutions.

Estimated Liabilities

We have already discussed various forms of known liabilities, also referred to as determinable liabilities, which are debts taken on by a company for which the terms are readily known. However, some company liabilities exist for which the exact terms are not precisely known and cannot be determined until future events occur. These unknown liabilities are referred to as non-determinable liabilities, and can be divided further into estimated liabilities and contingent liabilities.

Estimated liabilities are financial obligations that a company cannot exactly quantify. Examples include employee benefits, product warranties and customer loyalty programs. A company needs to adhere to the expense recognition principle when it makes an estimate of the amount of the upcoming liability.

Employee Benefits

In the section on payroll accounting, we briefly discussed voluntary deductions. These are additional deductions that an employee can authorize the employer to withhold from the employee's gross pay for pensions, medical and dental coverage, and other benefits known as **employee benefits**. Employee benefits are an expense to the employer. According to the matching principle, the cost of these benefits must be estimated and recorded in the period in which they are incurred—that is, in the period in which the employee earns the benefits. Next, we will look at some common employee benefits in more detail: paid vacations, pension benefits, health benefits and employee bonuses.

Vacation Pay

Many employers offer their employees paid vacations, also referred to as *compensated absences*. The employer estimates and records the amount to pay for employee vacations as an accrued liability for the period, either by pay period or at the end of the year. For example, assume that a company's salaried employee has earned an estimated $560 in vacation pay for the month of January. The company accrues its estimated vacation pay liabilities at the end of each month. On January 31, the employer makes the journal entry shown in Figure 13.38.

JOURNAL			
Date	**Account Title and Explanation**	**Debit**	**Credit**
Jan 31	Vacation Pay Expense	560	
	Vacation Pay Payable		560
	To accrue estimated vacation pay payable for the month		

FIGURE 13.38

In many cases, whether by personal choice or by employer policy, the employee uses the vacation entitlement within the year. In this case, any accrued vacation pay at the end of the year is reported on the company's balance sheet as a current liability. Sometimes, employees are allowed to accumulate vacation entitlement and carry it over into another period. If the employee does not take the vacation entitlement within the next year, the estimated vacation pay payable is reported on the company's balance sheet as a long-term liability.

When the employee in our example takes her vacation, the employer records a journal entry to debit vacation pay payable and credit cash. The employer must also record the normal entries related to taxes and withholdings in the payroll records.

Pension Benefits

Some employers contribute to *pension plans* for their employees, which allows employees to receive cash payments from the company after they retire. Employee pension rights are accrued during the period of time that the employee works for the company. There are several basic types of pension plans, known as defined contribution and defined benefit plans. Details of these plans are beyond the scope of this textbook. However, in simple terms, the employer accrues employee pensions each period (assume one year) as shown in Figure 13.39.

When the employee retires and the former employer starts paying out the pension benefits, the company records the payments by decreasing (debiting) employee pensions payable and crediting the cash account.

JOURNAL				
Date	**Account Title and Explanation**		**Debit**	**Credit**
Dec 31	Employee Benefits Expense		5,000	
	Employee Pensions Payable			5,000
	To record accrued pension benefits			

FIGURE 13.39

Health Benefits

Some employers provide continuing health benefits to their employees after they retire by paying for their medical and dental insurance coverage. The journal entry to record the accrued benefits for the period is shown in Figure 13.40.

JOURNAL				
Date	**Account Title and Explanation**		**Debit**	**Credit**
Dec 31	Employee Benefits Expense		2,000	
	Employee Medical Insurance Payable			2,000
	To record accrued medical insurance benefits			

FIGURE 13.40

When the medical insurance premiums are paid, the company records the payments by decreasing (debiting) employee medical insurance payable and crediting the cash account.

Employee Bonuses

Some employers offer employee bonuses based on a percentage of the company's net income for a period. Assume an employer plans to pay its staff a bonus equal to 5% of the company's net income. It estimates the total amount of the bonus as $5,000. The company records an accrual with the journal entry shown in Figure 13.41.

JOURNAL			
Date	**Account Title and Explanation**	**Debit**	**Credit**
Dec 31	Employee Bonus Expense	5,000	
	Employee Bonus Payable		5,000
	To record accrued employee bonus payable		

FIGURE 13.41

When the bonuses are paid, the company records the payments by decreasing (debiting) employee bonus payable and crediting the cash account.

Product Warranties

Just as a company needs to estimate how much bad debt it will have in the upcoming period, when a company sells products with warranties it needs to estimate how much warranty liability it will have. Warranties are one way a company reassures customers that its products are free of defects for a certain period of time, and any defects during that period are the responsibility of the company. By estimating the warranty liability, the company can expense this liability in the period in which related revenues are generated. Any errors in estimation can be adjusted once the actual figures are known.

There are two types of product warranties: basic and extended. A basic warranty is included in the price of the product. For example, when you buy a brand new cell phone, the price already includes a one-year warranty. There may be an option to purchase an extended warranty separately. This extended warranty will cover a specific period after the basic warranty expires. Basic warranties and extended warranties are accounted for differently. A basic warranty must be accounted for using the Expense Warranty Approach, which we will now discuss using the example of a company called Star Machines.

Star Machines manufactures industrial labeling machines. A basic warranty of three years is included with the purchase of each machine. If a machine breaks down during this warranty period, Star Machines is obliged to repair it, provide parts and, if necessary, replace the machine.

On the basis of an analysis of historical company trends, the company's accountant determines that an average of $100 per machine is paid out in warranty obligations. The company has sold

50 labeling machines during the 2018 fiscal year; therefore, the journal entry in Figure 13.42 is made to recognize the warranty expense for 2018.

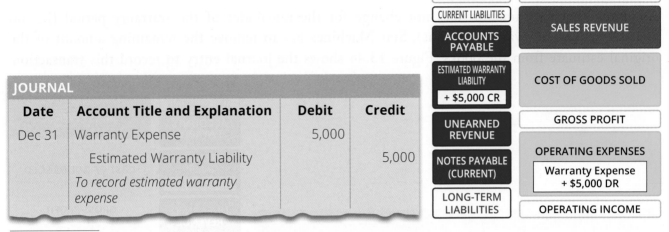

FIGURE 13.42

The $5,000 is expensed for this period on the income statement since this estimate covers expected warranties for the year. The estimated warranty liability of $5,000 is credited to the corresponding liability account.

During the next year, Star Machines receives some warranty claims and has actual expenditures in meeting those claims. Let us assume that Star Machines uses $500 in parts from its own inventory, and maintenance staff reports $1,500 worth of billable hours related to warranty claims. Figure 13.43 illustrates how Star's accountant records these transactions.

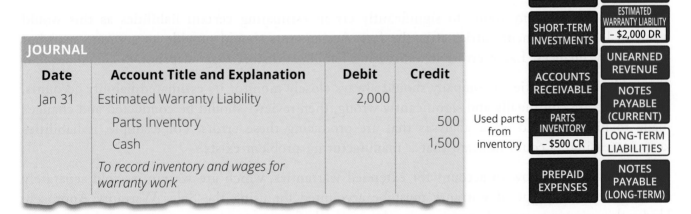

FIGURE 13.43

The estimated warranty liability account is debited with $2,000, leaving a balance of $3,000 to satisfy warranty claims over the remaining two-year period. On the credit side, $500 worth of inventory is taken off the books, and $1,500 is recorded as a decrease to cash.

There is no change to the income statement since the estimated warranty was expensed in the year the machine was sold. The company calculates and records a debit to warranty expense and a credit to estimated warranty liability accounts on the basis of the number of machines sold that year.

Assuming that this amount does not change for the remainder of the warranty period (i.e. no one else makes any warranty claims), Star Machines has to remove the remaining amount of the original estimate from the books. Figure 13.44 shows the journal entry to record this transaction.

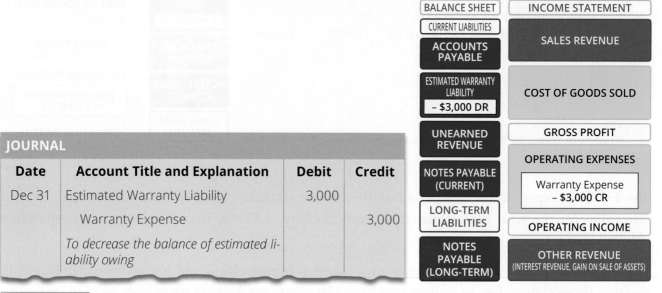

FIGURE 13.44

The remaining $3,000 in the estimated warranty liability account is removed with a debit. On the income statement, $3,000 in expenses is removed from the books with a credit (decrease) for that amount. The company is reversing the original expense for the amount that remains in the estimated warranty liability account.

Of course, no company wants to significantly err in estimating certain liabilities as this would result in large adjustment entries after the fact. Accountants should provide an accurate snapshot of company finances. Large errors in estimating liabilities distort that snapshot.

To avoid such difficulties, a company should always closely monitor its estimated liability accounts. If estimates are continually and significantly wrong, then reviews should be conducted and changes made to historical and other analyses that are producing these errors. For example, if liabilities keep increasing, it could indicate that a manufacturing problem exists.

Now let us look at how to account for extended warranties, which are warranties sold separately to customers. This type of warranty must be accounted for using the Sales Warranty Approach. Under this approach, journal entries are made separately for the warranty revenues and the warranty expenses.

Let us assume that Star Machines sold $60,000 worth of three-year warranties as a separate product to its customers on June 1, 2018. Figure 13.45 illustrates how the transaction is recorded in the company's books.

The receipt of $60,000 is recorded as a debit to cash and a credit to unearned warranty revenue. Since this is a three-year warranty, $20,000 is recognized at the end of each year. At the end of the first year, the company records the appropriate adjustment (see Figure 13.46).

JOURNAL			
Date	**Account Title and Explanation**	**Debit**	**Credit**
Jun 1	Cash	60,000	
	Unearned Warranty Revenue		60,000
	Record the sale of three-year warranties		

FIGURE 13.45

The $20,000 is recorded as a debit to the unearned warranty revenue and as a credit to the warranty revenue account. The rest of the revenue is earned as the warranty periods elapse. At present, the unearned warranty revenue account has

JOURNAL			
Date	**Account Title and Explanation**	**Debit**	**Credit**
May 31	Unearned Warranty Revenue	20,000	
	Warranty Revenue		20,000
	Recognize one year unearned warranty revenue as earned		

FIGURE 13.46

a $40,000 balance because there are two years left in the warranty period. Note that only the unearned revenue in the next 12 months is reported on the balance sheet as a current liability.

The journal entries in Figures 13.45 and 13.46 are for the revenue side of the warranty. On the expense side, the journal entries that have to be made are quite similar to what was already shown in Figures 13.42 and 13.43. For example, if Star Machines' customers make warranty claims in 2018 that cost the company $8,000 in total (including $3,000 worth of inventory parts and $5,000 cash paid for labor), Star Machines would record a credit to Parts Inventory for $3,000, a credit to Cash for $5,000, and a debit to Warranty Expense for $8,000.

Pause & Reflect

Exercise 13-4

Crystal Cleaners sells high-end vacuum cleaners. Every vacuum comes with a two-year warranty on parts and labor. The accountant estimates that an average of $50 worth of warranty work is done on each vacuum sold. During the year ending December 31, 2018, 8,000 vacuums were sold. Prepare the journal entry to record the estimated warranty expense.

JOURNAL			
Date	**Account Title and Explanation**	**Debit**	**Credit**

See Appendix I for solutions.

Customer Loyalty Programs

Customer loyalty programs have gained popularity in recent years as companies look for creative ways to retain or attract customers. Such programs require a business to record an estimated liability for the amount the customers receive in the future if they use up their accumulated rewards. The rewards are often in the form of points, store currencies or travel miles. Reward redemption by a customer represents a reduction in future sales. Therefore, when rewards are issued to a customer, a sales discounts account is normally debited instead of an expense account, and a redemption rewards liability account is credited. The dollar amount of redemption rewards liability recognized is estimated based on past redemption history.

For example, assume that Zen Gen is a teahouse chain that offers a customer loyalty program. Customers are rewarded one loyalty point for every dollar of tea and other refreshments purchased. One hundred loyalty points can be redeemed for a one-dollar discount toward a future purchase. In June 2018, Zen Gen sold $150,000 worth of refreshments. Historically, an average of 70% of the points issued are redeemed. Following past experience, Zen Gen's accountant recognizes a redemption rewards liability of $1,050 ($150,000 × 70% × $0.01). Figure 13.47 shows the journal entry to record Zen Gen's customer loyalty points issued in June 2018.

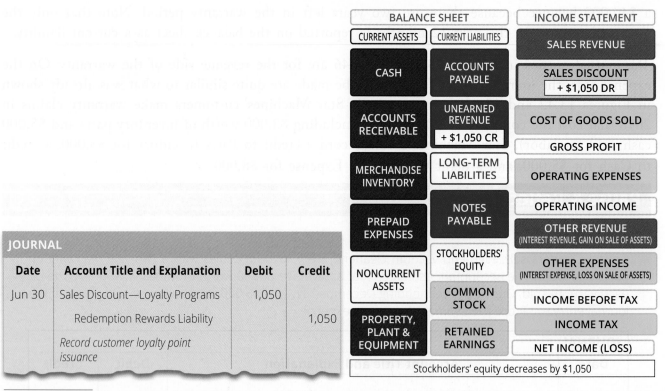

FIGURE 13.47

As a result of this transaction, net sales (and thus equity) decrease, and liabilities increase. Similar to the sales returns and allowances account, the sales discount account is a contra account linked to the sales revenue account. Both sales discounts and sales returns and allowances are deducted from sales revenue to reveal the net sales amount on an income statement.

Redemption rewards liability is a current liability. The redemption rewards liability account is considered unearned revenue because issuing loyalty points based on a current transaction's sales dollar amount is similar to Zen Gen accepting money from a customer in advance in exchange for a potential future discount. Once loyalty points are redeemed, Zen Gen's obligation or liability is nullified, and its unearned revenue becomes earned.

Zen Gen's sales transaction in July is used to illustrate an example of a loyalty point redemption journal entry. Assume that the total value of sales in July was $180,000, of which $179,250 was received in cash, and $750 was redeemed in points. Figure 13.48 shows the journal entry to record the sales through cash and loyalty point redemption in July. For simplicity, the cost of refreshments is ignored.

JOURNAL			
Date	**Account Title and Explanation**	**Debit**	**Credit**
Jul 31	Redemption Rewards Liability	750	
	Cash	179,250	
	Sales Revenue		180,000
	Record July sales through cash and loyalty point redemption		

FIGURE 13.48

From Figure 13.48, you can see that even though Zen Gen sold $180,000 worth of refreshments in July, the company received only $179,250 in cash due to the sales discount through loyalty points. Because sales discount was recorded at the time of loyalty point issuance in June, the difference between sales amount and cash receipt of $750 in July is recorded as a reduction in redemption rewards liability. The redemption rewards liability account should be reviewed regularly and adjusted as needed to make sure that the balance always reflects the company's best estimate based on past redemption rates.

Contingent Liabilities

Unlike estimated liabilities, a company's **contingent liabilities** involve a financial obligation that occurs only if a certain event takes place in the future. As a result, not only are contingent liabilities estimated, but they are also dependent upon another event taking place.

Since it is difficult to determine what is and is not possible, and how much of a contingency should be estimated, these items usually involve discretion and judgment by the accountants on behalf of the company.

According to the accounting rules, the accounting treatment of contingent liabilities depends on the following two factors.

- the likelihood that the event will occur, which is classified as probable, reasonably possible or remote
- whether the amount of the liability is estimable (measurable) or not estimable

GAAP vs IFRS

The financial obligation that occurs if a certain event takes place is referred to as a "contingent liability." Both GAAP and IFRS require the contingent liability to be recognized as an actual liability when the company determines that the payment is probable. However, IFRS defines the word *probable* as "more likely than not," whereas GAAP defines it as "likely to occur."

By assessing these two factors, accountants can determine the appropriate accounting treatment for the contingent liabilities.

- **Probable and Estimable**—If the likelihood of the future event is probable and the amount of the liability is estimable, the contingent liability is recorded in a journal entry and disclosed in the notes to the financial statements. The journal entry debits the related expense account and credits the related payable account.
- **Probable and Not Estimable**—If the likelihood of the future event is probable but the amount of the liability is not estimable, the contingent liability is disclosed in the notes to the financial statements according to the principle of full disclosure.
- **Reasonably Possible**—If the likelihood of the future event is reasonably possible, the contingent liability is disclosed in the notes to the financial statements according to the principle of full disclosure.
- **Remote**—If the likelihood of the future event is remote (unlikely), the contingent liability is neither recorded in the accounting records nor disclosed in the notes to the financial statements.

Figure 13.49 summarizes the accounting treatment for contingent liabilities.

	Likelihood of Future Event	Amount of Liability	Accounting Treatment
Contingent Liability	Probable	Estimable	Record in accounting records Disclose in notes to financial statements
		Not Estimable	Disclose in notes to financial statements
	Reasonably Possible		Disclose in notes to financial statements
	Remote		None required

FIGURE 13.49

Perhaps the most common reason to establish a contingent liability is to anticipate a costly lawsuit. If the company is found guilty in a lawsuit, it could seriously affect a company's bottom line. If the likelihood of losing the case is probable and the amount of liability is estimable, in addition to disclosing the contingency in the notes, the company will also debit a related expense account, such as litigation expense, and credit a related liability account, such as litigation liability, for the estimated amount. If the likelihood of losing the case is either probable or reasonably possible, and the amount of liability is not estimable, then the company must include in the notes to its financial statements any contingencies that may lead to a liability.

In summary, Figure 13.50 shows an example of how both determinable and non-determinable liabilities appear in the current liabilities section of a business' balance sheet. The note 4 beside the contingent liability refers to an explanation in the notes to the financial statements.

Red Carpet Inc. Balance Sheet (partial) As at December 31, 2018	
Current Liabilities	
Accounts Payable & Accrued Liabilities	$15,760
Unearned Revenue	2,500
Notes Payable, Current Portion	10,000
Salaries & Wages Payable	10,000
Payroll Taxes Payable	5,960
Estimated Warranty Liabilities	3,457
Contingent Liabilities (Note 4)	28,500
Total Current Liabilities	76,177

FIGURE 13.50

Internal Controls Relating to Current Liabilities

One of the first, basic controls over a company's liabilities involves a simple principle: keep track of company bills and budget well enough to pay them on time. The inability to pay suppliers can cause serious inventory shortages. Even more importantly, not paying suppliers risks a company's reputation and ability to do business with others. Controls are implemented to ensure that the right bills are paid at the right time. To that end, all relevant documents are gathered, such as purchase orders, receipts and original invoices, to verify the legitimacy of the invoices.

After an invoice is paid, it is marked as such and kept on file for verification purposes. A company never wants to pay the wrong bills or pay the same bills more than once. Controls related to invoices should prevent this from happening.

Accounting controls also safeguard that a company's resources are used efficiently and economically. This includes paying bills on time and making use of any payment discounts that are available. Automated systems can alert the appropriate personnel when payments should be made. Manual systems can make use of "tickler files," which allow placement of time-sensitive documents in labeled folders that are quickly and easily accessible.

The amount of current liabilities in a company can play a part in applying for a bank loan. Too many current liabilities compared to current assets may prevent the company from securing a loan. The comparison of current assets to current liabilities is called the current ratio and is an indicator of how liquid the company is. A higher current ratio indicates better liquidity.

WORTH REPEATING

Current ratio was introduced in Chapter 6. If a company has a current ratio of 1.5, this means they have $1.50 in current assets for every $1 in current liabilities.

If the company is showing poor liquidity, this might lead management to either hide current liabilities by not recording them or to reclassify them as long-term liabilities. Both actions are unethical and could lead to fines if discovered.

Payroll Controls

The payroll system must be carefully monitored to prevent abuse. There must be rules established by the business to ensure that an employee actually exists and is getting paid properly.

- Ensure the person hiring employees is not the same person paying employees. An employee start package should be created to collect important information about the employee, including the employee's social security number. This package should be passed to the person who prepares payroll checks. If the person hiring employees also pays them, it is possible to create a phantom employee and collect those paychecks.
- Monitor the hours worked by employees. Management should be responsible for ensuring that employees work the hours they claim they work. A time clock with punch cards or electronic swipe cards can track exactly how much time employees work. It is good practice for managers to physically see the individuals checking in and out to verify that they are actually starting work after checking in and that one person is not checking in many people.
- There should be proper authorization for pay increases or employee termination.
- If manual checks are being created, the person creating them should not be the same person signing them.
- A special payroll bank account could be set up for payroll. This is a separate bank account from the main bank account of the business. All payroll checks are cashed against the special payroll bank account, and only enough cash is available in the special payroll account to cover the payroll checks. This makes reconciliation easier and helps prevent theft through payroll.

In Summary

LO 1 Define and differentiate between determinable and non-determinable liabilities

▶ The listing order of liabilities on the balance sheet is dictated by the timing of the amount owed.

▶ A company's known liabilities, or determinable liabilities, are financial obligations with fixed terms that can be traced using documentation (e.g. accounts payable).

▶ Non-determinable liabilities include estimated liabilities for amounts that are not known as of the balance sheet date.

LO 2 Record accounts payable

▶ An accounts payable is the flip side of an accounts receivable. Instead of sending a customer a bill, an accounts payable involves receiving an invoice for goods or services received.

LO 3 Record transactions with sales tax

▶ Sales taxes are charged on sales. The amount collected by the business must be sent to the government.

LO 4 Record unearned revenue

▶ Unearned revenue relates to the way revenues are reconciled with the revenue recognition principle. Even though an amount may have been paid by customers, the revenue itself can only be recognized in a later period when goods or services are delivered.

LO 5 Record short-term notes payable

▶ Notes payable are the flip side of a promissory note from a customer. They represent a more formal contract between a company and a supplier after a sale has been made, as opposed to a standard bill or invoice.

LO 6 Record transactions related to the current portion of long-term liabilities

▶ If a liability will be paid out over several years, the amount to be paid within 12 months is separated on the balance sheet and called the current portion of long-term liabilities.

LO 7 Record payroll liabilities

▶ An accrued liability is how expenses are reconciled with the expense recognition principle. Even though an expense, such as an employee's salary, may not be paid until the next period, the expense itself must be recognized in the current period with an accrual.

▶ Payroll accounting involves three types of payroll liabilities: (1) the net pay owed to an employee, (2) employee payroll deductions, and (3) employer payroll contributions.

LO 8 **Record estimated liabilities**

▶ Estimated liabilities, such as product warranties, represent financial obligations whose specific amount will not be known until some future time.

LO 9 **Explain the accounting treatment for contingent liabilities**

▶ Contingent liabilities represent a financial obligation that needs to be met only if a certain event occurs. The possibility of a lawsuit might necessitate the establishment of a contingent liability.

LO 10 **Apply internal controls relating to current liabilities**

▶ Controls related to current liabilities should include proper tracking and monitoring of invoices and all related documentation. This ensures that the correct bills are paid on time, which is a crucial part of maintaining the company's finances.

▶ A company should not attempt to understate current liabilities by not recording them or by reclassifying them as long-term.

Review Exercise 13-1

Elnora Yearby Limited buys and resells machines. During the year, the following transactions took place.

Jan 15   Bought a machine for resale for $105,000 plus 6% sales tax. The amount is payable in 30 days. The company uses a perpetual inventory system.

Jan 30   Sold the machine for $214,000 plus 6% sales tax cash including a five-year warranty. Based on past experience, the accountant determines that an amount of $20,000 will be paid out in warranty obligations.

Jan 30   Paid the sales tax amount owing.

Feb 15   Paid for the machine purchased on Jan 15.

Mar 27   Elnora Yearby must repair the machine under warranty. The company uses $200 in parts from its own inventory.

Record the journal entries for the above transactions.

JOURNAL			
Date	Account Title and Explanation	Debit	Credit

See Appendix I for solutions.

Chapter 14
Partnerships

Learning Objectives

LO 1 **Describe the characteristics, advantages and disadvantages of a partnership**
- Characteristics of a Partnership
- Advantages of a Partnership
- Disadvantages of a Partnership

LO 2 **Describe different types of partnerships**
- General Partnership
- Limited Partnership
- Limited Liability Partnership
- Limited Liability Company
- S Corporations
- Partnerships, Proprietorships and LLCs—A Summary of Characteristics

LO 3 **Record the formation of a partnership**

LO 4 **Record the division of income or loss**
- Dividing Profits Equally
- Dividing Profits According to an Agreed-Upon Ratio

- Dividing Profits According to the Capital Contribution of Each Partner
- Dividing Profits According to Agreed-Upon Salary and Interest Allocations, Plus a Share of the Remainder
- When Allowances Exceed Net Income

LO 5 **Record partners' withdrawals**

LO 6 **Prepare financial statements for a partnership**

LO 7 **Account for the addition or withdrawal of a partner**
- Addition of a Partner
- Withdrawal of a Partner
- Death of a Partner
- Partner Bonuses

LO 8 **Record the liquidation of a partnership**
- Liquidation with No Capital Deficiency
- Liquidation with a Capital Deficiency

AMEENGAGE *Access **ameengage.com** for integrated resources including tutorials, practice exercises, the digital textbook and more.*

The Partnership Form of Business

In previous chapters, you learned about the three primary options for structuring the ownership of a business.

1. In a sole proprietorship, only one person owns the business and keeps all the profits, which are taxed at the personal level. The owner is personally responsible for all the liabilities of the business. This means that if creditors are looking for payment, they will pursue the owner's personal assets.

2. A **partnership** is an association of two or more people who jointly own a business, its assets and liabilities, and share in its gains or losses; profits are taxed personally. In the US, most states adhere to the *Uniform Partnership Act (UPA)*, which governs the formation, operation and dissolution of business partnerships. Some partners may be brought in for their technical expertise and others for their ability to raise capital. There are many similarities in accounting for partnerships and sole proprietorships.

3. In a corporation, there can be a large number of owners known as stockholders, many of whom may not participate in the running of the business. A corporation has many rights and duties because it is a legal entity distinct from its owners. All profits are taxed at the corporate level when they are earned and at the personal level when dividends are distributed to stockholders. Corporations can raise funds from the general public by issuing stock. The stockholders (owners) of a corporation are not personally responsible for the company's debt.

While other chapters of this textbook focus on sole proprietorships and corporations, this chapter examines the characteristics of partnerships in detail. We will explore business partnerships and demonstrate the effect of transactions and financial reporting on the asset, liability and partners' equity accounts and how various accounting principles are applied.

Figure 14.1 shows a simple comparison of the equity component of a proprietor's balance sheet to that of a partnership. In a sole proprietorship, the owner's capital account records the total equity of the business (shown on the left). The total investment by the owner, plus any profit or loss, is reported in this one account. In a partnership, each partner has a separate capital account (shown on the right). Details on each partner's investment and share of profit or loss is recorded separately.

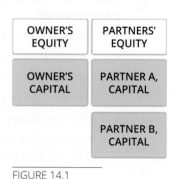

FIGURE 14.1

Many professional businesses are structured as partnerships, such as consulting firms, law firms and accounting firms. Regardless of which industries they operate in, all partnerships have certain characteristics in common that govern the duties, rights and responsibilities of all partners. Certain advantages and disadvantages are associated with conducting a business as a partnership. The characteristics, advantages and disadvantages of partnership will be discussed in detail.

Characteristics of a Partnership

Legal Entity

As with a sole proprietorship, a partnership can sue or be sued. Although a partnership is considered a legal entity, for some purposes it is not considered legally separate from its owners. While the partnership itself does not pay taxes, it must still file a report on the profits of the partnership, as well as each partner's share of profits. Each partner is then required to report his or her share of profits (or losses) on an individual tax return, and (as with a sole proprietorship) they must pay taxes at a specific personal tax rate regardless of whether the profits were actually withdrawn from the partnership.

Division of Profit and Losses

Even though it is not required for a partnership, it is generally advisable for partners to draw up a *legal partnership agreement* that specifies the division of partnership profits and losses. If partners consent to change the terms of the agreement, a new one is drawn up, which cancels and replaces the previous agreement. The division of profits and losses are discussed later in this chapter.

Right to Own Property

A partnership can own assets in its name, such as property, plant and equipment. In fact, partners often bring existing individual assets into the partnership for use by the business. The partnership's assets are jointly owned by all partners. This means that if a partner brings an existing individual asset into the partnership, the asset becomes the partnership's, and it is not legally returnable to the partner who contributed it. If the partnership dissolves, the asset is sold along with other partnership assets and the proceeds (or losses) are divided according to the terms of the original partnership agreement. Also, just as in a sole proprietorship, the accounting records for all partnership assets, liabilities and business activities are kept separately from the partners' personal accounting records. The treatment of partnership assets will be discussed in more detail later in the chapter.

Advantages of a Partnership

Instead of one person owning and operating a business as with a sole proprietorship, a partnership involves two or more people combining resources, both human and financial. This provides two advantages. First, the combination of human resources means that the business benefits from the skills and experience of each partner. To illustrate, assume two lawyers, Helen White and Greg Harris, form the partnership White & Harris, Attorneys-at-Law. Helen specializes in family law and Greg specializes in criminal law. Together, they are able to service twice as many clients in two different areas of law. Second, due to their combined financial resources, they are more likely than a sole proprietorship to provide sufficient cash flow to the business without having to rely on external financing.

Another advantage of the partnership form of business is the relative ease of formation. Some small partnerships of two or more individuals may be based on just a verbal agreement or a handshake. On the other hand, many professional partnerships, such as those of legal and accounting firms, may have hundreds of partners located in offices all over the world. Regardless of the number of partners, it is always wise to have a legal partnership agreement setting out the rights and obligations of all partners. A legal partnership agreement formalizes the arrangement for sharing profits and losses and for other eventualities, such as the addition or withdrawal of a partner, or the dissolution of the partnership. In the absence of a written agreement, individuals could be liable for the actions of other partners, regardless of their involvement in decisions made on behalf of the partnership. Partnership agreements are discussed in more depth later in the chapter.

Disadvantages of a Partnership

Perhaps the most serious disadvantage of the partnership form of business is that each partner is responsible for the liabilities of the business, referred to as unlimited liability (introduced in Chapter 3). Consider our legal partnership, White & Harris, Attorneys-at-Law. Assume that Helen White has no personal assets other than what she invested in the partnership. Greg Harris, on the other hand, owns his own home, rental property, cottage, sailboat and several valuable paintings. The business suffered losses for several years and was then sued for $1.5 million by a dissatisfied client. As the partnership had very little remaining cash or assets, the partners were personally liable for the $1.5 million liability. Since Helen had no assets, Greg, because of unlimited liability, was required to pay the debt on behalf of the partnership.

As with a sole proprietorship, one of the disadvantages of a partnership is its limited life. In the event of the death of one of the partners, bankruptcy or the addition or withdrawal of a partner, the existing partnership ends (although not necessarily the business). A new partnership can be formed based on the new circumstance, and with the agreement of all partners, the business can continue.

Another disadvantage is mutual agency, which means that each partner can authorize contracts and transactions on behalf of the partnership provided the activity is within the scope of the partnership's business. This is a disadvantage because it places the other partners at risk if the authorizing partner does not act in the best interests of the partnership.

To overcome the most serious disadvantage of the partnership form of business, which is unlimited liability, different types of partnerships have been introduced to limit liability. These are known as limited partnerships, and limited liability partnerships. In addition to the general form of partnership, these two special types of partnership are discussed in detail in the following section.

Types of Partnerships

There are several different types of partnerships that a business can form. Each one has a different way of dealing with liability issues. Owners must determine the type of partnership that best suits their business.

General Partnership

A **general partnership** means that all partners share the responsibility for the liabilities of the business; that is, they have unlimited liability.

Limited Partnership

Businesses are sometimes legally obligated to pay other parties a considerable amount of money. These obligations can include debt owed to creditors or financial sums awarded to other parties in a lawsuit. Sole proprietorships and partnerships generally extend unlimited liability to all the owners of the business. Unlimited liability in a partnership can be particularly damaging because if one partner is unable to meet liability obligations related to the partnership, the other partners are legally required to pay. This could mean having to sell off personal assets such as houses, cars and investments. Limited partnerships resolve the potential problem of unlimited liability by creating two categories of partners within the business: the general partner and the limited partner.

Unlimited liability is assigned to a **general partner**, who is legally authorized to manage the day-to-day operations of the business and to make decisions on behalf of the business. Each partnership must have at least one general partner.

Limited liability is a type of liability that extends only to the amount a person has invested in a partnership or limited liability company. Limited liability is assigned to a **limited partner**, who is responsible only for providing the capital to finance the business. This partner should not be involved in day-to-day operations and is therefore not considered liable for decisions made by the business that can lead to a liability. Limited partners are liable only for the amount they have invested in the business.

Limited Liability Partnership

Another business legal entity—the **limited liability partnership** or **LLP**—has been developed in some jurisdictions to deal with liability. Unlike a limited partnership, the limited partners in an LLP usually participate in managing the business. LLPs are primarily used in professional partnerships to protect one partner from another partner's negligence. For example, if a lawyer is sued for negligence, other lawyers in the firm are not automatically considered liable; however, as with limited partnerships, partners usually cannot escape liability entirely. In the case of LLPs, this means that all partners are still liable for any unpaid debts to creditors. Although the details of an LLP vary from state to state, generally an LLP can protect partners from some forms of liability, but not all.

Limited Liability Company

A newer form of business entity is the **limited liability company** or **LLC**, which has some characteristics of a corporation and some characteristics of a limited partnership. Accounting for an LLC is the same as for a partnership, but the LLC uses the terms "member" and "member equity" instead of "partner" and "partners' capital." The limited liability feature of this form of business organization, as well as the greater ability to raise funds, makes it an attractive choice over a partnership. For income tax purposes, a limited liability company can elect to be treated like a partnership. This means that income flows through the LLC and is reported by individual members on their personal tax returns.

Like a corporation, the LLC provides limited liability to its members; their personal assets are protected against claims of creditors, although their investments in the company are not. Unlike the limited partners of a limited partnership, members of an LLC are allowed to take an active management role in the LLC, despite having limited liabilities. This form of business organization can also have an unlimited life if specified in the original operating agreement, so the business can continue despite the addition or withdrawal of members.

In a limited liability company, management must comply with the obligations and regulations agreed to by the members in the operating agreement. This business form also requires that the accounting system provides the information required to comply with federal and state tax laws.

S Corporations

A corporation that elects to be taxed under *Subchapter S* of the Internal Revenue Code becomes classified as an S corporation (also called an *S corp*). An **S corporation** is a special type of corporation that does not pay federal income tax, but rather allocates its profits and losses to the individual members (owners) to be reported on their personal tax returns. To become an S corporation, the business must first file as a corporation by chartering the business in the state where its headquarters are located. The newly-formed corporation must then file a special election with the Internal Revenue Service (IRS) to become an S corporation.

S corporations share many characteristics of LLCs. Like an LLC, an S corp has both advantages and disadvantages. On the positive side, the business itself is not taxed and so the members benefit from tax savings by avoiding double taxation (that is, being taxed as a business and then again at the individual level). As a corporation, the business is considered by law to be an entity separate and apart from its members, providing its members with the additional protection of limited liability. In addition, an S corporation benefits from independence from its members, so that the business continues to operate undisturbed if a member leaves, or another member is added.

The major disadvantages are the additional complexity of recordkeeping, the legal requirements to hold stockholder meetings, and regularly assessing and updating by-laws and stockholder records. There may also be certain restrictions on the amounts of compensation that are considered reasonable, as well as the need for stricter accounting controls and audits.

Partnerships, Proprietorships, and LLCs—A Summary of Characteristics

Figure 14.2 summarizes the characteristics of partnerships and compares them with the characteristics of sole proprietorships and limited liability companies. You will notice both similarities and differences between the three forms of business ownership.

Characteristics	Sole Proprietorship	Partnership	Limited Liability Company (LLC)
# of Owners	One	Two or more	One or more (called "members")
Control	Owner has complete control	Decisions are shared among partners, with possibility of disagreement and conflict	Members are allowed to take an active management role in the LLC
Raising Capital	Small—since only one person is raising money	Moderate to Large—since more than one person is responsible for raising money	Small—if a single-member LLC, since only one person is raising money Moderate to Large—if more than one member, since more members are responsible for raising money
Profits	Proprietor receives 100% of profits	Partners share profits in proportion to terms of the partnership agreement	Members share profits in proportion to terms of the operating agreement
Formation	Relatively simple to set up	Simple to set up, but details require close attention	Moderately complex to set up; details require close attention when drawing up operating agreement
Liability	Proprietor is responsible for all debts and/or legal obligations	Partners are responsible jointly and individually for actions of other partners	Limited liability protects personal assets of members from creditor claims; liability for business debts limited to member's investment in company
Skills	Reliance on the skills of the proprietor alone	Partners offer different skills in various areas of the business	In a single-member LLC, there is reliance on the skills of that member; if more than one member, members offer different skills in various areas of the business
Dissolution	Relatively simple to dissolve	May be dissolved upon death or withdrawal of a partner; partnership has limited life	May continue despite addition, withdrawal, or death of member if specified in operating agreement; business can have unlimited life
Taxation	Profits are taxed whether or not cash is withdrawn from the business	Partners share profits and are taxed whether or not cash is withdrawn	Members can elect to be taxed as a partnership so income flows through the LLC and is reported by the individual members on their personal tax returns

FIGURE 14.2

Formation of a Partnership

In the formation stage of a partnership, all partners should collectively draw up a legal partnership agreement as a written contract. A partnership agreement lessens the chance of legal and ethical conflicts between the partners, and specifies the purpose of the business as well as the relationships between the partners. In the absence of a partnership agreement, individuals could find themselves liable for the actions of their partners. Also, without an agreement, all partnership profits and losses must be shared equally, which may not be what the partners intended.

A partnership agreement should normally include the following elements.

- date of inception of the partnership
- legal name and address of the business
- purpose of the business
- names and addresses of all partners
- contribution of each partner
- duties, rights and responsibilities of the partners
- terms for sharing profits and losses
- procedures for addition or withdrawal of a partner
- terms of withdrawal of assets from the business
- provisions for the death of a partner
- terms for liquidation of the partnership

Partnership agreements can be as varied as the businesses themselves, but any contract should include clear provisions for a full range of eventualities.

Once the partnership agreement has been drawn up, the next step is to record the initial journal entries to set up the asset, liability and equity accounts. The partners may have assets (other than cash) and liabilities that they would like to bring into the business. An independent market evaluation, or appraisal, of the items is required. Assume that on January 1, 2018, Lee Wang and Kim Chow decide to form the partnership Wang & Chow. Figure 14.3 is a summary of the amounts contributed by each partner.

Lee Wang		Kim Chow	
Cash	$8,000	Cash	$10,000
Accounts Receivable	10,000	Building	170,000
Allowance for Doubtful Accounts	890	Notes Payable	100,000
Equipment	18,000		
Accumulated Depreciation—Equipment	2,000		
Accounts Payable	1,800		
Notes Payable	6,000		

FIGURE 14.3

An independent appraiser determined that the allowance for doubtful accounts should be $1,200 and the market value of the equipment is $11,000. All other assets are recorded at the values presented. Notice that assets are recorded in the partnership's books at their market value and that their accumulated depreciation is not carried over when the partnership is formed. The journal entries to set up assets, liabilities and equity accounts based on Wang's and Chow's initial investments in the partnership are shown in Figure 14.4.

JOURNAL			
Date	**Account Title and Explanation**	**Debit**	**Credit**
Jan 1	Cash	8,000	
	Accounts Receivable	10,000	
	Equipment	11,000	
	Allowance for Doubtful Accounts		1,200
	Accounts Payable		1,800
	Notes Payable		6,000
	Wang, Capital		20,000
	To record Wang's investment in the partnership		
Jan 1	Cash	10,000	
	Building	170,000	
	Notes Payable		100,000
	Chow, Capital		80,000
	To record Chow's investment in the partnership		

FIGURE 14.4

Figure 14.5 shows the journal entry if Wang and Chow formed a limited liability company (LLC) instead.

JOURNAL			
Date	**Account Title and Explanation**	**Debit**	**Credit**
Jan 1	Cash	8,000	
	Accounts Receivable	10,000	
	Equipment	11,000	
	Allowance for Doubtful Accounts		1,200
	Accounts Payable		1,800
	Notes Payable		6,000
	Wang, Member Equity		20,000
	To record Wang's investment in the limited liability company		
Jan 1	Cash	10,000	
	Building	170,000	
	Notes Payable		100,000
	Chow, Member Equity		80,000
	To record Chow's investment in the limited liability company		

FIGURE 14.5

Each owner's opening capital (in the case of a partnership) or member equity (in the case of an LLC) is calculated by deducting the total amount of liabilities from the total amount of assets.

Lee Wang, Capital (or Member Equity) = ($8,000 + $10,000 + $11,000) − ($1,200 − $1,800 − $6,000)

= $20,000

Kim Chow, Capital (or Member Equity) = ($10,000 + $170,000) − $100,000

= $80,000

Pause & Reflect

Exercise 14-1

On September 1, 2018, Miko Akazi and Gayle Warren formed a general partnership for their bakery. They each brought to this new partnership the following assets and liabilities.

Miko Akazi	
Cash	$5,000
Building	250,000
Accumulated Depreciation—Building	120,000
Notes Payable	80,000

Gayle Warren	
Cash	$15,000
Equipment	60,000
Accumulated Depreciation—Equipment	25,000
Accounts Payable	10,000

An independent appraiser determined that the market value of the building is $275,000 and the market value of the equipment is $20,000. Prepare the journal entries to set up the partnership.

JOURNAL			
Date	Account Title and Explanation	Debit	Credit

See Appendix I for solutions.

Division of Income or Loss

A key difference between a sole proprietorship, partnership and corporation is the way in which profits are distributed. In a sole proprietorship, the proprietor simply receives all the profits. In a corporation, profits are distributed in the form of dividend payments (profits paid out to stockholders). If all the assets are sold and all debts are paid, the remaining cash is distributed among the stockholders in proportion to the amount of stock owned. For example, a stockholder with 10 times more stock than another stockholder receives 10 times more of the remaining cash. (Stocks and dividends are discussed in more detail in Chapter 15.)

In a partnership, profits are distributed differently than they are in a sole proprietorship or corporation. Since partners are involved, profits must be shared, but not necessarily on an equal basis. A partnership agreement sets out the terms of ownership, including how profits are divided. In the absence of a partnership agreement, all profits and losses are shared equally among the partners. A partnership's equity account on the balance sheet is referred to as the capital account. Figure 14.6 shows an example of how partnership equity changes over a period of time.

	J. Witner	R. Pierce	Total
Capital Balance (beginning)	$25,000	$50,000	$75,000
Add: Additional Contribution	0	0	0
Share of Partnership Net Income for the Period	75,000	75,000	150,000
Subtotal	100,000	125,000	225,000
Less: Withdrawals	40,000	80,000	120,000
Capital Balance (ending)	$60,000	$45,000	$105,000

FIGURE 14.6

The partnership's capital account is broken down by partner. In this case, J. Witner had a beginning capital balance of $25,000 and R. Pierce had a beginning capital balance of $50,000. During the year, they did not contribute additional capital to the business. At the end of the year, J. Witner's share of net income is $75,000 and $40,000 was withdrawn. R. Pierce's share of net income is $75,000 and $80,000 was withdrawn. The closing capital account balance is the net worth of the partnership.

One of the primary purposes of a partnership agreement is to stipulate how earnings are divided. Each partner's share of profits and losses is determined by the partnership's profit and loss ratio. In Figure 14.6, it is assumed that the partner's share of net income is split equally between the partners.

Profit and loss ratios can take many forms including, but not limited to, the following.

- by dividing equally among all partners
- according to an agreed-upon ratio, such as 2:1, or 60% to 40%
- according to the capital contribution of each partner
- according to agreed-upon salary and interest allocations, plus a share of the remainder

Each of these methods will be examined separately.

Dividing Profits Equally

The simplest method of dividing profits is on an equal basis. For example, assume L. Wang and K. Chow earned $46,000 in net income for the year. The net income is credited to the income summary account after the revenue and expense accounts have been closed. For the partners to share the profits equally, a debit is then made to the income summary account for the entire amount, while a credit of $23,000 ($46,000 ÷ 2) is made to the capital account of each partner, as shown in the journal entry in Figure 14.7.

JOURNAL			
Date	**Account Title and Explanation**	**Debit**	**Credit**
Dec 31	Income Summary	46,000	
	Wang, Capital		23,000
	Chow, Capital		23,000
	To adjust partners' capital accounts for their share of net income		

FIGURE 14.7

WORTH REPEATING

Closing the books for a company transfers the values in the revenue and expense accounts to the income summary account, leaving the revenue and expense accounts with a zero balance. The income summary account is then closed to the capital account. If the company had a net income for the year, the income summary account is debited and the capital account is credited, leaving the income summary account with a zero balance.

Dividing Profits According to an Agreed-Upon Ratio

The allocation of business profits can be done according to an agreed-upon ratio. For example, if L. Wang receives 60% of the profits and K. Chow receives 40%, the split is recorded in the books as shown in Figure 14.8.

JOURNAL			
Date	**Account Title and Explanation**	**Debit**	**Credit**
Dec 31	Income Summary	46,000	
	Wang, Capital		27,600
	Chow, Capital		18,400
	To adjust partners' capital accounts for their share of net income		

FIGURE 14.8

As a result of the $46,000 net income, L. Wang's capital balance increases by $27,600 ($46,000 × 60%), and K. Chow's capital balance increases by $18,400 ($46,000 × 40%).

Dividing Profits According to the Capital Contribution of Each Partner

Another method of allocating the profits among partners is to base it on the amount that each partner invested in the business. For example, L. Wang and K. Chow contributed a total of $100,000 to the partnership. L. Wang contributed $20,000 (one-fifth or 20%) of the capital and K. Chow contributed $80,000 (four-fifths or 80%). Therefore, L. Wang and K. Chow are entitled to 20% and 80% of the profits, respectively. The journal entry to record this is shown in Figure 14.9.

JOURNAL			
Date	**Account Title and Explanation**	**Debit**	**Credit**
Dec 31	Income Summary	46,000	
	Wang, Capital		9,200
	Chow, Capital		36,800
	To adjust partners' capital accounts for their share of net income		

FIGURE 14.9

To allocate the $46,000 net income, L. Wang's capital balance increases by $9,200 ($46,000 × 20%), and K. Chow's capital balance increases by $36,800 ($46,000 × 80%).

Dividing Profits According to Agreed-Upon Salary and Interest Allocations, Plus a Share of the Remainder

Profits can also be divided by using a fixed salary allocation, interest allocation, or both for each partner, and then dividing the remaining profits equally. For example, if the partnership agreement stipulates that L. Wang's salary is $18,000, K. Chow's salary is $20,000, and interest allowance is

5% of each partner's capital balance at the beginning of the year, then those are the first amounts to be deducted from the net income of the business and distributed to the partners. These amounts are shown in orange in Figure 14.10.

	Total	L. Wang	K. Chow
Net Income	$46,000		
Salary to Wang	−18,000	$18,000	
Salary to Chow	−20,000		$20,000
Interest allowance to Wang (20,000 × 5%)	−1,000	1,000	
Interest allowance to Chow (80,000 × 5%)	−4,000		4,000
Remainder	3,000		
Share of profit to Wang (3,000 × 50%)	−1,500	1,500	
Share of profit to Chow (3,000 × 50%)	−1,500		1,500
Transferred to partners' capital accounts	−$46,000	$20,500	$25,500

FIGURE 14.10

The $3,000 remaining after the salaries are distributed is divided equally between the partners. These amounts are shown in green on the chart.

If the distributed amounts are added up for each partner, the totals come to $20,500 ($18,000 + $1,000 + $1,500) for L. Wang and $25,500 ($20,000 + $4,000 + $1,500) for K. Chow, as shown in red on the chart. Figure 14.11 shows how the allocations are recorded to each partner's capital account.

	JOURNAL		
Date	**Account Title and Explanation**	**Debit**	**Credit**
Dec 31	Income Summary	46,000	
	Wang, Capital		20,500
	Chow, Capital		25,500
	To adjust partners' capital accounts for their share of net income		

FIGURE 14.11

The number of ways that profits can be divided between partners is unlimited. For example, interest can first be allocated (out of net income) at a fixed rate on each partner's capital account. The remaining amount of net income can then be divided according to a predetermined ratio or salary. The method chosen should meet the needs and interests of the partners involved and be clearly stated in the partnership agreement. The salary and interest allocations are not expenses and are not to be deducted from the partnership's revenues in determining net income for the period.

It is important to note that the method of distributing the earnings is just allocation, not actual payments and not actual expenses. Even the salary and interest amounts are allocations. The allocation is to assign to each partner's capital account their share of the earnings. If they wish to take money from the business, it is considered a withdrawal, which is discussed in the next section.

When Allowances Exceed Net Income

The preceding example was based on a net income of $46,000 for the year. The total salary was $38,000 ($18,000 for Wang, and $20,000 for Chow). The total interest allowance was $5,000 ($1,000 for Wang, and $4,000 for Chow). This means that the net income exceeded the salary and interest allowances.

If the partners have agreed to allocate salary and interest, then salary and interest are allocated regardless of whether or not the net income can cover all the salary and interest amounts. Suppose the net income was only $40,000. In this case the remainder is -$3,000, indicating an over allocation of salary and interest. To compensate for the over allocation, $1,500 is subtracted from each partner, reducing the total allocation of income to their capital accounts.

Figure 14.12 shows the final allocation of net income between Wang and Chow.

	Total	L. Wang	K. Chow
Net Income	$40,000		
Salary to Wang	−18,000	$18,000	
Salary to Chow	−20,000		$20,000
Interest allowance to Wang (20,000 × 5%)	−1,000	1,000	
Interest allowance to Chow (80,000 × 5%)	−4,000		4,000
Remainder	−3,000		
Less excess of allowance over net Income, Wang (−3,000 × 50%)	1,500	−1,500	
Less excess of allowance over net Income, Chow (−3,000 × 50%)	1,500		−1,500
Transferred to partners' capital accounts	−$40,000	$17,500	$22,500

FIGURE 14.12

In this case, the allocations are recorded to each partner's capital account as shown in Figure 14.13.

JOURNAL			
Date	**Account Title and Explanation**	**Debit**	**Credit**
Dec 31	Income Summary	40,000	
	Wang, Capital		17,500
	Chow, Capital		22,500
	To adjust partners' capital accounts for their share of net income		

FIGURE 14.13

If Wang and Chow experience a net loss for the year, the partners share the net loss in the same way, only they begin their calculations with a negative amount. They still allocate the salary and interest allowances, except this adds to the negative balances. The total negative balance *after* these allocations are divided equally between Wang and Chow.

Pause & Reflect

Exercise 14-2

Eric Banner and David Martin operate a general partnership. At year end on December 31, 2018, the partnership reported a net income of $90,000. In the partnership agreement, Eric receives a salary allowance of $45,000 per year and David receives a salary allowance of $35,000 per year. Any excess is shared equally between the two.

a) Calculate how much each partner is allocated from the net income.

	Total	Eric Banner	David Martin
Net Income			

b) Prepare the journal entry to close the income summary to the capital accounts.

JOURNAL				
Date	Account Title and Explanation		Debit	Credit

See Appendix I for solutions.

Partner Withdrawals

During the year, partners may withdraw cash or other assets from the business for personal use. This amount is reported as the amount that has been withdrawn from the partner's equity. Assume that on November 5, 2018, L. Wang and K. Chow withdrew from the partnership $8,000 and

$15,000, respectively. The journal entries to record the withdrawals are shown on the left side of Figure 14.14. The journal entries to record the related year-end closing entries for the Wang & Chow partnership are shown on the right side.

JOURNAL				JOURNAL			
Date	Account Title and Explanation	Debit	Credit	Date	Account Title and Explanation	Debit	Credit
Nov 5	Wang, Withdrawals	8,000		Dec 31	Wang, Capital	8,000	
	Chow, Withdrawals	15,000			Chow, Capital	15,000	
	Cash		23,000		Wang, Withdrawals		8,000
					Chow, Withdrawals		15,000
	To record partners' withdrawals during the year				*To close each partner's withdrawals account*		

FIGURE 14.14

Partnership Financial Statements

There are four basic financial statements that are prepared by partnerships: the income statement, statement of partners' equity, the balance sheet and the statement of cash flows. Partnership financial statements are quite similar to those of sole proprietorships. The main difference is that a partnership is an association of two or more people, and so there is a bit more involved in accounting for equity and the division of profits and losses of the partners.

For instance, Figure 14.15 shows an income statement for Wang & Chow. We have assumed all the balances in the statement simply for demonstration purposes.

Wang & Chow Income Statement For the Year Ended December 31, 2018		
Revenue		
Service Revenue		$60,000
Expenses		
Depreciation	$1,000	
Bank Charges	230	
Insurance	425	
Professional Fees	945	
Property Taxes	1,300	
Repairs and Maintenance	100	
Salaries	10,000	
Total Expenses		(14,000)
Net Income		$46,000

FIGURE 14.15

Notice that the partnership income statement is almost identical to a sole proprietorship income statement. Partners' share of the income is divided according to the terms in the partnership agreement. Any detailed calculations for the distribution of profit (or losses) is usually included as a separate schedule in notes to the income statement.

Partnerships must also prepare a **statement of partners' equity** (or a **statement of members' equity** for an LLC), which is a statement explaining the changes to the balance of each partner's capital account from the beginning to the end of the year. Changes are normally in the form of withdrawals from the business, investments added to the business and each partner's share of profit or loss.

Now look at a statement of partners' equity for Wang & Chow. Using the partners' beginning capital balance information from the journal entry in Figure 14.4, a statement can be prepared for Wang & Chow for the year ended December 31, 2018 (Figure 14.16). For simplicity, assume the following events occurred.

- the partnership was formed on January 1, 2018
- Lee Wang added an investment of $4,500 during the year
- the two partners share profits and losses equally
- Lee Wang withdrew $8,000 and Kim Chow withdrew $15,000 from the business in 2018

Note that net income is taken from the partnership's income statement in Figure 14.15.

Wang & Chow Statement of Partners' Equity For the Year Ended December 31, 2018			
	Lee Wang	Kim Chow	Total
Partners' Capital, January 1	$0	$0	$0
Add: Investments	24,500	80,000	104,500
Net Income	23,000	23,000	46,000
Subtotal	47,500	103,000	150,500
Less: Withdrawals	8,000	15,000	23,000
Partners' Capital, December 31	$39,500	$88,000	$127,500

FIGURE 14.16

The information for the statement of partners' equity is taken from the partnership income statement, the partners' capital accounts and the partners' withdrawals accounts. The opening balance of the partners' capital is $0 since the partnership formed this year. For next year, the opening balance of the partners' capital will be equal to the December 31 balance shown in Figure 14.16.

A partnership balance sheet is very similar to that of a sole proprietorship. The main difference is that a partnership's balance sheet shows the balance of each partner's capital account in a section called Partners' Capital. Using the partners' ending capital balance information from the statement of partners' equity in Figure 14.16, a balance sheet can be prepared for Wang & Chow for December 31, 2018, as shown in Figure 14.17.

Wang & Chow Balance Sheet As at December 31, 2018				
Assets		**Liabilities and Partners' Capital**		
Cash	$32,500	**Liabilities**		
Accounts Receivable	16,750	Accounts Payable		$40,500
Equipment	11,000	Notes Payable		52,000
Accumulated Depreciation—Equipment	(1,500)	**Total Liabilities**		92,500
Building	170,000	**Partners' Capital**		
Accumulated Depreciation—Building	(8,750)	Wang, Capital		39,500
		Chow, Capital		88,000
Total Assets	$220,000	**Total Liabilities and Partners' Capital**		$220,000

FIGURE 14.17

The partnership's statement of cash flows is omitted in this section because it is similar to that of a sole proprietorship's. Preparation of the statement of cash flows is covered in Chapter 19.

Addition and Withdrawal of a Partner

The legal basis for any partnership is the partnership agreement. Once a partner leaves, or another is added, a new partnership agreement should be prepared and signed by all parties. However, this does not mean that the business needs to open a new set of books. Instead, adjustments can be made to the current set of books to reflect any change in partner status.

Addition of a Partner

An existing partnership may want to add a new partner if they require additional capital or another skilled person. The new partner will either invest assets in the partnership (similar to Figure 14.4), or can purchase part of an existing partner's equity. To help illustrate the transactions to add or remove a partner from a partnership, we will examine a sample partnership with three existing partners, A, B and C.

In Figure 14.18, the first row shows the existing capital balances of the three partners before the addition of Partner D.

	Partner A	Partner B	Partner C	Partner D	Total
Capital balance before admitting new partner (includes all earnings to date)	$120,000	$150,000	$50,000		$320,000
Admission of new partner				$100,000	100,000
Capital balance after admitting new partner	$120,000	$150,000	$50,000	$100,000	$420,000

FIGURE 14.18

Partner D is the new addition; therefore, her opening balance is zero. The total of Partners A, B and C opening balances is $320,000. On January 1, 2018, Partner D contributes $100,000 to the partnership, which creates a new balance of $420,000 (shown in the second and third rows).

Figure 14.19 shows how the admission of the new partner is recorded as a journal entry.

JOURNAL

Date	Account Title and Explanation	Debit	Credit
Jan 1	Cash	100,000	
	Partner D, Capital		100,000
	To record admission of new partner		

FIGURE 14.19

The receipt of $100,000 is debited to the company's cash account, and a corresponding credit of $100,000 is added to Partner D's capital account.

Another way a partner can be added is if they purchase part of the equity of one or more existing partners. In this scenario, part of the capital of one or more partners is transferred to the new partner. In Figure 14.20, $100,000 of Partner A's capital is transferred to Partner D.

	Partner A	Partner B	Partner C	Partner D	Total
Capital balance before admitting new partner (includes all earnings to date)	$120,000	$150,000	$50,000		$320,000
Admission of new partner	−100,000			$100,000	0
Capital balance after admitting new partner	$20,000	$150,000	$50,000	$100,000	$320,000

FIGURE 14.20

In the second row, $100,000 is deducted from Partner A's balance, and added to Partner D's balance. The journal entry is shown in Figure 14.21.

JOURNAL			
Date	**Account Title and Explanation**	**Debit**	**Credit**
Jan 1	Partner A, Capital	100,000	
	Partner D, Capital		100,000
	To record admission of new partner		

FIGURE 14.21

Note that the above transaction did not involve cash of the business. In cases like this, any cash that changes hands between Partner A and Partner D is done personally between the two partners; that is, it is done outside of the partnership's books. In fact, the amount of cash paid by Partner D could be more or less than $100,000, however from the partnership's books perspective, that is irrelevant. Only the transfer of capital is what is recorded.

Since equity was simply transferred from Partner A to Partner D, no additional equity was brought into the partnership. Therefore, the partnership's total net assets after the transfer remain at $320,000.

Withdrawal of a Partner

At times, a partner may wish to leave the partnership, or the others may wish a partner to leave. When a partner leaves, his or her capital account is closed and the partner receives a cash payout. The cash payout can either be a private transaction between partners, or the partnership itself can pay the leaving partner. Figure 14.22 illustrates a private cash transaction between partners. Partners A and B each use their personal cash to pay Partner C for a portion of his capital.

	Partner A	**Partner B**	**Partner C**	**Total**
Capital balance before withdrawal of Partner C	$120,000	$150,000	$50,000	$320,000
Withdrawal of Partner C	25,000	25,000	−50,000	0
Capital balance after withdrawal of Partner C	$145,000	$175,000	$0	$320,000

FIGURE 14.22

After the withdrawal of Partner C, the total partnership capital of the business remains the same. It is important to understand that the cash payment to Partner C is not recorded using the cash account because Partner C's shares were paid by Partners A and B personally, and not from the business. Assuming Partners A and B each receive an equal share of Partner C's capital, the capital of both Partners A and B increases by $25,000 and the capital of Partner C decreases by $50,000.

Figure 14.23 shows how the withdrawal of Partner C is recorded as a journal entry..

JOURNAL			
Date	**Account Title and Explanation**	**Debit**	**Credit**
Jan 1	Partner C, Capital	50,000	
	Partner A, Capital		25,000
	Partner B, Capital		25,000
	To record withdrawal of Partner C		

FIGURE 14.23

If the withdrawal of Partner C was paid from partnership assets, this reduces both net assets and total partnership capital, as shown in Figure 14.24.

	Partner A	Partner B	Partner C	Total
Capital balance before withdrawal of Partner C	$120,000	$150,000	$50,000	$320,000
Withdrawal of Partner C			−50,000	−50,000
Capital balance after withdrawal of Partner C	$120,000	$150,000	$0	$270,000

FIGURE 14.24

Figure 14.25 shows how the withdrawal of Partner C is recorded as a journal entry.

JOURNAL			
Date	**Account Title and Explanation**	**Debit**	**Credit**
Jan 1	Partner C, Capital	50,000	
	Cash		50,000
	To record withdrawal of Partner C		

FIGURE 14.25

Death of a Partner

As you learned earlier in this chapter, when a partner dies the existing partnership ends (but not necessarily the business). The remaining partners have two choices: (1) liquidate the business, or (2) form a new partnership agreement and continue the business. No matter the decision, several things must happen upon a partner's death. First, the partnership accounts must be closed as of the date of the partner's death in order to determine the net income or loss for the current period. The net income or loss must then be divided among all partners' capital accounts. The assets and liabilities should be adjusted to their current market values, and the amount of any adjustments must be divided among all partners' capital accounts. The deceased partner's estate is entitled to that partner's equity. Therefore, the remaining partners and the deceased partner's estate must come to an agreement about the settlement of that partner's equity. Once a settlement amount has been established, a journal entry is made to close (debit) the deceased partner's capital account and record (credit) a liability for the amount payable to the partner's estate. This entire process can go much more smoothly if the original partnership agreement and legal contract include detailed provisions for such circumstances.

Partner Bonuses

The discussion so far has assumed that the cash received from a new partner or paid to a leaving partner is the same as the value shown in the capital account. However, sometimes the cash amount is different from the capital amount. When new partnership agreements are negotiated, the partners usually come to an understanding of what the business is really worth, relative to its stated book value. This understanding then forms the foundation of how much of a *bonus* (or premium) new partners must pay to the existing partners in order to receive a share of ownership in the business or, conversely, how much the existing partners are willing to pay to a new partner to join the partnership.

Let us build upon two examples that were already looked at in this chapter. Figure 14.26 shows the original opening balances for Partners A, B and C. The following examples will illustrate the *bonus method* of adding a partner.

	Partner A	Partner B	Partner C	Partner D	Total
Capital balance before admitting new partner (includes all earnings to date)	$120,000	$150,000	$50,000		$320,000

FIGURE 14.26

Bonus to Existing Partners

In the first example, assume that Partner D (the new partner) is willing to pay a bonus to the existing partners for a share of the business. He would be willing to do this if the business has a value that is not reflected in the capital account, such as an increase in the value of the good name of the business (goodwill), or a higher market value for assets, such as land or copyright.

After negotiating the new partnership agreement, Partner D agrees to pay $200,000 on January 1, 2018 to receive a $130,000 share of the business' book value, which amounts to a quarter of the business. Figure 14.27 shows how each partner's capital is affected by the admission of Partner D.

	Partner A	Partner B	Partner C	Partner D	Total
Capital balance before admitting new partner (includes all earnings to date)	$120,000	$150,000	$50,000		$320,000
Admission of new partner	23,334	23,333	23,333	$130,000	200,000
Capital balance after admitting new partner	$143,334	$173,333	$73,333	$130,000	$520,000

FIGURE 14.27

Partner D's $200,000 contribution increases the total net assets from $320,000 to $520,000. One quarter of the new total is $130,000, which is Partner D's new share. The remaining balance of Partner D's $200,000 investment, $70,000, is divided equally as a bonus among the other three partners, as shown in Figure 14.28. We assume the bonus is divided equally in this example, but it would be divided however the partnership agreement states.

JOURNAL			
Date	Account Title and Explanation	Debit	Credit
Jan 1	Cash	200,000	
	Partner A, Capital		23,334
	Partner B, Capital		23,333
	Partner C, Capital		23,333
	Partner D, Capital		130,000
	To record admission of new partner		

FIGURE 14.28

Bonus to New Partner

In our second example, assume that Partner D adds value to the business, perhaps by bringing with him a client list, or an area of expertise that the partnership is looking for. Figure 14.29 shows what happens when Partner D pays $100,000 on January 1, 2018 to receive a quarter share of the business, for a value of $105,000.

	Partner A	Partner B	Partner C	Partner D	Total
Capital balance before admitting new partner (includes all earnings to date)	$120,000	$150,000	$50,000		$320,000
Admission of new partner	−1,666	−1,667	−1,667	$105,000	100,000
Capital balance after admitting new partner	$118,334	$148,333	$48,333	$105,000	$420,000

FIGURE 14.29

The $100,000 contribution made by Partner D increases total net assets to $420,000. One quarter of the new total is $105,000, which is Partner D's share. Since Partner D only paid $100,000 for this share, the $5,000 difference is a bonus to the new partner, paid for by the capital of the original partners. Therefore, approximately $1,667 is deducted from the account balances of Partners A, B and C, as shown in Figure 14.30.

JOURNAL			
Date	**Account Title and Explanation**	**Debit**	**Credit**
Jan 1	Cash	100,000	
	Partner A, Capital	1,666	
	Partner B, Capital	1,667	
	Partner C, Capital	1,667	
	Partner D, Capital		105,000
	To record admission of new partner		

FIGURE 14.30

The withdrawal of a partner can also be accomplished when the cash given to a leaving partner is not equal to the capital in his or her account. Suppose Partner D has never joined the partnership, and instead Partner C wants to leave the business. This could be due to unresolved conflict with the other partners, unexpected life changes or any other reason. The desire to leave immediately may lead Partner C to accept a lesser amount of cash than what his capital account says should be received.

Suppose Partner C decides to leave and accepts $40,000 cash. In this scenario, both of the remaining partners receive a bonus based on the amount of Partner C's capital that was not paid out. This bonus to the remaining partners is split evenly. The impact on capital is shown in Figure 14.31.

	Partner A	**Partner B**	**Partner C**	**Total**
Capital balance before withdrawal of Partner C	$120,000	$150,000	$50,000	$320,000
Withdrawal of Partner C	5,000	5,000	−50,000	−40,000
Capital balance after withdrawal of Partner C	$125,000	$155,000	$0	$280,000

FIGURE 14.31

Equity and net assets decrease by $40,000, which is the amount of cash received by the departing partner. The remaining $10,000 is divided equally between Partners A and B. The journal entry to record this transaction is shown in Figure 14.32.

JOURNAL			
Date	**Account Title and Explanation**	**Debit**	**Credit**
Jan 1	Partner C, Capital	50,000	
	Cash		40,000
	Partner A, Capital		5,000
	Partner B, Capital		5,000
	To record the withdrawal of a partner		

FIGURE 14.32

Alternatively, a partner may be leaving because the remaining partners want him or her out of the business. In this case, the incentive to Partner C to leave is cash payment in excess of the stated value of his capital.

Suppose Partner C is willing to leave if he receives $58,000 cash. In this scenario, both remaining partners give a bonus to the leaving partner. This bonus to the leaving partner is split evenly between the remaining partners. The impact on capital is shown in Figure 14.33.

	Partner A	**Partner B**	**Partner C**	**Total**
Capital balance before withdrawal of Partner C	$120,000	$150,000	50,000	$320,000
Withdrawal of Partner C	−4,000	−4,000	−50,000	−58,000
Capital balance after withdrawal of Partner C	$116,000	$146,000	$0	$262,000

FIGURE 14.33

Equity and net assets decrease by $58,000, which is the amount of cash received by the departing partner. Partners A and B must each give $4,000 of their capital to Partner C as a bonus, so their capital accounts are debited for that amount. The journal entry to record this transaction is shown in Figure 14.34.

JOURNAL			
Date	**Account Title and Explanation**	**Debit**	**Credit**
Jan 1	Partner C, Capital	50,000	
	Partner A, Capital	4,000	
	Partner B, Capital	4,000	
	Cash		58,000
	To record the withdrawal of a partner		

FIGURE 14.34

Pause & Reflect

Exercise 14-3

Kelsey and Zac run a general partnership together. Kelsey has a capital balance of $110,000 and Zac has a capital balance of $150,000. They are looking to expand and want to bring in a new partner to help them grow the company. They find an interested person, Yelena, who has a good client list. They offer Yelena a one-third share in the partnership for an investment of $100,000. Any bonus will be shared evenly between Kelsey and Zac. Calculate the new balances of all three partners after the admission.

	Kelsey	Zac	Yelena	Total
Capital balance before admission				
Admission of new partner				
Capital balance after admission				

See Appendix I for solutions.

Liquidation of a Partnership

A partnership has a limited life. If the partnership changes due to the addition or withdrawal of a partner, the existing partnership ends. Similarly, if the partners decide to end or sell the business, or if the partnership dissolves due to bankruptcy or other factors, a process known as a **partnership liquidation** takes place. Liquidation means that the partnership as a business entity will legally cease to exist. The liquidation process involves selling off any partnership assets, paying off liabilities, and distributing any remaining proceeds to the partners according to their individual profit and loss ratios.

As with the end of any business, the accounting cycle must first be completed to determine a starting point for the liquidation process. By now you have a firm understanding of the entire accounting cycle: journalizing and posting transactions, preparing a trial balance, preparing the financial statements, and preparing closing entries and the post-closing trial balance. Once these tasks are complete, the liquidation process can begin. This involves the following steps.

ⓐ Sell off the partnership's noncash assets for cash, and realize a gain or loss

ⓑ Allocate any gain or loss to the partners according to their individual profit and loss ratios

ⓒ Pay partnership liabilities (in cash) to creditors

ⓓ Distribute remaining proceeds to partners based on the balances in their capital accounts

The last step is to distribute the remaining proceeds to partners according to their capital account balances. In many cases, all partners will have credit balances in their capital accounts. However, one or more partners may have a debit balance in their capital account, known as a **capital deficiency**. Both situations will be examined, starting with the most straightforward situation, where there is no capital deficiency.

Liquidation with No Capital Deficiency

First, consider a partnership liquidation based on the simplified balance sheet for ABC Partnership, in which there is no capital deficiency.

Suppose that before liquidation, ABC Partnership had assets valued at $700,000 and liabilities valued at $600,000, as shown on the balance sheet in Figure 14.35. Thus, net assets are equal to $100,000.

ABC Partnership Balance Sheet As at December 31, 2018			
Assets		**Liabilities and Partners' Capital**	
Cash	$100,000	**Liabilities**	
Land	600,000	Notes Payable	$200,000
		Accounts Payable	400,000
		Total Liabilities	600,000
		Partners' Capital	
		Partner A, Capital	35,000
		Partner B, Capital	40,000
		Partner C, Capital	25,000
		Total Partners' Capital	100,000
Total Assets	$700,000	**Total Liabilities and Partners' Capital**	$700,000

FIGURE 14.35

For this example, we will assume that profits and losses are divided equally amongst the three partners, that is, one-third each. The steps for liquidation are as follows.

ⓐ Sell off the partnership's noncash assets for cash, and realize a gain or loss

Assume that on December 31, the business sells its noncash asset, land, for $570,000. This represents a loss of $30,000 ($570,000 – $600,000). The journal entry for the sale is shown in Figure 14.36.

JOURNAL

Date	Account Title and Explanation	Debit	Credit
Dec 31	Cash	570,000	
	Loss on Sale of Assets	30,000	
	Land		600,000
	Sold land at a loss		

FIGURE 14.36

After the sale, the balance in the cash account is $670,000 ($100,000 + $570,000).

b **Allocate any gain or loss to the partners according to their individual profit and loss ratios.**

The $30,000 loss is allocated as one-third ($10,000) to each partner. The journal entry for the allocation of the loss is shown in Figure 14.37.

JOURNAL

Date	Account Title and Explanation	Debit	Credit
Dec 31	Partner A, Capital	10,000	
	Partner B, Capital	10,000	
	Partner C, Capital	10,000	
	Loss on Sale of Assets		30,000
	To allocate loss on sale of assets		

FIGURE 14.37

c **Pay partnership liabilities (in cash) to creditors**

From the existing cash balance of $670,000, the partnership pays its liabilities as in the journal entry in Figure 14.38.

JOURNAL

Date	Account Title and Explanation	Debit	Credit
Dec 31	Notes Payable	200,000	
	Accounts Payable	400,000	
	Cash		600,000
	To pay liabilities		

FIGURE 14.38

After paying the partnership liabilities, the balance in the cash account is $70,000 ($670,000 – $600,000). With the noncash assets sold and the liabilities paid, Figure 14.39 shows the effects on the partners' capital accounts and the balance of each before the cash is distributed to the partners.

INCREASE		DECREASE	DECREASE		INCREASE	DECREASE		INCREASE
+	PARTNER A. CAPITAL	+	–	PARTNER B, CAPITAL	+	–	PARTNER C, CAPITAL	+
		$35,000 Opening Balance			$40,000 Opening Balance			$25,000 Opening Balance
Dec 31	10,000		Dec 31	10,000		Dec 31	10,000	
		$25,000			$30,000			$15,000

FIGURE 14.39

d) Distribute remaining proceeds to partners according to the capital contribution of each partner

The entry to distribute the remaining cash to the partners is shown in Figure 14.40.

JOURNAL			
Date	Account Title and Explanation	Debit	Credit
Dec 31	Partner A, Capital	25,000	
	Partner B, Capital	30,000	
	Partner C, Capital	15,000	
	Cash		70,000
	To record cash distribution among partners		

FIGURE 14.40

Figure 14.41 summarizes the steps involved in the liquidation. The numbers in blue circles correspond with the steps already described.

		Assets		=		Liabilities + Partners' Capital			
		Cash	Land	Loan Payable	Accounts Payable	Partner A, Capital	Partner B, Capital	Partner C, Capital
	Before liquidation	$100,000	$600,000	$200,000	$400,000	$35,000	$40,000	$25,000
a b	Sell assets and realize loss	570,000	–600,000			–10,000	–10,000	–10,000
c	Pay partnership liabilities	670,000	0	200,000	400,000	25,000	30,000	15,000
		–600,000		–200,000	–400,000			
d	Distribute remaining proceeds to partners	70,000	0	0	0	25,000	30,000	15,000
		–70,000				–25,000	–30,000	–15,000
	Final balances	$ 0	$ 0	$ 0	$ 0	$ 0	$ 0	$ 0

FIGURE 14.41

This example involved allocating a loss on sale of assets. Any gain is allocated in the same manner—equally, unless otherwise provided for—and the cash is divided according to each partner's final balance of equity in the business.

Pause & Reflect

Exercise 14-4

On November 30, 2018, Diana and Kate liquidated their general partnership. Before the liquidation, Diana had a capital balance of $70,000 and Kate had a capital balance of $90,000. The partnership has a cash balance of $30,000, noncash assets worth $240,000 and liabilities worth $110,000. The noncash assets are sold for $200,000. Any gain or loss on the sale of assets is split evenly between Diana and Kate.

Prepare the journal entries to liquidate the partnership and distribute any remaining cash to the partners.

JOURNAL			
Date	Account Title and Explanation	Debit	Credit

See Appendix I for solutions.

Liquidation with a Capital Deficiency

Sometimes, one or more partners have a debit balance in their capital account, known as a capital deficiency. Capital deficiencies occur for many reasons, including normal business losses, cash withdrawals that exceed a partner's capital account balance, or a negative balance that arises during the process of liquidation. Let us look again at the previous example, but under different circumstances.

We will assume that the noncash assets have been sold and the liabilities have been paid. Prior to distributing the remaining proceeds to the partners, the balances of the partners' capital accounts are as follows: Partner A, $25,000; Partner B, $30,000; and Partner C, ($2,500). Partner C's account has a capital deficiency of $2,500, and so Partner C owes the partnership that amount. Legally, Partner A and Partner B have a claim against Partner C's personal assets. One of two situations can exist: (1) Partner C has enough personal cash to pay the $2,500, or (2) Partner C is unable to pay what is owed.

Partner Can Pay Deficiency

If Partner C has sufficient personal cash to pay the $2,500 deficit to the partnership, the journal entry in Figure 14.42 is made to record the payment. This payment brings Partner C's capital account balance to zero, thereby fulfilling his obligation to the partnership and completing the liquidation process.

JOURNAL			
Date	**Account Title and Explanation**	**Debit**	**Credit**
Dec 31	Cash	2,500	
	Partner C, Capital		2,500
	To record the payment of capital deficit by Partner C		

FIGURE 14.42

Partner Cannot Pay Deficiency

What if Partner C does not have enough cash to pay the $2,500 owed to the partnership? The partnership characteristic of unlimited liability means that if one partner is unable to meet obligations related to the partnership, the other partners are obligated to pay. Partner A and Partner B must absorb the loss according to their agreement—in this case, equally. Partner A and Partner B each need to decrease their own capital by $1,250 to cover the $2,500 capital deficiency, bringing Partner C's capital account balance to zero. The journal entry for this transaction is shown in Figure 14.43.

JOURNAL			
Date	**Account Title and Explanation**	**Debit**	**Credit**
Dec 31	Partner A, Capital	1,250	
	Partner B, Capital	1,250	
	Partner C, Capital		2,500
	To record the payment of Partner C's capital deficiency by Partner A and Partner B		

FIGURE 14.43

The partners are now able to close the partnership accounts and complete the liquidation process. Beyond this, Partners A and B may decide to pursue Partner C legally to get back the money they lost, although if Partner C cannot pay the partnership the amount owed, it is unlikely he would be able to pay Partners A and B.

In Summary

LO 1 Describe the characteristics, advantages and disadvantages of a partnership

▶ A partnership is an association of two or more people who jointly own a business, for which earnings are taxed at a personal level only.

▶ A partnership is a legal entity, however partners generally have unlimited liability.

▶ Partnership advantages include raising more capital and having more expertise, since more people are involved in creating the business. Partnerships can also be easy to create.

▶ Disadvantages can include unlimited liability and mutual agency.

LO 2 Describe different types of partnerships

▶ A general partnership means that all partners have unlimited liability.

▶ A limited partnership divides a company's partners into two categories: general partners and limited partners. Unlimited liability extends to general partners because they are involved in the day-to-day decision-making of the business. Limited partners, on the other hand, are only liable for the amount of capital they invest in the business. This is known as limited liability.

▶ A limited liability partnership, or LLP, is a legal ownership structure, used in some jurisdictions, that usually protects professionals from a partner's negligence. If one of the partners is sued, the others are not necessarily liable. However, all the partners are liable for any debts owed to regular day-to-day creditors.

▶ A limited liability company, or LLC, has some characteristics of a corporation and some characteristics of a limited partnership. Accounting for an LLC is the same as for a partnership, but the LLC uses the terms "member" and "member's equity" instead of "partner" and "partners' capital." An LLC provides limited liability to its members and it can continue despite the addition or withdrawal of members.

▶ A corporation that elects to be taxed under Subchapter S of the Internal Revenue Code becomes classified as an S corporation, a special type of corporation that does not pay federal income tax, but rather allocates its profits and losses to the individual members (owners) to be reported on their personal tax returns.

LO 3 Record the formation of a partnership

▶ Even though a partnership agreement in the form of a legal written contract is not required to form a partnership, having a partnership agreement lessens the chance of legal and ethical conflict between partners and specifies the purpose of the business and the relationships between the partners.

▶ Assets that partners bring into the business are recorded at their fair market values. Each partner's opening capital is calculated by deducting the total amount of liabilities from the total amount of assets that each partner brings into the business.

LO 4 Record the division of income or loss

▶ A partnership's earnings can be divided in a number of different ways; these are usually outlined in the partnership agreement. Four common methods of dividing earnings are the following: equally; based on a ratio; based on the capital contribution of each partner; and withdrawing salaries and interest before dividing the rest.

▶ To record the division of income, the income summary account is debited and the partners' capital accounts are credited. To record the division of loss, the partners' capital accounts are debited and the income summary account is credited.

LO 5 Record partners' withdrawals

▶ When a partner withdraws cash from the business for personal use, the partners' withdrawals account is debited and cash is credited.

▶ The partners' withdrawals account is closed at the end of each accounting period by debiting the partners' capital account and crediting the partners' withdrawals account.

LO 6 Prepare financial statements for a partnership

▶ There are four basic financial statements that are prepared by partnerships: the income statement, statement of partners' equity, the balance sheet and the statement of cash flows. Partnership financial statements are quite similar to those of sole proprietorships, except that they include capital accounts for each partner.

LO 7 Account for the addition or withdrawal of a partner

▶ A new partner can simply add in a new portion of partner's equity, or purchase some or all of another partner's share.

▶ When a partner withdraws from a partnership, the capital of the withdrawn partner can be bought out using either the existing partners' personal assets or the partnership's assets. If the personal assets of the existing partners are used, a credit or an increase in the existing partners' capital is recorded in the partnership's journal. If the partnership's assets are used, a credit or a decrease in the partnership's assets is recorded.

▶ If the amount of capital allocated to a new partner is different than the cash invested, a bonus is either allocated to the existing partners or the new partner.

▶ If the amount of cash paid to a departing partner is different than their capital account, a bonus is either allocated to the existing partners or the leaving partner.

LO 8 Record the liquidation of a partnership

▶ The partnership agreement should stipulate how the liquidation should be done. If assets are sold above or below book value, the corresponding gains or losses are shared among the partners. The remaining cash can be distributed according to each partner's proportion of equity in the business.

 *Access **ameengage.com** for integrated resources including tutorials, practice exercises, the digital textbook and more.*

Review Exercise 14-1

On January 1, 2018, Zelma Rapoza, Serena Dennen and Sharon Thorne have decided to set up a spa and operate it as a general partnership. They will each contribute $10,000 to buy equipment and help pay for lease expenses. Zelma is also contributing $25,000 of her own equipment.

They agree to pay themselves an annual salary of $5,000 each. Since Zelma contributed the equipment, she expects $3,000 "rent" per year on the equipment for ten years. Each partner is to earn 5% on her investment (cash contribution). The net income for the year 2018 was $25,000. The profit remaining after salaries, rent and interest is to be distributed at a ratio of each partner's cash contribution.

Required

a) Prepare a schedule showing the changes in capital during 2018.

b) Prepare journal entries for the following transactions.

Jan 1   The initial cash contribution

Jan 1   The equipment contribution

Dec 31   The division of partnership income assuming that revenues and expenses have already been closed to the income summary account

Jan 2, 2019   Sharon retires from the partnership. To buy Sharon's shares, Zelma and Serena contribute $10,000 and $7,333 of their personal assets, respectively.

JOURNAL			
Date	**Account Title and Explanation**	**Debit**	**Credit**

See Appendix I for solutions.

Chapter 15
Corporations: Stock and Dividends

Learning Objectives

LO 1 Describe the characteristics of corporations
- Characteristics of a Corporation
- Comparison between Corporations and LLCs
- Organization Expenses
- Classification of Corporations

LO 2 Describe differences between public and private corporations
- Public and Private Corporations: US and Non-US SEC Registrants

LO 3 Explain stockholders' equity
- The Classes of Stock: Common and Preferred
- Par Value Stock and No-Par Value Stock
- Stated Value

LO 4 Record the issuance of stock
- Issuing Stock at Par
- Issuing Stock at a Premium
- Issuing Stated Value Stock
- Issuing No-Par Value Stock
- Issuing Stock in Exchange for Noncash Assets or Services

LO 5 Record the payment of cash dividends
- On the Date of Declaration
- On the Date of Record
- On the Date of Payment
- Dividends in Arrears

LO 6 Record stock splits and stock dividends
- Stock Split
- Stock Dividend
- Restrictions on the Use of Retained Earnings

LO 7 Record treasury stock
- Purchasing Treasury Stock
- Reissuing Treasury Stock
- Retiring Treasury Stock

LO 8 Record income tax expense
- Recording Income Tax Liabilities
- Deferred Income Tax Liabilities

LO 9 Explain the importance of ethics for corporate reporting

 *Access **ameengage.com** for integrated resources including tutorials, practice exercises, the digital textbook and more.*

557

The Corporate Form of Organization

So far we have demonstrated accounting practices related to sole proprietorships and partnerships. These two types of business are usually operated and managed by their owners. In sole proprietorships and partnerships, the owners provide their own funding for the business. They can fund the business with their personal assets or by taking out a loan and incurring debt. Whether the owners use their own assets or borrow money, they are personally liable for all debts of the business. A sole proprietorship or a partnership exists as long as the owners are alive and decide to continue its operation.

There is a different type of business known as a corporation. A **corporation** is a legal entity that is separate from its owners. In a corporation, the owners are known as **stockholders,** or *shareholders,* because they hold **stock,** or shares, of equity in the corporation. A corporation is granted a *charter,* or *articles of incorporation*, under state law, which formally creates the corporation. The corporation's management and board of directors then establish a set of *bylaws*, the rules and procedures that govern how the corporation's affairs are to be conducted. State incorporation laws differ, and a corporation is not required to have an office in its state of incorporation. This is why many companies choose to be incorporated in states with the most favorable laws (i.e. Delaware). Figure 15.1 shows how sole proprietorships and partnerships differ from corporations in terms of equity.

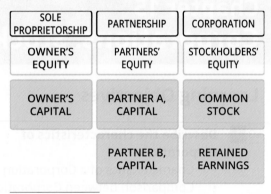

FIGURE 15.1

Characteristics of a Corporation

All corporations have certain characteristics in common that govern their duties, rights and responsibilities, and we will look at each one in more detail.

Separate Legal Existence

A corporation is a separate legal entity that has the rights and responsibilities of a person. This means that the corporation is legally separate from its owners, known as stockholders. A corporation can enter into its own contracts and buy and sell property. It is responsible for its own actions and for its own debts. It has the right to sue and can be sued.

Limited Liability of Stockholders

Because a corporation is legally separate from its owners, the stockholders are not responsible for any actions or debts of the business. Stockholders are only liable for the amount that they have invested in the company, giving them what is called limited liability. This is the same concept that was discussed in Chapter 14 regarding limited liability for a partnership.

Formal Organizational Structure

At the heart of a corporation is the separation of ownership and management. In a large corporation, the company's stockholders may have very little to do with managing the business. As owners of the business, stockholders are responsible for electing a board of directors to oversee the business on their behalf. The board of directors is responsible for deciding on the corporation's operational policies. The board also appoints the external auditors and an executive management team. The executive management team acts as the company's legal agents and is usually headed by a chief executive officer (CEO). Figure 15.2 shows the typical organizational structure of a corporation.

Organizational Structure of a Corporation

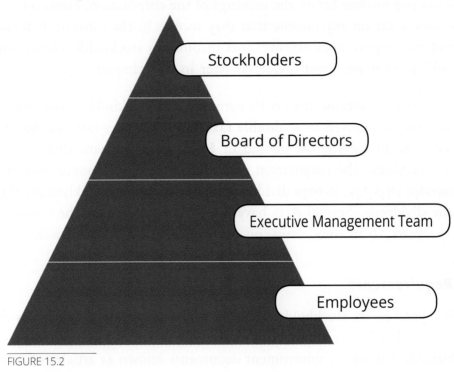

- Stockholders
- Board of Directors
- Executive Management Team
- Employees

FIGURE 15.2

Unlimited Life

A corporation is considered a *going concern*, which means that it remains an entity regardless of the comings and goings of stockholders.

Ability to Raise Capital

When a corporation needs to raise capital for day-to-day operations or to invest in property and equipment, it can issue stock. Stocks are an attractive investment for stockholders because they offer limited liability and have the potential to increase in value. They also offer liquidity, which is the investor's ability to quickly buy and sell them.

When an investor buys stock, the corporation sometimes issues a stock certificate as proof of the stockholder's ownership in the corporation. The stock certificate is a printed document that includes the company's name, the stockholder's name and the amount of stock owned. It may also show the par value per stock if there is one. Printed stock certificates are not always issued unless requested by the investor, because many investors now maintain accounts with brokerages who keep these records electronically for their clients.

Income Tax Treatment

As a separate legal entity, a corporation must file a tax return and pay income tax on its earnings. Stockholders do not pay income tax on the earnings of the corporation. However, they are required to pay personal income tax on any income that they receive in the form of dividends. A **dividend** is a distribution of the corporation's earnings (net income) to stockholders based on the stock that they own. You will learn more about dividends later in this chapter.

Because a corporation pays income tax on its earnings and stockholders pay personal income tax on their dividends, this is referred to as **double taxation**. This does not necessarily mean that the government receives $2 in income tax instead of $1. It simply means that tax is paid twice (at different rates) on earnings. The corporation earns income, pays corporate income tax, and from the remaining income after tax, it pays dividends to stockholders. Stockholders then pay personal income tax on the dividends. Several Acts have been passed to reduce the amount of tax paid on dividends over the years, so in some cases, no tax is paid at all on dividends.

Government Requirements

A corporation is owned by its stockholders, and it is responsible to them for its financial results. In the US, each state has its own laws, fees and requirements to set up a corporation. When a corporation is formed, it must file government documents known as articles of incorporation. The **articles of incorporation** (or corporate charter) contain the operational details of the corporation, including its name, purpose and general objectives.

Corporations must also meet certain requirements for issuing stock and distributing income to stockholders. They must regularly report on their financial results and operations and conduct formal stockholder meetings. Although the corporate structure has many advantages, it also has legal obligations that require lawyers to be hired, forms to be completed and documents to be prepared and filed.

Figure 15.3 compares the characteristics of a sole proprietorship, a partnership and a corporation.

Characteristics of Business Organizations			
	Sole Proprietorship	**Partnership**	**Corporation**
Owners	One individual	Two or more individuals	One or more stockholders
Owner liability	Unlimited	Unlimited	Limited
Life of business	Limited	Limited	Unlimited
Taxation of earnings	• Taxed at the individual's personal tax rate • Paid by owner	• Taxed at each partner's personal tax rate • Paid by partners	• Taxed at corporate tax rate • Paid by corporation
Example	Indra's Bookkeeping Services	PricewaterhouseCoopers	General Electric

FIGURE 15.3

The corporate form of organization allows businesses to do things on a larger scale and in a formally structured way. It also has certain duties, rights and responsibilities that can be viewed as advantages and disadvantages, as shown in Figure 15.4.

Advantages of a Corporation	Disadvantages of a Corporation
• Separate legal existence • Limited liability of stockholders • Formal organizational structure • Unlimited life • Ability to raise capital	• Strict government requirements • Double taxation of corporation and stockholders

FIGURE 15.4

Comparison between Corporations and LLCs

In Chapter 14, we discussed the characteristics of a limited liability company (LLC). You may recall that an LLC has some characteristics of a corporation. Both LLCs and corporations are formed under state law. An LLC is considered by law to be an entity separate from its owners, as is a regular (or "C") corporation. Like a corporation, the LLC provides limited liability to its members (owners), meaning that their personal assets are protected against claims of creditors. Both an LLC and a corporation may have an unlimited number of owners, and both forms of organization can have an unlimited life.

In an LLC, the members can share profits in proportion to the terms of their operating agreement. In a corporation, profits are distributed to owners (stockholders) in the form of dividends in proportion to the number of shares the stockholders own. An LLC can choose to be treated like a partnership for income tax purposes, in which case its profits pass through the company to be taxed only at the individual taxpayer level. A corporation, on the other hand, is subject to double taxation, as described earlier.

Organization Expenses

Organization expenses (or *organization costs*) are the initial costs incurred to organize or form a corporation, such as incorporation fees, legal fees, taxes and license fees. These costs are recorded as a debit to an expense account called Organization Expenses. Figure 15.5 illustrates the journal entry for a corporation's organization expenses of $1,500 on September 1, 2018.

JOURNAL			
Date	**Account Title and Explanation**	**Debit**	**Credit**
Sep 1	Organization Expenses	1,500	
	Cash		1,500
	To record costs incurred in organizing the corporation		

FIGURE 15.5

Classification of Corporations

Corporations can be classified by their purposes into for-profit corporations and nonprofit organizations. **For-profit corporations** are formed for the purpose of generating profits for their stockholders. Examples of for-profit corporations include McDonald's, American Airlines and Facebook. **Nonprofit organizations** are formed for the purpose of improving or benefiting communities by taking profits and redistributing them as services or products. Examples of nonprofit organizations include the World Wildlife Fund, the American Museum of Natural History, and the Breast Cancer Research Foundation. The accounting practices of for-profit corporations are different from those of nonprofit organizations. This textbook focuses on the accounting practices of for-profit corporations, which are discussed in the next section.

Public vs. Private Corporations

As a separate legal entity, a corporation has the right to be formed as either a public or private corporation. A **public corporation** is one that trades its stock on a stock exchange, such as the New York Stock Exchange (NYSE) or the Chicago Stock Exchange (CHX). Trading simply means buying or selling stock. That is, its stock is available to be traded publicly from one member of the general public (the seller) to another (the purchaser).

A **private corporation** is one that does not offer its stock to the public. The company's stock is instead owned and exchanged privately. For example, a private corporation may have a single owner who wishes never to sell the stock publicly. Or a private corporation may be a company with several owners who have no intention of selling stock on a stock exchange. A private corporation can also be referred to as a closed corporation or a privately held corporation.

The financial reporting requirements for private companies are different from those of public companies. The reporting standards for public corporations are generally more strict and detailed than those for private companies, since more external users depend on the financial statements of public corporations.

Public and Private Corporations: US and Non-US SEC Registrants

In the US, companies that offer and sell securities to the public must register with the Securities and Exchange Commission (SEC); these companies are referred to as *US SEC registrants*. The Securities Exchange Act also requires registrants to periodically file financial and other business documents with the SEC. Foreign (non-US) companies that offer and sell securities to US residents must also register with the SEC, and these companies are known as *non-US SEC registrants*.

As you learned in Chapter 3, the increased need for global comparability in accounting information resulted in International Financial Reporting Standards (IFRS). Issued by the International Accounting Standards Board (IASB), IFRS aims to provide a unified set of standard accounting practices for companies around the world. Currently, not all countries have chosen to adopt IFRS. Some countries require adherence to IFRS, while others allow companies to choose whether or not to follow IFRS. In the US, there are two sets of accepted accounting principles.

1. **US GAAP**. As US SEC registrants, American public companies must follow a standard version of US GAAP. American private companies that are unlisted with the SEC may also choose to follow US GAAP. However, these companies can choose to report under a simplified version of US GAAP that is designed specifically to provide relief to private companies. The simplified version was developed by the Private Company Council (PCC), which is an advisory body to the Financial Accounting Standards Board (FASB). In addition, foreign companies (both private companies that operate in the US and public companies that are non-US SEC registrants) can also choose to follow US GAAP.

2. **IFRS**. While US SEC registrants are not allowed to follow IFRS, American private companies that are unlisted with the SEC are allowed to report under IFRS if they do not want to follow US GAAP. Foreign companies (both public and private) that do not want to follow US GAAP may use IFRS.

In conclusion, all US SEC registrants must follow US GAAP. Both non-US SEC registrants and private companies that are not SEC registrants may choose to follow either US GAAP or IFRS.

Accounting for Stockholders' Equity

In a sole proprietorship, owner's equity is a simple figure that represents the net worth of the business. In a partnership, equity is divided into separate capital accounts for each partner's stake in the business. With a corporation, as the ownership structure gets more complicated, so does the recording and reporting of equity on the company's balance sheet. In the simplest terms, equity represents the owners' claims on the net assets of the business.

In a corporation, the stockholders actually own the company and so owners' equity is called **stockholders' equity**. Stockholders' equity is comprised of two components: paid-in capital (sometimes referred to as contributed capital) and retained earnings. These components are reported as two separate items in the stockholders' equity section of the financial statements.

Paid-in capital refers to the total amount of assets that stockholders contribute to the corporation in order to receive the corporation's stock in return. It is generally comprised of two sub-categories: capital stock (sometimes referred to as share capital and will contain common and preferred stock), and additional paid-in capital (sometimes referred to as paid-in capital in excess of par or contributed surplus), as shown in Figure 15.6. These two sub-categories will be explained in detail later in the chapter.

Retained earnings are the earnings that are kept and accumulated by the company after *dividends* have been paid to the stockholders. Dividends are distributions of the company's earnings to stockholders and the earnings not paid out to stockholders are retained in the business. Net income is added to the retained earnings; net loss and dividends of the company are subtracted from the retained earnings. Since most companies generate net income and do not pay out all their earnings in dividends, the account of retained earnings generally has a credit balance. If the retained earnings account has a debit balance, it is called a *deficit*.

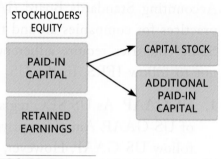

FIGURE 15.6

The articles of incorporation specify the number of shares of stock a corporation will issue, the types of stock to be issued and the rights of the stockholders for each type of stock. A corporation can offer for sale an unlimited number of shares of stock, or it can specify a particular number of shares of stock. Regardless of the stipulation in the articles of incorporation, a company will decide on the maximum number of shares of stock that can legally be issued, known as the company's **authorized shares**. If the company later decides it needs to issue more stock, additional authorization is required.

When authorized shares are sold to stockholders, they become **issued shares**. Once shares have been issued, they can be sold by or transferred from one investor to other investors without involving the corporation. This is known as trading on the secondary market. **Outstanding shares** are shares that are still held by the stockholders, and may be equal to the number of issued shares. However, a corporation may decide to buy back some of its stock to hold as *treasury stock*. This treasury stock is no longer held by the stockholders and therefore is not outstanding. In this case, the number of outstanding shares will be less than the number of issued shares. Treasury stock is discussed later in this chapter.

In the secondary market, stock is sold at a price known as its **market value**. The market value is determined by the amount that investors are willing to pay for it. This means that the stock may be sold at a higher or lower price than what the original holder paid for it.

When we examine the balance sheet of a corporation, the stock figure shows the total amount of money received by the corporation when it initially sold the stock to stockholders. This value is the book value of the stock and has no bearing on the market value of the stock. If the company is doing well, the market value is likely higher than the book value. If the company is not doing well, the market value is likely lower than the book value.

Figure 15.7 shows the stockholders' equity section of a balance sheet, illustrating how the classes of shares are typically presented. Each component of this statement is explained in detail throughout this chapter.

Standard Corporation Balance Sheet (partial) As at December 31, 2018	
Stockholders' Equity	
Paid-In Capital	
Preferred stock, 7% noncumulative, $20 par value, 4,000 shares authorized and issued	$80,000
Common stock, $10 par value, unlimited shares authorized, 50,000 shares issued, 49,000 shares outstanding	500,000
Additional Paid-In Capital	70,000
Total Paid-In Capital	650,000
Retained Earnings	300,000
Total Paid-In Capital and Retained Earnings	950,000
Less: Treasury Stock (1,000 shares at cost)	12,000
Total Stockholders' Equity	$938,000

FIGURE 15.7

The Classes of Stock: Common and Preferred

All public corporations must issue common stock. **Common stock** is a type of equity that gives stockholders ownership in the corporation, along with voting rights to elect a board of directors and the potential to receive a portion of the company's earnings in the form of dividends. Investors buy common stock with the expectation that the corporation will remain or become profitable, although the payment of dividends is not guaranteed. A corporation may offer several different classes of common stock with different voting rights in order for a specific group of investors to be able to maintain control within the company without having to buy more stock. For example, a corporation that has two classes of common stock may give 10 voting rights to a holder of each Class A stock versus only one voting right to a holder of each Class B stock.

A corporation may also issue preferred stock, a type of stock with features that are not available with common stock. **Preferred stock** receives preference because dividends must first be paid on it before any dividends are paid on common stock. This preference, however, does not guarantee that dividends will be paid.

In the event of a company liquidation, preferred stockholders also have priority over common stockholders regarding the assets of the liquidating company. However, preferred stockholders have no voting rights to influence the direction of the company. In this sense, it is only common stockholders that maintain this specific right of company ownership, and it is an important one.

Cumulative stock is a type of preferred stock that gives stockholders the right to be paid the current year's dividends and to accumulate any unpaid dividends from previous years. With cumulative preferred stock, if no dividend is declared by the board of directors, or if a dividend payment is otherwise missed, the dividends owing will accumulate and must be paid before any dividends are paid to the common stockholders. With cumulative preferred stock, any unpaid dividends from prior periods are known as **dividends in arrears**. Preferred stock that does not have the right to receive any accumulated unpaid dividends is known as **noncumulative stock.**

As you just learned, preferred stockholders must receive dividends before any dividends are paid on common stock. Preferred stockholders are entitled to the dividend percentage stated on the preferred stock certificates. In terms of dividend entitlement, preferred stock can be stated as either participating or nonparticipating. **Participating preferred stock** entitles preferred stockholders to share with common stockholders any dividends paid in excess of the percentage stated on the preferred stock certificates. For example, if a company declares a 6% dividend on its 2% participating preferred stock, the preferred stockholders are entitled to the stated dividend of 2%. In addition, the remaining dividend of 4% is split between the preferred and common stockholders. It should be noted that participating preferred stock are not often issued by companies.

Nonparticipating preferred stock limits the dividends that can be issued to preferred stockholders to preferred stockholders each year. The limit (or maximum) is stated on the stock certificates as a percentage of the stock's par value, or as a specific dollar amount. This ensures that any dividend declared goes to the preferred stockholders first, protecting their entitlement. For example, suppose a company has 2,000 common shares outstanding, and 200 nonparticipating preferred shares with a stated dividend of $12 per share. The board of directors declares a dividend of $4,000. First, the preferred stockholders receive dividends of $2,400 (200 shares × $12 per share maximum). The common stockholders then receive the remaining dividends of $1,600 ($4,000 − $2,400).

Figure 15.8 summarizes the most important features of common and preferred stock.

Features of Common Stock	Features of Preferred Stock
• Represent ownership in the corporation • Owners elect the board of directors • Owners vote on corporate policy • Owners rank after creditors and preferred stockholders in the event of a liquidation • Owners have a right to receive dividends only if declared by the board of directors	• In the case of a company liquidation, owners have a higher claim on assets than do common stockholders • If dividends are declared, owners are paid first before any dividends are paid to common stockholders • Cumulative preferred stock has the right to accumulate unpaid dividends from previous years

FIGURE 15.8

Par Value Stock and No-Par Value Stock

Both common and preferred stock may or may not have a par value. **Par value stock** is stock that is issued with an assigned value. **No-par value stock** is stock issued with no assigned value. In some jurisdictions, only par value stock is allowed to be issued. Preferred stock usually indicates the amount of dividends that each share of stock will receive. The dividend rights of preferred stock can be stated either as dollars per share or as a percent of par. To illustrate, a share of preferred stock with a $20 par value and a $2 per share dividend could be expressed as having dividends of either (1) preferred $2 stock at $20 par or (2) preferred 10% stock at $20 par.

When par value stock is issued, normally the company cannot sell the stock below its par value. Thus, the par value dictates the minimum amount of assets that stockholders are legally required to contribute to the company. This amount is known as the **minimum legal capital**. Minimum legal capital ensures that the company's equity does not fall below a certain level so that there is capital available to pay the corporation's creditors.

Stated Value

Some states require corporations that issue no-par value stock to determine a **stated value** for each share of stock they are authorized to issue. The purpose of assigning a stated or "legal" value, similar to the purpose of assigning a par value, is to establish the minimum legal capital to protect creditors from the board of directors declaring and paying out dividends to the point where insufficient equity remains to cover company's liabilities. Having a stated value ensures the corporation must maintain this minimum amount of stockholders' equity so that in the event of liquidation, the creditor claims are somewhat protected.

Issuing Stock

One of the advantages of the public corporate form of ownership is the company's ability to raise cash by selling stock to the public. We will look at the different ways a corporation can issue stock and how the transactions are recorded in the company's accounting records. Par value stock can be issued at or above its par value. When the stock issue price is above its par value, the excess over the par value is recorded as additional paid-in capital. When no-par value stock is issued, the entire proceeds of the sale are recorded as capital stock. In addition to monetary exchanges, stock can also be issued in non-monetary exchanges for noncash assets or services.

Issuing Stock at Par

The most common reason for issuing stock is to raise financial capital. If the cash proceeds from selling common and preferred stock are exactly equal to their par values, the proceeds are recorded in the respective capital stock account. Suppose that on February 8, 2018, a corporation issues

1,000 shares of common stock at $10 per share (par value), and 5,000 shares of $50 preferred stock to raise a total of $260,000 cash.

Figure 15.9 shows how the transaction is recorded in the journal, and how it affects the balance sheet accounts.

JOURNAL			
Date	**Account Title and Explanation**	**Debit**	**Credit**
Feb 8	Cash	260,000	
	Preferred Stock		250,000
	Common Stock		10,000
	To record issue of preferred stock and common stock at par for cash		

BALANCE SHEET

CURRENT ASSETS	CURRENT LIABILITIES
CASH + $260,000 DR	**ACCOUNTS PAYABLE**
ACCOUNTS RECEIVABLE	**UNEARNED REVENUE**
MERCHANDISE INVENTORY	**LONG-TERM LIABILITIES**
PREPAID EXPENSES	**BONDS PAYABLE**
	STOCKHOLDERS' EQUITY
NONCURRENT ASSETS	**PREFERRED STOCK** + $250,000 CR
PROPERTY, PLANT & EQUIPMENT	**COMMON STOCK** + $10,000 CR
	RETAINED EARNINGS

FIGURE 15.9

The receipt of $260,000 is recorded as a debit to the cash account. The corresponding credits are made to the common stock account ($10,000) and the preferred stock account ($250,000). Both of these amounts are reported in the stockholders' equity section of the balance sheet.

In reality, stock is usually issued at a price that is higher than its par value. This is referred to as issuing stock at a premium.

Issuing Stock at a Premium

Par value stock is often sold at a price other than its par value. If the stock is sold for a price more than its par value, it is sold at a **premium**. For example, if common stock with a par value of $20 per share is sold on March 31, 2018, for $23 per share, a premium of $3 ($23 − $20) per share has been received. To illustrate, suppose a company sells 20,000 shares of $20 par value common stock at a price of $23 per share. The cash account is increased (debited) for the amount received, $460,000 (20,000 shares × $23 per share). The common stock account is increased (credited) for the par amount of the stock. The excess amount received over par value is credited to the account called Paid-In Capital in Excess of Par, Common Stock, which is reported as additional paid-in capital on the balance sheet. Figure 15.10 shows the journal entry for this transaction.

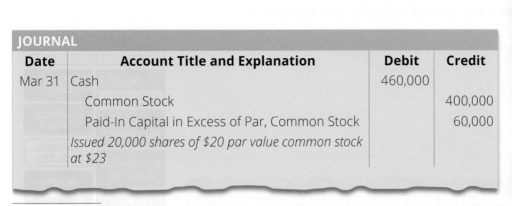

FIGURE 15.10

If a stock is sold for a price less than its par value, it is sold at a **discount**. However, selling stock at a discount is not permitted in most states. Therefore, the journal entry for selling stock at a discount is not illustrated.

Issuing Stated Value Stock

The accounting treatment for stated value stock is similar to that for par value stock. Most commonly, stock is issued at an amount in excess of the stated value. Therefore, the excess is credited to the additional paid-in capital account called Paid-In Capital in Excess of Stated Value, Common Stock. To illustrate, suppose that on April 12, 2018, a corporation issues 1,000 shares of no-par value common stock with a stated value of $18 per share, and sells it for $20 per share. Figure 15.11 shows the journal entry for the transaction.

BALANCE SHEET

CURRENT ASSETS	CURRENT LIABILITIES
CASH + $20,000 DR	ACCOUNTS PAYABLE
ACCOUNTS RECEIVABLE	UNEARNED REVENUE
	LONG-TERM LIABILITIES
MERCHANDISE INVENTORY	BONDS PAYABLE
PREPAID EXPENSES	STOCKHOLDERS' EQUITY
	COMMON STOCK + $18,000 CR
NONCURRENT ASSETS	ADDITIONAL PAID-IN CAPITAL + $2,000 CR
PROPERTY, PLANT & EQUIPMENT	RETAINED EARNINGS

JOURNAL

Date	Account Title and Explanation	Debit	Credit
Apr 12	Cash	20,000	
	Common Stock		18,000
	Paid-In Capital in Excess of Stated Value, Common Stock		2,000
	Issued 1,000 shares of $18 per share stated value common stock at $20 per share		

FIGURE 15.11

Issuing No-Par Value Stock

When no-par value stock is issued, the common stock account (or the preferred stock account if preferred stock is issued) is credited for the entire proceeds of the sale. To illustrate, suppose that on April 10, 2018, a corporation issues 20,000 shares of no-par value common stock for $20 per share. Figure 15.12 shows the journal entry for the transaction.

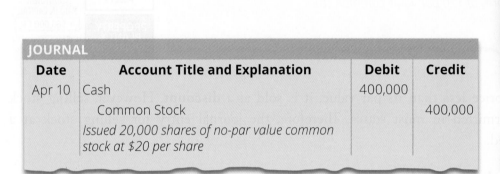

JOURNAL			
Date	**Account Title and Explanation**	**Debit**	**Credit**
Apr 10	Cash	400,000	
	Common Stock		400,000
	Issued 20,000 shares of no-par value common stock at $20 per share		

FIGURE 15.12

Issuing Stock in Exchange for Noncash Assets or Services

If a corporation has limited cash, it may offer stock to a supplier in exchange for noncash assets, such as property, plant and equipment. Suppliers may be willing to make the exchange since stocks offer liquidity, which is the ability to trade them at their market value, and there is potential for the market value to increase.

In a non-monetary exchange, the parties involved with the transaction still need to determine the value of assets that are being exchanged. Most importantly, the corporation needs to know the dollar amount at which the transaction will be recorded. Accountants and other professionals determine this amount using the concept of **fair value**, which is the amount that the asset could be sold for in the open market. If the fair value of the asset cannot be determined, then the stock issuance transaction is recorded at the fair value of the stock being exchanged. The fair market value of the stock of a public corporation can usually be taken from the stock market on the day of the transaction.

Suppose that on February 25, 2018, the corporation issues 20,000 shares of $20 par value common stock at its current market value (the fair value) of $40 each in exchange for some equipment. The corporation cannot readily determine the fair value of the equipment. Figure 15.13 shows how the transaction is recorded.

JOURNAL

Date	Account Title and Explanation	Debit	Credit
Feb 25	Equipment	800,000	
	Common Stock		400,000
	Paid-In Capital in Excess of Par, Common Stock		400,000
	Issue 20,000 shares of $20 par common stock for equipment		

FIGURE 15.13

If no-par value common stock is issued in exchange for a noncash asset, and if the fair value of the asset cannot be determined, then the common stock account is credited at its market value. To illustrate, assume that on February 25, 2018, the corporation issues 20,000 shares of no-par value common stock at its current market value of $40 in exchange for the equipment. Figure 15.14 shows how this transaction is recorded.

JOURNAL

Date	Account Title and Explanation	Debit	Credit
Feb 25	Equipment	800,000	
	Common Stock		800,000
	To record issue of 20,000 shares of common stock for equipment		

FIGURE 15.14

A private corporation may not have a stock value that is easy to determine since a private corporation does not sell stock on a stock exchange. In this case, it is likely easier to determine the fair value of the asset or service and use that as the value used in the transaction.

For example, on March 18, 2018, a private corporation issues 1,000 shares of no-par value common stock in exchange for land that is appraised at $1,000,000. The transaction is recorded as shown in Figure 15.15.

The purchase increases land, a noncurrent asset account, with a debit. The corresponding $1,000,000 credit is recorded in the common stock account, and reported in the stockholders' equity section of the balance sheet.

JOURNAL				
Date	Account Title and Explanation	Debit	Credit	
Mar 18	Land	1,000,000		
	Common Stock		1,000,000	
	To record issue of 1,000 shares of common stock for land valued at $1,000,000			

FIGURE 15.15

The concept and determination of fair value can also be used if a corporation wants to issue stock in exchange for professional services.

Suppose that a new corporation requires the services of an accountant. The accounting services total $10,000. The corporation considers this expenditure costly and hard on its cash flow. On March 21, 2018, the company offers to issue to the accountant 1,000 no-par value common stock at their current market value of $10 per share, to equal the fair value of $10,000. The accountant accepts the offer of stock in exchange for her accounting services. Figure 15.16 shows how the transaction is recorded on the company's books.

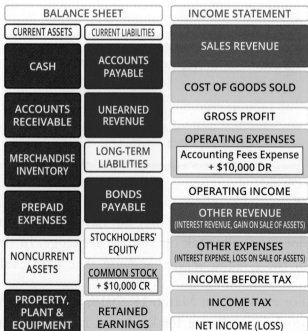

JOURNAL			
Date	Account Title and Explanation	Debit	Credit
Mar 21	Accounting Fees Expense	10,000	
	Common Stock		10,000
	To record issue of 1,000 shares of common stock in exchange for accounting services		

FIGURE 15.16

On the income statement, $10,000 is debited to an operating expense account, and the corresponding credit is made to the common stock account and reported in the stockholders' equity section of the balance sheet. Given the nature of such a transaction, the cash account remains untouched.

Pause & Reflect

Exercise 15-1

On January 7, 2018, Ketona Corporation issued 4,000 shares of $1 par value common stock at $8 per share and 1,000 shares of $10 par value preferred stock at $25 per share. The next day on January 8, the corporation purchased land that was appraised at $400,000 by issuing 50,000 shares of common stock. Prepare the journal entries for the stock issuance.

JOURNAL			
Date	Account Title and Explanation	Debit	Credit

See Appendix I for solutions.

Accounting for Cash Dividends

Corporations are able to raise capital by offering several attractive investment options to potential investors. Investors are not only attracted by the potential for increased market value of their stock, but also by an opportunity to receive a portion of the company's profits in the form of dividends. Dividends are commonly paid annually, biannually and quarterly. There are no set calendar dates to pay dividends; it depends on each individual company's fiscal calendar. Corporations commonly issue two types of dividends: cash dividends and stock dividends. We will discuss cash dividends first, and stock dividends in a later section.

There are three important dates related to the accounting treatment of dividends:

- The **date of declaration** is the date on which the board of directors announces (declares) that dividends will be paid to stockholders.
- The **date of record** is the date on which the corporation lists all those who currently hold stock and are therefore eligible to receive dividend payments.
- The **date of payment** is the date on which the company actually makes the dividend payment to eligible stockholders.

Figure 15.17 demonstrates the time line of these dates and the related journal entries (in green) if a cash dividend is announced and paid.

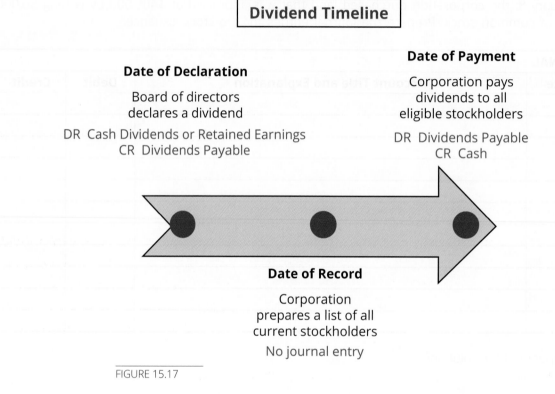

FIGURE 15.17

To illustrate the relationship between these three dates, suppose Zuti Corporation's board of directors declares a cash dividend on its common stock on March 31, 2018, and the dividend is to be paid on June 30, 2018. The board announces that all stockholders who hold common stock as of April 30, 2018 are eligible to receive the dividend. We would express this as follows: On March 31, 2018, Zuti Corporation declared a cash dividend to be distributed on June 30, 2018 to all stockholders of record as of April 30, 2018.

Next, we will examine Zuti Corporation's accounting responsibilities related to each of these dates.

A CLOSER LOOK

Before cash dividends can be paid, three important conditions must be met.

1. The board of directors must declare that a dividend will be paid.

2. The corporation must have enough cash to cover its ongoing operations and other obligations.

3. The corporation must have enough legal capital; that is, it must maintain enough assets to fulfill its obligations to creditors, and ensure that any dividend payments would not result in a deficit to retained earnings.

On the Date of Declaration

Suppose that Zuti Corporation's board of directors declares on March 31, 2018 that a dividend payment of $1 per share will be paid to stockholders of all 10,000 outstanding shares of common stock.

Although the dividends are not paid right away, the company must record the obligation to pay them on the date that the dividends are declared. The accounting entry for a dividend declaration can be done in one of two ways: using a cash dividends account, or using the retained earnings account.

Using the Cash Dividends Account

When the dividend is declared, a debit is made to a temporary account known as the cash dividends account, and a credit is made to the dividends payable account. The cash dividends account reduces the equity of the corporation and behaves like owner withdrawals in a sole proprietorship. It is used to accumulate all of the dividends declared for the period. Note that in the accounting records and financial statements, dividends must be divided between common stock and preferred stock. This example deals only with common stock.

Figure 15.18 shows the related accounting entry for Zuti Corporation. In this example, a debit of $10,000 is made to cash dividends. The debit to the cash dividends account eventually decreases the balance of retained earnings as part of the closing process on the balance sheet where retained earnings would be debited and the cash dividends would be credited at the end of the period. The credit appears on the balance sheet as an increase of $10,000 to the dividends payable account, which is considered a current liability; the dividend payment is accrued until the payment is finally made.

JOURNAL			
Date	**Account Title and Explanation**	**Debit**	**Credit**
Mar 31	Cash Dividends—Common	10,000	
	Dividends Payable		10,000
	To record declaration of cash dividend on 10,000 shares of common stock at $1 per share		

FIGURE 15.18

Using the Retained Earnings Account

Some companies choose an alternative method to record dividends on the date of declaration. Dividends eventually decrease the balance of retained earnings when the cash dividends account is closed to retained earnings at the end of the period. To save time and simplify their accounting entries, some companies choose to forego using the cash dividends account, and immediately debit the retained earnings account for the amount of the dividends. This method has the same effect on the balance sheet as the method that uses the cash dividends account. The related journal entry is shown in Figure 15.19.

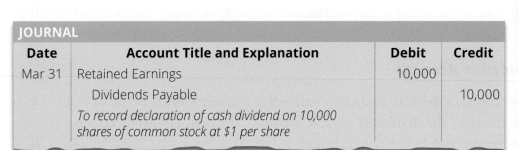

JOURNAL			
Date	**Account Title and Explanation**	**Debit**	**Credit**
Mar 31	Retained Earnings	10,000	
	Dividends Payable		10,000
	To record declaration of cash dividend on 10,000 shares of common stock at $1 per share		

FIGURE 15.19

Whichever method is used, this transaction does not involve the income statement. This is because dividend payments are not an operating expense, but a distribution of the corporation's earnings to its stockholders.

On the Date of Record

The date of record is the date on which the corporation determines who the existing stockholders are and how many shares each stockholder owns. The company must do this so that it knows who is eligible for the declared dividend payment.

No accounting entry is made for the date of record, but the corporation does keep detailed records of all stockholders. The person responsible for this is the corporate secretary, who is in charge of all official company documentation. Among other duties, the corporate secretary maintains the company's stock register, which is much like a subledger. Some large corporations use the services of a transfer agent to record changes in ownership of stock as a result of trading on the stock market.

On the Date of Payment

On the payment date, dividend payments are made to the stockholders by check or electronic transfer to their investment account at a financial institution. Using our previous example, assume that on June 30, 2018, Zuti Corporation pays the dividends that were declared on March 31, 2018. Figure 15.20 shows the related journal entry for this transaction.

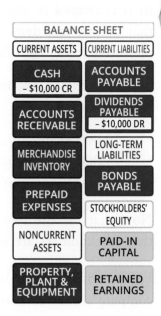

JOURNAL			
Date	**Account Title and Explanation**	**Debit**	**Credit**
Jun 30	Dividends Payable	10,000	
	Cash		10,000
	To record payment of cash dividend declared on March 31, 2018		

FIGURE 15.20

The debit to dividends payable decreases the current liability on the balance sheet. The credit to cash decreases the current assets on the balance sheet. Note that this accounting entry will be the same no matter which method—the cash dividends method or the retained earnings method—was used to record the dividend declaration. This is because both methods originally set up the liability as a credit to dividends payable.

Liquidating Dividends

In some states, the law allows a corporation to pay cash dividends using contributed capital. This type of cash dividend is known as a **liquidating dividend**, or *liquidating cash dividend*, because it returns some of the stockholders' original contributions to the stockholders. Liquidating dividends may (although rarely) be distributed if a corporation is downsizing its operations or preparing to close the business. The declaration of a liquidating dividend requires a journal entry to decrease (debit) paid-in capital and decrease (credit) the cash account. In such a case, the transaction does not affect the retained earnings account.

The preceding examples show the accounting entries for cash dividends on common stock. This was done to keep the examples easy to follow. The accounting entries are done in a similar manner if cash dividends were only paid out to preferred stockholders.

Dividends in Arrears

Cumulative preferred stock entitles stockholders to receive any unpaid dividends from prior periods—that is, dividends in arrears. Preferred stock without this cumulative feature is known as noncumulative stock. Noncumulative preferred stock does not accumulate unpaid dividends, and so it is treated in the accounting records much the same way as common stock. The discussion that follows will demonstrate the accounting treatment for all three types of stock: noncumulative preferred stock, cumulative preferred stock and common stock.

Suppose that on December 31, 2017, Yarind Corporation had the following capital stock on its balance sheet.

- 10,000 shares of cumulative preferred $2 stock at $6 par with a total book value of $60,000
- 25,000 shares of noncumulative preferred $2 stock at $4 par with a total book value of $100,000
- 100,000 shares of $1 par value common stock originally sold for a total price of $200,000

Note that for the two types of preferred shares, the $2 refers to the annual dividend per share that stockholders are entitled to receive when dividends are declared.

Figure 15.21 shows how the capital stock appears in the stockholders' equity section of the company's balance sheet on December 31, 2017.

Yarind Corporation Balance Sheet (partial) As at December 31, 2017	
Stockholders' Equity	
Paid-In Capital	
Preferred stock, $2 cumulative, $6 par value, 15,000 shares authorized, 10,000 shares issued and outstanding	$60,000
Preferred stock, $2 noncumulative, $4 par value, 30,000 shares authorized, 25,000 shares issued and outstanding	100,000
Common stock, $1 par value, unlimited shares authorized, 100,000 shares issued and outstanding	100,000
Additional Paid-In Capital	100,000
Total Paid-In Capital	360,000
Retained Earnings	500,000
Total Stockholders' Equity	860,000

FIGURE 15.21

Suppose that before the year 2018, Yarind Corporation paid dividends every year. However, during the year 2018, the company's board of directors neither declared nor paid any dividends. Then, on December 15, 2019, the board of directors declares $100,000 in dividends, payable on February 10, 2020 to the stockholders of record on December 31, 2019. No other dividends have been declared to date.

For the year ended December 31, 2018, dividends declared: $0
For the year ended December 31, 2019, dividends declared: $100,000

When dividends on cumulative preferred stock remain unpaid from prior periods, the corporation must keep track of the amount that is still owing to the cumulative preferred stockholders. This means the corporation owes the cumulative preferred stockholders a total of $40,000.

Dividends in arrears on cumulative preferred shares	
from 2018 ($2 × 10,000)	$20,000
Dividends on cumulative preferred shares for 2019 ($2 × 10,000)	20,000
Total cumulative preferred dividends	$40,000

For 2019, the corporation also owes the noncumulative preferred stockholders an amount equal to the dividends of 2019 only for a total of $50,000 ($2 × 25,000).

WORTH REPEATING

Dividends accumulate for cumulative preferred stock, regardless of whether or not cash dividends were actually declared for that year. When dividends are declared and paid out, the corporation must first determine how much it owes cumulative preferred stockholders for dividends in arrears.

After the preferred stockholders are paid, the remainder of the dividends are paid to the common stockholders, as follows.

Dividends declared (December 15, 2019)		$100,000
Payable on cumulative preferred shares (2018 and 2019)	$40,000	
Payable on noncumulative preferred shares (2019)	50,000	
Total preferred dividends payable		90,000
Remainder of dividends—payable to common stockholders		$10,000

The journal entry to record the declaration of dividends on December 15, 2019 is shown in Figure 15.22. This accounting entry shows the cash dividends method of accounting for the dividend declaration, but Yarind Corporation could also use the retained earnings method.

JOURNAL			
Date	**Account Title and Explanation**	**Debit**	**Credit**
Dec 15	Cash Dividends—Preferred, cumulative	40,000	
	Cash Dividends—Preferred, noncumulative	50,000	
	Cash Dividends—Common	10,000	
	Dividends Payable		100,000
	To record declaration of cash dividends on common and preferred shares		

FIGURE 15.22

The journal entry to record the subsequent payment of the dividends on February 10, 2020, and the effect on the balance sheet, is shown in Figure 15.23.

BALANCE SHEET	
CURRENT ASSETS	CURRENT LIABILITIES
CASH – $100,000 CR	ACCOUNTS PAYABLE
ACCOUNTS RECEIVABLE	DIVIDENDS PAYABLE – $100,000 DR
MERCHANDISE INVENTORY	LONG-TERM LIABILITIES
PREPAID EXPENSES	BONDS PAYABLE
NONCURRENT ASSETS	STOCKHOLDERS' EQUITY
PROPERTY, PLANT & EQUIPMENT	PAID-IN CAPITAL
	RETAINED EARNINGS

JOURNAL

Date	Account Title and Explanation	Debit	Credit
Feb 10	Dividends Payable	100,000	
	Cash		100,000
	To record payment of cash dividends declared		

FIGURE 15.23

As before, the payment reduces both the dividend liability and cash balances.

Pause & Reflect

Exercise 15-2

SP Inc. has the following reported in the stockholders' equity section of its balance sheet.

- Preferred stock, 10% cumulative, $40 par value, 20,000 shares authorized, 5,000 issued and outstanding
- Preferred stock, 20% noncumulative, $25 par value, 15,000 shares authorized, 10,000 issued and outstanding
- Common stock, unlimited shares authorized, 50,000 issued and outstanding

SP Inc. last paid dividends in 2016. In May 25, 2018, the board of directors declared $120,000 in cash dividends, to be distributed on July 15, 2018 to all stockholders of record on June 20, 2018. The company uses the cash dividends method to record dividends. Prepare the required journal entries.

JOURNAL

Date	Account Title and Explanation	Debit	Credit

See Appendix I for solutions.

Stock Splits and Stock Dividends

Among the advantages of the corporate form of organization is the right of a corporation to manage and reorganize its equity structure. For various reasons, a corporation's board of directors may decide to retain cash and, rather than declare a cash dividend, offer stockholders a different type of payment. This payment might be in the form of either a stock split or a stock dividend.

Stock Split

A **stock split** is an action that increases the number of a corporation's outstanding shares, which in turn decreases the individual price of each share traded on the stock market. For example, if a corporation declares a 2-for-1 stock split, it calls in all outstanding shares of existing stockholders, and exchanges each share for two shares. The stockholder now owns two shares for every one share previously held in the company; however, the value of each share is reduced by half. Stock splits can be done with any ratio that the corporation decides on, such as 3-for-1 or 4-for-1. Consider this example of a stock split.

Suppose that as of December 31, 2018, Standard Corporation has 10,000 shares of $5 par value common stock outstanding, and the stock is currently traded at $40 per share on the stock market. The book value of the common stock on the balance sheet is $50,000. On January 15, 2019, the company's board of directors declares a 2-for-1 stock split. The stock split results in twice as many shares (10,000 shares × 2 = 20,000 shares) and the par value has been cut in half to $2.50, but the book value remains the same at $50,000. Each stockholder now owns two shares for every one that they originally held, but the market responds by dropping the market value from $40 per share to $20 per share.

Figure 15.24 shows the effect on Standard Corporation's stockholders' equity if it declares a stock split. As shown, a stock split increases the number of common shares issued with no impact on the total stockholders' equity. The overall result is that there is no change in each stockholder's percentage ownership and the total values of both capital stock and stockholders' equity remain the same after the stock split.

Standard Corporation Balance Sheet (partial) December 31, 2018 (before stock split)		Standard Corporation Balance Sheet (partial) January 15, 2019 (after stock split)	
Stockholders' Equity		**Stockholders' Equity**	
Paid-In Capital		Paid-In Capital	
Common stock, $5 par value, unlimited shares authorized, 10,000 shares issued and outstanding	$50,000	Common stock, $2.50 par value, unlimited shares authorized, 20,000 shares issued and outstanding	$50,000
Additional Paid-In Capital	150,000	Additional Paid-In Capital	150,000
Total Paid-In Capital	200,000	Total Paid-In Capital	200,000
Retained Earnings	500,000	Retained Earnings	500,000
Total Stockholders' Equity	700,000	**Total Stockholders' Equity**	700,000

FIGURE 15.24

One of the main reasons for splitting shares is to increase their liquidity. If a stock price is too high on the stock market, some investors may feel the shares are too expensive or unaffordable. A lower stock price makes the shares attractive to more investors, which can potentially benefit all the investors. Because the total book value of the stock outstanding is not affected, no journal entry is needed to account for a stock split. A memorandum (note) is usually recorded to indicate the increased number of shares outstanding.

> **A CLOSER LOOK**
>
> A corporation can also do a stock split on preferred stock in addition to common stock. The increasing or decreasing of the amounts of preferred stock is handled the same as common stock. The difference is how the dividends for preferred stock are handled. Suppose a corporation is going to issue a 2-for-1 preferred stock split, and there are 20,000 preferred shares that currently pay $4 dividends. After the stock split, there will be 40,000 preferred shares that will pay $2 dividends. The preferred stock split has to be mentioned in the notes to the financial statements.

If a company wants to decrease its number of outstanding shares, it may decide to do a **reverse stock split**. In a 2-for-1 reverse stock split, each current stockholder receives one share for every two shares they held in the company; however, the market value of each share doubles.

Figure 15.25 shows the effect on Standard Corporation's stockholders' equity if it declares a reverse stock split. A reverse stock split reduces the number of common shares issued from 10,000 to 5,000. The par value increases from $5 per share to $10 per share. The market responds by increasing the market price from $40 per share to $80 per share. As with a regular stock split, there is zero overall effect on stockholders' equity and no change in each stockholder's percentage ownership. Reverse stock splits may be done when a company's stock price is becoming too low to be listed on a particular stock exchange.

Standard Corporation Balance Sheet (partial) December 31, 2018 (before reverse stock split)		Standard Corporation Balance Sheet (partial) January 15, 2019 (after reverse stock split)	
Stockholders' Equity		**Stockholders' Equity**	
Paid-In Capital		Paid-In Capital	
Common stock, $5 par value, unlimited shares authorized, 10,000 shares issued and outstanding	$50,000	Common stock, $10 par value, unlimited shares authorized, 5,000 shares issued and outstanding	$50,000
Additional Paid-In Capital	150,000	Additional Paid-In Capital	150,000
Total Paid-In Capital	200,000	Total Paid-In Capital	200,000
Retained Earnings	500,000	Retained Earnings	500,000
Total Stockholders' Equity	700,000	**Total Stockholders' Equity**	700,000

FIGURE 15.25

Stock Dividend

A **stock dividend** may be issued in lieu of a cash dividend for several reasons. First, a company may wish to retain its cash in order to expand the business, which eventually increases the value for stockholders. Another reason is to keep the share price affordable for new investors; the company can increase the number of outstanding shares to reduce the market price per share. A stock dividend can also satisfy investors with a dividend, even though cash will not be paid. Stock dividends are normally issued to common stockholders only.

The accounting for a stock dividend depends upon its classification. There are two classifications of stock dividends.

- A **small stock dividend** is one that distributes additional shares equal to 25% *or less* of currently outstanding shares at the date of declaration. Small stock dividends are recorded at market value.

- A **large stock dividend** is one that distributes additional shares equal to *more than* 25% of currently outstanding shares at the date of declaration. Large stock dividends are recorded at par or stated value.

To demonstrate a stock dividend, return to Standard Corporation. Figure 15.26 shows the stockholders' equity section of the company's balance sheet before the stock dividend is declared. On December 31, 2018, Standard Corporation has 10,000 outstanding common shares. The current market price is $40 per share. Note that the balance of the additional paid-in capital is $150,000, which shows that the original market price of the common stock was $20 per share at the time of issuance (($20 - $5) × 10,000 shares).

Standard Corporation Balance Sheet (partial) As at December 31, 2018 (before stock dividend)	
Stockholders' Equity	
Paid-In Capital	
Common stock, $5 par value, unlimited shares authorized,	
10,000 shares issued and outstanding	$50,000
Additional Paid-in Capital	150,000
Total Paid-In Capital	200,000
Retained Earnings	500,000
Total Stockholders' Equity	700,000

FIGURE 15.26

Small Stock Dividend

On January 15, 2019, the company's board of directors decides to declare a 20% stock dividend on all 10,000 outstanding shares, which classifies this as a small stock dividend. The transaction is therefore recorded at market value on the date of declaration. The dividend is to be distributed on February 20, 2019 to all stockholders of record as of January 31, 2019. The value of the stock in this stock dividend, assuming the market price on the date of declaration is $40 per share, is calculated as shown below.

Total number of outstanding common shares = 10,000

20% stock dividend on 10,000 shares = 10,000 × 0.20 = 2,000 shares

2,000 shares at the par value of $5 per share = 2000 × $5 = $10,000

2,000 shares at a current market price of $40 per share = 2,000 × $40 = $80,000

The journal entry to record a small stock dividend is similar to the journal entry to record stock issuance, except that the retained earnings account is debited instead of the cash account. Figure 15.27 shows the journal entry to record the declaration of the stock dividend.

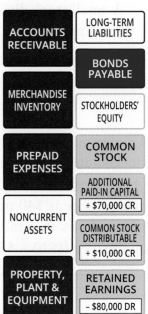

JOURNAL			
Date	Account Title and Explanation	Debit	Credit
Jan 15	Retained Earnings	80,000	
	Common Stock Dividends Distributable		10,000
	Paid-In Capital in Excess of Par, Common Stock		70,000
	To record declaration of 20% common stock dividends		

FIGURE 15.27

The Retained Earnings account is debited at the total market value of stock to be distributed as dividends. The Common Stock Dividends Distributable account is credited for the par value of the stock to be distributed as dividends. The Paid-In Capital in Excess of Par, Common Stock account is credited for the excess of market value over par value.

Stock dividends distributable is an equity account, not a liability, but it is used in a similar way that the dividends payable account is used for cash dividends. It keeps track of the amount that will be distributed to the stockholders. The end result of a stock dividend is a rearrangement of the components of stockholders' equity; some of the value of retained earnings is shifted to the common stock account. Stock dividends are never considered a liability, because the company does not actually owe stockholders a stock dividend.

Figure 15.28 shows the journal entry to record the distribution of the stock dividend on February 20, 2019, and the effect on the stockholders' equity section of the balance sheet. The Common

Stock Dividends Distributable account is debited and the Common Stock account is credited at the par value of the common stock dividends distributed.

JOURNAL			
Date	**Account Title and Explanation**	**Debit**	**Credit**
Feb 20	Common Stock Dividends Distributable	10,000	
	Common Stock		10,000
	To record distribution of 20% stock dividends on common stock		

FIGURE 15.28

This distribution of the stock dividend completes the transfer of part of retained earnings to the value of common stock. Figure 15.29 shows the stockholders' equity section of the balance sheet for Standard Corporation before the stock dividend was declared and after the stock dividend was distributed. Notice that total stockholders' equity has not changed, just the values of retained earnings, common stock and the number of common shares issued and outstanding.

Standard Corporation Balance Sheet (partial) December 31, 2018 (before stock dividend)		Standard Corporation Balance Sheet (partial) February 20, 2019 (after stock dividend)	
Stockholders' Equity		**Stockholders' Equity**	
Paid-In Capital		Paid-In Capital	
Common stock, $5 par value, unlimited shares authorized, 10,000 shares issued and outstanding	$50,000	Common stock, $5 par value, unlimited shares authorized, 12,000 shares issued and outstanding	$60,000
Additional Paid-In Capital	150,000	Additional Paid-In Capital	220,000
Total Paid-In Capital	200,000	Total Paid-In Capital	280,000
Retained Earnings	500,000	Retained Earnings	420,000
Total Stockholders' Equity	700,000	**Total Stockholders' Equity**	700,000

FIGURE 15.29

Large Stock Dividend

When a company declares a stock dividend that is more than 25%, it is considered a large stock dividend. Large stock dividends are recorded at the par value of the stock being distributed as dividend.

To illustrate, assume that on January 15, 2019, Standard Corporation's board of directors decides to declare a 40% stock dividend instead of the 20% stock dividend in the previous example. The par value of the stock being distributed as dividend is calculated as shown below.

Total number of outstanding common shares = 10,000

40% stock dividend on 10,000 shares = 10,000 × 0.40 = 4,000 shares

4,000 shares at the par value of $5 per share = 4,000 × $5 = $20,000

The journal entry to record the declaration of the stock dividend on January 15 is shown in Figure 15.30. Because large stock dividend is recorded at par value, the Paid-In Capital in Excess of Par, Common Stock account is not affected.

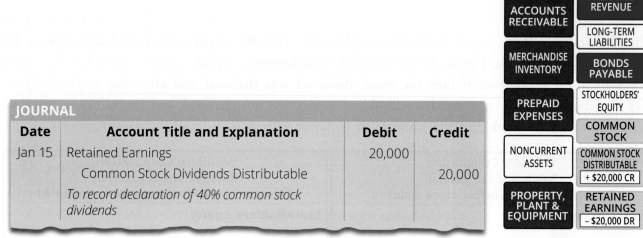

JOURNAL			
Date	Account Title and Explanation	Debit	Credit
Jan 15	Retained Earnings	20,000	
	Common Stock Dividends Distributable		20,000
	To record declaration of 40% common stock dividends		

FIGURE 15.30

When stock dividend is distributed on February 20, the company makes a journal entry that is similar to what was shown in Figure 15.28. The Common Stock Dividends Distributable account is debited for $20,000 and the Common Stock account is credited for $20,000.

All of the above transactions illustrate how public corporations account for issuing stock and recording dividends. For private corporations, issuing stock is recorded in the same manner. However, the recording and payment of dividends is usually less formal for private corporations because the stock is not publicly traded and the list of stockholders is usually quite short. Figure 15.31 shows the impact of cash dividends, stock dividends and stock splits.

	Common Stock		Retained Earnings	Stockholders' Equity	Assets
	Value	**Quantity**			
Cash Dividend	No Change	No Change	Decrease	Decrease	Decrease[(1)]
Stock Dividend	Increase	Increase	Decrease	No Change	No Change
Stock Split	No Change[(2)]	Increase	No Change	No Change	No Change
Reverse Stock Split	No Change[(3)]	Decrease	No Change	No Change	No Change

[(1)] Cash is reduced only when the declared cash dividend is paid out.

[(2)] For a stock split, the par value per share and market value per share decrease, but the book value of the shares remains the same.

[(3)] For a reverse stock split, the par value per share and market value per share increase, but the book value of the shares remains the same.

FIGURE 15.31

Restrictions on the Use of Retained Earnings

Sometimes a company's board of directors places restrictions on the use of retained earnings for the payment of dividends. *Restricted retained earnings* can be of several types.

- *Statutory restrictions* are those required by state law. One example is limiting the amount of dividends to the amount of retained earnings minus the cost of treasury stock currently held by the company so that legal capital is not used to pay dividends.

- *Contractual restrictions* are those limited by legal contracts. A common example is a loan agreement that requires the company to restrict retained earnings so that money is available to repay the loan, rather than to pay out dividends.

- *Discretionary restrictions* are those voluntarily imposed by the company's board of directors. Such restrictions may be put in place so that retained earnings can be used to expand the company rather than pay out dividends.

Restrictions on retained earnings must be disclosed in the notes to the financial statements.

IN THE REAL WORLD

 In a stock split, a corporation divides its existing outstanding shares into multiple shares. You may often see news of a company offering a 2-for-1 stock split, or perhaps a 3-for-1 stock split. The result is an increase in the number of shares outstanding by double (2-for-1) or triple (3-for-1).

Starbucks' Corporation (NASDAQ: SBUX), one of the world's leading specialty coffee retailers, has a long history of declaring stock splits. Since 1993, the company has offered six 2-for-1 stock splits on its common shares—the most recent of which was announced in March 2015. The 2-for-1 stock split reduced the company's stock from a then-current $94 per share (which was becoming too high for many investors) to a much more attractive price of about $47 per share. This also means that if you purchased 100 shares of Starbucks' stock in 1992 and held onto your shares until March 18, 2015, you would have 6,400 shares, a 160-fold increase in your holdings.

At the other end of the spectrum, Berskhire Hathaway, Inc. (NYSE: BRK.A)—a diverse company headed by investor Warren Buffett, with holdings in a wide variety of businesses including insurance, energy, transportation, manufacturing and retailing—has never offered a stock split. As of late 2016, Berkshire's stock was priced at over $200,000 per share.

Pause & Reflect

Exercise 15-3

StraightLine Industries has 400,000, $3 par value common shares issued and outstanding, worth $1,200,000 in its books. Retained earnings has a value of $5,600,000. StraightLine is planning to issue a 2-for-1 stock split when the market price is $80 per share.

a) After completing the stock split, what will be the impact on the quantity and value of the common stock in the books?

_____

_____

b) What will be the impact on retained earnings?

_____

_____

c) What will be the impact on the stock price and its par value?

_____

_____

See Appendix I for solutions.

Treasury Stock

LO 7

In addition to issuing stock, a corporation can also buy back its own stock from stockholders, which then becomes **treasury stock**. Treasury stock has no voting rights and does not receive any dividends. It can be held by the corporation indefinitely, reissued to the public, or canceled.

The reacquisition of stock may take place for a number of different reasons. For example, a corporation may purchase its stock to reduce the number of shares outstanding, hence increasing the stock's market price. A company may also purchase its own stock to create a larger trading volume in the stock market, which may attract interest in its stock. When they have enough cash on hand, some corporations may also reacquire stock to pay it to employees in the form of bonuses, to give back cash to stockholders or to remove a specific group of stockholders.

There are two allowable methods of accounting for treasury stock under US GAAP: the cost method, and the par value method. The cost method of accounting for treasury stock is shown in this chapter. The par value method is covered in advanced courses.

Both the purchase and resale of treasury stock are most commonly accounted for using the cost method. According to the cost method, the treasury stock account is debited for the cost (or original purchase price) of the stock. When the stock is reissued, the treasury stock account is credited for the cost. Any difference between the cost and the selling price of the stock is adjusted to either the Retained Earnings account or the account called Paid-In Capital, Treasury Stock. We will look at examples for each of these situations.

Purchasing Treasury Stock

Assume that on January 15, 2018, a corporation bought back 1,000 shares of its own stock at a price of $25 per share. The journal entry to record the purchase based on the cost method is shown in Figure 15.32.

JOURNAL			
Date	**Account Title and Explanation**	**Debit**	**Credit**
Jan 15	Treasury Stock	25,000	
	Cash		25,000
	Purchased 1,000 shares of the corporation's own common stock at $25 per share		

FIGURE 15.32

Treasury stock is not reported as an asset on the balance sheet but is instead deducted from the stockholders' equity section as shown in Figure 15.33.

Paid-In Capital	
Common stock, $10 par value 1,000,000 shares authorized, 40,000 shares issued, 39,000 shares outstanding	$400,000
Additional Paid-In Capital	815,000
Retained Earnings, $25,000 restricted by purchase of treasury stock	875,000
Less: Treasury Stock (1,000 shares at cost)	25,000
Total Stockholders' Equity	2,065,000

FIGURE 15.33

The purchase of treasury stock has decreased total stockholders' equity (and the balance of the cash account) by $25,000, but it has not affected the common stock account or the balance of retained earnings. However, notice in Figure 15.33 that the stockholders' equity section discloses two important pieces of information: (1) that 39,000 shares are outstanding, indicating that 1,000 of the 40,000 issued shares are now in the treasury; and (2) that retained earnings is now restricted by the amount of the treasury stock purchase, $25,000 (as discussed in the section on stock splits and stock dividends).

Reissuing Treasury Stock

As mentioned, shares held as treasury stock can be reissued at a later date. Treasury stock can be reissued (sold) *at cost*, *above cost*, or *below cost*. If the stock is sold at cost (i.e. at $25 per share in the above example), the journal entry is a straightforward increase (debit) to cash, and an increase (credit) to treasury stock for the same amount. The accounting is different when the stock is sold either above or below cost. We will look at these two situations in more detail.

Selling Above Cost

Recall that the corporation bought back 1,000 shares of its own stock at $25 per share. On April 30, the corporation reissued 500 shares of its treasury stock for $27 per share, for total proceeds of $13,500. Even though the shares were reissued for $2 more per share than they were originally purchased, no gain is recorded since a corporation cannot earn revenue by selling its own stock. Instead, the stockholders' equity account called Paid-In Capital, Treasury Stock, is credited for the excess. Figure 15.34 shows the journal entry to record the reissuance of the stock.

JOURNAL			
Date	**Account Title and Explanation**	**Debit**	**Credit**
Apr 30	Cash	13,500	
	Treasury Stock		12,500
	Paid-In Capital, Treasury Stock		1,000
	Sold 500 shares of treasury stock for $27 per share		

FIGURE 15.34

Assuming that the paid-in capital account has a beginning balance of zero, the surplus of $1,000 is presented under paid-in capital in the stockholders' equity section of the balance sheet.

Selling Below Cost

Now, let us assume the remaining treasury stock is reissued on June 7, 2018 for $21 per share, for total proceeds of $10,500. As with gains, the corporation is not allowed to record a loss on the sale of treasury stock; therefore, the difference is first debited to clear out any balance in the Paid-In Capital, Treasury Stock account and then, if needed, retained earnings is debited for any amount in excess of the balance. Due to the earlier sale of treasury stock above cost, the Paid-In Capital, Treasury Stock account has a credit balance of $1,000, which is insufficient to absorb the entire difference of $2,000. The paid-in capital account is therefore debited for $1,000, and the remaining balance of $1,000 is debited to retained earnings. The entry to record this sale is shown in Figure 15.35.

JOURNAL			
Date	**Account Title and Explanation**	**Debit**	**Credit**
Jun 7	Cash	10,500	
	Paid-In Capital, Treasury Stock	1,000	
	Retained Earnings	1,000	
	Treasury Stock		12,500
	Sold 500 shares of treasury stock for $21 per share		

FIGURE 15.35

Retiring Treasury Stock

When a company purchases treasury stock, it can choose to later resell the stock or retire it permanently. Retirement of treasury stock decreases the number of issued shares. In other words, retired treasury stock is the same as stock that has been authorized but unissued. Under state law, corporations can purchase treasury stock and retire it if approved by the board of directors, and if the retirement does not adversely affect stockholders' and creditors' interests.

To illustrate, assume a company's board of directors authorizes the retirement of 2,000 shares of treasury stock on April 30 that were originally purchased at a cost of $25 per share. The par value of common stock was $15 per share and the common stock was originally issued at $20 per share.

The company must record the retirement by removing any capital amounts related to the retired shares. When the 2,000 shares are retired, the common stock account is decreased (debited) by $30,000 (2,000 shares × $15 par value). The $5 excess amount paid ($20 – $15) on the initial issue of the shares must be removed from the paid-in capital in excess of par account. This amount is $10,000 (2,000 shares × $5). According to the cost method, the treasury stock account is decreased (credited) for the original cost of the reacquisition, $50,000 (2,000 shares × $25 per share). Since the treasury stock was purchased as a price greater than the issuance price, the excess will reduce retained earnings. This amount is $10,000 ($50,000 – $30,000 – $10,000). The journal entry for the retirement of the 2,000 shares under the cost method is shown in Figure 15.36.

JOURNAL			
Date	**Account Title and Explanation**	**Debit**	**Credit**
Apr 30	Common Stock	30,000	
	Paid-In Capital in Excess of Par, Common Stock	10,000	
	Retained Earnings	10,000	
	Treasury Stock		50,000
	To retire 2,000 shares of treasury stock		

FIGURE 15.36

Income Tax Expense and Liabilities

Unlike a sole proprietorship or partnership, a corporation is considered a separate legal entity from its owners. A corporation must therefore file and pay taxes on its net income; the amount that the corporation is obligated to pay is known as **income tax**. Federal income tax laws require that income tax be paid quarterly. A corporation must estimate its income tax liability based on the income earned, and record the liability periodically. This amount is then recorded as its income tax expense, and its income tax payable.

Recording Income Tax Liabilities

Suppose that Star Company prepares financial statements on a monthly basis. For the month ended January 31, 2018, Star Company reported a net income before tax of $266,000. Assume the company is subject to income tax at a rate of 30% on its net income for the period. Based on the net income according to its accounting records, Star Company would record an estimated income tax expense of $79,800 ($266,000 × 30%) for the month ended January 31, 2018. Figure 15.37 shows the recorded transaction, and the effects on the balance sheet and income statement.

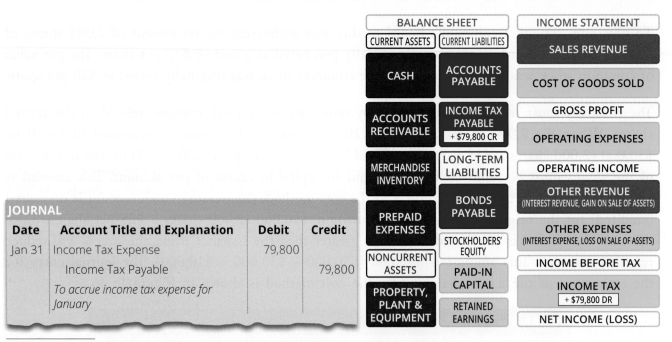

FIGURE 15.37

Note that the transaction is recorded with an increase to an expense and an increase to a liability. A similar tax liability is recorded at the end of each month until the next quarterly tax installment is paid to the government.

Assume that by March 31, 2018, Star Company has recorded the following monthly estimated income tax expenses and the corresponding liabilities for the first quarter (of the calendar year).

January 31, 2018, estimated tax expense/liability, based on net income of $266,000		$79,800
February 28, 2018, estimated tax expense/liability, based on net income of $285,000		$85,500
March 31, 2018, estimated tax expense/liability, based on net income of $225,000		$67,500
Total estimated income tax expense/liability for first quarter		$232,800

When the company pays its quarterly income tax installment to the government on April 1, 2018, it makes the journal entry shown in Figure 15.38.

JOURNAL

Date	Account Title and Explanation	Debit	Credit
Apr 1	Income Tax Payable	232,800	
	Cash		232,800
	To pay estimated income taxes based on first quarter 2018 income		

FIGURE 15.38

This procedure is repeated throughout the year until the company's year-end financial statements have been prepared and the actual amount of income tax payable is known. This allows the company to record any necessary adjustments during the fourth quarter so that the actual amount of income tax expense equals the amount paid to the government.

Deferred Income Tax Liabilities

There is a difference between the way that GAAP and the income tax laws measure and calculate taxable income. This can lead to different amounts of tax being calculated based on which income figures are used, and explains why the amount of income before taxes reported on a company's income statement often differs from the income reported on its income tax return.

Some of these differences between GAAP and the tax laws are simply timing differences, which are known as *temporary differences*. Timing differences occur when a revenue, or an expense such as depreciation, is based on a different calculation for GAAP than it is for tax purposes. If the income tax expense reported on the company's income statement under GAAP is higher than the income tax payable reported on its income tax return, this difference is known as a **deferred income tax liability**.

For example, suppose that Star Company estimates and records a fourth-quarter income tax expense of $250,000. However, when it determines that the actual amount of income tax due for this period is $245,500, the corporation records the difference of $4,500 as a deferred income tax liability, as shown in Figure 15.39.

JOURNAL			
Date	**Account Title and Explanation**	**Debit**	**Credit**
Dec 31	Income Tax Expense	250,000	
	Income Tax Payable		245,500
	Deferred Income Tax Liability		4,500
	To record income tax expense and deferred income tax liability		

FIGURE 15.39

This journal entry records the income tax payment to be deferred to a future year, when the temporary difference is reversed. A difference might also arise from the payment of an income tax amount before it has been reported on the income statement. In this case, the difference is recorded as a debit to a balance sheet account known as Deferred Income Tax Asset.

Income tax expense is one of the many things covered in this chapter that affects stockholders' equity, particularly retained earnings. The formula for calculating retained earnings is shown in Figure 15.40.

Ending Retained Earnings = Beginning Retained Earnings + Net Income – Dividends

FIGURE 15.40

The changes in the balance of retained earnings are outlined in a corporation's statement of retained earnings, which is illustrated in Chapter 16.

An Ethical Approach to Corporations and Insider Trading

One of the most important ethical principles for all businesses, large or small, is the need to maintain the integrity of information released publicly, which is why insider trading is considered one of the worst violations at the corporate level.

The stock market can be unpredictable at the best of times. Market trends can fluctuate, speculation can run rampant, and even the most informed investors can have a difficult time making the right decisions.

Nevertheless, one of the basic foundations of the stock market is fair and public access to all company-related information; if current or potential stockholders have a right to information about a company, then it should be disclosed to the public in a timely fashion. **Insider trading** occurs when anyone who has access to the company's private information uses such information to trade in the stock market for one's own gain before the information is released publicly.

For example, imagine that a secretary in a company overhears information about an upcoming announcement of better-than-expected company earnings for the year. The secretary passes on this confidential information to a close friend. Knowing that the announcement will increase the price, the friend buys a large quantity of stock and even tells a few more friends, who also purchase the stock.

By the time the announcement is finally made, the price of the stock increases dramatically, and the friends who bought stock before the announcement make a substantial amount of money. This, of course, is highly illegal. Everyone involved, including the secretary and the friends, should be charged with insider trading. The crime is very serious and comes with some harsh penalties.

The purpose of insider trading laws is to give everyone the same amount of information at the same time, and a fair chance to make profits on the stock market. That is why securities regulators go to great lengths to detect the spread of information by way of insider activity. As tempting as it might be to act on private company information before anyone else knows, doing so violates the principle of fairness and openness that exists in world markets. Anything less threatens the way that capitalism and free markets should work.

IN THE REAL WORLD

 Celebrity homemaking and insider trading are two concepts that do not often come to mind at the same time. However, Martha Stewart rose to fame and fortune by way of the stock market. In the late 1990s, she took Martha Stewart Living Omnimedia Inc. public and made a fortune on the subsequent rise of the company's stock.

Stewart's success with the stock market, however, started to unravel in late 2001 with events surrounding the stock of a company called ImClone, a biopharmaceutical corporation. During that period, ImClone stock took a tumble as a result of regulatory procedures that were detrimental to the company. Records show that Stewart sold almost 4,000 shares in the company, making her a gain of $229,000, shortly before public disclosure about the regulations.

It appears that Stewart was good friends with Samuel Waksel, the CEO of ImClone. Investigations revealed that Stewart was advised by her stockbroker to sell her stock, based on information he was privy to regarding Waksel. The situation was a clear case of insider trading.

As is often the case with insider trading, however, it is very hard to prove who knew what and when. The investigators therefore focused on the cover-up, and discovered that Stewart had deceived investigators numerous times as they tried to gather information on insider activity in this case. In July of 2004, she was found guilty of obstructing justice and served a five-month prison sentence.

In Summary

LO 1 Describe the characteristics of corporations

▶ A corporation is a legal entity that is separate from its owners, known as stockholders.

▶ Some characteristics of corporations include limited liability of stockholders, formal organizational structure, unlimited life and the ability to raise capital.

LO 2 Describe differences between public and private corporations

▶ Public corporations sell a portion of their stock to the public through stock markets. Private corporations do not sell their stock to the public.

▶ Public corporations that are registered with the SEC must use GAAP. A private corporation not registered with the SEC may use GAAP or IFRS.

LO 3 Explain stockholders' equity

▶ Stockholders' equity is made up of two components: paid-in capital and retained earnings.

▶ Paid-in capital generally consists of two sub-categories, called capital stock and additional paid-in capital.

▶ There are two types of capital stock: common stock and preferred stock.

▶ Common stock constitutes ownership in the company, but does not come with guaranteed dividend payments.

▶ Preferred stock does not come with voting rights, but generally does come with regular dividend payments and a higher claim to company assets than common stock.

▶ Par value stock is stock that is issued with an assigned value. No-par value stock is stock issued with no assigned value. Some states require no-par value stock to have a stated value, which has the same purpose as the par value.

▶ The par value dictates the minimum amount of assets that stockholders are legally required to contribute to the company. This amount is known as the minimum legal capital.

▶ Retained earnings are the earnings that are kept and accumulated by the company after dividends have been paid to the stockholders.

LO 4 Record the issuance of stock

▶ A company can issue stock in exchange for cash, assets owned or services rendered.

▶ Issuing stock in exchange for noncash assets or services must be recorded at the fair value of the assets or services received. If the fair value of assets or services cannot be determined, then the transaction is recorded at the fair value of the stock being exchanged.

▶ When the stock is sold for a higher price than its par value, it is sold at a premium. The common stock (or preferred stock) account is credited for the par amount of the stock. The excess amount received is credited to Paid-In Capital in Excess of Par.

▶ If no-par value stock is issued, the common stock (or preferred stock) account is credited for the entire proceeds of the sale.

LO 5   Record the payment of cash dividends

- ▶ There are three important dates related to the accounting treatment of dividends: the date of declaration, the date of record and the date of payment.

- ▶ The accounting entry for a dividend declaration can be made in one of two ways: using a cash dividends account, or using the retained earnings account.

- ▶ A cash dividend paid from the stockholders' original contributed capital is known as a liquidating dividend.

- ▶ The declared dividends must first go to preferred stockholders, including both the current year's dividends and dividends in arrears. Then, the remaining amount goes to common stockholders.

LO 6   Record stock splits and stock dividends

- ▶ A stock split is a corporate action that increases the number of a corporation's outstanding shares, which in turn decreases the individual price of each share. No journal entry is required for a stock split.

- ▶ A stock dividend may be issued in lieu of a cash dividend if a company wants to retain its cash in order to expand the business, or to keep the share price affordable for new investors.

- ▶ A stock dividend of 25% or less of current outstanding shares is considered a small stock dividend and is recorded at market value. A stock dividend of more than 25% of current outstanding shares is considered a large stock dividend and is recorded at par or stated value.

LO 7   Record treasury of stock

- ▶ The reacquisition of stock means that a corporation buys back its own stock from stockholders. The reacquired stock, known as treasury stock, can be held for an indefinite period of time, reissued (sold) or retired permanently.

- ▶ A corporation reacquires its stock for a number of different reasons, including reducing the number of shares outstanding, increasing share market price or giving back cash to stockholders.

- ▶ Treasury stock can be resold at cost, below cost or above cost. Both the purchase and resale of treasury stock are most commonly accounted for using the cost method.

- ▶ According to the cost method, the treasury stock account is debited for the cost (or original purchase price) of the stock. When the stock is reissued, the treasury stock account is credited for the cost. Any difference between the cost and the selling price of the stock is adjusted.

LO 8   Record income tax expense

- ▶ A corporation must file and pay taxes on its net income; the amount that the corporation is obligated to pay is known as income tax.

- ▶ Income tax expense is recorded in a corporation's accounting records periodically on an accrual basis.

LO 9   Explain the importance of ethics for corporate reporting

- ▶ Insider trading laws enforce the principle that everyone is given the same amount of information at the same time, and a fair chance to make profits on the stock market.

 *Access **ameengage.com** for integrated resources including tutorials, practice exercises, the digital textbook and more.*

Review Exercise 15-1

Marcel Campos and Felicity Feisthamel have operated their company as a general partnership for several years. Over the years the company has grown, and the partners believe it is appropriate to incorporate their company as Camphamel Inc., a publicly traded company, and raise more capital to expand.

Accordingly, Marcel and Felicity engaged a qualified bookkeeper to provide accounting services for their new corporation. The corporate charter authorized the company to issue an unlimited number of $1 par value common shares and 200,000, 30%, $10 par value noncumulative preferred shares. On March 3, 2018, the partners transferred assets worth $2,000,000 and liabilities worth $1,250,000 to the company in exchange for 20,000, $1 par value common shares.

Then, Marcel and Felicity sought investment capital from investors. On April 15, 2018, a group of investors agreed to buy an additional 20,000 shares of common stock for $1,000,000 cash.

Instead of paying the accountant $100,000 of fees in cash, Marcel and Felicity gave her 10,000, 30%, $10 par value noncumulative preferred shares on April 30, 2018. The corporation cannot readily determine the fair value of the preferred shares.

To inject more capital into the business, on May 10, 2018, the company issued 5,000 additional shares of common stock at their current market value of $50 each in exchange for equipment. The fair value of the equipment cannot be readily determined.

On September 15, 2018, the company declared a 5% stock dividend on all the common shares outstanding. The market value of each common share was $60 on this date. (For this transaction, use the retained earnings account to record the journal entry.) The stock dividend was later distributed to stockholders on October 2, 2018.

On October 7, the corporation bought back 1,000 shares of its own common stock at a price of $55 per share.

At the directors' meeting on October 15, 2018, Marcel, Felicity, and a director appointed by the stockholders decided to pay cash dividends of $180,000 to preferred and common stockholders of record on November 30, 2018. (For this transaction, use the cash dividends account to record the journal entry.) The cash dividend is paid on December 15, 2018.

On December 20, the corporation reissued 500 shares of its treasury stock at a price of $53 per share.

On December 31, the company estimated and recorded an accrual-based income tax expense of $320,000. However, based on the income tax form to the government, the actual amount of income tax due to be paid at the beginning of next year is $290,000. For the year ended December 31, 2018, the newly incorporated company made a net income (after deducting income tax expenses) of $900,000.

Required

a) Record the required journal entries for 2018 and 2019.

JOURNAL			
Date	**Account Title and Explanation**	**Debit**	**Credit**

JOURNAL			
Date	Account Title and Explanation	Debit	Credit

b) Prepare the stockholders' equity section of the balance sheet as at December 31, 2018.

See Appendix I for solutions.

Chapter 16
Corporations: The Financial Statements

Learning Objectives

LO 1 Explain the different requirements under US GAAP and IFRS when presenting financial statements

LO 2 Prepare an income statement and a statement of comprehensive income
- US GAAP
- IFRS

LO 3 Prepare a statement of retained earnings and a statement of changes in equity
- US GAAP
- IFRS

LO 4 Record and report on prior period adjustments
- Correction of Prior Period Errors

LO 5 Prepare a balance sheet and a statement of financial position
- US GAAP
- IFRS

LO 6 Calculate and explain earnings per share

LO 7 Calculate ratios used to evaluate earnings and dividend performance
- Book Value per Common Share
- Dividend Yield
- Price-Earnings Ratio

AMEENGAGE™ *Access **ameengage.com** for integrated resources including tutorials, practice exercises, the digital textbook and more.*

601

Preparation of Financial Statements

In the news, you may come across articles about large companies, such as Google or Microsoft, releasing their quarterly or annual reports. These companies are presenting their financial performances for the last period. Most stock exchanges require public companies to prepare financial statements every three months in addition to their annual reports.

You have already learned how to prepare financial statements for a sole proprietorship and partnership. The logic behind preparing statements for a corporation is the same, although these statements are generally more complex than those of a sole proprietorship. Corporations have access to more sources of financing, so the debt and equity sections of the balance sheet may appear to be quite different. Additionally, a corporation may offer more diverse products and services, which can make the income statement more complex.

One reason for the complexity is because a corporation's financial statements serve a much wider audience group. While a sole proprietorship may have a few financial statement users, a corporation can have hundreds or thousands of financial statement users. Corporation ownership is determined by stock, so all stockholders are users of the financial statements. Also, a public corporation has potential investors—that is, potential stockholders—who may purchase the corporation's stock. These investors are also users of the financial information. Users of a corporation's financial statements want different financial information for different purposes, so the corporation is subject to more complex disclosure requirements.

This chapter illustrates how a corporation's financial statements can be prepared to satisfy disclosure requirements. Financial disclosure requirements for a corporation can be found in US Generally Accepted Accounting Principles (US GAAP) and International Financial Reporting Standards (IFRS). As explained in previous chapters, public companies are required to use US GAAP in preparing their financial statements. However, as the economy is becoming more globalized and an increasing number of companies around the world are adopting IFRS, it is important to understand IFRS statements in addition to US GAAP statements.

US GAAP requires disclosure for the current year and prior two years for the income statement, statement of cash flows and statement of retained earnings, while IFRS requires disclosure for the current year and the prior year. Disclosure of accounting policies includes the description of accounting principles and methods used by the reporting company, and the basis for any significant judgments that have been used in preparing the statements.

As we progress through this chapter, we will prepare two sets of financial statements for a fictitious public company, Darma Corporation. The first set of financial statements presented in each section will be prepared according to US GAAP. The second set of financial statements in each section will be prepared according to IFRS.

Figure 16.1 shows the adjusted trial balance for Darma Corporation, as at its year end, December 31, 2018. All financial statements prepared in this chapter will use figures from this trial balance; however, terms may differ depending on if US GAAP or IFRS is used.

Darma Corporation Adjusted Trial Balance December 31, 2018		
Account Title	**Debit**	**Credit**
Cash and Cash Equivalents	$87,650	
Trading Investments (at Cost)	278,880	
Valuation Allowance for Trading Investments	8,700	
Accounts Receivable	685,725	
Merchandise Inventory	1,652,840	
Prepaid Expenses	16,840	
Property, Plant and Equipment	5,174,000	
Accumulated Depreciation		$1,967,260
Goodwill	777,185	
Accounts Payable		556,890
Salaries Payable		15,845
Notes Payable*		612,620
Deferred Tax Liabilities		24,800
Common Stock		1,000,000
Additional Paid-In Capital		3,000,000
Treasury Stock	100,000	
Retained Earnings		1,340,000
Cash Dividends	400,000	
Sales Revenue		2,505,750
Sales Discounts	1,200	
Sales Returns & Allowances	3,800	
Gain on Sale of Assets		4,500
Foreign Currency Translation Adjustments		5,200
Unrealized Gain on Trading Investments		8,700
Income from Operating Discontinued Operations		125,000
Gain on Sale of Discontinued Operations		45,000
Cost of Goods Sold	1,100,000	
Interest Expense	21,000	
Sales Salaries Expense	150,000	
Office Salaries Expense	125,000	
Depreciation Expense—Store Equipment	23,000	
Depreciation Expense—Office Equipment	21,000	
Advertising Expense	230,000	
Miscellaneous Administrative Expenses	70,000	
Income Tax Expense	284,745	
Total	**$11,211,565**	**$11,211,565**

*Notes payable balance consists of current and noncurrent portions of $43,870 and $568,750, respectively.

FIGURE 16.1

Income Statement and Statement of Comprehensive Income

Recall from previous chapters that the purpose of an income statement is to display the company's profitability during a specific period. The income statement shows the amount of revenue, and the expenses that are deducted to provide the net income figure for the period. When comprehensive income is shown in the same statement as net income, the statement is called the **statement of comprehensive income**. This section will first show the requirements for the statement of comprehensive income under US GAAP, followed by the requirements under IFRS.

WORTH REPEATING

Chapter 15 discussed the different types of companies and which ones must follow US GAAP, and which ones can choose to follow either US GAAP or IFRS. American public companies are SEC registrants and must follow US GAAP. American private companies not registered with the SEC may choose to follow US GAAP, a simplified version of US GAAP, or IFRS.

Foreign companies (both private companies operating in the US and public companies that are non-US SEC registrants) may choose to follow either US GAAP or IFRS.

As you work through this section, notice some of the most significant differences between reporting under US GAAP and IFRS.

1. IFRS provides more flexibility than US GAAP and other prescribed regulations with regard to line items, headings and subtotals on the income statements. In particular, two sets of prescribed regulations for financial reporting are *Regulation S–X*, which specifies the format and content of financial statements; and *Regulation S–K*, which specifies reporting requirements of SEC filings for public companies. IFRS does, however, require some specific disclosures on both the actual financial statements and the notes to those financial statements. IFRS has a list of minimum line items that is less prescriptive than the requirements under Regulation S-X. For example, financial costs (interest expense) and income tax expense are on the list of minimum line items that must be disclosed separately on the face of the statement of comprehensive income.

2. IFRS statements often group together amounts that are additions and subtractions; therefore, amounts to be subtracted are displayed in parentheses on the statements. GAAP statements do not always show subtracted amounts in parentheses. Because more numbers tend to be grouped together on the same line under IFRS, the IFRS statements often appear more compact than US GAAP statements.

3. Both US GAAP and IFRS specify the income statement treatment of continuing and discontinued operations. US GAAP defines discontinued operations as components that are held for sale or disposed of *provided there are no continuing cash flows expected* from those components. IFRS, on the other hand, defines discontinued operations as components that are held for sale or disposed of *that relate to a separate line of business, a separate geographical location, or a subsidiary that has been acquired in order to be resold.* We will discuss the differences between continuing operations and discontinued operations in more detail later in this section.

4. US GAAP income statements tend to use the term "net income," while IFRS income statements tend to use the term "profit" or "profit for the year."

5. IFRS permits expenses on the statement of comprehensive income to be presented either by their function or their nature (but not a combination of the two). Under IFRS, if a functional classification of expenses is used, a note to the statement of comprehensive income must show the natural classification of expenses. US GAAP provides no direction on a specific format (by function or by nature) for the income statement, but the SEC requires presentation by function for public companies.

6. IFRS and US GAAP use different terminologies for similar items. For example, US GAAP uses the term "interest expense," but IFRS uses the term "finance costs," which includes interest expense.

7. IFRS permits alternative income measures on the income statement, whereas US GAAP does not permit non-GAAP financial measures, such as earnings before interest, taxes, depreciation and amortization (EBITDA) or free cash flow.

Let us now look at how to prepare a statement of comprehensive income under US GAAP.

US GAAP

Similar to IFRS, companies reporting under US GAAP must present comprehensive income either in a single continuous financial statement (often called the one-step format) or in two separate but consecutive financial statements (the two-step format). A company reporting comprehensive income in a single continuous statement must present its components in two sections: net income and other comprehensive income. For our purposes, we will demonstrate the single continuous financial statement format, which separately presents net income and other comprehensive income.

The statement of comprehensive income for Darma Corporation under US GAAP is shown in Figure 16.2. Both US GAAP and IFRS require companies to separate continuing operations from discontinued operations in their income statement presentation. Therefore, Darma Corporation's statement of comprehensive income is divided into two major components: continuing operations and discontinued operations.

Darma Corporation
Statement of Comprehensive Income
For the Year Ended December 31, 2018

Sales Revenue			$2,505,750
Less: Sales Returns & Allowances		$3,800	
Sales Discounts		1,200	5,000
Net Sales			2,500,750
Cost of Goods Sold			1,100,000
Gross Profit			1,400,750
Operating Expenses			
Selling Expenses			
Sales Salaries Expense		$150,000	
Depreciation Expense—Store Equipment		23,000	
Advertising Expense		230,000	
Total Selling Expenses		403,000	
Administrative Expenses			
Office Salaries Expense		125,000	
Depreciation Expense—Office Equipment		21,000	
Miscellaneous Administrative Expenses		70,000	
Total Administrative Expenses		216,000	
Total Operating Expenses			619,000
Income from Operations			ⓐ 781,750
Other Income and Expenses			
Gain on Sale of Assets		4,500	
Unrealized Gain on Trading Investments		8,700	
Interest Expense		(21,000)	(7,800)
Income (Loss) from Continuing Operations before Income Tax Expense			ⓑ 773,950
Income Tax Expense			ⓒ 232,185
Income (Loss) from Continuing Operations			ⓓ 541,765
Discontinued Operations			
Income from Operating Discontinued Operations (net of $37,500 tax)		87,500	
Gain on Sale of Discontinued Operations (net of $13,500 tax)		31,500	ⓔ 119,000
Net Income (Loss)			ⓕ 660,765
Other Comprehensive Income, Net of Tax			
Foreign Currency Translation Adjustments (net of $1,560 tax)			3,640
Total Comprehensive Income			ⓖ $664,405
Basic and Diluted Earnings per Share			
Continuing Operations			2.74
Discontinued Operations			0.60
Net Income (Loss)			3.35

FIGURE 16.2

As we discuss how to complete the statement of comprehensive income, we will refer to the lettered items in Figure 16.2.

Continuing Operations

Continuing operations refers to a business' normal day-to-day activities, such as the process required to make a product or service and deliver it to a customer. These operations are expected to continue in the near future.

Income (loss) from continuing operations shows the results of the company's operations that are ongoing. It is the component of the income that is from the continuing operations only. A large corporation may have several different lines of business that serve different types of customers or provide different goods and services. Each of these different operations is known as a **business segment**. Occasionally, a company may sell or discontinue a business segment. The requirement under US GAAP and IFRS is to separately report the results of discontinued operations, as will be discussed later. The income (loss) from continuing operations represents the results of only business segments that have not been sold or discontinued.

The income (loss) from continuing operations can be calculated in multiple steps. The first step is to calculate gross profit using the formula shown in Figure 16.3.

Gross Profit = Net Sales – Cost of Goods Sold

FIGURE 16.3

Using values for net sales and COGS from the statement of comprehensive income, gross profit is calculated as follows.

Gross Profit = $2,500,750 – $1,100,000

= $1,400,750

Figure 16.4 shows the formula to calculate income from operations.

Income from Operations = Gross Profit – Total Operating Expenses

FIGURE 16.4

Using the value for gross profit already calculated, and the value for total operating expenses from the statement of comprehensive income, we can calculate income from operations.

Income from Operations = $1,400,750 – $619,000

= $781,750 **ⓐ**

The next step is to calculate income (loss) from continuing operations before income tax expense, using the formula shown in Figure 16.5.

Income (Loss) from Continuing Operations before Income Tax Expense = Income from Operations + Other Income – Other Expenses

FIGURE 16.5

For this calculation, other income is added to, and other expenses are subtracted from, income from operations. **Other income (expenses)** includes items that are not part of the company's regular day-to-day operations. For example, any gain or loss on the sale of property, plant and equipment is listed as other income or expenses. In Darma's case, there are two gains and one loss from the other income (expenses) category. The calculation is shown here, with the value for income from operations taken from the calculation above.

$$\text{Income (Loss) from Continuing Operations before Income Tax Expense} = \$781{,}750 + (\$4{,}500 + \$8{,}700) - \$21{,}000$$

$$= \$773{,}950 \ \text{\textbf{b}}$$

Next we will look at calculating continuing operations' taxes, which must be reported separately from discontinued operations' taxes. Continuing operations' income tax expense appears on the statement of comprehensive income following the income (loss) from continuing operations before income tax expense. Corporate income tax calculation in the real world can be quite complex and is beyond the scope of this textbook. For illustrative purposes, income tax presentation will be simply calculated by multiplying a tax percentage by an income figure. The formula to calculate income (loss) from continuing operations is shown in Figure 16.6.

Income (Loss) from Continuing Operations = Income (Loss) from Continuing Operations before Income Tax Expense – Income Tax Expense

FIGURE 16.6

Assume Darma must pay income tax at 30%. Darma's income tax expense based on its income before taxes and discontinued operations is $232,185 (**c**) ($773,950 × 30%). This income tax expense is deducted from the income (loss) from continuing operations before income tax expense to determine the income (loss) from continuing operations, as shown here.

$$\text{Income (Loss) from Continuing Operations} = \$773{,}950 - \$232{,}185$$

$$= \$541{,}765 \ \text{\textbf{d}}$$

Discontinued Operations

A **discontinued operation** is a business segment that is no longer part of the company's regular operating activities.

The formula to calculate income from discontinued operations is shown in Figure 16.7.

Income (Loss) from Discontinued Operations = Income (Loss) from Operating Discontinued Operations, Net of Income Tax Expense (Benefit) + Gain (Loss) on Disposal of Discontinued Operations, Net of Income Tax Expense (Benefit)

FIGURE 16.7

During the year, Darma discontinued a segment of its business operations. This segment generated an income from operations of $125,000 before its disposal and a $45,000 gain on the sale of the assets. Darma must pay 30% tax on both the income and gain. These taxes are not reported as a separate line item; therefore, income from operating discontinued operations is reported as $87,000 ($125,000 − $37,500 in tax). The gain on disposal of discontinued operations is reported as $31,500 ($45,000 − $13,500 in tax). Using these values, income (loss) from discontinued operations is calculated as shown.

$$\text{Income (Loss) from Discontinued Operations} = (\$125,000 - \$37,500) + (\$45,000 - \$13,500)$$
$$= \$119,000 \ \textbf{ⓔ}$$

We can now calculate net income (loss) using the formula shown in Figure 16.8.

Net Income (Loss) = Income (Loss) from Continuing Operations + Income (Loss) from Discontinued Operations

FIGURE 16.8

For Darma Corporation, we use values that were just calculated to determine the total net income (loss), as shown here.

$$\text{Net Income (Loss)} = \$541,765 + \$119,000$$
$$= \$660,765 \ \textbf{ⓘ}$$

The after-tax income from continuing operations and the after-tax income from discontinued operations leave Darma with a total net income of $660,765.

If the discontinued segment showed a loss from its operations or from the sale of assets, Darma would recognize a savings of income tax. For example, suppose Darma has an operating loss from the discontinued operations and the assets are sold at a loss for a total of $100,000. Darma saves 30% (or $30,000) of that in income tax, so the net loss is $70,000.

Another scenario is that Darma has income from operations from the discontinued segment but incurs a loss from the sale of assets. Suppose Darma has income from operations of $100,000 from the discontinued segment but the assets are sold at a loss of $30,000. Darma needs to pay an income tax expense of $30,000 ($100,000 × 30%) but also has an income tax benefit of $9,000 ($30,000 × 30%). The net effect is paying tax of $21,000 ($30,000 − $9,000) for this discontinued segment.

It is important to report the income from continuing operations and from discontinued operations separately because investors and creditors rely on this accounting information to make decisions. Reporting separately allows the users of financial information to identify what is not relevant to the company's ongoing performance. This especially helps users predict future results, such as how much profit the company will make in the following year and how competitive the company will be after eliminating a segment.

Comprehensive Income

Comprehensive income is the total of net income plus other comprehensive income (or loss). **Other comprehensive income (OCI)** is a category of income resulting from transactions that are beyond the owners' or management's control. Other comprehensive income can arise from adjustments in the fair value of available-for-sale investments, pension, or property, plant and equipment, and also differences arising from foreign currency translation transactions. Neither US GAAP nor IFRS allow these items to be reported as a part of net income, but they do affect the equity accounts. In our example, Darma Corporation has a gain of $5,200 that results from exchange differences arising from the translation of its foreign operation's financial statements. The amount of foreign currency translation adjustments is reported net of $1,560 tax in the other comprehensive income section. As shown in Figure 16.2, a section called Other Comprehensive Income, Net of Tax appears below net income. Other comprehensive income (or loss) is added to net income to arrive at total comprehensive income. For Darma Corporation, its total comprehensive income is reported as $664,405 (**❾**). The details of the items in other comprehensive income are beyond the scope of this textbook.

Both US GAAP and IFRS require that other comprehensive income (or loss) be reported either

1. in its own section on the statement of comprehensive income; or
2. in a separate statement that accompanies the traditional income statement.

This textbook presents other comprehensive income in its own section on the statement of comprehensive income. Similar to income from discontinued operations, each item listed under other comprehensive income is reported net of income tax. If the company chooses to report the total comprehensive income as one line item, the number shown must be net of income tax. This is why the sample statement in Figure 16.2 includes the heading "Other Comprehensive Income, Net of Tax."

Presentation of Earnings per Share

Both US GAAP and IFRS require the presentation of earnings per share (EPS) on the statement of comprehensive income. A company with a complex capital structure must report two EPS figures: basic earnings per share, and diluted earnings per share. EPS should be reported separately for discontinued operations. The earnings per share values for Darma Corporation are presented at the bottom of the statement in Figure 16.2. Earnings per share and its calculation are discussed in more detail later in this chapter.

IFRS

If Darma Corporation was planning to expand further internationally and borrow from foreign banks, it may want to prepare another set of financial statements under IFRS to be presented to foreign banks and other stakeholders. Thus, it would prepare a statement of comprehensive income under IFRS guidelines. Some of the IFRS requirements on how to present the statement of comprehensive income are similar to US GAAP's requirements. For example, both must separate continuing operations income from discontinued operations. However, a major difference is that whereas the SEC requires public companies to present their expenses by function, IFRS allows presentation of expenses by function or by nature.

Presentation of Expenses by Function

IFRS requires that expenses be analyzed and presented on the statement of comprehensive income either by function or by nature. A corporation is allowed to choose the more suitable of the two methods for its statement presentation, based on which format is considered most reliable and relevant to its users. IFRS also allows the expenses to be listed in any order within each classification.

Classifying expenses **by function** means that expenses are presented on the statement according to the various functions of the company, such as selling expenses and administrative expenses.

When a company uses the "by function" presentation for its income statement, it must still disclose the individual expenses by nature in notes to the statement. Figure 16.9 demonstrated how Darma Corporation presents its statement of comprehensive income with expenses analyzed by function.

Darma Corporation **Statement of Comprehensive Income (by function)** **For the Year Ended December 31, 2018**	
Sales (Net)	$2,500,750
Cost of Goods Sold	(1,100,000)
Gross Profit	1,400,750
Selling Expenses	(403,000)
Administrative Expenses	(216,000)
Other Income (Expenses)[1]	13,200
Operating Profit	794,950
Finance Costs	(21,000)
Profit before Income Tax	773,950
Income Tax Expense	(232,185)
Profit for the Year from Continuing Operations	541,765
Profit for the Year from Discontinued Operations[2]	119,000
Profit for the Year	660,765
Other Comprehensive Income, Net of Tax	
Foreign Currency Translation Adjustments (net of $1,560 tax)[3]	3,640
Total Comprehensive Income	$664,405
Basic and Diluted Earnings per Share	
Continuing Operations	2.74
Discontinued Operations	0.60
Net Income (Loss)	3.35

[1] $4,500 Gain on Sale of Assets + $8,700 Unrealized Gain on Trading Investments = $13,200
[2] ($125,000 + $45,000) − 30% tax = $119,000
[3] $5,200 − 30% tax = $3,640

FIGURE 16.9

Presentation of Expenses by Nature

Classifying expenses **by nature** means that expenses are presented on the statement according to their natural classification, such as salary expense, employee benefits, advertising expense, depreciation, and so on. Expenses analyzed by nature are *not* allocated to the different functions of the business. Figure 16.10 demonstrates how Darma Corporation presents its statement of comprehensive income with expenses analyzed by nature.

Darma Corporation Statement of Comprehensive Income (by nature) For the Year Ended December 31, 2018	
Sales (Net)	$2,500,750
Cost of Goods Sold	(1,100,000)
Gross Profit	1,400,750
Salaries Expense	(275,000)
Depreciation Expense	(44,000)
Advertising Expense	(230,000)
Miscellaneous Administrative Expenses	(70,000)
Other Income (Expenses)	13,200
Operating Profit	794,950
Finance Costs	(21,000)
Profit before Income Tax	773,950
Income Tax Expense	(232,185)
Profit for the Year from Continuing Operations	541,765
Profit for the Year from Discontinued Operations	119,000
Profit for the Year	660,765
Other Comprehensive Income, Net of Tax	
Foreign Currency Translation Adjustments (net of $1,560 tax)	3,640
Total Comprehensive Income	$664,405
Basic and Diluted Earnings Per Share	
Continuing Operations	2.74
Discontinued Operations	0.60
Net Income (Loss)	3.30

FIGURE 16.10

The net income figure from the income statement or the statement of comprehensive income is added to the beginning retained earnings balance in the statement of retained earnings or the statement of stockholders' equity (under US GAAP) or the statement of changes in equity (under IFRS), as explained in the next section.

Statement of Retained Earnings and Statement of Changes in Equity

Similar to how sole proprietorships report the changes to owner's equity on the statement of owner's equity, all corporations are required to report on the changes to retained earnings during the accounting period. Net income from the income statement is added to, and dividends are subtracted from, the beginning balance of retained earnings to determine the ending balance of retained earnings. Both US GAAP and IFRS require the changes in stockholders' equity to be presented. However, US GAAP allows changes in stockholders' equity to be presented in a note to the financial statements, while IFRS requires the changes in stockholders' equity to be presented as a separate statement. You will learn more about the requirements under IFRS later in this chapter. For now, we will discuss the requirements under US GAAP.

US GAAP

Under US GAAP, the changes in stockholders' equity can be presented either in a statement or in the footnotes to the financial statements. When the changes are reported in the footnotes and only changes in retained earnings are presented, the statement is referred to as the **statement of retained earnings**, also called the *retained earnings statement*. Retained earnings are the earnings that are kept and accumulated by the company after dividends have been paid to the stockholders. Note that the income statement must be prepared before the statement of retained earnings because the net income from the income statement must be added to (or the net loss subtracted from) the retained earnings at the beginning of the period. Retained earnings increase if the company reported a net income and decrease if the company reported a net loss or paid out dividends.

Assume Darma had an opening balance of retained earnings of $1,340,000 and paid $400,000 in cash dividends. As shown in Figure 16.11, the statement of retained earnings is prepared in a similar way to the statement of owner's equity in a sole proprietorship. The net income is taken from the income statement that was already prepared.

Darma Corporation Statement of Retained Earnings For the Year Ended December 31, 2018	
Retained Earnings, January 1, 2018	$1,340,000
Net Income	660,765
Less: Common Stock Dividends	400,000
Retained Earnings, December 31, 2018	$1,600,765

FIGURE 16.11

Alternatively, some companies that follow US GAAP present the changes in all stockholders' equity accounts in a **statement of stockholders' equity**. Darma's statement of stockholders' equity is shown in Figure 16.12. Both the net income and other comprehensive income figures are transferred from the statement of comprehensive income to the statement of stockholders' equity. Similar to how the net income figure is added to (or the net loss figure is deducted from) the beginning retained earnings balance, other comprehensive income is added to (or loss is subtracted from) the beginning balance of accumulated other comprehensive income. Darma's accumulated other comprehensive income account has a zero beginning balance. US GAAP requires that treasury stock be disclosed separately from common stock and any other equity accounts.

Darma Corporation Statement of Stockholders' Equity For the Year Ended December 31, 2018						
	Common Stock	Additional Paid-In Capital	Retained Earnings	Accumulated Other Comprehensive Income	Treasury Stock	Total
Balance, January 1, 2018	$1,000,000	$3,000,000	$1,340,000	$0	($100,000)	$5,240,000
Net Income			660,765			660,765
Dividends on Common Stock			(400,000)			(400,000)
Foreign Currency Translation Adjustments				3,640		3,640
Balance, December 31, 2018	$1,000,000	$3,000,000	$1,600,765	$3,640	($100,000)	$5,504,405

FIGURE 16.12

IFRS

IFRS requires that all changes to the equity accounts be shown on a **statement of changes in equity**. This statement must include changes in retained earnings, the changes in capital stock and any other items that affected equity during the period.

The statement of changes in equity has a column for each item that makes up stockholders' equity. Net income from the statement of comprehensive income is added to retained earnings, and dividends are subtracted from retained earnings. Any issuance of common stock and preferred stock are added to capital stock and preferred stock, respectively.

There are some differences in terminologies between US GAAP and IFRS. While the stock issuance price in excess of par value is referred to by US GAAP as additional paid-in capital, it is referred to by IFRS as share premium. In addition, companies that report under IFRS usually refer to some parts of stockholders' equity that are not common stock, share premium and retained earnings under the title called "reserves." Treasury stock, for example, can be reported as part of the reserves. Under IFRS, an alternative is to report treasury stock as a separate item, although unlike US GAAP, doing so is not required. In Darma's example, the company reports treasury stock as "reserve for own shares" and reports foreign currency translation adjustment, which is a part of other comprehensive income, as "foreign currency translation reserve." A total column combines all values and shows how equity changed from the beginning of the period to the end.

Figure 16.13 shows the statement of changes in equity under IFRS for Darma Corporation for the year ended December 31, 2018.

Darma Corporation Statement of Changes in Equity For the Year Ended December 31, 2018				Reserves		
	Common Stock	Share Premium	Retained Earnings	Foreign Currency Translations Reserve	Reserve for Own Shares	Total Equity
Balance, January 1, 2018	$1,000,000	$3,000,000	$1,340,000	$0	($100,000)	$5,240,000
Profit for the Year			660,765			660,765
Other Comprehensive Income						
Currency Translation Adjustments				3,640		3,640
Total Comprehensive Income			660,765	3,640		664,405
Transactions with Owners						
Dividends on Common Stock			(400,000)			(400,000)
Total Transactions with Owners	0	0	(400,000)	0	0	(400,000)
Balance, December 31, 2018	$1,000,000	$3,000,000	$1,600,765	$3,640	($100,000)	$5,504,405

FIGURE 16.13

The statements in Figures 16.11, 16.12 and 16.13 are prepared based on the assumption that no adjustment needs to be made to the beginning retained earnings balance. Sometimes, this balance needs to be adjusted due to prior period adjustments, which is discussed next.

Prior Period Adjustments

Sometimes errors are discovered in the accounting records. A correcting entry can be made, but it must be journalized and posted before the closing entries at the end of that period. That way, the information is included in the period to which it belongs. For example, if a company's accounting clerk discovers an error in a journal entry that was made on June 15, 2018, and corrects it on June 22, 2018, the financial statements for June will be accurate.

But what happens when an error is found after the period has been closed? The error must be corrected so that the information is included in the period to which it belongs, and it remains comparable from one period to the next. A correcting entry that is made to a previous period is known as a **prior period adjustment**. Prior period adjustments are particularly important because they can affect net income (or loss) of the prior period, and therefore affect the beginning retained earnings balance for the current period.

The mechanics of how the prior period adjustments are made and how they are presented on the statement of retained earnings will be discussed.

Correction of Prior Period Errors

Correction of prior period errors are actions taken to correct errors made in previous financial statements by the business. Suppose a $25,000 purchase of equipment was mistakenly recorded as a maintenance expense. The original entry was made in 2017 but is not discovered until 2018. Since the error overstated the repairs and maintenance expenses, income for 2017 was understated. Simply transferring $25,000 from maintenance expense to equipment is not appropriate because maintenance expense would be understated for 2018. The transfer would also not address the fact that retained earnings should be increased when this error is corrected.

The solution is to increase the balance of the equipment account by $25,000 so that the asset is properly recorded. The balance in retained earnings should also increase; however, we must also take into account income taxes that are now owed on the extra amount of income. If Darma pays 30% income tax, it will owe $7,500 in taxes based on the increase of $25,000 in income. The journal entry to record the correction is shown in Figure 16.14. Notice that this entry only affects balance sheet accounts and does not affect the income statement.

JOURNAL			Page 1
Date	**Account Title and Explanation**	**Debit**	**Credit**
Jan 31	Equipment	25,000	
	Retained Earnings		17,500
	Income Tax Payable		7,500
	To record correction for error in June 15, 2017 journal entry, expensed to Maintenance		

FIGURE 16.14

The error caused net income for 2017 to be understated by $17,500 ($25,000 less the income tax at a rate of 30%). By crediting retained earnings for the net effect of the error, this account was corrected to reflect the income that would have been recorded. Income tax payable is also corrected to reflect the actual amount owing on the income earned.

When a company has a prior period error, adjustments to retained earnings must be included in the statement of retained earnings or the statement of stockholders' equity if the company uses US GAAP, or the statement of changes in equity if the company uses IFRS. Specifically, the adjustment to retained earnings is listed before any other items are added or subtracted. Figure 16.15 shows the statement of retained earnings, Figure 16.16 shows the statement of stockholders' equity, and Figure 16.17 shows the statement of change in equity, all with the prior period adjustment.

Darma Corporation Statement of Retained Earnings For the Year Ended December 31, 2018	
Retained Earnings, January 1, 2018, as Originally Reported	$1,340,000
Prior Period Adjustment	
Cost of Equipment Incorrectly Expensed (net of $7,500 tax)	17,500
Retained Earnings, January 1, 2018, as Adjusted	1,357,500
Net Income	660,765
Less: Common Stock Dividends	400,000
Retained Earnings, December 31, 2018	$1,618,265

FIGURE 16.15

Darma Corporation Statement of Stockholders' Equity For the Year Ended December 31, 2018						
	Common Stock	Additional Paid-In Capital	Retained Earnings	Accumulated Other Comprehensive Income	Treasury Stock	Total
Balance, January 1, 2018	$1,000,000	$3,000,000	$1,340,000	$0	($100,000)	$5,240,000
Prior Period Adjustment (net of $7,500 tax)			17,500			17,500
Net Income			660,765			660,765
Dividends on Common Stock			(400,000)			(400,000)
Foreign Currency Translation Adjustments				3,640		3,640
Balance, December 31, 2018	$1,000,000	$3,000,000	$1,618,265	$3,640	($100,000)	$5,521,905

FIGURE 16.16

Darma Corporation Statement of Changes in Equity For the Year Ended December 31, 2018				Reserves		
				Foreign Currency Translations Reserve	Reserve for Own Shares	
	Common Stock	Share Premium	Retained Earnings			Total Equity
Balance, January 1, 2018	$1,000,000	$3,000,000	$1,340,000	$0	($100,000)	$5,240,000
Adjustment for Errors			17,500			17,500
Restated Balance	1,000,000	3,000,000	1,357,500	0	(100,000)	5,257,500
Changes in Equity for 2018						
Profit for the Year			660,765			660,765
Other Comprehensive Income						
Currency Translation Adjustments				3,640		3,640
Total Comprehensive Income			660,765	3,640		664,405
Contributions by and Distributions to Stockholders						
Dividends on Common Stock			(400,000)			(400,000)
Total Contributions by and Distributions to Stockholders	0	0	(400,000)	0	0	(400,000)
Balance, December 31, 2018	$1,000,000	$3,000,000	$1,618,265	$3,640	($100,000)	$5,521,905

FIGURE 16.17

Balance Sheet and Statement of Financial Position

LO 5

The three statements we have just looked at—statement of retained earnings, statement of stockholders' equity, and statement of changes in equity—all link the income statement and the balance sheet together. The net income figure from the income statement is used in the statement of retained earnings to calculate the ending balance of retained earnings. This ending balance is then presented under the stockholders' equity section on the balance sheet. The ending balances of other stockholders' equity accounts from the statement of stockholders' equity and statement of changes in equity are also presented under the stockholders' equity section on the balance sheet. As you work through this section, notice some of the most significant differences between reporting under US GAAP and IFRS.

1. US GAAP requires separate disclosure of treasury stock on the balance sheet. Under IFRS, treasury stock can be reported as a separate item, but it can also be reported as a reduction of a reserve, or a reduction of a stock premium.

2. US GAAP and IFRS use different terminology when reporting a company's financial position.

   • Under US GAAP, the heading Stockholders' Equity appears on the balance sheet, whereas under IFRS, the statement of financial position refers to Equity Attributable to Owners, or sometimes Capital and Reserves.

   • US GAAP refers to stock sold in excess of par value as "additional paid-in capital," but IFRS uses the term "share premium."

   • US GAAP refers to "long-term liabilities," whereas IFRS uses the term "noncurrent liabilities."

   • When presenting changes in equity for a period, US GAAP refers to "accumulated other comprehensive income," whereas IFRS uses the term "reserves."

   • US GAAP uses the term "salaries payable," whereas under IFRS the term "provisions" is used.

US GAAP

A classified balance sheet prepared under US GAAP looks very similar to a sole proprietorship's balance sheet. Assets and liabilities are listed on the basis of liquidity from most liquid to least liquid (i.e. the current items are listed first). US GAAP allows a company the flexibility to call this statement either a balance sheet or a statement of financial position. The normal presentation of a balance sheet includes an asset section with the following classifications of assets.

• Current Assets
• Long-Term Investments
• Property, Plant and Equipment
• Intangible Assets
• Goodwill

The liabilities section includes both current and long-term liabilities.

The stockholders' equity section includes the following sections.

• Paid-In Capital
• Retained Earnings
• Accumulated Other Comprehensive Income
• Treasury Stock

Figure 16.18 shows the classified balance sheet for Darma Corporation prepared according to US GAAP.

Darma Corporation Balance Sheet As at December 31, 2018		
Assets		
Current Assets		
Cash and Cash Equivalents		$87,650
Trading Investments (at Cost)	$278,880	
Plus Valuation Allowance for Trading Investments	8,700	287,580
Accounts Receivable (net)		685,725
Merchandise Inventory		1,652,840
Prepaid Expenses		16,840
Total Current Assets		2,730,635
Property, Plant and Equipment (net)		3,206,740
Goodwill		777,185
Total Assets		$6,714,560
Liabilities		
Current Liabilities		
Accounts Payable	$556,890	
Notes Payable, Current Portion	43,870	
Salaries Payable	15,845	
Total Current Liabilities		$616,605
Long-Term Liabilities		
Notes Payable, Long-Term Portion	568,750	
Deferred Tax Liabilities	24,800	
Total Long-Term Liabilities		593,550
Total Liabilities		1,210,155
Stockholders' Equity		
Paid-In Capital		
Common stock, $5 par value, unlimited shares authorized,		
200,000 shares issued, 197,500 shares outstanding	1,000,000	
Additional Paid-In Capital	3,000,000	
Total Paid-In Capital	4,000,000	
Retained Earnings	1,600,765	
Accumulated Other Comprehensive Income	3,640	
Total	5,604,405	
Less: Treasury Stock (2,500 shares at cost)	100,000	
Total Stockholders' Equity		5,504,405
Total Liabilities and Stockholders' Equity		$6,714,560

FIGURE 16.18

The balance sheet shows the common practice of presenting the individual items under each classification ordered by liquidity (most liquid to least liquid).

As you saw in the previous section, changes in stockholders' equity can also be reported in separate statements: in the statement of retained earnings and the statement of stockholders' equity under US GAAP. Significant changes to stockholders' equity can also be presented in notes to the financial statements, along with information about the individual classes of stocks, such as their rights and privileges.

IFRS

Preparing a balance sheet under IFRS involves some similarities to, as well as some notable differences from, US GAAP.

- IFRS allows the balance sheet to be called a balance sheet or, more often, the statement of financial position.

- Assets and liabilities are still classified as current and long-term; however the term "noncurrent" is used instead of "long-term."

- As with US GAAP, there is currently no specific requirement regarding the order of items on the balance sheet. However, the typical order under IFRS is to list noncurrent items before current items, and to list equity before liabilities.

- Similar to the US GAAP balance sheet, the statement of financial position under IFRS must show the number of shares authorized and the number of shares issued.

- Under IFRS, treasury stock can be reported as a separate item, or it can be reported as a reduction of a reserve or a reduction of a stock premium.

Figure 16.19 shows the statement of financial position for Darma Corporation under IFRS guidelines. Note that it shows an item called "Reserves" under the section Equity Attributable to Owners, and this is where Darma's treasury stock and foreign currency translation reserve are reported.

Darma Corporation Statement of Financial Position As at December 31, 2018		
Assets		
Noncurrent Assets		
Property, Plant and Equipment (net)		$3,206,740
Goodwill		777,185
Total Noncurrent Assets		3,983,925
Current Assets		
Prepaid Expenses	$16,840	
Merchandise Inventory	1,652,840	
Accounts Receivable (net)	685,725	
Financial Assets at Fair Value through		
Profit or Loss	287,580	
Cash and Cash Equivalents	87,650	
Total Current Assets		2,730,635
Total Assets		$6,714,560
Equity Attributable to Owners		
Common stock, $5 par value, unlimited shares authorized,		
200,000 shares issued, 197,500 shares outstanding	$1,000,000	
Share Premium	3,000,000	
Reserves	(96,360)	
Retained Earnings	1,600,765	
Total Equity Attributable to Owners		$5,504,405
Liabilities		
Noncurrent Liabilities		
Notes Payable, Noncurrent Portion	568,750	
Deferred Tax Liabilities	24,800	
Total Noncurrent Liabilities		593,550
Current Liabilities		
Accounts Payable	556,890	
Notes Payable, Current Portion	43,870	
Employee Provisions	15,845	
Total Current Liabilities		616,605
Total Liabilities		1,210,155
Total Equity and Liabilities		$6,714,560

FIGURE 16.19

621

Earnings per Share

Chapter 15 discussed how corporations raise capital by offering their stock to the public. For investors, or stockholders, there are two monetary reasons to buy stock in a company. One reason is the potential of making a profit from an increase in the stock price (what is known as a *capital gain*). The other reason to buy stock is the anticipation of regular payments of cash dividends.

WORTH REPEATING

Stocks are an attractive investment for stockholders because they offer limited liability and have the potential to increase in value. They also offer liquidity, which is the ability to sell or transfer stocks at their market value. The market value of stocks is determined by the amount that investors are willing to pay for them at that particular point in time. This means that the stock may be sold at a higher or lower price than the current holder paid for them.

Every corporation issues common stock. Common stock is a type of equity that gives stockholders ownership in the corporation, along with voting rights to elect a board of directors, and the potential to receive a portion of the company's equity in the form of dividends. Investors buy common stock with the expectation that the corporation will remain or become profitable, although the payment of dividends is not guaranteed. Some corporations also offer another class of stock known as preferred stock.

When potential investors are deciding which company's stock to buy, they first want to know something about the company's profitability. One key indicator of a company's profitability is a value known as earnings per share. **Earnings per share** (**EPS**) is a ratio that indicates the profit earned by each common share. EPS enables stockholders to evaluate the potential return on their investment. We will look at the formula for calculating earnings per share.

First, recall the discussion about dividends from Chapter 15. When a company issues both preferred and common shares, dividends must be paid to preferred stockholders first. The remainder of profits available for dividends is then declared to the common stockholders. Because EPS is only calculated on common shares, the current year's preferred dividends are subtracted from net income, and then divided by the weighted average number of common shares outstanding. The **weighted average number of common shares outstanding** is determined by taking the number of shares outstanding multiplied by the fraction of the year during which those shares were outstanding. This ensures that the number of shares outstanding is matched to the amount of income that was earned on them.

The formula for calculating earnings per share is presented in Figure 16.20.

$$\text{Earnings per Share} = \frac{\text{Net Income} - \text{Preferred Dividends}}{\text{Weighted Average Number of Common Shares Outstanding}}$$

FIGURE 16.20

All calculations in this section are based on the example of Darma Corporation. From Figures 16.2, 16.9 or 16.10, Darma's 2018 net income of $660,765 is used. Note that other comprehensive income is not included in this calculation. Assume that Darma has 197,500 common shares outstanding on December 31, 2018, and no preferred shares outstanding. For now, assume that there were no changes to the number of shares outstanding for 2018; that is, all 197,500 common shares were outstanding for the entire year. Darma's earnings per share (EPS) is calculated as follows.

$$\text{Earnings per Share} = \frac{(\$660,765 - \$0)}{197,500}$$

$$= \frac{\$660,765}{197,500}$$

$$= \$3.35$$

For the year ended December 31, 2018, Darma Corporation had earnings per share (EPS) of $3.35, which means the company is earning a profit of $3.35 for every common share outstanding. The general interpretation is that the larger the EPS, the more profitable the company. Figures 16.2 and 16.10 showed how the earnings per share figure is presented on Darma's statement of comprehensive income for 2018.

A CLOSER LOOK

When examining corporate financial statements, it is common to see two earnings per share figures: basic earnings per share and fully diluted earnings per share. **Basic earnings per share** is based on actual shares that have been issued to stockholders, and it is shown in this textbook. **Fully diluted earnings per share** is based on actual and potential shares that have or could be issued. Potential shares can arise from a few places.

- Management compensation—Some corporations give senior management options to purchase company stock at a reduced price.
- Convertible bonds—Corporations can sell bonds that are convertible into stock in the company.
- Convertible preferred shares—Corporations may issue preferred shares with the "convertible" feature, which allows preferred stockholders to convert their preferred shares into common shares.

The fully diluted EPS is calculated as if all existing management options, convertible bonds and convertible preferred shares were converted into common shares. This causes the fully diluted EPS to be a smaller figure than the basic EPS. The concept of fully diluted EPS is covered in more advanced accounting courses.

When earnings per share was calculated for the statement of comprehensive income, it was assumed that there was no change in the number of outstanding common shares for the entire year. That is, Darma had 197,500 common shares outstanding on January 1, 2018 and 197,500 common shares outstanding on December 31, 2018. What if Darma had 200,000 shares of common stock outstanding on January 1, 2018, and issued an additional 10,000 common shares on July 1, 2018, which would mean 10,000 additional shares were outstanding for six months, from July 1 to December 31? This is where the calculation of weighted average number of shares comes into play.

Figure 16.21 summarizes the numbers needed to calculate EPS for this situation.

Date 2018	Actual Number of Shares	Fraction of Year	Weighted Average Number of Shares
Jan 1	200,000	x 12 months/12 months	200,000
Jul 1	10,000	x 6 months/12 months	5,000
Total	210,000		205,000

FIGURE 16.21

In addition, assume that Darma Corporation has preferred shares and declared preferred dividends of $50,000 for 2018. The calculation of earnings per share for 2018 using the formula from Figure 16.19 is shown here.

$$\text{Earnings per Share} = \frac{(\$660,765 - \$50,000)}{205,000}$$

$$= \frac{\$610,765}{205,000}$$

$$= \$2.98$$

For the year ended December 31, 2018, Darma Corporation had earnings per share (EPS) of $2.98. Under these changed conditions, the company is earning a profit of $2.98 for every common share outstanding.

Under both GAAP and IFRS, corporations must disclose earnings per share (EPS) on their statement of comprehensive income, or on the income statement if it is presented separately. EPS must also be explained in notes to the financial statements.

Pause & Reflect

Exercise 16-1

The December 31, 2018 statement of comprehensive income for Digit Corporation shows profit from continuing operations was $850,000 and profit for the year was $925,000.

The company had 100,000 common shares outstanding on December 31, 2018, and no preferred shares outstanding. There were no changes to the number of shares during the year. Calculate the company's earnings per share from continuing operations, and basic earnings per share.

Earnings per share from continuing operations	
Basic earnings per share	

See Appendix I for solutions.

Calculation of Financial Ratios

Earnings per share (EPS) is a financial ratio that is used to evaluate a company's profitability. In addition to EPS, there are several other ratios of interest to potential investors, stockholders and other users of financial information: book value per share, dividend yield ratio and the price-earnings (P/E) ratio. These three ratios and how they are used to evaluate a company's earnings and dividend performance is discussed in this section.

Book Value per Common Share

Like earnings per share (EPS), book value per share is considered a profitability ratio. It enables stockholders to evaluate the potential return on their investment. **Book value per share** is a value that indicates what a share would be worth to stockholders if the company were to be liquidated (dissolved).

A company's stock can be valued at either its market value or book value. Market value represents the price at which shares are publicly traded on the stock market. Book value represents the theoretical value of a share based on a stockholder's claim to the company's assets.

Theoretically, a stock's market value should mirror its book value. What the company is worth according to its financial statements should be reflected in the price at which its stock is trading. However, stock is often bought and sold for a very different price than what is reflected on the company's financial statements; the book value does not usually match the market value.

Book value per common share is calculated using the formula in Figure 16.22.

$$\text{Book Value per Common Share} = \frac{\text{Stockholders' Equity} - \text{Preferred Stock}}{\text{Number of Common Shares Outstanding}}$$

FIGURE 16.22

From Figure 16.19, the stockholders' equity section of Darma's December 31, 2018 statement of financial position is used. The value of stockholders' equity (listed as total equity attributable to owners) is $5,504,405 and Darma does not have any preferred shares. The number of common shares outstanding is 197,500. Darma's book value per common share is calculated as follows.

$$\text{Book Value per Common Share} = \frac{\$5,504,405}{197,500}$$

$$= \$27.87$$

Therefore, as of December 31, 2018, Darma Corporation's book value per common share is $27.87. This figure is of interest to investors and others who want to evaluate a stock's value against its market price; that is, as a comparison against what a share in the company is currently selling for.

Dividend Yield

The **dividend yield** shows potential investors what percentage of market value of a common share is paid out to stockholders in cash dividends. In fact, this ratio calculates a rate of return on investment in common stock. This helps investors evaluate which company they want to invest in. A stable dividend yield indicates that a company's board of directors has a consistent record of paying out dividends. For this reason, the dividend yield is considered a good market analysis tool. Having a low dividend yield is not necessarily a bad sign of a company's profitability; a company could be profitable but decides to mainly invest its profits in the growth of the company rather than paying it out to investors. In addition, some stockholders are more interested in the price increase of their stock than receiving cash dividends, and consider that a better indication of a company's future success.

The dividend yield is calculated using the formula shown in Figure 16.23.

$$\text{Dividend Yield} = \frac{\text{Cash Dividends per Common Share}}{\text{Market Price per Common Share}}$$

FIGURE 16.23

Darma's statement of changes in equity shows that the company paid $400,000 in dividends to stockholders during 2018 and there were 197,500 common shares outstanding. This gives us the numerator, which is a cash dividend per common share of $2.03 ($400,000 ÷ 197,500). Assume on December 31, 2018, Darma's common stock was selling at $24 per share, which is the denominator. Darma's dividend yield is calculated as follows.

$$\text{Dividend Yield} = \frac{\$2.03}{\$24}$$

$$= 0.085 \text{ or } 8.5\%$$

The company is paying out 8.5% of a share market price in the form of cash dividends to common stockholders.

Price-Earnings Ratio

Another good indicator of company performance is the **price-earnings (P/E) ratio**, which divides the market price per common share by earnings per share. The P/E ratio is considered a good market analysis tool that provides an investor with an indicator of future growth, as well as risk, of the company's earnings. It is often used by investors and investment advisors as an indicator to buy, sell or hold on to stock.

The P/E ratio is calculated using the formula shown in Figure 16.24.

$$\text{Price-Earnings (P/E) Ratio} = \frac{\text{Market Price per Share}}{\text{Earnings per Share}}$$

FIGURE 16.24

Darma had 2018 earnings per common share of $3.35. As mentioned previously, on December 31, 2018, Darma's common stock was selling at $24 per share. Darma's P/E ratio is calculated as follows.

$$\text{Price-Earnings (P/E) Ratio} = \frac{\$24.00}{\$3.35}$$

$$= 7.16$$

This price-earnings ratio indicates that, as of December 31, 2018, Darma's common stock was selling at 7.16 times its earnings. If it is assumed that Darma always reports comparative numbers (statements for two or more years) on its financial statements, then its P/E ratio can be compared from one period to the next. Investors generally look at a high P/E ratio as an indicator of earnings growth in the future. It can be useful to compare a company's ratio from one period to another, to the ratios of other companies within the same industry or to ratios in the market in general.

It is important to note that no one particular financial ratio tells the whole story about a company's performance. Investors and other users of financial information must evaluate a combination of factors when deciding whether and when to invest in a company.

Pause & Reflect

Exercise 16-2

a) The December 31, 2018 statement of stockholders' equity for Benning Corporation showed a net income of $1,462,000 and dividends paid on common stock in the amount of $300,000 for 100,000 common shares outstanding during the year. Each share has a market price of $50. Calculate the dividend yield.

b) If Alpha company has earnings per share of $3.15 and the current market price per share is $17.42, calculate the price-earnings ratio.

See Appendix I for solutions.

In Summary

LO 1 Explain the different requirements under US GAAP and IFRS when presenting financial statements

▶ US GAAP and IFRS have different financial statement presentation requirements.

▶ US GAAP requires disclosure for the current year and prior two years for the income statement, statement of cash flows and statement of retained earnings, while IFRS requires disclosure for the current year and the prior year.

LO 2 Prepare an income statement and a statement of comprehensive income

▶ Both US GAAP and IFRS require other comprehensive income to be reported separately from net income. Other comprehensive income can be reported in the same statement as the net income but in a separate section, or in a separate statement.

▶ Both US GAAP and IFRS require companies to present income (or loss) and taxes from continuing operations separately from those from discontinued operations.

▶ Whereas the SEC requires public American companies to present their expenses by function, IFRS allows presentation of expenses by function or by nature (but not a combination of the two). There are also some terminology differences. For example, US GAAP uses the term "interest expense," but IFRS uses the term "finance costs," which includes interest expense.

LO 3 Prepare a statement of retained earnings and a statement of changes in equity

▶ In both the statement of retained earnings and the statement of stockholders' equity under US GAAP, and the statement of changes in equity under IFRS, net income from the income statement is added to, and dividends are subtracted from, the beginning balance of retained earnings to determine the ending balance of retained earnings.

▶ Under US GAAP, the changes in stockholders' equity can be presented either in the statement of stockholders' equity or in the footnotes to the financial statements. When the changes are reported in the footnotes and only changes in retained earnings are presented in the statement, the statement is referred to as the statement of retained earnings.

▶ In a statement of changes in equity under IFRS, changes in all equity accounts are presented on the face of the statement.

LO 4 Record and report on prior period adjustments

▶ If prior period adjustments are needed, adjustments to retained earnings must be listed before any other items are added or subtracted on the statement of retained earnings or the statement of stockholders' equity under US GAAP or on the statement of changes in equity under IFRS.

LO 5 Prepare a balance sheet and a statement of financial position

▶ A statement that lists a company's assets, liabilities and stockholders' equity is called a balance sheet under US GAAP and a statement of financial position under IFRS.

▶ Both US GAAP and IFRS currently do not specify how items should be listed on a balance sheet or a statement of financial position. Companies that use US GAAP tend to list assets and liabilities on the basis of liquidity from most liquid to least liquid, while companies that use IFRS tend to list items in the reverse order.

▶ Treasury stock must be reported separately under US GAAP. However, under IFRS, treasury stock can be reported in a number of ways, such as included with other equity items in "reserves."

LO 6 Calculate and explain earnings per share

▶ Earnings per share (EPS) can be calculated by dividing the net income available for common stockholders by weighted average number of common shares outstanding.

▶ EPS measures dollars of profit for every common share outstanding. The larger the EPS, the more profitable the company.

LO 7 Calculate ratios used to evaluate earnings and dividend performance

▶ Book value per common share is calculated by dividing equity net of preferred shares by number of common shares outstanding. It is a value that indicates what a common share would be worth to common stockholders if the company were to be liquidated (dissolved).

▶ Dividend yield is calculated by dividing dividends paid for the year by a share market price. It shows what percentage of market value of a common share paid out to stockholders in dividends.

▶ The price to earnings (P/E) ratio is calculated by dividing market price per share by earnings per share. It compares a company's current stock price to its EPS.

Review Exercise 16-1

The following information was taken from the accounting records of a US public corporation called Shah Company at December 31, 2018. Assume the tax rate is 35%. Also assume that Shah's preferred stock is not convertible, and that Shah does not have any outstanding securities that can be converted into common stock.

FINANCIAL STATEMENT ITEMS	Amount
Prior-year error—debit to retained earnings	$7,500
Income tax expense on operating income from discontinued operations	12,250
Total dividends	25,000
Common stock, $10 par value unlimited shares authorized, 15,500 shares issued and outstanding	155,000
Sales revenue	710,000
Interest expense	30,000
Operating income, discontinued operations	35,000
Loss due to lawsuit	11,000
Sales discounts	15,000
Income tax savings on sale of discontinued operations (sold at a loss)	14,000
Selling Expenses	42,000
Administrative Expenses	20,000
Income tax expense on continuing operations	74,200
Preferred stock, non-cumulative, 10%, $50 par value, 10,000 shares authorized, 1,000 shares issued	50,000
Retained earnings, January 1, 2018 (prior to adjustment)	110,000
Loss on sale of discontinued operations	40,000
Cost of goods sold	380,000

Required

a) Prepare an income statement for the year ended December 31, 2018.

b) Prepare a statement of retained earnings for Shah Company for the year ended December 31, 2018.

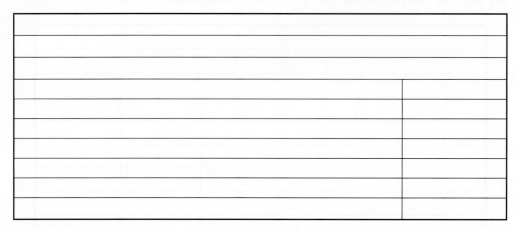

c) Prepare a partial balance sheet that shows only the stockholders' equity portion as at December 31, 2018.

d) Calculate the EPS ratio.

See Appendix I for solutions.

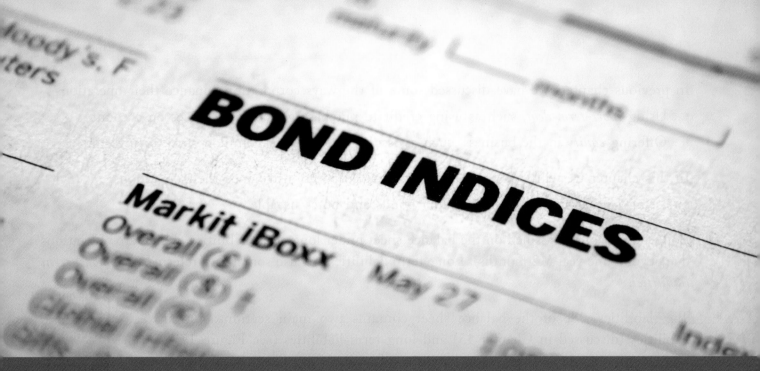

Chapter 17
Long-Term Liabilities

Learning Objectives

LO 1 State the characteristics and different types of bonds
- Bond Issuance

LO 2 Apply the concept of present value
- Time Value of Money and Bonds Payable

LO 3 Record bonds issued at par

LO 4 Record bonds issued at a discount or a premium
- Issuing Bonds at a Discount
- Issuing Bonds at a Premium

LO 5 Record the retirement of bonds

LO 6 Record installment notes payable

LO 7 Describe how long-term liabilities are analyzed and presented on the balance sheet
- Notes Payable on the Financial Statements

- Bonds Payable on the Financial Statements
- Debt-to-Total-Assets Ratio
- Debt-to-Equity Ratio

LO 8 Apply controls and ethics related to long-term liabilities

Appendix

LO 9 Describe the effective interest amortization method
- Amortization of Bond Discount by the Effective-Interest Method
- Amortization of Bond Premium by the Effective-Interest Method

In previous chapters we have discussed some of the ways corporations finance their operations.

- Using *short-term debt*, such as using credit to purchase goods and services on account
- Offering *equity* in the business, such as issuing preferred or common stock to investors

In this chapter we will look at another way that corporations finance their operations.

- Using *long-term debt*, such as issuing bonds and notes payable

Long-term debt is classified on the balance sheet under long-term liabilities, which are obligations due beyond one year (12 months). Long-term liabilities are also sometimes referred to as *noncurrent liabilities*.

The liabilities side of the balance sheet contains two main sections: current liabilities (discussed in Chapter 13) and long-term liabilities (see Figure 17.1). Some common types of long-term liabilities of business organizations are bonds payable and notes payable with a due date longer than one year.

The most common form of long-term financing used by a company is signing a note payable to borrow a bank loan. Notes payable were partly covered in the current liabilities chapter because the portion of the note due within one fiscal period is presented as a current liability on the balance sheet.

An alternative to borrowing money from a bank is to borrow money from private investors. This is done by issuing bonds, which can be sold to raise cash for the business. In the next section, we will discuss bonds in detail, and see how they compare to other financing options when a corporation seeks funding for operations.

CURRENT LIABILITIES

ACCOUNTS PAYABLE

INTEREST PAYABLE

UNEARNED REVENUE

NOTES PAYABLE (CURRENT)

LONG-TERM LIABILITIES

NOTES PAYABLE (LONG-TERM)

BONDS PAYABLE

FIGURE 17.1

Characteristics and Types of Bonds   LO 1

Companies cannot always secure sufficient financing from a bank or by selling stock. Instead, a large company may choose to borrow money by offering investors a type of long-term debt in the form of an interest-bearing note known as a **bond**. A bond represents a promise to pay a specified amount to the investor on a specific date, known as the bond's maturity date.

The company that issues the bond is called the **bond issuer**. The investor who purchases the bond is known as the **bondholder**. The contract between the bond issuer and the bondholder is called a **bond indenture**. Like a company's stock, bonds are sold to investors on the stock (or securities) exchange. Bonds are typically sold in small denominations, in multiples of $1,000. Bond investors are often large organizations, such as pension funds, but can also include smaller institutions or individuals. The primary difference between a bond and a note is that there is a market in which bonds are actively traded. A note is usually a private agreement between two parties that is non-tradeable.

There are several types of bonds.

- **Term bonds** mature on a specific date, whereas **serial bonds** are a set of bonds that mature at different intervals.

- **Debenture bonds**, often just referred to as "debentures," are unsecured bonds that are backed only by the bondholder's faith in the company's good reputation.

- **Redeemable bonds**, or callable bonds, have a callable feature whereby the bond issuer has the right to buy back the bonds before maturity at a set or "call" price.

- **Mortgage bonds**, or secured bonds, can be issued when a company puts up specific assets as collateral in the event that it defaults on interest or principal repayments.

- **Convertible bonds** give bondholders the option of converting or exchanging the bonds for a specific number of the company's shares.

- **Registered bonds** list the bondholders as registered owners who receive regular interest payments on the interest payment dates.

- **Coupon bonds** contain detachable coupons that state the amount and due date of the interest payment. These coupons can be removed and cashed by the holder separately.

Bond Issuance

Similar to a company's stock, a bond issue must first be authorized by the corporation's board of directors. To authorize a bond issue, the board of directors must determine the following.

- the total number of bonds to authorize and issue
- the **face value** of the bonds, which is the amount to be paid to the investor upon maturity date; the face value is also sometimes referred to as the bond's par value; the *bond price* is quoted as a percentage of the bond's face value.
- the **contractual interest rate**, which is the annual percentage rate of interest the investor receives on the face value of each bond; the contractual rate is also sometimes referred to as the bond's coupon rate
- the **maturity date**, which is the date on which the final payment is due to the investor

All of these details are stated in a **bond certificate**, a document that is issued as an official record to investors when they purchase their bonds.

A bond is an interest-bearing investment vehicle whereby money is received from investors in exchange for interest payments. Interest payments are determined by the bond's contractual interest rate, which is written on the bond. The contractual interest rate is an annual rate. For example, if an investor buys a $100,000 bond with a 10% interest rate, the investor earns $10,000 every year ($100,000 × 10%). However, most bonds pay out interest semi-annually (twice a year). To calculate this, the annual interest is simply divided by two. So the semi-annual interest for the above bond is $5,000 ($10,000 ÷ 2).

When deciding whether to finance its operations using debt or equity, a company must assess the potential effects of the various alternatives. In other words, is it more advantageous for the company to seek financing through long-term liabilities, or by issuing equity (i.e. stock) to investors? One way of assessing the various options is calculating earnings per share (EPS). As you learned in Chapter 16, EPS is calculated as shown in Figure 17.2.

$$\text{Earnings per Share (EPS)} = \frac{\text{Net Income} - \text{Preferred Dividends}}{\text{Weighted Average Number of Common Shares Outstanding}}$$

FIGURE 17.2

Using earnings per share as an indicator, a company seeks to earn a higher EPS with the borrowed funds than the amount of interest that must be paid on those funds. When a company finances additional assets with liabilities, this is known as *financial leverage*. With higher financial leverage comes higher risk, because the related liabilities must be repaid, which often includes interest as well. Despite the higher risk, stockholders get a higher return if the rate of return that the company receives is higher than the interest rate the company has to pay.

To illustrate, suppose that a corporation needs $800,000 to expand its manufacturing plant. The company expects the expanded plant to yield $100,000 in additional income (before paying interest and income tax). The company's current net income is $200,000 per year, and it has $1,500,000 in equity, consisting of 100,000, $10 par value shares of common stock and $500,000 in retained earnings. (The company does not have any preferred stock or additional paid-in capital.) The company is considering the following options.

- Plan 1—Raise $800,000 by issuing 80,000 shares of $10 par value common stock to investors
- Plan 2—Raise $800,000 by issuing bonds that pay 10% annual interest
- Plan 3—Do not expand

The three options, and their potential effects on net income, equity and earnings per share, are shown in Figure 17.3. Assume that stock is issued on the first day of the fiscal year for Plan 1, and that bonds are issued on the first day of the fiscal year for Plan 2. The tax rate is assumed to be 30%.

	Plan 1 Equity Financing	Plan 2 Debt Financing	Plan 3 Do Not Expand
Income before Interest Expense and Income Tax	$300,000	$300,000	$200,000
Less: Interest Expense	0	80,000	0
Income before Income Tax	300,000	220,000	200,000
Income Tax	90,000	66,000	60,000
Net Income	$210,000	$154,000	$140,000
Weighted Average Number of Common Shares Outstanding	180,000	100,000	100,000
Earnings per Share (EPS)	$1.17	$1.54	$1.40

FIGURE 17.3

As Figure 17.3 indicates, the company can earn the highest earnings per share if it expands through debt financing by issuing the 10% bonds. This is why many companies choose debt financing over equity financing, especially when they are confident that they can meet interest payment obligations.

Companies that issue bonds want to pay the lowest interest possible, but must remain competitive with other investment opportunities or potential buyers will invest elsewhere. That is why companies generally issue bonds at the going or **market interest rate**, which is the interest rate that investors can demand in return for lending their money. For example, if the market rate is 10%, the company is likely to issue the bond with a 10% interest rate; this is known as issuing a bond at par (face value). But, since it can take several months to arrange the printing and distribution of bonds, rates of existing bonds can differ significantly from current market rates. If the bonds' coupon rate differs from the market rate when the bonds are issued, the market responds by adjusting the prices of the bonds up or down from the bonds' face value, depending on whether the bonds' coupon rate is higher or lower than the market rate. Calculating the market price of bonds involves a concept known as the time value of money, which is discussed next.

IN THE REAL WORLD

 When potential investors want to purchase bonds, they need to be able to assess the creditworthiness of the issuer and the securities that they are offering. They often rely on information from bond rating agencies such as Moody's, Standard & Poor's (S&P), and Fitch Group.

Bond rating agencies review and assign ratings to the issuers of bonds and other debt instruments. A company's credit grade indicates its financial health and how likely it will continue to pay interest and return the bond's principal at maturity. Each agency uses its own evaluation and grading system. For instance, S&P uses a rating grade system ranging from AAA (highest quality) to D (in default). Bonds rated from AAA to BBB are known as *investment grade* because they are of high to medium quality and considered safe investments. (These grades often include a plus (+) or a minus (−) to indicate their standing within their category.)

Ratings that range from BB+ and lower are considered *non-investment grade* or *junk bonds* because of their higher risk level or potential to default on payments. Some investors, however, may be attracted to these lower-grade bonds because of their much higher market rates of interest that they pay—that is, if the company behind them survives to pay its obligations.

The Concept of Present Value

LO 2

The value of money changes over time due to interest. If money is lent, it is repaid with interest. When you deposit money in your bank account, you are essentially loaning your money to the bank. The bank pays you interest to "borrow" your money. Conversely, if you borrow money from the bank, you must pay back the principal you borrowed, plus interest as payment for the loan. Therefore, if you are given a choice whether to receive $100 today or $100 one year from now, receiving $100 today is always a better choice because you can deposit $100 today, and if the annual interest rate is 10%, the money will grow into $110 by the end of the year. In other words, $100 today is worth more than $100 in the future.

The world of finance often refers to this phenomenon as the **time value of money**. It is important for accountants to be familiar with this because it is a basic principle of economics and finance. Furthermore, it affects the amounts in transactions that an accountant records over time. If a company keeps money in a bank, its value will change even if nothing is done to it.

Here is a simple example to show how the value of money changes over a longer period of time. Suppose Samuel has one dollar and invests it for one year at an interest rate of 10%. At the end of the year, Samuel has made 10 cents in interest and has a total of $1.10.

At the start of the second year, Samuel starts with $1.10. The interest for the year amounts to 11 cents ($1.10 × 10%) for a year-end balance of $1.21.

There is a pattern developing. The more money that is left in an interest-bearing account, the more the interest grows each year. In the first year, interest was 10 cents. In the second year, it was 11 cents. Figure 17.4 shows the interest that would accumulate in the account over a period of 10 years.

This phenomenon is referred to as **compound interest**, which is the piling on effect that applying the same interest rate has on an account over a period of time. With each passing period, the interest rate is applied to interest on top of the principal. The amount

Year	Opening Balance	Interest at 10%	Closing Balance
1	1.0000	0.1000	1.1000
2	1.1000	0.1100	1.2100
3	1.2100	0.1210	1.3310
4	1.3310	0.1331	1.4641
5	1.4641	0.1464	1.6105
6	1.6105	0.1611	1.7716
7	1.7716	0.1772	1.9487
8	1.9487	0.1949	2.1436
9	2.1436	0.2144	2.3579
10	2.3579	0.2358	2.5937

FIGURE 17.4

of interest earned in Year 10 is over 23 cents, more than double the amount of interest earned in Year 1.

The closing balance in the second row of the chart ($1.21) is the value of the money in the account after Year 2, also referred to as the **future value**. Following this basic logic, the future value of the money after Year 5 is $1.61; after Year 10, it is $2.59.

Calculating the value of money can work in reverse, too. An accountant can try to calculate what amount needs to be invested today to produce a certain amount in the future. This is known as the **present value**.

Figure 17.5 shows the present values of $1.00 over 10 years, given an interest rate of 10%. The factors are calculated using a formula that is beyond the scope of this book. However, these factors can be found in many mathematical textbooks, and are commonly included as tables in professional accounting exams. Most business calculators include functions which use the factors, as do common spreadsheet programs.

The chart provides answers for the following question: What amount needs to be invested now to create $1 in x number of years, with x representing Years 1 to 10 and assuming an interest rate of 10%?

Year	Factor
1	0.9091
2	0.8264
3	0.7513
4	0.6830
5	0.6209
6	0.5645
7	0.5132
8	0.4665
9	0.4241
10	0.3855

FIGURE 17.5

An investor requiring $1.00 after one year would have to invest about 91 cents (as indicated on the first line of the chart). If the investor wanted $1 after 10 years, 39 cents would have to be invested now (as shown on the last line of the chart). The difference between the amounts is a testament to the power of compound interest. Waiting nine years to get the same payoff means initially investing less than half the money. The greater the interest rate, and the longer this interest rate is applied, the more compound interest is earned.

It should be noted that Figure 17.5 applies only to an interest rate calculation of 10%. Separate charts need to be used when other interest rates are involved in calculating present and future values.

Time Value of Money and Bonds Payable

In the context of the current discussion of bonds payable, the time value of money matters because it helps determine the price the bonds will sell for. The price of the bonds can be determined by calculating the present value of the principal and future interest payments. In the previous calculations, interest was stated at an annual rate and paid once per year. Interest on bonds is normally paid semi-annually. Therefore, when applying present value concepts, the number of periods is doubled and the interest rate is divided by two.

Some corporations also issue what are known as *zero-coupon bonds*, which pay zero interest but pay the full face value of the bond at maturity. These bonds sell at a discount (i.e. the buyer pays lower than face value), at an amount equal to the present value of their face value.

A $100,000 bond issued with 10% interest payable semi-annually over the next five years is used for the following calculations.

$$\text{Future Value } (FV) = \$100{,}000$$
$$\text{Semi-Annual Interest Rate } (i) = 10\% \times \tfrac{1}{2} = 5\%$$
$$\text{Semi-Annual Interest Payments } (PMT) = \$100{,}000 \times 5\% = \$5{,}000$$
$$\text{Number of Periods } (n) = 5 \times 2 = 10$$

Using the period 10 factor from Figure 17.6, which is 0.6139, the present value of the $100,000 principal repayment is calculated as follows.

$$\$100{,}000 \times 0.6139 = \$61{,}390$$

The interest payments are different from the principal repayment in that they represent an **annuity** because they are periodic and recurring fixed payments. One of two methods can be used to calculate the present value of the interest payment annuity.

Periods	Factor
1	0.9524
2	0.9070
3	0.8638
4	0.8227
5	0.7835
6	0.7462
7	0.7107
8	0.6768
9	0.6446
10	0.6139

FIGURE 17.6

1. The present value of each interest payment can be calculated individually. For example, the first interest payment of $5,000 in six months is multiplied by the period 1 factor from Figure 17.6 to determine the present value of that particular payment. To this amount, add the second $5,000 payment in 12 months and multiply it by the period 2 factor. After this, add the third $5,000 payment in 18 months and multiply it by the period 3 factor. This goes on for all 10 interest payments, which can get tedious and is prone to error. For a five-year bond, this calculation would be repeated 10 times (once for each semi-annual interest payment) to determine the present value of all the interest payments.

2. Since annuities are a common occurrence in the financial industry, tables containing factors for annuities have been developed (see Figure 17.7). Using this table, the present value of *all* interest payments can be made in just one calculation.

Periods	Factor
1	0.9524
2	1.8594
3	2.7232
4	3.5460
5	4.3295
6	5.0757
7	5.7864
8	6.4632
9	7.1078
10	7.7217

FIGURE 17.7

Calculate the present value of the future interest payments.

Present Value of $5,000 payments (annuity) made over 10 periods
= $5,000 x 7.7217
= $38,608.50 (round to $38,610)

Summary

Present value of principal	$61,390
Present value of interest payments	$38,610
Total proceeds	$100,000

Note: The present value of the interest payments is rounded to $38,610 for illustrative purposes.

A spreadsheet or financial calculator with the present value function would not require rounding. This text uses the tables at the end of the chapter for illustration and exercise purposes. Figures may be slightly different if a spreadsheet or financial calculator are used.

It is important to note that the present value of the principal and interest payments equal the face value of the bond ($100,000). This occurred because we have discounted the 5% bond using the 5% interest rate. This shows that the face value of the bond is equal to the present value of the payments when the market rate is equal to the interest rate of the bond.

A CLOSER LOOK

Present value (*PV*) and future value (*FV*) can also be calculated using either a business or financial calculator, or a spreadsheet program. These tools use the same factors found in charts or tables, but they allow you to eliminate steps in calculations. Rather than separately calculating the PV or FV of the bond's face value and then its interest, these tools enable you to find the total value using one calculation. All you need to know are the input values: the bond's face value, the market rate of interest per period (*i*), the number of periods (*n*), and the interest payment (*PMT*). You may find that you get slightly different answers using the tables than you do using a digital tool; this is simply due to rounding factors used in the PV and FV tables. Different calculators may vary in their method of operation, but they are based on the same concepts and use the same inputs. Check the user manual or help file for your calculator or spreadsheet.

Issuing Bonds at Par

LO 3

Business Time Inc., a publisher of investment-related books, magazines and newspapers, wants to raise money for long-term financing by issuing bonds. On December 31, 2018, the company issues 1,000, 10-year bonds at par, at a price of $100 each with 5% annual interest. Figure 17.8 shows the journal entry for the transaction.

BALANCE SHEET	
CURRENT ASSETS	**CURRENT LIABILITIES**
CASH + $100,000 DR	ACCOUNTS PAYABLE
ACCOUNTS RECEIVABLE	INTEREST PAYABLE
MERCHANDISE INVENTORY	UNEARNED REVENUE
PREPAID EXPENSES	NOTES PAYABLE (CURRENT)
NONCURRENT ASSETS	LONG-TERM LIABILITIES
LONG-TERM INVESTMENTS	NOTES PAYABLE (LONG-TERM)
PROPERTY, PLANT & EQUIPMENT	BONDS PAYABLE + $100,000 CR
INTANGIBLE ASSETS	STOCKHOLDERS' EQUITY
	PAID-IN CAPITAL
GOODWILL	RETAINED EARNINGS

JOURNAL			
Date	**Account Title and Explanation**	**Debit**	**Credit**
Dec 31	Cash	100,000	
	Bonds Payable		100,000
	Issue of $100,000 worth of bonds at par (due in 2028)		

FIGURE 17.8

The total amount of $100,000 is debited to the cash account. A corresponding liability shows a credit increase of $100,000 in the bonds payable account. Since the principal for the bonds is due in 10 years, the liability is classified as long-term and placed in that section of the balance sheet.

Issuing the bond for a 10-year term means that a company has to make interest payments to its bondholders every year for 10 years. Most bonds call for semi-annual (twice per year) interest payments. For simplicity, interest is paid annually in this illustration.

When an interest payment is made, a $5,000 credit represents a decrease in cash, while a $5,000 debit represents an increase in interest expense. This is illustrated in Figure 17.9.

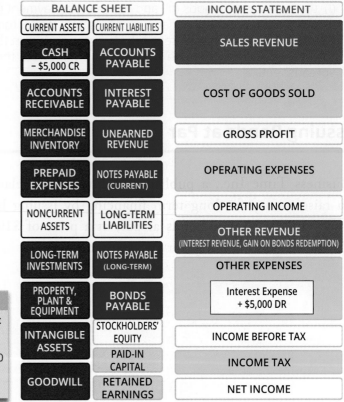

JOURNAL			
Date	Account Title and Explanation	Debit	Credit
Dec 31	Interest Expense	5,000	
	Cash		5,000
	Pay interest on bonds		

FIGURE 17.9

During the 10-year term that Business Time Inc. is making interest payments to its bondholders, the year end may occur before the payment is made. A portion of the interest must be accrued, even though the interest is actually paid in the following period.

The company is therefore required to expense the interest during the period in which it was incurred; this is regarded as an accrual and represents a decrease in the company's equity for the period. Recognizing the interest expense in the same period as when the bond proceed is used to generate revenue follows the expense recognition principle under the accrual basis of accounting. If the interest expense is not properly accrued, the current period's liability would be understated and equity would be overstated.

Assume for a moment that the company's year end is October 31, but the bond anniversary date is December 31. On October 31, when the company prepares its financial statements, it will accrue only 10/12 of the annual interest, as shown in Figure 17.10.

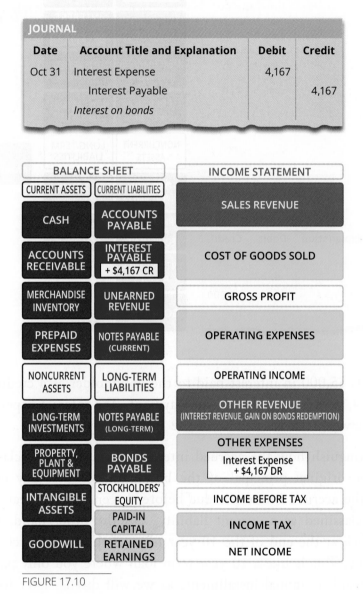

FIGURE 17.10

As with the other interest payments on the bond, $4,167 is expensed as a debit (increase) to bond interest on October 31. However, unlike the previous transaction, interest payable (accrued liabilities) is credited instead of cash.

Continuing the above example, when interest is paid on December 31, the payment is recorded as shown in Figure 17.11.

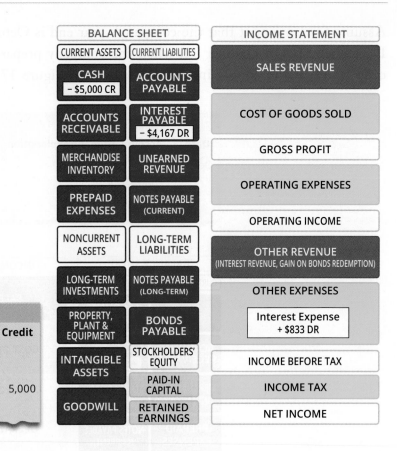

JOURNAL			
Date	Account Title and Explanation	Debit	Credit
Dec 31	Interest Expense	833	
	Interest Payable	4,167	
	Cash		5,000
	Interest paid		

FIGURE 17.11

This transaction records $5,000 in interest paid to the bondholder as a credit to cash. The interest accrued at year end ($4,167) is cleared with the payment. The interest expense ($833) is recorded for the two months between the year end and the interest payment date.

It is important to distinguish how the accrued interest on the bonds is classified on the balance sheet compared to the original principal of the bond: on the first day of the fiscal year, the company knows that the accrued interest is due before the end of the year. Therefore, that year's interest payable gets classified as a current liability. On the other hand, the original principal (which will be paid back at the end of the 10-year term of the bond) is classified as a long-term liability by the company. This is like a 10-year term loan where you only pay the interest; that is, the principal is not repaid in annual installments as we will discuss later for a note payable.

A bond's face value is printed on the face of the bond. The face value is the same as the principal. The principal amount gets paid back to the bondholder, regardless of any changes in market price. In other words, *regardless of the price paid for the bond*, the business needs to pay the full face value of the bond to the bondholder when the bond matures.

JOURNAL			
Date	Account Title and Explanation	Debit	Credit
Dec 31	Bonds Payable	100,000	
	Cash		100,000
	Payment of bond principal on maturity date		

FIGURE 17.12

For example, Figure 17.12 shows the journal entry when Business Time repays the bond principal on December 31, 2028.

In the next section, we will look at what happens when the market value and the face value of a bond are not the same.

Pause & Reflect

Exercise 17-1

On January 1, 2018, Decorum Inc. issues 1,500 five-year bonds at par at a price of $200 each, with 9% interest paid annually. Show how the bond issuance transaction is recorded.

JOURNAL			
Date	Account Title and Explanation	Debit	Credit

See Appendix I for solutions.

Issuing Bonds at a Discount or a Premium

We have demonstrated how a bond issue is treated at par. However, the period from the time that a business decides to issue the bonds to the time they are printed for distribution can be several months. In the meantime, the market rate is likely to have changed. This means that the interest rate on the bond may end up being higher—or lower—than that of the market. This affects the demand for the company's bonds. The price of the bond must, therefore, be adjusted accordingly.

There are two scenarios to consider when such situations occur.

Scenario 1: Market value is less than face value. The bond will be sold at a discount.

Scenario 2: Market value is more than face value. The bond will be sold at a premium.

Issuing Bonds at a Discount

When bonds are sold at par (or face value), the resulting transaction is relatively simple. From the previous example, Business Time Inc. received a lump sum of $100,000 and established a bonds payable for that same amount.

Things change when market interest rates rise above the interest rate attached to the bond. When that happens, investors can receive higher interest payments from other bonds and market investments.

To deter investors from those other investments and to attract them to the issuer's bonds, the company should offer the bonds at a more attractive price—at a discount. The **discount** is the difference between the price paid and the par value.

But what should that discount price be? The company sets a discount price which compensates the investor for the money lost with the bond's lower interest rate. Here is a demonstration of how this is done.

Assume on January 1, 2018, Energy Bite Inc. issued bonds with a maturity value of $100,000 when the market rate of interest was 12%. The bonds have an annual contractual interest rate of 10% and mature in five years. Interest on the bonds is payable semi-annually on July 1 and January 1 of each year. The company's year end is September 30. The principal is $100,000, which means that the semi-annual interest payment is $5,000 ($100,000 × 10% × ½).

However, since the market rate is 12%, receiving an interest payment of 10% is not high enough to attract investors. In that case, the company must lower the price of the bond to below face value so that the buyer gets an *effective interest rate* of 12%. It is important to understand that the buyer still expects to get $100,000 for the bond when it matures plus the $5,000 interest every period regardless of what was initially paid. Using the same present value concepts already discussed, here is how the price of the bond is determined.

> Note: Use Table 17-1 and Table 17-2 at the end of the chapter for factors used in the following calculations.

Future Value *(FV)* = $100,000

Semi-Annual Payment *(PMT)* = (10% × ½) × $100,000 = $5,000

Semi-Annual Market Interest Rate *(i)* = 12% × ½ = 6%

Number of Periods *(n)* = 5 × 2 = 10

Present Value of the Principal *(PV)* = $100,000 × 0.5584 = $55,840
(Semi-Annual Market Interest Rate *(i)* of 6%, 10 periods *(n)*)

Present Value of Future Interest Payments *(PV)* = $5,000 × 7.3601 = $36,800
(6% Semi-Annual Market Interest Rate *(i)*, 10 periods *(n)*)

Total price bondholders are willing to pay for their investment = $55,840 + $36,800 = $92,640

Remember to always use the market interest rate to determine the present value factor because that is what investors use to determine what they should pay for the bonds. However, the bond contractual rate should be used to determine the interest payment as that is the rate attached to the bond. The price investors are willing to pay is lower than the par value because the market rate is 12%, meaning investors can easily get a return higher than 10% elsewhere in the market. Therefore, the price they are willing to pay will be lower.

The difference between the price for the bond paid and its par value is known as the *discount*. Accounting for the bond discount requires the use of a contra account. As you learned in your previous accounting studies, a contra account is linked to another account and records decreases in the value of that other account. This is done so that the original value of the related account remains unchanged. For example, a contra account is used when accounting for the depreciation of an asset such as property, plant and equipment.

Figure 17.13 shows how this receipt of $92,640 for the issue of Energy Bite Inc. bonds (at discount) is recorded by the company using the contra account called Discount on Bonds Payable.

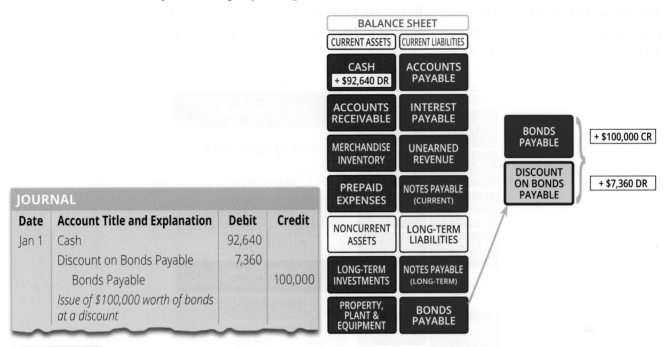

JOURNAL			
Date	Account Title and Explanation	Debit	Credit
Jan 1	Cash	92,640	
	Discount on Bonds Payable	7,360	
	Bonds Payable		100,000
	Issue of $100,000 worth of bonds at a discount		

FIGURE 17.13

So although Energy Bite has issued a $100,000 bond, and this amount must be paid when the bond matures, it only received $92,640 from the bondholder.

Because of the discount, issuing bonds below the market rate makes it more costly for the company to borrow money. At the maturity date, the company needs to repay the face value of $100,000, rather than the issue price of $92,640; the discount itself ($7,360) is an additional cost of borrowing. Over the life of the bonds, the total cost of borrowing (interest and discount) must be allocated to the interest expense account. This process is called **amortizing the discount** and increases the amount of interest expense reported in each period. We will amortize the discount using two different methods. One method of amortization (*straight-line amortization method*) is illustrated in this section. The other method (the *effective-interest amortization method*) is illustrated in Appendix 17A.

GAAP vs IFRS

Although companies are strictly required to use the effective-interest amortization method (also called the "interest method") under IFRS, GAAP also specifies the use of the effective-interest method, but allows the straight-line method if the results are not significantly different from the effective-interest method.

In the real world, companies most often choose the effective-interest method. This is because the calculation for the straight-line method does not accurately reflect the change in value of an item over time. This is true with regard to the value of assets, and is also true with regard to the value of bonds issued at a discount or premium.

The bond discount is amortized semi-annually using the **straight-line amortization method**, which means the same amount of bond discount is recorded each period. The bond discount is recorded as an interest expense. The principle involved is similar to accounting for the depreciation of an asset, such as property, plant and equipment, in that the discount on a bond is also amortized over the life of the bond. At the end of five years (10 semi-annual periods), the discount on the bond reaches a zero balance. In this example, the discount is amortized as $736 per period ($7,360 ÷ 10), as shown in Figure 17.14.

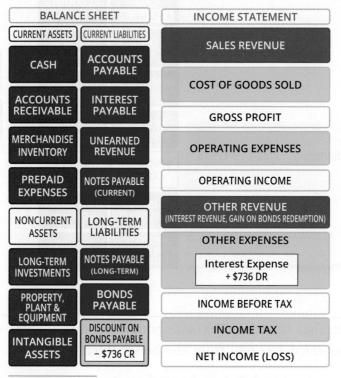

FIGURE 17.14

Figure 17.15 shows an amortization table of the bond for the 10 periods. Notice how the discount balance decreases while the bond book value increases.

Straight-Line Amortization Table of Bond Discount					
Semi-Annual Interest Period	A Interest Payment ($100,000 × 5%)	B Discount Amortization (D / 10 periods)	C Interest Expense (A + B)	D Discount Balance (D [Previous Period] – B)	E Bond Book Value ($100,000 – D)
0				$7,360	$92,640
1	$5,000	$736	$5,736	6,624	93,376
2	5,000	736	5,736	5,888	94,112
3	5,000	736	5,736	5,152	94,848
4	5,000	736	5,736	4,416	95,584
5	5,000	736	5,736	3,680	96,320
6	5,000	736	5,736	2,944	97,056
7	5,000	736	5,736	2,208	97,792
8	5,000	736	5,736	1,472	98,528
9	5,000	736	5,736	736	99,264
10	5,000	736	5,736	0	100,000
Total	$50,000	$7,360	$57,360	-	-

FIGURE 17.15

At the end of the first period when the interest payment is made, the company records the total interest expense for the bond, $5,736, the amortization on the discount, $736, and the cash paid to the bondholder, $5,000. The journal entry and the effects on the company's account balances are shown in Figure 17.16.

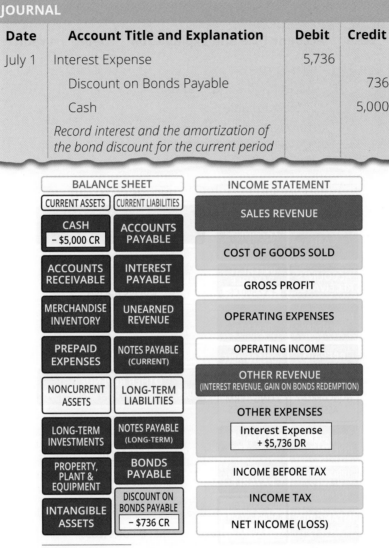

FIGURE 17.16

Over five years (10 semi-annual periods), interest is paid to the bond holder and the discount is amortized. As this happens, the value of the discount on the bonds decreases and the book value (or carrying value) of the bonds increases. By the end of the five years, the discount is reduced to zero and the book value of the bond is equal to its face value, $100,000.

Since the year end is September 30, 2018, Energy Bite needs to accrue interest expense before the second payment date on January 1, 2019. Figure 17.17 shows that at each year end for the next five years, the interest expense is accrued and the discount is amortized for three months, from July 1 to September 30. The interest expense and the amortized discounts for period 2 (six months) can be found in the table from Figure 17.15. These numbers must be adjusted to reflect only three months instead of six months. As shown in Figure 17.17, the interest payable is credited for $2,500 ($5,000 × ³⁄₆), discount on bond payable is amortized (credited) for $368 ($736 × ³⁄₆) and interest expense is debited for 2,868 ($2,500 + $368).

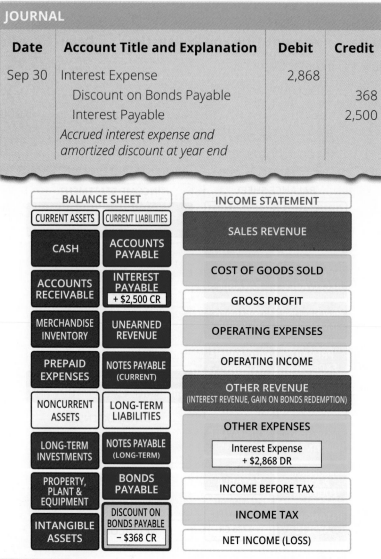

FIGURE 17.17

As shown in Figure 17.18, on January 1, 2019, the cash payment is made for $5,000. Interest payable is debited for $2,500 and interest expense is also debited for the remaining balance of period 2, which is $2,868 ($5,736 - $2,868). The rest of the discount on bonds payable of period 2 is also amortized and credited for $368 ($736 - $368).

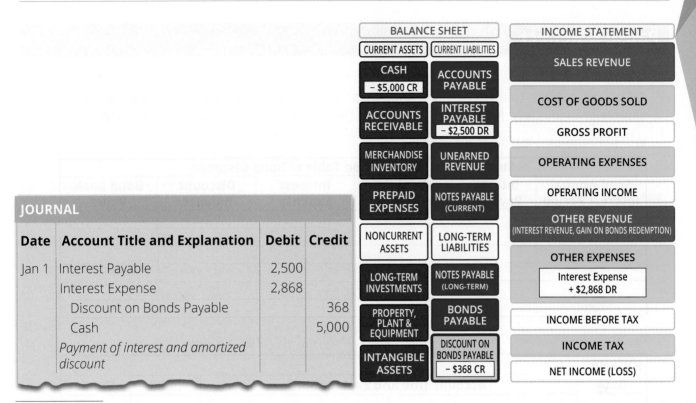

FIGURE 17.18

At the end of the five-year term, cash is credited in the amount of $100,000, and the same amount is debited to bonds payable, thereby clearing the liability. Assume that any outstanding interest has already been paid and recorded in a separate transaction. When the last interest payment is made, the discount on bonds payable is also fully amortized and thus has a zero balance remaining. The journal entry is presented in Figure 17.19.

JOURNAL

Date	Account Title and Explanation	Debit	Credit
Jan 1	Bonds Payable	100,000	
	Cash		100,000
	Repay $100,000 to bondholder		

FIGURE 17.19

Pause & Reflect

Exercise 17-2

On January 1, 2018, Draper Corporation issues $100,000 worth of 8%, two-year bonds with interest payable semi-annually. Just prior to issuing the bonds, the market interest rate increases to 10%.

a) Fill in the amortization table below.

Straight-Line Amortization Table of Bond Discount					
Semi-Annual Interest Period	Interest Payment	Discount Amortization	Interest Expense	Discount Balance	Bond Book Value
0					
1					
2					
3					
4					
Total					

b) Show how Draper Corporation records the bond issuance transaction.

JOURNAL			
Date	Account Title and Explanation	Debit	Credit

See Appendix I for solutions.

Issuing Bonds at a Premium

We have already discussed why companies issue bonds at a discount. The higher market interest rate makes the bond's interest rate less competitive, so the selling price is reduced to make up the difference with potential investors.

Of course, there is a flip side to that scenario. By the time a company's bond issue reaches the market, the market interest rate may decline. This means that the bond's interest rate would be higher than that of the market, and produce a higher rate of return for an investor than what the market is currently offering. This creates a greater demand for the company's bond, which means the company can now sell the bond at a premium (at a price that is higher than its face value).

A company that issues bonds at a premium takes the same steps in recording the transaction as it would with a discount, except in reverse. Let us review those steps with an example using Energy Bite Inc. again.

On January 1, 2018, Energy Bite Inc. issued bonds with a maturity value of $100,000. The bonds have an annual contractual interest rate of 10% and mature in five years. Interest on the bonds is payable semi-annually on July 1 and January 1 of each year. The company's year end is September 30. A market rate of 10% means that the bonds could be issued at par. A market rate of 12% means that the bonds were issued at discount. What happens when the market rate is 8%?

> Note: Use Table 17-1 and Table 17-2 at the end of the chapter for factors used in the following calculations.

$$\text{Future Value } (FV) = \$100{,}000$$
$$\text{Semi-Annual Payment } (PMT) = 5\% \times \$100{,}000 = \$5{,}000$$
$$\text{Semi-Annual Market Interest Rate } (i) = 8\% \times \tfrac{1}{2} = 4\%$$
$$\text{Number of Periods } (n) = 5 \times 2 = 10$$

$$\text{Present Value of the Principal } (PV) = \$100{,}000 \times 0.6756 = \$67{,}560$$
$$\text{(Semi-Annual Market Interest Rate } (i) \text{ of } 4\%, \text{ 10 periods } (n))$$

$$\text{Present Value of Future Interest Payments} = \$5{,}000 \times 8.1109 = \$40{,}555$$
$$\text{(4\% Semi-Annual Market Interest Rate } (i), \text{ 10 Periods } (n))$$

$$\text{Total price bondholders are willing to pay for their investment} = \$67{,}560 + \$40{,}555 = \$108{,}115$$

The price investors are willing to pay is higher than the par value because the market rate is 8%, meaning it is difficult for investors to get a return as high as 10% elsewhere in the market.

Figure 17.20 shows how this bond issue is recorded on the company's books.

As always, proceeds from the sale are deposited and recorded as a debit to cash. On the other side of the balance sheet, the principal amount of the bond ($100,000) is credited to bonds payable (a long-term liability). Finally, the premium on the bond of $8,115 is recorded as a credit in an account called Premium on Bonds Payable. Premium on bonds payable appears directly below the bonds payable account on the balance sheet. So far, there is no change to equity; therefore, the income statement is not impacted.

BALANCE SHEET

CURRENT ASSETS	CURRENT LIABILITIES
CASH + $108,115 DR	ACCOUNTS PAYABLE
ACCOUNTS RECEIVABLE	INTEREST PAYABLE
MERCHANDISE INVENTORY	UNEARNED REVENUE
PREPAID EXPENSES	NOTES PAYABLE (CURRENT)
NONCURRENT ASSETS	LONG-TERM LIABILITIES
LONG-TERM INVESTMENTS	NOTES PAYABLE (LONG-TERM)
PROPERTY, PLANT & EQUIPMENT	BONDS PAYABLE + $100,000 CR
INTANGIBLE ASSETS	PREMIUM ON BONDS PAYABLE + $8,115 CR

JOURNAL

Date	Account Title and Explanation	Debit	Credit
Jan 1	Cash	108,115	
	Premium on Bonds Payable		8,115
	Bonds Payable		100,000
	Issue of $100,000 worth of bonds at a premium		

FIGURE 17.20

Unlike the discount on a bond, which is recorded in a contra-liability account, the premium is recorded in an adjunct liability account. The nature of an adjunct account is opposite to that of a contra account. The balance of Discount on Bonds Payable account, which is a contra liability account, is deducted from the Bonds Payable balance on the balance sheet. The balance of Premium on Bonds Payable account, which is an adjunct liability account, is added to the Bonds Payable balance on the balance sheet. When the discount on bond is amortized, it increases the interest expense. On the contrary, when the premium on bond is amortized, it decreases the interest expense.

Because of the premium, issuing bonds above the market rate makes it less costly for the company to borrow money. At the maturity date, the company needs to repay the face value of $100,000, rather than the issue price of $108,115. In other words, the premium itself ($8,115) is reducing the cost of borrowing. Over the life of the bonds, the total cost of borrowing (interest payment less premium) must be allocated to the interest expense account. This process of allocating the premium is called **amortizing the premium**, which decreases the amount of interest expense reported in each period.

Similar to the discount on a bond issue, a bond premium is amortized each period when the interest payments are made. In other words, the premium liability of $8,115 is amortized over the term of the bond. Using the straight-line amortization method, this amount comes to $812 ($8,115 ÷ 10, rounded to the nearest dollar) over each of the 10 semi-annual periods. Therefore, $812 is debited to an account called Premium on Bonds Payable every period until the amount is zero upon maturity of the bond.

Figure 17.21 shows an amortization table of the bond for 10 periods. Notice how the premium balance and the bond book value decrease.

Straight-Line Amortization Table of Bond Premium					
Semi-Annual Interest Period	A Interest Payment ($100,000 × 5%)	B Premium Amortization (D / 10 periods)	C Interest Expense (A − B)	D Premium Balance (D [Previous Period] − B)	E Bond Book Value ($100,000 + D)
0				$8,115	$108,115
1	$5,000	$812	$4,188	7,303	107,303
2	5,000	812	4,188	6,491	106,491
3	5,000	812	4,188	5,679	105,679
4	5,000	812	4,188	4,867	104,867
5	5,000	812	4,188	4,055	104,055
6	5,000	812	4,188	3,243	103,243
7	5,000	812	4,188	2,431	102,431
8	5,000	812	4,188	1,619	101,619
9	5,000	812	4,188	807	100,807
10	5,000	807*	4,193	0	100,000
Total	$50,000	$8,115	$41,885	-	-

*$807 is due to rounding

FIGURE 17.21

Figure 17.22 shows how the transaction is recorded at the end of the first period if the straight-line method is used.

The $5,000 interest payment is recorded each period with a credit to cash. The expense to the company is $4,188 and the rest of the debit is taken care of by the $812 amortization of the premium calculated using the straight-line method.

JOURNAL			
Date	Account Title and Explanation	Debit	Credit
July 1	Interest Expense	4,188	
	Premium on Bonds Payable	812	
	Cash		5,000
	Payment of interest and amortization of the bond premium		

FIGURE 17.22

When financial statements are prepared, the premium on bonds is added to the face value of the bonds. The partial balance sheet at the end of the first period is shown in Figure 17.23, after 1/10 of the premium is applied.

Bonds Payable	$100,000
Added: Unamortized Premium	7,303
Book Value	$107,303

FIGURE 17.23

Since the year end is September 30, 2018, Energy Bite needs to accrue interest expense before the second payment date on January 1, 2019. At each year end for the next five years, the interest expense is accrued and the premium is amortized for three months, from July 1 to September 30. The interest expense and the amortized premium for period 2 (six months) can be found in the table from Figure 17.21. These numbers must be adjusted to reflect only three months instead of six months. As shown in Figure 17.24, the interest payable is credited for $2,500 ($5,000 × 3/6), premium on bonds payable is amortized (debited) for $406 ($812 × 3/6) and interest expense is debited for $2,094 ($2,500 - $406).

JOURNAL			
Date	Account Title and Explanation	Debit	Credit
Sep 30	Interest Expense	2,094	
	Premium on Bonds Payable	406	
	Interest Payable		2,500
	Accrued interest expense and amortized premium at year end		

FIGURE 17.24

As shown in Figure 17.25, on January 1, 2019, the cash payment is made for $5,000. Interest payable is debited for $2,500 and interest expense is also debited for the

JOURNAL			
Date	Account Title and Explanation	Debit	Credit
Jan 1	Interest Payable	2,500	
	Interest Expense	2,094	
	Premium on Bonds Payable	406	
	Cash		5,000
	Payment of interest and amortized discount		

FIGURE 17.25

remaining balance of period 2, which is $2,094 ($4,188 − $2,094). The rest of the premium on bonds payable of period 2 should also be amortized and debited for $406 ($812 − $406).

At the end of five years, the company pays the bondholder $100,000 instead of the $108,115 that was originally received.

Over the 10 periods, the journal entry shown in Figure 17.22 is repeated. As this happens, the value of the premium on the bonds decreases and the book value (or carrying value) of the bond decreases. By the end of the 10 periods, the premium is reduced to zero and the book value of the bond is the face value, $100,000.

Similar to Figure 17.13 from the discount discussion, on the maturity date, cash is credited in the amount of $100,000, and the same amount is debited to bonds payable to remove the debt from the books.

As mentioned earlier in this section, the effective-interest amortization method for a bond premium is illustrated in Appendix 17A.

A CLOSER LOOK

Recording the bond premium or discount using a separate Premium on Bonds Payable or Discount on Bonds Payable account is called the gross method. Alternatively, a bond issuer can account for bond premiums or discounts using the net method by recording them directly in the Bonds Payable account. This method eliminates the use of separate accounts to track premiums or discounts. To illustrate the differences between the two methods, the transactions below compare how issuing bonds at a discount is recorded under the net method and the gross method.

Net Method		
Jan 1	Cash	92,640	
	Bonds Payable		92,640

Gross Method		
Jan 1	Cash	92,640	
	Discount on Bonds Payable	7,360	
	Bonds Payable		100,000

The transactions below compare how the interest payment and discount amortization are recorded under the net and gross methods.

Net Method		
July 1	Interest Expense	5,558	
	Bonds Payable		558
	Cash		5,000

Gross Method		
July 1	Interest Expense	5,558	
	Discount on Bonds Payable		558
	Cash		5,000

If the bonds are issued at a premium, the differences between the two methods of accounting are still similar. The premium amount is included in the Bonds Payable account on the date of bond issuance, making the balance of bonds payable higher than the par value. When the premium is amortized, instead of debiting the Premium on Bonds Payable account, the bond issuer debits the Bonds Payable account, thus lowering its balance.

Pause & Reflect

Exercise 17-3

On January 1, 2018, The Kitchen Company issues $200,000 worth of 12%, two-year bonds with interest payable semi-annually. Just prior to issuing the bonds, the market interest rate decreases to 10%.

a) Fill in the premium amortization table below.

Straight-Line Amortization Table of Bond Premium					
Semi-Annual Interest Period	Interest Payment	Premium Amortization	Interest Expense	Premium Balance	Bond Book Value
0					
1					
2					
3					
4					
Total					

b) Show how The Kitchen Company records the bond issuance transaction.

JOURNAL			
Date	Account Title and Explanation	Debit	Credit

See Appendix I for solutions.

Retiring Bonds

Regardless of the price at which a bond was issued, whether at par, discount or premium, the underlying terms of the bond remain the same. This means that an interest payment is made regularly according to the rate on the bond. It also means that the principal amount is paid back in full. The original investor essentially loans the issuing company the principal amount.

When the bond matures, that principal amount is paid back to the current owner of the bond. This transaction is also referred to as redeeming the bond, or buying it back.

Using our example of Energy Bite Inc., let us look at how the final bond redemption is recorded. Cash is credited in the amount of $100,000. The original bonds payable, created five years earlier at the time of bond issue, is finally taken off the books with a $100,000 debit to that account. This transaction of bonds redemption is identical to what was shown earlier in Figures 17.12 and 17.19.

This transaction (shown in Figure 17.26) takes care of the redemption of the bond. However, a company sometimes issues what are known as redeemable bonds, also called callable bonds. These give the issuing company the option to buy back the bonds before the stated maturity date. The issuer might want to do this to take advantage of lower market interest rates, which would allow for the issuance of new bonds to match those lower rates. The company would then make lower annual interest payments on its bonds.

When the bonds are redeemed, in addition to removing the bonds from the books, any remaining premium or discount must also be removed.

Consider our earlier example of Energy Bite Inc. bonds, which were issued at a discount. If the company exercises a call option on the bonds at the end of Year 4 (which includes eight periods of paid interest), then according to the amortization table in Figure 17.15, the unamortized discount at the end of semi-annual interest period 8 amounts to $1,472.

JOURNAL			
Date	**Account Title and Explanation**	**Debit**	**Credit**
Jan 1	Bonds Payable	100,000	
	Cash		100,000
	Redemption of $100,000 worth of bonds		

FIGURE 17.26

The book value of the bond on this date is $98,528 ($100,000 – $1,472); however, it is likely that the amount of cash paid to redeem this bond early will be different from the book value. If the amount of cash paid is greater than the book value, a loss must be recognized. If the amount of cash paid is less than the book value, a gain must be recognized.

If Energy Bite pays $99,000 to redeem the bonds early, it records a loss of $472, as shown in Figure 17.27.

JOURNAL			
Date	**Account Title and Explanation**	**Debit**	**Credit**
Jan 1	Bonds Payable	100,000	
	Loss on Bond Redemption	472	
	Discount on Bonds Payable		1,472
	Cash		99,000
	Redemption of $100,000 worth of bonds		

FIGURE 17.27

The debit to bonds payable and the credit to discount on bonds payable are to remove both items from the balance sheet. The loss is reported on the income statement under other income and expenses. If the cash paid is less than the bond's book value, a gain is recorded and also reported on the income statement.

If we use the bonds that were issued at a premium, then the same type of transaction takes place, except that a debit is recorded to the Premium on Bonds Payable to close the account. Any gain or loss on the redemption is recorded in the same manner illustrated.

Pause & Reflect

Exercise 17-4

On June 30, 2018, The Goldstar Group has the following bond issue on its books.

Face value of bonds:	$2,000,000 of callable bonds
Premium on bonds payable:	$80,000

The company decides to redeem one-half of the bonds ($1,000,000) early. It pays $950,000 to redeem the bonds. Show how the company's accountant records the transaction.

JOURNAL			
Date	Account Title and Explanation	Debit	Credit

See Appendix I for solutions.

Notes Payable

A note payable is a legally binding document that represents money owed to the bank, an individual, corporation or other lender. In Chapter 13 you learned about short-term notes payable, which represent a current liability due within 12 months of the date of issue. Short-term notes payable are shown as current liabilities on the balance sheet at the end of the period.

Long-term notes payable, on the other hand, represent a long-term liability due beyond 12 months of the date of issue. Long-term notes payable are repayable in periodic payments, such as monthly, quarterly or semi-annually. These periodic payments on the notes are usually referred to as **installments**. A note that is used to purchase a particular asset, such as equipment or a building, is usually *secured* by the asset being purchased, meaning that the asset can be sold for cash by the lender if the borrower defaults on payment. A note secured by an asset is known as a **mortgage note**.

Notes payable are similar to bonds payable in some respects. Like bonds, notes represent the borrower's promise to repay the principal to the lender. Also, both bonds and notes require interest payments. However, whereas bonds have a stated contractual interest rate (or coupon rate), notes can have two types of interest rates. The first, a **fixed interest rate**, is a rate that remains constant for the entire term of the note. The second type of rate is a **variable interest rate**, also referred to as a "floating" rate because it fluctuates according to market interest rates. Another difference between bonds and notes is that a bond's principal is repaid all at once on a single maturity date (except in the case of serial bonds), but a note's principal is repaid in installments.

When the periodic payments, or installments, are paid on notes payable, the amount consists of both a payment toward the note's principal (its face value), and interest on the unpaid balance of the note. Let us look at an example using a company called Trigraph Inc. Suppose that Trigraph issues a $300,000 five-year, 5% note payable on January 1, 2018. The journal entry to record the issue of the note payable is shown in Figure 17.28.

JOURNAL			
Date	**Account Title and Explanation**	**Debit**	**Credit**
Jan 1	Cash	300,000	
	Notes Payable		300,000
	Issue five-year, 5% note payable (due in 2023)		

FIGURE 17.28

According to the terms of the note, the note is repayable in 60 monthly installments. Therefore, the blended payments include the interest on the outstanding principal. This type of payment is often used for mortgages, car loans, student loan payments, and so on.

The installments are made in equal monthly payments that consist of both the reduction of the principal and the monthly interest expense of 0.417% (5% × $\frac{1}{12}$) on the outstanding principal. Therefore, the interest expense decreases with each period. However, the portion of the payment that is applied to the principal increases with each period. Let us look at how this happens.

The first monthly installment on February 1 is calculated as follows.

Principal:	$300,000
Payment Terms:	60 equal installment payments of $5,661
Interest (5%):	($300,000 × 5% × $\frac{1}{12}$) = $1,250
Reduction of Principal:	$5,661 − $1,250 = $4,411

The equal installment payments can be calculated using a calculator, or by applying the present value (*PV*) concepts you used earlier in the chapter. To illustrate, we can calculate the dollar value of the monthly installment payments using the concept of present value of an annuity. The formula to calculate monthly installment payment is shown in Figure 17.29.

$$\text{Monthly Installment Payment} = \frac{\text{Note Payable Amount}}{\text{Present Value of an Annuity of \$1 for } n \text{ periods at } i\%}$$

FIGURE 17.29

The amount of the monthly installment payment is calculated by dividing the total amount of the note principal ($300,000) by the present value of an annuity of $1 for 60 periods at 0.417% compound interest (which is 52.99071). (To determine the present value factor, you can use a calculator or a spreadsheet application. The calculation is shown here.

$$\text{Monthly Installment Payment} = \frac{\$300,000}{52.99071}$$

$$= \$5,661$$

The key is determining how much of the installment payment of $5,661 is interest and how much is principal. Figure 17.30 shows an installment payment schedule for Trigraph Inc.'s note payable for the first four payment periods.

Date	A Cash Payment	B Interest Expense $(D \times 5\% \times \frac{1}{12})$	C Reduction of Principal $(A - B)$	D Principal Balance $(D - C)$
Jan 1				$300,000
Feb 1	$5,661	$1,250	$4,411	295,589
Mar 1	5,661	1,232	4,429	291,160
Apr 1	5,661	1,213	4,448	286,712

FIGURE 17.30

Column A represents the total cash payment which is fixed on each interest period and equals $5,661. The interest expense (column B) is calculated by multiplying the interest rate by the outstanding principal (column D of the previous period). The principal reduction (column C) is equal to the difference between the fixed cash payment and the interest expense. As the payments are made, the principal balance (column D) decreases.

Looking at the 2nd row in Figure 17.30, the principal balance after the February 1 payment is as follows.

$$\$300,000 - \$4,411 = \$295,589$$

The journal entry to record the first installment payment on the note payable is shown in Figure 17.31. Interest expense and notes payable are both debited for $1,250 and $4,411, respectively. Cash is also credited for $5,661. As shown in the Accounting Map, the interest expense for the period is shown on the income statement under other expenses. On the balance sheet, the principal amount of $4,411 reduces the current portion of the notes payable.

A similar journal entry is made monthly for the remainder of the term of the note, but it is based on the decreasing interest expense as the portion of the payment that is applied to the principal increases with each period.

As more payments are made, the amount going toward reducing the principal increases while the amount of interest decreases.

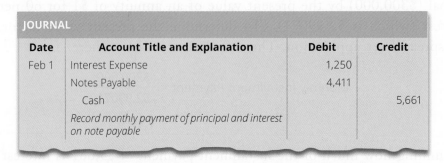

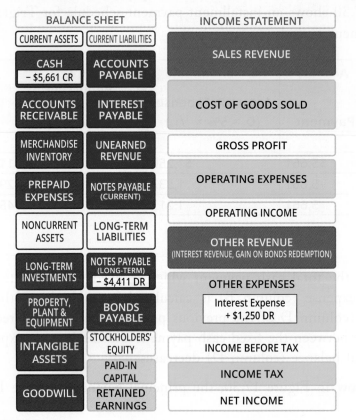

Pause & Reflect

Exercise 17-5

The table below shows a portion of the installment payment schedule for Trigraph Inc.'s note payable that relates to 2019.

Date	A Cash Payment	B Interest Expense (D x 5% x 1/12)	C Reduction of Principal (A – B)	D Principal Balance (D – C)
Jan 1, 2019	$5,661	$1,044	$4,617	$245,840
Feb 1	5,661	1,024	4,637	241,203
Mar 1	5,661	1,005	4,656	236,547
Apr 1	5,661	986	4,675	231,872
May 1	5,661	966	4,695	227,177
Jun 1	5,661	947	4,714	222,463
Jul 1	5,661	927	4,734	217,729
Aug 1	5,661	907	4,754	212,975
Sep 1	5,661	887	4,774	208,201
Oct 1	5,661	867	4,794	203,408
Nov 1	5,661	848	4,813	198,594
Dec1	5,661	827	4,834	193,761
Total	$67,932	$11,236	$56,696	-

Show how the July 1, 2019 interest payment is recorded.

JOURNAL			
Date	Account Title and Explanation	Debit	Credit

See Appendix I for solutions.

Financial Statement Presentation and Analysis

In the normal presentation of a balance sheet, assets and liabilities are classified as current and long-term. This level of detail is required by users of the financial statements so that they can fully understand and assess a company's financial position and its ability to pay its debts.

We have just discussed the concept of separately reporting current and long-term portions of notes payable on the balance sheet. This same practice applies to bonds payable, which was covered earlier in this chapter. Let us look at an example of financial statement presentation for both types of long-term liabilities, starting with notes payable.

Notes Payable on the Financial Statements

By now you are quite familiar with the difference between current and long-term (or noncurrent) liabilities: current liabilities are those payable within 12 months of the balance sheet date, while long-term liabilities are those payable beyond 12 months. Using this concept, the amount of a note payable must be reported on the balance sheet in its respective categories: the amount of principal to be reduced over the next 12 months from the balance sheet date is reported as Notes Payable, Current Portion, and the balance of the principal to be reduced beyond the 12-month period is reported as Notes Payable, Long-Term Portion.

The example of the notes payable of Trigraph Inc. will be used to illustrate the balance sheet presentation. Fast-forward to the end of the first 12 months after the note was issued, to the balance sheet date of December 31, 2018. First, determine the current and long-term portions of the note as of December 31. Based on the installment payment schedule in Figure 17.30, the schedule for the year 2018 is shown in Figure 17.32.

Date	A Cash Payment	B Interest Expense (D × 5% × $^1/_{12}$)	C Reduction of Principal (A − B)	D Principal Balance (D − C)
Jan 1, 2018				$300,000
Feb 1	$5,661	$1,250	$4,411	295,589
Mar 1	5,661	1,232	4,429	291,160
Apr 1	5,661	1,213	4,448	286,712
May 1	5,661	1,195	4,466	282,246
Jun 1	5,661	1,176	4,485	277,761
Jul 1	5,661	1,157	4,504	273,257
Aug 1	5,661	1,139	4,522	268,735
Sep 1	5,661	1,120	4,541	264,194
Oct 1	5,661	1,101	4,560	259,634
Nov 1	5,661	1,082	4,579	255,055
Dec 1	5,661	1,063	4,598	250,457
Total	$62,271	$12,728	$49,543	-

FIGURE 17.32

In Column C, the reduction of principal increases each month, with a total of $49,543 for 2018. Figure 17.33 shows the installment payment schedule over the five-year term of the note (for simplicity, this has already been calculated and condensed).

Year	A Beginning Balance	B Cash Payment	C Interest Expense	D Reduction of Principal	E Principal Balance
2018	$300,000	$62,271	$12,728	$49,543	$250,457
2019	250,457	$67,932	11,236	56,696	193,761
2020	193,761	$67,932	8,333	59,599	134,162
2021	134,162	$67,932	5,283	62,649	71,513
2022	71,513	$67,932	2,080	65,852	5,661
2023	5,661	5,661	0	5,661	0
Total	-	$339,660	$39,660	$300,000	-

FIGURE 17.33

So, as of December 31, 2018, the current portion of the note payable, the amount to be paid over the next 12 months, is $56,696 (from Column D). As of December 31, 2018, the long-term portion of the note payable, the amount to be paid beyond the next 12 months, is calculated as follows.

Long-Term Portion of Note Payable = Principal Balance (Dec 31, 2018) – Reduction of Principal Over Next 12 Months

= $250,457 – $56,696

= $193,761

Figure 17.34 presents the partial balance sheet for Trigraph Inc., focusing on the liabilities section of the statement. Note that all other amounts in the partial balance sheet are assumed for illustration purposes.

Trigraph Inc. Balance Sheet (partial) As at December 31, 2018		
Current Liabilities		
Accounts Payable	$70,000	
Interest Payable	10,000	
Notes Payable, Current Portion	56,696	
Total Current Liabilities		$136,696
Long-Term Liabilities		
Notes Payable, Long-Term Portion	193,761	
Total Long-Term Liabilities		193,761
Total Liabilities		330,457

FIGURE 17.34

Bonds Payable on the Financial Statements

Bonds payable affect the balance sheet accounts in different ways, depending on whether the bonds are issued at par, at a discount or at a premium. Generally, the presentation of bonds payable on the balance sheet can be summarized as follows.

- Bonds issued at par—The balance sheet reports the long-term liability (as of the end of the period) equal to the bonds' face value, until the bonds' maturity.

- Bonds issued at a discount—The balance sheet reports the long-term liability (as of the end of the period) equal to the bonds' carrying value (its book value), until the bond's maturity. For bonds issued at a discount, the carrying value is the bonds' face value minus the total unamortized discount. Each year, the bond's carrying value increases until the amount reported on the balance sheet equals the bond's face value.

- Bonds issued at a premium—The balance sheet reports the long-term liability (as of the end of the period) equal to the bonds' carrying value (its book value), until the bond's maturity. For bonds issued at a premium, the carrying value is the bond's face value plus the total unamortized premium. Each year, the bond's carrying value decreases until the amount reported on the balance sheet equals the bond's face value.

To illustrate the balance sheet presentation, we will use an example of bonds issued at a discount. Return to the earlier example in which Energy Bite issued $100,000 five-year, 10% interest bonds on January 1, 2018. At the then-current market interest rate of 12% with semi-annual interest payments, the bonds were issued at a discount for $92,640; this is the carrying value of the bonds on their issue date. Referring to the amortization table in Figure 17.15, at the end of the first fiscal year of September 30 (half way between semi-annual interest periods 1 and 2), the unamortized discount on the bonds payable is $6,256 ($7,360 - $736 - $368). Notice that since the year end is September 30, only three months of period 2 should be accounted for when it comes to calculating the year-end adjustments ($736 × ½ = $368) We know that the face value of the bonds is $100,000. Energy Bite's partial balance sheet for September 30, 2018 is shown in Figure 17.35.

Energy Bite Inc. Balance Sheet (partial) As at September 30, 2018	
Long-Term Liabilities	
Bonds Payable, 10%, due January 1, 2023	$100,000
Discount on Bonds Payable	6,256
Total Long-Term Liabilities	93,744

FIGURE 17.35

Note that as of September 30, 2018, the bonds' carrying value is now $93,744, which represents its amortized cost.

If Energy Bite issues the same bonds on January 1, 2018, at a then-current market interest rate of 8% with semi-annual interest payments, the bonds are issued at a premium for $108,115; this is the carrying value of the bonds on their issue date. Referring to the amortization table in Figure 17.21, at the end of the first fiscal year (half way between semi-annual interest periods 1 and 2), the unamortized premium on the bonds payable is $6,897 ($8,115 - $812 - $406). Since the year end is September 30, only three months of period 2 are accounted for when calculating the year-end adjustments ($812 × ½ = $406) We know that the face value of the bonds is $100,000. Energy Bite's partial balance sheet for September 30, 2018 is shown in Figure 17.36.

Energy Bite Inc. Balance Sheet (partial) As at September 30, 2018	
Long-Term Liabilities	
Bonds Payable, 10%, Due January 1, 2023	$100,000
Premium on Bonds Payable	6,897
Total Long-Term Liabilities	$106,897

FIGURE 17.36

Interest expense, and the amortization of bond discount and premium, affect the income statement accounts in different ways, depending on whether the bonds are issued at par, at a discount or at a premium. Generally, the presentation of interest expense from the bonds payable on the income statement can be summarized as follows.

- Bonds issued at par—The income statement reports interest expense for the period equal to the bond's contractual interest rate.

- Bonds issued at a discount—The income statement reports interest expense for the period equal to the bond's contractual interest rate plus the amortized portion of the discount.

- Bonds issued at a premium—The income statement reports interest expense for the period equal to the bond's contractual interest rate minus the amortized portion of the premium.

As the Accounting Maps showed in the section on bonds payable, the income statement includes interest expense for the period under other expenses.

At the beginning of this section, you learned that users of the financial statements require this level of detail. Creditors and investors require complete and accurate financial information so that they can make informed business decisions. This is why accounting standards require full disclosure of all current and long-term debt.

In the next section we will look at financial ratios related to liabilities, and how to calculate the different ratios.

Debt-to-Total-Assets Ratio

The **debt-to-total-assets ratio** measures how much of a company's assets are financed through total liabilities. This ratio is an indicator of a company's financial leverage, a concept discussed at the beginning of this chapter. The higher the ratio, the greater the difficulty a company has in repaying its creditors. A high debt-to-total-assets ratio indicates that the company is at a greater risk of being unable to meet debt obligations. A low debt-to-total-assets ratio indicates that a company is in a favorable position to meet debt obligations, which is more desirable to creditors.

The debt-to-total-assets ratio is calculated by dividing a company's total liabilities by its total assets, as shown in Figure 17.37.

$$\text{Debt-to-Total-Assets Ratio} = \frac{\text{Total Liabilities}}{\text{Total Assets}}$$

FIGURE 17.37

To illustrate, assume that a corporation has $10,000,000 in total assets, $4,000,000 in total liabilities, and $6,000,000 in stockholders' equity. Its debt-to-total-assets ratio is calculated as follows.

$$\text{Debt-to-Total-Assets Ratio} = \frac{\$4,000,000}{\$10,000,000}$$

$$= 0.4 \text{ or } 0.4 \text{ to } 1$$

This means that 40% of the company's assets are financed by debt, and therefore 60% of the assets are financed by equity (its owners, or stockholders). To determine if this is an acceptable level of financial leverage, decision-makers often compare a company's debt-to-total-assets ratio to the industry ratio (i.e. against that of competitors in the same industry).

Debt-to-Equity Ratio

The **debt-to-equity ratio** is used to assess how much of a company is being financed by lenders, and how much is being financed by the owners or stockholders; it measures the extent to which a business is indebted to lenders. Generally, owners or stockholders are expected to take a higher risk than lenders.

The debt-to-equity ratio is calculated by dividing a company's total liabilities by its total stockholders' equity, as shown in Figure 17.38.

$$\text{Debt-to-Equity Ratio} = \frac{\text{Total Liabilities}}{\text{Total Stockholders' Equity}}$$

FIGURE 17.38

To illustrate, we can use the information from the corporation in our previous example. The corporation's debt-to-equity ratio is calculated as follows.

$$\text{Debt-to-Equity Ratio} = \frac{\$4,000,000}{\$6,000,000}$$

$$= 0.67 \text{ or } 0.67 \text{ to } 1$$

This means that the company has 67 cents of debt for every $1 in equity. Ideally, a business should have a debt-to-equity ratio of 1:2, which would mean that the company has $1 of debt for every $2 of equity. Like other ratios, though, make note that the debt-to-equity ratio must be compared to industry benchmarks to draw sound conclusions.

Controls and Ethics Related to Long-Term Liabilities

Long-term liabilities play a key role in helping a company finance its business. At the same time, lenders and investors want assurance that they will receive their money back by the payment dates. That is why a company needs to monitor the level of debt and its accompanying interest expense. Taking too much debt can jeopardize a company's ability to maintain a good credit rating and may consequently limit future borrowing. For the same reasons, banks and other creditors use various measurement tools to confirm whether or not a company can handle its obligations.

In general, different financial measurements can be applied to control a company's ability to pay off its long-term debt. For example, analysts can look at the amount of a company's total assets financed by creditors or the amount of interest obligations compared to its earnings. In addition to the ratios illustrated in the previous section, other financial ratios used for long-term liabilities and solvency analysis are discussed in detail in Chapter 20.

A company must comply with all relevant policies, plans, procedures, laws and regulations. With regard to loans, this means that all documents pertaining to the loan should be reviewed by legal counsel. Strong controls surrounding the negotiation of long-term liabilities should result in obtaining the best possible interest rates. A lower interest rate increases cash flow, which can then be used for other activities of the business. In addition, robust cash controls ensure that interest and principal payments are made on time. Other controls include verifying that interest and principal payments have been received by lenders.

We will now examine ethical violations related to long-term liabilities.

Companies assume long-term liabilities, such as term loans and bond issues, to finance large items and projects that often take years to complete. The sheer magnitude of these transactions makes them vulnerable to abuse.

Management is often closely involved when large sums of money are dealt with. Since at this level there can be fewer internal controls, those in place must be thorough and complete. Reviews by top-level executives and audits should be performed internally and externally.

Individuals may be tempted to siphon off or redirect money when dealing with large amounts. Staying alert and attentive to these risks is one of the primary responsibilities of those who own and run the company.

Additionally, it is necessary to be vigilant with transactions conducted with financial institutions, where unauthorized commissions may exist. Some part of the loan money might end up in the hands of individuals who work out a side deal for themselves. That is why it is always important for companies to keep track of all the money.

Another type of fraud is off-balance sheet financing. Some businesses engage in accounting practices that keep some large financing schemes off the books. This allows a business to keep its debt-to-equity and leverage ratios low, which might artificially inflate stock prices by overstating a company's equity position. Examples include joint ventures, research and development partnerships and operating leases.

A **lease** is a contract between the owner of an asset and another party who uses the asset for a given period of time. One form is an **operating lease**, such as a car rental, where the ownership is not transferred to another party over the term of the agreement.

Operating leases were once a common example of off-balance sheet financing. Instead of owning the asset, a company could lease it and expense any rental fees. Accounting rules have been changed so that some leases, depending on their terms, are treated as a form of financing. This forces the company to record an asset and the accompanying liability on its balance sheet. This increases its debt-to-equity ratio and gives users of its financial statements a more accurate picture of the company's financial position.

IN THE REAL WORLD

In the fall of 2008, the world was hit by the worst financial crisis since the Depression. Global financial institutions had too much money invested in bad credit, especially sub-prime mortgages. The economy started to slow down when these bad debts went unpaid and the credit market crashed as a result.

In the aftermath of the crash, leading financial minds looked for solutions to problems that had gone unsolved for years. Although many experts looked for ways to better regulate the markets, some analysts started pointing fingers at the accounting profession.

Specifically, a long-running criticism of accounting standards is that they do not require an appropriate level of disclosure. A perfect example of this is off-balance-sheet financing—the practice of keeping some forms of long-term financing off the company books.

Another example of poor disclosure is reporting pension fund assets and liabilities only in footnote form. Recent standards are now forcing companies to disclose a net amount on the balance sheet itself.

Critics of the accounting profession believe that it is only through fair and open reporting that companies can gain the trust of investment markets in general. How can companies expect people to trust them with money if they are not fully open about what is reported in the financial statements?

Open and fair accounting practices can help bring back some stability and trust in world markets at a time when it is most needed.

In Summary

LO 1 **State the characteristics and different types of bonds**

▸ The company that issues the bond is called the bond issuer. The investor who purchases the bond is the bondholder.

▸ The investor provides a principal loan to the issuing company. In return, the company makes interest payments to the investor, in addition to eventually repaying the principal.

▸ There are several types of bonds, such as term bonds, debenture bonds, redeemable bonds, mortgage bonds, convertible bonds, registered bonds and coupon bonds.

LO 2 **Apply the concept of present value**

▸ The time value of money involves the concept that interest is earned on top of interest year after year. This is called compound interest.

▸ Future value determines the value of an investment in the future if an amount is invested today. Present value determines the amount invested today to produce a certain amount in the future.

LO 3 **Record bonds issued at par**

▸ When the bond interest rate equals the market interest rate, the company can sell the bond at par.

LO 4 **Record bonds issued at a discount or a premium**

▸ When the bond interest rate is lower than the market interest rate, the company sells the bond at a discount.

▸ When the bond interest rate is higher than the market interest rate, the company can sell the bond at a premium.

▸ Both the discount and premium attached to the bond price should be amortized over the term of the bond until maturity.

LO 5 **Record the retirement of bonds**

▸ When the bond reaches maturity, it is time for the issuing company to repay the principal to whoever holds the bond at the time. This is also called bond redemption.

▸ The issuing company may have the option to redeem a bond early. Such securities are referred to as redeemable bonds, or callable bonds.

LO 6 **Record installment notes payable**

▸ A company usually has three basic options when it comes to long-term financing: bank loans, bond issues and notes payable.

▸ Long-term notes payable are repayable in periodic payments, such as monthly, quarterly or semi-annually.

▸ A long-term note payable represents a long-term liability that is due beyond 12 months of the date of issue.

Describe how long-term liabilities are analyzed and presented on the balance sheet

▶ Long-term liabilities must be split into a current portion (amount owed in the next 12 months) and a long-term portion (amount owed beyond 12 months). These amounts are reported on the balance sheet in the current liabilities and long-term liabilities sections respectively.

Apply controls and ethics related to long-term liabilities

▶ Controls related to long-term liabilities should ensure that all documents are in order and that cash flow planning accommodates future payments for loans and bonds.

▶ Ethics related to long-term liabilities should ensure the integrity of large amounts of cash that upper management has the responsibility of handling.

▶ Unauthorized commissions are always a risk when dealing with financial institutions.

▶ Off-balance-sheet financing is also a practice that can skew the way in which company finances are reported to the public.

Table 17-1
Present Value of $1

Periods	1%	2%	3%	4%	5%	6%
1	0.9901	0.9804	0.9709	0.9615	0.9524	0.9434
2	0.9803	0.9612	0.9426	0.9246	0.9070	0.8900
3	0.9706	0.9423	0.9151	0.8890	0.8638	0.8396
4	0.9610	0.9238	0.8885	0.8548	0.8227	0.7921
5	0.9515	0.9057	0.8626	0.8219	0.7835	0.7473
6	0.9420	0.8880	0.8375	0.7903	0.7462	0.7050
7	0.9327	0.8706	0.8131	0.7599	0.7107	0.6651
8	0.9235	0.8535	0.7894	0.7307	0.6768	0.6274
9	0.9143	0.8368	0.7664	0.7026	0.6446	0.5919
10	0.9053	0.8203	0.7441	0.6756	0.6139	0.5584
11	0.8963	0.8043	0.7224	0.6496	0.5847	0.5268
12	0.8874	0.7885	0.7014	0.6246	0.5568	0.4970
13	0.8787	0.7730	0.6810	0.6006	0.5303	0.4688
14	0.8700	0.7579	0.6611	0.5775	0.5051	0.4423
15	0.8613	0.7430	0.6419	0.5553	0.4810	0.4173

Table 17-2
Present Value of Annuity $1

Periods	1%	2%	3%	4%	5%	6%
1	0.9901	0.9804	0.9709	0.9615	0.9524	0.9434
2	1.9704	1.9416	1.9135	1.8861	1.8594	1.8334
3	2.9410	2.8839	2.8286	2.7751	2.7232	2.6730
4	3.9020	3.8077	3.7171	3.6299	3.5460	3.4651
5	4.8534	4.7135	4.5797	4.4518	4.3295	4.2124
6	5.7955	5.6014	5.4172	5.2421	5.0757	4.9173
7	6.7282	6.4720	6.2303	6.0021	5.7864	5.5824
8	7.6517	7.3255	7.0197	6.7327	6.4632	6.2098
9	8.5660	8.1622	7.7861	7.4353	7.1078	6.8017
10	9.4713	8.9826	8.5302	8.1109	7.7217	7.3601
11	10.3676	9.7868	9.2526	8.7605	8.3064	7.8869
12	11.2551	10.5753	9.9540	9.3851	8.8633	8.3838
13	12.1337	11.3484	10.6350	9.9856	9.3936	8.8527
14	13.0037	12.1062	11.2961	10.5631	9.8986	9.2950
15	13.8651	12.8493	11.9379	11.1184	10.3797	9.7122

Review Exercise 17-1

Hohl Company is planning to expand its facilities by constructing a new building and installing new machines. To complete this project, the company has decided to issue $2,000,000 worth of 20-year, 4% callable bonds, with interest paid every six months.

On April 1, 2018 the company completed all the necessary paperwork, and is now ready to issue the bonds. Fortunately, just as Hohl Company was issuing its bonds, the current market rate dropped to 3.5%. Their financial advisor recommended issuing the bonds at a premium of $142,968.

On March 31 of 2023, interest rates dropped to 2%. At this point, the company issued $2,200,000 of 10-year, 2% bonds at par to redeem all outstanding 4% bonds. The company paid $2,110,000 to redeem the 4% bonds.

Required

a) Prepare the bond premium amortization table from period 1 to period 10 (covers 2018 to 2023).

Semi-Annual Interest Period	A Interest Payment	B Premium Amortization	C Interest Expense	D Premium Balance	E Bond Book Value

b) Record the journal entries for the following transactions.

- The issuance of bonds on April 1, 2018
- Any required entries as of the company year end, February 28, 2019 (note that the company pays interest semi-annually)
- The retirement of the 4% bonds and issue of the new 2% bonds
- The first interest payment on the 2% bonds

JOURNAL			
Date	Account Title and Explanation	Debit	Credit

See Appendix I for solutions.

Review Exercise 17-2

On April 1, 2018, Hohl Company issued a two-year notes payable of $200,000 for purchasing equipment from one of the company's suppliers. The interest rate is 4% and payments are made semi-annually. Assume all other conditions remain unchanged and the company's year end is February 28.

Required

a) Using the table below, calculate cash payment, interest expense, reduction of principal and principal balance on each payment date, with an equal installment payment of $52,525 using the blended payment method.

Date	A Cash Payment	B Interest Expense	C Reduction of Principal	D Principal Balance

b) Record journal entries of issuing day, first payment day, first year end and second payment day, using the blended payment method from part a).

JOURNAL			
Date	**Account Title and Explanation**	**Debit**	**Credit**

See Appendix I for solutions.

Appendix 17A: Effective Interest Amortization Method

In Chapter 17 you learned about amortization of bond discount using the straight-line method. In this section, we will look at amortization of bond discount using the effective-interest method.

We will illustrate this method using data from the chapter example of Energy Bite Inc. (in the section Issuing Bonds at a Discount). Keep in mind the following summary points.

- Face value of 10%, five-year bonds, interest paid semi-annually: $100,000

- Present value of bonds at market interest rate (effective rate) of 12%: $92,640

- Discount on bonds payable: $7,360

Amortization of Bond Discount by the Effective-Interest Method

Figure 17A.1 shows how the receipt of $92,640 for the issue of Energy Bite Inc. bonds (at discount) is recorded by the company using the contra account called Discount on Bonds Payable.

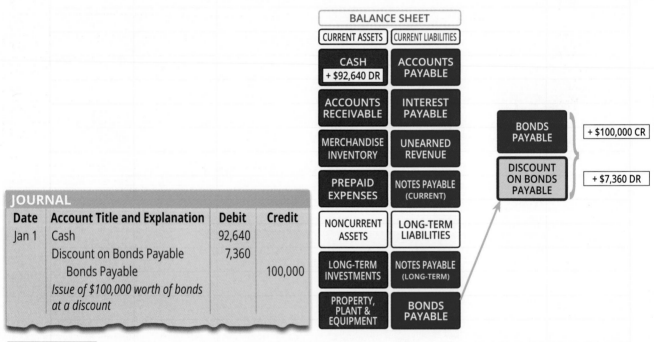

FIGURE 17A.1

So although Energy Bite has issued a $100,000 bond, and this amount must be paid when the bond matures, they only received $92,640 from the bondholder.

The bond discount is amortized using the **effective interest amortization method**, which uses the market interest rate at the date the bonds are issued as the basis to calculate the interest expense. The effective interest rate is applied to the amortized cost of the bonds payable and reflects the actual cost of borrowing.

Figure 17A.2 shows the amortization table of the bond over five years (10 periods). Column A shows the interest payment of $5,000, which is fixed in each period since the semi-annual contractual interest rate of 5% and the face value of $100,000 stay the same. Column B shows the interest expense, which is calculated by multiplying the semi-annual interest market rate of 6% and the bond's amortized cost at the end of the previous period. The values in this column increase over time since although the market rate is fixed, the bond's amortized cost increases over time. Column C shows the amount of discount amortized over the periods by calculating the difference between the interest expense and the interest payment. The values in this column increase as well since the interest expense increases. Column D shows the bond's amortized cost. Note that this continues to increase by the amount of discounts amortized each period until it reaches the face value of $100,000.

Effective Interest Amortization Table of Bond Discount				
Semi-Annual Interest Period	A Interest Payment ($100,000 × 5%)	B Interest Expense (D × 6%)	C Discount Amortization (B – A)	D Bond Amortized Cost (D + C)
0				$92,640
1	$5,000	$5,558	$558	93,198
2	5,000	5,592	592	93,790
3	5,000	5,627	627	94,418
4	5,000	5,665	665	95,083
5	5,000	5,705	705	95,788
6	5,000	5,747	747	96,535
7	5,000	5,792	792	97,327
8	5,000	5,840	840	98,167
9	5,000	5,890	890	99,057
10	5,000	5,943	943	100,000
Total	$50,000	$57,360	$7,360	-

FIGURE 17A.2

On July 1, 2018, the first payment of interest is recorded as shown in Figure 17A.3. Going back to the table in Figure 17A.2, in period 1, the interest expense is debited for $5,558 (column B). The discount on bonds payable is also amortized and credited for $558 (column C). The cash is credited for the interest payment of $5,000 (column A).

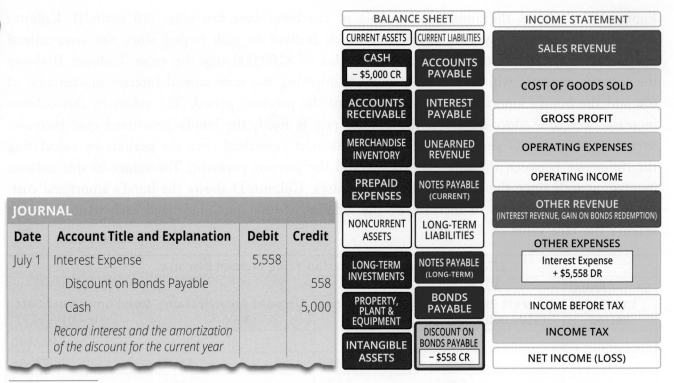

FIGURE 17A.3

On July 1 and January 1 in each of the next five years, the bond issuer will pay $5,000 interest on the bond in cash to the bondholder. The amortization of the discount is just an adjustment and calculated as a difference between the interest payment and the interest expense. After each period, the value of the discount on the bonds decreases and the book value (or carrying value) of the bond increases. By the end of the five years, the discount is reduced to zero and the book value of the bond is the face value, $100,000.

Since the year end is September 30, 2018, Energy Bite needs to accrue interest expense before the second payment date on January 1, 2019. Figure 17A.4 shows that at each year end for the next five years, the interest expense is accrued and the discount is amortized for three months, from July 1 to September 30. The interest expense and the amortized discounts for period 2 (six months) can be found in the table from Figure 17A.2. These numbers must be adjusted to reflect only three months instead of six months. As shown in Figure 17A.4, the interest expense is debited for $2,796 ($5,592 × ³⁄₆), discount on bonds payable is amortized (credited) for $296 ($592 × ³⁄₆) and interest payable is credited for $2,500 ($2,796 − $296).

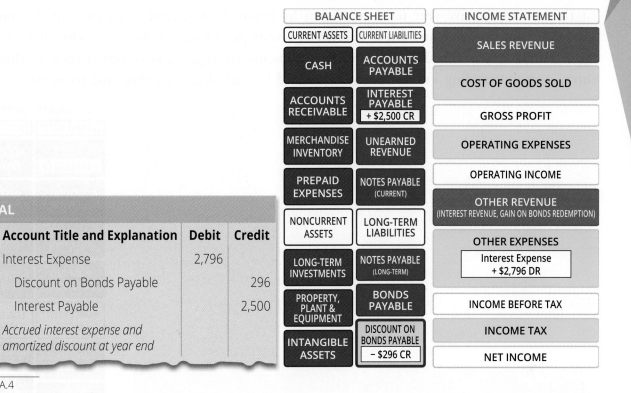

BALANCE SHEET		INCOME STATEMENT
CURRENT ASSETS	CURRENT LIABILITIES	SALES REVENUE
CASH	ACCOUNTS PAYABLE	COST OF GOODS SOLD
ACCOUNTS RECEIVABLE	INTEREST PAYABLE + $2,500 CR	GROSS PROFIT
MERCHANDISE INVENTORY	UNEARNED REVENUE	OPERATING EXPENSES
PREPAID EXPENSES	NOTES PAYABLE (CURRENT)	OPERATING INCOME
NONCURRENT ASSETS	LONG-TERM LIABILITIES	OTHER REVENUE (INTEREST REVENUE, GAIN ON BONDS REDEMPTION)
LONG-TERM INVESTMENTS	NOTES PAYABLE (LONG-TERM)	OTHER EXPENSES — Interest Expense + $2,796 DR
PROPERTY, PLANT & EQUIPMENT	BONDS PAYABLE	INCOME BEFORE TAX
INTANGIBLE ASSETS	DISCOUNT ON BONDS PAYABLE − $296 CR	INCOME TAX
		NET INCOME

JOURNAL

Date	Account Title and Explanation	Debit	Credit
Sep 30	Interest Expense	2,796	
	Discount on Bonds Payable		296
	Interest Payable		2,500
	Accrued interest expense and amortized discount at year end		

FIGURE 17A.4

As shown in Figure 17A.5, on January 1, 2019, the cash payment is made for $5,000. Interest payable is debited for $2,500 and interest expense is also debited for the remaining balance of period 2, which is $2,796 ($5,592 – $2,796). The rest of the discount of period 2 is also amortized and credited for $296 ($592 – $296).

BALANCE SHEET		INCOME STATEMENT
CURRENT ASSETS	CURRENT LIABILITIES	SALES REVENUE
CASH − $5,000 CR	ACCOUNTS PAYABLE	COST OF GOODS SOLD
ACCOUNTS RECEIVABLE	INTEREST PAYABLE − $2,500 DR	GROSS PROFIT
MERCHANDISE INVENTORY	UNEARNED REVENUE	OPERATING EXPENSES
PREPAID EXPENSES	NOTES PAYABLE (CURRENT)	OPERATING INCOME
NONCURRENT ASSETS	LONG-TERM LIABILITIES	OTHER REVENUE (INTEREST REVENUE, GAIN ON BONDS REDEMPTION)
LONG-TERM INVESTMENTS	NOTES PAYABLE (LONG-TERM)	OTHER EXPENSES — Interest Expense + $2,796 DR
PROPERTY, PLANT & EQUIPMENT	BONDS PAYABLE	INCOME BEFORE TAX
INTANGIBLE ASSETS	DISCOUNT ON BONDS PAYABLE − $296 CR	INCOME TAX
		NET INCOME

JOURNAL

Date	Account Title and Explanation	Debit	Credit
Jan 1	Interest Payable	2,500	
	Interest Expense	2,796	
	Discount on Bonds Payable		296
	Cash		5,000
	Payment of interest and amortized discount		

FIGURE 17A.5

At the end of the five-year term, as shown in Figure 17A.6, cash is credited in the amount of $100,000, and the same amount is debited to bonds payable as a long-term debt, thereby clearing the liability. It is assumed that all interest payments are made and recorded prior to this journal entry. Any outstanding interest payments would be included with this final payment.

JOURNAL			
Date	**Account Title and Explanation**	**Debit**	**Credit**
Jan 1, 2023	Bonds Payable	100,000	
	Cash		100,000
	Repay $100,000 to bondholder		

FIGURE 17A.6

In Chapter 17 you learned about amortization of bond premium using the straight-line method. We will now look at how to amortize bond premiums using the effective-interest method.

Amortization of Bond Premium by the Effective-Interest Method

We will illustrate this method using data from the chapter example of Energy Bite Inc. (in the section Issuing Bonds at a Premium). Keep in mind the following summary points.

- Face value of 8%, five-year bonds, interest paid semi-annually: $100,000

- Present value of bonds at market interest rate (effective rate) of 10%: $108,115

- Premium on bonds payable: $8,115

Similar to a discount on a bond issue, a premium must be amortized as periodic interest payments are made. In other words, the premium liability of $8,115 should be amortized over the term of the bond using the effective-interest method. Figure 17A.7 shows the amortization table of the bond over five years.

Effective-Interest Amortization Table of Bond Premium				
Semi-Annual Interest Period	A Interest Payment ($100,000 × 5%)	B Interest Expense (D × 4%)	C Premium Amortization (A – B)	D Bond Amortized Cost (D – C)
0				$108,115
1	$5,000	$4,325	$675	107,440
2	5,000	4,298	702	106,738
3	5,000	4,270	730	106,008
4	5,000	4,240	760	105,248
5	5,000	4,210	790	104,458
6	5,000	4,178	822	103,636
7	5,000	4,145	855	102,781
8	5,000	4,111	889	101,892
9	5,000	4,076	924	100,968
10	5,000	4,032*	968	100,000
Total	$50,000	$41,885	$8,115	-

* $7 difference due to rounding. The final interest expense is adjusted due to rounding to ensure the final bond amortized cost is equal to $100,000.

FIGURE 17A.7

Column A shows the interest payment of $5,000, which is fixed over five years (10 periods) since the semi-annual contractual interest rate of 5% and the face value of $100,000 stay the same. Column B shows the interest expense, which is calculated by multiplying the semi-annual interest market rate of 4% and the bond's amortized cost from the end of the previous period. The values in this column decrease over time since although the market rate is fixed, the bond's amortized cost decreases over time. Column C shows the amount of premium amortized over the periods by calculating a difference between the interest expense and the interest payment. The values in this column increase since the interest expense decreases while the interest payment remains constant. Column D shows the bond's amortized cost. Note that the bond's amortized cost continues to decrease by the amount of premium amortized each period until it reaches the face value of $100,000.

Figure 17A.8 shows how that transaction is recorded for the first year if the effective-interest rate method is used.

On July 1, 2018, the first payment date, the $5,000 interest payment (column A) is recorded and is represented by a credit to cash. The expense to the company is only $4,325 (column B) and the rest of the debit is taken care of by the $675 first period's amortization (column C) of the premium calculated using the effective-interest rate method.

JOURNAL			
Date	Account Title and Explanation	Debit	Credit
July 1	Interest Expense	4,325	
	Premium on Bonds Payable	675	
	Cash		5,000
	Payment of interest and amortization of premium		

FIGURE 17A.8

On July 1 and January 1 in each of the next five years, the bond issuer pays $5,000 interest on the bond in cash to the bondholder. The amortization of the premium is just an adjustment and calculated as a difference between the interest payment and the interest expense.

When financial statements are prepared, the premium on bonds payable is added to the face value of the bonds. The balance sheet at the end of the first period is shown in Figure 17A.9, after the amortization of the premium.

Bonds Payable	$100,000
Add: Unamortized Premium	7,440
Book Value	$107,440

FIGURE 17A.9

Since the year end is September 30, 2018, Energy Bite needs to accrue interest expense before the second payment date on January 1, 2019. Figure 17A.10 shows that at each year end for the next five years, the interest expense is accrued and the premium is amortized for three months, from July 1 to September 30. The interest expense and the amortized premium for period 2 (six months) can be found in the table from Figure 17A.7. These numbers must be adjusted to reflect only three months instead of six months. As shown in Figure 17A.10, the interest expense is debited for $2,149 ($4,298 × 3⁄6), premium is amortized (debited) for $351 ($702 × 3⁄6) and interest payable is credited for $2,500 ($2,149 + $351).

JOURNAL

Date	Account Title and Explanation	Debit	Credit
Sep 30	Interest Expense	2,149	
	Premium on Bonds Payable	351	
	Interest Payable		2,500
	Accrued interest expense and amortized premium at year end		

FIGURE 17A.10

As shown in Figure 17A.11, on January 1, 2019, the cash payment is made for $5,000. Interest payable is debited for $2,500 and interest expense is debited for the remaining balance of period 2, which is $2,149 ($4,298 − $2,149). The rest of the premium of period 2 is also amortized and debited for $351 ($702 − $351).

JOURNAL

Date	Account Title and Explanation	Debit	Credit
Jan 1	Interest Payable	2,500	
	Interest Expense	2,149	
	Premium on Bonds Payable	351	
	Cash		5,000
	Payment of interest and amortized discount		

FIGURE 17A.11

In Summary

LO 9   **Describe the effective interest amortization method**

> ►   In contrast to the straight-line amortization method (which records the same amount of interest expense each period), effective interest amortization records interest expense based on the amortized cost of the bond—that is, on the bond's book value at the end of the previous period.

> ►   When amortizing a bond discount, the bond's amortized cost increases each period as the interest expense increases. Conversely, when amortizing a bond premium, the bond's amortized cost decreases each period as the interest expense increases.

AMEENGAGE   *Access **ameengage.com** for integrated resources including tutorials, practice exercises, the digital textbook and more.*

Review Exercise 17A-1

The following information was gathered from the records of Danbury Inc. after a bond issue on January 1, 2017. Interest is paid semi-annually on June 30 and December 31.

- Face value of 8%, five-year bonds, interest compounded semi-annually: $200,000

- Present value of bonds at market interest rate (effective rate) of 10%: $184,557

- Discount on bonds payable: $15,443

Required

a) Prepare the bond discount amortization table for periods 1 to 10 using the effective interest amortization method.

Semi-Annual Interest Period (Date)	A Interest Payment	B Interest Expense	C Discount Amortization	D Bond Amortized Cost

b) Record the journal entry for the issuance of the bonds.

JOURNAL			
Date	Account Title and Explanation	Debit	Credit

c) Record the journal entry for the first interest payment date.

JOURNAL			
Date	**Account Title and Explanation**	**Debit**	**Credit**

d) Record the journal entry for the end of the five-year term of the bonds. Assume the last interest expense payment has already been recorded.

JOURNAL			
Date	**Account Title and Explanation**	**Debit**	**Credit**

See Appendix I for solutions.

Notes

Chapter 18
Investments

Learning Objectives

LO 1 Describe and classify different types of investments
- Debt Investments
- Equity Investments

LO 2 Prepare journal entries for debt investments
- Trading Securities
- Available-for-Sale Securities
- Held-to-Maturity Securities

LO 3 Prepare journal entries for equity investments
- Investments with Insignificant Influence
- Investments with Significant Influence

LO 4 Describe how the different types of investments are presented in the financial statements
- Debt Investments
- Equity Investments

Investments: An Introduction and Classification

LO 1

Cash is the lifeblood of a business; cash management is therefore of the utmost importance, not only to ensure that the business has enough cash to cover its operations and debt obligations, but also that the business is able to maximize returns on its excess cash. When a company has more cash on hand than it immediately needs for general operations and debt repayment, the company can invest the surplus to generate investment income rather than leaving it in a bank account and receiving a much lower return. This chapter covers how to account for and report on these investments.

The Accounting Map in Figure 18.1 shows how investments appear on the balance sheet. The balance sheet presentation of an investment depends on whether the investment is considered short-term or long-term. A **short-term investment**, or *temporary investment*, is intended to be held for less than a year and is reported in the current assets section of the balance sheet. A **long-term investment** is intended to be held for longer than a year, and is reported in the noncurrent (or long-term) assets section of the balance sheet.

There are two types of investments a business can make. One is lending money to someone else (debt). The other is buying a stake (equity) in the ownership of another company.

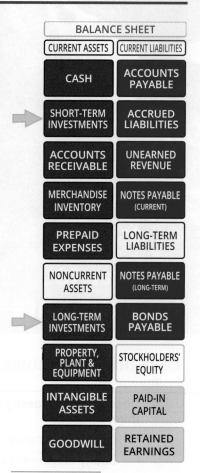

FIGURE 18.1

When a company loans excess cash to someone else, this is known as investing in **debt instruments** (or *debt securities*). The company that purchases the debt instruments is the **investor**. The company that issues (sells) the debt instruments is the **investee**. The investee is obligated to pay back the principal amount of the loan, plus any interest, to the investor. Examples of debt instruments include money market funds, term deposits, treasury bills and bonds. The different types of debt investments are discussed later in this section.

When a company invests excess cash by buying a stake in the ownership of another organization, this is known as investing in **equity instruments** (or *equity securities*), which include preferred and common stock of another company (discussed in Chapter 15). Similar to debt instruments, the company that purchases the equity is the investor. The company that issues (sells) the equity is the investee. This chapter focuses on investments mostly from the investor's point of view.

On the investor's books, an investment is first classified based on the investor's *intent*. Investors may invest with either of the following intentions.

1. An investor may simply try to generate investment income without intending to establish a long-term business relationship with, or to influence or control, the investee. Such an investment is classified as a **non-strategic investment**.

2. Alternatively, an investor may intend to establish a long-term business relationship with, or to influence or control, the investee. Such an investment is classified as a **strategic investment**.

The classification of investments is summarized in Figure 18.2. Notice that debt instruments are always considered a non-strategic investment. This is because purchasing debt instruments does not give the investor ownership rights in the investee. Equity instruments can be either non-strategic or strategic investments. For example, investors with ownership rights through investee's stock (particularly common stock) can vote on important matters, such as electing the investee's board of directors, and thus have an opportunity to establish and maintain a long-term relationship with, or influence or control, the investee.

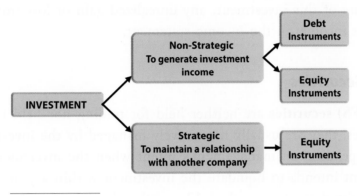

FIGURE 18.2

Let us explain the concept of intent in more detail. A company has a plan, or *strategy*, when it comes to investing. It may want to invest its money for a few months, or may plan on getting long-term returns or having a long-term relationship with the investee. The plan of the company highlights its intent. It is important to note that the intent at the time the investment is purchased may not always be the actual outcome. For example, a company may plan to invest for the long term, but an unexpected event happens that causes it to sell its investment early to get the cash. In accounting, the intent at the purchase date determines how the investment is initially classified. Specifically, how an investment is accounted for is based on both the investor's intent (strategic or non-strategic and short-term or long-term) and the type of instruments (debt or equity).

Debt Investments

GAAP classifies debt investments into three different types: (1) trading securities, (2) available-for-sale securities, and (3) held-to-maturity securities. Although all debt instruments are non-strategic investments, each of these three types has its own characteristics and associated method of accounting.

WORTH REPEATING

Debt involves lending money to someone else in return for interest. Debt generally has a fixed maturity.

Equity involves investing in another organization in the form of ownership, with the expectation that its value will increase over time while profits are shared in the form of dividends. Unlike debt, equity does not have a maturity.

Trading Securities

Trading securities are intended to be held for the short term (typically up to one year) and then sold for a profit. Trading securities are actively managed because the investor hopes to take advantage of changes in the market price. The investor may receive interest while holding the investment. Trading securities are reported as current assets on the balance sheet. The investment's value may fluctuate during the time it is held; therefore, at the end of each period, the investment value must be adjusted to its fair value, or market price. This revaluation results in unrealized gains or losses for the period. The term *unrealized* is used because the investment has not yet been sold. The gain or loss is only shown on paper and is not realized until the investment is sold. Because of the short-term nature of this investment, any unrealized gain or loss from trading securities is reported as part of net income on the income statement.

Available-for-Sale Securities

Available-for-sale (AFS) securities are neither held for trading nor held to maturity. Therefore, unlike trading securities, they are usually not actively managed by the investor. They can be short term or long term, depending on management's intent when the investment was purchased. For example, if management intends to liquidate the investment within a year, even though the AFS securities have a maturity date of more than 12 months, this investment is classified as a current asset on the balance sheet. Similar to trading securities, the book value of AFS securities must be adjusted to match the securities' market value at the end of the period. However, unlike unrealized gains or losses from trading securities, the unrealized gains or losses from AFS securities are not reported as part of net income. Instead, they are reported as part of other comprehensive income in the statement of comprehensive income. The financial statement presentation of unrealized gains or losses from AFS securities is explained in more detail later in the chapter.

Held-to-Maturity Securities

Held-to-Maturity (HTM) securities are intended to be held until maturity in order to earn interest revenue. Held-to-maturity securities that will mature within one year are reported as current assets on the balance sheet. Those due to mature beyond one year are reported as noncurrent assets. Unlike trading and AFS securities, the book value of HTM securities is not adjusted to the securities' fair value at the end of each period; therefore, unrealized gains or losses are never recorded for HTM securities. If the company later decides to sell the investment before the maturity date, any gain or loss on the sale of investments is recorded as part of net income on the income statement.

Equity investments

GAAP classifies equity investments into two main types: (1) non-strategic and (2) strategic. Each type has its own characteristics and associated method of accounting.

Non-Strategic Equity Investments

When investors purchase common stock in a company, they become part-owner of that company. For many stockholders, the level of ownership is minimal because they own such a small percentage of the total stock outstanding. For instance, if you own 10 shares out of 1,000,000 common shares outstanding, your vote does little to elect a board of directors or influence the operation of the company you have invested in. Accordingly, you have an insignificant influence on the investee corporation. This applies to any stockholder who owns less than 20% of the common stock outstanding and is usually considered a non-strategic investment.

Non-strategic equity investments can be either short-term or long-term depending upon management's intent when the securities are purchased and will be recorded on the balance sheet based on the intent. Accounting for non-strategic equity investments is similar to accounting for debt trading instruments. The main difference for equity instruments is that they pay out dividends, not interest, to the investor for as long as the investor holds the equity instrument. Any gain or loss on the sale of the investment is recorded under the other income and expenses section of the income statement. Similar to trading debt securities, unrealized gains or losses from non-strategic equity securities are reported as part of net income on the income statement. This practice follows the FASB's amendment made in 2016, which requires corporations using US GAAP to recognize the changes of non-strategic equity securities' fair value in net income starting in the fiscal year ending December 15, 2017 onwards.

Non-strategic equity securities and trading debt securities share the same accounting method, called the fair value through net income method, which is discussed later in the chapter.

Strategic Equity Investments

A company may choose to invest in another corporation for strategic reasons. For example, the investor may want to build a long-term relationship with a key customer or vendor by investing in it. The company may want to venture into a new industry by investing in another company that is already established in that industry. Alternatively, the company may invest strategically in common stock of another company in the same industry because it wants to expand its market base, tap into new technologies used by another company or eliminate competition.

Equity instruments that are held for strategic purposes are always considered long-term investments. Strategic investments can be further classified into equity investments with significant influence and equity investments with controlling influence. The accounting method required for strategic investments depends on which type of influence the investor has over the investee.

Investments with Significant Influence

A company that owns between 20% to 50% of another company's common stock outstanding has a **significant influence** on the investee corporation. This gives the investor the right to participate in decisions over the investee's operating and financial policies. At this level of influence, the investor has a non-controlling interest in the investee company.

Investments with Controlling Influence

If one stockholder or investor owns more than 50% of a company's outstanding common stock, that investor has a **controlling influence**, which means that the investor company has control over how the investee company operates. At this level of stock ownership, the investor has the right to direct the operating and financial activities of the investee.

When one company purchases more than 50% of the outstanding stock of another company, the transaction is known as a **business combination**. Such an arrangement is usually made in order to maximize the investor company's operating efficiency, expand its product offerings or minimize competition. The investor then becomes known as the **parent company**, and the investee becomes the **subsidiary company**.

Investments with controlling influence are accounted for using the *consolidation method*. This means that although the parent and the subsidiary usually maintain separate accounting records and financial statements during the accounting period, at the end of the year the parent company combines all the financial statements into a set of **consolidated financial statements**. Consolidated financial statements are considered more meaningful to investors than if the companies were to report separately. The specifics of the consolidation method are beyond the scope of this textbook.

How a security is classified determines how it should be valued and presented on the financial statements. We will discuss how to account for investments in debt first, followed by investments in equity.

Investments in Debt   LO 2

A debt instrument (or security) is classified and reported according to its maturity and its purpose. A debt instrument that will mature within 12 months is considered a **short-term debt instrument**. A short-term debt instrument is usually a highly liquid, low-risk **money market instrument** such as a treasury bill, term deposit or money market fund.

A debt instrument that will take more than 12 months to mature is considered a **long-term debt instrument**. A common example of a long-term debt instrument is bonds, which provide a steady source of interest income.

Recall that GAAP classifies debt investments as trading securities, AFS securities, and HTM securities. The accounting method for each classification of debt investment is illustrated

GAAP vs IFRS

While GAAP refers to trading securities and available-for-sale securities, under IFRS these are normally referred to as "financial assets at fair value through profit or loss" and "available-for-sale financial assets," respectively.

in Figure 18.3. In this section, we will look at how to account for each of these classifications in more detail.

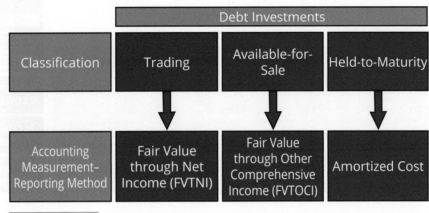

FIGURE 18.3

Trading Securities

Similar to equity instruments, some debt instruments can be readily bought and sold on the open market, making them good trading investments. When debt instruments are purchased for the primary purpose of trading, they are reported at their fair value. Fair value is the amount that an asset can be sold for in the public market. Recording investments at fair value enables investors to evaluate the issuer's financial solvency and predict its future cash flows.

There are several important events during the lifetime of a debt instrument that must be accounted for. These include the following.

- Acquisition, at the fair value of the securities

- Recording interest earned

- Fair value adjustments, to record changes from the original cost to the current market value

The accounting method used to report trading securities is called the **fair value through net income method (FVTNI)**. We will demonstrate this method with an example.

Fair Value through Net Income Method

Suppose that on October 1, 2018, Vinyl Sound Company pays $9,500, including broker's fees, to purchase a *portfolio* (or group) of debt securities. Vinyl Sound records the acquisition of the securities as in Figure 18.4. Note that all the individual securities are combined into one total portfolio cost of $9,500.

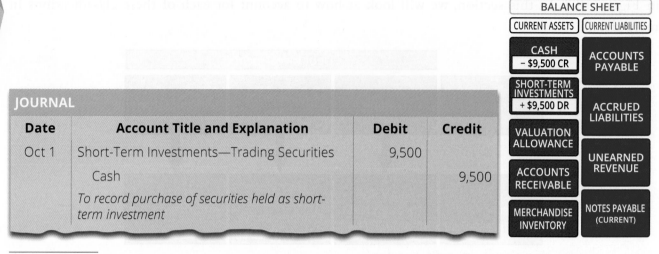

FIGURE 18.4

Assuming Vinyl Sound has a year end of December 31, the entry in Figure 18.5 is made to accrue the interest receivable on the bonds that make up the securities portfolio.

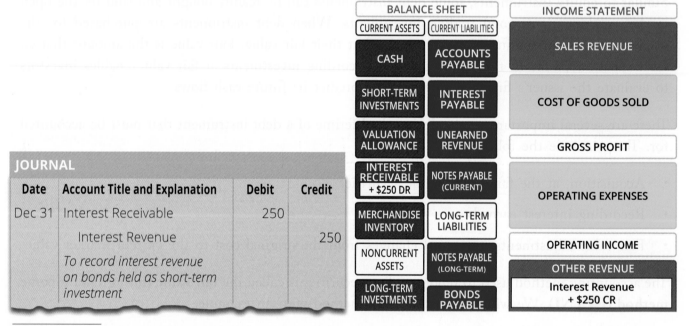

FIGURE 18.5

Note that for as long as the company owns these investments, regular journal entries must be made for any interest earned. Interest revenue is reported under the other income and expenses section of the income statement.

Now, assume that on December 31, the portfolio has a fair value of $10,500, representing a gain of $1,000 ($10,500 – $9,500). The gain is so far unrealized, because the securities have not actually been sold. Therefore, the entry in Figure 18.6 is needed to record what is known as a **fair value adjustment**.

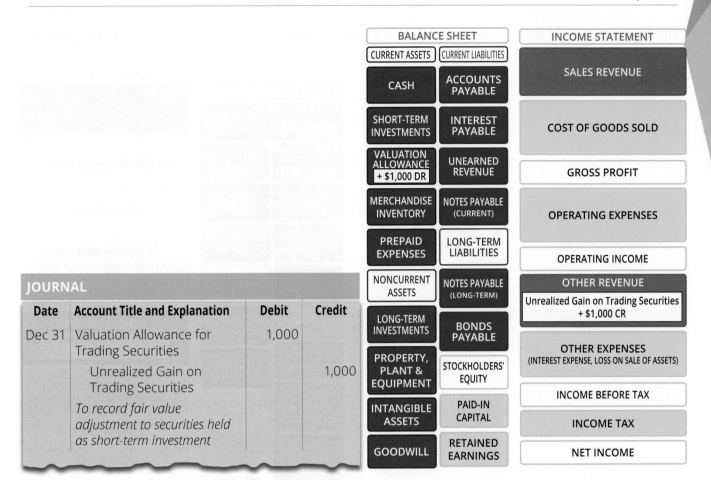

FIGURE 18.6

The account Unrealized Gain (or Loss) on Trading Securities is a temporary account, and its balance must be reported under the other income and expenses section on the income statement. Valuation Allowance for Trading Securities is a permanent account and its balance is reported on the balance sheet to adjust the book value of the investment to its fair value of $10,500. As shown on the Accounting Map in Figure 18.6, the Valuation Allowance for Trading Securities account is debited by $1,000 as the end of period's fair value adjustment resulted in an unrealized gain. Instead of debiting the investment account directly, the valuation allowance account is debited so that the original cost of the investment is always kept on record on the balance sheet. If an unrealized loss is incurred instead of the unrealized gain, Unrealized Loss on Trading Securities would be debited and Valuation Allowance for Trading Securities would be credited. Therefore, the valuation allowance account could have either a debit or credit balance depending on the fair value adjustment required at the end of the period. If the fair value of the security turns out to be more than its original cost, the valuation allowance method would have a debit balance, which adds to the cost of the investment and vice versa.

Now, suppose that on January 15, 2019, Vinyl Sound sells some of the trading securities in its portfolio. The securities originally cost $1,800, and they are sold for $2,100. Vinyl Sound Company therefore realizes a gain of $300 ($2,100 − $1,800), which is recorded as shown in the journal entry in Figure 18.7.

BALANCE SHEET		INCOME STATEMENT

BALANCE SHEET

CURRENT ASSETS	CURRENT LIABILITIES
CASH + $2,100 DR	ACCOUNTS PAYABLE
SHORT-TERM INVESTMENTS − $1,800 CR	INTEREST PAYABLE
VALUATION ALLOWANCE	UNEARNED REVENUE
ACCOUNTS RECEIVABLE	NOTES PAYABLE (CURRENT)
MERCHANDISE INVENTORY	LONG-TERM LIABILITIES
NONCURRENT ASSETS	NOTES PAYABLE (LONG-TERM)
LONG-TERM INVESTMENTS	BONDS PAYABLE
PROPERTY, PLANT & EQUIPMENT	STOCKHOLDERS' EQUITY
INTANGIBLE ASSETS	PAID-IN CAPITAL
GOODWILL	RETAINED EARNINGS

INCOME STATEMENT

SALES REVENUE	
COST OF GOODS SOLD	
GROSS PROFIT	
OPERATING EXPENSES	
OPERATING INCOME	
OTHER REVENUE Gain on Sale of Investment + $300 CR	
OTHER EXPENSES (INTEREST EXPENSE, LOSS ON SALE OF ASSETS)	
INCOME BEFORE TAX	
INCOME TAX	
NET INCOME	

JOURNAL

Date	Account Title and Explanation	Debit	Credit
Jan 15	Cash	2,100	
	Short-Term Investment— Trading Securities		1,800
	Gain on Sale of Investment		300
	To record sale of securities held as short-term investment		

FIGURE 18.7

Note that the journal entry records the difference between the sale price and the original cost of the securities, but does not include any amounts related to previous fair value adjustments. This is because the fair value adjustment in Figure 18.6 was applied to the value of the *entire* portfolio and not to the individual trading securities. At the end of the accounting period, the balance of the valuation allowance account would be adjusted so that the investment value would match its fair value. For example, if at Vinyl Sound's year end of December 31, 2019, the remaining investment, which had an original cost of $7,700 ($9,500 − $1,800), has a fair value of $8,000, Vinyl Sound will adjust its valuation allowance account to have a debit balance of $300 so that the value of the investment on the balance sheet (original cost of $7,700 plus valuation allowance of $300) is equal to the investment's fair value of $8,000.

Available-for-Sale Securities

When accounting for available-for-sale (AFS) securities, we use the **fair value through other comprehensive income method (FVTOCI)**. Under this method, the important events that require journal entries are as follows.

- Acquisition, at the fair value of the securities

- Recording interest earned

- Fair value adjustments, to record a gain or loss due to changes in fair value

We will demonstrate the FVTOCI method with an example.

Fair Value through Other Comprehensive Income Method

Suppose that Vinyl Sound Company pays $400,000 to purchase a portfolio of debt securities on January 1, 2018. Because the securities are purchased with the intent to hold onto them for longer than one year and the bonds have a maturity date beyond 12 months, they are considered long-term investments. Let us first look at how to account for the acquisition.

1. **Acquisition**. If the investor buys AFS securities with an intention to sell them within one year, then the short-term investment account is debited at cost. However, because Vinyl Sound intends to hold onto the investments for longer than one year, the long-term investment account is debited at cost on the purchase date, as shown in Figure 18.8.

   As an investment made for the long term, it is reported on Vinyl Sound's balance sheet as a noncurrent asset.

BALANCE SHEET	
CURRENT ASSETS	CURRENT LIABILITIES
CASH – $400,000 CR	ACCOUNTS PAYABLE
SHORT-TERM INVESTMENTS	INTEREST PAYABLE
ACCOUNTS RECEIVABLE	UNEARNED REVENUE
MERCHANDISE INVENTORY	NOTES PAYABLE (CURRENT)
PREPAID EXPENSES	LONG-TERM LIABILITIES
NONCURRENT ASSETS	NOTES PAYABLE (LONG-TERM)
LONG-TERM INVESTMENTS + $400,000 DR	BONDS PAYABLE
VALUATION ALLOWANCE	STOCKHOLDERS' EQUITY
PROPERTY, PLANT & EQUIPMENT	PAID-IN CAPITAL
INTANGIBLE ASSETS	RETAINED EARNINGS

JOURNAL			
Date	**Account Title and Explanation**	**Debit**	**Credit**
Jan 1	Long-Term Investment—Available-for-Sale Securities	400,000	
	Cash		400,000
	To record purchase of AFS securities held as a long-term investment		

FIGURE 18.8

2. **Recording interest revenue**. Suppose Vinyl Sound receives $2,000 in interest on the bonds held in the portfolio on March 31, 2018. The journal entry to record the interest revenue is shown in Figure 18.9. Similar to the interest received from a trading investment, the interest revenue from an AFS investment is also reported as other income on the income statement.

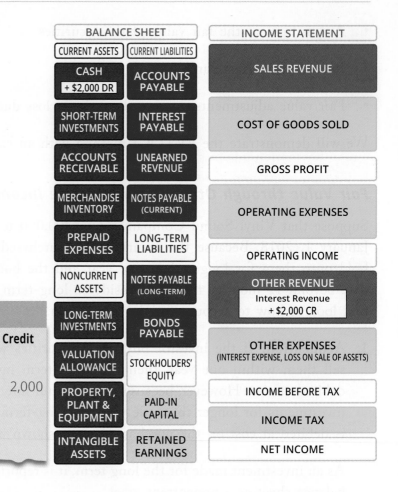

JOURNAL			
Date	**Account Title and Explanation**	**Debit**	**Credit**
Mar 31	Cash	2,000	
	Interest Revenue		2,000
	To record receipt of interest on securities held as a long-term investment		

FIGURE 18.9

3. **Fair value adjustments**. By Vinyl Sound's year end, December 31, 2018, the portfolio has a fair value of $425,000 due to a decrease in market interest rate. This represents an overall gain of $25,000 over the original cost of the investment ($425,000 – $400,000). The gain is so far unrealized, because the securities have not actually been sold. Therefore, the journal entry in Figure 18.10 is made to record the fair value adjustment.

NONCURRENT ASSETS	STOCKHOLDERS' EQUITY
LONG-TERM INVESTMENTS	PAID-IN CAPITAL
VALUATION ALLOWANCE **+ $25,000 DR**	RETAINED EARNINGS
PROPERTY, PLANT & EQUIPMENT	AOCI **+ $25,000 CR**

JOURNAL			
Date	**Account Title and Explanation**	**Debit**	**Credit**
Dec 31	Valuation Allowance for Available-for-Sale Securities	25,000	
	Unrealized Gain on Available-for-Sale Securities		25,000
	To record fair value adjustment to securities held as a long-term investment		

FIGURE 18.10

Similar to the Valuation Allowance for Trading Securities account, Valuation Allowance for Available-for-Sale Securities is a permanent account and its balance is reported together with its related short- or long-term investments on the balance sheet. However, unlike the Unrealized Gain (or Loss) on Trading Securities account, Unrealized Gain (or Loss) on Available-for-Sale Securities is a permanent account. Its balance is not reported as part of the net income. Instead, it is reported as part of Accumulated Other Comprehensive Income (AOCI) in the stockholders' equity section of the balance sheet. Because it is a permanent account, its balance accumulates and is carried forward to the next accounting period. If the beginning balance of the Unrealized Gain on Available-for-Sale Securities is $0 in 2018, its ending balance after the journal entry in Figure 18.10 would be $25,000 on December 31, 2018. Then in 2019, this account will have an opening balance of $25,000, which is carried forward from 2018. The increase in the balance of this account from $0 at the beginning of 2018 to $25,000 at the end of 2018 is also reported as other comprehensive income in the statement of comprehensive income in 2018. The financial statement presentation of available-for-sale securities and the associated valuation allowance and unrealized gain or loss will be illustrated later.

Selling available-for-sale securities requires the same type of journal entries as those used for selling trading securities.

Held-to-Maturity Securities

In the first section of this chapter, you learned that held-to-maturity (HTM) securities are debt instruments (e.g. notes or bonds) that are intended to be held by the investor until they mature in order to earn interest revenue. Securities that will mature within one year are classified as current assets, and those due to mature beyond one year are classified as noncurrent assets.

At acquisition, HTM securities are recorded at cost. Interest revenue on the debt is recorded as it is earned. The purchase and interest revenue transactions are recorded in the same manner that was covered in the trading securities section. As you know from Chapter 17, bonds are often issued at a discount or a premium, which must be amortized during the term of the bond.

Held-to-maturity securities are accounted for using the *amortized cost method*, which means that they are reported on the balance sheet at their amortized cost. The journal entries related to a discount or a premium under the amortized cost method are beyond the scope of this textbook.

Pause & Reflect

Exercise 18-1

On January 21, 2019, Jolly Inc. sells some of the trading securities in its portfolio. The securities were originally purchased for $5,000, and they are sold for $5,550. Show how the company's accountant records the sale transaction in the journal.

JOURNAL			
Date	**Account Title and Explanation**	**Debit**	**Credit**

See Appendix I for solutions.

Investments In Equity LO 3

As you learned in the first section of this chapter, non-strategic equity investments are typically investments in stock where less than 20% of the common stock is owned by the investor. A strategic investment means an investment of 20% or more of the common stock issued by an investee. Strategic investments are further classified into investments with significant influence and investments with controlling influence. Figure 18.11 shows the classification of equity investments and the accounting methods used for each.

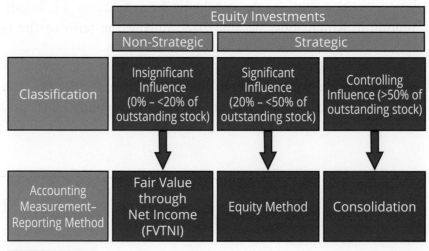

FIGURE 18.11

Investments with Insignificant Influence

Notice that the non-strategic equity investment of insignificant influence uses the fair value through net income method. This is the same method for debt trading instruments. Thus, the transactions to acquire, record fair value adjustments and sell the investment are similar to what we have learned already.

Assume Vinyl Sound Company purchases 500 shares of common stock in Wonder Company on January 1, 2018 at $30 per share. The 500 shares of common stock represent only 1% of Wonder's outstanding common stock, which means Vinyl Sound has insignificant influence over Wonder and this is a non-strategic investment. Vinyl intends to hold this stock for more than one year; therefore, this investment is considered long-term. If Vinyl's intention were to sell this stock within a year, then this investment would be considered short-term and reported under current assets on the balance sheet.

1. **Acquisition**. The stock is recorded in a noncurrent asset account called Investment in Wonder Company Stock. The entry to record the acquisition is shown in Figure 18.12.

JOURNAL			
Date	**Account Title and Explanation**	**Debit**	**Credit**
Jan 1	Investment in Wonder Company Stock	15,000	
	Cash		15,000
	To record purchase of 500 shares of Wonder Company common stock		

FIGURE 18.12

2. **Recording dividend revenue**. Suppose Vinyl received $400 in cash dividends from Wonder Company on August 31, 2018. The journal entry to record the dividend revenue is shown in Figure 18.13.

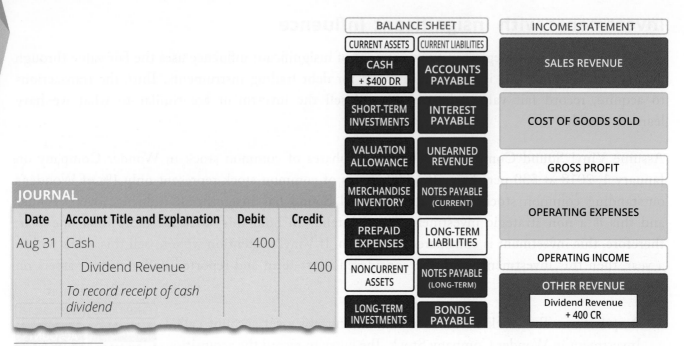

JOURNAL

Date	Account Title and Explanation	Debit	Credit
Aug 31	Cash	400	
	Dividend Revenue		400
	To record receipt of cash dividend		

FIGURE 18.13

3. **Fair value adjustment**. By Vinyl Sound's year end, December 31, 2018, the market value of Wonder Company's stock has increased to $35 per share. This represents an increase of $2,500 in the value of the investment. As with debt trading investments, this is an unrealized gain since the stock has not been sold. The journal entry in Figure 18.14 is made to record the fair value adjustment.

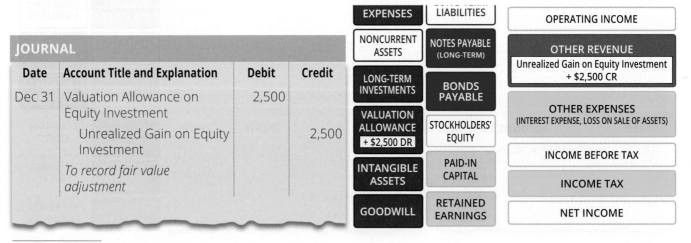

JOURNAL

Date	Account Title and Explanation	Debit	Credit
Dec 31	Valuation Allowance on Equity Investment	2,500	
	Unrealized Gain on Equity Investment		2,500
	To record fair value adjustment		

FIGURE 18.14

The reporting of the change in value of the investment is treated the same way as was done for debt trading investments. The unrealized gain (or loss) is reported under the other income and expenses section of the income statement. The valuation allowance is reported in the asset section of the balance sheet and is added or subtracted from the investment account to arrive at the fair value of $17,500.

Investments with Significant Influence

Strategic investments are equity instruments purchased with the intention to build a long-term relationship with the investee company. Specifically, the investor intends to participate in or control the investee's decisions on how the investee company operates its business. Recall that strategic equity investments can be classified as investments with significant influence or investments with controlling influence. Investments with controlling influence are accounted for using the consolidation method. The specifics of this type of accounting method are beyond the scope of this textbook. This section will focus on accounting for investments with significant influence using the equity method.

The **equity method** is used to record and report strategic equity investments when the investor owns 20% to 50% of the investee's outstanding common stock. The equity method records the purchase of the investment at its original cost, including any broker's fees. Thereafter, the investor adjusts its investment account for its share of the investee's net income and dividends.

When accounting for strategic investments under the equity method, the important events that require journal entries are as follows.

- Acquisition, at cost (the purchase price) of the instrument on the date of purchase
- Recording investment revenue, the share of the investee's profit or loss, as an adjustment to the investor's equity account
- Recording dividends received, recognized when the investor becomes entitled to the dividend

We will once again use the example of Vinyl Sound Company, but this time we will apply the equity method for recording and reporting the investment. For this purchase, there are some transaction costs (i.e. brokerage fees) for purchasing the stock, but assume that these costs are included in the price per share. The main point is that under all methods presented in this chapter, including the equity method, any transaction costs must be included to record the purchase "at cost."

Assume that Vinyl Sound Company purchases 1,000 shares of common stock in Dempton Corporation on January 1, 2018 at $400 per share.

JOURNAL			
Date	**Account Title and Explanation**	**Debit**	**Credit**
Jan 1	Investment in Dempton Corporation Stock	400,000	
	Cash		400,000
	To record purchase of 1,000 shares of Dempton Corporation common stock		

FIGURE 18.15

The 1,000 shares of common stock represent 25% of Dempton's total outstanding common stock, which means that Vinyl Sound has a significant influence over Dempton.

1. **Acquisition.** When the stock is initially purchased, it is recorded at cost in a noncurrent asset account. In this case, the account is called Investment in Dempton Corporation Stock. It is listed on the balance sheet under the category of long-term investments. The entry to record the acquisition is shown in Figure 18.15.

2. **Recording Investment Revenue and Dividends Received.** Assume that for the year ended December 31, 2018, Dempton Corporation has a profit of $200,000. It also declares and pays a $20,000 cash dividend. Vinyl Sound Company owns a 25% stake in Dempton's total outstanding common stock. Vinyl Sound must first calculate its share of Dempton's profit, which is $50,000 ($200,000 × 25%). Then, Vinyl Sound calculates the cash dividend it received, which is $5,000 ($20,000 × 25%). The cash dividend of $5,000 is a reduction of Vinyl Sound's investment since Dempton Corporation's net assets are reduced as a result of the dividends paid. Vinyl Sound records the investment revenue and dividend received as in Figure 18.16.

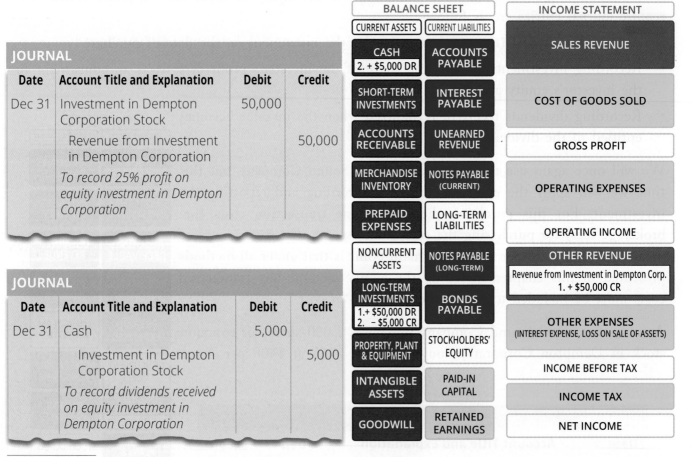

FIGURE 18.16

As a result of these transactions, the Investment in Dempton Corporation Stock balance on Vinyl Sound Company's books as of December 31, 2018 is calculated as follows.

Investment in Dempton Stock = Initial Investment + Revenue from Investment – Cash Dividend Received

= $400,000 + $50,000 – $5,000

= $445,000

Summary

Figure 18.17 summarizes the levels of influence that investors can have, the portions of investees' stock that investors generally own in order to obtain those levels of influence and the associated reporting requirements.

Portion of Outstanding Common Stock Owned by Investor	Investor's Level of Influence on Investee	Method of Accounting and Reporting Required
Less than 20%	Insignificant Influence	Fair Value through Net Income (FVTNI) method
20% to 50%	Significant Influence	Equity method
More than 50%	Controlling Influence	Consolidation method

FIGURE 18.17

Note that in the real world, an investor's level of influence can often be affected by other circumstances, such as "hostile takeovers," or legal issues. However, such situations are beyond the scope of this textbook.

Pause & Reflect

Exercise 18-2

During 2018, Andover Company purchased $250,000 worth of common stock in Blackstar Limited. This represents 30% of the outstanding common stock of Blackstar. For the year ended December 31, 2018, Blackstar made a profit of $200,000. Also during 2018, Blackstar declared and paid a cash dividend of $10,000.

Calculate Andover's net investment in Blackstar Limited as of December 31, 2018.

See Appendix I for solutions.

Presentation of Investments on the Financial Statements

In the first section of this chapter, we discussed the importance of *intent* when determining how to classify and account for investments in debt and equity securities. In other words, an investor's intent at the purchase date determines an investment's accounting treatment—its classification, its valuation and its presentation on the financial statements. Referring once again to Figure 18.3 and Figure 18.11, we can get a visual summary of the investor's intent by looking across the classifications row. In this section, we will illustrate how the different classifications of investments are presented in the financial statements using our examples of Vinyl Sound Company. We will look at the financial statement presentation for debt investments first.

Debt Investments

We have already discussed that GAAP classifies debt investments as trading securities, available-for-sale securities, and held-to-maturity securities. To demonstrate how each class of securities is reported on the balance sheet and income statement (or statement of comprehensive income), we will return to the Vinyl Sound Company examples from earlier in the chapter. (Note that some accounts displayed on the financial statements that follow, such as cash and cash equivalents, income from operations and paid-in capital, have been added simply to show where they fit into the statement format.)

Trading Securities

The following is a reminder of the accounting events that occurred during the year ended December 31, 2018.

- On October 1, 2018, Vinyl Sound Company paid $9,500 to purchase a portfolio of debt and equity securities. Vinyl Sound intends to hold the securities for a short time and then sell them to make a profit.

- On its December 31, 2018 year end, Vinyl Sound recorded $250 in interest revenue on the bonds in its trading portfolio.

- By its December 31, 2018 year end, Vinyl Sound's portfolio of debt and equity securities had a fair value of $10,500, representing an unrealized gain of $1,000, and requiring a fair value adjustment in that amount.

Recall that trading securities are accounted for using the fair value through net income method (FVTNI).

Income Statement

Both interest revenue and unrealized gain on trading securities are temporary accounts, and their balances must be reported in the other income and expenses section on the income statement (see Figure 18.18).

Vinyl Sound Company Income Statement (partial) For the Year Ended December 31, 2018		
Income from Operations		$765,000
Other Income and Expenses		
Interest Revenue	$250	
Unrealized Gain on Trading Securities	1,000	1,250
Income before Income Taxes		766,250

FIGURE 18.18

Balance Sheet

Vinyl Sound's December 31, 2018 partial balance sheet is shown in Figure 18.19. Note that valuation allowance for trading securities is reported on the balance sheet to show the calculation of the assets' fair value, which is $10,500.

Vinyl Sound Company Balance Sheet (partial) As at December 31, 2018		
Current Assets		
Cash and Cash Equivalents		$70,000
Trading Securities (at Cost)	$9,500	
Valuation Allowance for Trading Securities	1,000	
Trading Securities (at Fair Value)		10,500
Interest Receivable		250

FIGURE 18.19

Available-for-Sale Securities

The following is a reminder of the accounting events that occurred during the year ended December 31, 2018.

- On January 1, 2018, Vinyl Sound Company paid $400,000 to purchase a portfolio of debt securities. Vinyl Sound intends to hold onto the securities for longer than one year.

- On its December 31, 2018 year end, Vinyl Sound recorded $2,000 in interest revenue on interest received from the bonds.

- By its December 31, 2018 year end, Vinyl Sound's portfolio of debt securities had a fair value of $425,000, representing an unrealized gain of $25,000, and requiring a fair value adjustment in that amount.

Recall that available-for-sale securities are accounted for using the fair value through other comprehensive income method (FVTOCI).

Statement of Comprehensive Income

Interest Revenue is a temporary account, and its balance must be reported in the other income and expenses section on the statement of comprehensive income. The Unrealized Gain on Available-for-Sale Securities for the current year is reported as other comprehensive income, which is reported net of tax on the statement of comprehensive income, as shown in Figure 18.20. For illustrative purposes, the income tax effect of other comprehensive income is ignored in this figure. The presentation of the unrealized gain (loss) on available-for-sale securities' tax effects and reclassification to net income is beyond the scope of this textbook.

Vinyl Sound Company Statement of Comprehensive Income (partial) For the Year Ended December 31, 2018	
Income from Operations	$765,000
Other Income and Expenses	
Interest Revenue	2,000
Income Before Income Tax Expense	767,000
Income Tax Expense	230,100
Net Income	536,900
Other Comprehensive Income	
Unrealized Gain on Available-for-Sale Securities	25,000
Total Comprehensive Income	$561,900

FIGURE 18.20

WORTH REPEATING

Comprehensive income is the total of net income plus other comprehensive income. Other Comprehensive Income (OCI) is a category of income and expense that GAAP defines as resulting from transactions that are beyond company owners' or management's control, such as an increase or decrease in market value of available-for-sale investments. These items are not allowed by GAAP to be reported as a part of net income, but they do affect the equity accounts. Similar to how revenue and expense accounts are ultimately transferred to the retained earnings account at the end of the accounting period, the OCI account is transferred to the Accumulated Other Comprehensive Income (AOCI) account at period end. AOCI is reported separately from retained earnings in the stockholders' equity section of the balance sheet.

Balance Sheet

Similar to trading securities, available-for-sale securities are also reported at their market value. Valuation Allowance for Available-for-Sale Securities is a permanent account and its balance is reported together with its related short- or long-term investments on the balance sheet to adjust the value of the investment from its original cost to its fair value as at the balance sheet date. Because Vinyl Sound intends to hold this investment for longer than one year, the investment and its valuation allowance are reported under the long-term investments section of the balance sheet, as shown in Figure 18.21. The long-term investments section is located below current assets and above property, plant and equipment. If, on the other hand, Vinyl Sound plans to sell the available-for-sale securities within less than a year, the investment together with its valuation allowance would be reported under the current assets section of the balance sheet instead.

Vinyl Sound Company Balance Sheet (partial) As at December 31, 2018		
Long-Term Investments		
Long-Term Investments—Available-for-Sale Securities (at Cost)	$400,000	
Valuation Allowance for Available-for-Sale Securities	25,000	
Long-Term Investments—Available-for-Sale Securities (at Fair Value)		$425,000

FIGURE 18.21

Net income for the year is added to the existing balance of retained earnings under stockholders' equity on the balance sheet. The $25,000 unrealized gain on available-for-sale securities for the current year, as reported on the statement of comprehensive income, is added to the existing balance of accumulated other comprehensive income, which is also reported under stockholders' equity on the balance sheet. If the retained earnings and accumulated other comprehensive income balances at the beginning of the year were equal to zero, and if no dividend was paid to stockholders during the year, the retained earnings and accumulated other comprehensive income for the year 2018 would be reported as shown in Figure 18.22. Because the Unrealized Gain on Available-for-Sale Securities account is a permanent account, its balance is carried forward to the next year. In the year 2019, this account, which is reported under accumulated other comprehensive income on the balance sheet, will have an opening balance of $25,000, and any unrealized gain (loss) on available-for-sale securities in 2019 will be added to (subtracted from) this amount.

Vinyl Sound Company Balance Sheet (partial) As at December 31, 2018	
Stockholders' Equity	
Common Stock	$70,000
Additional Paid-In Capital	5,000
Retained Earnings	536,900
Accumulated Other Comprehensive Income	25,000
Total Stockholders' Equity	636,900

FIGURE 18.22

Held-to-Maturity Securities

If Vinyl Sound Company had classified its $400,000 investment in debt securities as held-to-maturity securities instead of AFS securities, the company would report this investment on its financial statements using the amortized cost method, as shown below.

Income Statement

Under the amortized cost method, the investment is not adjusted to its market value. Therefore, unrealized gain or loss is not recorded in the journal and thus not reported on the income statement. Interest revenue is reported on the income statement as shown in Figure 18.23.

Vinyl Sound Company Income Statement (partial) For the Year Ended December 31, 2018	
Income from Operations	$765,000
Other Income and Expenses	
Interest Revenue	2,000

FIGURE 18.23

Balance Sheet

Unlike trading and AFS securities, HTM securities are reported on the balance sheet at their amortized cost instead of at their market value. Figure 18.24 shows how the HTM securities are reported on the balance sheet. If their maturity date is longer than one year from the balance sheet date, they are classified as long-term investments.

Vinyl Sound Company **Balance Sheet (partial)** **As at December 31, 2018**	
Long-Term Investments	
Long-Term Investments—Held-to-Maturity Securities (at Amortized Cost)	$400,000

FIGURE 18.24

Equity Investments

Insignificant Influence

As mentioned earlier, non-strategic equity investments of less than 20% are accounted for similarly to how debt trading investments are accounted for. Thus, the presentation on the income statement would be similar to Figure 18.18, except Dividend Revenue would be reported instead of Interest Revenue. The balance sheet would also be similar to Figure 18.19, showing the valuation allowance as an increase or decrease to the cost of the initial investment. However, because equity investments do not generate interest, interest receivable would not appear on the company's balance sheet. The equity investment would be classified either as a short-term investment or a long-term investment, depending on management's intent whether to hold the investment for less than or longer than one year. If management intends to liquidate the investment within one year, then the investment is classified as a short-term investment and reported under the current assets section of the balance sheet. If management intends to hold the investment for longer than one year, then the investment is reported under the long-term investments section of the balance sheet.

Significant Influence

When an investor owns 20% to 50% of the investee's outstanding stock, the equity method records the purchase of the investment at its original cost. We will return to the Vinyl Sound Company example when we discussed the equity method earlier in the chapter.

The following is a reminder of the accounting events that occurred during the year ended December 31, 2018.

*   On January 1, 2018, Vinyl Sound Company purchased 1,000 shares of common stock from Dempton Corporation at $400 per share. The 1,000 shares represent 25% of Dempton's total outstanding common stock, giving Vinyl Sound a significant influence over Dempton's business.

*   For the year ended December 31, 2018, Dempton Corporation had a profit of $200,000. Vinyl Sound's share of Dempton's profit was $50,000.

*   During the year ended December 31, 2018, Dempton declared and paid a cash dividend of $20,000. Vinyl Sound's share of the cash dividend was $5,000.

Income Statement

Vinyl Sound's income statement will include its share of Dempton's profits, which is reported as part of other income, as shown in Figure 18.25.

Vinyl Sound Company Income Statement (partial) For the Year Ended December 31, 2018	
Income from Operations	$765,000
Other Income and Expenses	
Equity Income in Dempton Corporation	50,000

FIGURE 18.25

Balance Sheet

Recall that as a result of these transactions, Vinyl Sound's *net* equity investment in Dempton as of December 31, 2018 was $445,000 ($400,000 + $50,000 − $5,000). The investment is reported on Vinyl Sound's balance sheet at cost, along with any other long-term investments, as shown in Figure 18.26.

Vinyl Sound Company Balance Sheet (partial) As at December 31, 2018	
Long-Term Investments	
Investment in Dempton Corporation (Equity Method)	$445,000

FIGURE 18.26

As previously mentioned, investments with controlling influence are reported in a set of consolidated financial statements, which are beyond the scope of this textbook.

In Summary

LO 1 Describe and classify different types of investments

▶ Investments can be made by purchasing debt instruments (or debt securities) such as money market funds, term deposits, treasury bills and bonds. Investments can also be made by purchasing equity instruments (or equity securities) such as preferred and common stock of another company.

▶ Investors can purchase debt and equity instruments with an intention to generate investment income only (a non-strategic investment) or to establish a long-term relationship with another company (a strategic investment).

▶ Equity instruments held for strategic purposes are always considered long-term investments.

▶ A stockholder owning less than 20% of an investee's common stock outstanding has an insignificant influence on the investee corporation.

▶ A significant influence exists if one stockholder owns between 20% and 50% of the common stock outstanding.

▶ An investor owning more than 50% of the common stock outstanding has a controlling influence.

LO 2 Prepare journal entries for debt investments

▶ Debt securities purchased with the intent of selling them in the short term at a gain are known as trading investments, or trading securities.

▶ A debt instrument that will mature within 12 months is considered a short-term debt instrument.

▶ Trading securities are accounted for using the fair value through net income method.

▶ Available-for-sale securities are accounted for using the fair value through other comprehensive income method.

▶ Held-to-maturity securities are accounted for using the amortized cost method.

LO 3 Prepare journal entries for equity investments

▶ Investments with insignificant influence are considered non-strategic investments and are accounted for using the fair value through net income method.

▶ Investments with significant influence are accounted for using the equity method.

▶ The equity method records the purchase of the investment at its original cost.

▶ The investor's investment account must be adjusted to account for its share of the investee's net income and dividends.

▶ Investments with controlling influence are accounted for using the consolidation method.

LO 4 **Describe how the different types of investments are presented in the financial statements**

▶ Trading investments are always classified as current assets on the investor's balance sheet.

▶ Available-for-sale securities that mature within 12 months are classified as current assets on the investor's balance sheet. AFS securities with maturity dates longer than 12 months can be classified as either current or noncurrent assets based on management's intent.

▶ When long-term debt instruments, such as bonds, are purchased as held-to-maturity investments, they are classified on the balance sheet according to their time to maturity: any investments that are due to mature within 12 months are classified as current assets, while any investments maturing beyond 12 months are classified as noncurrent assets.

▶ Equity investments with insignificant influence can be classified as either current or noncurrent assets based on management's intent.

▶ Gain or loss from fair value adjustment is reported as part of net income for trading securities and part of other comprehensive income for AFS securities. Fair value adjustment is not reported for HTM securities.

 *Access **ameengage.com** for integrated resources including tutorials, practice exercises, the digital textbook and more.*

Review Exercise 18-1

Benita Sikorsky is the controller for Travel Time Inc., a medium-sized enterprise that has a December 31 year end. From time to time, her company has surplus cash on hand that it uses to make short-term and long-term investments. The types of investments vary from period to period, depending on which investments produce the highest return for the company.

During the past year, the company completed the following transactions.

Jan 1   Paid $450,000 to purchase 6,000 shares of common stock in Tamalie Inc. for strategic reasons. The 6,000 shares of common stock represent 30% of Tamalie's total outstanding common stock.

Apr 1   Paid $101,500 to purchase a portfolio of debt securities with an intention to sell them for profit after holding them for longer than a year but before the debt securities mature.

May 10   Paid $50,000 to purchase 4% of the outstanding common stock in Pergola Inc. Management hopes that their prices will rise quickly and that the stock can be sold for a gain within one year.

Jul 1   Received $3,000 in interest revenue from the debt securities purchased on April 1

Jul 10   Received a $100 cash dividend from the equity securities purchased on May 10

Jul 31   Tamalie Inc. announced that its net income for the year ended July 31, 2018 was $80,000

Aug 20   Tamalie Inc. declared and paid a $10,000 cash dividend to its common stockholders

Oct 1   Sold 10% of the portfolio that was purchased on April 1, 2018 for $10,000

Dec 15   Sold half of the stock that was purchased on May 10, 2018 for $26,800

Dec 31   At the company's year end, the market values of the portfolio purchased on April 1 is $92,000 and the value of the stock in Pergola Inc. is worth $24,000.

Record journal entries for each of the above transactions.

JOURNAL			
Date	Account Title and Explanation	Debit	Credit

JOURNAL			
Date	Account Title and Explanation	Debit	Credit

See Appendix I for solutions.

Chapter 19
The Statement of Cash Flows

Learning Objectives

LO 1 Classify operating, investing and financing activities

- Three Categories of Cash Flow Activities

LO 2 Prepare a statement of cash flows using the indirect method

- A Step-by-Step Approach to the Statement of Cash Flows
- Noncash and Non-Operating Items from the Income Statement
- Changes in Operating Assets and Liabilities
- Analysis of the Statement of Cash Flows

LO 3 Calculate book value and cash received for selling noncurrent assets

- Property, Plant and Equipment with Depreciation
- Long-Term Investments

LO 4 Explain the concept of free cash flow and its importance for potential investors

LO 5 Discuss ethical issues related to cash flow

Appendix

LO 6 Prepare a statement of cash flows using the direct method

- Cash Receipts
- Cash Payments

LO 7 Prepare a statement of cash flows in a spreadsheet using the indirect method

- Preparing the Spreadsheet
- Analyzing Account Changes
- Preparing the Statement of Cash Flows

AMEENGAGE™ *Access **ameengage.com** for integrated resources including tutorials, practice exercises, the digital textbook and more.*

719

The Importance of Cash Flow

Most of our discussion of accounting procedures and principles so far has focused on two types of financial statements: the balance sheet and the income statement. When people think about business finance, they usually think about these financial statements.

However, analyzing the income statement and balance sheet does not provide all the information needed by users. This is because balance sheets and income statements are prepared on an accrual basis. Revenue and expense recognition dictate that revenues and expenses be recorded for the period in which they are earned or incurred. However, these types of transactions do not always involve an actual exchange of cash or cash equivalents. Conversely, other transactions, such as borrowing or repaying loans, affect cash but do not affect net income.

Why is cash so important? Without cash, a company cannot pay its bills. Without cash, a company cannot purchase and pay for new inventory or other assets required to run the business. Thus, determining how cash is generated and spent is an important way to assess how well the company is performing.

To some extent, recording accruals masks the sources and uses of cash in a business. Thus, accounting standards require the preparation of a **statement of cash flows**, sometimes also referred to as a cash flow statement, to track the sources and uses of cash in a business. The statement of cash flows was briefly introduced in Chapter 2. This chapter examines the statement in more depth and discusses how to prepare it.

The statement of cash flows ignores accruals and just focuses on cash. As you learned in Chapter 16 on corporate financial statements, a corporation can have hundreds or thousands of financial statement users. Internal users (e.g. company managers and executives) rely on the statement of cash flows to help them evaluate operations, and to make financing and investing decisions. These decisions include whether the company can pay for expenses in its day-to-day operations or whether the company must borrow cash to make large asset purchases. External users (e.g. stockholders, potential investors, creditors and lenders) use the statement of cash flows to assess the company's overall cash position and potential to make a profit. They make decisions such as whether the company can pay its debts as they mature (to lenders and creditors), or whether it will be able to pay dividends (to investors and stockholders).

Three Categories of Cash Flow Activities

A business generates and consumes cash in one of the following three ways.

- operating activities
- investing activities
- financing activities

In fact, all statements of cash flow have three sections showing how cash flows in and out of a company.

Cash Flow from Operating Activities

Cash flow from operating activities is the movement of cash within a business as a result of day-to-day activities. All items in this section are directly related to items on the income statement (revenue and expenses) and the current assets and current liabilities on the balance sheet. This includes transactions involving customers, suppliers, inventory, and so on. It is the most important section because the future of a business largely depends on operating activities.

Cash Flow from Investing Activities

Cash flow from investing activities is the movement of cash in a business on the basis of the purchases and sales of noncurrent assets. This section shows how the business is investing cash back into itself. For example, if a truck was sold during the year, cash flow would have increased. Alternatively, if the business purchased land, cash flow would have decreased, since the business had to use cash to invest in the land.

Cash Flow from Financing Activities

Cash flow from financing activities is cash received from investors and lenders to help run, or finance, the business. It is also cash paid back to the investors (dividends) and lenders (principal repayment). This section shows financing that generally deals with long-term liabilities, such as notes payable, and equity financing, such as selling stock. Payments toward notes payable and dividend payments to stockholders are also reported here.

Figure 19.1 summarizes the events that are recorded in each of the three sections of the statement of cash flows.

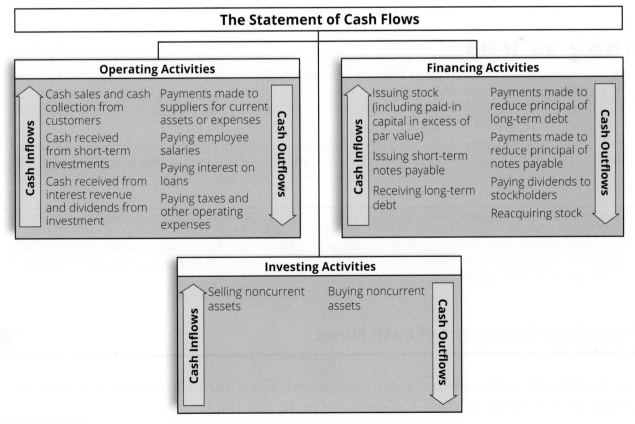

FIGURE 19.1

Figure 19.2 shows the format of the statement of cash flows. The individual cash inflow and outflow items, similar to those shown in Figure 19.1, are listed below their respective headings. There may also be noncash investing and financing transactions, such as the company issuing stock to pay off a note payable, or buying assets in exchange for stock. These noncash transactions must be disclosed in a separate schedule either at the bottom of the statement of cash flows, as shown in Figure 19.2, or in the notes to the financial statements. Illustration of the noncash investing and financing transactions is beyond the scope of this textbook.

ABC Company Statement of Cash Flows For the Year Ended MM-DD-YYYY		
Cash Flow from Operating Activities		
(Individual cash inflows and outflows are listed here)	$xxx	
Net Cash Provided (Used) by Operating Activities		$xxx
Cash Flow from Investing Activities		
(Individual cash inflows and outflows are listed here)	xxx	
Net Cash Provided (Used) by Investing Activities		xxx
Cash Flow from Financing Activities		
(Individual cash inflows and outflows are listed here)	xxx	
Net Cash Provided (Used) by Financing Activities		xxx
Net Increase (Decrease) in Cash		xxx
Cash at the Beginning of the Year		xxx
Cash at the End of the Year		$xxx
Noncash Investing and Financing Activities		$xxx

FIGURE 19.2

GAAP vs IFRS

Although both standards require the creation of the statement of cash flows, IFRS does allow for some options on how a few items are reported. Under GAAP, interest or dividends received from a short- or long-term investment are reported as operating activities. IFRS, however, allows the option to report them as either operating or investing activities.

Under GAAP, interest paid on loans is an operating activity. Dividends paid to stockholders are a financing activity. IFRS, however, allows the option to report them either as operating or financing activities. Of course for IFRS statements to be consistent, once a decision is made about where to report interest and dividends, they must always be reported in that manner.

Under IFRS, cash flows to pay taxes are reported as a separate line in the operating activities, in contrast to GAAP, which does not require a separate line disclosure. According to IAS 7.35, "Cash flows arising from taxes on income shall be separately disclosed and shall be classified as cash flows from operating activities unless they can be specifically identified with financing and investing activities." GAAP requires that cash outflows for income tax always be classified as operating activities.

Preparing a Statement of Cash Flows

Two methods are used to prepare a statement of cash flows: the indirect method and the direct method. Both methods are allowed under both GAAP and IFRS.

There are some similarities between the indirect method and the direct method. Both methods break down the three ways of generating and using cash into operating, investing and financing activities. The investing activities and financing activities sections are prepared in exactly the same way under both methods. Specifically, investing activities and financing activities are determined by analyzing the noncurrent assets, long-term liabilities and equity portion of the balance sheet.

The only difference between the indirect method and the direct method is how the cash flow from operating activities section is prepared. The **indirect method** *indirectly* analyzes cash flow from operating activities by starting with accrual-based net income, and then adding or subtracting certain items from the income statement as well as changes in current assets and current liabilities from the balance sheet.

Unlike the indirect method, the direct method calculates cash flow from operating activities by *directly* analyzing cash received from sales and collections and *directly* analyzing cash spent on expenses. As you will learn by the end of this chapter, the net cash flow from operating activities is the same no matter which method is used; it is simply the way of calculating and presenting the information that differs, not the actual amount. The indirect method is most commonly used since it is generally easier to prepare. Preparation of the statement of cash flows using the direct method is illustrated in Appendix 19A. In this section, we will demonstrate the step-by-step approach to creating the statement of cash flows using the indirect method.

IN THE REAL WORLD

Academic studies have shown that if two versions of the statement of cash flows are shown (i.e. direct and indirect method), investors can make better decisions. By disclosing both the direct and indirect methods, a company improves its accounting transparency. Through statistical studies, it has been shown that the indirect method is more useful than the direct method. However, a reason for this discrepancy was not revealed by the studies. On the other hand, the direct method is usually more easily understood by users than the indirect method.

A Step-by-Step Approach to the Statement of Cash Flows

The statement of cash flows is easiest to prepare using the following six steps.

Step 1. Calculate the net increase (decrease) in cash during the period.

Step 2. Calculate the net cash provided (or used) by operating activities using the indirect method.

Step 3. Calculate the net cash provided (or used) by investing activities.

Step 4. Calculate the net cash provided (or used) by financing activities.

Step 5. Calculate the total net cash provided (or used) by operating, investing and financing activities combined.

Step 6. Verify that this total net cash flow equals the ending cash balance less the beginning cash balance.

We will follow this process using the example of Soho Supplies, a manufacturer of office supplies with a year end of December 31, 2018. Before preparing the statement of cash flows, we must examine Soho's balance sheet and income statement.

Step 1. Calculate the net increase (decrease) in cash during the period.

Figure 19.3 on the next page is a comparative balance sheet for two periods and shows both periods' cash balances. We will use this specific balance sheet for Soho Supplies for the remainder of the chapter, and keep referring to it as we move along.

The last column of the balance sheet shows the difference between 2017 and 2018 period-end account balances. This difference is used when preparing the statement of cash flows. The first line of the balance sheet shows that the cash account decreased from $396,142 in 2017 to $349,935 in 2018. Therefore, the net decrease in cash for the year was $46,207, as shown in blue on the first line. Alternatively, we could say that Soho's net cash flow was ($46,207).

Step 2. Calculate the net cash provided (or used) by operating activities using the indirect method.

The indirect method of analyzing cash flows from operating activities begins with the period's net income (from the income statement), which is then adjusted as necessary. These adjustments include adding back noncash expenses to net income, and deducting noncash increases from net income.

At this point, some additional information will help in our cash flow analysis. The indirect method of preparing a statement of cash flows follows the logic of the basic accounting equation.

$$\text{Assets} = \text{Liabilities} + \text{Stockholders' Equity}$$

The basic accounting equation enables us to analyze changes in one balance sheet account by examining changes in the other balance sheet accounts. Even by analyzing noncash balance sheet accounts, we can determine indirectly how they affect the cash account (hence, the term indirect method). To demonstrate, we can also express the basic accounting equation as follows.

$$\text{Cash} + \text{Noncash Assets} = \text{Liabilities} + \text{Stockholders' Equity}$$

and therefore,

$$\text{Cash} = \text{Liabilities} + \text{Stockholders' Equity} - \text{Noncash Assets}$$

It then follows that any changes in the cash balance can be determined from changes in liabilities, stockholders' equity and noncash assets.

$$\text{Changes in Cash} = \text{Changes in Liabilities} + \text{Changes in Stockholders' Equity} - \text{Changes in Noncash Assets}$$

This relationship will become apparent as we work through the example in this section.

Soho Supplies Balance Sheet As at December 31, 2018			
	2018	**2017**	**Change**
Assets			
Current Assets			
Cash	$349,935	$396,142	**($46,207)**
Accounts Receivable	1,286,138	1,065,812	220,326
Merchandise Inventory	1,683,560	840,091	843,469
Prepaid Insurance	48,612	42,625	5,987
Total Current Assets	3,368,245	2,344,670	1,023,575
Noncurrent Assets			
Land[1]	0	50,000	(50,000)
Equipment[2]	322,518	120,000	202,518
Accumulated Depreciation	(79,262)	(36,000)	(43,262)
Total Noncurrent Assets	243,256	134,000	109,256
Total Assets	$3,611,501	$2,478,670	$1,132,831
Liabilities			
Current Liabilities			
Accounts Payable	$783,602	$475,645	$307,957
Salaries Payable	25,000	50,000	(25,000)
Interest Payable	15,650	23,500	(7,850)
Income Taxes Payable	280,117	250,000	30,117
Notes Payable, Current Portion	380,000	240,000	140,000
Total Current Liabilities	1,484,369	1,039,145	445,224
Long-Term Liabilities			
Notes Payable, Long-Term Portion	420,000	356,000	64,000
Bonds Payable[3]	170,000	200,000	(30,000)
Total Long-Term Liabilities	590,000	556,000	34,000
Total Liabilities	2,074,369	1,595,145	479,224
Stockholders' Equity			
Paid-In Capital			
Preferred Stock	8,000	0	8,000
Common Stock	5,000	5,000	0
Additional Paid-In Capital	2,000	0	2,000
Total Paid-In Capital	15,000	5,000	10,000
Retained Earnings[4]	1,522,132	878,525	643,607
Total Stockholders' Equity	1,537,132	883,525	653,607
Total Liabilities and Stockholders' Equity	$3,611,501	$2,478,670	$1,132,831

Additional Information

[1] During 2018, land that cost $50,000 was sold for $60,000, resulting in a $10,000 gain on sale. The gain is reported on the Income Statement in the Other Income and Expenses section.

[2] During 2018, Soho made purchases of equipment for $202,518.

[3] The bonds were issued at par.

[4] Soho declared and paid $10,000 in dividends in 2018.

FIGURE 19.3

Soho's income statement is shown in Figure 19.4.

Soho Supplies Income Statement For the Year Ended December 31, 2018	
Sales Revenue	$8,685,025
Cost of Goods Sold	5,998,612
Gross Profit	2,686,413
Operating Expenses	
Salaries Expense	1,416,135
Depreciation Expense	43,262
Insurance Expense	16,000
Other Operating Expenses	235,417
Total Operating Expenses	1,710,814
Income from Operations	975,599
Other Income and Expenses	
Gain on Sale of Land	10,000
Interest Expense	(51,875)
Income before Income Taxes	933,724
Income Tax Expense	280,117
Net Income	**$653,607**

FIGURE 19.4

The company's net income is $653,607 for 2018. This income statement will be used for the remainder of the chapter, so refer to it as we assemble the statement of cash flows for 2018.

Remember that cash flow from operating activities under the indirect method starts with net income and then adds or subtracts certain items from the income statement and from changes on the balance sheet. In the current example, the company's net income for 2018 is $653,607, shown in blue on the income statement in Figure 19.4. However, in reality, not all revenues and expenses involve cash due to the accrual basis of accounting required under GAAP and IFRS. Since the focus is on cash flow instead of accruals, only the money that actually changes hands during a period needs to be accounted for. Therefore, in the cash flow from operating activities section, we begin with net income and add or subtract noncash items that appear on the income statement.

Noncash and Non-Operating Items from the Income Statement

Noncash and non-operating items from the income statement include things such as depreciation and amortization, gains (losses) from the sale of assets, and gains (losses) on the retirement of debt (discussed in Chapter 17 in the section on retiring bonds). These and other such noncash or non-operating items either have no effect on actual cash inflows or outflows or are not classified as operating activities; therefore, their amounts must be canceled by adjusting net income. In our example, there are two noncash or non-operating items affecting Soho's cash flow from operating activities: depreciation, and gain on the sale of land.

To help illustrate how the cash balance changes using the indirect method, we will start with the opening cash balance in 2018 (or the ending cash balance in 2017). Figure 19.5 shows a partial statement of cash flows that includes cash flow from operating activities. At the top of the statement is the opening cash balance, which is $396,142. If the whole amount of net income was received in cash, then cash would be increased by the net income amount. This is why net income (a) is added to the opening cash balance in Figure 19.5. At this point, cash is updated to $1,049,749, which is equal to the opening cash balance of $396,142 plus the net income amount of $653,607. However, not all components of the net income are cash, and not all components are classified as operating activities. To prepare the cash flow from operating activities section of the statement of cash flows, items that are noncash or unrelated to operating activities must be taken out. Consequently, as shown in Figure 19.5, depreciation (b) is added to net income, and gain on sale of land (c) is subtracted from net income in order to adjust accrual-based net income to cash-based operating income.

Soho Supplies Statement of Cash Flows (partial) For the Year Ended December 31, 2018		
	Amount	**Updated Cash Balance**
Opening Cash Balance		$396,142
Cash Flow from Operating Activities		
Net Income	$653,607 (a)	1,049,749
Adjustments to Reconcile Net Income to Net Cash Provided (Used) by Operating Activities		
Depreciation	43,262 (b)	1,093,011
Gain on Sale of Land	(10,000) (c)	1,083,011

The Updated Cash Balance column is used to calculate the updated cash balance to help you understand the process. **You will not see this theoretical column illustrated in a proper statement of cash flows. It is a learning tool only.**

FIGURE 19.5

Depreciation

Depreciation is a noncash expense that simply decreases the book value of an asset without any change to cash. Therefore, depreciation must be excluded from any equations involving cash flow. To illustrate this point, a journal entry for depreciation debits depreciation expense, and credits accumulated depreciation for the particular asset—neither the debit nor the credit involves cash. Therefore, Soho Supplies' depreciation expense of $43,262 from the income statement in Figure 19.4 is added to the net income, item (a) on the statement of cash flows, as shown in Figure 19.5, item (b).

Gain on Sale of Land

In 2018, Soho Supplies' land with a book value of $50,000 was sold for $60,000. This means that the company made a profit (or gain) of $10,000, which appears in the other income and expenses section of Soho Supplies' income statement.

Soho Supplies' net income of $653,607 includes the $10,000 gain on sale of land. However, because the gain is not part of day-to-day operating activities, it must be removed from the cash flow from operating activities section of the statement of cash flows. This is why the $10,000 gain on sale of land is deducted from net income in the cash flow from operating activities section, in item (c). Although the gain is removed from this section, the $60,000 proceeds from the sale of land is reported in the cash flow from investing activities section, which is explained later. *Therefore, the $10,000 gain is deducted from net income in the cash flow from operating activities section to avoid double counting.* If, instead, Soho incurred a *loss* from the sale of land, the amount is added back to net income in the cash flow from operating activities section.

Changes in Operating Assets and Liabilities

The next step is to add or subtract changes in items related to operating activities that do not flow through the income statement. These items include all the current assets and current liabilities (except the current portion of long-term debt) on the balance sheet.

Figure 19.6 shows the rest of the cash flow from operating activities with all the changes in current assets and current liabilities, items (d) to (k). A discussion of these items follows after the figure.

Soho Supplies Statement of Cash Flows (partial) For the Year Ended December 31, 2018		
	Amount	**Updated Cash Balance**
Opening Cash Balance		$396,142
Cash Flow from Operating Activities		
Net Income	$653,607	1,049,749
Adjustments to Reconcile Net Income to Net Cash Provided (Used) by Operating Activities		
Depreciation	43,262	1,093,011
Gain on Sale of Land	(10,000)	1,083,011
Changes in Operating Assets and Liabilities		
Increase in Accounts Receivable	(220,326) (d)	862,685
Increase in Prepaid Insurance	(5,987) (e)	856,698
Increase in Merchandise Inventory	(843,469) (f)	13,229
Increase in Accounts Payable	307,957 (g)	321,186
Decrease in Salaries Payable	(25,000) (h)	296,186
Decrease in Interest Payable	(7,850) (i)	288,336
Increase in Income Taxes Payable	30,117 (j)	318,453
Net Cash Provided (Used) by Operating Activities	($77,689) (k)	

FIGURE 19.6

(d) The first listed current asset in the comparative balance sheet (after cash) is accounts receivable. The balance sheet in Figure 19.3 showed that this account increased by $220,326 from 2017 to 2018. Remember that since accounts receivable increased, it will decrease cash because it is yet to be collected. We therefore deduct this amount from the cash balance of $1,083,011. As indicated in Figure 19.6, the updated cash balance is $862,685.

(e) Prepaid insurance increased by $5,987, decreasing the cash balance to $856,698 because the prepaid insurance must have been paid with cash.

(f) Merchandise inventory increased by $843,469, decreasing the cash balance to $13,229 because cash must have been used to pay for the additional inventory.

(g) Accounts payable increased by $307,957. This resulted in more cash in the bank since Soho deferred paying their suppliers, increasing the cash balance to $321,186.

(h) Salaries payable decreased by $25,000. This means Soho paid out cash owing for salaries, decreasing the cash balance to $296,186.

(i) Interest payable also decreased by $7,850, meaning Soho used cash to pay for the interest owed. The cash balance decreased to $288,336.

(j) Income taxes payable increased by $30,117. This means Soho has deferred payment of income taxes and therefore has more cash. This increases the cash balance to $318,453.

(k) The updated cash balance has gone from the beginning balance of $396,142 to $318,453. This indicates that cash decreased by $77,689 due to operating activities.

Under the indirect method of preparing a statement of cash flows, Figure 19.7 outlines the impact an increase or decrease to current assets or current liabilities has on the statement of cash flows.

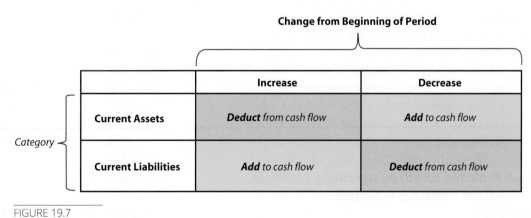

Impact on Statement of Cash Flows:
Change in Current Assets and Current Liabilities

FIGURE 19.7

Step 3. Calculate the net cash provided (or used) by investing activities.

Changes in the value of noncurrent assets (i.e. property, plant and equipment) affect cash flow. However, measuring the effect is not as straightforward as observing the change in the property, plant and equipment balance from one year to the next.

This section of the statement of cash flows deals with the way cash flow changes through the investment in or sale of noncurrent assets. In the current example with Soho Supplies, the information required to complete the cash flow from investing activities section is provided in the Additional Information portion below Soho's balance sheet (Figure 19.3). We will analyze the items from this additional information and show them in Figure 19.8, items (l) to (n).

(l) The proceeds from the sale of the land in the amount of $60,000 are added to the updated cash balance since the transaction represents a cash inflow. The proceeds include the $10,000 gain, which was previously deducted from the operating activities section of the statement of cash flows.

(m) The $202,518 purchase of equipment is deducted from the updated cash balance because it represents a cash outflow.

(n) The updated cash balance has dropped from $318,453 to $175,935. This indicates that net cash provided (used) by investing activities was ($142,518).

In Figure 19.8, the cash flow from the investing activities section is added to the illustrative statement of cash flows.

Soho Supplies Statement of Cash Flows (partial) For the Year Ended December 31, 2018		
	Amount	Updated Cash Balance
Opening Cash Balance		$396,142
Cash Flow from Operating Activities		
Net Income	$653,607	1,049,749
Adjustments to Reconcile Net Income to Net Cash Provided (Used) by Operating Activities		
Depreciation	43,262	1,093,011
Gain on Sale of Land	(10,000)	1,083,011
Changes in Operating Assets and Liabilities		
Increase in Accounts Receivable	(220,326)	862,685
Increase in Prepaid Insurance	(5,987)	856,698
Increase in Merchandise Inventory	(843,469)	13,229
Increase in Accounts Payable	307,957	321,186
Decrease in Salaries Payable	(25,000)	296,186
Decrease in Interest Payable	(7,850)	288,336
Increase in Income Taxes Payable	30,117	318,453
Net Cash Provided (Used) by Operating Activities	(77,689)	
Cash Flow from Investing Activities		
Sale of Land	60,000 (l)	378,453
Purchase of Equipment	(202,518) (m)	$175,935
Net Cash Provided (Used) by Investing Activities	($142,518) (n)	

FIGURE 19.8

The updated partial statement of cash flows now shows the net cash used by operating activities, which is $77,689, and the net cash used by investing activities, which is $142,518.

Step 4. Calculate the net cash provided (or used) by financing activities.

The last section prepared for the statement of cash flows is cash flow from financing activities. This section includes borrowing money or receiving cash as a result of a stock issue. It also includes any payments involved with financing, such as dividend payments or loan repayments. Therefore, the cash flow in this section is affected by changes in liabilities, based on which interest must be paid, such as notes payable (current and long-term portions), and changes related to preferred stock, common stock and additional paid-in capital as a result of stock being sold in excess of par value.

The liabilities and stockholders' equity portion of Soho Supplies' balance sheet from Figure 19.3 is shown in Figure 19.9.

Soho Supplies Balance Sheet (partial) As at December 31, 2018			
	2018	**2017**	**Change**
Liabilities			
Current Liabilities			
Accounts Payable	$783,602	$475,645	$307,957
Salaries Payable	25,000	50,000	(25,000)
Interest Payable	15,650	23,500	(7,850)
Income Taxes Payable	280,117	250,000	30,117
Notes Payable, Current Portion	380,000	240,000	**140,000**
Total Current Liabilities	1,484,369	1,039,145	445,224
			Sum = $204,0000
Long-Term Liabilities			
Notes Payable, Long-Term Portion	420,000	356,000	**64,000**
Bonds Payable	170,000	200,000	(30,000)
Total Long-Term Liabilities	590,000	556,000	34,000
Total Liabilities	2,074,369	1,595,145	479,224
Stockholders' Equity			
Paid-In Capital			
Preferred Stock	8,000	0	8,000
Common Stock	5,000	5,000	0
Additional Paid-In Capital	2,000	0	2,000
Total Paid-In Capital	15,000	5,000	10,000
Retained Earnings	1,522,132	878,525	643,607
Total Stockholders' Equity	1,537,132	883,525	653,607
Total Liabilities and Stockholders' Equity	$3,611,501	$2,478,670	$1,132,831

FIGURE 19.9

For our Soho Supplies example, the following account balances changed between 2017 and 2018: notes payable, bonds payable, dividends (included in retained earnings) and preferred stock (including any paid-in capital in excess of par). We will look at each of these items, labeled (o) to (r), to correspond to the statement of cash flows in Figure 19.11.

(o) First, we will look at notes payable. As shown in Figure 19.9, the notes payable is reported in two areas of the balance sheet: in the current portion under Current Liabilities, and in the noncurrent portion under Long-Term Liabilities. From 2017 to 2018, the current portion of the notes payable increased by $140,000. The noncurrent portion of the notes payable increased by $64,000. Therefore, the total increase in the notes payable balance is $204,000 ($140,000 + $64,000). This amount is an increase to cash— or a cash inflow—since Soho received additional money.

(p) The decrease in bonds payable of $30,000 indicates that cash also decreased by $30,000 from 2017 to 2018 due to principal repayment. Since the notes indicate that the bonds were sold at par, there is no discount or premium to be included in the statement of cash flows.

(q) Dividends are considered next. In the Additional Information section under Soho's balance sheet (Figure 19.3), it is mentioned that Soho declared and paid $10,000 in dividends during 2018. This represents a decrease to cash because it is a cash outflow.

Although there is a note regarding the amount of dividends paid, the amount of dividends paid can be calculated by examining the financial statements.

Previous chapters explained that the retained earnings account will increase if there is a net income for the year and decrease if there is a net loss for the year. Additionally, dividends are paid out of the retained earnings account, decreasing its value. The partial balance sheet in Figure 19.9 shows that the retained earnings account increased by $643,607 in 2018, however the income statement shows that net income was $653,607. Therefore, the difference of $10,000 must be the dividends paid, as illustrated in the T-account in Figure 19.10. This represents a decrease in cash flow in the financing section of the statement of cash flows.

DECREASE				INCREASE
−		RETAINED EARNINGS		+
			$878,525	Opening Balance
Dividends	10,000		653,607	2018 Net Income
			$1,522,132	Closing Balance

FIGURE 19.10

(r) The balance of preferred stock increased by $8,000 from 2017 to 2018. The stock was issued in excess of its par value—1,000 shares of $8 preferred stock for $10 per share—therefore, $8,000 is recorded as preferred stock and $2,000 is recorded as additional paid-in capital. The cash receipt of $10,000 from the sale of preferred stock is reported in the financing section of the cash flow statement as an increase to cash.

(s) Net cash provided (used) by financing activities accounts for an increase to the cash account of $174,000 ($204,000 − $30,000 − $10,000 + $10,000). The cash flow from financing activities section is added to the statement of cash flows in Figure 19.11.

Soho Supplies Statement of Cash Flows (partial) For the Year Ended December 31, 2018		
	Amount	**Updated Cash Balance**
Opening Cash Balance		$396,142
Cash Flow from Operating Activities		
Net Income	$653,607	1,049,749
Adjustments to Reconcile Net Income to Net Cash		
Provided (Used) by Operating Activities		
Depreciation	43,262	1,093,011
Gain on Sale of Land	(10,000)	1,083,011
Changes in Operating Assets and Liabilities		
Increase in Accounts Receivable	(220,326)	862,685
Increase in Prepaid Insurance	(5,987)	856,698
Increase in Merchandise Inventory	(843,469)	13,229
Increase in Accounts Payable	307,957	321,186
Decrease in Salaries Payable	(25,000)	296,186
Decrease in Interest Payable	(7,850)	288,336
Increase in Income Taxes Payable	30,117	318,453
Net Cash Provided (Used) by Operating Activities	(77,689)	
Cash Flow from Investing Activities		
Sale of Land	60,000	378,453
Purchase of Equipment	(202,518)	175,935
Net Cash Provided (Used) by Investing Activities	(142,518)	
Cash Flow from Financing Activities		
Proceeds from Notes Payable[1] (o)	204,000 [2]	349,935
Payment toward Bonds Payable (p)	(30,000)	145,935
Payment of Cash Dividend (q)	(10,000) [3]	339,935
Issuance of Preferred Stock (r)	10,000	349,935
Net Cash Provided (Used) by Financing Activities	$174,000 (S)	

[1] Soho Supplies did not borrow any additional notes payable during the year.
[2] The $204,000 proceeds from the notes payable is from the calculation in Figure 19.9.
[3] Increase in preferred stock $8,000 + Increase in additional paid-in capital $2,000

FIGURE 19.11

Step 5. Calculate the *total* net cash provided (or used) by operating, investing and financing activities combined.

Three sections of the statement of cash flows have been completed: net cash provided (or used) from operating activities, investing activities and financing activities. They can now be put all together to form one complete statement of cash flows in proper format for 2018, as shown in Figure 19.12.

Soho Supplies Statement of Cash Flows For the Year Ended December 31, 2018		
Cash Flow from Operating Activities		
Net Income	$653,607	
Adjustments to Reconcile Net Income to Net Cash		
Provided (Used) by Operating Activities		
Depreciation	43,262	
Gain on Sale of Land	(10,000)	
Changes in Operating Assets and Liabilities		
Increase in Accounts Receivable	(220,326)	
Increase in Prepaid Expenses	(5,987)	
Increase in Merchandise Inventory	(843,469)	
Increase in Accounts Payable	307,957	
Decrease in Salaries Payable	(25,000)	
Decrease in Interest Payable	(7,850)	
Increase in Income Taxes Payable	30,117	
Net Cash Provided (Used) by Operating Activities		($77,689)
Cash Flow from Investing Activities		
Sale of Land	60,000	
Purchase of Equipment	(202,518)	
Net Cash Provided (Used) by Investing Activities		(142,518)
Cash Flow from Financing Activities		
Proceeds from Notes Payable[1]	204,000	
Payment toward Bonds Payable	(30,000)	
Payment of Cash Dividends	(10,000)	
Issuance of Preferred Stock	10,000	
Net Cash Provided (Used) by Financing Activities		174,000
Net Increase (Decrease) in Cash		(46,207)
Cash at the Beginning of the Year		396,142
Cash at the End of the Year		$349,935

[1] Soho Supplies did not borrow any additional notes payable during the year.

FIGURE 19.12

Step 6. Verify that the total net cash flow equals the ending cash balance less the beginning cash balance.

To finish the process, we must verify that the net cash provided (or used) by operating, investing, and financing activities combined, or the Net Increase (Decrease) in Cash, equals the difference between the cash balance at the beginning of the year and the cash balance at the end of the year. The bottom three lines on the statement of cash flows in Figure 19.12 verify that the net decrease in cash of $46,207 accounts for the difference.

Analysis of the Statement of Cash Flows

Once the statement of cash flows is completed, it is analyzed to see if there are any concerns. The first item to note is that cash decreased during the year even though there was a net income. Part of that decrease was due to an outflow of cash from operating activities of $77,689. This can be a problem for the company, since it indicates that day-to-day operations are not generating a cash inflow. In other words, the company is not being self-sufficient with its operations.

The two major contributors to this cash outflow from operations were an increase in accounts receivable and an increase in inventory. Both can indicate trouble for the company. An increase in accounts receivable can result from an increase in sales on account instead of cash, or from customers taking longer to pay their bills. Either situation means the company is not receiving cash on a timely basis. The large increase in inventory can indicate that the company is buying too much inventory, which eventually has to be paid with cash. Alternatively, it could mean that inventory is not turning into cost of goods sold, which would mean that the quantity of sales has decreased.

The company purchased some new equipment during the year and also sold some land. Both can be considered normal, assuming the equipment is needed and the plan was to sell the land. However, considering the cash flow problems from operations, the question may be asked whether the sale of land was simply to raise some cash to pay for operating expenses. Financing operations by selling noncurrent assets is not a sustainable practice.

The financing activities section of the statement of cash flows is the only one showing a cash inflow. This is primarily due to a large bank loan. The bank loan may have been borrowed to pay for the equipment. Overall, there are concerns due to the negative cash flow from operations and the apparent financing of operating activities by selling assets and taking loans.

Pause & Reflect

Exercise 19-1

For each item in the below schedule, indicate in the space provided in the right-hand column whether the amount should be *added to*, or *subtracted from*, net income to reconcile it to the net cash provided (used) by operating activities.

Reconciliation of Net Income to Net Cash Provided (Used) by Operating Activities	Add or Subtract?
Net Income	
Adjustments to Reconcile Net Income to Net Cash Provided (Used) by Operating Activities	
Depreciation	_____
Amortization	_____
Loss on Sale of Land	_____
Gain on Retirement of Debt	_____
Changes in Current Assets and Current Liabilities	
Increase in Accounts Receivable	_____
Increase in Prepaid Expenses	_____
Decrease in Merchandise Inventory	_____
Decrease in Accounts Payable	_____
Increase in Salaries Payable	_____
Decrease in Interest Payable	_____
Increase in Income Taxes Payable	_____
Net Cash Provided (Used) by Operating Activities	

See Appendix I for solutions.

Selling Noncurrent Assets

In the example of Soho Supplies, land was sold and reported in the investing activities section of the statement of cash flows. Since land does not depreciate, the decrease in the value of land was equal to the book value of the land. A gain is reported if the amount received is greater than the book value of the land, and a loss is reported if the amount is less than the book value of the land.

When selling equipment or any other noncurrent asset that depreciates in value, determining the book value of the item is an important step in calculating cash flow. Figure 19.13 presents the assets section of the balance sheet for Soho Supplies. For demonstration purposes, information regarding the noncurrent assets section has been changed. It is now different from Figure 19.3.

Soho Supplies Balance Sheet (partial) As at December 31, 2018			
	2018	**2017**	**Change**
Assets			
Current Assets			
Cash	$349,935	$396,142	($46,207)
Accounts Receivable	1,286,138	1,065,812	220,326
Merchandise Inventory	1,683,560	840,091	843,469
Prepaid Insurance	48,612	42,625	5,987
Total Current Assets	3,368,245	2,344,670	1,023,575
Noncurrent Assets			
Long-Term Investments[1]	400,000	500,000	(100,000)
Equipment[2]	420,000	170,000	250,000
Accumulated Depreciation	(61,262)	(36,000)	(25,262)
Total Noncurrent Assets	758,738	634,000	124,738
Total Assets	$4,126,983	$2,978,670	$1,148,313

Additional Information

[1] During 2018, Soho did not purchase any long-term investments.
[2] During 2018, Soho made purchases of equipment for $375,000.

FIGURE 19.13

The additional information indicates that there were no purchases of long-term investments, so the decrease in that account is due only to the sale of investments. However, the actual cash received does not necessarily match the decrease in value. Also, Soho purchased equipment worth $375,000; however, the value of that account only increased by $250,000. This indicates that some equipment was sold. The income statement in Figure 19.14 provides more information about these accounts. For demonstration purposes, the other income and expenses section has been changed. It is now different from Figure 19.4.

Soho Supplies Income Statement For the Year Ended December 31, 2018	
Sales Revenue	$8,685,025
Cost of Goods Sold	5,998,612
Gross Profit	2,686,413
Operating Expenses	
Salaries Expense	1,416,135
Depreciation Expense	43,262
Insurance Expense	16,000
Other Operating Expenses	235,417
Total Operating Expenses	1,710,814
Income from Operations	975,599
Other Income and Expenses	
Loss on Sale of Investments	(5,000)
Gain on Sale of Equipment	16,000
Income before Income Tax Expense	986,599
Income Tax Expense	(280,117)
Net Income	$706,482

FIGURE 19.14

Property, Plant and Equipment with Depreciation

The cash involved for both sale of long-term investments and the sale and purchase of equipment is reported in the investing activities section. In this example, the income statement (from Figure 19.14) indicates that some equipment has been sold for a gain. To determine how much cash was actually received, the book value of the asset must be determined. This is done by examining the changes in the balance sheet accounts. Figure 19.15 helps illustrate this.

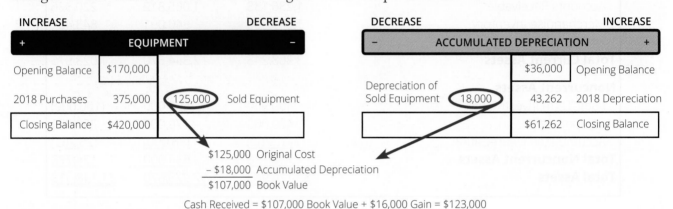

FIGURE 19.15

The balance sheet shows that equipment increased by $250,000; however, the additional information indicates that $375,000 was purchased during the year. The $125,000 difference represents the original cost of the equipment that was sold in 2018. Also from the balance sheet, accumulated depreciation increased by $25,262; however, depreciation expense on the income statement was $43,262. This means that $18,000 was removed from accumulated depreciation when the equipment was sold.

The difference between the cost of the equipment and the associated accumulated depreciation indicates the equipment had a book value of $107,000 when it was sold. The income statement tells us that the equipment was sold at a gain of $16,000, which means the total amount of cash received was $123,000 ($107,000 + $16,000). If there was a loss instead of a gain on the sale of the equipment, the cash received is calculated by deducting the loss from the book value of the equipment. The proceeds from the sale of equipment represents an increase in cash flow in the investing activities section of the statement of cash flows.

Long-Term Investments

Long-term investments held at cost were also sold during the year, as shown by the account's decrease on the balance sheet in Figure 19.13.

However, the $100,000 decrease represents the cost of the investment, not necessarily the amount of cash received. The income statement indicates there was a loss of $5,000 when the investment was sold. Thus, the amount of cash received, as shown in Figure 19.16, was $95,000 ($100,000 - $5,000), representing an increase in cash flow in the investing activities section of the statement of cash flows. Note

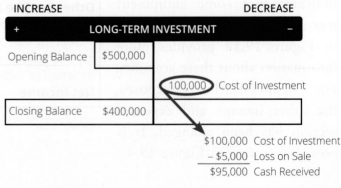

FIGURE 19.16

that a gain on the sale would be added to the cost of the investment for calculating the amount of cash received on the sale.

In this example for long-term investments, it was assumed that there were no additional purchases in the year. If there were any purchases of long-term investments during the year, the amount would be added to the debit side of the investment account and then the amount (cost) of investment sold would be calculated. The calculation is similar to the example shown in the equipment account from Figure 19.15.

Based on the information given in Figures 19.13 and 19.14, the investing activities section of the statement of cash flows would be reported as in Figure 19.17.

Soho Supplies **Statement of Cash Flows (partial)** **For the Year Ended December 31, 2018**		
Cash Flow from Investing Activities		
Sale of Equipment	$123,000	
Sale of Investments	95,000	
Purchase of Equipment	(375,000)	
Net Cash Provided (Used) by Investing Activities		($157,000)

FIGURE 19.17

Pause & Reflect

Exercise 19-2

Altitude Sportswear Inc. is preparing a statement of cash flows for the year ended December 31, 2018. The accountant needs to determine the company's net cash provided (used) by investing activities. The accounting records show the following events that occurred during 2018.

- The company purchased office equipment for $250,000 cash

- Long-term investments had an opening balance of $155,000 and a closing balance of $70,000. Altitude's income statement reports a loss on sale of investments of $5,000. No investment was purchased during the year.

- Land that cost $850,000 was sold for cash. The gain on sale of land was $50,000.

- The company sold its old production equipment for cash and did not purchase any production equipment during the year. The production equipment had an original cost of $200,000. The accumulated depreciation related to this equipment had an opening balance of $130,000 and a closing balance of $0. Altitude's 2018 income statement shows the production equipment's depreciation expense of $30,000 and a loss on its sale of $25,000.

Use the above information and the template below to prepare the cash flows from investing activities section for Altitude's statement of cash flows.

Altitude Sportswear Inc. **Statement of Cash Flows (partial)** **For the Year Ended December 31, 2018**	
Cash Flow from Investing Activities	
_____	$ _____
_____	_____
_____	_____
_____	_____
Net Cash Provided (Used) by Investing Activities	$ _____

See Appendix I for solutions.

Free Cash Flow

Throughout this course, it is continually emphasized that the fundamental objective of accounting is to provide financial information that readers can use to make appropriate decisions. A group of readers—the external users—is made up of those outside the organization, primarily existing of current and potential investors, creditors and lenders. These external users want to ensure that their investment or loan is protected, and so they require information on the company's economic resources and any claims on those resources. Some of the information most crucial to their decisions can be found on the statement of cash flows, in a concept known as *free cash flow*.

Free cash flow is the amount of cash remaining after a business has covered its operating activities and capital expenditures (investing in noncurrent assets) that are required to maintain the company's existing production capacity. This remaining cash is available for uses such as reducing debt, buying back shares or paying dividends. Free cash flow relies partly on the company's cash from operating activities, which in turn is based on the company's net income. However, the investing activities section of the statement of cash flows does not separate capital expenditures that are required to maintain the current capacity versus those that are additional investments to expand the capacity. Since it can be difficult to determine exactly which items in the investing section are only related to the maintenance of the existing capacity, companies quite often just use net cash from investing activities in the calculation of free cash flow.

Free cash flow is calculated by deducting the net cash used by investing activities from the net cash provided by operating activities. If the net cash provided (used) by investing activities is negative, it means that cash has been spent on assets. This number must be subtracted from the cash flow from operating activities. If the net cash provided (used) by investing activities is positive, it means that cash was received from selling assets. This number must be added to the cash flow from operating activities. The equation to calculate free cash flow is shown in Figure 19.18.

Free Cash Flow = Net Cash Provided by Operating Activities – Net Cash Used by Investing Activities

FIGURE 19.18

The information from Soho's statement of cash flows in Figure 19.12 can be used to calculate free cash flow. Soho Supplies' statement of cash flows for the year ended December 31, 2018 reported a decrease in cash due to operations of $77,689, and a decrease in cash due to investments of $142,518. Using the equation from Figure 19.18, Soho's free cash flow can be calculated as follows.

$$\text{Free Cash Flow} = -\$77,689 - \$142,518$$

$$= -\$220,207$$

The negative free cash flow is an unfavorable indicator of Soho's financial health. Investors and lenders often use free cash flow as a measure of a business' ability to grow its capacity and to pay them back in the form of loan repayment and dividends. Therefore, they are looking for a positive or increasing cash flow. Despite generating over half a million dollars in net income, Soho has a negative free cash flow mainly due to inventory and equipment purchases. Because the income statement does not include such transactions as asset purchase, financial statement users should not look at a company's financial wellbeing only from the income statement. The statement of cash flows provides additional insight into Soho's activities during the year.

External users of the financial statements must be aware of the many factors that affect a company's reported cash flow, and that different companies may interpret accounting guidelines differently. As well, companies can influence their cash flow in various ways, and external users need to be particularly well informed before making any decisions.

Pause & Reflect

Exercise 19-3

Pacific Property Management Inc. has just prepared its statement of cash flows for December 31, 2018. It shows an increase in cash from operations of $235,000 and a decrease in cash due to investments of $78,000.

a) Calculate Pacific's free cash flow.

b) Is Pacific's free cash flow a favorable or unfavorable indicator of the company's financial health? Explain.

_____

_____

_____

_____

_____

_____

_____

_____

_____

See Appendix I for solutions.

Ethics

The accounting scandals that began in 2001 with Enron served as a warning to much of the financial community that income statements and balance sheets can be manipulated to present a false financial picture of a business. As a result, an increasing number of people started using the statement of cash flows as a more revealing snapshot of a company's financial well-being.

Indeed, the motivation behind relying more on a statement of cash flows to analyze company performance is understandable. Statements of cash flows are supposed to show where the money is coming from and where it is going. However, no financial statement is immune from flaws, and this is certainly also the case with statements of cash flows.

The following three situations should be viewed with caution when analyzing the statement of cash flows of a business.

- **Some companies may stretch out their payables.** One way of artificially enhancing a company's cash position from operations is to deliberately delay paying bills. In fact, some companies will even go so far as to institute such a policy and label it as a form of good cash flow decision-making. Of course, the company has not improved its underlying cash flow, but has simply manipulated it.

- **Some companies may finance their payables.** Some companies try to manipulate their statement of cash flows by having a third party pay their payables for them, although regulators have tried to crack down on this practice. This means that the company itself shows no payments in its cash flow and, instead, pays a fee to the third party at a later date. Picking and choosing the periods in which this is done artificially manipulates the statement of cash flows.

- **Some companies may shorten their collection of receivables.** While not necessarily a bad decision to collect faster from customers, this can have implications if it is done just to improve perceived cash flow. If collections that would normally happen in the next fiscal year are collected immediately to improve the cash flow in the current fiscal year, then the next fiscal year may show poor cash flow. This type of action merely delays reporting a poor cash flow.

In Summary

LO 1 **Classify operating, investing and financing activities**

▶ Balance sheets and income statements are prepared on an accrual basis, which involves recording transactions that do not necessarily involve any exchange of money. Statements of cash flows differ in that they reveal both the sources and uses of cash within a business.

▶ The statement of cash flows contains three sections: cash flow from operating activities, cash flow from investing activities and cash flow from financing activities.

▶ The cash flow from operating activities tracks the movement of cash related to day-to-day activities of the business.

▶ The cash flow from investing activities tracks the movement of cash on the basis of the purchases and sales of noncurrent assets.

▶ The cash flow from financing activities tracks the movement of cash related to the way a company receives money for financing purposes and pays it back.

LO 2 **Prepare a statement of cash flows using the indirect method**

▶ The indirect method of preparing a statement of cash flows starts with accrual-based net income from the income statement and adjusts it by adding or subtracting noncash items and changes in current assets and current liabilities to reveal net cash flow from operating activities.

▶ The indirect method tends to be more commonly used in preparing a statement of cash flows, since the direct method takes a more burdensome approach to tracking cash receipts and payments.

LO 3 **Calculate book value and cash received for selling noncurrent assets**

▶ When selling noncurrent assets, the accumulated depreciation must also be cleared out. Accumulated depreciation, along with an assets' book value and gain (or loss) on disposal must be taken into account in calculating cash proceeds from the disposal.

LO 4 **Explain the concept of free cash flow and its importance for potential investors**

▶ Free cash flow is the amount of cash remaining after a business has covered its operating activities and capital expenditures.

▶ Investors often use free cash flow as a measure of a business' cash-generating ability and its overall financial health.

LO 5 **Discuss ethical issues related to cash flow**

▶ Three situations should be viewed with caution when analyzing the statement of cash flows of a business: some companies may stretch out their payables; some companies may finance their payables; and some companies may shorten their collections.

AMEENGAGE *Access **ameengage.com** for integrated resources including tutorials, practice exercises, the digital textbook and more.*

Review Exercise 19-1

Shown below is the balance sheet, income statement and notes for Dellray Inc.

Dellray Inc. Balance Sheet As at December 31		
	2018	**2017**
Assets		
Current Assets		
Cash	$1,085,700	$27,000
Accounts Receivable	370,000	400,000
Merchandise Inventory	290,000	250,000
Prepaid Expenses	29,000	21,000
Total Current Assets	1,774,700	698,000
Noncurrent Assets		
Long-Term Investments[1]	560,000	600,000
Equipment[2]	1,300,000	1,100,000
Accumulated Depreciation	(206,000)	(156,000)
Total Noncurrent Assets	1,654,000	1,544,000
Total Assets	$3,428,700	$2,242,000
Liabilities		
Current Liabilities		
Accounts Payable	$461,000	$342,000
Notes Payable, Current Portion[3]	75,000	65,000
Total Current Liabilities	536,000	407,000
Long-Term Liabilities		
Notes Payable, Long-Term Portion[3]	275,000	215,000
Bonds Payable[4]	96,000	90,000
Total Long-Term Liabilities	371,000	305,000
Total Liabilities	907,000	712,000
Stockholders' Equity		
Common Stock	400,000	320,000
Retained Earnings	2,121,700	1,210,000
Total Stockholders' Equity	2,521,700	1,530,000
Total Liabilities and Stockholders' Equity	$3,428,700	$2,242,000

Additional Information

[1] During 2018, Dellray Inc. did not purchase any long-term investments.
[2] During 2018, Dellray Inc. made purchases of equipment for $400,000.
[3] Dellray Inc. did not repay any notes payable during the year.
[4] The bonds were issued at par.

Dellray Inc. Income Statement For the Year Ended December 31, 2018	
Sales Revenue	$5,600,000
Cost of Goods Sold	2,968,000
Gross Profit	2,632,000
Operating Expenses	
Selling Expenses	
Depreciation Expense	80,000
Insurance Expense	8,000
Other Operating Expenses	367,300
Total Selling Expenses	455,300
Administrative Expenses	
Salaries Expense	766,000
Total Administrative Expenses	766,000
Total Operating Expenses	1,221,300
Income from Operations	1,410,700
Other Income and Expenses	
Gain on Sale of Investments	8,000
Loss on Sale of Factory Equipment	(10,000)
Income before Income Tax Expense	1,408,700
Income Tax Expense	422,000
Net Income	$986,700

Required

a) Prepare the statement of cash flows for 2018 using the indirect method. Include any notes if
    necessary.

Notes:

_____

_____

_____

_____

_____

_____

_____

_____

_____

_____

_____

_____

_____

b) Calculate and analyze Dellray's free cash flow for 2018.

_____

_____

_____

_____

_____

_____

_____

_____

_____

See Appendix I for solutions.

Appendix 19A: The Direct Method

Earlier in this chapter, a statement of cash flows was assembled using the indirect method. As you learned, the net cash flow from operating activities is the same whether the indirect method or the direct method is used—it is simply the way of calculating and presenting the information that differs, not the actual amount. The term "indirect" refers to tracking the changes to cash without direct reference to cash receipts or payments. The indirect method analyzes cash flow by starting with accrual-based net income and making related adjustments for changes on the balance sheet and income statement.

The direct method is the other way to prepare the statement of cash flows. Like the indirect method, the direct method breaks down the three ways of generating and using cash into operating activities, investing activities and financing activities. The difference is that the direct method prepares the operating activities section so that each income statement item is reported on a cash-basis; that is, each item is adjusted to remove any accruals and just report cash. Therefore, the only difference in the step-by-step approach to preparing the statement of cash flows is step 2, as follows.

Step 1. Calculate the net increase (decrease) in cash during the period.

Step 2. Calculate the net cash provided (or used) by operating activities using the direct method.

Step 3. Calculate the net cash provided (or used) by investing activities.

Step 4. Calculate the net cash provided (or used) by financing activities.

Step 5. Calculate the *total* net cash provided (or used) by operating, investing, and financing activities combined.

Step 6. Verify that this total net cash flow equals the ending cash balance less the beginning cash balance.

To illustrate the direct method, we will use the same Soho Supplies balance sheet and income statement that were used for the indirect method. The balance sheet is shown in Figure 19A.1 and the income statement is shown in Figure 19A.2.

Soho Supplies **Balance Sheet** **As at December 31**			
	2018	**2017**	**Change**
Assets			
Current Assets			
Cash	$349,935	$396,142	**($46,207)**
Accounts Receivable	1,286,138	1,065,812	220,326
Merchandise Inventory	1,683,560	840,091	843,469
Prepaid Insurance	48,612	42,625	5,987
Total Current Assets	3,368,245	2,344,670	1,023,575
Noncurrent Assets			
Land[(1)]	0	50,000	(50,000)
Equipment[(2)]	322,518	120,000	202,518
Accumulated Depreciation	(79,262)	(36,000)	(43,262)
Total Noncurrent Assets	243,2566	134,000	109,256
Total Assets	$3,611,501	$2,478,670	$1,132,831
Liabilities			
Current Liabilities			
Accounts Payable	$783,602	$475,645	$307,957
Salaries Payable	25,000	50,000	(25,000)
Interest Payable	15,650	23,500	(7,850)
Income Taxes Payable	280,117	250,000	30,117
Notes Payable, Current Portion	380,000	240,000	140,000
Total Current Liabilities	1,484,369	1,039,145	445,224
Long-Term Liabilities			
Notes Payable, Long-Term Portion	420,000	356,000	64,000
Bonds Payable[(3)]	170,000	200,000	(30,000)
Total Long-Term Liabilities	590,000	556,000	34,000
Total Liabilities	2,074,369	1,595,145	479,224
Stockholders' Equity			
Paid-In Capital			
Preferred Stock	8,000	0	8,000
Common Stock	5,000	5,000	0
Additional Paid-In Capital	2,000	0	2,000
Total Paid-In Capital	15,000	5,000	10,000
Retained Earnings[(4)]	1,522,132	878,525	643,607
Total Stockholders' Equity	1,537,132	883,525	653,607
Total Liabilities and Stockholders' Equity	$3,611,501	$2,478,670	$1,132,831

Additional Information

[(1)] During 2018, land that cost $50,000 was sold for $60,000, resulting in a $10,000 gain on sale. The gain is reported on the Income Statement in the Other Income and Expenses section.

[(2)] During 2018, Soho made purchases of equipment for $202,518.

[(3)] The bonds were issued at par.

[(4)] Soho declared and paid $10,000 in dividends in 2018.

FIGURE 19A.1

Soho Supplies Income Statement For the Year Ended December 31, 2018	
Sales Revenue	$8,685,025
Cost of Goods Sold	5,998,612
Gross Profit	2,686,413
Operating Expenses	
Salaries Expense	1,416,135
Depreciation Expense	43,262
Insurance Expense	16,000
Other Operating Expenses	235,417
Total Operating Expenses	1,710,814
Income from Operations	975,599
Other Income and Expenses	
Gain on Sale of Land	10,000
Interest Expense	(51,875)
Income before Income Tax Expense	933,724
Income Tax Expense	280,117
Net Income	**$653,607**

FIGURE 19A.2

For the operating activities section, the focus is on operating items that affect cash. Thus, depreciation is ignored, since depreciation is a transaction that does not affect cash. Also, the gain on the sale of land is ignored, since the sale of land is an investing activity. All other items on the income statement are examined and recorded on the statement of cash flows. Each of these items are labeled, (a) to (g), to correspond with the final statement of cash flows in Figure 19A.11.

Cash Receipts

(a) Cash Receipts

The first item on the statement of cash flows prepared using the direct method is cash receipts. For simplicity, let us assume that Soho Supplies' only source of cash receipts is from sales to its customers. Also assume that all sales are credit sales. For the purpose of statement of cash flows preparation, the credit sales balance has to be converted to the actual amount of cash collected from customers during 2018. The amount of sales revenue from Soho's income statement and the beginning and ending accounts receivable balances from Soho's balance sheet can be used to calculate the amount of cash collection from customers.

An analysis of the T-account in Figure 19A.3 will help visualize the calculation.

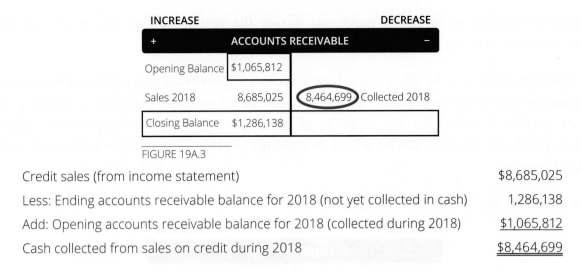

FIGURE 19A.3

Credit sales (from income statement)	$8,685,025
Less: Ending accounts receivable balance for 2018 (not yet collected in cash)	1,286,138
Add: Opening accounts receivable balance for 2018 (collected during 2018)	$1,065,812
Cash collected from sales on credit during 2018	$8,464,699

We now know that $8,464,699 cash was collected from sales during 2018.

Cash Payments

Next, Soho's cash payments are calculated by analyzing the changes to each of the expenses listed on the income statement and their related balance sheet accounts.

(b) Cash Payments for Merchandise Inventory

There are two steps involved in calculating the cash payments for inventory purchased.

First, the amount of inventory purchased during the year must be calculated. From the balance sheet, we know the beginning and ending balances of inventory. The income statement tells us the amount of COGS. Based on COGS and inventory balances, the amount of purchases can be calculated by solving the missing number in the merchandise inventory T-account, as shown in Figure 19A.4.

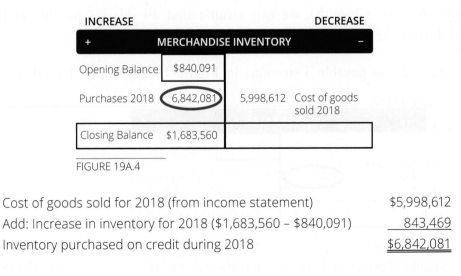

FIGURE 19A.4

Cost of goods sold for 2018 (from income statement)	$5,998,612
Add: Increase in inventory for 2018 ($1,683,560 – $840,091)	843,469
Inventory purchased on credit during 2018	$6,842,081

Now that the amount of inventory purchased during the year is known, this figure can be used to determine the cash payments for inventory.

A few assumptions have to be made about how inventory is purchased and paid for. One assumption is that inventory is purchased on credit and paid for at a later date. Another assumption is that accounts payable is only used for suppliers of inventory. With two assumptions in place, the inventory purchases for 2018 can be added to accounts payable to determine how much cash was paid for inventory.

This is shown in the T-account in Figure 19A.5.

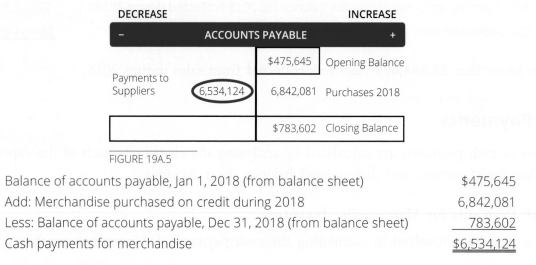

FIGURE 19A.5

Balance of accounts payable, Jan 1, 2018 (from balance sheet)	$475,645
Add: Merchandise purchased on credit during 2018	6,842,081
Less: Balance of accounts payable, Dec 31, 2018 (from balance sheet)	783,602
Cash payments for merchandise	$6,534,124

(c) Cash Payments to Employees

To analyze Soho's cash payment to employees for salaries expense for the year, start with the expense on the income statement. Next, adjust this amount by the change in salaries payable during the year. Because salaries are normally paid within a short time period of when they are accrued (usually weeks or a month), we can assume that all salaries payable at January 1, 2018 were fully paid during the year.

The analysis of the salaries payable T-account in Figure 19A.6 shows the calculation.

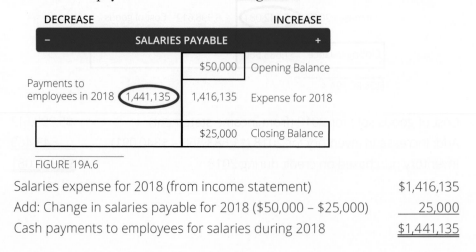

FIGURE 19A.6

Salaries expense for 2018 (from income statement)	$1,416,135
Add: Change in salaries payable for 2018 ($50,000 – $25,000)	25,000
Cash payments to employees for salaries during 2018	$1,441,135

(d) Cash Payments for Other Operating Expenses

The next expense on the income statement is other operating expenses. None of the remaining current assets or current liabilities are related to this item on the income statement. For example, prepaid insurance is related to insurance expense and interest payable is related to interest expense.

Thus, there are no adjustments to the amount of cash for other operating expenses and the amount shown on the income statement ($235,417) is the amount reported as cash payments on the statement of cash flows.

(e) Cash Payments for Insurance

Cash paid for insurance is based on the insurance expense reported on the income statement and adjusted by the change in prepaid insurance on the balance sheet. Recall that insurance premiums that are paid in advance are recorded in the prepaid insurance account until the amount has been used. Since the prepaid insurance account increased, we can assume that more cash was paid for prepaid insurance over the year. This is added to the amount of the insurance expense.

The analysis of the prepaid insurance T-account in Figure 19A.7 shows the calculation.

INCREASE			DECREASE	
+	**PREPAID INSURANCE**			−
Opening Balance	$42,625			
Paid during 2018	21,987	16,000	Insurance expense 2018	
Closing Balance	$48,612			

FIGURE 19A.7

Insurance expense incurred during 2018 (from income statement)	$16,000
Add: Change in prepaid insurance for 2018 ($48,612 − $42,625)	5,987
Cash payments for insurance during 2018	$21,987

(f) Cash Payments for Interest

Interest expense is the next cash item on the income statement. The amount reported as an expense is adjusted by the change in interest payable. The decrease in interest payable indicates that more cash was paid to cover interest owed during the year. This decrease is added to the interest expense.

The analysis of the interest payable T-account in Figure 19A.8 shows the calculation.

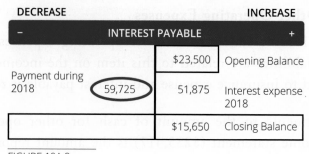

FIGURE 19A.8

Interest expense incurred during 2018 (from income statement)	$51,875
Add: Change in interest payable for 2018 ($23,500 – $15,650)	7,850
Cash payments for interest during 2018	$59,725

(g) Cash Payments for Income Taxes

The last cash expense is income taxes. The balance sheet account, income tax payable, is used to adjust the expense to determine the actual cash amount paid. Since income tax payable increased over the year, it indicates that the company was able to defer paying income taxes. This saves cash, thus reducing the amount of cash paid for income tax during 2018 to $250,000.

The analysis of the income tax payable T-account in Figure 19A.9 shows the calculation.

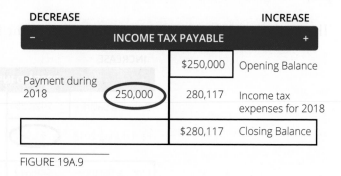

FIGURE 19A.9

Income tax expense for 2018 (from income statement)	$280,117
Less: Change in income tax payable for 2018 ($250,000 – $280,117)	(30,117)
Cash payments for income tax during 2018	$250,000

Now that all the cash-related income statement items are complete, the operating activities section of the statement of cash flows can be prepared, as shown in Figure 19A.10. The section is divided into the cash receipts and the cash payments, which matches with the adjusted sales and adjusted expenses from the income statement.

Soho Supplies Statement of Cash Flows For the Year Ended December 31, 2018		
Cash Flow from Operating Activities		
Cash Receipts		
Cash Received from Customers (a)		$8,464,699
Cash Payments		
Payments for Merchandise Inventory (b)	$6,534,124	
Payments to Employees (c)	1,441,135	
Payments for Other Operating Expenses (d)	235,417	
Payments for Insurance (e)	21,987	
Payments for Interest (f)	59,725	
Payments for Income Taxes (g)	250,000	
Total Cash Payments		8,542,388
Net Cash Provided (Used) by Operating Activities		($77,689)

FIGURE 19A.10

You will notice that the decrease in cash from operating activities of $77,689 matches the statement of cash flows prepared under the indirect method in Figure 19.12.

The investing and financing activities of the statement of cash flows under the direct method are analyzed and prepared in the same manner as for the indirect method. These two sections are explained in Chapter 19. The completed statement of cash flows prepared using the direct method is shown in Figure 19A.11. Notice that the bottom part of the statement provides a schedule reconciling net income to the net cash flows from operating activities. This schedule is similar to the cash flow from operating activities section in the statement of cash flows prepared by the indirect method (see Figure 19.12).

Soho Supplies		
Statement of Cash Flows		
For the Year Ended December 31, 2018		
Cash Flow from Operating Activities		
Cash Receipts		
Cash Received from Customers		$8,464,699
Cash Payments		
Payments for Merchandise Inventory	$6,534,124	
Payments to Employees	1,441,135	
Payments for Other Operating Expenses	235,417	
Payments for Insurance	21,987	
Payments for Interest	59,725	
Payments for Income taxes	250,000	
Total Cash Payments		8,542,388
Net Cash Provided (Used) by Operating Activities		(77,689)
Cash Flow from Investing Activities		
Sale of Land	60,000	
Purchase of Equipment	(202,518)	
Net Cash Provided (Used) by Investing Activities		(142,518)
Cash Flow from Financing Activities		
Proceeds from Notes Payable[1]	204,000	
Payments toward Bonds Payable	(30,000)	
Payment of Cash Dividends	(10,000)	
Issuance of Preferred Stock	10,000	
Net Cash Provided (Used) by Financing Activities		174,000
Net Increase (Decrease) in Cash		(46,207)
Cash at the Beginning of the Year		396,142
Cash at the End of the Year		$349,935
Reconciliation of Net Income with Net Cash Provided (Used) by Operating Activities		
Cash Flow from Operating Activities		
Net Income	$653,607	
Adjustments to Reconcile Net Income to Net Cash Provided (Used) by Operating Activities		
Depreciation	43,262	
Gain on Sale of Land	(10,000)	
Changes in Operating Assets and Liabilities		
Increase in Accounts Receivable	(220,326)	
Increase in Prepaid Expenses	(5,987)	
Increase in Merchandise Inventory	(843,469)	
Increase in Accounts Payable	307,957	
Decrease in Salaries Payable	(25,000)	
Decrease in Interest Payable	(7,850)	
Increase in Income Taxes Payable	30,117	
Net Cash Provided (Used) by Operating Activities	($77,689)	

Additional Notes

[1] Soho Supplies did not borrow any additional notes payable during the year.

FIGURE 19A.11

Summary of the Statement of Cash Flows—Direct Method

This appendix demonstrates many of the adjustments made to net income in order to arrive at the net cash provided (used) by operating activities under the direct method. Figure 19A.12 summarizes these adjustments.

Income Statement Adjustments to Cash Flows from Operating Activities—Direct Method		
Income Statement Item	**Adjustments**	**Cash Flows from Operating Activities**
Sales	Increase (–) or decrease (+) in Accounts Receivable	Cash Received from Customers
Cost of Goods Sold	Increase (+) or decrease (–) in Merchandise Inventory and Increase (–) or decrease (+) in Accounts Payable	Cash Payments for Merchandise Inventory
Salaries Expense	Increase (+) or decrease (–) in Salaries Payable	Cash Payments to Employees
Other Operating Expenses	Increase (+) or decrease (–) in Prepaid Expenses and Increase (–) or decrease (+) in Accrued Liabilities	Cash Payments for Other Operating Expenses
Insurance Expense	Increase (+) or decrease (–) in Prepaid Insurance	Cash Payments for Insurance
Interest Expense	Increase (+) or decrease (–) in Interest Payable	Cash Payments for Interest
Income Tax Expense	Increase (–) or decrease (+) in Income Tax Payable	Cash Payments for Income Taxes

FIGURE 19A.12

Note that two of the items on the income statement do not appear as adjustments to cash flows from operating activities: depreciation, and gain on sale of land. As you learned earlier in the chapter, depreciation does not involve a cash outflow so it is not reported in the statement of cash flows prepared using the direct method. The gain on the sale of land is not an operating activity; however, the proceeds from the sale of land are an investing activity and are therefore reported in the cash flow from investing activities section.

GAAP vs IFRS

Under GAAP, net income must be reconciled to net cash provided (used) by operating activities under both direct and indirect methods.

Under IFRS, net income must be reconciled to net cash provided (used) by operating activities only under the indirect method.

In Summary

LO 6 **Prepare a statement of cash flows using the direct method**

▶ The direct method applies only to the operating activities section of the statement of cash flows.

▶ Under the direct method, all cash items on the income statement are reported separately on the statement of cash flows, after being adjusted by changes in related accounts from the balance sheet.

Review Exercise 19A-1

The balance sheet, income statement and notes for Harmony Inc. are shown as follows.

Harmony Inc. Balance Sheet As at December 31		
	2018	**2017**
Assets		
Current Assets		
Cash	$1,085,700	$27,000
Accounts Receivable	370,000	400,000
Merchandise Inventory	290,000	250,000
Prepaid Insurance	29,000	21,000
Total Current Assets	1,774,700	698,000
Noncurrent Assets		
Long-Term Investments[1]	560,000	600,000
Equipment[2]	1,300,000	1,100,000
Accumulated Depreciation	(206,000)	(156,000)
Total Noncurrent Assets	1,654,000	1,544,000
Total Assets	$3,428,700	$2,242,000
Liabilities		
Current Liabilities		
Accounts Payable[3]	$461,000	$342,000
Notes Payable, Current Portion	75,000	65,000
Total Current Liabilities	536,000	407,000
Long-Term Liabilities		
Notes Payable, Long-Term Portion	275,000	215,000
Bonds Payable[4]	96,000	90,000
Total Long-Term Liabilities	371,000	305,000
Total Liabilities	907,000	712,000
Stockholders' Equity		
Common Stock	400,000	320,000
Retained Earnings	2,121,700	1,210,000
Total Stockholders' Equity	2,521,700	1,530,000
Total Liabilities and Stockholders' Equity	$3,428,700	$2,242,000

Additional Information

[1] During 2018, Harmony Inc. did not purchase any long-term investments.

[2] During 2018, Harmony Inc. made purchases of equipment for $400,000.

[3] Assume accounts payable is only used for suppliers of inventory.

[4] The bonds were issued at par.

Harmony Inc. Income Statement For the Year Ended December 31, 2018	
Sales Revenue	$5,600,000
Cost of Goods Sold	2,968,000
Gross Profit	2,632,000
Operating Expenses	
Salaries Expense	766,000
Depreciation Expense	80,000
Insurance Expense	8,000
Other Operating Expenses	376,300
Total Operating Expenses	1,221,300
Income from Operations	1,410,700
Other Income and Expenses	
Gain on Sale of Investments	8,000
Loss on Sale of Factory Equipment	(10,000)
Income before Income Tax Expense	1,408,700
Income Tax Expense	422,000
Net Income	$986,700

Prepare the statement of cash flows for 2018 using the direct method. Show your calculations on a separate piece of paper.

See Appendix I for solutions.

Appendix 19B: Preparing a Statement of Cash Flows Using a Spreadsheet—Indirect Method

This appendix shows how to use a spreadsheet (work sheet) to prepare a statement of cash flows under the indirect method. A spreadsheet is a valuable tool to help organize and verify all the transactions that affect a company's cash balance.

To illustrate, we will once again use the example of Soho Supplies. We will use Soho's comparative balance sheet from Figure 19.3 (including the Additional Information), and its income statement from Figure 19.4. We will also identify all the transaction items in the spreadsheet using the same alphabetical codes that we used throughout the chapter examples.

- Cash flows from operating activities, items (d) to (k)

- Cash flows from investing activities, items (l) to (n)

- Cash flows from financing activities, items (o) to (s)

Soho's transactions for the year ended December 31, 2018 are shown below. (They include the additional information that accompanies Soho's balance sheet in Figure 19.3.)

(a) Net income for the year, $653,607

(b) Depreciation expense, $43,262

(c) Gain on sale of land, $10,000

(d) Increase in accounts receivable, $220,326

(e) Increase in prepaid insurance, $5,987

(f) Increase in merchandise inventory, $843,469

(g) Increase in accounts payable, $307,957

(h) Decrease in salaries payable, $25,000

(i) Decrease in interest payable, $7,850

(j) Increase in income taxes payable, $30,117

(k) Net cash provided (used) by operating activities, ($77,689)

Additional Information from Balance Sheet (Figure 19.3)

(l) During 2018, land that cost $50,000 was sold for $60,000, resulting in a $10,000 gain on sale.

(m) During 2018, Soho made purchases of equipment for $202,518.

(n) Net cash provided (used) by investing activities, ($142,518)

(o) Increase in (i.e. proceeds from) notes payable (total), $204,000: current portion, $64,000; noncurrent portion, $140,000

(p) Decrease in (i.e. payment toward) bonds payable, $30,000

Additional Information from Balance Sheet (Figure 19.3)

(q) Soho declared and paid $10,000 in cash dividends in 2018

(r) Increase in (i.e. issuance of) preferred stock, $8,000 par value plus $2,000 additional paid-in capital

(s) Net cash provided (used) by financing activities, $174,000

Preparing the Spreadsheet

To prepare the spreadsheet using a spreadsheet application, refer to Figure 19B.1 and use the following steps.

Step 1. Set up a spreadsheet with separate columns for the following items: the names of the balance sheet accounts; the December 31, 2017 balances of those accounts; a column for changes that are debits; a column for changes that are credits; and the December 31, 2018 balances of the balance sheet accounts. It is also a good idea to add some narrow columns in which to enter alphabetical codes (as in Figure 19B.1), so that you can track and cross-reference the entries that you make.

Step 2. In the first column, list the name of each balance sheet account.

Step 3. In the second column, enter the balance for each balance sheet account as at December 31, 2017. In the last column, enter the corresponding balances as at December 31, 2018. Use parentheses for all credit balances. Total each of these columns, ensuring that each one totals zero.

Step 4. Start a statement of cash flows section below the balance sheet accounts. Enter the amount of net income (debit) as your first entry, and make a corresponding (credit) entry to retained earnings.

Step 5. Analyze the change in each noncash account to determine the net increase (decrease) in cash flows. Enter the amount of the change as an adjustment in the appropriate Change column under either "Debit" or "Credit." In the statement of cash flows section, enter a corresponding entry for each adjustment under the appropriate classification: an operating, investing, financing, or noncash investing and financing activity (if any). (Note that Soho does not have any noncash investing and financing activities—this is simply mentioned for completeness.)

Step 6. When all changes have been analyzed and entered, calculate the net increase (decrease) in cash, and enter the amount of the change in the cash account.

Step 7. Total each Changes column (debit and credit) for the balance sheet accounts. These two totals should be equal. Do the same for the debit and credit columns for the statement of cash flows section, and ensure that they too are equal.

Analyzing Account Changes

When you begin to analyze the accounts, you may notice that many of the changes are fairly straightforward while some are a bit more complex. Just as we used T-account analysis to help explain some of the account changes earlier in the chapter, it may help to practice with something similar to journal entries when working through some of the adjustments in the spreadsheet approach. The following items are some of the more complex adjustments.

Retained earnings increased by $643,607 during 2018, which breaks down as follows.

(a) Net Income (operating activities)...653,607

      Retained Earnings...653,607

(q) Retained Earnings...10,000

      Payment of Cash Dividend (financing activities) 10,000

During 2018, land that cost $50,000 was sold for $60,000, resulting in a $10,000 gain on sale.

(c)(l) Proceeds from sale of land (investing activities)................................60,000

      Land.. 50,000

      Gain on sale of land (operating activities).. 10,000

Preparing the Statement of Cash Flows

Once you have completed all of the steps to prepare the spreadsheet, the statement of cash flows can be prepared using the information from the bottom section of the spreadsheet. In fact, if you compare the spreadsheet in Figure 19B.1 you will notice that it is the same as the statement of cash flows in Figure 19.12.

	A	B	C	D	E	F	G
1		Soho Supplies					
2		Spreadsheet for Statement of Cash Flows					
3		For the Year Ended December 31, 2018					
4		Balance		Changes			Balance
5		Dec 31, 2017		Debit		Credit	Dec 31, 2018
6	**Balance Sheet Accounts**						
7	Cash	396,142			(s)	46,207	349,935
8	Accounts Receivable	1,065,812	(d)	220,326			1,286,138
9	Merchandise Inventory	840,091	(f)	843,469			1,683,560
10	Prepaid Insurance	42,625	(e)	5,987			48,612
11	Land	50,000			(c)	50,000	0
12	Equipment	120,000	(m)	202,518			322,518
13	Accumulated Depreciation	(36,000)			(b)	43,262	(79,262)
14	Accounts Payable	(475,645)			(g)	307,957	(783,602)
15	Salaries Payable	(50,000)	(h)	25,000			(25,000)
16	Interest Payable	(23,500)	(i)	7,850			(15,650)
17	Income Taxes Payable	(250,000)			(j)	30,117	(280,117)
18	Notes Payable	(596,000)			(o)	204,000	(800,000)
19	Bonds Payable	(200,000)	(p)	30,000			(170,000)
20	Preferred Stock	0			(r)	8,000	(8,000)
21	Common Stock	(5,000)					(5,000)
22	Additional Paid-In Capital	0			(r)	2,000	(2,000)
23	Retained Earnings	(878,525)	(q)	10,000	(a)	653,607	(1,522,132)
24	Totals			1,345,150		1,345,150	
25							
26	**Statement of Cash Flows**						
27	Operating Activities						
28	Net Income		(a)	653,607			
29	Depreciation		(b)	43,262			
30	Gain on Sale of Land				(c)	10,000	
31	Increase in Accounts Receivable				(d)	220,326	
32	Increase in Prepaid Insurance				(e)	5,987	
33	Increase in Merchandise Inventory				(f)	843,469	
34	Increase in Accounts Payable		(g)	307,957			
35	Decrease in Salaries Payable				(h)	25,000	
36	Decrease in Interest Payable				(i)	7,850	
37	Increase in Income Taxes Payable		(j)	30,117			
38	Investing Activities						
39	Sale of Land		(c)	60,000			
40	Purchase of Equipment				(m)	202,518	
41	Financing Activities						
42	Proceeds of Bank Loan		(o)	204,000			
43	Payment on Notes Payable				(p)	30,000	
44	Payment of Cash Dividend				(q)	10,000	
45	Issuance of Preferred Stock		(r)	8,000			
46	Additional Paid-In Capital		(r)	2,000			
47	Net Increase (Decrease) in Cash		(s)	46,207			
48	Totals			1,355,150		1,355,150	

FIGURE 19B.1

In Summary

LO 7 **Prepare a statement of cash flows in a spreadsheet using the indirect method.**

► A spreadsheet is a valuable tool to help organize and verify all the transactions that affect a company's cash balance. It is divided into two sections: the balance sheet accounts, and the statement of cash flows.

► A spreadsheet allows you to analyze the change in each noncash account to determine the net increase (decrease) in cash flows.

► The statement of cash flows is prepared using the information from the bottom section of the spreadsheet, which shows the net increase (decrease) in cash from operating, investing and financing activities.

AMEENGAGE™ *Access **ameengage.com** for integrated resources including tutorials, practice exercises, the digital textbook and more.*

Chapter 20
Financial Statement Analysis

Learning Objectives

LO 1 Explain the importance of analyzing financial statements

LO 2 Conduct a horizontal and vertical analysis of financial statements
- Horizontal Analysis—Balance Sheet
- Vertical Analysis—Balance Sheet
- Horizontal Analysis—Income Statement
- Vertical Analysis—Income Statement

LO 3 Calculate and apply liquidity ratios
- Working Capital
- Current Ratio
- Quick Ratio

LO 4 Calculate and apply profitability ratios
- Gross Profit Margin
- Net Profit Margin
- Return on Equity
- Return on Common Stockholders' Equity
- Return on Assets
- Asset Turnover

LO 5 Calculate and apply operations management and solvency ratios
- Operations Management Analysis
- Inventory Turnover Ratio
- Days' Sales in Inventory
- Days' Sales Outstanding
- Accounts Receivable Turnover Ratio
- Solvency Analysis
- Debt-to-Equity Ratio
- Times-Interest-Earned
- Debt-to-Total-Assets Ratio

LO 6 Calculate and apply capital market ratios
- Book Value per Common Share
- Dividend Yield
- Earnings per Share
- Price-Earnings Ratio

LO 7 Identify the limitations of financial statement analysis

 *Access **ameengage.com** for integrated resources including tutorials, practice exercises, the digital textbook and more.*

The Importance of Financial Statement Analysis

In this textbook, you have learned how to prepare the financial statements for sole proprietorships, partnerships and corporations. These statements provide the basic set of information about a company and are used in decision-making processes internally and externally. Internal users, such as managers and executives, analyze financial information to correct negative results and take advantage of positive results. External users, such as investors and suppliers, analyze financial information to determine whether to invest money or extend credit terms. Analyzing financial statements focuses on four areas of information that are critical to decision-making.

- Liquidity—a company's ability to convert current assets into cash
- Profitability—a company's ability to generate profits
- Operations Management—a company's ability to manage its assets, such as inventory and accounts receivable
- Solvency—a company's ability to cover its long-term debt obligations as they become due

Financial statement analysis also uses *capital market ratios* to assess a company's potential to generate positive returns for stockholders.

All of these areas of financial statement analysis are related. For instance, a company's ability to convert its current assets into cash (liquidity) can affect its ability to take advantage of profit-generating opportunities (profitability). Liquidity also affects the company's ability to purchase assets or inventory (operations management), and to cover its debts as they become due (solvency). If the company is unable to purchase inventory or expand its operations, this can affect its profitability. Furthermore, if the company cannot meet its debt obligations, this affects its credit standing, and hence its ability to obtain any necessary financing.

There are different ways to analyze a company's financial statements. One way is to perform a horizontal or vertical analysis of the financial statements. Another way is to calculate ratios based on the numbers from a company's financial statements. While each ratio has its own merits, one ratio alone does not provide users with the complete picture of a company's financial health.

Other key information comes from several official sources. The first source is **Management's Discussion and Analysis (MD&A)**, a special section that is included in a company's annual report filed with the SEC. In the MD&A, management provides stockholders with an analysis of the company's past and current performances, and a discussion of its future plans and projected performance. The second source is the *report on internal control* by management, which is required for corporate governance under the Sarbanes-Oxley Act of 2002. This report requires that the CEO and CFO certify to the fairness of the financial statements and the effectiveness of the company's internal controls. A report on internal control must be accompanied by formal verification made by a public accounting firm; both must be included in the company's annual report.

This chapter illustrates how to calculate important ratios and how to analyze them to better understand the complex nature of a corporation's financial status. We will begin our discussion with horizontal and vertical analyses of the statements.

Horizontal and Vertical Analyses

LO 2

We will inspect the balance sheet of Star Hotel, a fictitious hotel corporation. Suppose this company is planning to renovate to offer more rooms and services. It has contacted the bank to secure a note payable, but the bank must determine whether the company is profitable and can afford the note and interest payments. The bank has asked for Star Hotel's financial statements for the last three years. Star Hotel's comparative balance sheet is presented in Figure 20.1. A **comparative balance sheet** is a balance sheet that shows the balances for multiple years for easy comparison. For readability, a single column is used for each year.

Star Hotel Comparative Balance Sheet As at December 31, 2016–2018			
	2018	**2017**	**2016**
Assets			
Current Assets			
Cash and Cash Equivalents	$8,000	$20,000	$32,000
Accounts Receivable	100,000	70,000	40,000
Food Inventory	40,000	28,000	16,000
Prepaid Expenses	12,000	12,000	12,000
Total Current Assets	160,000	130,000	100,000
Total Noncurrent Assets	440,000	455,000	470,000
Total Assets	$600,000	$585,000	$570,000
Liabilities			
Current Liabilities			
Accounts Payable	$50,000	$60,000	$80,000
Unearned Revenue	30,000	25,000	20,000
Total Current Liabilities	80,000	85,000	100,000
Total Liabilities	80,000	85,000	100,000
Stockholders' Equity			
Capital Stock			
Common Stock—10,000 shares outstanding	100,000	100,000	100,000
Preferred Stock—5,000 shares outstanding	20,000	10,000	10,000
Retained Earnings	400,000	390,000	360,000
Total Stockholders' Equity	520,000	500,000	470,000
Total Liabilities and Stockholders' Equity	$600,000	$585,000	$570,000

FIGURE 20.1

Horizontal Analysis—Balance Sheet

The comparative balance sheet is a tool used to perform a **horizontal analysis** because it compares information from one accounting period to another, usually from year to year. This means that you can compare similar line items to see how that item has changed from year to year, providing what is known as a **trend analysis**. Trend analysis compares line items in terms of two things:

- the *dollar change* (increase or decrease) compared to a base year; and

- the *percentage change* (increase or decrease) compared to a base year.

A **base year** is usually the earliest year shown and is used as the basis for comparison.

Figure 20.2 summarizes some key financial information for Star Hotel's previous three years.

Star Hotel Key Figures As at December 31, 2016–2018			
	2018	**2017**	**2016**
Cash	$8,000	$20,000	$32,000
Total Current Assets	160,000	130,000	100,000
Total Noncurrent Assets	440,000	455,000	470,000
Total Assets	600,000	585,000	570,000
Total Current Liabilities	80,000	85,000	100,000
Total Stockholders' Equity	520,000	500,000	470,000

FIGURE 20.2

In this example, 2016 (the earliest year shown) is the base year. If we start our comparison with the cash balance of the current year (2018), we can see that compared to 2016, the following things happened:

- cash decreased by $24,000 ($8,000 − $32,000)

- total assets increased by $30,000 ($600,000 − $570,000)

- total current liabilities decreased by $20,000 ($80,000 − $100,000)

- total stockholders' equity increased by $50,000 ($520,000 − $470,000)

Using the comparative balance sheet, the bank can easily see the increases and decreases in assets and liabilities. Specifically, total assets have increased while total liabilities have decreased, which is a good sign. We can see that the company's cash balance is dwindling while accounts receivable significantly increased, indicating that there may be some cash or collection issues. However, just examining dollar amounts may not reveal trends in the company. To make its decision, the bank needs more in-depth information. The values can be expressed as percentages, or more specifically, *trend percentages*.

To perform a trend analysis, we can calculate trend percentages using the formula in Figure 20.3.

$$\text{Trend Percentage} = \frac{\text{New Account Balance} - \text{Base Year Account Balance}}{\text{Base Year Account Balance}}$$

FIGURE 20.3

As before, 2016 is selected as the base year. For cash, we subtract $32,000 from the year we are examining and divide the result by $32,000. For example, the balance of cash in 2018 was $8,000.

$$\frac{\$8,000 - \$32,000}{\$32,000} = -0.75 \text{ or } -75\%$$

A way to describe this trend is that the cash balance decreased by 75% between 2016 and 2018. This could be the reason why Star Hotel needs a loan, because the company does not have enough cash to pay for renovations. Figure 20.4 shows the trend percentages for Star Hotel, based on the key figures from its comparative balance sheet.

Star Hotel Trend Percentage As at December 31, 2016–2018			
	2018	**2017**	**2016**
Cash	−75%	−38%	0%
Total Current Assets	60%	30%	0%
Total Noncurrent Assets	−6%	−5%	0%
Total Assets	5%	3%	0%
Total Current Liabilities	−20%	−15%	0%
Total Stockholders' Equity	11%	6%	0%

FIGURE 20.4

One item to note in Figure 20.4 is the 0% changes for 2016. There is no percent change from the base year figure, because there is no previous year to compare it to.

Using this method, the bank can see trends emerging in the data. Despite cash significantly decreasing over time, total current assets have been steadily increasing. Liabilities have been reduced while stockholders' equity has been increasing since 2016. There are no major concerns with these observations.

Vertical Analysis—Balance Sheet

The balance sheet can also be used to perform a **vertical analysis**, in which a line item is compared to a base figure within the same year. This type of analysis provides information on the *relationship* between the balance sheet components. Usually, the **base figure** is a total dollar amount, such as total assets.

To calculate the percentages, we use the formula shown in Figure 20.5.

$$Percentage = \frac{Line\ Item\ Account\ Balance}{Base\ Figure\ Account\ Balance}$$

FIGURE 20.5

To start, a base figure must be selected. In 2018, Star Hotel had a total asset balance of $600,000; this amount is the base figure. Next, divide all line items in the 2018 balance sheet by the base figure. For example, for cash, divide the balance of $8,000 by the total assets. The result is 0.01 or 1%.

$$\frac{\$8,000}{\$600,000} = 0.01\ or\ 1\%$$

Figure 20.6 shows a horizontal analysis in which the individual line items are stated as a percentage of total assets.

Star Hotel Key Percentages As at December 31, 2016–2018			
	2018	**2017**	**2016**
Cash	1%	3%	6%
Total Current Assets	27%	22%	18%
Total Noncurrent Assets	73%	78%	82%
Total Assets	100%*	100%	100%
Total Current Liabilities	13%	15%	18%
Total Stockholders' Equity	87%	85%	82%

*$600,000 ÷ $600,000 = 100%

FIGURE 20.6

This type of analysis reveals that cash currently represents 1% of total assets. Star Hotel should consider holding more cash in case of unexpected events. Fortunately, current assets represent 27% of total assets and have grown to more than double that of current liabilities. Using this information, the bank decides that Star Hotel is in an overall healthy financial position.

Horizontal Analysis—Income Statement

The next step is to use the same tools to analyze the company's income statement. Horizontal analysis is done in much the same way on the income statement as it is on the balance sheet.

The comparative income statement allows the bank to quickly see which revenue and expenses have increased or decreased and whether net income is rising or falling. Star Hotel has seen a large increase in revenue, perhaps attributable to an increased advertising budget. The company's net income has doubled since 2017, which is a good sign of profitability. However, if the bank grants a loan, Star Hotel will incur an interest expense, which reduces the profitability of the company. The bank decides to look at other trends in the company.

Star Hotel's comparative income statement for the past three years is shown in Figure 20.7.

Star Hotel Comparative Income Statement For the Year Ended December 31, 2016–2018			
	2018	**2017**	**2016**
Revenue			
Service Revenue	$270,000	$200,000	$180,000
Sales Revenue	80,000	50,000	40,000
Total Revenue	350,000	250,000	220,000
Cost of Goods Sold	50,000	30,000	25,000
Gross Profit	300,000	220,000	195,000
Operating Expenses			
Selling Expense	200,000	150,000	140,000
Administration Expense	80,000	60,000	47,500
Total Operating Expenses	280,000	210,000	187,500
Net Income	$20,000	$10,000	$7,500

FIGURE 20.7

Figure 20.8 lists the key figures from the income statement for the previous three years as dollars, percentage of, as well as percentage changed from the base year of 2016.

Star Hotel Key Figures For the Year Ended December 31, 2016–2018			
	2018	**2017**	**2016**
Total Revenue	$350,000	$250,000	$220,000
Cost of Goods Sold	50,000	30,000	25,000
Gross Profit	300,000	220,000	195,000
Total Operating Expenses	280,000	210,000	187,500
Net Income	20,000	10,000	7,500

Star Hotel Percentage of 2016 Base Year For the Year Ended December 31, 2016–2018			
	2018	**2017**	**2016**
Total Revenue	160%	114%	100%
Cost of Goods Sold	200%	120%	100%
Gross Profit	154%	113%	100%
Total Operating Expenses	150%	112%	100%
Net Income	267%	133%	100%

Star Hotel Percentage Changed with 2016 Base Year For the Year Ended December 31, 2016–2018			
	2018	**2017**	**2016**
Total Revenue	60%	14%	0%
Cost of Goods Sold	100%	20%	0%
Gross Profit	54%	13%	0%
Total Operating Expenses	50%	12%	0%
Net Income	167%	33%	0%

FIGURE 20.8

Star Hotel's sales have been increasing at a faster rate than its expenses, resulting in higher net income. After seeing these trends, the bank decides that the company is likely to continue operating profitably into the future.

Vertical Analysis—Income Statement

Finally, the bank can also perform a vertical analysis on Star Hotel's income statement by converting everything to a percentage of total revenue for each year, as shown in Figure 20.9.

Star Hotel Percentage of Base Figure Total Revenue For the Year Ended December 31, 2016–2018			
	2018	**2017**	**2016**
Total Revenue	100%	100%	100%
Cost of Goods Sold	14%	12%	11%
Gross Profit	86%	88%	89%
Total Operating Expenses	80%	84%	85%
Net Income	6%	4%	3%

FIGURE 20.9

This analysis reveals that gross profit has remained quite steady, but operating expenses have been gradually falling in relation to total revenue. This indicates that sales have risen without causing much of an increase to operating expenses, allowing for more net income per dollar of sales.

Considering all of the conclusions, the bank approves the loan to Star Hotel because it has been growing steadily over the past three years and is in a healthy enough financial position to expand operations without much risk.

The Star Hotel example used horizontal and vertical analysis tools to make a decision. While these tools provide some insight regarding a company's financial position, there are limitations to what they can actually show. The tools do not consider errors in the figures. Also, the trends may not continue because businesses change and evolve constantly. Fortunately, there are many other analysis tools available to users. These will be discussed next.

Pause & Reflect

Exercise 20-1

The following summarizes key financial information for Industrial Furnishing's previous four years.

	2018	2017	2016	2015
Total Revenue	$610,000	$600,000	$525,000	$500,000
Cost of Goods Sold	155,000	150,000	110,000	100,000
Gross Profit	455,000	450,000	415,000	400,000
Total Operating Expenses	385,000	375,000	325,000	315,000
Net Income	70,000	75,000	90,000	85,000

a) Calculate the trend precentage for each account, using 2015 as the base year.

Industrial Furnishings Percentage of 2015 Base Year For the Year Ended December 31, 2015–2018				
	2018	**2017**	**2016**	**2015**
Total Revenue				
Cost of Goods Sold				
Gross Profit				
Total Operating Expenses				
Net Income				

b) Based on the trend percentage calculated in part a), analyze why net income has been decreasing in the past two years.

_____

_____

_____

See Appendix I for solutions.

Liquidity Analysis

For the next type of analysis, we will use the financial statements of Dunkin' Brands Group, Inc. (Dunkin' Donuts), an American corporation that sells specialty coffee and baked goods. We will compare the analysis of these financial statements to an analysis of a fictitious company in the same industry: Best Coffee Company (Best Coffee).

The comparative balance sheet for Dunkin' Donuts is shown in Figure 20.10. The comparative balance sheet is not only an important tool in conducting horizontal and vertical analyses, but it also allows users to easily calculate various financial ratios for a company to better understand its finances. Note that throughout the chapter, all of Dunkin' Donuts' and Best Coffee's data is presented in thousands, with the exception of share data.

DUNKIN' BRANDS GROUP, INC. AND SUBSIDIARIES
Consolidated Balance Sheets
(In thousands, except share data)

	December 26, 2015	December 27, 2014
Assets		
Current assets:		
Cash and cash equivalents	$ 260,430	208,080
Restricted cash	71,917	—
Accounts receivable, net	53,142	55,908
Notes and other receivables, net	75,218	49,152
Restricted assets of advertising funds	38,554	34,300
Prepaid income taxes	23,899	24,861
Prepaid expenses and other current assets	34,664	21,101
Total current assets	557,824	393,402
Property and equipment, net	182,614	182,061
Equity method investments	106,878	164,493
Goodwill	889,588	891,370
Other intangible assets, net	1,401,208	1,425,797
Other assets	59,007	67,277
Total assets	$ 3,197,119	3,124,400
Liabilities, Redeemable Noncontrolling Interests, and Stockholders' Equity (Deficit)		
Current liabilities:		
Current portion of long-term debt	$ 25,000	3,852
Capital lease obligations	546	506
Accounts payable	18,663	13,814
Liabilities of advertising funds	50,189	48,081
Deferred income	31,535	30,374
Other current liabilities	292,859	258,892
Total current liabilities	418,792	355,519
Long-term debt, net	2,420,600	1,795,623
Capital lease obligations	7,497	7,575
Unfavorable operating leases acquired	12,975	14,795
Deferred income	15,619	14,935
Deferred income taxes, net	476,510	498,814
Other long-term liabilities	65,869	62,189
Total long-term liabilities	2,999,070	2,393,931
Commitments and contingencies (note 17)		
Redeemable noncontrolling interests	—	6,991
Stockholders' equity (deficit):		
Preferred stock, $0.001 par value; 25,000,000 shares authorized; no shares issued and outstanding	—	—
Common stock, $0.001 par value; 475,000,000 shares authorized; 92,668,211 shares issued and 92,641,044 shares outstanding at December 26, 2015; 104,630,978 shares issued and outstanding at December 27, 2014	92	104
Additional paid-in capital	876,557	1,093,363
Treasury stock, at cost; 27,167 shares at December 26, 2015	(1,075)	—
Accumulated deficit	(1,076,479)	(711,531)
Accumulated other comprehensive loss	(20,046)	(13,977)
Total stockholders' equity (deficit) of Dunkin' Brands	(220,951)	367,959
Noncontrolling interests	208	—
Total stockholders' equity (deficit)	(220,743)	367,959
Total liabilities, redeemable noncontrolling interests, and stockholders' equity (deficit)	$ 3,197,119	3,124,400

FIGURE 20.10

We will dissect sections of the balance sheet to perform our initial analysis: the calculation of ratios. Ratios measure four different aspects of a company's financial situation: liquidity, profitability, operations management and solvency. For a public company, we can also measure corporate performance. By comparing ratios of Dunkin' Donuts to a similar company in the same industry (i.e. Best Coffee Company), or to industry averages, we can assess if the company is performing relatively well or relatively poorly. Industry averages are available online through many financial research websites. Industry financial ratios are grouped by a four-digit code known as a *standard industrial classification* (SIC). SICs are used by government agencies to classify business entities by industry. For instance, Dunkin' Brands Group is classified as SIC-5810 (Retail – Eating & Drinking Places), as is our fictitious Best Coffee Company.

In our discussion of Dunkin' Donuts, we will compare its ratios from one year to the next, to Best Coffee Company's ratios and to sample industry averages. Both Best Coffee's ratios and the industry averages are presented here for illustrative purposes only.

Liquidity refers to the ability of a company to convert current assets into cash in order to repay its short-term debt obligations. The more liquid a company is, the easier it is to cover obligations, such as accounts payable and loan payments. There are several ways to measure liquidity: working capital, current ratio and quick ratio, which were discussed in Chapter 6.

Working Capital

Working capital is a measure of liquidity that assesses the adequacy of a company's current assets to cover its current liabilities. The formula for working capital is shown in Figure 20.11.

$$\text{Working Capital} = \text{Current Assets} - \text{Current Liabilities}$$

FIGURE 20.11

A positive working capital indicates that the company has enough liquid assets to pay off its upcoming debts. Specifically, the positive working capital is the amount of money leftover from paying short-term debt that can be used to expand the business. On the other hand, a negative working capital indicates that current assets alone are not enough to pay off short-term debt, and that the company may have to sell some noncurrent assets in order to meet short-term debt obligations. If the company is forced to sell noncurrent assets that are necessary for generating sales, it may lead to a decrease in revenue and net income, which can put the company's long-term prospects in jeopardy.

The working capital of Dunkin' Donuts is calculated in Figure 20.12 for 2014 and 2015.

	2015	2014
Total Current Assets	$557,824	$393,402
Total Current Liabilities	$418,792	$355,519
Total Revenue	$810,933	$748,709
Working Capital—Dunkin' Donuts	**$139,032**	**$37,883**
Working Capital—Best Coffee (in millions)	**$699**	**$1,130**
Industry Average	**$30,000**	**$20,000**

FIGURE 20.12

Dunkin' Donuts had enough current assets to cover its current liabilities, as evident by its positive working capital in both 2014 and 2015. Its working capital increased from 2014 to 2015, indicating improved liquidity. In fact, it exceeded the industry average for both years. However, because working capital is calculated in dollars rather than in the form of a ratio, it may not provide a very meaningful comparison. For this reason, it is better to also calculate current and quick ratios in order to more clearly understand a company's liquidity and be able to compare it against those of the industry average or a specific competitors'.

Current Ratio

The current ratio is a useful ratio for determining a company's ability to repay its upcoming debts and obligations. The current ratio is calculated as shown in Figure 20.13.

$$\text{Current Ratio} = \frac{\text{Current Assets}}{\text{Current Liabilities}}$$

FIGURE 20.13

The current ratio assesses a business' liquidity by determining the extent to which current assets can cover current liabilities. This means establishing the business' ability to pay off its debt due within one year. No business wants to find itself in a position of having to sell noncurrent assets to pay current bills. A current ratio of 1.0 indicates that the business has just enough current assets to pay for its current liabilities.

Depending on the industry, the higher the current ratio, the more assurance that the business can afford to pay off its current liabilities without being forced to liquidate its noncurrent assets to do so. However, a very high current ratio could indicate poor management of current assets. For example, if the current ratio of a business is 5.0, it has $5.00 in current assets for every dollar that it owes in the next 12 months. This indicates that the business may have too much cash. Money in a bank account earning 0.1% interest is not an efficient use of assets, especially if the business can earn a better rate of return elsewhere. Cash should either be invested in new noncurrent assets or perhaps a short-term investment until a better use for the cash can be established.

The chart in Figure 20.14 calculates the current ratio using the numbers provided in Dunkin' Donuts' financial statements.

	2015	2014
Total Current Assets	$557,824	$393,402
Total Current Liabilities	$418,792	$355,519
Current Ratio—Dunkin' Donuts	**1.33**	**1.11**
Current Ratio—Best Coffee	**1.19**	**1.37**
Industry Average	**1.19**	**0.88**

FIGURE 20.14

In this case, the ratio indicates a healthy situation. Not only is the ratio above 1 for both years, but it has increased from 2014 to 2015, in keeping with the increase in the industry as a whole. Dunkin' Donuts' ratio is also above the industry average for both years.

In 2014, Best Coffee's current ratio was 1.37, which is higher than Dunkin' Donuts' 2014 current ratio of 1.11. However, in 2015, Best Coffee's current ratio of 1.19 is significantly lower than that for Dunkin' Donuts, although it is in line with the industry average. Compared overall, the ratios suggest that of the two companies, Dunkin' Donuts had a healthier liquidity over that time period with its current ratio increasing, whereas Best Coffee experienced a decrease in its current ratio over the same time period.

Quick Ratio

Another ratio that is relevant to the analysis of a business' liquidity is the quick ratio (also known as the acid test). This ratio measures the adequacy of highly liquid assets (including cash, short-term investments and accounts receivable) to cover current liabilities. The formula for the quick ratio is shown in Figure 20.15.

$$\text{Quick Ratio} = \frac{\text{Cash} + \text{Short-Term Investments} + \text{Accounts Receivable}}{\text{Current Liabilities}}$$

FIGURE 20.15

The quick ratio is much like the current ratio; the only difference is that the quick ratio excludes some current assets that cannot be quickly converted to cash (e.g. inventory and prepaid expenses). Short-term investments occur when a company has excess cash and wishes to invest it. This cash can be invested in debt and equity instruments, such as bonds and stock of other companies.

The quick ratio assesses the ability of the business to meet its most immediate debt obligations without relying on the liquidation of inventory (which may take some time to sell). A quick ratio of 1 indicates that the business has just enough liquid assets to pay for its current liabilities. Anything below 1 might mean the business has too much of its money tied up in inventory or other less liquid assets and may be unable to pay its short-term bills.

Quick ratios have been calculated in Figure 20.16 using the numbers from Dunkin' Donuts' balance sheet. Note that Dunkin' Donuts' 2015 cash amount excludes the "restricted cash" reported on its consolidated balance sheets. The company has designated that amount for a specific purpose; it is therefore not considered as part of its highly liquid assets when calculating the quick ratio.

	2015	2014
Cash + Short-Term Investments + Accounts Receivable	$388,790	$313,140
Total Current Liabilities	$418,792	$355,519
Quick Ratio—Dunkin' Donuts	**0.93**	**0.88**
Quick Ratio—Best Coffee	**0.64**	**0.81**
Industry Average	**1.26**	**0.86**

FIGURE 20.16

In 2014, Dunkin' Donuts had a better short-term liquidity than Best Coffee since Dunkin' Donuts' quick ratio of 0.88 was slightly higher than Best Coffee's quick ratio of 0.81. However, Best Coffee's quick ratio dropped considerably in 2015 to 0.64, while Dunkin' Donuts' quick ratio increased further to 0.93. This means that Best Coffee has gone from a nearly adequate short-term liquidity position to a riskier one, while Dunkin' Donuts has increased to a nearly adequate liquidity position. Still, both companies have remained below the industry average over that time period.

Best Coffee's liquidity situation could have worsened if the company had invested even more money in inventory or fixed assets. To address any potential problems here, and since the balance sheet provides only a snapshot of business finances, further analyses should be performed over the next few months on the specific assets and liabilities of the business. A review should be performed to address the situation and rectify any problems found. This is to ensure that bills can be paid on time.

IN THE REAL WORLD

Liquidation is a process in which a company ceases to operate. In general, a liquidator is appointed, by either the stockholders (in the case of a voluntary liquidation) or a court of law (in the case of a compulsory liquidation). The liquidator is a third-party who represents the interests of the creditors and supervises the liquidation. First, the company's assets are collected and turned into cash. The company's liabilities are then paid off, first to secured creditors (i.e. banks), then to unsecured creditors (including suppliers, bondholders, taxes owed to the government, and any unpaid wages or other obligations to current employees). Finally, any funds left over are distributed to stockholders according to the articles of incorporation, with preferred stockholders having priority over common stockholders. After these steps are complete, a company is formally dissolved.

Pause & Reflect

Exercise 20-2

Stellar Corporation includes the following items on its December 31 comparative balance sheet.

Stellar Corporation Comparative Balance Sheet (partial) As at December 31, 2017-2018		
	2018	**2017**
Cash	$10,918	$6,501
Short-Term Investments	$81	$220
Accounts Receivable	$4,026	$4,368
Merchandise Inventory	$221	$123
Prepaid Expenses	$485	$190
Deferred Income Tax Asset	$699	-
Current Liabilities	$23,684	$11,061

a) Calculate the company's working capital for both years.

b) Calculate the company's current ratio for both years.

See Appendix I for solutions.

Profitability Analysis

Profitability refers to the ability of a company to generate profits. The greater the profitability, the more valuable the company is to stockholders. A consistently unprofitable company is likely to go bankrupt. There are several ratios available to help analyze the profitability of a company. They are calculated using figures from the income statement as well as the balance sheet. Dunkin' Donuts income statement (statement of operations) in Figure 20.17 allows users to easily compare the financial results of the company over the years.

DUNKIN' BRANDS GROUP, INC. AND SUBSIDIARIES
Consolidated Statements of Operations
(In thousands, except per share data)

	Fiscal year ended		
	December 26, 2015	December 27, 2014	December 28, 2013
Revenues:			
Franchise fees and royalty income	$ 513,222	482,329	453,976
Rental income	100,422	97,663	96,082
Sales of ice cream and other products	115,252	117,484	112,276
Sales at company-operated restaurants	28,340	22,206	24,976
Other revenues	53,697	29,027	26,530
Total revenues	810,933	748,709	713,840
Operating costs and expenses:			
Occupancy expenses—franchised restaurants	54,611	53,395	52,097
Cost of ice cream and other products	76,877	83,129	79,278
Company-operated restaurant expenses	29,900	22,687	24,480
General and administrative expenses, net	243,796	226,301	230,847
Depreciation	20,556	19,779	22,423
Amortization of other intangible assets	24,688	25,760	26,943
Long-lived asset impairment charges	623	1,484	563
Total operating costs and expenses	451,051	432,535	436,631
Net income (loss) of equity method investments:			
Net income, excluding impairment	12,555	14,846	19,243
Impairment charge	(54,300)	—	(873)
Net income (loss) of equity method investments	(41,745)	14,846	18,370
Other operating income, net	1,430	7,838	9,157
Operating income	319,567	338,858	304,736
Other income (expense), net:			
Interest income	424	274	404
Interest expense	(96,765)	(68,098)	(80,235)
Loss on debt extinguishment and refinancing transactions	(20,554)	(13,735)	(5,018)
Other losses, net	(1,084)	(1,566)	(1,799)
Total other expense, net	(117,979)	(83,125)	(86,648)
Income before income taxes	201,588	255,733	218,088
Provision for income taxes	96,359	80,170	71,784
Net income including noncontrolling interests	105,229	175,563	146,304
Net income (loss) attributable to noncontrolling interests	2	(794)	(599)
Net income attributable to Dunkin' Brands	$ 105,227	176,357	146,903
Earnings per share:			
Common—basic	$ 1.10	1.67	1.38
Common—diluted	1.08	1.65	1.36
Cash dividends declared per common share	1.06	0.92	0.76

FIGURE 20.17

For example, we can instantly see that Dunkin' Donuts has generated increasing sales for the past two years. We can also see that expenses have correspondingly increased overall, although an impairment charge of $54,300 (primarily due to the termination of leasehold agreements) in 2015 resulted in a drop in operating income to below that of 2014. The impairment charge was an adjustment related to foreign joint ventures, and is not a regular occurrence. In addition to these observations, several more ratios can be calculated to assess profitability: gross profit margin, net profit margin, return on equity, return on common stockholders' equity, return on assets and asset turnover.

Gross Profit Margin

The gross profit margin is used to demonstrate the impact of cost of goods sold on the income statement (discussed in Chapter 7). In other words, the gross profit margin subtracts cost of goods sold from sales revenue, the result of which is divided by net sales. The formula is shown in Figure 20.18.

$$\text{Gross Profit Margin (\%)} = \frac{\text{Gross Profit*}}{\text{Net Sales}}$$

*Gross Profit = Sales Revenue − Cost of Goods Sold

FIGURE 20.18

Gross profit margin reveals the percentage of revenue left after the costs that are directly involved in producing the goods or services (for manufacturers) or in buying the goods for resale (for retailers) are deducted. That is, the amount of profit remaining after deducting the cost of goods sold. The remaining profit is used to pay for operating and other expenses. Figure 20.19 calculates the gross profit margin related to the sale and cost of ice cream and other products using figures from Dunkin' Donuts' income statement for 2014 and 2015.

	2015	2014
Gross Profit[1]	$38,375	$34,355
Net Sales	$115,252	$117,484
Gross Profit Margin—Dunkin' Donuts	**0.33 or 33%**	**0.29 or 29%**
Gross Profit Margin—Best Coffee	**59%**	**58%**
Industry Average	**27%**	**32%**

[1] Gross Profit for 2014: $117,484 − $83,129 = $34,355
   Gross Profit for 2015: $115,252 − $76,877 = $38,375

FIGURE 20.19

Compared with Best Coffee's gross profit margin, Dunkin' Donuts' lower gross profit margin means that the company may have a more difficult time covering its expenses and is less likely to be profitable. A decline in the gross profit margin could indicate that the company is either not generating enough revenue, has experienced an increase in inventory costs or both. Fortunately for Dunkin' Donuts, this is not the case. Its gross profit margin increased from 2014 to 2015, and for both periods it was above the industry average.

The industry averages in 2014 and 2015 indicate that the industry has experienced a decrease in gross profit margin. This could indicate that there is an increase in the cost of coffee and other items being sold across the industry. It could also indicate that prices are driven down by an increase in competition as a whole. Despite an increase in gross profit margin from 2014 to 2015, Dunkin' Donuts still has a much lower margin than Best Coffee. The relatively lower gross profit margin could be due to the high competitive pressure. Dunkin' Donuts could also intentionally keep the gross profit margin low as part of its marketing strategy to gain a bigger market share.

Net Profit Margin

The **net profit margin** assesses a company's profitability after all expenses have been deducted. This is the amount of net profit or loss per dollar of revenue. The formula is shown in Figure 20.20.

$$\text{Net Profit Margin} = \frac{\text{Net Income}}{\text{Total Revenue}}$$

FIGURE 20.20

As with the gross profit margin, a higher net profit margin is generally considered a better sign than a lower one, although it should always be compared to an industry average and previous results. Figure 20.21 calculates the net profit margins for Dunkin' Donuts for both 2014 and 2015.

	2015	2014
Net Income (Loss)	$105,227	$176,357
Total Revenue	$810,933	$748,709
Net Profit Margin—Dunkin' Donuts	**0.13 or 13%**	**0.24 or 24%**
Net Profit Margin—Best Coffee	**14%**	**13%**
Industry Average	**9%**	**5%**

FIGURE 20.21

Although total revenue has increased since 2014, net income has dropped since then. This was partially due to the impairment charge of $54,300 in 2015, mentioned earlier. This could be a bad sign for the stockholders because earnings on their investments have dropped from 2014 to 2015. To perform a complete analysis of net profit margins, comparisons should be made on a monthly and yearly basis to historical company performance, industry averages and direct competitors. Conclusions can only be drawn when net incomes figures are placed in context.

The industry and Best Coffee are showing positive net profit margins for both years, with Best Coffee's net profit margin increasing slightly from 13% in 2014 to 14% in 2015. This is of concern to Dunkin' Donuts, since it has posted a drop in its net profit margin from 2014 to 2015. However, such a decrease in a company's net profit margin does not necessarily mean the company is performing poorly, or that it is not achieving its goals. Perhaps it intentionally took a lower margin to gain market share, particularly if the income statement shows the company has increased its sales and its bottom line. If the company's net profit margin is down from the previous year (but the company still makes a profit), this could signal that it was necessary to increase market share or expand its territory in order to remain competitive.

Return on Equity

Return on equity (ROE) is a measure of what the owners are getting out of their investment in the company. It is often the most important ratio for investors because it has a large impact on the value of an investment. This ratio requires calculations using information from both the balance sheet and income statement. The formula is shown in Figure 20.22.

$$\text{Return on Equity (ROE)} = \frac{\text{Net Income}}{\text{Average Stockholders' Equity}}$$

FIGURE 20.22

Notice that the calculation requires average stockholders' equity. Whenever a ratio is calculated that uses some information from the balance sheet and some from the income statement, the balance sheet information is always averaged. This is because the balance sheet represents a snapshot in time while the income statement represents an entire accounting period. By averaging the balance sheet accounts, we are simulating a figure that covers the same period of time as the income statement. This makes the ratio more comparable and reliable.

Although not shown in Figure 20.10, we need to know the balance of stockholders' equity at December 28, 2013 to calculate the average stockholders' equity for 2014. Assume that the balance on this date was $407,358. The calculations of ROE for Dunkin' Donuts in 2014 and 2015 are shown in Figure 20.23.

	2015	**2014**
Net Income (Loss)	$105,227	$176,357
Average Stockholders' Equity[1]	$73,608	$387,659
Return on Equity—Dunkin' Donuts	**1.43 or 143%**	**0.45 or 45%**
Return on Equity—Best Coffee	**50%**	**42%**
Industry Average	**40%**	**13%**

[1] Average Stockholders' Equity for 2014: ($407,358 + $367,959) ÷ 2 = $387,659
Average Stockholders' Equity for 2015: ($367,959 + ($220,743)) ÷ 2 = $73,608

FIGURE 20.23

A high ROE is desirable because it means that investors made a good decision to invest in the company. Stockholders like to see a return that is as good as or better than they could have received by investing elsewhere. A negative ROE indicates that stockholders lost money on their investments over the year. It deters investors from investing more money because of the risk of loss. Dunkin' Donuts' return on equity has approximately tripled from 2014 to 2015, as has the industry average over that same time period. Best Coffee's ROE has also increased over that period, although not as dramatically: from 42% in 2014 to 50% in 2015. Still, for both years it has exceeded the industry average. Based on its high ROE in 2015, Dunkin' Donuts would provide a more attractive investment than Best Coffee.

Return on Common Stockholders' Equity

Return on common stockholders' equity is a measure of the profits earned on the investment of common stockholders. This differs from the return on equity (ROE), which assumes that there is no preferred share equity included in stockholders' equity. As with ROE, this ratio requires information from both the balance sheet and income statement. If preferred equity exists, the correct formula is shown in Figure 20.24.

$$\text{Return on Common Stockholders' Equity} = \frac{\text{(Net Income − Preferred Dividends)}}{\text{Average Common Stockholders' Equity}}$$

FIGURE 20.24

In the numerator of this equation, preferred dividends are subtracted from net income. This takes into account that preferred stockholders have the first claim on earnings, before common stockholders. If the preferred stock is cumulative, dividends must be subtracted whether or not they have been declared or if they are in arrears. If the preferred stock is non-cumulative, dividends are subtracted only if they have been declared. The denominator of this calculation is average common stockholders' equity.

The stockholders' equity section of Dunkin' Donuts' consolidated balance sheets in Figure 20.10 indicates that, although 25,000,000 preferred shares are authorized, none are issued or outstanding at the end of either year. Therefore, the numerator in the equation will simply be equal to the net income for the respective periods. Therefore, in this particular example of Dunkin' Donuts, we will arrive at the same returns as we did for ROE.

IN THE REAL WORLD

One of the most important assessments business owners can make is to know if they are getting a decent return on their investment. How is this done?

Any determination of return on investment revolves around stockholders' equity. That is, how much cash would the owners have left if they sold all the assets of the business and paid off all its debt? Given that this is a hypothetical question, and that the owners do not have to sell everything to assess the return on investment, there are other ways of assessing the value of the investment in the business.

For example, the owners could ask themselves another practical question: Should we keep our money in the business, or put it elsewhere? Safe investments, such as fixed deposit accounts, come with relatively lower returns on investment. Investing in a friend's new business comes with a potentially much larger return on investment—but also with greater risk.

In fact, a general rule of thumb can be applied to assessing return on investment associated with certain levels of risk. Generally speaking, investments in publicly traded companies come with the expectation of a return ranging from 15%–25%. Alternatively, the rate of return associated with private companies is expected to be much higher. In fact, it is not unusual to expect a rate of return of 100% or more for an investment in a small private company.

As with most things in life, everything comes at a price. With return on investment, the price can be a matter of risk. If owners want a better return, they must have a greater tolerance for risk.

Return on Assets

Return on assets (ROA) provides an assessment of what the company does with what it has; it measures every dollar earned against each dollar's worth of assets. (Return on assets was introduced in Chapter 12.) A business invests in assets for the purpose of generating sales and making a profit. ROA is a measure of how effective the investment in assets is. Although assessing ROA depends on the type of business being analyzed, a higher ROA number is generally considered better than a lower one; it means the business is earning more money on its investment in assets. Figure 20.25 shows the equation to calculate ROA.

$$\text{Return on Assets (ROA)} = \frac{\text{Net Income}}{\text{Average Total Assets}}$$

FIGURE 20.25

Now calculate ROA for Dunkin' Donuts. The net income (loss) comes from the income statement. The total asset figures are found on the balance sheet. Assume that the balance of total assets at the year end in 2013 was $3,177,383. The calculation is shown in Figure 20.26.

	2015	2014
Net Income (Loss)	$105,227	$176,357
Average Total Assets[1]	$3,160,760	$3,150,892
Return on Assets—Dunkin' Donuts	**0.03 or 3%**	**0.06 or 6%**
Return on Assets—Best Coffee	**24%**	**19%**
Industry Average	**7%**	**12%**

[1] Average Total Assets for 2014: ($3,124,400 + $3,177,383) ÷ 2 = $3,150,892
Average Total Assets for 2015: ($3,124,400 + $3,197,119) ÷ 2 = $3,160,760

FIGURE 20.26

There was a slight drop in the ROA in 2015. What the ROA means is that in 2014, Dunkin' Donuts gained $0.06 for every $1 invested in assets. In 2015, the company's returns dropped to $0.03 for every $1 invested in assets. Although in this case it is likely the effect of the impairment charge of $54,300 taken during 2015, there are various other factors that might explain such a drop in ROA. For example, selling noncurrent assets (which would result in a smaller denominator in the ROA formula), or an increase in costs of goods sold or other expenses. Note from the industry averages, however, that the industry appears to have experienced a similar drop from 2014 to 2015, so there could be industry-wide factors affecting the returns. Ultimately, if resources are properly allocated and assets are efficiently used, ROA should increase. In comparison, Best Coffee reported an increase in ROA over the same period, with a return of 19% in 2014 and 24% in 2015, both of which are well above the industry average. This improvement is likely the result of the company's growth in net income.

As a general rule, a business in an industry with a low ROA usually indicates the business is capital-intensive or asset-heavy. This means that the business is investing a considerable amount in assets relative to profits. Industries that tend to display low ROA figures include manufacturers and large transportation companies such as railroads. Alternatively, a business in an industry with a high ROA is less capital-intensive or asset-heavy. Examples include professional practices, software companies and retailers.

Asset Turnover

Another way to assess how well business assets are being utilized is to calculate the asset turnover ratio, which measures a company's ability to generate sales revenue from asset investments. (Asset turnover was discussed in Chapter 12.) This is calculated by dividing revenue by average total assets, as shown in Figure 20.27.

$$\text{Asset Turnover} = \frac{\text{Total Revenue}}{\text{Average Total Assets}}$$

FIGURE 20.27

Since this is a measurement of generating sales, the higher the number, the better. Figure 20.28 shows the asset turnover for Dunkin' Donuts.

	2015	2014
Total Revenue	$810,933	$748,709
Average Total Assets[1]	$3,160,760	3,150,892
Asset Turnover—Dunkin' Donuts	**0.26 times**	**0.24 times**
Asset Turnover—Best Coffee	**1.65 times**	**1.48 times**
Industry Average	**0.80 times**	**0.80 times**

[1] Average Total Assets for 2014: ($3,124,400 + $3,177,383) ÷ 2 = $3,150,892
Average Total Assets for 2015: ($3,197,119 + $3,124,400) ÷ 2 = $3,160,760

FIGURE 20.28

For 2015, an asset turnover of 0.26 means Dunkin' Donuts generated $0.26 of revenue for every dollar tied up in assets. This is a slight increase from the previous year. This indicates the business has become more efficient at generating revenue with its assets. Despite this improvement, Dunkin' Donuts did not perform as well as the industry overall. For both years, its asset turnover fell significantly below the $0.80 per dollar industry average.

When compared to Best Coffee, Dunkin' Donuts performed worse in both years. Best Coffee was able to generate $1.48 and $1.65 of revenue for every dollar tied up in assets in 2014 and 2015, respectively. Best Coffee's asset turnover figures for both 2014 and 2015 were many times that of Dunkin' Donuts, and almost twice the industry average.

Pause & Reflect

Exercise 20-3

Vernacular Inc. reports the following key items on its comparative income statement for the year ended December 31, 2018.

Vernacular Inc. Comparative Income Statement For the Period Ended December 31, 2017–2018		
	2018	**2017**
Sales Revenue	$28,172	$27,188
Cost of Goods Sold	7,679	4,054
Gross Profit	20,493	23,134
Operating Expenses	47,525	30,503
Net Income (Loss)	($27,032)	($7,369)

a) Calculate the company's gross profit margin for both years.

b) Calculate the company's net profit margin for both years.

See Appendix I for solutions.

Operations Management and Solvency Analyses

Operations Management Analysis

Operations management refers to the ability of a company to manage its assets, such as inventory and accounts receivable. Accounts receivable may be a large source of cash for a company, but it is not worth anything if it cannot be collected. As well, inventory is converted into cash by selling it, but it must be managed properly to ensure that it can be sold in a timely manner. To determine whether inventory is being managed properly, there are two ratios that can be calculated: inventory turnover ratio and days' sales in inventory, both of which were covered in Chapter 8.

Inventory Turnover Ratio

Management is often concerned with the company's ability to sell, or *turn over*, inventory. In industries that deal with food and beverage sales, it is especially important because of the short shelf life of the inventory. Throwing away expired products is just like throwing away cash. The inventory turnover ratio is calculated as shown in Figure 20.29.

$$\text{Inventory Turnover Ratio} \ = \ \frac{\text{Cost of Goods Sold}}{\text{Average Inventory}}$$

FIGURE 20.29

The inventory turnover ratio represents the number of times that the company sold its entire inventory. The industry the company is in determines the desirable value for this ratio. For example, hardware stores may only turn over inventory once or twice per year because the goods do not expire or become obsolete very quickly. The fashion industry may turn over inventory four times per year because fashion trends tend to change quickly and with the seasons.

Dunkin' Brands Group, Inc. is made up of several subsidiary companies—including Dunkin' Donuts and the ice cream company Baskin-Robbins—and so it reports using consolidated financial statements. Although Dunkin' Donuts does not report its inventories, the Baskin-Robbins division reports its ice cream inventories while they are in transit to international markets—however, it includes such inventories in "prepaid expenses and other current assets," shown on its consolidated balance sheets. For *illustrative purposes* we will use the figures reported for that line item on Dunkin' Donuts' balance sheets.

Dunkin' Donuts' inventory turnover ratio is calculated in Figure 20.30. Assume that the inventory balance at December 28, 2013 was $21,409.

	2015	2014
Cost of Goods Sold	$76,877	$83,129
Average Inventory[(1)]	$27,883	$21,255
Inventory Turnover—Dunkin' Donuts	**2.76 times**	**3.91 times**
Inventory Turnover—Best Coffee	**6.50 times**	**6.20 times**
Industry Average	**27.49 times**	**27.49 times**

[(1)] Average Inventory for 2014: ($21,409 + $21,101) ÷ 2 = $21,255
Average Inventory for 2015: ($21,101 + $34,664) ÷ 2 = $27,883

FIGURE 20.30

Dunkin' Donuts' very low inventory turnover ratio reflects Dunkin' Brands' accounting practices with regard to reporting inventories, and it also implies a departure from the overall conditions within the industry.

Best Coffee's inventory turnover increased slightly from 6.2 in 2014 to 6.5 in 2015. Still, this is well below the industry average of 27.49, suggesting that Best Coffee may have a buildup of inventory.

To get a better understanding of what this ratio means in a more general sense, we can also calculate the days' sales in inventory.

Days' Sales in Inventory

This ratio states the same thing as the inventory turnover ratio but in a different way. Days' sales in inventory is equal to the average number of days that it took to turn over inventory during the year. Some users prefer this ratio because they are familiar with working in units such as days and months. Figure 20.31 shows two different ways to calculate days' sales in inventory.

$$\text{Days' Sales in Inventory} = \frac{\text{Average Inventory}}{\text{Cost of Goods Sold}} \times 365$$

or

$$\text{Days' Sales in Inventory} = \frac{365}{\text{Inventory Turnover Ratio}}$$

FIGURE 20.31

This ratio converts the number of times inventory is turned over into the average number of days it took to turn over inventory. For example, a company that sells its entire inventory twice a year has an inventory turnover ratio of 2 and a days' sales in inventory of 182.5 days. The ratio is calculated for Dunkin' Donuts in Figure 20.32.

	2015	2014
Average Inventory[1]	$27,883	$21,255
Cost of Goods Sold	$76,877	$83,129
Days in a Year	365	365
Days' Sales in Inventory—Dunkin' Donuts	**132.4 days**	**93.3 days**
Days' Sales in Inventory—Best Coffee	**56.2 days**	**58.6 days**
Industry Average	**14.1 days**	**15.8 days**

[1] Average Inventory for 2014: ($21,409 + $21,101) ÷ 2 = $21,255
Average Inventory for 2015: ($21,101 + $34,664) ÷ 2 = $27,883

FIGURE 20.32

The lower the number, the faster inventory is sold on average. However, as we saw with industry turnover, Dunkin' Donuts' very high days' sales in inventory for 2014 and 2015 reflect Dunkin' Brands' accounting practices with regard to reporting inventories, and it also implies a departure from the overall conditions within the industry.

Best Coffee's days' sales in inventory decreased slightly from 58.6 in 2014 to 56.2 in 2015. This is well above the industry averages of 15.8 and 14.1, respectively, once again suggesting that Best Coffee may have a buildup of inventory.

The other aspect of operating management is the ability to collect on its bills. Sales have to result in cash. If customers are buying a product or service on credit, they have to pay within a reasonable amount of time to ensure proper cash flow and good financial health for the business. To determine whether accounts receivable is being managed properly, there are two ratios that can be calculated: days' sales outstanding and accounts receivable turnover, both of which were covered in Chapter 11.

Days' Sales Outstanding

Days' sales outstanding (DSO) measures the average number of days that a company takes to collect its receivables. The formula for DSO is shown in Figure 20.33.

$$\text{Days' Sales Outstanding (DSO)} = \frac{\text{Average Net Accounts Receivable}}{\text{Net Credit Sales}} \times 365$$

FIGURE 20.33

Dunkin' Donuts' accounts receivable is primarily comprised of franchise fees, royalty income and rental income owed from franchisees. From an external point of view, we do not know what portion of the total revenue of Dunkin' Donuts is cash versus credit. For our discussion, we will assume that all revenue is on credit except for rental income. The DSO provides an indication of how many days it takes for customers (in this case, franchisees) to pay their bills. This number is important because late payments can cost a business lost interest from cash deposits in a bank, or additional administration costs required to collect payments from customers.

The calculation of DSO for Dunkin' Donuts is shown in Figure 20.34. Assume that the accounts receivable balance at the year end in 2013 was $47,162.

	2015	2014
Average Accounts Receivable[1]	$54,525	$51,535
Net Credit Sales (Total Revenue)[2]	$710,511	$651,046
Number of Days in the Year	365	365
Days' Sales Outstanding—Dunkin' Donuts	**28 days**	**29 days**
Days' Sales Outstanding—Best Coffee	**64 days**	**62 days**
Industry Average	**55 days**	**57 days**

[1] Average Accounts Receivable for 2014: ($47,162 + $55,908) ÷ 2 = $51,535
  Average Accounts Receivable for 2015: ($55,908 + $53,142) ÷ 2 = $54,525
[2] Net Credit Sales for 2014: $748,709 − $97,663 = $651,046
  Net Credit Sales for 2015: $810,933 − $100,422 = $710,511

FIGURE 20.34

As you can see, the business is improving its ability to collect from customers. The DSO decreased slightly from 29 days in 2014, to 28 days in 2015. This is lower than, but keeping in line with the industry values, and lower than Best Coffee's DSO (over 60 days for both 2014 and 2015). Dunkin' Donuts is performing much better than both the industry and Best Coffee in collecting from customers. If the DSO increased, it might be an indication of disputes with customers, a slowdown in sales resulting in slower payments to the company, or problems in the billing and credit function of the company. None of these reasons would be considered favorably by owners, investors or analysts.

However, there are some cautionary notes to keep in mind related to the DSO. First, the revenue figure used in the ratio should exclude all cash sales, since only sales on account (credit sales) are of concern, relative to collecting customer payments. Second, outliers in sales data, such as sales to a major customer who was given a different credit policy from other customers, should be kept out of the total revenue figure used to calculate DSO, because they can skew the ratio. While data such as Best Coffee's and Dunkin' Donuts' credit sales as a percentage of total sales and credit policies to franchisees are not available on the public financial statements, Dunkin' Donuts' and Best Coffee's management should track and analyze their credit sales and receivables data internally to be able to manage its DSO.

Accounts Receivable Turnover

The accounts receivable turnover ratio (ART) is similar to DSO. It involves dividing a company's net credit sales by the average amount of accounts receivable. Figure 20.35 shows the formula to calculate accounts receivable turnover.

$$\text{Accounts Receivable Turnover (ART)} = \frac{\text{Net Credit Sales}}{\text{Average Net Accounts Receivable}}$$

FIGURE 20.35

The calculation for Dunkin' Donuts is shown in Figure 20.36.

	2015	2014
Net Credit Sales (Total Revenue)[1]	$710,511	$651,046
Average Accounts Receivable[2]	$54,525	$51,535
Accounts Receivable Turnover—Dunkin' Donuts	**13.0 times**	**12.6 times**
Accounts Receivable Turnover—Best Coffee	**5.8 times**	**5.7 times**
Industry Average	**21.4 times**	**20.0 times**

[1] Net Credit Sales for 2014: $748,709 – $97,663 = $651,046
Net Credit Sales for 2015: $810,933 – $100,422 = $710,511
[2] Average Accounts Receivable for 2014: ($47,162 + $55,908) ÷ 2 = $51,535
Average Accounts Receivable for 2015: ($55,908 + $53,142) ÷ 2 = $54,525

FIGURE 20.36

Note that the *net credit sales* amount is not usually reported to external users of the financial statements; therefore, external users would simply use the *net sales* figure as the numerator in their ART calculations.

A higher ratio indicates a greater ability to convert accounts receivable into cash. If a business turns over its receivables 12 times per year, it is collecting the average balance of receivables every month. In Dunkin' Donuts' case, an accounts receivable turnover of 12.6 in 2014 means that it collected receivables once every 29 days on average. By 2015, Dunkin's ART had improved to 13.0 times, or nearly once every 28 days. By the same token, Best Coffee's ART of almost 6 for both 2014 and 2015 means that it takes slightly longer than two months on average to collect its receivables.

Solvency Analysis

There are two ways to finance a business: debt and equity. Debts are the liabilities of the business, such as bank loans and accounts payable. Equity is generated by selling stock and generating profits. **Solvency** refers to the company's ability to cover its long-term debt obligations, and it relates to the amount of debt and risk the company has. Companies often take on debt to finance the purchase of large assets. They then use these assets to expand operations and generate sales. However, there is usually a high cost of debt in the form of interest expense, which is where the risk comes in. A company must be able to increase profits by more than the interest expense to benefit the stockholders. There are three measurements of solvency: debt-to-equity ratio (from Chapter 17), times-interest-earned, and debt-to-total assets ratio (from Chapter 17).

Debt-to-Equity Ratio

The debt-to-equity (D/E) ratio is used to assess the balance of debt and equity in a business. The debt-to-equity ratio is calculated as shown in Figure 20.37.

$$\text{Debt-to-Equity (D/E) Ratio} = \frac{\text{Total Liabilities}}{\text{Total Stockholders' Equity}}$$

FIGURE 20.37

It is not healthy for a business to borrow too much relative to what it is worth. This is because there is a cost of debt in the form of interest. The industry a business is in usually influences how much should be borrowed. For example, capital-intensive industries, such as auto manufacturers, have higher debt-to-equity ratios than software developers. Dunkin' Donuts' debt-to-equity ratios for the years 2014 and 2015 are calculated in Figure 20.38. The industry averages are also shown for comparison purposes.

WORTH REPEATING

Acquiring loans or paying back loan principals has no effect on equity. However, paying interest on a loan has a negative effect on equity.

	2015	**2014**
Total Liabilities[(1)]	$3,417,862	$2,749,450
Stockholders' Equity	($220,743)	$367,959
Debt-to-Equity Ratio—Dunkin' Donuts	**-15.5**	**7.5**
Debt-to-Equity Ratio—Best Coffee	**1.14**	**1.04**
Industry Average	**0.06**	**0.85**

(1) Total Liabilities for 2014: $2,393,931 + $355,519 = $2,749,450
     Total Liabilities for 2015: $2,999,070 + $418,792 = $3,417,862

FIGURE 20.38

As you can see, the debt-to-equity ratio dropped drastically from 2014 to 2015. By the end of 2015, Dunkin' Donuts had a deficit in stockholders' equity, which significantly affected its D/E ratio. This is due to a deficit accumulated over a period of about four years as the company repurchased its common stock and subsequently retired blocks of its treasury stock. In fact, for 2015, Dunkin' Donuts was reported to have one of the lowest D/E ratios in the industry. Dunkin' Donut's 2014 D/E ratio of 7.5 is significantly higher than the industry average, while Best Coffee's was much lower at 1.04 and 1.14 for 2014 and 2015, respectively. Even so, Best Coffee was higher than the industry average for both years.

There are a few ways a business can improve its debt-to-equity ratio. First, but not easy, making more profit directly results in an increase to stockholders' equity. Second, the business might consider issuing more stock in exchange for cash.

Times-Interest-Earned

There is a cost to borrowing money. The **times-interest-earned ratio** is used to determine whether the company is able to cover the interest charged on its debt. This ratio divides earnings before interest expense and income tax by the interest expense. Figure 20.39 shows the formula to calculate times-interest-earned.

$$\text{Times-Interest-Earned} = \frac{\text{Earnings before Interest Expense and Income Tax}}{\text{Interest Expense}}$$

FIGURE 20.39

For example, times-interest-earned of only 1 time means that the business has just enough earnings (before interest and tax expenses are deducted) to cover the amount of interest paid during the year.

For Dunkin' Donuts' the calculation of the times-interest-earned ratio is shown in Figure 20.40. Earnings before interest and taxes is simply adding back income taxes and interest expense to net income.

	2015	2014
Earnings before Interest Expense and Income Tax	$298,353	$323,831
Interest Expense	$96,765	$68,098
Times-Interest-Earned—Dunkin' Donuts	**3.1 times**	**4.8 times**
Times-Interest-Earned—Best Coffee	**28 times**	**24 times**
Industry Average	**17 times**	**6 times**

FIGURE 20.40

The actual amount of interest to be paid in 2015 has increased from the previous year, and the company has significantly lower earnings before interest expense and income tax. However, the company is still able to cover its interest expenses despite the drop in times-interest-earned since

2014. Notice, though, that for both years (particularly 2015) Dunkin' Donuts falls below the industry average. This is a key ratio that a lender would be interested in when making a decision to lend money to a company. A poor times-interest-earned, or a continual drop in that figure from year to year, may mean the company will have difficulty securing loans in the future. Best Coffee had a healthy times-interest-earned for 2014 and 2015, at 24 and 28, respectively. This is significantly higher than the industry average for both years, which means that Best Coffee earned more than enough in both of those years to cover its interest expense.

Debt-to-Total-Assets Ratio

The debt-to-total-assets ratio shows how much debt a company has as a percentage of assets. The formula to calculate the debt-to-total-assets ratio is shown in Figure 20.41.

$$\text{Debt-to-Total-Assets Ratio} \ = \ \frac{\text{Total Liabilities}}{\text{Total Assets}}$$

FIGURE 20.41

The calculation for Dunkin' Donuts is shown in Figure 20.42.

	2015	2014
Total Liabilities[1]	$3,417,862	$2,749,450
Total Assets	$3,197,119	$3,124,400
Debt-to-Total-Assets Ratio—Dunkin' Donuts	**1.07 or 107%**	**0.88 or 88%**
Debt-to-Total-Assets Ratio—Best Coffee	**53%**	**51%**
Industry Average	**42%**	**40%**

[1] Total Liabilities for 2014: $2,393,931 + $355,519 = $2,749,450
   Total Liabilities for 2015: $2,999,070 + $418,792 = $3,417,862

FIGURE 20.42

As the debt-to-total-assets ratio increases, this indicates that more debt is being used to finance the business relative to its assets. This increases the risk the company takes on. Debt accrues interest and interest must be paid. Failure to pay interest or debt can lead to bankruptcy in worst-case scenarios.

Different industries have different tolerances for the amount of debt the business should incur. In 2014, Dunkin' Donuts had a debt-to-total-assets ratio over twice the industry average, and by 2015 it had increased significantly to 2.5 times the industry average. This indicates a high and increasing rate of risk. Best Coffee was also higher than the industry average, at 51% and 53% for 2014 and 2015, respectively.

Pause & Reflect

Exercise 20-4

Reaper Company reports the following key items on its comparative financial statements for the year ended December 31, 2018.

Reaper Company	2018	2017
Average Inventory	$172	$130
Cost of Goods Sold	$7,679	$4,054

Calculate the company's days' sales in inventory for each of the two years.

See Appendix I for solutions.

Capital Market Performance Analysis

In addition to calculating financial ratios for internal measurements, some ratios are used by investors to determine whether a public corporation's stock is a desirable purchase. The ratios that measure the stock performance of a public corporation—book value per common share, dividend yield, earnings per share, and price-earnings ratio—were covered in Chapter 16 and are reviewed here.

Stock that is publicly traded on the stock markets can experience price changes daily, hourly or even by the minute. The changes in market value affect investors as they buy and sell stock but the corporation does not record any of these changes in its books.

Dunkin' Donuts does not have any preferred stock; however, its consolidated balance sheet shows that it had 104,630,978 common shares outstanding at the year end of 2015. The company ended 2016 with 92,641,044 common shares outstanding.

Book Value per Common Share

Book value per common share represents the theoretical value of a common share based on a stockholder's claim to the company assets. This assumes that all assets would be sold for their book value and all liabilities would be paid off. However, book value will not necessarily match the market value of the stock. The calculation of book value per common share is shown in Figure 20.43.

$$\text{Book Value per Common Share} = \frac{\text{Stockholders' Equity} - \text{Preferred Stock}}{\text{Number of Common Shares Outstanding}}$$

FIGURE 20.43

Note that preferred stock includes preferred dividends if there are any preferred dividends outstanding. The formula calculates the amount of money that a holder of each common share would receive if all the company's assets were immediately liquidated.

For Dunkin' Donuts, the book value per common share at the end of 2015 is calculated below.

$$\text{Book Value per Common Share} = \frac{-\$220{,}743{,}000}{92{,}641{,}044}$$

$$= -\$2.38$$

Dunkin' Donuts' stockholder deficit for 2015 results in a negative book value per common share. This indicates that if Dunkin' Donuts were to liquidate immediately, it is highly unlikely stockholders would receive anything for their shares since they are a last priority. In comparison, Best Coffee's common stockholders could expect to receive about $3.92 per share if the company liquidates.

Dividend Yield

Since dividends, or at least the potential for dividends, must form part of an analysis of a company, the investing community developed a ratio to assess just how much in dividends a corporation is paying out to stockholders. This is called the dividend yield and calculates dividends paid as a percentage of market price per share. Figure 20.44 shows how to calculate the dividend yield.

$$\text{Dividend Yield} = \frac{\text{Cash Dividends per Common Share}}{\text{Market Price per Common Share}}$$

FIGURE 20.44

Dunkin' Donuts paid $1.06 per common share in dividends in 2015, when the current stock price was $42.36. The calculation of the dividend yield is shown below.

$$\text{Dividend Yield} = \frac{\$1.06}{\$42.36}$$

$$= 0.025 \text{ or } 2.5\%$$

The dividend yield for Dunkin' Donuts in 2015 was 2.5%. This means that if the investor paid $42.36 to purchase a share of Dunkin' Donuts' common stock and in turn received a cash dividend of $1.06, then the investor's rate of return for investing in Dunkin' Donuts' stock in the form of a dividend would be 2.5% in 2015. In comparison, Best Coffee had a 2015 dividend yield of 1.2%. Dunkin' Donuts' higher dividend yield means that in 2015, Dunkin' Donuts' stockholders received a higher rate of return than Best Coffee's stockholders in the form of cash dividends. While a higher dividend yield provides investors with a higher return on investment, paying too high of a dividend may not leave enough cash for the company to grow its operations. Therefore, a high dividend yield may not always be interpreted positively by investors. While some investors may prefer to invest in a stock that gives a higher dividend yield in order to get a higher return on investment, other investors may prefer to make a long-term investment in a company that currently pays a lower dividend yield but has a higher growth potential.

Earnings per Share

Earnings per share (EPS) is a key corporate measure for investors. This measures how much profit is earned for each outstanding common share. The formula for earnings per share is shown in Figure 20.45.

$$\text{Earnings per Share (EPS)} = \frac{\text{Net Income} - \text{Preferred Dividends}}{\text{Weighted Average Number of Common Shares Outstanding}}$$

FIGURE 20.45

Dunkin' Donuts' financial statements present the weighted average number of common shares for 2015 as 97,131,674. We will use this number in our calculation.

$$\text{Earnings per Share} \ = \ \frac{\$105{,}229{,}000}{97{,}131{,}674}$$

$$= \ \$1.08$$

Although Dunkin' Donuts had a positive EPS of $1.08, Best Coffee had a positive EPS of $1.82 in 2015, making it more attractive for investors compared to Dunkin' Donuts.

We learned in Chapter 16 how to calculate the weighted average number of common shares; however, companies may use slightly different variations in their calculation. Thus, since Dunkin' Donuts provided its weighted number of common shares, we used that in our calculation. If we had to calculate the weighted number based on the information given, we might end up with a slightly different weighted average and a different EPS.

Price-Earnings Ratio

Another ratio commonly used by stockholders to evaluate their investment in a corporation is the price-earnings ratio (P/E), which provides the investor with a measurement of share price to actual earnings of the corporation. It is used as an indicator of company growth and risk. It can be used as an indicator to buy, sell or hold shares. P/E ratios and dividend yields are found in the daily stock market quotations listed in many publications, such as the Wall Street Journal, and from numerous online sources, such as Yahoo Finance. The formula is shown in Figure 20.46.

$$\text{Price-Earnings (P/E) Ratio} \ = \ \frac{\text{Market Price per Share}}{\text{Earnings per Share}}$$

FIGURE 20.46

Dunkin' Donuts had a year end of December 26, 2015. On that date, the market value of its shares was $42.36 per share. Thus, the price-earnings ratio for Dunkin' Donuts is calculated below.

$$\text{Price-Earnings Ratio} \ = \ \frac{\$42.36}{\$1.08}$$

$$= 39.22$$

When a company has a positive P/E ratio, as Dunkin' Donuts does, the ratio indicates the shares are selling for a multiple of its earnings. For example, Best Coffee's P/E ratio of 30.58 in 2015 indicates the company's shares on the market are selling 30.58 times its EPS of $1.82 per share. The fact that Dunkin' Donuts has a higher P/E ratio than Best Coffee reflects the market's expectation that Dunkin' Donuts growth potential may be higher than Best Coffee's. This may explain why the investors were willing to pay more for each dollar of Dunkin' Donuts' earnings than for each dollar of Best Coffee's earnings. However, if Dunkin' Donuts' future earnings do not match the market's expectations, then the investors may take its relatively high P/E ratio as an indicator that Dunkin' Donuts' stock is overpriced, thus will sell the stock, which will result in a lower stock price and a lower P/E ratio in the future.

We have just examined many different ratios. Examining only one ratio does not provide a complete picture of the financial status of a company. Many values are needed to form a proper picture. Figure 20.47 summarizes the formulas used to determine different valuations and indicates whether a higher or lower value is desirable for each ratio.

Ratio	Formula	Is a measure of
Liquidity		
Working Capital	Current Assets − Current Liabilities	Ability to cover current liabilities using current assets
Current Ratio	$\dfrac{\text{Current Assets}}{\text{Current Liabilities}}$	Ability to cover current liabilities using current assets
Quick Ratio	$\dfrac{\text{Cash + Short-Term Investments + Accounts Receivable}}{\text{Current Liabilities}}$	Ability of *highly liquid* assets to cover current liabilities
Profitability		
Gross Profit Margin	$\dfrac{\text{Gross Profit}}{\text{Net Sales}}$	Percentage of profit remaining after deducting cost of goods sold
Net Profit Margin	$\dfrac{\text{Net Income}}{\text{Total Revenue}}$	Percentage of profit remaining after deducting all expenses
Return on Equity	$\dfrac{\text{Net Income}}{\text{Average Stockholders' Equity}}$	Profitability of stockholders' investments
Return on Common Stockholders' Equity	$\dfrac{\text{(Net Income − Preferred Dividends)}}{\text{Average Common Stockholders' Equity}}$	Profits earned on investment of common stockholders
Return on Assets	$\dfrac{\text{Net Income}}{\text{Average Total Assets}}$	Effectiveness of the company's investment in assets
Asset Turnover	$\dfrac{\text{Total Sales}}{\text{Average Total Assets}}$	Ability to generate sales revenue from asset investments
Operations Management		
Inventory Turnover Ratio	$\dfrac{\text{Cost of Goods Sold}}{\text{Average Inventory}}$	Efficiency of inventory management
Days' Sales in Inventory	$\dfrac{\text{Average Inventory}}{\text{Cost of Goods Sold}} \times 365$	Average number of days to turn over inventory during the year
Days' Sales Outstanding	$\dfrac{\text{Average Net Accounts Receivable}}{\text{Net Credit Sales}} \times 365$	Average number of days to collect accounts receivable
Accounts Receivable Turnover Ratio	$\dfrac{\text{Net Credit Sales}}{\text{Average Net Accounts Receivable}}$	Efficiency of accounts receivable collections
Solvency		

Ratio	Formula	Is a measure of
Debt-to-Equity Ratio	$\dfrac{\text{Total Liabilities}}{\text{Total Stockholder's Equity}}$	Relative amount of debt vs stockholders' equity that is being used to finance a company's assets
Times-Interest-Earned	$\dfrac{\text{Earnings before Interest Expense and Income Tax}}{\text{Interest Expense}}$	Ability to cover interest on debt
Debt-to-Total-Assets Ratio	$\dfrac{\text{Total Liabilities}}{\text{Total Assets}}$	Amount of debt being financed by creditors
Capital Market Performance		
Book Value per Common Share	$\dfrac{\text{Stockholders' Equity} - \text{Preferred Equity}}{\text{Number of Common Shares Outstanding}}$	Theoretical value of a share based on stockholders' claims to a company's assets
Dividend Yield	$\dfrac{\text{Cash Dividends per Common Share}}{\text{Market Price per Common Share}}$	Rate of return to common stockholders
Earnings per Share	$\dfrac{\text{Net Income} - \text{Preferred Dividends}}{\text{Weighted Average Number of Common Shares Outstanding}}$	Profit earned by investors per share of common stock
Price-Earnings Ratio	$\dfrac{\text{Market Price per Share}}{\text{Earnings per Share}}$	Market value of a share of common stock related to its earnings

FIGURE 20.47

Keep in mind that an extremely high value on a ratio where higher is better, or an extremely low value on a ratio where a lower value is better may not always be a good outcome. For example, if days' sales in inventory is too low, it could indicate a situation where the company is always running out of products. A quick ratio that is too high may indicate the company is not re-investing cash into the business to improve operations.

Pause & Reflect

Exercise 20-5

Peach Tree Company does not have any preferred shares. However, the company's financial statement notes show that it had 9,903,045 common shares outstanding at its 2017 year end. Toward the end of 2018, the company issued an additional 2,927,900 common shares and ended 2018 with 12,830,945 common shares outstanding. The company reported total stockholders' equity of $24,994,000 in its balance sheet as at December 31, 2018. Calculate the company's book value per common share at the end of 2018.

See Appendix I for solutions.

Limitations of Financial Analysis

Although financial analysis of a company's statements can be beneficial, there are several instances where the comparison will not be entirely accurate, or the information provided may not be useful.

For example, when comparing results between companies, different accounting policies can alter the values and make a comparison more difficult. Different accounting policies could include how inventory is valued (specific identification, FIFO, LIFO or weighted average), and how property, plant and equipment is depreciated (straight-line, declining-balance, double-declining-balance or units-of-production). Also, US corporations following US GAAP may find it difficult to compare with international competitors that follow IFRS.

To work around this challenge, accountants may adjust the stated values in the financial statements *for comparison purposes only*. The statements are not re-issued; this is simply an internal process for ratio comparison. By changing the account values based on similar accounting policies, a more accurate comparison can be made.

A second limitation arises from how IFRS presents certain information. Comprehensive income is not usually included in profitability or other ratios. In most cases, using net income instead of comprehensive income will not cause any significant change in the ratios presented. For example, a change in the profitability ratio from 6.3% to 6.6% due to including comprehensive income will not affect decision makers. However, if comprehensive income makes up a large portion of the income reported by a company, the company may wish to include comprehensive income in the ratio calculations so the relevant information is available to users.

Lastly, the economy and other external factors can affect how ratios are interpreted. For example, if a company is affected by a recession and reports a net loss for the year, comparing the current year to previous years really does not provide much useful information. A net loss can also cause other ratios to lose their meanings. For example, a company may have a negative price earnings ratio and a negative dividend yield, but that information alone does not mean much.

When a company experiences a loss, in which case some ratios and analyses are not productive, it may be more beneficial to examine what caused the loss. If the loss is due to an economic downturn, is the company able to survive the loss and is it positioned to bounce back once the economy recovers? If the loss is due to selling off a portion of the company and restructuring, does the company have a sound plan in place to maximize remaining resources to begin generating a profit again? Financial statement analysis can begin to provide a better understanding of a company's financial position and performance. Still, it is just a starting point in the decision-making process, and does not eliminate or replace the need for sound expert judgment.

In Summary

LO 1 Explain the importance of analyzing financial statements

▶ There are different ways to analyze a company's financial statements, such as horizontal analysis, vertical analysis and financial ratio analysis.

▶ Internal users, such as managers and executives, analyze financial information to correct negative results and take advantage of positive results.

▶ External users, such as investors and suppliers, analyze financial information to determine whether to invest money or extend credit terms.

LO 2 Conduct a horizontal and vertical analysis of financial statements

▶ The comparative balance sheet is used to perform a horizontal analysis because it compares information from one accounting period to another.

▶ One way of conducting a horizontal analysis is by calculating the succeeding years' balance sheet items as a percentage of the base year's number. Another way is by calculating the percentage change from a base year to show the percentage increase or decrease of each balance sheet item over time.

▶ A vertical analysis is conducted by converting each separate line item in a financial statement into a percentage of the base figure within the specific year.

LO 3 Calculate and apply liquidity ratios

▶ A company's liquidity can be assessed using working capital, current ratio and quick ratio.

▶ Working capital measures a company's ability to cover current liabilities using current assets.

▶ Current ratio assesses business liquidity by determining the extent to which current assets can cover current debts.

▶ Quick ratio assesses the ability of the business to meet its short-term debt obligations using only highly liquid assets.

LO 4 Calculate and apply profitability ratios

▶ A company's profitability can be assessed using gross profit margin, net profit margin, return on equity, return on common stockholders' equity, return on assets and asset turnover.

▶ Gross profit margin measures the percentage of sales revenue left after deducting cost of goods sold.

▶ Net profit margin assesses a company's profitability after deducting all expenses.

▶ Return on equity is a measure of what the stockholders are getting out of their investment in the company.

▶ Return on common stockholders' equity is a measure of the profitability of stockholders' investments.

▸ Return on assets measures every dollar of net income earned against each dollar's worth of assets.

▸ Asset turnover is a measure of a company's ability to generate sales revenue from asset investments.

LO 5 Calculate and apply operations management and solvency ratios

▸ A company's operations management can be assessed using inventory turnover, days' sales in inventory, days' sales oustanding and accounts receivable turnover.

▸ Inventory turnover measures the efficiency of inventory management.

▸ Days' sales in inventory measures the average number of days a company turns over inventory during the year.

▸ Days' sales outstanding measures the average number of days a company takes to collect accounts receivable.

▸ Accounts receivable turnover measures the efficiency of accounts receivable collections.

▸ A company's solvency can be assessed using debt-to-equity ratio, times-interest-earned and debt-to-total-assets ratio.

▸ Debt-to-equity measures the relative amount of debt versus stockholders' equity being used to finance a company's assets.

▸ Times-interest-earned measures a company's ability to cover interest on its debt.

▸ Debt-to-total-assets measures the amount of debt being financed by creditors.

LO 6 Calculate and apply capital market ratios

▸ Public corporations can be analyzed to determine if they are desirable as investments.

▸ Book value per common share measures the theoretical value of a share based on stockholders' claims to a company's assets.

▸ Dividend yield measures the rate of return to common stockholders.

▸ Earnings per share measures profit earned by investors per share of common stock.

▸ Price-earnings ratio measures the market value of a share of common stock related to its earnings.

LO 7 Identify the limitations of financial statement analysis

▸ Ratio analysis may not present an accurate picture if the companies being compared use different accounting policies, or if one follows US GAAP while another follows IFRS.

▸ Under IFRS, comprehensive income is usually not included in ratio analysis. Comprehensive income may need to be included if the amount is significant.

▸ Economic situations, or losses, can cause some ratios to lose their meaning. A closer look at the cause of a loss may be beneficial in addition to ratio analysis.

AMEENGAGE *Access **ameengage.com** for integrated resources including tutorials, practice exercises, the digital textbook and more.*

Review Exercise 20-1

Basil's Bakery has provided you with the following financial statements.

Basil's Bakery Balance Sheet As at December 31		
	2018	**2017**
Assets		
Current Assets		
Cash	$1,605	$987
Accounts Receivable	1,175	573
Inventory	396	256
Other Current Assets	301	103
Total Current Assets	3,477	1,919
Property, Plant and Equipment	2,034	1,170
Total Assets	$5,511	$3,089
Liabilities		
Current Liabilities	$1,474	$547
Long-Term Liabilities	104	58
Total Liabilities	1,578	605
Stockholders' Equity	3,933	2,484
Total Liabilities and Equity	$5,511	$3,089

*Note: The numbers in this financial statement are expressed in thousands of dollars.

Basil's Bakery Income Statement For the Year Ended December 31, 2018	
Sales Revenue	$6,009
Cost of Goods Sold	2,928
Gross Profit	3,081
Operating Expenses	
Depreciation	108
Interest Expense	518
Other Operating Expenses	723
Total Operating Expenses	1,349
Income from Operations	1,732
Investment Income	79
Operating Income before Tax	1,811
Income Tax	516
Net Income	$1,295

*Note: The numbers in this financial statement are expressed in thousands of dollars.

Assume all sales are credit sales.

In addition to the financial statements, the following data is known. Basil's Bakery does not have preferred stock. The bakery industry average for gross profit margin is 49.47% for 2018, and the industry average for net profit margin is 20.36% for the same time period.

In 2017, Basil's Bakery had a gross profit margin of 52.13% and a net profit margin of 21.95%.

Required

a) Perform a horizontal and vertical analysis of Basil's Bakery.

Basil's Bakery Percentage Change and Vertical Analysis As at December 31				
	2018	2017	% Change	% of Base Figure 2018
Cash	$1,605	$987		
Accounts Receivable	1,175	573		
Merchandise Inventory	396	256		
Other Current Assets	301	103		
Total Current Assets	3,477	1,919		
Property, Plant and Equipment	2,034	1,170		
Total Assets	$5,511	$3,089		
Current Liabilities	$1,474	$547		
Long-Term Liabilities	104	58		
Total Liabilities	1,578	605		
Stockholders' Equity	3,933	2,484		
Total Liabilities and Equity	$5,511	$3,089		

b) Calculate the financial ratios and figures for 2018.

Financial Ratio or Figure	Calculation	Result
Working Capital		
Current Ratio		
Quick Ratio		
Gross Profit Margin		
Net Profit Margin		
Return on Equity		
Return on Common Stockholders' Equity		

Financial Ratio or Figure	Calculation	Result
Return on Assets		
Asset Turnover		
Inventory Turnover Ratio		
Days' Sales in Inventory		
Days' Sales Outstanding		
Accounts Receivable Turnover		
Debt-to-Equity Ratio		
Times-Interest-Earned		
Debt-to-Total-Assets		

c) For each ratio, comment on the result. In your explanation, state whether or not the result is favorable for the company and include your reasons.

_____

_____

_____

_____

_____

_____

_____

_____

_____

_____

See Appendix I for solutions.

Appendix I

CHAPTER 1 SOLUTIONS

Pause & Reflect Exercise 1-1

a), b) and c)

	Assets	=	Liabilities	+	Net Worth
Beginning Balances	$1,500	=	$300	+	$1,200
1. Paid $100 toward credit card balance	−100		−100		
2. Paid $25 for a meal using cash	−25				−25
3. Deposited $300 in wages	+300			+	+300
Ending Balances	$1,675	=	$200	+	$1,475

d) Closing Balance of Cash = $200 − $100 − $25 + $300 = $375

Review Exercise 1-1

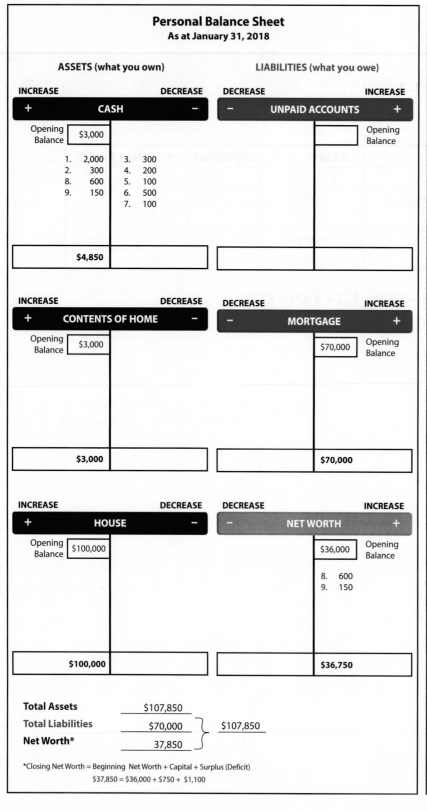

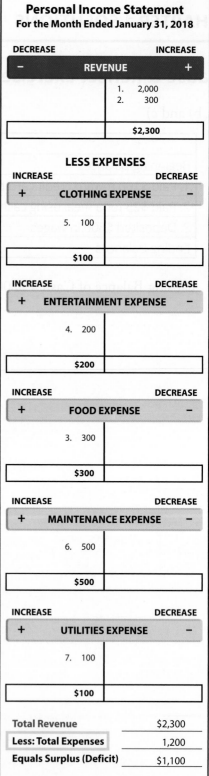

Personal Balance Sheet
As at January 31, 2018

ASSETS (what you own)

INCREASE — CASH — DECREASE (+ / −)

Opening Balance	$3,000		
1.	2,000	3.	300
2.	300	4.	200
8.	600	5.	100
9.	150	6.	500
		7.	100

$4,850	

INCREASE — CONTENTS OF HOME — DECREASE (+ / −)

Opening Balance	$3,000	

$3,000	

INCREASE — HOUSE — DECREASE (+ / −)

Opening Balance	$100,000	

$100,000	

LIABILITIES (what you owe)

DECREASE — UNPAID ACCOUNTS — INCREASE (− / +)

	Opening Balance

DECREASE — MORTGAGE — INCREASE (− / +)

	$70,000	Opening Balance

	$70,000

DECREASE — NET WORTH — INCREASE (− / +)

	$36,000	Opening Balance
	8.	600
	9.	150

	$36,750

Total Assets	$107,850	
Total Liabilities	$70,000	} $107,850
Net Worth*	37,850	

*Closing Net Worth = Beginning Net Worth + Capital + Surplus (Deficit)
$37,850 = $36,000 + $750 + $1,100

Personal Income Statement
For the Month Ended January 31, 2018

DECREASE — REVENUE — INCREASE (− / +)

1.	2,000
2.	300

$2,300	

LESS EXPENSES

INCREASE — CLOTHING EXPENSE — DECREASE (+ / −)

5.	100

$100	

INCREASE — ENTERTAINMENT EXPENSE — DECREASE (+ / −)

4.	200

$200	

INCREASE — FOOD EXPENSE — DECREASE (+ / −)

3.	300

$300	

INCREASE — MAINTENANCE EXPENSE — DECREASE (+ / −)

6.	500

$500	

INCREASE — UTILITIES EXPENSE — DECREASE (+ / −)

7.	100

$100	

Total Revenue	$2,300
Less: Total Expenses	1,200
Equals Surplus (Deficit)	$1,100

CHAPTER 2 SOLUTIONS

Pause & Reflect Exercise 2-1

	Name of the Account Affected	Category of Account	Increase or Decrease
2.	Cash	Asset	Increase
	Service Revenue	Revenue	Increase
3.	Cash	Asset	Increase
	Unearned Revenue	Liability	Increase

Pause & Reflect Exercise 2-2

	Name of the Account Affected	Category of Account	Increase or Decrease
2.	Telephone Expense	Expense	Increase
	Accounts Payable	Liability	Increase
3.	Prepaid Insurance	Asset	Increase
	Cash	Asset	Decrease

Pause & Reflect Exercise 2-3

	Name of the Account Affected	Category of Account	Increase or Decrease
2.	Cash	Asset	Increase
	Graham, Capital	Owner's Capital	Increase
3.	Furniture (Property, Plant and Equipment)	Asset	Increase
	Accounts Payable	Liability	Increase
4.	Cash	Asset	Increase
	Notes Payable	Liability	Increase
5.	Graham, Withdrawals	Owner's Withdrawal	Increase
	Cash	Asset	Decrease

Review Exercise 2-1

a)

Style House
Balance Sheet
As at January 31, 2018

ASSETS (what you own)

INCREASE				DECREASE
+		**CASH**		**–**

Opening Balance	$3,000		2.	8,000
			3.	333
1.	12,000		4.	50
6.	8,000		5.	600
14.	100		7.	4,000
			10.	2,000
			11.	1,000
			12.	3,000

$4,117

INCREASE		DECREASE
+	**ACCOUNTS RECEIVABLE**	**–**

Opening Balance	
13.	400

$400

INCREASE		DECREASE
+	**PREPAID MAINTENANCE**	**–**

Opening Balance	
5.	600

$600

INCREASE		DECREASE
+	**EQUIPMENT**	**–**

Opening Balance	$12,000
2.	8,000

$20,000

LIABILITIES (what you owe)

DECREASE			INCREASE
–	**ACCOUNTS PAYBLE**		**+**

		$5,000	Opening Balance
11.	1,000	8.	250
		9.	800

	$5,050

DECREASE		INCREASE
–	**UNEARNED REVENUE**	**+**

	Opening Balance
	14.	100

$100

DECREASE			INCREASE
–	**NOTES PAYABLE**		**+**

			Opening Balance
3.	333	1.	12,000

	$11,667

DECREASE		INCREASE
–	**JONES, CAPITAL**	**+**

	$10,000	Opening Balance

	$10,000

DECREASE		INCREASE
–	**JONES, WITHDRAWALS**	**+**

12.	3,000

$3,000

Total Assets	$25,117	
Total Liabilities	16,817	} $25,117
Owner's Equity*	8,300	

*Ending Owner's Equity Balance = Begining Owner's Equity Balance + Owner's Contributions + Net Income (Loss) - Owner's Withdrawals

$8,300 = $10,000 + $0 + $1,300 - $3,000

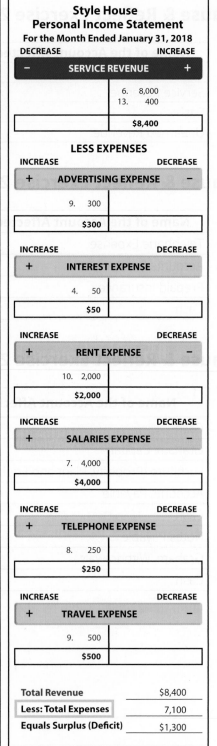

Style House
Personal Income Statement
For the Month Ended January 31, 2018

DECREASE			INCREASE
–	**SERVICE REVENUE**		**+**

	6.	8,000
	13.	400

$8,400

LESS EXPENSES

INCREASE		DECREASE
+	**ADVERTISING EXPENSE**	**–**

9.	300

$300

INCREASE		DECREASE
+	**INTEREST EXPENSE**	**–**

4.	50

$50

INCREASE		DECREASE
+	**RENT EXPENSE**	**–**

10.	2,000

$2,000

INCREASE		DECREASE
+	**SALARIES EXPENSE**	**–**

7.	4,000

$4,000

INCREASE		DECREASE
+	**TELEPHONE EXPENSE**	**–**

8.	250

$250

INCREASE		DECREASE
+	**TRAVEL EXPENSE**	**–**

9.	500

$500

Total Revenue	$8,400
Less: Total Expenses	7,100
Equals Surplus (Deficit)	$1,300

b)

Style House Income Statement For the Month Ended March 31, 2018		
Revenue		
Service Revenue		$8,400
Expenses		
Advertising Expense	$300	
Interest Expense	50	
Rent Expense	2,000	
Salaries Expense	4,000	
Telephone Expense	250	
Travel Expense	500	
Total Expenses		7,100
Net Income		$1,300

c)

Style House Statement of Owner's Equity For the Month Ended March 31, 2018	
Jones, Capital, March 1, 2018	$10,000
Add: Net Income	1,300
Less: Withdrawals	3,000
Jones, Capital, March 31, 2018	$8,300

d)

Style House Balance Sheet As at March 31, 2018			
Assets		**Liabilities**	
Cash	$4,117	Accounts Payable	$5,050
Accounts Receivable	400	Unearned Revenue	100
Prepaid Maintenance	600	Notes Payable	11,667
Equipment	20,000	**Total Liabilities**	16,817
		Owner's Equity	
		Jones, Capital	8,300
Total Assets	$25,117	**Total Liabilities and Owner's Equity**	$25,117

e)

Transaction	Cash Flow Section
Borrowed $12,000 from the bank	Financing
Purchased chairs and dryers with $8,000 cash	Investing
Paid $333 cash toward the principal of the bank loan	Financing
Paid $50 cash for interest on the bank loan	Operating
Prepaid $600 cash for a six-month maintenance contract	Operating
Provided services to customers and received $8,000	Operating
Paid $4,000 cash to employees for salaries	Operating
Paid monthly rent with $2,000 cash	Operating
Paid $1,000 owing to a supplier	Operating
Miranda withdrew $3,000 cash from the business	Financing

CHAPTER 3 SOLUTIONS

Pause and Reflect Exercise 3-1

	Description	Terminology	Characteristic, Assumption, Principle or Constraint
2.	A company is believed to stay in business for the foreseeable future and not go bankrupt any time soon.	Going concern	Assumption
3.	Revenue must be recorded or recognized when goods are sold or when services are performed.	Revenue recognition	Principle
4.	The financial statements of a company must be prepared in a similar way year after year.	Comparability	Characteristic
5.	Information is free from significant error and bias.	Reliability	Characteristic
6.	The value of reported financial information outweighs the costs incurred to report it.	Cost constraint	Constraint
7.	An expense must be recorded in the same accounting period in which it was used to produce revenue.	Expense recognition	Principle
8.	Accounting records are expressed in a single currency, such as US dollars.	Monetary unit	Assumption

Review Exercise 3-1

a) HRI has failed to apply three qualitative characteristics.

Relevance

- A particular piece of information is relevant if its omission may cause the users of the financial information to make decisions differently. In the financial statements, the company did not disclose that two different currencies were used in the comparative balance sheet (one for 2018 and another for 2017). This omission can potentially affect users' (investors') decisions.

- A component of relevance is timeliness. HRI only prepares financial statements on an annual basis. However, the company's hundreds of stockholders would benefit from more timely financial statements (e.g. quarterly or monthly).

Reliability

- A component of reliability is verifiability. Since several invoices did not match the cost amounts listed in HRI's accounting records, the reported costs are not verifiable. Therefore, the amount of total expenses in the company's income statement is not a reliable number.

Comparability

- Even though the company provided balance sheet amounts from the previous year, two different currencies are used from one year to the next. Because one currency is stronger than the other, it is not straightforward to compare the financial information of HRI through time.

b) HRI has violated the following assumptions and principles.

The Business Entity Assumption

- The HRI cash account includes the personal savings of some of the stockholders. This indicates that the accounting for the business was not kept separate from the personal affairs of the owners.

The Monetary Unit Assumption

- HRI has included values in two different currencies on its financial statements.

Measurement

- Except in rare cases, which will be discussed in later chapters, assets must be recorded at their historical cost. However, HRI has valued its purchases at fair market value.

Disclosure

- HRI did not disclose the justification for changing the depreciation method.

- HRI did not disclose the information related to changing the location of the headquarters and the inconsistent measures of currency.

The Going Concern Assumption *(requires critical thinking)*

- There is evidence that the company may not exist and operate in the foreseeable future.

  o HRI has experienced a significant net loss for each of the past three years (even before adjusting for the unverified expense amounts).
  o The cash and merchandise inventory balances are extremely low in 2018.

- o The company's property, plant and equipment balance in 2018 declined significantly from 2017 (even after adjusting for exchange rates). It is possible some of these assets were sold during 2018.
- o The above examples of HRI's poor financial performance occurred during a time when the economy was booming. HRI's performance is normally aligned with the state of economy. This discrepancy should cause stockholders to question the going concern assumption with respect to HRI.

CHAPTER 4 SOLUTIONS

Pause & Reflect Exercise 4-1

	Name of the Account Affected	Category	Increase or Decrease	Debit or Credit
1.	Cash	Asset	Increase	Debit
	Lee, Capital	Owner's Capital	Increase	Credit
2.	Cash	Asset	Increase	Debit
	Service Revenue	Revenue	Increase	Credit
3.	Furniture (Property, Plant and Equipment)	Asset	Increase	Debit
	Accounts Payable	Liability	Increase	Credit
4.	Accounts Receivable	Asset	Increase	Debit
	Service Revenue	Revenue	Increase	Credit
5.	Advertising Expense	Expense	Increase	Debit
	Cash	Asset	Decrease	Credit
6.	Prepaid Rent	Asset	Increase	Debit
	Cash	Asset	Decrease	Credit

Pause & Reflect Exercise 4-2

JOURNAL				Page 1
Date	Account Title and Explanation	PR	Debit	Credit
2018				
Apr 18	Cash		600	
	Accounts Receivable		400	
	Service Revenue			1,000
	Completed work for client			

Pause & Reflect Exercise 4-3

JOURNAL					Page 2
Date	Account Title and Explanation	PR	Debit	Credit	
2018					
Sep 28	Cash		5,000		
	Interest Expense			5,000	
	To reverse incorrect entry				
Sep 28	Notes Payable		5,000		
	Cash			5,000	
	To correctly record bank loan principal repayment				

Review Exercise 4-1

a)

JOURNAL					Page 1
Date	Account Titles and Explanation	PR	Debit	Credit	
2018					
Jun 1	Rent Expense	540	900		
	Cash	101		900	
	Paid cash for month's rent				
Jun 3	Prepaid Insurance	110	1,200		
	Cash	101		1,200	
	Prepaid a one-year insurance policy				
Jun 6	Cash	101	2,100		
	Service Revenue	400		2,100	
	Received cash for services				
Jun 11	Advertising Expense	500	450		
	Accounts Payable	200		450	
	Received invoice for advertising				
Jun 13	Cash	101	3,000		
	Gordon, Capital	300		3,000	
	Owner invested cash in business				
Jun 16	Cash	101	300		
	Unearned Revenue	210		300	
	Received deposit from customer				

JOURNAL — **Page 1**

Date	Account Titles and Explanation	PR	Debit	Credit
Jun 18	Accounts Receivable	105	1,500	
	Service Revenue	400		1,500
	Provided services on account			
Jun 23	Notes Payable	215	950	
	Cash	101		950
	Paid notes payable principal			
Jun 30	Gordon, Withdrawals	310	1,000	
	Cash	101		1,000
	Owner withdrawal for personal use			

b)

GENERAL LEDGER

Account: Cash — **GL No: 101**

Date	Description	PR	DR	CR	Balance	
2018						
Jun 1	Opening Balance				4,200	DR
Jun 1		J1		900	3,300	DR
Jun 3		J1		1,200	2,100	DR
Jun 6		J1	2,100		4,200	DR
Jun 13		J1	3,000		7,200	DR
Jun 16		J1	300		7,500	DR
Jun 23		J1		950	6,550	DR
Jun 30		J1		1,000	5,550	DR

Account: Accounts Receivable — **GL No: 105**

Date	Description	PR	DR	CR	Balance	
2018						
Jun 1	Opening Balance				3,100	DR
Jun 18		J1	1,500		4,600	DR

Account: Prepaid Insurance — **GL No: 110**

Date	Description	PR	DR	CR	Balance	
2018						
Jun 1	Opening Balance				0	DR
Jun 3		J1	1,200		1,200	DR

Account: Equipment — **GL No: 120**

Date	Description	PR	DR	CR	Balance	
2018						
Jun 1	Opening Balance				6,000	DR

Account: Accounts Payable — GL No: 200

Date	Description	PR	DR	CR	Balance	
2018						
Jun 1	Opening Balance				2,300	CR
Jun 11		J1		450	2,750	CR

Account: Unearned Revenue — GL No: 210

Date	Description	PR	DR	CR	Balance	
2018						
Jun 1	Opening Balance				600	CR
Jun 16		J1		300	900	CR

Account: Notes Payable — GL No: 215

Date	Description	PR	DR	CR	Balance	
2018						
Jun 1	Opening Balance				4,000	CR
Jun 23		J1	950		3,050	CR

Account: Gordon, Capital — GL No: 300

Date	Description	PR	DR	CR	Balance	
2018						
Jun 1	Opening Balance				6,400	CR
Jun 13		J1		3,000	9,400	CR

Account: Gordon, Withdrawals — GL No: 310

Date	Description	PR	DR	CR	Balance	
2018						
Jun 30		J1	1,000		1,000	DR

Account: Service Revenue — GL No: 400

Date	Description	PR	DR	CR	Balance	
2018						
Jun 6		J1		2,100	2,100	CR
Jun 18		J1		1,500	3,600	CR

Account: Advertising Expense — GL No: 500

Date	Description	PR	DR	CR	Balance	
2018						
Jun 11		J1	450		450	DR

Account: Rent Expense — GL No: 540

Date	Description	PR	DR	CR	Balance	
2018						
Jun 1		J1	900		900	DR

c)

CG Accounting		
Trial Balance		
June 30, 2018		
Account Title	**DR**	**CR**
Cash	$5,550	
Accounts Receivable	4,600	
Prepaid Insurance	1,200	
Equipment	6,000	
Accounts Payable		$2,750
Unearned Revenue		900
Notes Payable		3,050
Gordon, Capital		9,400
Gordon, Withdrawals	1,000	
Service Revenue		3,600
Advertising Expense	450	
Rent Expense	900	
Total	**$19,700**	**$19,700**

Review Exercise 4-2

JOURNAL				Page 2
Date	**Account Title and Explanation**	**PR**	**Debit**	**Credit**
2018				
Jun 28	Cash		400	
	Automobile			400
	To reverse incorrect entry			
Jun 28	Maintenance Expense		400	
	Cash			400
	To correctly pay for automobile maintenance			
Jun 28	Cash		200	
	Equipment			200
	To reverse incorrect entry			
Jun 28	Office Supplies		200	
	Cash			200
	To correctly pay for office supplies			

CHAPTER 5 SOLUTIONS

Pause & Reflect Exercise 5-1

JOURNAL				Page 2
Date	Account Title and Explanation	PR	Debit	Credit
2018				
Dec 31	Accounts Receivable		480	
	Service Revenue			480
	To accrue revenue on contract			
	(8 days × $60 per day)			
2019				
Jan 2	Cash		600	
	Accounts Receivable			480
	Service Revenue			120
	To record collection from client			

Pause & Reflect Exercise 5-2

JOURNAL				Page 1
Date	Account Title and Explanation	PR	Debit	Credit
2018				
Jan 31	Salaries Expense		330	
	Salaries Payable			330
	To accrue salaries owing			
	(3 days × $110 per day)			
Jan 31	Interest Expense		40	
	Interest Payable			40
	To accrue interest owing			
	($8,000 × 6% × 1/12)			

Pause & Reflect Exercise 5-3

Armadillo Property Management's Journal Entries

JOURNAL				Page 1
Date	Account Title and Explanation	PR	Debit	Credit
2018				
Aug 1	Cash		36,000	
	Unearned Revenue			36,000
	Receive cash for 12 months' rent			
Dec 31	Unearned Revenue		15,000	
	Rent Revenue			15,000
	To adjust for 5 months rent earned			
	($3,000 per month × 5 months)			

Beaver Company's Journal Entries

JOURNAL				Page 1
Date	Account Title and Explanation	PR	Debit	Credit
2018				
Aug 1	Prepaid Rent		36,000	
	Cash			36,000
	Pay cash for 12 months rent			
Dec 31	Rent Expense		15,000	
	Prepaid Rent			15,000
	To adjust for 5 months rent used			

Pause & Reflect Exercise 5-4

JOURNAL				Page 2
Date	Account Title and Explanation	PR	Debit	Credit
2018				
Dec 31	Depreciation Expense		2,000	
	Accumulated Depreciation—Equipment			2,000
	To adjust for depreciation			
	[($20,000 − $4,000) ÷ 8 years]			

Review Exercise 5-1

a)

CG Accounting Spreadsheet June 30, 2018						
	Unadjusted Trial Balance		Adjustments		Adjusted Trial Balance	
Account Titles	DR	CR	DR	CR	DR	CR
Cash	$5,550				$5,550	
Accounts Receivable	4,600		$900		5,500	
Prepaid Insurance	1,200			$100	1,100	
Equipment	6,000				6,000	
Accumulated Depreciation—Equipment		$0		100		$100
Accounts Payable		2,750				2,750
Interest Payable		0		25		25
Unearned Revenue		900	450			450
Notes Payable		3,050				3,050
Gordon, Capital		9,400				9,400
Gordon, Withdrawals	1,000				1,000	
Service Revenue		3,600		1,350		4,950
Advertising Expense	450				450	
Depreciation Expense	0		100		100	
Insurance Expense	0		100		100	
Interest Expense	0		25		25	
Rent Expense	900				900	
Total	$19,700	$19,700	$1,575	$1,575	$20,725	$20,725

b)

JOURNAL				Page 2
Date	**Account Title and Explanation**	**PR**	**Debit**	**Credit**
2018				
Jun 30	Insurance Expense	515	100	
	Prepaid Insurance	110		100
	Recognized one month of insurance used			
Jun 30	Unearned Revenue	210	450	
	Service Revenue	400		450
	Recognized revenue previously unearned			
Jun 30	Interest Expense	520	25	
	Interest Payable	205		25
	Accrued interest on notes payable			
Jun 30	Depreciation Expense	510	100	
	Accumulated Depreciation—Equipment	125		100
	Recorded depreciation of equipment			
Jun 30	Accounts Receivable	105	900	
	Service Revenue	400		900
	Record accrued revenue			

GENERAL LEDGER

Account: Cash					GL No:	101
Date	**Description**	**PR**	**DR**	**CR**	**Balance**	
2018						
Jun 1	Opening Balance				4,200	DR
Jun 1		J1		900	3,300	DR
Jun 3		J1		1,200	2,100	DR
Jun 6		J1	2,100		4,200	DR
Jun 13		J1	3,000		7,200	DR
Jun 16		J1	300		7,500	DR
Jun 23		J1		950	6,550	DR
Jun 30		J1		1,000	5,550	DR

Account: Accounts Receivable					GL No:	105
Date	Description	PR	DR	CR	Balance	
2018						
Jun 1	Opening Balance				3,100	DR
Jun 18		J1	1,500		4,600	DR
Jun 30	Adjusting Entry	J2	900		5,500	DR

Account: Prepaid Insurance					GL No:	110
Date	Description	PR	DR	CR	Balance	
2018						
Jun 1	Opening Balance				0	DR
Jun 3		J1	1,200		1,200	DR
Jun 30	Adjusting Entry	J2		100	1,100	DR

Account: Equipment					GL No:	120
Date	Description	PR	DR	CR	Balance	
2018						
Jun 1	Opening Balance				6,000	DR

Account: Accumulated Depreciation—Equipment					GL No:	125
Date	Description	PR	DR	CR	Balance	
2018						
Jun 30	Adjusting Entry	J2		100	100	CR

Account: Accounts Payable					GL No:	200
Date	Description	PR	DR	CR	Balance	
2018						
Jun 1	Opening Balance				2,300	CR
Jun 11		J1		450	2,750	CR

Account: Interest Payable					GL No:	205
Date	Description	PR	DR	CR	Balance	
2018						
Jun 30	Adjusting Entry	J2		25	25	CR

Account: Unearned Revenue					GL No:	210
Date	Description	PR	DR	CR	Balance	
2018						
Jun 1	Opening Balance				600	CR
Jun 16		J1		300	900	CR
Jun 30	Adjusting Entry	J2	450		450	CR

Account: Notes Payable					GL No:	215
Date	**Description**	**PR**	**DR**	**CR**	**Balance**	
2018						
Jun 1	Opening Balance				4,000	CR
Jun 23		J1	950		3,050	CR

Account: Gordon, Capital					GL No:	300
Date	**Description**	**PR**	**DR**	**CR**	**Balance**	
2018						
Jun 1	Opening Balance				6,400	CR
Jun 13		J1		3,000	9,400	CR

Account: Gordon, Withdrawals					GL No:	310
Date	**Description**	**PR**	**DR**	**CR**	**Balance**	
2018						
Jun 30		J1	1,000		1,000	DR

Account: Service Revenue					GL No:	400
Date	**Description**	**PR**	**DR**	**CR**	**Balance**	
2018						
Jun 6		J1		2,100	2,100	CR
Jun 18		J1		1,500	3,600	CR
Jun 30	Adjusting Entry	J2		450	4,050	CR
Jun 30	Adjusting Enry	J2		900	4,950	CR

Account: Advertising Expense					GL No:	500
Date	**Description**	**PR**	**DR**	**CR**	**Balance**	
2018						
Jun 11		J1	450		450	DR

Account: Depreciation Expense					GL No:	510
Date	**Description**	**PR**	**DR**	**CR**	**Balance**	
2018						
Jun 30	Adjusting Entry	J2	100		100	DR

Account: Insurance Expense					GL No:	515
Date	**Description**	**PR**	**DR**	**CR**	**Balance**	
2018						
Jun 30	Adjusting Entry	J2	100		100	DR

Account: Interest Expense					GL No:	520	
Date	Description	PR	DR	CR	Balance	
2018						
Jun 30	Adjusting Entry	J2	25		25	DR

Account: Rent Expense					GL No:	540	
Date	Description	PR	DR	CR	Balance	
2018						
Jun 1		J1	900		900	DR

CHAPTER 6 SOLUTIONS

Pause & Reflect Exercise 6-1

JOURNAL				Page 5
Date	Account Title and Explanation	PR	Debit	Credit
2018				
Aug 31	Service Revenue		9,400	
	Income Summary			9,400
	Close revenue accounts			
Aug 31	Income Summary		4,990	
	Depreciation Expense			290
	Insurance Expense			260
	Interest Expense			70
	Rent Expense			1,870
	Salaries Expense			2,250
	Telephone Expense			250
	Close expense accounts			
Aug 31	Income Summary		4,410	
	ZooTak, Capital			4,410
	Close income summary account			
Aug 31	ZooTak, Capital		3,050	
	ZooTak, Withdrawals			3,050
	Close owner's withdrawals			

Pause & Reflect Exercise 6-2

Working Capital	($120,000 + $90,000 + $65,000) – ($101,000 + $80,000) = $94,000
Current Ratio	($120,000 + $90,000 + $65,000) ÷ ($101,000 + $80,000) = 1.52
Quick Ratio	($120,000 + $90,000) ÷ ($101,000 + $80,000) = 1.16

Pause & Reflect Exercise 6-3

a) Both systems have special sections or journals to enter similar types of transactions. They both have a general journal for adjusting entries and other specific types of transactions. Some differences are that entries for computerized accounting systems do not have to be entered in chronological order.

b) One benefit of a computerized accounting system is that it automatically orders transactions chronologically, so they can be entered in any order. Another benefit is posting to the general ledger, preparing reports, and preparing journal entries are all done automatically.

Review Exercise 6-1

a)

CG Accounting Income Statement For the Month Ended June 30, 2018		
Service Revenue		$4,950
Expenses		
Advertising Expense	$450	
Depreciation Expense	100	
Insurance Expense	100	
Interest Expense	25	
Rent Expense	900	
Total Expenses		1,575
Net Income (Loss)		$3,375

CG Accounting Statement of Owner's Equity For the Month Ended June 30, 2018		
Gordon, Capital at June 1		$6,400
Add:		
Additional Investment	$3,000	
Net Income	3,375	6,375
Subtotal		12,775
Less:		
Gordon, Withdrawals		1,000
Gordon, Capital at June 30		$11,775

CG Accounting Classified Balance Sheet As at June 30, 2018		
Assets		
Current Assets		
Cash	$5,550	
Accounts Receivable	5,500	
Prepaid Insurance	1,100	
Total Current Assets		$12,150
Property, Plant & Equipment		
Equipment	6,000	
Accumulated Depreciation	(100)	
Total Property, Plant & Equipment		5,900
Total Assets		$18,050
Liabilities		
Current Liabilities		
Accounts Payable	$2,750	
Interest Payable	25	
Unearned Revenue	450	
Notes Payable, Current Portion	800	
Total Current Liabilities		$4,025
Long-Term Liabilities		
Notes Payable, Long-Term Portion	2,250	
Total Long-Term Liabilities		2,250
Total Liabilities		6,275
Owner's Equity		
Gordon, Capital		11,775
Total Owner's Equity		11,775
Total Liabilities and Owner's Equity		$18,050

b)

JOURNAL				Page 3
Date	Account Title and Explanation	PR	Debit	Credit
2018				
Jun 30	Service Revenue	400	4,950	
	Income Summary	315		4,950
	Close revenue to income summary			
Jun 30	Income Summary	315	1,575	
	Advertising Expense	500		450
	Depreciation Expense	510		100
	Insurance Expense	515		100
	Interest Expense	520		25
	Rent Expense	540		900
	Close expenses to income summary			
Jun 30	Income Summary	315	3,375	
	Gordon, Capital	300		3,375
	Close income summary to capital			
Jun 30	Gordon, Capital	300	1,000	
	Gordon, Withdrawals	310		1,000
	Close owner withdrawals to capital			

GENERAL LEDGER

Account: Cash					GL No: 101	
Date	Description	PR	DR	CR	Balance	
2018						
Jun 1	Opening Balance				4,200	DR
Jun 1		J1		900	3,300	DR
Jun 3		J1		1,200	2,100	DR
Jun 6		J1	2,100		4,200	DR
Jun 13		J1	3,000		7,200	DR
Jun 16		J1	300		7,500	DR
Jun 23		J1		950	6,550	DR
Jun 30		J1		1,000	5,550	DR

Account: Accounts Receivable — GL No: 105

Date	Description	PR	DR	CR	Balance	
2018						
Jun 1	Opening Balance				3,100	DR
Jun 18		J1	1,500		4,600	DR
Jun 30	Adjusting Entry	J2	900		5,500	DR

Account: Prepaid Insurance — GL No: 110

Date	Description	PR	DR	CR	Balance	
2018						
Jun 1	Opening Balance				0	DR
Jun 3		J1	1,200		1,200	DR
Jun 30	Adjusting Entry	J2		100	1,100	DR

Account: Equipment — GL No: 120

Date	Description	PR	DR	CR	Balance	
2018						
Jun 1	Opening Balance				6,000	DR

Account: Accumulated Depreciation—Equipment — GL No: 125

Date	Description	PR	DR	CR	Balance	
2018						
Jun 30	Adjusting Entry	J2		100	100	CR

Account: Accounts Payable — GL No: 200

Date	Description	PR	DR	CR	Balance	
2018						
Jun 1	Opening Balance				2,300	CR
Jun 11		J1		450	2,750	CR

Account: Interest Payable — GL No: 205

Date	Description	PR	DR	CR	Balance	
2018						
Jun 30	Adjusting Entry	J2		25	25	CR

Account: Unearned Revenue — GL No: 210

Date	Description	PR	DR	CR	Balance	
2018						
Jun 1	Opening Balance				600	CR
Jun 16		J1		300	900	CR
Jun 30	Adjusting Entry	J2	450		450	CR

Account: Notes Payable   **GL No: 215**

Date	Description	PR	DR	CR	Balance	
2018						
Jun 1	Opening Balance				4,000	CR
Jun 23		J1	950		3,050	CR

Account: Gordon, Capital   **GL No: 300**

Date	Description	PR	DR	CR	Balance	
2018						
Jun 1	Opening Balance				6,400	CR
Jun 13		J1		3,000	9,400	CR
Jun 30	Closing Entry	J3		3,375	12,775	CR
Jun 30	Closing Entry	J3	1,000		11,775	CR

Account: Gordon, Withdrawals   **GL No: 310**

Date	Description	PR	DR	CR	Balance	
2018						
Jun 30		J1	1,000		1,000	DR
Jun 30	Closing Entry	J3		1,000	0	DR

Account: Income Summary   **GL No: 315**

Date	Description	PR	DR	CR	Balance	
2018						
Jun 30	Closing Entry	J3		4,950	4,950	CR
Jun 30	Closing Entry	J3	1,575		3,375	CR
Jun 30	Closing Entry	J3	3,375		0	CR

Account: Service Revenue   **GL No: 400**

Date	Description	PR	DR	CR	Balance	
2018						
Jun 6		J1		2,100	2,100	CR
Jun 18		J1		1,500	3,600	CR
Jun 30	Adjusting Entry	J2		450	4,050	CR
Jun 30	Adjusting Entry	J2		900	4,950	CR
Jun 30	Closing Entry	J3	4,950		0	CR

Account: Advertising Expense   **GL No: 500**

Date	Description	PR	DR	CR	Balance	
2018						
Jun 11		J1	450		450	DR
Jun 30	Closing Entry	J3		450	0	DR

Account: Depreciation Expense   GL No: 510

Date	Description	PR	DR	CR	Balance	
2018						
Jun 30	Adjusting Entry	J2	100		100	DR
Jun 30	Closing Entry	J3		100	0	DR

Account: Insurance Expense   GL No: 515

Date	Description	PR	DR	CR	Balance	
2018						
Jun 30	Adjusting Entry	J2	100		100	DR
Jun 30	Closing Entry	J3		100	0	DR

Account: Interest Expense   GL No: 520

Date	Description	PR	DR	CR	Balance	
2018						
Jun 30	Adjusting Entry	J2	25		25	DR
Jun 30	Closing Entry	J3		25	0	DR

Account: Rent Expense   GL No: 540

Date	Description	PR	DR	CR	Balance	
2018						
Jun 1		J1	900		900	DR
Jun 30	Closing Entry	J3		900	0	DR

c)

CG Accounting		
Post-Closing Trial Balance		
June 30, 2018		
Account Title	**DR**	**CR**
Cash	$5,550	
Accounts Receivable	5,500	
Prepaid Insurance	1,100	
Equipment	6,000	
Accumulated Depreciation—Equipment		$100
Accounts Payable		2,750
Interest Payable		25
Unearned Revenue		450
Notes Payable		3,050
Gordon, Capital		11,775
Total	**$18,150**	**$18,150**

Review Exercise 6A-1

CG Accounting Spreadsheet
June 30, 2018

Account Titles	Unadjusted Trial Balance DR	Unadjusted Trial Balance CR	Adjustments DR	Adjustments CR	Adjusted Trial Balance DR	Adjusted Trial Balance CR	Income Statement DR	Income Statement CR	Balance Sheet & Equity DR	Balance Sheet & Equity CR
Cash	$5,550				$5,550				$5,550	
Accounts Receivable	4,600		$900		5,500				5,500	
Prepaid Insurance	1,200			$100	1,100				1,100	
Equipment	6,000				6,000				6,000	
Accumulated Depreciation—Equipment		$0		100		$100				$100
Accounts Payable		2,750				2,750				2,750
Interest Payable		0		25		25				25
Unearned Revenue		900	450			450				450
Notes Payable		3,050				3,050				3,050
Gordon, Capital		9,400				9,400				9,400
Gordon, Withdrawals	1,000				1,000				1,000	
Service Revenue		3,600		1,350		4,950		$4,950		
Advertising Expense	450				450		$450			
Depreciation Expense	0		100		100		100			
Insurance Expense	0		100		100		100			
Interest Expense	0		25		25		25			
Rent Expense	900				900		900			
Total	$19,700	$19,700	$1,575	$1,575	$20,725	$20,725	1,575	4,950	19,150	15,775
Net Income (Loss)							3,375			3,375
Total							$4,950	$4,950	$19,150	$19,150

CHAPTER 7 SOLUTIONS

Pause & Reflect Exercise 7-1

Sales Revenue	$10,500	(300 clocks × $35)
COGS	$4,200	(300 clocks × $14)
Gross Profit	$6,300	($10,500 − $4,200)
Net Income	$1,300	($6,300 − $5,000)

Pause & Reflect Exercise 7-2

Caterpy Company

JOURNAL			
Date	**Account Title and Explanation**	**Debit**	**Credit**
2018			
May 10	Cash	5,000	
	Sales Revenue		5,000
	To record product sales		
May 10	Cost of Goods Sold	3,000	
	Merchandise Inventory		3,000
	Sold inventory to a customer		

Weezle Company

JOURNAL			
Date	**Account Title and Explanation**	**Debit**	**Credit**
2018			
May 10	Merchandise Inventory	5,130	
	Cash		5,130
	Purchased inventory and paid freight costs		

Pause & Reflect Exercise 7-3

a) Gross Profit Margin = ($400,000−$220,000)÷ $400,000 = 0.45 or 45%

b) To keep the same level of gross profit margin as in 2018, Cochran's 2019 gross profit will be $225,000 ($500,000 × 45%). This means that its COGS cannot exceed $275,000 ($500,000 net sales − $225,000 gross profit).

Pause & Reflect Exercise 7-4

JOURNAL			
Date	Account Title and Explanation	Debit	Credit
2018			
Dec 31	Cost of Goods Sold	3,000	
	Merchandise Inventory		3,000
	Adjust inventory to physical count		

Review Exercise 7-1

Part 1

a)

JOURNAL			
Date	Account Title and Explanation	Debit	Credit
2018			
Dec 3	Merchandise Inventory	50,000	
	Accounts Payable		50,000
	Purchased inventory on account		
Dec 6	Merchandise Inventory	200	
	Cash		200
	Paid freight charges		
Dec 8	Accounts Payable	2,000	
	Merchandise Inventory		2,000
	Purchase return		
Dec 11	Accounts Payable	48,000	
	Merchandise Inventory		960
	Cash		47,040
	Paid supplier and took discount		

b)

JOURNAL			
Date	Account Title and Explanation	Debit	Credit
2018			
Dec 3	Accounts Receivable	50,000	
	Sales Revenue		50,000
	Sold inventory on account		
Dec 3	Cost of Goods Sold	35,000	
	Merchandise Inventory		35,000
	Cost of goods sold for above sale		
Dec 6	Delivery Expense	200	
	Cash		200
	Paid freight charges		

JOURNAL			
Dec 8	Sales Returns & Allowances	2,000	
	Accounts Receivable		2,000
	Customer returned incorrect merchandise		
Dec 8	Merchandise Inventory	700	
	Cost of Goods Sold		700
	Inventory returned to stock		
Dec 11	Cash	47,040	
	Sales Discounts	960	
	Accounts Receivable		48,000
	Received payment from customer		

Part 2

a)

George's Gardening Supplies		
Income Statement		
For the Year Ended December 31, 2018		
Revenues		
Sales Revenue		$113,500
Less: Sales Returns & Allowances	$1,000	
Sales Discounts	1,580	(2,580)
Interest Revenue		6,500
Total Revenues		117,420
Expenses		
Cost of Goods Sold	44,700	
Depreciation Expense	5,000	
Insurance Expense	2,500	
Interest Expense	2,600	
Rent Expense	6,000	
Salaries Expense	11,000	
Supplies Expense	4,500	
Utilities Expense	750	
Total Expenses		77,050
Net Income		$40,370

b) Gross Profit Margin $= \dfrac{\text{Gross Profit}}{\text{Net Sales}}$

$= \dfrac{\$66,220}{\$110,920}$

$= 0.60$ or 60%

c)

George's Gardening Supplies			
Income Statement			
For the Year Ended December 31, 2018			
Sales Revenue			$113,500
Less: Sales Returns & Allowances		$1,000	
Sales Discounts		1,580	(2,580)
Net Sales			110,920
Cost of Goods Sold			44,700
Gross Profit			66,220
Operating Expenses			
Selling Expenses			
Depreciation Expense	$5,000		
Insurance Expense—Retail	1,750		
Rent Expense—Retail	4,200		
Salaries Expense—Retail	7,700		
Utilities Expense—Retail	525		
Total Selling Expenses		19,175	
Administrative Expenses			
Insurance Expense—Office	750		
Rent Expense—Office	1,800		
Salaries Expense—Office	3,300		
Supplies Expense	4,500		
Utilities Expense—Office	225		
Total Administrative Expenses		10,575	
Total Operating Expenses			29,750
Income from Operations			36,470
Other Income and Expenses			
Interest Revenue		6,500	
Interest Expense		(2,600)	3,900
Net Income			$40,370

d)

JOURNAL			
Date	Account Title and Explanation	Debit	Credit
2018			
Dec 31	Sales Revenue	113,500	
	Interest Revenue	6,500	
	Income Summary		120,000
	Close revenue accounts		

JOURNAL			
Date	Account Title and Explanation	Debit	Credit
Dec 31	Income Summary	79,630	
	Sales Returns & Allowances		1,000
	Sales Discounts		1,580
	Cost of Goods Sold		44,700
	Depreciation Expense		5,000
	Insurance Expense		2,500
	Interest Expense		2,600
	Rent Expense		6,000
	Salaries Expense		11,000
	Supplies Expense		4,500
	Utilities Expense		750
	Close expense and debit accounts		
Dec 31	Income Summary	40,370	
	Gregg, Capital		40,370
	Close income summary		
Dec 31	Gregg, Capital	5,000	
	Gregg, Withdrawals		5,000
	Close withdrawals account		

Review Exercise 7A-1

Part 1

a)

JOURNAL			
Date	Account Title and Explanation	Debit	Credit
2018			
Dec 3	Purchases	50,000	
	Accounts Payable		50,000
	Purchased inventory on account		
Dec 6	Freight-In	200	
	Cash		200
	Paid freight charges		
Dec 8	Accounts Payable	2,000	
	Purchase Returns & Allowances		2,000
	Purchase return		
Dec 11	Accounts Payable	48,000	
	Purchase Discounts		960
	Cash		47,040
	Paid supplier and took discount		

b)

JOURNAL			Page 1
Date	**Account Title and Explanation**	**Debit**	**Credit**
2018			
Dec 3	Accounts Receivable	50,000	
	Sales Revenue		50,000
	Sold inventory on account		
Dec 6	Freight Out	200	
	Cash		200
	Paid freight charges		
Dec 8	Sales Returns & Allowances	2,000	
	Accounts Receivable		2,000
	Customer returned incorrect merchandise		
Dec 11	Cash	47,040	
	Sales Discounts	960	
	Accounts Receivable		48,000
	Received payment from customer		

Part 2

a)

George's Gardening Supplies				
Income Statement				
For the Year Ended December 31, 2018				
Sales Revenue				$113,500
Less: Sales Returns & Allowances			$1,000	
Sales Discounts			1,580	(2,580)
Net Sales				110,920
Cost of Goods Sold				
Merchandise Inventory, January 1, 2018			16,140	
Purchases		$70,000		
Less: Purchase Returns & Allowances	$5,800			
Purchase Discounts	3,200	(9,000)		
Net Purchases		61,000		
Freight-In		1,000	62,000	
Cost of Goods Available for Sale			78,140	
Merchandise Inventory, December 31, 2018			33,440	
Cost of Goods Sold				44,700
Gross Profit				66,220
Operating Expenses				
Depreciation Expense			5,000	
Insurance Expense			2,500	
Rent Expense			6,000	
Salaries Expense			11,000	
Supplies Expense			4,500	
Utilities Expense			750	
Total Operating Expenses				29,750
Income from Operations				36,470
Other Income and Expenses				
Interest Revenue			6,500	
Interest Expense			(2,600)	3,900
Net Income				$40,370

b) Gross Profit Margin $= \dfrac{\text{Gross Profit}}{\text{Net Sales}}$

$= \dfrac{\$66,220}{\$110,920}$

$= 0.60$ or 60%

c)

JOURNAL			
Date	**Account Title and Explanation**	**Debit**	**Credit**
2018			
Dec 31	Sales Revenue	113,500	
	Interest Revenue	6,500	
	Merchandise Inventory	33,440	
	Purchase Returns & Allowances	5,800	
	Purchase Discounts	3,200	
	Income Summary		162,440
	Close revenue and credit accounts and update inventory balance		
Dec 31	Income Summary	122,070	
	Merchandise Inventory		16,140
	Sales Returns & Allowances		1,000
	Sales Discounts		1,580
	Purchases		70,000
	Freight-In		1,000
	Depreciation Expense		5,000
	Insurance Expense		2,500
	Interest Expense		2,600
	Rent Expense		6,000
	Salaries Expense		11,000
	Supplies Expense		4,500
	Utilities Expense		750
	Close expense and debit accounts and update inventory balance		
Dec 31	Income Summary	40,370	
	Gregg, Capital		40,370
	Close income summary		
Dec 31	Gregg, Capital	5,000	
	Gregg, Withdrawals		5,000
	Close owner withdrawals account		

CHAPTER 8 SOLUTIONS

Pause & Reflect Exercise 8-1

Method	Ending Merchandise Inventory	Cost of Goods Sold
FIFO	(640 − 630) × $8.50 = $85	$5,322 − $85 = $5,237
LIFO	(640 − 630) × $8.15 = $81.50	$5,322 − $81.50 = $5,240.50
Weighted-Average Cost	(640-630) × [{(20 × $8.15) + (300 × $8.20) + (210 × $8.40) + (110 × $8.50)} / 640] = $83.20	$5,322 − $83.20 = $5,238.80

Pause & Reflect Exercise 8-2

a) The company's COGS in 2018 would be <u>overstated</u>.

b) The company's gross profit in 2018 would be <u>understated</u>.

c) The company's opening balance of merchandise inventory in 2019 would be <u>understated</u>.

d) The company's COGS in 2019 would be <u>understated</u>.

e) The company's gross profit in 2019 would be <u>overstated</u>.

Pause & Reflect Exercise 8-3

a)

	Cost	NRV	LCNRV (Individual)
Cat Eye	$6,000	$7,500	$6,000
Rimless	10,000	9,000	9,000
Total	$16,000	$16,500	$15,000

b)

JOURNAL			
Date	Account Title and Explanation	Debit	Credit
2018			
Dec 31	Cost of Goods Sold	1,000	
	Merchandise Inventory		1,000
	Adjust inventory to LCNRV		
	($16,000 − $15,000)		

Pause & Reflect Exercise 8-4

a)

	Nado	Vaporen
Average Inventory	120,000	240,000
Inventory Turnover	5	4
Days' Sales in Inventory	73	91

b) Nado Company has more favorable ratios.

Review Exercise 8-1

a)

Date	Purchases			Sales			Balance		
	Quantity	Unit Cost	Value	Quantity	Unit Cost	Value	Quantity	Unit Cost	Value
June 1							100	$12	$1,200
June 3							100	$12	$1,200
	500	$15	$7,500				500	$15	$7,500
June 10				100	$12	$1,200			
				100	$15	$1,500	400	$15	$6,000
June 12							400	$15	$6,000
	300	$18	$5,400				300	$18	$5,400
June 20				300	$15	$4,500	100	$15	$1,500
							300	$18	$5,400
Ending Inventory									$6,900

b)

Mike's Tikes Toys	
Income Statement (partial)	
For the Month Ended June 30, 2018	
Sales Revenue*	$24,000
Cost of Goods Sold**	7,200
Gross Profit	16,800

*$24,000 = (200 × $45) + (300 × $50)

**$7,200 = $1,200 + $1,500 + $4,500

c)

Date	Purchases			Sales			Balance		
	Quantity	Unit Cost	Value	Quantity	Unit Cost	Value	Quantity	Unit Cost	Value
June 1							100	$12	$1,200
June 3							100	$12	$1,200
	500	$15	$7,500				500	$15	$7,500
June 10							100	$12	$1,200
				200	$15	$3,000	300	$15	$4,500
June 12							100	$12	$1,200
							300	$15	$4,500
	300	$18	$5,400				300	$18	$5,400
June 20							100	$12	$1,200
							300	$15	$4,500
				300	$18	$5,400	0	-	-
Ending Inventory									$5,700

d)

Mike's Tikes Toys	
Income Statement (partial)	
For the Month Ended June 30, 2018	
Sales Revenue	$24,000
Cost of Goods Sold*	8,400
Gross Profit	15,600

*$8,400 = $3,000 + $5,400

e)

Date	Purchases			Sales			Balance		
	Quantity	Unit Cost	Value	Quantity	Unit Cost	Value	Quantity	Unit Cost	Value
June 1							100	$12.00	$1,200
June 3	500	$15	$7,500				600	$14.50	$8,700
June 10				200	$14.50	$2,900	400	$14.50	$5,800
June 12	300	$18	$5,400				700	$16.00	$11,200
June 20				300	$16.00	$4,800	400	$16.00	$6,400
Ending Inventory									$6,400

f)

Mike's Tikes Toys	
Income Statement (partial)	
For the Month Ended June 30, 2018	
Sales Revenue	$24,000
Cost of Goods Sold*	7,700
Gross Profit	16,300

* $7,700 = $2,900 + $4,800

Review Exercise 8A-1

a)

Date	Purchases			Sales			Balance		
	Quantity	Unit Cost	Value	Quantity	Unit Cost	Value	Quantity	Unit Cost	Value
Mar 1							100	$12	$1,200
Mar 3							100	$12	$1,200
	500	$15	$7,500				500	$15	$7,500
Mar 12							100	$12	$1,200
							500	$15	$7,500
	300	$18	$5,400				300	$18	$5,400
Sales for the Month				50	$12	$600	50	$12	$600
				350	$15	$5,250	150	$15	$2,250
				100	$18	$1,800	200	$18	$3,600
Ending Inventory									$6,450

b)

Date	Purchases			Sales			Balance		
	Quantity	Unit Cost	Value	Quantity	Unit Cost	Value	Quantity	Unit Cost	Value
Mar 1							100	$12	$1,200
Mar 3							100	$12	$1,200
	500	$15	$7,500				500	$15	$7,500
Mar 12							100	$12	$1,200
							500	$15	$7,500
	300	$18	$5,400				300	$18	$5,400
Sales for the Month				100	$12	$1,200			
				400	$15	$6,000	100	$15	$1,500
							300	$18	$5,400
Ending Inventory									$6,900

c)

Date	Purchases			Sales			Balance		
	Quantity	Unit Cost	Value	Quantity	Unit Cost	Value	Quantity	Unit Cost	Value
Mar 1							100	$12	$1,200
Mar 3							100	$12	$1,200
	500	$15	$7,500				500	$15	$7,500
Mar 12							100	$12	$1,200
							500	$15	$7,500
	300	$18	$5,400				300	$18	$5,400
Sales for the Month							100	$12	$1,200
				200	$15	$3,000	300	$15	$4,500
				300	$18	$5,400	0	-	-
Ending Inventory									$5,700

d)

Date	Purchases			Sales			Balance		
	Quantity	Unit Cost	Value	Quantity	Unit Cost	Value	Quantity	Unit Cost	Value
Mar 1							100		$1,200
Mar 3	500	$15	$7,500				600		$8,700
Mar 12	300	$18	$5,400				900		$14,100
Average Inventory for the Month							900	$15.67	$14,100
Sales for the Month				500	$15.67	$7,835	400	$15.67	$6,265
Ending Inventory									$6,265

Note: numbers may vary due to rounding

CHAPTER 9 SOLUTIONS

Pause & Reflect Exercise 9-1

Simmons Inc. June 30, 2018 General Ledger	
Accounts Receivable	$1,025

Simmons Inc. Schedule of Accounts Receivable June 30, 2018	
Derek Smith *($1,200 – $700)*	$500
Soft Cell Enterprises *($800 – $800*	0
Bill Waites	525
Total Accounts Receivable	$1,025

Simmons Inc. June 30, 2018 General Ledger	
Accounts Payable	$140

Simmons Inc. Schedule of Accounts Payable June 30, 2018	
Buzz Electronics	$140
Supply Depot *($75 – $75)*	0
Total Accounts Payable	$140

Review Exercise 9-1

a)

Cash Receipts Journal									Page 1
Date	Account	PR	Cash (DR)	Sales (CR)	Accounts Receivable (CR)	Interest Revenue (CR)	Notes Payable (CR)	Other (CR)	COGS/ Merchandise Inventory (DR/CR)
Jun 4	Cash Sale		4,000	4,000					2,015
Jun 6	B. Didley	✓	480		480				
Jun 9	Cash Sale		2,160	2,160					1,050
Jun 10	K. Domino		25			25			
Jun 15	Bank Loan		2,400				2,400		
	Total		9,065	6,160	480	25	2,400		3,065

Sales Journal					Page 1
Date	Account	Invoice #	PR	Accounts Receivable/Sales (DR/CR)	COGS/ Merchandise Inventory (DR/CR)
Jun 18	Richard Starkey	10022	✓	3,000	2,000
Jun 28	Pete Best	10023	✓	5,000	3,700
	Total			8,000	5,700

Purchases Journal							Page 1
Date	Account	Invoice #	PR	Repairs Expense (DR)	Office Supplies (DR)	Purchases (DR)	Accounts Payable (CR)
Jun 5	Stapl-EZ	4053	✓		100		100
Jun 9	Building Services Inc.	124	✓	350			350
Jun 26	Brick & Mortar	404241	✓			3,500	3,500
	Total			350	100	3,500	3,950

Cash Payments Journal							Page 1
Date	Account	Chq #	PR	Other (DR)	Purchases (DR)	Accounts Payable (DR)	Cash (CR)
Jun 12	Stapl-EZ Inc.	465	✓			100	100
Jun 21	Noel's Inc.	466			4,000		4,000
Jun 22	Building Services Inc.	467	✓			350	350
Jun 25	SKG Inc.	468		175			175
	Total			175	4,000	450	4,625

b)

Accounts Receivable Subsidiary Ledger Bo Didley					
Date	PR	DR	CR	Balance	
Opening Bal				2,000 DR	DR
Jun 6	CR1		480	1,520 DR	DR

Accounts Receivable Subsidiary Ledger Richard Starkey					
Date	PR	DR	CR	Balance	
Opening Bal				1,000	DR
Jun 18	SJ1	3,000		4,000	DR

Accounts Receivable Subsidiary Ledger Pete Best					
Date	PR	DR	CR	Balance	
Opening Bal				1,500	DR
Jun 28	SJ1	5,000		6,500	DR

Account: Accounts Receivable					GL No: 110	
Date	Description	PR	DR	CR	Balance	
Opening Bal					4,500 DR	DR
Jun 30		CRI		480	4,020 DR	DR
Jun 30		SJ1	8,000		12,020 DR	DR

Lin-Z June 30, 2018 General Ledger	
Accounts Receivable	$12,020

Lin-Z Schedule of Accounts Receivable June 30, 2018	
Bo Didley	$1,520
Richard Starkey	4,000
Pete Best	6,500
Total Accounts Receivable	$12,020

c)

Accounts Payable Subsidiary Ledger Stapl-EZ Inc.					
Date	PR	DR	CR	Balance	
Opening Bal				500	CR
Jun 5	PJ1		100	600	CR
Jun 12	CP1	100		500	CR

Accounts Payable Subsidiary Ledger Building Services Inc.					
Date	PR	DR	CR	Balance	
Opening Bal				750	CR
Jun 9	PJ1		350	1,100	CR
Jun 22	CP1	350		750	CR

Accounts Payable Subsidiary Ledger Brick & Mortar Inc.					
Date	PR	DR	CR	Balance	
Opening Bal				2,500	CR
Jun 26	PJ1		3,500	6,000	CR

Account: Accounts Payable					GL No: 200	
Date	Description	PR	DR	CR	Balance	
Opening Bal					3,750	CR
Jun 30		PJ1		3,950	7,700	CR
Jun 30		CP1	450		7,250	CR

Lin-Z June 30, 2018 General Ledger	
Accounts Receivable	$7,250

Lin-Z Schedule of Accounts Payable June 30, 2018	
Stapl-EZ Inc.	$500
Building Services Inc.	750
Brick & Mortar Inc.	6,000
Total Accounts Payable	$7,250

Review Exercise 9A-1

a)

Cash Receipts Journal								Page 1
Date	Account	PR	Cash (DR)	Sales (CR)	Accounts Receivable (CR)	Interest Revenue (CR)	Notes Payable (CR)	Other (CR)
Jun 4	Cash Sale		4,000	4,000				
Jun 6	B. Didley	✓	480		480			
Jun 9	Cash Sale		2,160	2,160				
Jun 10	K. Domino		25			25		
Jun 15	Bank Loan		2,400				2,400	
	Total		9,065	6,160	480	25	2,400	

Sales Journal				Page 1
Date	Account	Invoice #	PR	Accounts Receivable/Sales (DR/CR)
Jun 18	Richard Starkey	10022	✓	3,000
Jun 28	Pete Best	10023	✓	5,000
	Total			8,000

Purchases Journal							Page 1
Date	Account	Invoice #	PR	Repairs Expense (DR)	Office Supplies (DR)	Purchases (DR)	Accounts Payable (CR)
Jun 5	Stapl-EZ	4053	✓		100		100
Jun 9	Building Services Inc	124	✓	350			350
Jun 26	Brick & Mortar	404241	✓			3,500	3,500
	Total			350	100	3,500	3,950

Cash Payments Journal							Page 1
Date	Account	Chq #	PR	Other (DR)	Purchases (DR)	Accounts Payable (DR)	Cash (CR)
Jun 12	Stapl-EZ Inc.	465	✓			100	100
Jun 21	Noel's Inc.	466			4,000		4,000
Jun 22	Building Services Inc.	467	✓			350	350
Jun 25	SKG Inc.	468		175			175
	Total			175	4,000	450	4,625

b)

Accounts Receivable Subsidiary Ledger **Bo Didley**					
Date	**PR**	**DR**	**CR**	**Balance**	
Opening Bal				2,000	DR
Jun 6	CR1		480	1,520	DR

Accounts Receivable Subsidiary Ledger **Richard Starkey**					
Date	**PR**	**DR**	**CR**	**Balance**	
Opening Bal				1,000	DR
Jun 18	SJ1	3,000		4,000	DR

Accounts Receivable Subsidiary Ledger **Pete Best**					
Date	**PR**	**DR**	**CR**	**Balance**	
Opening Bal				1,500	DR
Jun 28	SJ1	5,000		6,500	DR

Account: Accounts Receivable					**GL No: 110**	
Date	**Description**	**PR**	**DR**	**CR**	**Balance**	
Opening Bal.					4,500	DR
Jun 30		CRI		480	4,020	DR
Jun 30		SJ1	8,000		12,020	DR

Lin-Z **June 30, 2018** **General Ledger**	
Accounts Receivable	$12,020

Lin-Z **Schedule of Accounts Receivable** **June 30, 2018**	
Bo Didley	$1,520
Richard Starkey	4,000
Pete Best	6,500
Total Accounts Receivable	$12,020

c)

Accounts Payable Subsidiary Ledger **Stapl-EZ Inc.**					
Date	**PR**	**DR**	**CR**	**Balance**	
Opening Bal.				500	CR
Jun 5	PJ1		100	600	CR
Jun 12	CP1	100		500	CR

Accounts Payable Subsidiary Ledger
Building Services Inc.

Date	PR	DR	CR	Balance	
Opening Bal.				750	CR
Jun 9	PJ1		350	1,100	CR
Jun 22	CP1	350		750	CR

Accounts Payable Subsidiary Ledger
Brick & Mortar Inc.

Date	PR	DR	CR	Balance	
Opening Bal.				2,500	CR
Jun 26	PJ1		3,500	6,000	CR

Account: Accounts Payable   **GL No: 200**

Date	Description	PR	DR	CR	Balance	
Opening Bal.					3,750	CR
Jun 30		PJ1		3,950	7,700	CR
Jun 30		CP1	450		7,250	CR

Lin-Z
June 30, 2018
General Ledger

Accounts Receivable	$7,250

Lin-Z
Schedule of Accounts Payable
June 30, 2018

Stapl-EZ Inc.	$500
Building Services Inc.	750
Brick & Mortar Inc.	6,000
Total Accounts Payable	$7,250

CHAPTER 10 SOLUTIONS

Pause & Reflect Exercise 10-1

Although this is a small store, Stacy should take a more active role in preparing and recording the cash from sales. She should prepare the float for each day, and compare the day's sales to the actual cash received at the end of the day. She should also count the money for each deposit and compare that to the deposit slip. By getting more involved in the cash sales part of the business, Stacy will have better control over cash receipts.

If cash sales are high during the day, the amount of cash in the cash drawer can become too high. It would be best to periodically take excess cash from the cash drawer and place it in a safe. This would then be deposited at the bank later in the day.

Although the cashier may be authorized to make the cash payments to suppliers that deliver and stock soda and chips, it would be better to pay by means of a check instead of cash. A check ensures that the correct amount is paid (no accidental miscount) and that the supplier company gets paid the full amount (no one is able to take cash for themselves). The invoice and the check would provide a better paper trail if questions of payment were to ever arise.

Pause & Reflect Exercise 10-2

Prescott Marketing					
Bank Reconciliation					
September 30, 2018					
Cash balance per bank statement		$8,570	Cash balance per books		$9,260
Add outstanding deposit		2,480	Add EFT deposit		1,560
Deduct outstanding checks			Deduct		
Check #287	650		Check returned NSF	1,240	
Check #291	870	1,520	Bank service charge	50	1,290
Adjusted bank balance		$9,530	Adjusted book balance		$9,530

Pause & Reflect Exercise 10-3

JOURNAL			
Date	Account Title and Explanation	Debit	Credit
Nov 1	Petty Cash	500	
	Cash		500
	To establish petty cash		
Nov 15	Postage Expense	58	
	Delivery Expense	94	
	Entertainment Expense	242	
	Maintenance Expense	46	
	Cash Over and Short	4	
	Cash		444
	To replenish petty cash		

Review Exercise 10-1

a) *Record cash immediately when received*

- Use sequential pre-numbered receipts.
- Purchase and use a cash register.
- Compare and reconcile the sum of sales amounts (office copy) to the cash on hand (cash drawer or cash register copy).

Protect cash when it is on the premises

- Lock the cash drawer or cash register when not in use.
- Remove the cash from the cash drawer or cash register at night. Lock it in a safe, or the office.
- Create a customer policy of free cleaning if no receipt is given by the counter clerk. This ensures the customer is always given a receipt when they pay cash.

Remove cash from the premises as soon as possible

- Deposit cash into the bank daily, multiple times if necessary.

b) The overall goal for cash controls is to ensure that the amount of cash received is the amount of cash recorded, which is the amount of cash deposited.

c) Contact authorities to report the counter clerk for fraudulent activities and theft, and provide information for their investigation.

- Terminate the employment of the counter clerk.
- JP can step in as the counter clerk until another employee is found.

Review Exercise 10-2

a)

Martin Furniture
Bank Reconciliation
June 30, 2018

Cash balance per bank statement	$2,000	Cash balance per books			$4,815
Add outstanding deposit	1,300	Add Interest			5
Deduct outstanding checks		Deduct charges			
Check #545	500				
		NSF Check		2,000	
		Bank charges for NSF Check		6	
		Bank service charge		14	2,020
Adjusted bank balance	$2,800	Adjusted book balance			$2,800

b)

JOURNAL

Date	Account Title and Explanation	Debit	Credit
2018			
Jun 30	Cash	5	
	Interest Revenue		5
	To record deposit of interest earned		
Jun 30	Accounts Receivable	2,000	
	Cash		2,000
	Reinstate accounts receivable for NSF check		

JOURNAL			
Jun 30	Bank Charges Expense	6	
	Cash		6
	To record NSF charges		
Jun 30	Bank Charges Expense	14	
	Cash		14
	To record payment of bank service charges		

Review Exercise 10-3

a)

JOURNAL			
Date	**Account Title and Explanation**	**Debit**	**Credit**
2018			
Apr 1	Petty Cash	200	
	Cash		200
	To establish petty cash fund		

b)

JOURNAL			
Date	**Account Title and Explanation**	**Debit**	**Credit**
2018			
Apr 16	Postage Expense	40	
	Delivery Expense	20	
	Travel Expense	25	
	Entertainment Expense	8	
	Office Expenses	7	
	Cash Over and Short	5	
	Cash		105
	To reimburse petty cash fund		

CHAPTER 11 SOLUTIONS

Pause & Reflect Exercise 11-1

JOURNAL			
Date	**Account Title and Explanation**	**Debit**	**Credit**
2018			
Dec 31	Bad Debt Expense	6,500	
	Allowance for Doubtful Accounts		6,500
	To record estimated bad debt		
2019			
Mar 5	Allowance for Doubtful Accounts	2,100	
	Accounts Receivable—Basil's Hotel		2,100
	To write off bad debt		

Pause & Reflect Exercise 11-2

a)

Aging Category	Bad Debt %	Balance of Accounts Receivable	Estimated Bad Debt
30 days	1%	$200,000	$2,000
31-60 days	5%	120,000	6,000
More than 60 days	10%	80,000	8,000
Total		$400,000	$16,000

b)

JOURNAL			
Date	**Account Title and Explanation**	**Debit**	**Credit**
Dec 31	Bad Debt Expense	12,600	
	Allowance for Doubtful Accounts		12,600
	To record bad debt expense		

Pause & Reflect Exercise 11-3

JOURNAL			
Date	**Account Title and Explanation**	**Debit**	**Credit**
2018			
Nov 1	Notes Receivable	6,000	
	Accounts Receivable		6,000
	Convert accounts receivable into notes receivable		
Dec 31	Interest Receivable	50	
	Interest Revenue		50
	Accrue interest on the note receivable		
2019			
Apr 30	Cash	6,150	
	Interest Receivable		50
	Interest Revenue		100
	Notes Receivable		6,000
	Received payment of note plus interest		

Pause & Reflect Exercise 11-4

a)

$$\text{Accounts Receivable Turnover Ratio} = \frac{\text{Net Credit Sales}}{\text{Average Net Accounts Receivable}}$$

$$= \frac{\$278,000}{\$23,000}$$

$$= 12 \text{ times}$$

The accounts receivable turnover is 12 times. This means that the company collects the entire amount of accounts receivable about 12 times a year, or approximately once a month.

b) $\text{Days' Sales Outstanding} = \dfrac{\text{Average Net Accounts Receivable}}{\text{Net Credit Sales}} \times 365$

$$= \frac{\$23,000}{\$278,000} \times 365$$

$$= 30 \text{ days}$$

The days' sales outstanding is 30 days. This means that the company collects the entire amount of accounts receivable in an average of 30 days, or approximately one month.

Review Exercise 11-1

a)

JOURNAL			
Date	Account Title and Explanation	Debit	Credit
Dec 31	Cash	70,000	
	Accounts Receivable	280,000	
	Sales Revenue		350,000
Dec 31	Cash	250,000	
	Accounts Receivable		250,000
Dec 31	Allowance for Doubtful Accounts	1,500	
	Accounts Receivable		1,500
Dec 31	Accounts Receivable	1,500	
	Allowance for Doubtful Accounts		1,500
Dec 31	Bad Debt Expense	2,500	
	Allowance for Doubtful Accounts		2,500

b)

Cash	
$70,000	
250,000	
$320,000	

Accounts Receivable	
Beg. Bal.: $250,000	
$35,000	1,500
280,000	
1,500	
$65,000	

Sales Revenue	
	$350,000

AFDA	
$1,500	Beg. Bal.:
	$2,500
	1,500
	2,500
	$5,000

Bad Debt Expense	
$2,500	

c)

ABC Company Balance Sheet (partial) As at December 31, 2018	
Accounts Receivable	$65,000
Less: Allowance for Doubtful Accounts	5,000
Net Accounts Receivable	$60,000

d)

JOURNAL			
Date	Account Title	Debit	Credit
Dec 31	Bad Debt Expense	2,800	
	Allowance for Doubtful Accounts		2,800
	To estimate bad debt for the year		

If the company uses the income statement approach, it does not take the AFDA beginning balance into account when it records the journal entry to estimate bad debt. Simply calculate 1% of credit sales (350,000 × 0.8 = 280,000), which is equal to $2,800, and use this number in the journal entry.

Review Exercise 11-2

JOURNAL			
Date	**Account Title and Explanation**	**Debit**	**Credit**
Jun 30	Accounts Receivable	5,000	
	Sales Revenue		5,000
	To record sale on credit		
Jul 31	Notes Receivable	5,000	
	Accounts Receivable		5,000
	Converted accounts receivable to a note receivable		
Aug 31	Interest Receivable	25	
	Interest Revenue		25
	To record accrued interest revenue		
	($5,000 × 6% × 1/12)		
Dec 31	Cash	5,125	
	Interest Receivable		25
	Interest Revenue		100
	Notes Receivable		5,000
	Receipt of note principal and interest		
Dec 31	Accounts Receivable	5,125	
	Interest Receivable		25
	Interest Revenue		100
	Notes Receivable		5,000
	To record a dishonored note		

CHAPTER 12 SOLUTIONS

Pause & Reflect Exercise 12-1

a)

Asset	Appraised Value	Percentage	Book Value
Building	$1,000,000	50%	$900,000
Land	600,000	30%	540,000
Parking Lot	400,000	20%	360,000
Total	$2,000,000	100%	$1,800,000

b)

JOURNAL			Page 2
Date	Account Title and Explanation	Debit	Credit
May 1	Building	900,000	
	Land	540,000	
	Parking Lot	360,000	
	Cash		1,800,000
	Purchased assets with cash		

Pause & Reflect Exercise 12-2

Year	Beginning of Year Book Value	Depreciation	Remaining Book Value
2018	$5,000,000	$2,000,000	$3,000,000
2019	$3,000,000	$1,200,000	$1,800,000
2020	$1,800,000	$720,000	$1,080,000
2021	$1,080,000	$432,000	$648,000
2022	$648,000	$248,000	$400,000

Pause & Reflect Exercise 12-3

JOURNAL			
Date	Account Title and Explanation	Debit	Credit
Dec 31	Depreciation Expense	260,000	
	Accumulated Depreciation—Equipment		260,000
	Record annual depreciation		
Dec 31	Cash	360,000	
	Accumulated Depreciation—Equipment	2,340,000	
	Loss on Disposal of Asset	300,000	
	Equipment		3,000,000
	Sold asset for cash		

Pause & Reflect Exercise 12-4

a) Depletion Rate = $\dfrac{(\$21,000,000 - \$1,000,000)}{57,000 \text{ ounces}}$

= $40/ounce

b)

JOURNAL			
Date	Account Title and Explanation	Debit	Credit
Dec 31	Depletion Expense—Mineral Deposit	560,000	
	Accumulated Depletion—Mineral Deposit		560,000
	Depletion of gold mine		

Review Exercise 12-1

a)

JOURNAL			
Date	**Account Title and Explanation**	**Debit**	**Credit**
Dec 31	Computer	3,000	
	Office Equipment	10,000	
	Cash		13,000
	Purchase of computer and office equipment for cash		

b) A reasonable life for a computer would be three years, and for equipment would be 5–10 years. Students will arrive at various numbers based on their research.

c) Because computers are upgraded quickly, a declining-balance method would be appropriate with large amounts of depreciation early on. For office equipment, straight-line depreciation would be reasonable.

d)

Year	Cost	Depreciation	Accumulated Depreciation	Net Book Value
2017	3,000.00	1,000.00	1,000.00	2,000.00
2018	2,000.00	666.67	1,666.67	1,333.33
2019	1,333.33	444.44	2,111.11	888.89

Year	Cost	Depreciation	Accumulated Depreciation	Net Book Value
2017	10,000	2,000	2,000	8,000
2018	10,000	2,000	4,000	6,000
2019	10,000	2,000	6,000	4,000
2020	10,000	2,000	8,000	2,000
2021	10,000	2,000	10,000	0

e) The profit or loss on disposal of a noncurrent asset is the difference between the amount received, and the net book value of the asset at the time of disposal.

Review Exercise 12-2

JOURNAL			
Date	**Account Title and Explanation**	**Debit**	**Credit**
Jan 1	Assets	500,000	
	Goodwill	50,000	
	Liabilities		300,000
	Cash		250,000
	Purchase of assets and liabilities of Regnier		
	company		
Jan 1	Patents	50,000	
	Cash		50,000
	Purchase of patents for cash		
Jan 1	Trademarks	20,000	
	Cash		20,000
	Purchase of trademarks for cash		
Jan 30	Mineral Deposit	100,000	
	Cash		100,000
	Purchase of mineral deposit for cash		
Jun 30	Impairment Loss	25,000	
	Goodwill		25,000
	To record impairment of goodwill		
Dec 31	Amortization Expense—Patents	6,250	
	Accumulated Amortization—Patents		6,250
	Amortization for the period		
	[(50,000 ÷ 4) 3½ year]		
Dec 31	Amortization Expense—Trademarks	1,244	
	Accumulated Amortization—Trademarks		1,244
	Amortization for the period		
	[((20,000 − 100) ÷ 8) 3½ year]		
Dec 31	Depletion Expense—Mineral Deposit	2,000	
	Accumulated Depletion—Mineral Rights		2,000
	Depletion for the period		
	[10,000 3 (100,000 ÷ 500,000)]		

Review Exercise 12A-1

a) The following shows both calculation methods, either of which is correct. Fair market value is shortened to FMV in the table below.

Exchange of Asset with Commercial Substance—Worksheet			
Method: Difference between FMV (new asset) and book value (old asset) plus cash paid on exchange			
Price (FMV) of New Machinery			$150,000
Less: Value of Assets Given Up in Exchange			
Book Value of Old Machinery ($125,000 – $103,750)		$21,250	
Cash Paid on Exchange		120,000	141,250
Gain on Exchange of Assets			$ 8,750
Method: Difference between FMV (trade-in allowance) of old asset *and* book value of old asset			
FMV (Trade-In Allowance) of Old Machinery			$30,000
Less: Book Value of Old Machinery ($125,000 – $103,750)			21,250
Gain on Exchange of Assets			$8,750

b)

JOURNAL			
Date	**Account Title and Explanation**	**Debit**	**Credit**
Nov 30	Machinery (new)	150,000	
	Accumulated Depreciation—Machinery (old)	103,750	
	Machinery (old)		125,000
	Cash		120,000
	Gain on Exchange of Assets		8,750
	To record exchange of old machinery and cash for		
	new machinery		

c)

JOURNAL			
Date	**Account Title and Explanation**	**Debit**	**Credit**
Nov 30	Machinery (new)	141,250	
	Accumulated Depreciation—Machinery (old)	103,750	
	Machinery (old)		125,000
	Cash		120,000
	To record exchange of old machinery and cash for		
	new machinery		

Review Exercise 12A-2

a)   The following shows both calculation methods, either of which is correct. Fair market value is shortened to FMV in the table below.

Exchange of Asset with Commercial Substance—Worksheet		
Method: Difference between FMV (new asset) *and* book value (old asset) plus cash paid on exchange		
Price (FMV) of New Delivery Vehicle		$60,000
Less: Value of Assets Given Up in Exchange		
Book Value of Old Delivery Vehicle *($45,000 – $39,000)*	$6,000	
Cash Paid on Exchange	55,000	61,000
Loss on Exchange of Assets		($1,000)
Method: Difference between FMV (trade-in allowance) of old asset *and* book value of old asset		
FMV (Trade-In Allowance) of Old Delivery Vehicle		$5,000
Less: Book Value of Old Delivery Vehicle *($45,000 – $39,000)*		6,000
Loss on Exchange of Assets		($1,000)

b)

JOURNAL			
Date	**Account Title and Explanation**	**Debit**	**Credit**
Apr 30	Delivery Vehicle (new)	60,000	
	Accumulated Depreciation—Delivery Vehicle (old)	39,000	
	Loss on Exchange of Assets	1,000	
	Delivery Vehicle (old)		45,000
	Cash		55,000
	To record exchange of old delivery vehicle and		
	cash for new delivery vehicle		

c)

JOURNAL			
Date	**Account Title and Explanation**	**Debit**	**Credit**
Apr 30	Delivery Vehicle (new)	61,000	
	Accumulated Depreciation— Delivery Vehicle (old)	39,000	
	Delivery Vehicle (old)		45,000
	Cash		55,000
	To record exchange of old delivery vehicle and		
	cash for new delivery vehicle		

CHAPTER 13 SOLUTIONS

Pause & Reflect Exercise 13-1

JOURNAL			
Date	**Account Title and Explanation**	**Debit**	**Credit**
Mar 13	Cash	52,500	
	Sales Tax Payable		2,500
	Sales Revenue		50,000
	Sold items for cash		
Mar 13	Cost of Goods Sold	22,000	
	Merchandise Inventory		22,000
	Record COGS		

Pause & Reflect Exercise 13-2

JOURNAL			
Date	**Account Title and Explanation**	**Debit**	**Credit**
2018			
Sep 1	Cash	20,000	
	Notes Payable		20,000
	Borrowed cash from the bank, due in six months		
Dec 31	Interest Expense	400	
	Interest Payable		400
	Accrued interest on note payable		
2019			
Feb 28	Notes Payable	20,000	
	Interest Payable	400	
	Interest Expense	200	
	Cash		20,600
	Paid note and interest on due date		

Pause & Reflect Exercise 13-3

			Deductions				
Gross Earnings	**Federal Income Tax**	**State Income Tax**	**FICA Tax**	**FUTA**	**SUTA**	**Total Contributions**	**Net Pay**
$10,000	$1,000	$500	$765	$60	$540	$1,365	$7,735

The net pay to employees is equal to gross earnings minus employee deductions.

Net Pay = $10,000 − $1,000 − $500 − $765
= $7,735

The employer payroll contributions are equal to adding FICA, FUTA, and SUTA together.

Total Employer Contributions = $765 + $60 + 540
= $1,365

Pause & Reflect Exercise 13-4

JOURNAL			
Date	Account Title and Explanation	Debit	Credit
Dec 31	Warranty Expense	400,000	
	Estimated Warranty Liability		400,000
	Record estimated warranty liability		

Review Exercise 13-1

JOURNAL			
Date	Account Title and Explanation	Debit	Credit
Jan 15	Merchandise Inventory	111,300	
	Accounts Payable		111,300
	Bought machine for resale		
Jan 30	Cash	226,840	
	Sales Tax Payable		12,840
	Sales Revenue		214,000
	Sold machine for cash		
Jan 30	Cost of Goods Sold	111,300	
	Merchandise Inventory		111,300
	Record COGS for above sale		
Jan 30	Warranty Expense	20,000	
	Estimated Warranty Liability		20,000
	Accrued for estimated warranty costs		
Jan 30	Sales Tax Payable	12,840	
	Cash		12,840
	Paid sales tax to the government		
Feb 15	Accounts Payable	111,300	
	Cash		111,300
	Paid for machine bought on account on Jan 15		
Mar 27	Estimated Warranty Liability	200	
	Parts Inventory		200
	To record inventory for warranty work		

CHAPTER 14 SOLUTIONS

Pause & Reflect Exercise 14-1

JOURNAL			
Date	Account Title and Explanation	Debit	Credit
Sep 1	Cash	5,000	
	Building	275,000	
	Notes Payable		80,000
	Akazi, Capital		200,000
	Investment by Miko into partnership		
Sep 1	Cash	15,000	
	Equipment	20,000	
	Accounts Payable		10,000
	Warren, Capital		25,000
	Investment by Gayle into partnership		

Pause & Reflect Exercise 14-2

a)

	Total	Eric Banner	David Martin
Net Income	$90,000		
Salary to Eric	−45,000	$45,000	
Salary to David	−35,000		$35,000
Remainder	10,000		
Share of profit to Eric	−5,000	5,000	
Share of profit to David	−5,000		5,000
Transferred to Capital	−$90,000	$50,000	$40,000

b)

JOURNAL			
Date	Account Title and Explanation	Debit	Credit
Dec 31	Income Summary	90,000	
	Banner, Capital		50,000
	Martin, Capital		40,000
	Allocate net income to capital accounts		

Pause & Reflect Exercise 14-3

	Kelsey	Zac	Yelena	Total
Capital balance before admission	$110,000	$150,000		$260,000
Admission of new partner	−10,000	−10,000	$120,000	100,000
Capital balance after admission	$100,000	$140,000	$120,000	$360,000

Pause & Reflect Exercise 14-4

JOURNAL			
Date	**Account Title and Explanation**	**Debit**	**Credit**
Nov 30	Cash	200,000	
	Loss on Sale of Assets	40,000	
	Assets		240,000
	Sold assets for a loss		
Nov 30	Diana, Capital	20,000	
	Kate, Capital	20,000	
	Loss on Sale of Assets		40,000
	Allocate loss to partners		
Nov 30	Liabilities	110,000	
	Cash		110,000
	Pay partnership liabilities		
Nov 30	Diana, Capital	50,000	
	Kate, Capital	70,000	
	Cash		120,000
	Distribute cash to partners		

Review Exercise 14-1

a)

	Total	Zelma	Serena	Sharron
Cash Contribution	$30,000	$10,000	$10,000	$10,000
Contribution of Equipment	25,000	25,000		
Partner Contributions	$55,000	$35,000	$10,000	$10,000
Net Income	$25,000			
Salaries	–15,000	5,000	5,000	5,000
Equipment Rental	–3,000	3,000		
Interest	–1,500	500	500	500
Division of Income	5,500	1,834	1,833	1,833
Addition to Partners' Capital		$10,334	$7,333	$7,333
Capital Balance, December 31, 2018	$80,000	$45,334	$17,333	$17,333

b)

JOURNAL			
Date	Account Title and Explanation	Debit	Credit
2018			
Jan 1	Cash	30,000	
	Rapoza, Capital		10,000
	Dennen, Capital		10,000
	Throop, Capital		10,000
	To record set up of partnership		
Jan 1	Equipment	25,000	
	Rapoza, Capital		25,000
	To record contribution of equipment		
Dec 31	Income Summary	25,000	
	Rapoza, Capital		10,334
	Dennen, Capital		7,333
	Throop, Capital		7,333
	To adjust partners' capital accounts for their		
	share of net income		
2019			
Jan 2	Throop, Capital	17,333	
	Rapoza, Capital		10,000
	Dennen, Capital		7,333
	To record Thorne's withdrawal from partnership		

CHAPTER 15 SOLUTIONS

Pause & Reflect Exercise 15-1

JOURNAL			
Date	Account Title and Explanation	Debit	Credit
Jan 7	Cash	57,000	
	Preferred Stock		10,000
	Paid-In Capital in Excess of Par, Preferred Stock		15,000
	Common Stock		4,000
	Paid-In Capital in Excess of Par, Common Stock		28,000
	Issued preferred and common stock for cash		
Jan 8	Land	400,000	
	Common Stock		50,000
	Paid-In Capital in Excess of Par, Common Stock		350,000
	Issued common stock in exchange for land		

Pause & Reflect Exercise 15-2

JOURNAL			
Date	**Account Title and Explanation**	**Debit**	**Credit**
May 25	Cash Dividends—Preferred, cumulative	40,000	
	Cash Dividends—Preferred, non-cumulative	50,000	
	Cash Dividends—Common	30,000	
	Dividends Payable		120,000
	To record declaration of cash dividends		
Jul 15	Dividends Payable	120,000	
	Cash		120,000
	To record cash payment of dividend		

Note: Preferred, cumulative dividends per year are: 10% × $40 par value × 5,000 shares = $20,000. Total cumulative preferred dividends for 2017 and 2018 are: $20,000× 2 years = $40,000. Preferred, non-cumulative dividends are 20% × $25 par value × 10,000 shares = $50,000.

Pause & Reflect Exercise 15-3

a)   The 2-for-1 stock split will double the quantity of common stock from 400,000 common shares to 800,000 common shares. The total book value of common stock will remain unchanged.

b)   The value of retained earnings will remain unchanged.

c)   The par value will be reduced by half from $3 per share to $1.50 per share. The stock price will also likely be halved, to approximately $40 per share.

Review Exercise 15-1

a)

JOURNAL			
Date	**Account Title and Explanation**	**Debit**	**Credit**
Mar 3	Assets	2,000,000	
	Liabilities		1,250,000
	Common Stock		20,000
	Paid-In Capital in Excess of Par, Common Stock		730,000
	Issued common stock for net assets of partnership		
Apr 15	Cash	1,000,000	
	Common Stock		20,000
	Paid-in Capital in Excess of Par, Common Stock		980,000
	Issued common stock for cash		
Apr 30	Accounting Fees Expense	100,000	
	Preferred Stock		100,000

JOURNAL			
Date	**Account Title and Explanation**	**Debit**	**Credit**
	Issued preferred stock for accounting services		
May 10	Equipment	250,000	
	Common Stock		5,000
	Paid-in Capital in Excess of Par, Common Stock		245,000
	Issued common stock for equipment		
Sep 15	Retained Earnings	135,000	
	Common Stock Dividends Distributable		2,250
	Paid-in Capital in Excess of Par, Common Stock		132,750
	Declared 5% common stock dividends		
	(5% × 45,000 outstanding common shares × $1 = $2,250)		
	(2,250 × $60 = $135,000)		
Oct 2	Common Stock Dividends Distributable	2,250	
	Common Stock		2,250
	Recorded distribution of stock dividends		
Oct 7	Treasury Stock	55,000	
	Cash		55,000
	Purchased treasury stock		
Oct 15	Cash Dividends—Preferred	30,000	
	Cash Dividends—Common	150,000	
	Dividends Payable		180,000
	Declared cash dividends on common and preferred		
	stock		
Dec 15	Dividends Payable	180,000	
	Cash		180,000
	Recorded payment of cash dividends declared		
Dec 20	Cash	26,500	
	Retained Earnings	1,000	
	Treasury Stock		27,500
	Sold 500 shares of treasury stock for $53 per share		
Dec 31	Income Tax Expense	320,000	
	Income Tax Payable		290,000
	Deferred Income Tax Liability		30,000
	To record tax expense and deferred income tax liability		

b)

Camphamel Inc.	
Balance Sheet (partial)	
As at December 31, 2018	
Stockholders' Equity	
Paid-In Capital	
Preferred stock, 30%, $10 par value, 200,000 shares authorized,	
10,000 shares issued	$100,000
Common stock, $1 par value, unlimited shares authorized,	
47,250 shares issued, 46,750 shares outstanding	47,250
Additional Paid-In Capital	2,087,750
Total Paid-In Capital	2,235,000
Retained Earnings	584,000
Total Paid-In Capital and Retained Earnings	2,819,000
Treasury Stock, Common (500 shares at cost)	(27,500)
Total Stockholders' Equity	$2,791,500

Notes:

Common Stock = $20,000 + $20,000 + $5,000 + $2,250 = $47,250

Additional Paid-In Capital = $730,000 + $980,000 + $245,000 + $132,750 = $2,087,750

Retained Earnings = Net Income − Stock Dividends − Cash Dividends − Selling Treasury Stock Below Cost
= $900,000 − $135,000 − $180,000 − $1,000
= $584,000

Treasury Stock = (1,000 shares − 500 shares) × $55 per share = $27,500

CHAPTER 16 SOLUTIONS

Pause & Reflect Exercise 16-1

Earnings per share from continuing operations	Earnings per Share $= \dfrac{(\$850,000 - \$0)}{100,000}$ $= \$8.50$
Basic earnings per share	Earnings per Share $= \dfrac{(\$925,000 - \$0)}{100,000}$ $= \$9.25$

Pause & Reflect Exercise 16-2

a) Dividend per common share = $300,000 ÷ 100,000 = $3

Dividend Yield = $\dfrac{\$3}{50}$ = 6%

b) Price-Earnings (P/E) Ratio = $\dfrac{\$17.42}{\$3.15}$ = 5.53

Review Exercise 16-1

a)

Shah Company		
Income Statement		
For the Year Ended December 31, 2018		
Sales Revenue		$710,000
Less: Sales Discounts		15,000
Net Sales		695,000
Cost of Goods Sold		380,000
Gross Profit		315,000
Operating Expenses		
Selling Expenses	$42,000	
Administrative Expenses	20,000	
Total Operating Expenses		62,000
Income from Operations		253,000
Other Income and Expenses		
Interest Expenses	(30,000)	
Loss Due to Lawsuit	(11,000)	(41,000)
Income (Loss) from Continuing Operations before Income Tax Expense		212,000
Income Tax Expense		74,200
Income (Loss) from Continuing Operations		137,800
Discontinued Operations		
Income from Operating Discontinued Operations (net of $12,250 tax)	22,750	
Loss on Sale of Discontinued Operations (net of $14,000 tax)	(26,000)	(3,250)
Net Income (Loss)		$134,550
Basic and Diluted Earnings per Share		$8.36

b)

Shah Company	
Statement of Retained Earnings	
For the Year Ended December 31, 2018	
Retained Earnings, January 1, 2018, as Originally Reported	$110,000
Prior Period Adjustment	
Retained Earnings Overstated	(7,500)
Retained Earnings, January 1, 2018, as Adjusted	102,500
Net Income	134,550
Less: Cash Dividends—Common	20,000
Cash Dividends—Preferred	5,000
Retained Earnings, December 31, 2018	$212,050

c)

Shah Company		
Balance Sheet (partial)		
As at December 31, 2018		
Stockholders' Equity		
Paid-In Capital		
Preferred stock, 10% non-cumulative, $50 par value,		
20,000 shares authorized, 1,000 shares issued	$50,000	
Common stock, $10 par value, unlimited shares authorized,		
15,500 shares issued and outstanding	155,000	
Total Paid-In Capital	205,000	
Retained Earnings	212,050	
Total Stockholders' Equity		$417,050

d) Since preferred dividends equal $5,000 ($5.00 × 1,000), and assuming the same number of shares has been outstanding throughout the year, earnings per share is calculated as follows.

$$\text{EPS} = \frac{\text{Net Income} - \text{Preferred Dividends}}{\text{Weighted Average Number of Common Shares Outstanding}}$$

$$= \frac{\$134,550 - \$5,000}{15,500}$$

$$= \$8.36$$

CHAPTER 17 SOLUTIONS

Pause & Reflect Exercise 17-1

JOURNAL			
Date	Account Title and Explanation	Debit	Credit
Jan 1	Cash	300,000	
	Bonds Payable		300,000
	Issued 1,500 five-year bonds at par		

Pause & Reflect Exercise 17-2

a)

Straight-Line Amortization Table of Bond Discount					
Semi-Annual Interest Period	Interest Payment	Discount Amortization	Interest Expense	Discount Balance	Bond Book Value
0				3,546	96,454[1]
1	4,000	887	4,887	2,659	97,341
2	4,000	887	4,887	1,772	98,228
3	4,000	887	4,887	885	99,115
4	4,000	885[2]	4,885	0	100,000
Total	16,000	3,546	19,546	0	-

[1] $96,454 = ($100,000 × 0.8227) + ($4,000 × 3.5460)
[2] $885 is due to rounding.

b)

JOURNAL			
Date	Account Title and Explanation	Debit	Credit
Jan 1	Cash	96,454	
	Discount on Bonds Payable	3,546	
	Bonds Payable		100,000
	Issued $100,000 worth of bonds at a discount		

Pause & Reflect Exercise 17-3

a)

Straight-Line Amortization Table of Bond Premium					
Semi-Annual Interest Period	Interest Payment	Premium Amortization	Interest Expense	Premium Balance	Bond Book Value
0				7,092	207,092[1]
1	12,000	1,773	10,227	5,319	205,319
2	12,000	1,773	10,227	3,546	203,546
3	12,000	1,773	10,227	1,773	201,773
4	12,000	1,773	10,227	0	200,000
Total	48,000	7,092	40,908	0	-

[1] $207,092 = ($200,000 × 0.8227) + ($12,000 × 3.5460)

b)

JOURNAL			
Date	**Account Title and Explanation**	**Debit**	**Credit**
Jan 1	Cash	207,092	
	Premium on Bonds Payable		7,092
	Bonds Payable		200,000
	Issued $200,000 worth of bonds at a premium		

Pause & Reflect Exercise 17-4

JOURNAL			
Date	**Account Title and Explanation**	**Debit**	**Credit**
Jun 30	Bonds Payable	1,000,000	
	Premium on Bonds Payable	40,000	
	Cash		950,000
	Gain on Bond Redemption		90,000
	Redemption of $1,000,000 worth of bonds		

Pause & Reflect Exercise 17-5

JOURNAL			
Date	**Account Title and Explanation**	**Debit**	**Credit**
Jul 1	Interest Expense	927	
	Notes Payable	4,734	
	Cash		5,661
	Record monthly payment of principal and interest on note payable		

Review Exercise 17-1

Premium bond price = $2,000,000 + $142,968 = $2,142,968

a)

Semi-Annual Interest Period	A Interest Payment ($2,000,000 – 2%)	B Premium Amortization (D/40 periods)	C Interest Expense (A – B)	D Premium Balance (D [Previous Period] – B)	E Bond Book Value ($2,000,000 + D)
0				$142,968	$2,142,968
1	$40,000	$3,574	$36,426	139,394	2,139,394
2	40,000	3,574	36,426	135,820	2,135,820
3	40,000	3,574	36,426	132,246	2,132,246
4	40,000	3,574	36,426	128,672	2,128,672
5	40,000	3,574	36,426	125,098	2,125,098
6	40,000	3,574	36,426	121,524	2,121,524
7	40,000	3,574	36,426	117,950	2,117,950
8	40,000	3,574	36,426	114,376	2,114,376
9	40,000	3,574	36,426	110,802	2,110,802
10	40,000	3,574	36,426	107,228	2,107,228

b)

JOURNAL			
Date	**Account Title and Explanation**	**Debit**	**Credit**
2018			
Apr 1	Cash	2,142,968	
	Premium on Bonds		142,968
	Bonds Payable		2,000,000
	Issue of $2 million worth of bonds at a premium, due in		
	20 years		
Sep 30	Interest Expense	36,426	
	Premium on Bonds	3,574	
	Cash		40,000
	Payment of interest and amortization of premium		
2019			
Feb 28	Interest Expense	30,355	
	Premium on Bonds	2,978	
	Interest Payable		33,333
	To accrued interest at year end		
2023			
Mar 31	Cash	2,200,000	
	Bonds Payable		2,200,000
	Issuance of new bonds		
Mar 31	Bonds Payable	2,000,000	
	Premium on Bonds	107,228	
	Loss on Bond Redemption	2,772	
	Cash		2,110,000
	Redemption of bonds		
Sep 30	Interest Expense	22,000	
	Cash		22,000
	To record interest		
	($2,200,000 × 2% × 6/12)		

Review Exercise 17-2

a)

Date	A Cash Payment	B Interest Expense (D × 4% × $^6/_{12}$)	C Reduction of Principal (A − B)	D Principal Balance (C − D)
Apr 1, 2018				$200,000
Oct 1, 2018	$52,525	$4,000	$48,525	151,475
Apr 1, 2019	52,525	3,030	49,495	101,980
Oct 1, 2019	52,525	2,040	50,485	51,495
Apr 1, 2020	52,525	1,030	51,495	0

b)

JOURNAL			
Date	Account Title and Explanation	Debit	Credit
Apr 1, 2018	Cash	200,000	
	Notes Payable		200,000
	Issue of note payable of $200,000, at 4%		
	annual interest rate, paid semi-annually		
Oct 1, 2018	Interest Expense	4,000	
	Notes Payable	48,525	
	Cash		52,525
	Installment payment of principal and interest		
Feb 28, 2019	Interest Expense	2,525	
	Interest Payable		2,525
	To recognize accrued interest at year end		
Apr 1, 2019	Interest Expense	505	
	Interest Payable	2,525	
	Notes Payable	49,495	
	Cash		52,525
	To record payments of interest and principal		

Review Exercise 17A-1

a)

Semi-Annual Interest Period (Date)	A Interest Payment ($200,000 × 4%)	B Interest Expense (D × 5%)	C Discount Amortization (B − A)	D Bond Amortized Cost (D + C)
0 (Jan 1, 2017)				$184,557
1 (Jun 30, 2017)	$8,000	$9,228	$1,228	185,785
2 (Dec 31, 2017)	8,000	9,289	1,289	187,074
3 (Jun 30, 2018)	8,000	9,354	1,354	188,428
4 (Dec 31, 2018)	8,000	9,421	1,421	189,849
5 (Jun 20, 2019)	8,000	9,492	1,492	191,341
6 (Dec 31, 2019)	8,000	9,567	1,567	192,908
7 (Jun 30, 2020)	8,000	9,645	1,645	194,553
8 (Dec 31, 2020)	8,000	9,728	1,728	196,281
9 (Jun 30, 2021)	8,000	9,814	1,814	198,095
10 (Dec 31, 2021)	8,000	9,905	1,905	$200,000
Total	$80,000	$95,443	$15,443	

b)

JOURNAL			
Date	Account Title and Explanation	Debit	Credit
2017			
Jan 1	Cash	184,557	
	Discount on Bonds Payable	15,444	
	Bonds Payable		200,000
	Issue of $200,000 worth of bonds at a discount		

c)

JOURNAL			
Date	Account Title and Explanation	Debit	Credit
2017			
Jun 30	Interest Expense	9,228	
	Discount on Bonds Payable		1,228
	Cash		8,000
	Record semi-annual interest and amortization		
	of the bond discount		

d)

JOURNAL			
Date	Account Title and Explanation	Debit	Credit
2021			
Dec 31	Bonds Payable	200,000	
	Cash		200,000
	Repayment of $200,000 to bondholders		

CHAPTER 18 SOLUTIONS

Pause & Reflect Exercise 18-1

JOURNAL			
Date	**Account Title and Explanation**	**Debit**	**Credit**
Jan 21	Cash	5,500	
	Short-Term Investment—Trading Securities		5,000
	Gain on Sale of Investment		550
	To record sale of trading securities		

Pause & Reflect Exercise 18-2

Initial investment: $250,000
Andover's share of Blackstar's profit: $200,000 × 30% = $60,000
Andover's share of cash dividend received: $10,000 × 30% = $3,000

Net Investment in Blackstar Limited = Initial Investment + Revenue from Investment – Cash Dividend Received

$$= \$250,000 + \$60,000 - \$3,000$$
$$= \$307,000$$

Review Exercise 18-1

JOURNAL			
Date	**Account Title and Explanation**	**Debit**	**Credit**
Jan 1	Investment in Tamalie Inc. Stock	450,000	
	Cash		450,000
	Purchased 6,000 shares of Tamalie Inc. common stock		
Apr 1	Long-Term Investment—Available-for-Sale Securities	101,500	
	Cash		101,500
	Purchased available-for-sale securities		
May 10	Investment in Pergola Inc. Stock	50,000	
	Cash		50,000
	Purchased common stock		
Jul 1	Cash	3,000	
	Interest Revenue		3,000
	Received interest from available-for-sale debt securities		

JOURNAL			
Date	**Account Title and Explanation**	**Debit**	**Credit**
Jul 10	Cash	100	
	Dividend Revenue		100
	Received dividend from trading equity securities		
Jul 31	Investment in Tamalie Inc. Stock	24,000	
	Revenue from Investment in Tamalie Inc.		24,000
	To record 30% profit on equity investment in Tamalie Inc.		
Aug 20	Cash	3,000	
	Investment in Tamalie Inc. Stock		3,000
	To record dividends received from Tamalie Inc.		
Oct 1	Cash	10,000	
	Loss on Sale of Investment	150	
	Long-Term Investment—Available-for-Sale Securities		10,150
	Sold 10% of available-for-sale securities		
Dec 15	Cash	26,800	
	Investment in Pergola Inc. Stock		25,000
	Gain on Sale of Investment		1,800
	Sold half of Pergola stock		
Dec 31	Valuation Allowance for Available-for-Sale Securities	650	
	Unrealized Gain on Available-for-Sale Securities		650
	Fair value adjustment for Available-for-Sale Securities		
	[$92,000 − ($101,500 − $10,150)]		
Dec 31	Unrealized Loss on Investment	1,000	
	Valuation Allowance for Investment		1,000
	Fair value adjustment for Pergola stock		
	[($50,000 − $25,000) − $24,000]		

CHAPTER 19 SOLUTIONS

Pause & Reflect Exercise 19-1

Reconciliation of Net Income to Net Cash Provided (Used) by Operating Activities	Add or Subtract?
Net Income	
Adjustments to Reconcile Net Income to Net Cash Provided (Used) by Operating Activities	
Depreciation	Add
Amortization	Add
Loss on Sale of Land	Add
Gain on Retirement of Debt	Subtract
Changes in Current Assets and Current Liabilities	
Increase in Accounts Receivable	Subtract
Increase in Prepaid Expenses	Subtract
Decrease in Merchandise Inventory	Add
Decrease in Accounts Payable	Subtract
Increase in Salaries Payable	Add
Decrease in Interest Payable	Subtract
Increase in Income Taxes Payable	Add
Net Cash Provided (Used) by Operating Activities	

Pause & Reflect Exercise 19-2

Altitude Sportswear Inc. Statement of Cash Flows (partial) For the Year Ended December 31, 2018	
Cash Flows from Investing Activities	
Cash paid for new office equipment	($250,000)
Cash received from sale of long-term investments	80,000[1]
Cash received from sale of land	900,000 [2]
Cash received from sale of old production equipment	15,000[3]
Net Cash Provided (Used) by Investing Activities	$745,000

[1] Cash received from sale of long-term investments = ($155,000 − $70,000) − $5,000 = $80,000

[2] Cash received from sale of land = $850,000 + $50,000 = $900,000

[3] Cash received from sale of old production equipment = $200,000 − ($130,000 + $30,000 − $0) − $25,000 = $15,000

Pause & Reflect Exercise 19-3

a) Pacific's free cash flow is $157,000, calculated as follows:

Free Cash Flow = Net Cash Provided by Operating Activities − Net Cash Used byInvesting Activities
= $235,000 − $78,000
= $157,000

b) This is a favorable indicator of the company's financial health. This indicates the company has $157,000 remaining after it has covered its operating activities and capital expenditures. It may choose to use the cash to reduce debt, buy back shares, or pay dividends.

Review Exercise 19-1

a)

Dellray Inc.		
Statement of Cash Flows		
For the Year Ended December 31, 2018		
Cash Flow from Operating Activities		
Net Income	$986,700	
Adjustments to Reconcile Net Income to Net Cash		
Provided (Used) by Operating Activities		
Depreciation	80,000	
Loss on Sale of Equipment	10,000	
Gain on Sale of Investments	(8,000)	
Changes in Operating Assets and Liabilities		
Decrease in Accounts Receivable	30,000	
Increase in Merchandise Inventory	(40,000)	
Increase in Prepaid Expenses	(8,000)	
Increase in Accounts Payable	119,000	
Net Cash Provided (Used) by Operating Activities		$1,169,700
Cash Flow from Investing Activities		
Sale of Equipment	160,000	
Sale of Investments	48,000	
Purchase of Equipment	(400,000)	
Net Cash Provided (Used) by Investing Activities		(192,000)
Cash Flow from Financing Activities		
Proceeds from Notes Payable	70,000	
Proceeds from Bonds Payable	6,000	
Payment of Cash Dividends	(75,000)	
Proceeds from Issuance of Common Stock	80,000	
Net Cash Provided (Used) by Financing Activities		81,000
Net Increase (Decrease) in Cash		1,058,700
Cash at the Beginning of the Year		27,000
Cash at the End of the Year		$1,085,700

Cost of equipment sold = $1,100,000 + $400,000 − $1,300,000
= $200,000

Depreciation of equipment sold = $156,000 + $80,000 − $206,000
= $30,000

Book value = $200,000 − $30,000
= $170,000 − $10,000 loss
= $160,000 cash received
on sale of equipment

Cost of investment = $600,000 − $560,000
= $40,000 + $8,000
= $48,000 cash received
on sale of investments

Proceeds from notes payable = ($75,000 + $275,000) - ($65,000 + $215,000)
= $70,000

Dividends paid = $1,210,000 + $986,700 − $2,121,700
= $75,000

b)

Free Cash Flow = Net Cash Provided by Operating Activities − Net Cash Used by Investing Activities

= $1,169,700 − $192,000

= $977,700

Dellray has a positive free cash flow, which means that the company generated more than enough cash from operations to cover its capital expenditures in 2018. It has $977,700 remaining cash that it could have used to reduce debt, buy back shares or pay dividends. In addition, Dellray's free cash flow is more than enough to cover its total current liabilities, which is equal to $632,000 at the end of 2018. Analysis of Dellray's free cash flow together with the income statement and balance sheet reveals favorable conditions for Dellray because the company is profitable and would not have a liquidity crisis even if it has to repay all of its current liabilities right away.

Review Exercise 19A-1

Harmony Inc.		
Statement of Cash Flows		
For the Year Ended December 31, 2018		
Cash Flow from Operating Activities		
Cash Receipts		
Cash Received from Customers		$5,630,000
Cash Payments		
Payments for Inventory	$2,889,000	
Payments for Insurance	16,000	
Payments to Employees	766,000	
Payments for Other Operating Expenses	367,300	
Payments for Income Taxes	422,000	
Total Cash Payments		4,460,300
Net Cash Provided (Used) by Operating Activities		1,169,700
Cash Flow from Investing Activities		
Sale of Equipment	160,000	
Sale of Investments	48,000	
Purchase of Equipment	(400,000)	
Net Cash Provided (Used) by Investing Activities		(192,000)
Cash Flow from Financing Activities		
Proceeds from Notes Payable	70,000	
Proceeds from Bonds Payable	6,000	
Payment of Cash Dividends	(75,000)	
Issuance of Common Stock	80,000	
Net Cash Provided (Used) by Financing Activities		81,000
Net Increase (Decrease) in Cash		1,058,700
Cash at the Beginning of the Year		27,000
Cash at the End of the Year		$1,085,700
Reconciliation of Net Income with Net Cash Provided		
(Used) by Operating Activities		
Cash Flow from Operating Activities		
Net Income		$986,700
Adjustments to Reconcile Net Income to Net Cash		
Provided (Used) by Operating Activities		
Depreciation		80,000
Gain on Sale of Investments		(8,000)
Loss on Sale of Factory Equipment		10,000

Changes in Operating Assets and Liabilities		
Decrease in Accounts Receivable		30,000
Increase in Merchandise Inventory		(40,000)
Increase in Prepaid Expenses		(8,000)
Increase in Accounts Payable		119,000
Net Cash Provided (Used) by Operating Activities		$1,169,700

*Note that the investing and financing sections are calculated the same way under both direct and indirect methods.

Calculations for the Operating Activities—Direct Method

Cash Received from Customers	
Sales of 2018	$5,600,000
Add: Increase of Account Payable Changes ($400,000 – $370,000)	30,000
Cash Received from Customers	$5,630,000
Payments for Inventory	
Cost of goods sold for 2018 (from income statement)	$2,968,000
Add: Increase in Inventory for 2018	40,000
Inventory purchased on credit during 2018	$3,008,000
Balance of Accounts Payable, Jan 1, 2018 (from balance sheet)	$342,000
Add: Merchandise purchased on credit during 2018	3,008,000
Less: Balance of Accounts Payable, Dec 31, 2018 (from balance sheet)	461,000
Cash payments for merchandise	$2,889,000
Payments for Insurance	
Insurance expense for 2018 (from income statement)	$8,000
Add: Change in prepaid insurance for 2018	8,000
Cash payments for insurance during 2018	$16,000
Payments to Employees	
Salaries expense for 2018 (from income statement)	$766,000
Add: Change in salaries payable for 2018	0
Cash payments to employees for salaries during 2018	$766,000
Payments for other operating expenses = Other Operating Expenses	$367,300
Payments made for Income taxes	
Income tax expense for 2018 (from income statement)	$422,000
Less: Change in Income Tax Payable for 2018	0
Cash payments for income tax during 2018	$422,000

Cost of equipment sold   = $1,100,000 + $400,000 − $1,300,000
       = $200,000

Depreciation of equipment sold   = $156,000 + $80,000 − $206,000
       = $30,000

Book value on sale of equipment   = $200,000 − $30,000 = $170,000

Proceed from sale of equipment   = $170,000 − $10,000 loss
       = $160,000

Cost of investment sold   = $600,000 − $560,000 = $40,000

Proceed from sale of investment   = $40,000 + $8,000
       = $48,000

Dividends paid   = $1,210,000 + $986,700 − $2,121,700
       = $75,000

Proceed from bank loan   = ($75,000 + $275,000) − ($65,000 + $215,000)
       = $75,000

CHAPTER 20 SOLUTIONS

Pause & Reflect Exercise 20-1

a)

Industrial Furnishings Percentage of 2015 Base Year For the Year Ended December 31				
	2018	**2017**	**2016**	**2015**
Total Revenue	122%	120%	105%	100%
Cost of Goods Sold	155%	150%	110%	100%
Gross Profit	114%	113%	104%	100%
Total Expenses	122%	119%	103%	100%
Net Income	82%	88%	106%	100%

b) Net income has been decreasing in 2017 and 2018 despite a steady increase in revenue because the expenses have been increasing more than the increase in revenue. While the cost of goods sold increased quite significantly from 110% in 2016 to 150% and 155% in 2017 and 2018, respectively, there was still a modest increase in gross profit year after year. The most important factor causing a decrease in net income is the increase in total expenses, which jumped from 103% in 2016 to 119% and 122% in 2017 and 2018, respectively.

Pause & Reflect Exercise 20-2

a) Working Capital (2017) = Current Assets − Current Liabilities
       = ($6,501 + $220 + $4,368 + $123 + $190 + $0) − $11,061
       = $11,402 − $11,061
       = $341

Working Capital (2018) = Current Assets – Current Liabilities

= ($10,918 + $81 + $4,026 + $221 + $485 + $699) – $23,684

= $16,430 – $23,684

= ($7,254)

b) Current Ratio (2017) $= \dfrac{\text{Current Assets}}{\text{Current Liabilities}}$

$= \dfrac{\$11,402}{\$11,061}$

= 1.03

Current Ratio (2018) $= \dfrac{\text{Current Assets}}{\text{Current Liabilities}}$

$= \dfrac{\$16,430}{\$23,684}$

= 0.69

Pause & Reflect Exercise 20-3

a) Gross Profit Margin (2017) $= \dfrac{\text{Gross Profit}}{\text{Sales Revenue}}$

$= \dfrac{\$23,134}{\$27,188}$

= 0.85 or 85%

Gross Profit Margin (2018) $= \dfrac{\text{Gross Profit}}{\text{Sales Revenue}}$

$= \dfrac{\$20,493}{\$28,172}$

= 0.73 or 73%

b) Net Profit Margin (2017) $= \dfrac{\text{Net Income}}{\text{Sales Revenue}}$

$= \dfrac{(\$7,369)}{\$27,188}$

= –0.27 or –27%

Net Profit Margin (2018) $= \dfrac{\text{Net Income}}{\text{Sales Revenue}}$

$= \dfrac{(\$27,032)}{\$28,172}$

= –0.96 or –96%

Pause & Reflect Exercise 20-4

$$\text{Days' Sales in Inventory (2017)} = \frac{\text{Average Inventory}}{\text{Cost of Goods Sold}} \times 365$$

$$= \frac{\$130}{\$4,054} \times 365$$

$$= 11.7 \text{ days}$$

$$\text{Days' Sales in Inventory (2018)} = \frac{\text{Average Inventory}}{\text{Cost of Goods Sold}} \times 365$$

$$= \frac{\$172}{\$7,679} \times 365$$

$$= 8.2 \text{ days}$$

Pause & Reflect Exercise 20-5

$$\text{Book Value per Common Share} = \frac{\text{Stockholders' Equity} - \text{Preferred Equity}}{\text{Number of Common Shares Outstanding}}$$

$$= \frac{\$24,994,000}{\$12,830,945}$$

$$= \$1.95$$

Review Exercise 20-1

a)

Basil's Bakery Percentage Change and Vertical Analysis As at December 31, 2018				
	2018	**2017**	**% Change**	**% of Base-Figure 2018**
Cash	$1,605	$987	62.61%	29.12%
Accounts Receivable	1,175	573	105.06%	21.15%
Merchandise Inventory	396	256	54.69%	7.13%
Other Current Assets	301	103	192.23%	5.42%
Total Current Assets	3,477	1,919	81.19%	63.09%
Property, Plant and Equipment	2,034	1,170	73.85%	36.61%
Total Assets	$5,511	$3,089	78.41%	100.00%
Current Liabilities	$1,474	$547	169.47%	26.53%
Long-Term Liabilities	104	58	79.31%	1.87%
Total Liabilities	1,578	605	160.83%	28.40%
Stockholders' Equity	3,933	2,484	58.33%	71.36%
Total Liabilities + Equity	$5,511	$3,089	78.41%	100.00%

b)

Financial Ratio or Figure	Calculation	Result
Working Capital	$3,477 – $1,474	$2,003
Current Ratio	$\dfrac{\$3,477}{\$1,474}$	2.36
Quick Ratio	$\dfrac{\$1,605 + \$1,175}{\$1,474}$	1.89
Gross Profit Margin	$\dfrac{\$3,081}{\$6,009}$	0.5127 or 51.27%
Net Profit Margin	$\dfrac{\$1,295}{\$6,009}$	0.2155 or 21.55%
Return on Equity	$\$1,295 \div \dfrac{(\$3,933 + \$2,484)}{2}$	0.4036 or 40.36%
Return on Common Stockholders' Equity	$\dfrac{(\$1,295 - 0)}{(\$3,933 + \$2,484) \div 2}$	0.4036 or 40.36%
Return on Assets	$\$1,295 \div \left(\dfrac{\$5,511 + \$3,089}{2}\right)$	0.3012 or 30.12%
Asset Turnover	$\dfrac{\$6,009}{(\$5,511 + \$3,089) \div 2}$	1.40 times
Inventory Turnover Ratio	$\$2,928 \div \left(\dfrac{\$396 + \$256}{2}\right)$	8.98
Days' Sales in Inventory	$\dfrac{(\$396 + \$256) \div 2}{\$2,928} \times 365$	40.64 days
Days' Sales Outstanding	$\dfrac{(\$1,175 + \$573) \div 2}{\$6,009} \times 365$	53.09 days
Accounts Receivable Turnover	$\$6,009 \div \left(\dfrac{\$1,175 + \$573}{2}\right)$	6.88
Debt-to-Equity Ratio	$\dfrac{\$1,578}{\$3,933}$	0.4012 or 40.12%
Times-Interest-Earned	$\dfrac{\$2,329}{\$518}$	4.50 times
Debt-to-Total-Assets Ratio	$\dfrac{\$1,578}{\$5,511}$	0.2863 or 28.63%

c) A positive **working capital** of $2,003 indicates that the company has enough liquid assets to pay off its upcoming short-term debts.

A **current ratio** of 2.36 indicates that the business has a little more than twice the amount of current assets to pay for its current liabilities. It could be argued that the bakery has enough of a cushion that it could afford to have more cash tied up in current assets, such as inventory and accounts receivable. It could also invest a small portion to earn more investment income.

A **quick ratio** of 1.89 which indicates that the business can meet its most immediate debt obligations without relying on the liquidation of inventory. In terms of liquidity as a whole, Basil's Bakery is highly liquid based on the above three financial ratios and figures, indicating a strong financial position in meeting short-term debt obligations.

A **gross profit margin** of 51.27% means that after deducting cost of goods sold from sales revenue, the company still has a little more than half of sales revenue left to cover other expenses. Compared to 2017, the gross profit margin declined, indicating that the company is either generating less revenue, has experienced an increase in inventory costs or both. This should be a point of concern, indicating a downward trend. Comparing 2018's gross profit margin to the industry average of 49.47% shows that the bakery is doing better than the average company in the same industry. It must work to ensure that it remains above this amount by setting appropriate prices and properly managing inventory costs.

A **net profit margin** of 21.55% which means that the company is earning 21 cents of net income for every one dollar of revenue earned. Compared to 2015, the net profit margin declined, indicating that the company's costs have increased. This should be a point of concern, indicating a downward trend. Comparing 2018's net profit margin to the industry average of 20.36% shows that the bakery is doing better than the average company in the same industry. It must work to ensure that it remains above this amount by managing costs and expenses.

Basil's Bakery has a positive 40.36% **return on equity (ROE)**, which is favorable for investors. As always, stockholders can compare the company's ROE with other companies' ROE to see whether the return from investing in Basil's Bakery provides at least as high of a return as they could have received if they had invested elsewhere. In terms of profitability, the company is doing well.

Because Basil's Bakery does not have preferred stock, its return on common stockholders' equity is equal to its ROE of 40.36%. Similar to the ROE, the return on common stockholders' equity indicates that approximately $0.40 of net income was earned for every $1 invested by the common stockholders. By comparing this rate of return to that of other companies in the industry, investors can determine if this is a good rate of return, and whether they made a good choice to invest in the company. Good returns can also attract potential investors to purchase shares and benefit the company's value.

Basil's Bakery had a **return on assets** of about 30%. This means the company made a profit of $0.30 for every dollar invested in assets in the business. This appears to be a good return, but can be compared to other bakeries for a more thorough assessment.

The **asset turnover** is 1.4 times. This means the bakery generates $1.40 of revenue for every one dollar of assets. This is a good indicator that the company is using its assets efficiently.

Basil's Bakery has an **inventory turnover ratio** of 8.98, which represents the number of times that the company sold its entire inventory within the year. Bakeries should have a higher turnover ratio because some of the input products they use can expire, such as milk and eggs. Once items are baked, they have a short shelf life as efficiently.

A days' sales in inventory of 40.64 days indicates that the inventory is sold rather slowly. This paired with the inventory turnover ratio, shows that the bakery could be selling inventory faster. This is a point of concern. In terms of operations management, inventory must be addressed immediately. Inventory should be turning over more quickly to ensure that the bakery is not throwing out expired products. A turnaround in operations management could mean more success in profitability and liquidity.

The **days' sales outstanding** and **accounts receivable turnover** ratios indicate the company collects its accounts receivable every 53 days, or turns over it accounts receivable almost seven times a year. This is not a very healthy ratio. Long collection periods can mean that the company's credit policy is too lenient, or that there are billing disputes, resulting in a delay in receivables collection from customers. It can lead to cash flow problems if cash is not being received in a timely manner.

A **debt-to-equity ratio** of 40.12% indicates that the total debt is significantly lower than equity. Having relatively low debt compared to equity is considered low risk because the company has a low cost of debt in the form of interest. Therefore, the company's leverage appears to be at an acceptable level.

The **times-interest-earned** appears healthy. Basil's Bakery has enough cash to cover its interest obligations 4.5 times. The bakery currently has a debt-to-equity ratio of 40%, but if the amount of debt were to increase, the bakery should still be able to cover the interest on the debt. This should be monitored to ensure the times-interest-earned does not get too low.

The **debt-to-total-assets ratio** is sitting at a little more than 28%. This may be a relatively low value for debt-to-total-assets, which would indicate the company is not relying too heavily on debt to finance its assets. A comparison with other bakeries would place this in perspective.

GLOSSARY

A

account allows a person to track detailed information about the values of individual items, such as cash and unpaid accounts

accountants people who measure, record and report on an individual's or a business' financial activities

accounting a system to identify, measure and communicate all the financial activities of an individual or a business

accounting cycle a series of steps required to complete the financial statements

accounting equation assets = liabilities + net worth

accounting ethics the standards by which an accountant judges that the financial status of a business is accurately reported

accounting period the time frame in which the financial statements are prepared

accounting system documents and procedures that are used to collect, classify, summarize and report on a business' transactions and operations

accounts payable the obligation a business owes to others

accounts receivable the amount owed to a business by its customers

accounts receivable turnover ratio (ART) measures how often during the year a company collects its entire accounts receivable amount

accrual-based accounting a type of accounting where revenue and expenses are recorded in the period in which they occur, regardless of when cash is received or paid

accruals accruals are related to net worth or equity and not necessarily to cash flow; they help in recognizing how much a person is worth at a point in time

accrued expenses expenses that have been incurred but have not yet been recorded and require an adjusted entry

accrued revenue revenue that has been earned but not yet recorded and requires an adjusted entry

accumulated depreciation the contra asset account for property, plant and equipment (PPE); reflects the decrease in the net book value of PPE without changing the original cost of the asset

adjusted trial balance the trial balance after adjustments are made

adjusting entries made at the end of the accounting period to record assets, liabilities, equity, revenue and expenses according to revenue and expense recognition principles

administrative expenses expenses related to running the business, which are not directly tied to selling inventory; also referred to as *general expenses* or *general and administrative expenses*

aging method a method to estimate bad debt by which percentages are applied to groupings based on the age of outstanding accounts receivable amounts

allowance for doubtful accounts (AFDA) a contra asset account that records bad debt in a way that satisfies the expense recognition principle

allowance method estimates an amount that will be bad debt and records it in the books

amortization the process of allocating the cost of intangible assets over their useful lives

amortizing the discount the process of allocating the total cost of borrowing (interest and discount) to the interest expense account over the life of a bond

amortizing the premium the process of allocating the total cost of borrowing (interest payment less premium) to the interest expense account over the life of a bond

annuity a stream of periodic and recurring fixed payments, such as interest payments, over a period of time

articles of incorporation government documents filed when a corporation is formed, containing the operational details of the corporation; also called a *corporate charter*

asset something that you own that will benefit you now and in the future

asset turnover measures how quickly a company converts total assets, including noncurrent assets, into revenue

authorized shares the maximum number of shares of stock that can be legally issued by a company

available-for-sale (AFS) securities debt or equity instruments that are neither held for trading nor held to maturity

B

bad debt an uncollectible account resulting from customers who will never pay their bills

balance sheet a permanent document used to record what you own (assets), what you owe (liabilities) and what you are worth (net worth) on a specific date

balance sheet approach a method by which a company calculates allowance for bad debt using either the percentage of total accounts receivable method or the aging method

bank overdraft a financial institution's extension of credit to cover the portion of cash withdrawal that is more than the account's balance

bank statement a record of all activities in a bank account for a given period, usually a month

base figure a total dollar amount used to determine the relationship between line items on a financial statement

base year the earliest year shown on a comparative balance sheet; used as a basis for comparison

basic earnings per share EPS that is based on actual shares that have been issued to stockholders

basket purchase buying property, plant and equipment from the same vendor in one transaction, as opposed to buying them separately from different vendors; also called a *lump sum purchase*

bond a type of long-term debt in the form of an interest-bearing note

bond certificate a document that is issued as an official record to investors when they purchase bonds

bond indenture a contract between a bond issuer and a bondholder

bond issuer a company that issues a bond

bondholder an investor who purchases a bond

book value per common share a value that indicates what a common share would be worth to common stockholders if the company were to be liquidated

book value per preferred share a value that indicates what a preferred share would be worth to preferred stockholders if the company were to be liquidated

book value per share a value that indicates what a share would be worth to stockholders if the company were to be liquidated

business combination a transaction that occurs when one company purchases more than 50% of the outstanding stock of another company

business entity assumption accounting for a business must be kept separate from the personal affairs of its owner or any other businesses

business segment different lines of business within a company that serve different types of customers or provide different goods and services

C

capital amounts that increase your net worth but are not earned, and therefore not considered revenue

capital deficiency a partner who has a debit balance in his or her capital account

capital expenditure expenses paid for a change to an asset resulting in benefits extending beyond the current period

cash currency, coins, checks, money orders and money on deposit in a bank account

cash discount offered by merchandisers to encourage prompt payment from customers, by which a percentage off the final bill is given if it is paid in a specified amount of time

cash equivalents highly liquid investments that can be easily converted into cash

cash flow the amount of cash flowing into and out of a bank account

cash flow from financing activities the movement of cash within a business received from investors and lenders to help run, or finance, a business; also cash paid back to investors and lenders

cash flow from investing activities the movement of cash in a business on the basis of purchases and sales of noncurrent assets

cash flow from operating activities the movement of cash within a business as a result of day-to-day activities

cash over and short the difference between the amount of petty cash on record and the actual amount on hand

cash payments journal a special journal used to record all cash payments made by a business

cash receipts journal a special journal used to record all cash deposits and collections

cash-based accounting a type of accounting in which revenue and expenses are recorded only when cash is received or paid

chart of accounts a list of all the accounts in the general ledger

closing balance the amount remaining in an account at the end of the current accounting period; also called *ending balance*

closing entries entries made to revenue, expenses and owner's withdrawals at the end of an accounting period to close out the accounts

closing the books updates owner's capital (the equity of the business) and starts a new income statement for the next accounting period

cloud accounting accounting software that is hosted remotely on a vendor's computer servers and accessed by users through the cloud; also called *cloud-based accounting*

Committee of Sponsoring Organizations (COSO) part of the Treadway Commission; provides a framework to help companies design and implement internal controls

common stock a type of equity that gives stockholders ownership in a corporation, voting rights to elect a board of directors and potential to receive dividends

comparability financial statements of a company must be prepared in a similar way year after year

comparative balance sheet a balance sheet that shows the balances for multiple years for easy comparison

compound interest the piling on effect of applying the same interest rate on an account over a period of time

compound journal entries journal entries that affect three or more accounts

comprehensive income the total of net income plus other comprehensive income (or loss)

conceptual framework the basis to determine how business transactions should be measured and reported

conservatism states that whenever an accountant has several options in applying an accounting standard, the least optimistic or least favorable option should be selected

consigned inventory merchandise that is carried and sold by the selling agent and not the owner in return for a commission

consignee a selling agent that resells merchandise for a commission on behalf of the owner

consignor the owner of merchandise that is being sold by a selling agent

consistency prevents businesses from changing accounting methods for the sole purpose of manipulating figures on the financial statements

consolidated financial statements combining the financial statements at the end of the year of both the parent and subsidiary companies

contingent liabilities financial obligations that occur only if a certain event takes place in the future

continuing operations a business' normal day-to-day activities that are expected to continue in the near future

contra account linked to another account and records decreases in the value of that account

contractual interest rate the annual percentage rate of interest an investor receives on the face value of a bond; also called the bond's *coupon rate*

controlling account an account in the general ledger that summarizes information and combines the balance of every related subsidiary ledger; also called a *control account*

controlling influence occurs if one stockholder or investor owns more than 50% of the outstanding common stock

convertible bonds bonds that give bondholders the option of converting or exchanging them for a specific number of the company's shares

copyright gives exclusive rights of ownership to a person or group that has created something

corporation a type of business that is a legal entity separate from its owners

cost constraint ensures that the value of reported financial information outweighs the costs incurred to report it, even if the information would improve the accuracy and completeness of the financial statements

cost of goods sold (COGS) the value of all the goods sold; it is subtracted from sales revenue to determine gross profit

coupon bonds contain detachable coupons that state the amount and due date of the interest payment

credit a credit is recorded on the right-hand side of a T-account; increases or decreases an account depending on the type of account

credit memorandum issued by the seller to inform the buyer that the accounts receivable balance has been credited in the seller's books; also called a *credit memo*

credit period the maximum number of days that a buyer can wait before paying the full amount of an invoice

credit terms the terms indicating when a buyer has to pay for the merchandise and whether there are any discounts for paying early

cumulative stock a type of preferred stock that gives stockholders the right to be paid the current year's dividends and to accumulate any unpaid dividends from previous years

current assets assets that are likely to be converted into cash or used up through the day-to-day operations of the business within the next 12 months or the operating cycle, whichever is longer

current liabilities amounts due to be paid within 12 months

current ratio measures a company's ability to pay off short-term debt

customer deposit occurs when a customer pays a business for goods before they are received or services before they are performed

customer loyalty programs rewards given to customers that can be redeemed in future for a product or service

D

date of declaration the date on which the board of directors announces dividends will be paid to stockholders

date of payment the date on which the company makes dividend payments to eligible stockholders

date of record the date on which the corporation lists all those who currently hold stock and are eligible to receive dividend payments

days' sales in inventory calculates how many days inventory will last given the current rate of sales; also called *inventory days on hand*

days' sales outstanding (DSO) tracks how long customers take to pay their bills

debenture bonds unsecured bonds that are backed only by a bondholder's faith in a company's reputation; also referred to as *debentures*

debit a debit is recorded on the left-hand side of a T-account; increases or decreases an account depending on the type of account

debit memorandum a notice issued when a buyer encounters undesirable goods and informs the seller about the purchase returns or allowances; also called a *debit memo*

debt instruments investing excess cash by lending money to someone else for interest income; also called *debt securities*

debt-to-equity ratio a measure of how much of a company is being financed by lenders, and how much is being financed by stockholders

debt-to-total-assets ratio a measure of how much of a company's assets are financed through total liabilities

declining-balance method applies an annual percentage to calculate depreciation against the net book value of an asset

deferred income tax liability occurs when the income tax expense reported on the company's income statement is higher than the income tax payable reported on its income tax return

depletion the process of allocating or expensing resources as they are harvested or mined and sold

depreciation allocating the cost of a noncurrent asset over its useful life

determinable liabilities liabilities with a precise value

disclosure states that any necessary information that enables financial statement users to make informed decisions must be included with the financial statements

discontinued operation a business segment that is no longer part of a company's regular operating activities

discount (bonds) the difference between the price paid and the par value of a bond

discount (stock) when stock is sold for a price less than its par value

discount period the number of days within which a buyer has to pay to receive a cash discount

dishonored note a note receivable that is not paid at maturity

dividend a distribution of a company's earnings to stockholders

dividend yield shows potential investors what percentage of company earnings is paid out to stockholders in cash dividends

dividends in arrears unpaid dividends on cumulative preferred stock from prior periods

double entry recording the same value on both debit and credit sides for every transaction

double taxation a situation in which a corporation pays income tax on its earnings and stockholders pay personal income tax on their dividends

double-declining-balance method doubles the declining-balance rate of depreciation

E

earnings per share (EPS) a ratio that indicates the profit earned by each common share

electronic funds transfer (EFT) a method of sending payment online directly from a customer's bank account into the bank account of a supplier

employee benefits compensation to employees in addition to their normal wages and salaries, such as pensions, medical and dental coverage, and other benefits

equity the net worth of a business, after all assets have been sold and all liabilities have been paid

equity instruments investing excess cash by buying a stake in the ownership of another organization; also called *equity securities*

equity method a method used to record and report strategic equity investments when the investor owns 20% to 50% of the investee's outstanding common stock

estimated liabilities financial obligations a company cannot exactly quantify

ethics a set of guidelines that define if a behavior is moral or not

event an occurrence in business where nothing of value is traded and no transaction is recorded

expense recognition states that an expense must be recorded in the same accounting period in which it is used to generate revenue

expenses a decrease to net worth caused by day-to-day activities; costs that are incurred or use up an asset, usually cash

expenses by function a method of classifying related expenses together, such as selling expenses or administrative expenses, and presenting them as such on the statement of comprehensive income

expenses by nature a method of classifying expenses in which they are presented based on their natural classification, such as salary expense or advertising expense, and presenting them as such on the statement of comprehensive income

external users people or organizations outside a business, such as suppliers, banks and external accountants, that use the business' financial statements in making their decisions

F

face value the amount on a bond to be paid to an investor upon maturity; also called the bond's *par value*

fair value adjustment recording changes in the carrying value of an investment due to changes in fair value

fair value the amount an asset could be sold for in the open market

fair value through net income method (FVTNI) an accounting method used to report trading securities

fair value through other comprehensive income method (FVTOCI) an accounting method used to report available-for-sale securities

faithful representation transactions must be presented as their true economic substance rather than their legal form

FICA tax the portion of an employee's earnings deducted in accordance with the Federal Insurance Contributions Act (FICA)

financial accounting a field of accounting concerned with keeping records of a business and preparing the financial statements

Financial Accounting Standards Board (FASB) a private, nonprofit organization designated by the SEC to develop guidelines that all public US companies are required to use in reporting their financial statements according to GAAP

first-in, first-out (FIFO) method an inventory valuation method that assumes the first items received in inventory are the first items moved out

fiscal year a period of time covered by the financial statements; usually a one-year time frame and not necessarily the same as a calendar year

fixed assets noncurrent assets used to help run the business and not purchased with an intention to resell as inventory

fixed interest rate an interest rate that remains constant for the entire term of a note

FOB destination indicates that ownership of the purchased items changes when the goods arrive at the buyer's place of business

FOB shipping point indicates that ownership of purchased items changes as soon as the goods leave the seller's place of business

Form W-2 a form called the Wage and Tax Statement that states an employee's gross pay and all statutory deductions for the year

Form W-4 a form called the Employee's Withholding Allowance certificate, used to determine the amount of tax a company withholds from an employee's earnings

for-profit corporations a business formed for the purpose of generate profits for its stockholders

franchise a contract that allows the franchisee to operate a branch using the franchisor's brand name and business model

fraud any illegal intentional act of deception that results in a financial benefit or gain

free cash flow the amount of cash remaining after a business has covered its operating activities and capital expenditures required to maintain a company's existing production capacity

fully diluted earnings per share EPS that is based on actual and potential shares that have or could be issued

future value the value of money that will be in an account after a number of years

G

general journal a book of original entry used to record transactions; all transactions are listed in one place and in chronological order; used to record any entry that does not belong in one of the special journals

general ledger a book used to record and organize all the accounts and balances of a business

general partner a partner with unlimited liability who is legally authorized to manage the day-to-day operations and make decisions on behalf of the business

general partnership all partners share responsibilities of the business; they have unlimited liability

generally accepted accounting principles (GAAP) standards created by the accounting profession, which provide guidance on how financial information should be reported

going concern assumption assumes that a business will continue to operate into the foreseeable future

goodwill arises when a company purchases another company at a cost that is greater than the market value of that company's net assets

gross pay represents the total amount earned by an employee before any deductions

gross profit the difference between sales revenue and cost of goods sold

gross profit margin the difference between sales revenue and COGS expressed as a percentage of sales; also called *gross margin*

H

held-to-maturity (HTM) securities debt instruments that have a maturity date and are intended to be held until maturity in order to earn interest revenue

horizontal analysis a method to compare information from one accounting period to another, usually from year to year

I

impairment occurs when an asset's fair value appears to permanently drop to a point that is below its net book value

income (loss) from continuing operations shows the results of the company's operations that are ongoing

income statement a temporary record used to show and summarize revenue and expenses

income statement approach a method that uses credit sales from the income statement as a basis to predict future bad debt

income summary a temporary holding account used to close the revenue and expense accounts, instead of debiting and crediting owner's capital or retained earnings directly

income tax the amount of taxes on its net income that a corporation is obligated to pay to the government

indirect method indirectly analyzes cash flow from operating activities by starting with accrual-based net income, then adding or subtracting certain items from the income statement as well as changes in current assets and current liabilities from the balance sheet; investing activities and financing activities are determined by analyzing the noncurrent assets, long-term liabilities and equity portions of the balance sheet

insider trading occurs when anyone uses a company's private information to trade in the stock market for personal gain before the information is released publicly

installments periodic payments made on a note payable

intangible assets conceptual assets that have no physical form and largely constitute intellectual property, such as patents and trademarks

internal controls policies and procedures a business uses to protect assets, operate efficiently, keep accurate accounting records and adhere to company practices and laws or regulations

internal users people who own a business and/or work in a business that use the business' financial information in making their decisions

International Accounting Standards Board (IASB) an independent organization that works with the Financial Accounting Standards Board (FASB) to establish the International Financial Reporting Standards (IFRS)

International Financial Reporting Standards (IFRS) standards created by the International Accounting Standards Board (IASB), which provide guidance on how financial information should be reported

inventory shrinkage occurs when there is a difference between accounting records and a physical inventory count

inventory turnover ratio an estimate of how many times a year a company is selling its entire inventory

inventory valuation methods the different methods a company can use to determine how inventory costs are handled

investee a company that issues (sells) the debt or equity to another company

investor a company that purchases and owns the debt or equity issued by another company

invoice a document issued by a seller to a buyer after a service is provided or a product is sold; includes details of the purchase, the amount owing, and terms of payment

issued shares authorized shares that are sold to stockholders

J

journal a book of original entry in which transactions are recorded

journalizing the act of recording in a journal

L

large stock dividend a stock dividend that distributes additional shares equal to more than 25% of currently outstanding shares at the date of declaration

last-in, first-out (LIFO) method an inventory valuation method that assumes the last items received in inventory are the first items moved out

lease a contract between the owner of an asset and another party who uses the asset for a given period of time

liabilities something that you owe and consider to be a financial obligation

license a contract that permits the licensee to use the licensor's product or brand name under specified terms and conditions

limited liability a type of liability that extends only to the amount a person has invested in a partnership, limited liability company or a corporation

limited liability company (LLC) provides limited liability to its members, who are allowed to take a management role in the LLC

limited liability partnership (LLP) a business legal entity used to protect one partner from another partner's negligence

limited partner a partner with limited liability who is responsible only for providing the capital to finance a business

liquid asset an asset that is cash or easily converted to cash; cash is the most liquid asset and is listed first on the balance sheet, followed by accounts receivable, inventory, and so on

liquidating dividend a cash dividend that returns some of the stockholders' original contributions to the stockholders; also called a *liquidating cash dividend*

liquidity the ease with which an asset can be converted to cash

long-term debt instrument a debt instrument that will take more than 12 months to mature

long-term investment an investment intended to be held for longer than a year that is reported under the noncurrent (or long-term) assets section of a balance sheet

long-term liabilities amounts due to be paid after 12 months

long-term notes payable a long-term liability due beyond 12 months of the date of issue

lower of cost and net realizable value (LCNRV) a method of recording merchandise inventory at the lower of its cost or net realizable value

lump sum purchase buying property, plant and equipment from the same vendor in one transaction, as opposed to buying them separately from different vendors; also called a *basket purchase*

M

maker a customer (borrower) of a note receivable who makes a promise to pay

Management's Discussion and Analysis (MD&A) a special section included in a company's annual report filed with the SEC; provides stockholders with an analysis of the company's past and current performances, and a discussion of its future plans and projected performance

managerial accounting a field of accounting that serves the internal users of the accounting information by preparing specialized reports to assist in decision-making inside a business

market interest rate the interest rate that investors can demand in return for lending their money

market value the price stock is sold for, determined by the amount investors are willing to pay for it

materiality refers to the significance of information to the users; a piece of information is material if it could influence or change a user's decision

maturity date the date on which the final payment of the bond is due to the investor

measurement the process of determining the amount at which an item is recorded in the financial statements

merchandise inventory a collection of physical goods that a company has purchased or manufactured to sell to customers; also called *inventory*

merchandiser a business that buys and sells products, referred to as merchandise or goods, to make a profit; also called a *merchandising business*

minimum legal capital the minimum amount of assets that stockholders are legally required to contribute to a company

Modified Accelerated Cost Recovery System (MACRS) depreciation rules under US federal income tax law

monetary unit assumption requires that accounting records are expressed in terms of money and in a single currency

money market instrument a short-term debt instrument that is highly-liquid and low-risk, such as a treasury bill, term deposit or money market fund

mortgage bonds issued when a company puts up specific assets as collateral in the event it defaults on interest or principal repayments

mortgage note a note secured by an asset

multiple-step income statement an income statement that further divides specific revenues and expenses to show subtotals like gross profit, operating expenses and income from operations

mutual agency in a partnership, each partner is able to speak for the other partner(s) and bind them to business contracts

N

natural business year an accounting period of time in which the fiscal year ends during a slow time of year

natural resources assets with a physical nature that are different from property, plant and equipment, such as metal ores, minerals timber or petroleum

net book value the original value of an asset less the total depreciation that has been recognized

net income occurs when revenue exceeds expenses for the period, which causes equity to increase

net loss occurs when expenses exceed revenue for the period, which causes equity to decrease

net pay the amount an employee is paid after various deductions have been made

net profit margin assesses a company's profitability after all expenses have been deducted

net realizable value (NRV) the price that a company can realistically expect to sell the item for, less any costs incurred to make the item ready for sale

net worth the amount remaining if you sell all your assets for cash and pay off all your liabilities

neutrality financial information must be free from bias

noncumulative stock preferred stock that does not have the right to receive any accumulated unpaid dividends

noncurrent assets used to operate a business and not expected to turn into cash or be used up within the next 12 months; also called *long-term assets*

non-determinable liabilities unknown liabilities including estimated and contingent liabilities

nonparticipating preferred stock stock with a limit to the dividends that can be issued each year

nonprofit organizations formed for the purpose of improving or benefiting communities by taking profits and redistributing them as services or products

non-strategic investment an investment where the purpose is to generate investment income without intending to establish a long-term business relationship with, or to influence or control, the investee

non-sufficient funds (NSF) checks payments made to a company by a customer who does not have sufficient funds in his or her bank account to cover the amount of the check

no-par value stock stock issued with no assigned value

normal balance corresponds to the side of a T-account that records the increase

note payable a legally binding document that obligates the borrower to certain terms, much like a loan

notes receivable makes an account receivable resemble a formal loan by adding precise terms of repayment and the customer's signature; also called a *promissory note*

O

opening balance the amount left over from the last accounting period carried over to the beginning of the current accounting period; also called *beginning balance*

operating cycle the time between the use of cash and the receipt of cash for the business

operating expenses expenses incurred as part of the main operations of the business that are beyond the cost of goods sold

operating lease a form of a lease where ownership is not transferred to another party over the term of the agreement, such as for a car rental

operating line of credit the maximum loan balance a business may draw upon at any time without having to visit or request approval from the bank

operations management the ability of a company to manage its assets, such as inventory and accounts receivable

organization expenses initial costs incurred to organize or form a corporation; also called *organization costs*

other comprehensive income (OCI) a category of income resulting from transactions that are beyond company owners' or management's control

other income (expenses) items that are not part of a company's regular day-to-day operations

outstanding shares shares that are still held by stockholders; may be equal to the number of issued shares

owner's capital account an account used to record the amount of an owner's equity including owner's contributions

owner's contributions the amount of cash or assets invested in a business by the owner

owner's withdrawals the amount of cash or assets taken by the owner for personal use

owner's withdrawals account an account used to record owner's withdrawals

P

paid-in capital the total amount of assets that stockholders contribute to the corporation to receive the corporation's stock in return; also called *contributed capital*

par value stock stock that is issued with an assigned value

parent company the investor in a business combination

participating preferred stock stock that entitles preferred stockholders to share with common stockholders any dividends paid in excess of the percentage stated on the preferred stock certificate

partnership an association of two or more people who jointly own a business, its assets and liabilities, and share in its gains or losses

partnership liquidation a process to dissolve a partnership; involves selling assets, paying off liabilities and distributing any proceeds to the partners according to individual profit and loss ratios

patent grants the patentee the exclusive right, for a set period of time, to prevent others from making, using, selling or distributing the patented invention without permission

payee a company (lender) of a note receivable to whom the note is payable

payment terms conditions by which a vendor expects to be paid by a customer

percentage of total accounts receivable method a method by which a company uses a percentage of receivables to estimate bad debt

periodic inventory system a method of keeping track of inventory in which the company's record of merchandise inventory is only updated after a physical count, usually at the end of the month or year

permanent accounts balance sheet items that have their balances carried forward from one accounting period to the next with no need of being closed; also called *real accounts*

perpetual inventory system a method of keeping track of inventory in which inventory levels are updated after every purchase and sale

plant assets property, plant and equipment that are noncurrent physical assets used to help run the business

post-closing trial balance a trial balance that only lists accounts that have a balance after the closing entries are completed

preferred stock a type of equity for which dividends must first be paid before those on common stock

premium when stock is sold for a price more than its par value

prepaid expense occurs when you pay cash for an expense before you use it

present value the amount that needs to be invested today to produce a specific amount in the future

price-earnings (P/E) ratio provides an investor with an indicator or future growth and potential risk of a company's earnings

prior period adjustment a correcting entry that is made to a previous period

private accounting the practice of accounting for a single organization

private corporation one that does not offer its stock to the public

private enterprise any business or organization in which ownership is restricted to a select group of people; the general public cannot acquire ownership of the business

profitability the ability of a company to generate profits

promissory note makes an account receivable resemble a formal loan by adding precise terms of repayment and the customer's signature; also called a *notes receivable*

property, plant and equipment equipment, buildings, land and other similar assets that provide a business with benefits for a long period of time

public accounting providing services, such as auditing and tax advice, to different companies or individuals

public corporation one that trades its stock on a stock exchange

purchase discounts cash discounts as referred to by a buyer

purchases journal a special journal used to record all purchases made on account

Q

quick ratio similar to the current ratio, but only counts assets that can easily be turned into cash

R

recognizing recording an expense or revenue on the income statement

redeemable bonds bonds issued that a company has the right to buy back before maturity; also called *callable bonds*

registered bonds list bondholders as registered owners who receive regular interest payments on interest payment dates

relevance all information useful for decision-making must be present in the financial statements

reliability information is free from significant error and bias, so different independent people looking at the evidence will arrive at the same values

remote deposit depositing checks directly into a bank account without having to physically deposit the check at a bank machine or bank branch

residual value estimated value of an asset at the end of its useful life

retailer a business that buys merchandise from a wholesaler or manufacturer to sell to end consumers

retained earnings earnings that are kept and accumulated by a company after dividends have been paid to stockholders

return on assets measures the relationship between net income and assets

return on common stockholders' equity a measure of the profits earned on an investment of common stockholders

revenue an increase to net worth caused by providing goods or services in exchange for an asset, usually cash

revenue expenditure expenses paid for a change to an asset that benefits the current period

revenue recognition states that revenue can only be recorded (recognized) when goods are sold or services are performed

reverse stock split an action that gives one share for every two shares a stockholder owns; doubles the market value of each share

S

S corporation a special type of corporation that does not pay federal income tax; it allocates its profits and losses to individual members to be reported on their personal tax returns

sales allowances occur when the customer decides to keep undesirable products at a reduced price

sales discount account a contra-revenue account to record sales discounts offered to customers

sales discounts cash discounts as referred to by a seller

sales journal a special journal used to record all sales made on account

sales returns occur when undesirable products are returned from the buyer to the seller

sales returns and allowances a contra-revenue account used to track the number of returns

sales revenue a type of revenue earned by a business for selling products to customers

sales tax a tax applied by the state government to goods or services that are sold

Sarbanes-Oxley Act (SOX) an act passed by the US Congress to prevent accounting practices from committing fraudulent activities

Section 404 a section of the Sarbanes–Oxley Act that requires a company's senior management and auditors to establish internal controls

Securities and Exchange Commission (SEC) a federal government agency whose mission is to protect investors; the development of GAAP is under its legal authority

selling expenses expenses related to selling inventory

serial bonds a set of bonds that mature at different intervals

service revenue a type of revenue earned by a business for providing service to customers, such as interest or fees earned

short-term debt instrument a debt instrument that will mature within 12 months

short-term investment an investment intended to be held for less than a year that is reported under the current assets section of a balance sheet; also called a *temporary investment*

short-term notes payable a short-term liability paid in full at its maturity date, usually within 12 months of the date of issue

significant influence exists if a company owns between 20% to 50% of another company's common stock outstanding

single-step income statement a format of the income statement in which revenue accounts are grouped together and expense accounts are grouped together, with no further categorizing; also called an *income statement*

small stock dividend a stock dividend that distributes additional shares equal to 25% or less of currently outstanding shares at the date of declaration

sole proprietorship a business that is owned and generally operated by one owner

solvency a company's ability to cover its long-term debt obligations; relates to the amount of debt and risk a company has

source documents evidence, such as sales receipts, bills, checks, bank statements, and so on, that proves a transaction happened

special journal a separate book to record regular transactions, such as sales, purchases, cash payments, cash receipts, and payroll

specific identification method an inventory valuation method that accurately tracks the unit cost and value of merchandise inventory

spreadsheet a work sheet prepared using programs like Excel, that can be used to display the trial balances before and after the adjustments are made

stated value a value assigned to no-par value stock that protects creditors from the company paying out dividends to the point where insufficient equity remains to cover the company's liabilities

statement of cash flows a statement that tracks the sources and uses of cash in a business; also called the *cash flow statement*

statement of changes in equity a statement required under IFRS reporting changes to all equity accounts

statement of comprehensive income a statement in which comprehensive income is reported as well as earnings per share; under IFRS, the statement can be presented by function or by nature

statement of members' equity an LLC's statement explaining changes to the balance of each member's capital account from the beginning to the end of a year

statement of owner's equity a formal statement that shows how owner's equity changed during the accounting period

statement of partners' equity a partnership's statement explaining changes to the balance of each partner's capital account from the beginning to the end of a year

statement of retained earnings a statement required under US GAAP reporting changes in the retained earning account; also called the *retained earnings statement*

statement of stockholders' equity a statement under US GAAP showing all changes to stockholders' equity accounts, as opposed to the information provided in the financial statement footnotes

stock a unit of equity in a corporation; also called *shares*

stock dividend issued in lieu of a cash dividend

stock split an action that increases the number of a corporation's outstanding shares, decreasing the individual price of each share traded on the stock market

stockholders owners of a corporation who own equity in a corporation in the form of stocks; also called *shareholders*

stockholders' equity the partial ownership of a stockholder in a company

straight-line amortization method a method in which the same amount of bond discount is recorded each period

straight-line method of depreciation produces an average depreciation expense, which is applied each year until the asset is sold or reaches the end of its useful life

strategic investment an investment where the investor intends to establish a long-term business relationship with, or to influence or control, the investee

subledgers a group of similar accounts used to keep track of specific information related to the general ledger account; also called *subsidiary ledgers*

subsidiary company the investee in a business combination

subsidiary ledgers a group of similar accounts used to keep track of specific information related to the general ledger account; also called *subledgers*

T

T-account a tool used to record transactions and keep the accounting equation balanced; it shows increases to the account on one side and decreases on the other

temporary accounts accounts that are brought back to a zero balance at the end of each period; also called *nominal accounts*

term bonds bonds that mature on a specific date

time period assumption requires that accounting takes place over specific time periods known as fiscal periods

time value of money a basic principle of economics and finance that shows how the value of money changes over time

timeliness information is timely if there is no delay in reporting crucial information

times-interest-earned ratio measures whether a company is able to cover the interest charged on its debt

trade discounts the discount from the manufacturer's suggested retail price that is usually given by manufacturers to merchandisers to resell their products

trade name grants exclusive rights to a name under which a company or product trades for commercial purposes, even though its legal or technical name might differ

trademark grants ownership rights for a recognizable symbol or logo

trading securities debt or equity instruments intended to be held for the short term and then sold for a profit

transaction a trade or exchange with someone else in order to receive something of value

treasury stock stock that is bought back from stockholders by the corporation

trend analysis comparing similar line items in a comparative balance sheet to see how an item has changed from year to year

trial balance lists all the accounts in the general ledger and their balances at a specific date

U

unadjusted trial balance the trial balance before adjusting entries are made

understandability financial information can be reasonably understood by its users if the users have knowledge of the business and a basic knowledge of accounting

unearned revenue an obligation a business has to provide products or services to a customer

units-of-production method uses an estimated number of units used for the entire life of the asset and bases each period's depreciation amount based on the actual units used for that period

unlimited liability if a business is unable to pay its debts, creditors of the business can force the owner to sell personal assets, suffer any net loss and be personally liable for all financial obligations of the business

useful life the length of time an asset can be used

V

variable interest rate an interest rate that fluctuates according to market interest rates; also called a *floating rate*

vertical analysis a method to compare a line item to a base figure within the same year

voucher documentation used to authorize and record a cash payment

voucher system a set of control procedures that a business uses to authorize, record and disburse cash payments

W

wage bracket method tables tables to help employers calculate the amount of federal income tax to withhold

weighted average number of common shares outstanding determined by taking the number of shares outstanding multiplied by the fraction of the year during which those shares were outstanding

weighted-average cost method an inventory valuation method in which a business applies an average unit cost to all units of a particular inventory item

wholesaler a business that buys mostly bulk merchandise from a manufacturer for reselling

working capital the difference between current assets and current liabilities

PHOTO AND INFORMATION CREDITS

Chapter 1, © Corepics Vof | Dreamstime.com

Chapter 2, © Monkey Business Images | Dreamstime.com

Chapter 3, © Dmitry Kalinovsky | Dreamstime.com, © The Financial Accounting Standards Board | Fasb.org, © 2017 IFRS Foundation. All rights reserved.

Chapter 4, © Herbert Kratky | Shutterstock.com

Chapter 5, © Evgeny Trofimov | Dreamstime.com

Chapter 6, © Stanislav Komogorov | Dreamstime.com, © Alistair Scott | Dreamstime.com

Chapter 7, © Edyta Pawlowska | Dreamstime.com

Chapter 8, © Marcin Balcerzak | Dreamstime.com, © Ultraone | Dreamstime.com

Chapter 9, © Rawpixelimages | Dreamstime.com

Chapter 10, © Cerbi | Dreamstime.com, © Dmitry Kalinovsky | Dreamstime.com, © Dave Bredeson | Dreamstime.com, © Alexey Stiop | Dreamstime.com, © 2016 Target Brands, Inc. Target, the Bullseye Design and Bullseye Dog are trademarks of Target Brands, Inc.

Chapter 11, © surasaki | Shutterstock.com

Chapter 12, © Gary Blakeley | Dreamstime.com, © Srki66 | Dreamstime.com, © Guryanov Andrey | Shutterstock, © 2016 Newmont Mining Corporation. All rights reserved.

Chapter 13, © Anthony Berenyi | Shutterstock, Dusan Petkovic, © Vlue | Dreamstime.com, © Catherine Lall | Dreamstime.com

Chapter 14, © Ammentorp | Dreamstime.com

Chapter 15, Rawpixel.com

Chapter 16, © Yong Hian Lim | Dreamstime.com, © Vinnstock | Dreamstime.com, © William Potter | Shutterstock.com

Chapter 17, © Alexskopje | Dreamstime.com

Chapter 18, © Ertem Osmanoglu | Dreamstime.com

Chapter 19, © Wisitporn Cheyasak | Dreamstime.com

Chapter 20, © Yurolaitsalbert | Dreamstime.com

INDEX

D

G

M

T